AdvancED Flex Application Development
Building Rich Media X

R Blank
Hasan Otuome
Omar Gonzalez
Chris Charlton

friendsof
DESIGNER TO DESIGNER™
an Apress® company

AdvancED Flex Application Development: Building Rich Media X

ISBN-13 (pbk): 978-1-59059-896-2

ISBN-10 (pbk): 1-59059-896-2

ISBN-13 (electronic): 978-1-4302-0441-1

ISBN-10 (electronic): 1-4302-0441-9

Distributed to the book trade worldwide by Springer-Verlag New York, Inc., 233 Spring Street, 6th Floor, New York, NY 10013. Phone 1-800-SPRINGER, fax 201-348-4505, e-mail orders-ny@springer-sbm.com, or visit www.springeronline.com.

For information on translations, please contact Apress directly at 2855 Telegraph Avenue, Suite 600, Berkeley, CA 94705. Phone 510-549-5930, fax 510-549-5939, e-mail info@apress.com, or visit www.apress.com.

The source code for this book is freely available to readers at www.friendsofed.com in the Downloads section.

Credits

Lead Editor	**Production Editor**
Ben Renow-Clarke	Jill Ellis
Technical Reviewer	**Compositor**
Lar Drolet	Dina Quan
Editorial Board	**Proofreader**
Steve Anglin, Ewan Buckingham,	Lisa Hamilton
Gary Cornell, Jonathan Gennick,	
Jason Gilmore, Jonathan Hassell,	**Indexer**
Chris Mills, Matthew Moodie,	Broccoli Information Management
Jeffrey Pepper, Ben Renow-Clarke,	
Dominic Shakeshaft, Matt Wade,	**Artist**
Tom Welsh	Kinetic Publishing Services, LLC
Project Manager	**Cover Image Designer**
Sofia Marchant	Bruce Tang
Copy Editor	**Interior and Cover Designer**
Ami Knox	Kurt Krames
Associate Production Director	**Manufacturing Director**
Kari Brooks-Copony	Tom Debolski

To my parents, Marion and Martin, and my brother, Jonathan, for all they have given me in life, especially the ability to communicate my thoughts fluently, the confidence to do so abundantly, and the drive to keep doing it. To my amazing team at Almer/Blank who make it possible for me to do everything I do, through their outstanding skills, vision, imagination, drive, and dedication. To Stephanie, who for years told me that I would write a book, whether I wanted to or not. And, of course, to Puck and Pippin, who never once complained when I stayed up writing till 4 a.m., even if that meant I forgot to feed them.

R Blank

To God and my mom for my life. I would not be here without you. To my beautiful wife for the understanding you showed. Your sacrifice will never be forgotten. To the best children a father could ever ask for. Daddy loves you more than you'll ever know.

Hasan Otuome

I dedicate this book to my parents, Juan and Maria Reyna Gonzalez. I cannot put in words the love and gratitude I have for everything you have ever done for me. I would not be here if it weren't for everything you've taught me—thank you.
Quisiera dedicar este libro a mis padres, Juan y Maria Reyna Gonzalez. No hay palabras para expresar el amor y agradecimiento por todo lo que han hecho por mi. No estaria aqui sin la educacion que me dieron ustedes—gracias.

Omar Gonzalez

To my loved ones—as always I share my love, dedication, and dreams.

Chris Charlton

CONTENTS AT A GLANCE

PART 3 BUILDING OUT NEW FEATURES

PART 4 SPECIAL TOPICS

CONTENTS

PART 2 BUILDING THE RMX CORE FUNCTIONS

Chapter 4 Preparing to Get to Work 95

PART 3 BUILDING OUT NEW FEATURES

Chapter 12 Building the Blog 319

Chapter 13 Building the Jobs Board 337

Chapter 14 Building the Event Calendar 371

Chapter 15 Ideas for the Future: Extending the RMX **391**

PART 4 SPECIAL TOPICS

Chapter 16 RSLs and Persistent Framework Caching **419**

FOREWORD

The world of Internet applications is changing. Using Adobe Flex technologies, web applications look great, are accessible and portable, and can completely move the end-user experience well beyond the page response/request model popularized by HTML. Best of all, the Flash Player is the most widely distributed piece of software in the history of the Internet. Never in history has "the experience" been more important in terms of web applications. Using Adobe Flash/Flex technology, programmers can create state-of-the-art enterprise web applications that enable experiences unlike anything else on the Web. Numerous organizations throughout the world have discovered the benefits of Rich Internet Application technology to create better experiences for end users, which in turn leads to greater productivity and enhanced social interaction, a primary goal of sites like YouTube and MySpace. The Rich Media Exchange, the building of which is detailed in this book, uses Rich Internet Application technology to foster a greater sense of community among Adobe User Groups worldwide.

Getting started with Flex can be simple; MXML tags are easy to learn and provide tremendous functionality right out of the box. Visual design mode and the host of components that ship with the product make building your first Flex applications straightforward. Taking this knowledge to the next level can be more difficult. ActionScript has a steeper learning curve, but experienced developers can pick up the basics with relative ease. This book, unlike any other on the market, details the internal workings of a large and complex application that utilizes best practices. You will see how a complex social networking site with a host of features, such as a calendar, communication among members, forums, and video, is made. This book shows you how a Flex application should and should not be built. Importantly, it will teach you when and how to utilize the existing Flex components and when to build your own. The application shows how to create code that is scalable, manageable, and reusable.

This book offers the reader an unparalleled insight into a complicated Flex project with a number of moving parts. Not only are Adobe Flex and the Flash Platform covered, but the book offers deep insight into the myriad details of planning, source control, documentation, and integrating with other technologies, including the server and Ajax. This comprehensive look into such a large Flash-based application provides a window unlike anything else available on the market. Most importantly, the book details firsthand how Rich Internet Application technology can enable organizations to better engage with end users and provide a great experience.

James Talbot
Principle Instructor/Developer
Partner Readiness
Adobe Systems Incorporated

ABOUT THE AUTHORS

R Blank is CTO of Almer/Blank, an Adobe Solution Partner based in Venice, California, that specializes in video and application development for the Flash Platform, for clients including E! Entertainment, Live Nation, Microsoft, Apple, and IKEA. For over 13 years, he has been an interactive designer, developer, consultant, teacher, and author, specializing in the planning, development, and release of rich interfaces; R has specialized in Flash since 1999.

R holds four Flash Certifications, was one of the first 50 certified Flash Developers in the world, is an author for the Flash MX 2004 Designer Certification Exam, and is a frequent contributor to the Adobe *Edge* newsletter. In 2003, he founded and continues to manage LAFlash.org, a community of over 3,000 Flash industry professionals and home to three Adobe User Groups for the Flash Platform. R also serves on the information technology faculty at the University of Southern California Viterbi School of Engineering.

Previously, R cofounded and served as director of product and design at Wildform, the makers of the first video encoder for Flash, where he cocreated Flix, the first video encoder for Flash (now owned by On2). R has an MBA in entrepreneurship from the UCLA Anderson School of Management and a BA in history from Columbia University, and has studied at Cambridge University (UK), the University of Salamanca (Spain), and the Nizhny Novgorod Institute of Foreign Languages (Russia).

Hasan Otuome is a senior application developer at Almer/Blank, where he can usually be found developing Rich Internet Applications for the company's clients. He is an Adobe Flex champion who espouses creative uses and combinations of Flash, Flex, AIR, PHP, MySQL, and ColdFusion for their benefits in creating unique user experiences.

When not immersed in client development, Hasan can be found lending a helping hand to the development community at sites such as LAFlash.org, gotoAndLearn.com, thesourcecode.org, and ActionScript.org.

Omar Gonzalez is a senior application developer at Almer/Blank who has been developing for the Web since 1997. He has acquired a strong sense for developing accessible sites employing web standards, open source projects, and frameworks like Drupal and CSS. During the quick rise of Flash, he began to incorporate the popular technology in the sites he worked on, adding Flash development as well as PHP and MySQL to his repertoire.

Omar has developed Flash video applications for companies like eHarmony and has spoken at conferences like FITC on such topics as Flash video, Motion XML, and AIR. Over the past two years he has been developing Flex applications, harnessing the power of Flash Platform technology to create cutting-edge Rich Internet Applications. Omar is on the resident faculty at the Rich Media Institute, teaching topics in Flex, HTML/CSS, and web development, and he is an active member of the LA Flash user groups.

Chris Charlton is a software architect at Almer/Blank and an Adobe Flex champion. He is a CSS and ActionScript expert who successfully cannonballed into web development in the late '90s and has been programming since childhood. Always caught up with the latest in Flash, Dreamweaver, Fireworks, and XML, Chris authored premium articles for the largest Dreamweaver/ Flash community, DMXzone (www.dmxzone.com), and produced WebDevDesign, a popular web design and development podcast featured on iTunes. Somehow, Chris finds time to run an authorized Adobe user group, LA AIR, focused around open source and Adobe technologies. As a community leader, Chris Charlton remains a resident faculty member of the Rich Media Institute and lends himself to speak at large industry events, like JobStock, NAB, and FITC Hollywood. Brain cycles from Chris are always web standards, the Flash Platform, and accessibility.

ABOUT THE TECHNICAL REVIEWER

Lar Drolet is a senior software engineer in Los Angeles where he develops Flex, AIR, and Flash applications. Lar is part of an ambitious team of developers and recently spoke at MAX and FITC on Flex and AIR topics. Not your typical engineer, Lar is an aspiring triathlete with a degree in economics and an MBA who will begin another graduate degree this spring.

ABOUT THE COVER IMAGE DESIGNER

Bruce Tang is a freelance web designer, visual programmer, and author from Hong Kong. His main creative interest is generating stunning visual effects using Flash or Processing.

Bruce has been an avid Flash user since Flash 4, when he began using Flash to create games, web sites, and other multimedia content. After several years of ActionScripting, he found himself increasingly drawn toward visual programming and computational art. He likes to integrate math and physics into his work, simulating 3D and other real-life experiences onscreen. His first Flash book was published in October 2005. Bruce's folio, featuring Flash and Processing pieces, can be found at www.betaruce.com, and his blog at www.betaruce.com/blog.

The cover image uses a high-resolution Henon phase diagram generated by Bruce with Processing, which he feels is an ideal tool for such experiments. Henon is a strange attractor created by iterating through some equations to calculate the coordinates of millions of points. The points are then plotted with an assigned color.

$$x_{n+1} = x_n \cos(a) - (y_n - x_n^P) \sin(a)$$

$$y_{n+1} = x_n \sin(a) + (y_n - x_n^P) \cos(a)$$

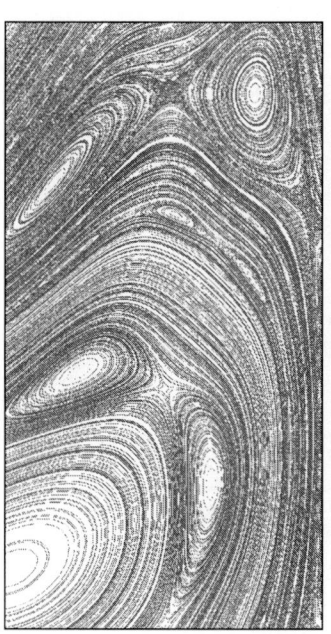

LAYOUT CONVENTIONS

To keep this book as clear and easy to follow as possible, the following text conventions are used throughout:

Important words or concepts are normally highlighted on the first appearance in **bold type**.

Code is presented in `fixed-width font`.

New or changed code is normally presented in **`bold fixed-width font`**.

Menu commands are written in the form Menu ➤ Submenu ➤ Submenu.

Where we want to draw your attention to something, we've highlighted it like this:

> *Ahem, don't say I didn't warn you.*

Sometimes code won't fit on a single line in a book. Where this happens, we use an arrow like this: ➡.

```
This is a very, very long section of code that should be written ➡
all on the same line without a break.
```

Part 1

PLANNING THE RMX

This book is about how we at Almer/Blank used Flex, along with other open source tech-nologies like Drupal and OpenAds, to help create a great application, the Rich Media Exchange, or RMX. Flex is a remarkable new way to build Internet-connected applica-tions; developers can now build Flash Platform projects of far larger scope and complex-ity than ever before. So many books on Flex cover the basics—we want to take this opportunity to extend that knowledge, to show you some of the techniques, code, and planning that goes into building an advanced Flex application.

We'll get into the heavy technical stuff pretty soon, but in these first three chapters, we discuss the state of Flash (where it's at, what it offers, and what Flex has added to the equation) and then introduce you to the RMX, what it is, what tools we used to build it, and how we planned for the process.

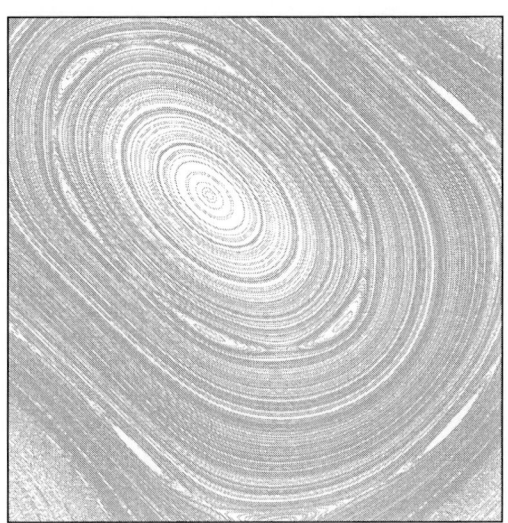

Chapter 1

INTRODUCTION TO FLEX 2 APPLICATIONS

By R Blank

What an amazingly exciting time for Flash! Flash technologies are now way more powerful than ever, and with Flex you now have a whole new way of creating content for the Flash Platform. To get you started on the road to excellence in Flex applications, this chapter gives you some background on the current state of the industry, what people are doing with Flash, and what Flex is adding to the mix.

Of course, the Internet isn't about technology—it is about experiences. Technology is simply the set of tools we developers use to create and deliver those experiences. Understanding how to create enjoyable, usable, and valuable Internet experiences involves knowing how to integrate multiple technologies to achieve your specific goals. Different developers have different opinions on this, and any community application must involve several technologies. Increasingly, Flash technology is adding vitality, power, and depth to more and more aspects of these experiences.

The Flash Platform and Web 2.0

The Flash Platform has evolved to a point of such power and flexibility that the creations now possible are awe-inspiring and available on an increasing variety of devices. From 2001, when my colleagues and I at Wildform created Flix, the first video encoder for Flash, we have come to the point where a business like YouTube, based entirely around Flash Platform video technology, is valued at over $1.5 billion,

3

and the entertainment industry has recognized the contributions of Adobe Flash video in the form of an Emmy award.

For those of us who have been working with Flash since the 1990s, through boom and bust and years in the wilderness, it is so gratifying to see this amazing technology receive the attention and investment that it deserves. And those new to the technology—like you reformed Java jockeys—are joining at a time of immense potential.

But, in order to comprehend just what's so exciting about the current scene, you should first understand what the current scene is. That scene is commonly referred to as **Web 2.0**.

Just what is this Web 2.0?

Web 2.0 is a term used so frequently now that it's very easy to lose sight of what it actually means. In fact, most people outside of Internet-related industries—and even many inside—don't have a working definition of Web 2.0.

While there is no single accepted definition of Web 2.0, in my mind it refers to a general sense of a quantum leap in the quality of Internet-based experiences in the past few years. In my opinion, Web 2.0 began the day Netflix changed their ratings widget so that users didn't have to refresh the page to rate a video—they can now do so simply and quickly, inline in the page without updating the URL. That might sound like a minor change, but in practice it allowed a Netflix user such as myself to rate dozens of movies—even on a slow connection—in the time that it previously took to rate just a few, which meant that Netflix could provide better recommendations for me (and, of course, the friends I now share those recommendations with will have deeper insight into my soul). The fact that I experienced the new ratings feature on a faster computer with a faster Internet connection meant that the value of the new ratings widget was that much greater. That is a major leap in the value of the service Netflix provides to consumers and content providers.

Of course, there really is nothing new, per se, represented by Web 2.0. But the various aspects that constitute Internet experiences—the software, the computers that run the software, and the connections that network those computers—have all individually evolved to a point where, when combined, they enable experiences that are vastly more powerful, varied, specialized, enjoyable, and productive.

In tangible terms, Web 2.0 manifests as video-sharing sites, wikis, blogs, and communities—technologies that enable user-generated content across a variety of media and forms—and RSS feeds, podcasts, and applications like Google Maps—technologies that improve user access to and interaction with the wide variety of media being generated. Other features, such as permalinks (permanent, bookmarkable URLs for dynamic content), taxonomies (editorial tagging), and folksonomies (user-generated tagging), are the mortar holding this Web 2.0 together.

But, in essence, Web 2.0 is just the proper execution of what we all wanted Web 1.0 to be—and what many, many Internet-focused startups failed while awaiting. Indeed, in Tim Berners-Lee's vision of the Web, he foresaw "editors," not "browsers," that enabled users to edit and add to the content with which they interacted; however, the initial Internet technologies did not adequately support this vision (with certain notable exceptions—for instance, Amazon's support for consumer reviews since its launch in 1995). It is interesting that Mr. Berners-Lee doubts the existence of Web 2.0—perhaps because he sees it as the natural evolution of usage of the basic architecture he created.

Now, however, the technological equation has shifted to the point where the "editor" can reside on the server, the content we generate and edit can be far more than just text, and we as a global society are beginning to understand what Mr. Berners-Lee was on about. The advances in technology widely referred to as Web 2.0 have, in reality, led to the creation of Internet experiences with real and immediate power to tangibly alter the dynamics, energy, and value of our lives.

What's Flash got to do with it?

Flash is a central component of Web 2.0 experiences. This is perhaps most obvious in the example of YouTube, but Flash is really everywhere. Without Flash—if only for its video features—Web 2.0 would lack much of the richness and enjoyment it now provides.

Once, when I was discussing a Flex project with a client, he asked me, "What do you think of Ajax?" I replied, "What do you think of the equator?" The equator, of course, doesn't really exist—it's a useful shortcut reference. Similarly, Ajax isn't a technology; just like Web 2.0 is the proper expression of what we wanted Web 1.0 to be, Ajax is really just the proper application of JavaScript to complement web-based experiences, employing XML for data and DHTML/CSS for interfaces.

This is not at all to diminish Ajax—but it is important to realize that it is not a technology, nor does it compete with the Flash Platform. Indeed, Flash, along with the set of technologies known as Ajax, are the essential and complementary building blocks of the vast majority of what we consider Web 2.0 to be.

Let's take a brief moment to see just what Flash contributes to this landscape. Ever since its release, Flash has brought three key benefits: ubiquity, reliability, and experience.

Ubiquity

Since version 3, Flash has really been everywhere. It is literally the most widely distributed software in the history of computing. The Flash Player is written for Windows, Mac, and Linux (as well as other platforms), and Macromedia created distribution deals with companies like Microsoft, AOL, Apple, and Netscape to ensure wide preinstalled distribution of the Flash Player. As well, Flash has always been tiny (Flash 4 was around 300K, and Flash 9 is still under 1MB), which meant that installing or upgrading it has always been a rapid and easy process, ensuring a wide market for any content created in Flash.

Whereas other tools, such as Adobe Director and Apple QuickTime, have long enabled rich interactive experiences, none ever had the global distribution of the Flash Player. That frictionless exchange between the user and the experience has always been a central component of every aspect of Flash's success: from character animation, banner ad production, e-learning development, e-commerce applications, and especially now its dominance in the video realm—whatever you create in Flash can be viewed immediately by almost anyone in the world with a computer.

Reliability

Not only does Flash run everywhere, but it does so reliably. Unlike any other browser-based technology, such as HTML or JavaScript or Java, Flash is the closest thing in God's creation to write-once, publish-everywhere technology. Indeed, this was the main reason I was initially attracted to the Flash Platform—I got sick of spending half my web-development time testing and recoding because Internet Explorer was rendering my content slightly differently than Netscape (whoops, have I dated myself? At least I didn't say Mosaic), or that my JavaScript would work on PC but not Mac. In the Flash world, you can basically assume that if it works on one computer, it will work on others, no matter what operating system or browser it is running (although you must, of course, always test!). This is a key fulfilling aspect of Flash development for those of us who do what we do for the thrill of the creation, not the testing and debugging (which, I will assume, is all of you). It's also a key driver behind the economic benefits of adopting Flash as the delivery platform for your content—reduced platform refactoring and testing requirements make the development process significantly faster and cheaper.

Experience

Flash provides a tremendous experience for one very specific reason: the makers of the technology allow you to create that experience entirely from whole-cloth, with no interference from them. The Flash Player runs transparently; once it's installed, web surfers don't ever need to know if they are experiencing a Flash application or something else. There is no Flash Player splash screen launched when Flash is invoked, and there is no Adobe-branded chrome anywhere to be found. It is truly transparent to the user. What's more, the flexibility provided by the design and coding features of Flash enable the creation of highly customized and engagingly beautiful interface designs and functionalities, most recently exemplified by the Nike Air project from Big Spaceship, shown in Figure 1-1. And the visual expressiveness of the Flash Platform has continued to improve, with a dramatic leap in Flash 8.

Figure 1-1. Big Spaceship's Nike Air project is an outstanding example of lush, immersive, interactive experiences possible on the Flash Platform.

More recently, the core values of the Flash Player expanded to include two key innovations: video and ActionScript 3.

Video

I have worked with online video since the mid-1990s, using formats like RealMedia and Vivo. Of course, those technologies, giving us the ability to deliver audio and video content over the Internet, were groundbreaking. But they were also quite limiting in the quality of the experience. In those days, video compression was still relatively young, and the connection speeds were measured in baud, so the quality of online video really did justify the oft-applied description "It's like watching a postage stamp." A truly satisfying on-demand delivery of video over the Internet did not really occur until around 2005, and 2006 saw the massive explosion in online video experiences and businesses fueled by Flash video technology.

And, of course, virtually all of these technologies required use of their own players, which launched outside of the browser (if it was even installed), was loaded up with the branding of the software maker, and was, more often than not, brute ugly. Heaven forbid you wanted some interaction between your media and the rest of your content. The frustration of attempting to build a custom audio player by embedding RealAudio controls with ActiveX in DHTML brought me directly to Flash and the creation of my first audio jukeboxes, as shown here in Figure 1-2.

Figure 1-2. An audio jukebox I built at Wildform

For years, the media capabilities of Flash were limited to audio (expanding to include MP3 in Flash 5). While some of us in the Flash community viewed this as a limitation affecting Flash, the advances of the past few years have revealed this was really a limitation affecting the entire entertainment industry.

Wildform created Flix in 2001. At that time, there was nothing like the current Flash Video format (FLV), and indeed Macromedia's own web site specifically indicated video in Flash was not possible. Soon after, other encoders appeared, and almost all encoded video to SWF using a glorified motion-JPEG scheme along with MP3 audio (with some additional enhancements in the SWF for memory management). Of course, the quality was nothing like it is today, but it represented the moment in time at which video could be seamlessly integrated into the completely customized Flash experiences already being created, as I did for Buddhist scholar Robert Thurman's web site in 2001, as shown in Figure 1-3.

Figure 1-3. Viewing a Flash video excerpt of "God and Buddha Dialog" on BobThurman.com in 2001

Macromedia released the first version of the FLV format for Flash 6, and improved its performance and usability for Flash 7. But, while that first version of FLV technology, based on the Sorenson Spark codec, was quite lightweight, its quality was lacking, discouraging many firms from adopting Flash video solutions. With Flash 8, and the introduction of the On2 VP6 codec into the FLV format, the quality improvements were so significant that within one year of the release of Flash 8, virtually every major-brand Hollywood entertainment firm switched its web-video system to a Flash Platform–based solution. With the first public versions of Flash Player 9, we have true full-screen video, with no JavaScript and no chrome whatsoever (from Flash, the browser, or the operating system). And with the release of Flash Player 9.0.6 we now have the amazingly powerful new ability to play any video encoded using the H.264 codec (and any AAC audio, as well), meaning that Flash can now play many of the same files that QuickTime can.

> For more information on what H.264 really is, I suggest visiting the Wikipedia entry at http://en.wikipedia.org/wiki/H.264.

Today, if you spend more than five minutes online, you will see Flash video everywhere, from popular video-sharing sites, to major-brand entertainment sites, to video-enabled banner ads. Simply stated, Flash is the most effective, efficient, and enjoyable method to deliver on-demand video over Internet connections. FLV has been a key aspect of Flash's success (as well as the explosion of Web 2.0), and its reach continues to expand. At my company, Almer/Blank, starting in 2005, developing and maintain Flash video applications has become a huge part of our business, beginning with custom video applications for firms including E! Entertainment (see Figure 1-4), Style Network, eHarmony, Live Nation, Comcast, Whiskas (see Figure 1-5), and Apple, and evolving to the point where we now have a reusable, licensable Flex-based social video and media network, FlexTube.tv, which we've applied to the Adobe User Group communities in the form of the Rich Media Exchange. We have a lot more information about using video in Flex throughout this book, especially in Chapter 10.

Figure 1-4. The Vine @ E! Online

Figure 1-5. The Whiskas Virtual Cat

ActionScript 3

All four of the preceding issues—ubiquity, reliability, experience, and video capability—combined to create a real problem. Flash was so cool, versatile, and universally viewable that developers kept pushing more and more into their projects. This forced many to the realization that, despite all its features and functionality, Flash just wasn't that powerful, for three main reasons:

- **Size**: The Flash Player is really, really small. Odds are, for any Flash video player, the combined size of the Flash Player and the Flash application delivering the video is much smaller than the first 30 seconds of video you watch. And there's just so much in there, including three video codecs, as you just read, and two ActionScript virtual machines, as well as tons of other goodies like an MP3 player and a video encoder (yes, encoder). The size of the Flash Player, given its agility, continues to be an amazing feat of software engineering.

- **Cross-platform performance**: Again, key benefits of Flash are its ubiquity and cross-platform reliability—which means that Flash, to a certain extent, must remain agnostic as to its host platform. Earlier in Flash's history, this led the team to shun plugging into certain platform-specific enhancements (such as MMX-processor calculations). Increasingly, this is not an issue, especially as Apple has moved to Intel.

- **Legacy architecture**: The early architecture of Flash wasn't designed to support the amazing breadth of applications now being created in it. But, because of the amazingly fluent backward compatibility that has always been a characteristic of Flash, that architecture has largely informed the design of all Flash Player versions, and the ActionScript language, through version 8.

Many of us—particularly Mac users—have been disappointed with the performance of web sites and Rich Internet Applications (RIAs) because the Flash Player can't really handle what many of us developers have asked it to do. While each version of the Flash Player has performed better than the previous, Flash 9 represents the first truly notable leap in Flash Platform strength, enabling the creation of Flash applications that run up to 30 times faster (that's times, not percent) than equivalent experiences delivered through previous versions of the Flash Player.

How did that happen? The masterminds at Adobe have created a new version of the ActionScript language, **ActionScript 3**, or **AS3**, which is a strict implementation of the ECMAScript specification (based on JavaScript). The new version of ActionScript runs in a new virtual machine (AVM, or ActionScript Virtual Machine), called **AVM2**. Any Flash project written in an earlier version of ActionScript will run in AVM1.

By including this new AVM in Flash Player 9, we get the major performance boost we can see in so many Flex 2 applications. But another result is that Flash 9 represents the first schism in the version history of Flash. In the simplest terms, Flash 9 content can load Flash 8 and earlier content, and vice versa, but, without hacks, they cannot communicate with each other! This is the same reason why content written in Flex 2 and 3 cannot work with content produced in earlier versions of Flex.

So, Flash 9/AS3 enables the creation of unprecedentedly powerful Flash applications, but unlike with the previous evolutions of ActionScript (from Flash 4 to 5, to ActionScript 1 to ActionScript 2), no baby steps are allowed. You can't mix and match as you feel comfortable until you get your footing. You have to jump in.

Despite the shock AS3 represents to the Flash development community, AS3 is a very important innovation in the Flash Platform, opening up a new horizon of robust applications that would previously have been unacceptably slow to create in Flash.

So, there you have it: the five key unique and glorious gifts Flash technology has given unto the world. What these gifts mean in practice is that it is possible for individuals or small groups of developers to create amazingly immersive, powerful, interactive experiences, laced with video, audio, and other media, that can run well and reliably on almost any Internet-connected device. And it can be done more satisfyingly, in far less time, with far less debugging and platform-specific refactoring, than is the case with alternative technologies, such as Ajax and Java. Many of the most entertaining aspects of the Web today exist because of Flash—from video-sharing sites like YouTube and major-branded video sites like NBC.com, to viral successes like Subservient Chicken and The Sith Sense, to tremendous web sites like NikeAir.com and MTV.com, to great animations like JibJab and Angry Alien's 30-Second Bunny Theater.

That's all well and good, but what does Flex have to do with that? What's Flex really bringing to the party that's so cool that we should let it in? Or, more professionally stated, what specific advances is Flex contributing to the Flash Platform? Well, to answer that, it is first useful to define precisely what Flex is.

What is Flex?

First and foremost, Flex is a Flash development framework, not an authoring tool or a player, designed from the ground up to facilitate the creation of RIAs on the Flash Platform.

The Flash authoring tool, or integrated development environment (IDE), is a tremendous application. Since the days when Macromedia purchased FutureSplash, Flash has been the dominant tool used to create Flash experiences. But, as I've said over and over again (and will no doubt repeat ad nauseam), Flash is such a flexible format that it is used to create an amazingly wide breadth of experiences. While Flash is a great format for delivering everything from banner ads, to animations, to web sites, to RIAs, it would be impossible for a single IDE to be optimized for the creation of all those experiences. That is, it is highly unreasonable to expect your animators and your application developers to use the same tool for the creation of such different experiences with such different workflows.

Over the past several years, the Flash development options have become more diverse and specialized. For instance, Adobe Captivate is a tremendous way to create simulation-based training modules. There is nothing you can do in Captivate that you couldn't effectively emulate in Flash, but packaging those specific features required for simulation training in a separate tool means that creating those experiences is *much* more rapid (and in the case of Captivate, designed for PowerPoint-level users, it is also easier for lower-level developers). Just as Captivate is designed to improve the development workflow for Flash-based simulation training, Flex is optimized for the development of Flash-based applications.

The Flex framework utilizes a mixture of a custom XML format called **MXML** and ActionScript 3—you cannot use any previous version of ActionScript with Flex 2 or 3. There are no timelines in the Flex world; it is structured entirely by components, driven by events, and held together with robust data binding. Even though developing applications is entirely different in Flex than in Flash, it is important to understand that both result in the creation of SWF files—the compiled format of the Flash Platform.

In the most childish (and therefore enjoyable) terms possible, Flex is like an Erector Set for Flash applications. To understand what I mean, it is important first to understand that all web-based applications share a similar language. When studying Russian at a summer immersion program, I remember a course offered in word roots, prefixes, and suffixes. There is a set of a few hundred keywords that form, in one way or another, a huge portion of the Russian lexicon. Many of the students who took that class could subsequently understand a large number of words (even really big and intimidating ones) they'd never previously encountered.

The world of Internet applications shares a similar concept, and indeed, it is the fundamental concept on which Flex is based. While your parents may not know the words "radio button," odds are they intuitively understand that the "circular check box" enables single selections, whereas traditional check boxes enable multiple selections. The fact that a check box is different from a radio button is not random—they represent distinct ways of interacting with information. And your parents were not taught these facts; they have learned them over a dozen years of consuming computer-based applications built around standards. These standards are called **user interface (UI) components**, or **components** for short. Both the radio button and the check box are components. Other components include the scrollbar, the combo box (or drop-down list), text fields, and text areas; they represent the fundamental information interactions that have evolved over 30+ years of GUI computing.

You may be surprised to discover that fewer than two dozen such components comprise the vast majority of web-based experiences; these components form the basis of the language of each and every Internet application, and as I say, are readily understood by an increasing majority of web users. If you understand the purpose of the UI components, you will understand how to use most any RIA interface you ever encounter—and you can also design most any required interaction.

What makes Flex so special is that it makes it incredibly easy to assemble applications out of these components—far, far easier than authoring custom applications in the Flash authoring tool or even using the Flash authoring tool to assemble applications from the functionally similar components that come with Flash Professional. Flex comes with these essential UI components, as well as additional ones to assist in laying out content. Flex also makes it incredibly simple to create your own custom components out of these components and has robust CSS support, making it quite easy to style your Flash applications and even consume the same CSS files that you might use elsewhere on your web site.

The Flex framework is free. You can download the Flex framework command-line compiler for Windows and create your own Flex applications for no cost. But that is not a practical option for most professional-level developers. So, to facilitate the use of the Flex framework, three tools from Adobe are included as a part of Flex:

- **Flex Builder**: The Eclipse-based IDE for the creation of Flash RIAs. Not only does the presence of an IDE significantly aid in the creation of Flex applications, but Flex Builder also has a design view and a code view, each with its own benefits, further improving ease-of-use and application development workflow.

- **Flex Charting**: A set of charting and graphing components, capable of generating Excel-style data representations, to aid in the visualization of data through Flex RIAs.

- **Live Cycle Data Services (LCDS)**: A server-side application that expedites the speed of data synchronization between your middleware and your Flex application SWF (formerly, Flex Data Services).

The topics in this book focus mainly on the use of the Flex framework through the Flex plug-in for Eclipse (which is functionally identical to the Flex Builder, as you'll read in Chapter 4).

To Flex or not to Flex . . .

OK, now you know what Flex is. So when do you use it?

As I've explained, Flash 9 represents a massive shift in the power of the Flash Platform. In part because of the Flash express-install scheme, and in part because sites like MySpace force-upgraded their users, Flash 9 achieved the most rapid penetration of any version of the Flash Player. But, for the first time in Flash history, the Flash Player was updated long before the Flash authoring tool. This meant that for a big chunk of time spanning 2006 and 2007, the only supported Adobe tool you could use to create Flash 9 content was Flex. Given the benefits of Flash 9, it was very easy to choose Flex as your authoring tool.

But now that the Flash CS3 authoring tool is out and available, it is important to select the proper tool, or mix of tools, to create your Flash projects. So, the question is, since Flash enables the creation of such a wide variety of experiences, which are suited to Flex?

I first heard of Flex in 2004. I had recently completed the IKEA PAX Wardrobe Configurator in Flash 7 (see Figure 1-6)—my first project I really felt had met the definition of this new term Macromedia was throwing around, Rich Internet Application.

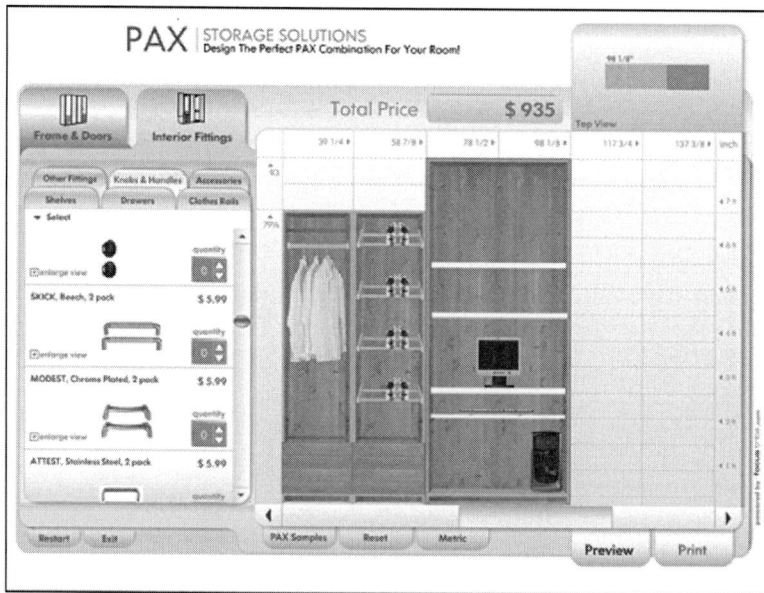

Figure 1-6. The IKEA PAX Wardrobe Configurator

And then Macromedia announced this new product, Flex 1, and it became clear that Macromedia really only considered a project an RIA if it were authored in Flex. As I considered myself to be a Flash developer creating RIAs, I was confused and a bit put off. But I think the real factor that put people like me off was the price tag of Flex 1 and 1.5. Until version 2, Flex was a server technology, requiring dynamic compilation and caching of your applications, with prices starting near $20,000. This meant that the only people who could play with RIAs were the big boys who could afford to lay out $20K for server software.

While Flex 1 and 1.5 did well as new products, the price tag led developers like me to continue with Flash as our tool of choice for Flash application development.

Then, of course, Flex 2 came along, with two major enhancements:

- **No required server software**: Flex Builder allows you to author and compile applications, and then place the resulting SWF on your web server, in much the same way that Flash does. No more $20,000 roadblocks to working with this amazing technology.

- **AS3**: The Flex framework is based entirely around ActionScript 3, and for almost a year it was the only officially released and supported tool that authored AS3. This means that applications created in Flex 2 and 3 are really much more powerful and snappy than those created in Flex 1 and 1.5.

Finally, along with the set of significant improvements to the framework in Flex 3, we also have **persistent framework caching** (or PFC—see Chapter 16 for more details). Flex, as I've just explained, is a framework. This means, effectively, Adobe builds a bunch of stuff into a structure, called the framework, which you can then utilize in your applications. It saves you time and effort, and makes development really easy. But, of course, a framework is not invisible—or, more relevantly stated, a framework is not weightless. All that cool stuff that Adobe builds for us into the framework must be downloaded by the users of your applications. One of the biggest drawbacks of Flex 2 was this download requirement, which in some cases approached 1.6MB. This one hurdle, which can radically increase download times, essentially restricted Flex's value to comprehensive applications, rather than web pages or widgets (such as RSS readers that can be easily added to any page). With PFC in Flash Player 9.0.6, the Flash Player effectively caches the Flex framework into the Flash Player itself (i.e., not the browser's cache), meaning that applications that had been, for example, 300KB, can now weigh in at 40KB! And another hurdle has been surmounted!

So, with the significant evolution in Flex since version 1, I guess the simple answer to whether or not Flex is right is that if it's an RIA, then use Flex; otherwise, do it in Flash. As we all know, Flash is used for more than just applications. The most obvious example is character animations or any other timeline-intensive artform. But, it is important to remember that Flash is Flash, and anything that can be created in Flex Builder can be replicated in the Flash CS3 authoring tool and vice versa. On many larger Flex projects, it will in fact be necessary to develop some assets and content in the Flash authoring tool. There will, of course, be boundary cases—projects that, for one set of reasons or another, could be equally well executed in Flash or Flex.

So, to determine whether or not Flex is the right tool for your project, you should answer these three questions:

Is it an application?

First and foremost, Flex is an application development tool. So is your project an application, like an e-commerce store or content management system, or more like a traditional animation or banner ad? Of course, this is a simplistic example with an obvious answer. When you are building something like a game or a richly designed movie web site, the lines are much blurrier, and you must approach such projects on a case-by-case basis, evaluating the functional and design requirements of the project as well as your skill-sets and those of your team.

Does it use components heavily?

This, too, may seem to be an obvious question—Flex is a component-driven environment, so it's clear that your application should also be component heavy. But adopting components may mean more than you think. For example, when you use a Flex combo box, you are implicitly adopting all the default behaviors of a combo box; as one simple example, the drop-down list is revealed on press, not on release, and by default reveals a standard scrolling list of repeated items, not a more complex interface such as a form.

It is certainly possible to create highly customized classes and components in Flex, as described later in this book, but depending on how much and what type of customization is actually required, it may not be easy to do so. Sometimes, given your specific functional requirements, it might in fact be easier to create your project (or at least a portion of it) in Flash.

How much custom skinning will be required?

Flex is very easy to style. But styling is different from skinning. **Styling** involves design settings, such as "make the text Arial 10 white" or "make the button a red-white gradient," that can be set with code, through the IDE, or through CSS. **Skinning** is the application of custom design elements—most often bitmaps, like PNGs, or vectors, like SWFs—to alter notably the look and feel of your components.

Styling alone may be insufficient to achieve your design requirements. While it is possible to skin heavily your Flex application, it can be very resource-consuming to do so—far, far more time intensive than you might expect if you have experience building similar applications in the Flash authoring tool. And, as awesome as Flex is, it should be noted that its support for styles and skins is imperfect, and sometimes executing precise design requirements can be impossible.

So, there you have it. Of course, whether to use Flex or Flash will often be a personal judgment. Hopefully these three rules of thumb will help you make the distinction. But, beyond the nature of the project, there is one more key consideration: the nature of the talent you have on hand.

Flexers are from Mars, Flashers are from Venus

Adobe and those of us involved in the Flash Platform have many challenges at the moment in terms of public and client conceptions of the technology, including decoupling the Flash Player from the Flash authoring tool, explaining the nature and role of Flex in the equation, and helping the existing Flash developer community make the leap from ActionScript 1 and 2 to AS3.

Among these challenges is the key one of communicating clearly the differences between Flash and Flex—not only in terms of capabilities, but also in terms of talent and workflow. For years, one of the difficulties in helping companies plan Flash projects was getting them to understand that, yes, Flash is Flash, but no, not every Flash developer can do everything in Flash. Even before Flash Player 9, the Flash Platform had evolved to the point where several distinct disciplines existed within it, including coding, design, motion design, character animation, and video and audio integration.

As the Flash Platform expands, many people will make similar mistakes with regard to Flex. Now that developers have an entirely new authoring tool, it becomes even more important to understand the nature of these individual tools, and who is right for which tool.

So, let's state it plainly and simply: Flash and Flex are fundamentally different tools. Knowing this, it should not be surprising that Flashers and Flexers are going to be, by and large, fundamentally different developers—maybe not quite as different as Photoshop and ColdFusion developers are, but in many cases that wouldn't be too far off.

While Flash enables a wide breadth of possible experiences, Flex was designed from the ground up to build applications. The emergence of Flex will likely lead to a cleaner differentiation between coding and noncoding roles of the Flash Platform, with a big chunk of the coding moving into Flex. Certainly, there will be people who continue to straddle the divide, knowing, and even mastering, both Flex and Flash. And it will continue to be unclear for some time how precisely this will play out—how much heavy-duty ActionScript will still be conducted in Flash, how much will separate cleanly out to Flex.

But in a general production context, because Flex and Flash are so different, with such different workflows, and because so many Flexers will have no knowledge of the Flash authoring tool, it is important to realize that your Flashers and your Flexers are going to be very different people, and you should not necessarily expect your developers to be able to be productive with both tools. Even if your developers are comfortable and experienced working in both (which will be highly unlikely), the difference in workflows means that switching frequently between the two will lead to some significant inefficiencies in progress.

As I just mentioned, Flex has no timeline. It has no drawing tools. It doesn't even have layers (I think they could have given us layers, just to help organize items in design view of the IDE, but they didn't). To really use Flex properly requires fluent switching between code and design view. Sure, you have all the same visual richness as in Flash (such as those cool filters and blend modes and neat transitions), but you need to know ActionScript or the Flex framework pretty well to apply them through Flex. Harnessing Flex also requires a deep understanding of event flows, data structures, and things like custom namespaces. While Flash makes basic hacking around with ActionScript quite simple, getting under the hood in Flex really requires some advanced coding knowledge. This means all but the higher-level programmers of the current crop of Flash developers will have little interest in or comfort with the idea of migrating any development to Flex. This is, it is important to understand, separate from the question of whether or not these Flash developers will migrate to ActionScript 3.

Flash, on the other hand, has a timeline. It has drawing tools—great ones. It makes it easy to design great experiences through a graphical, rather than code-driven, interface. It invites experimentation with, rather than forcing immersion into, ActionScript and the creation of dynamic experiences. And, of course, it is still the most economical animation option available.

And fortunately for all of us, we have the choice. Flash and Flex are entirely different tools, designed for the creation of very different experiences. Don't fight it—exploit it. Use the tool that's right for you—and odds are, if you've bought this book, you've already decided that Flex is for you. And you are in good company.

One of the great benefits of Flex, beyond all the development advantages it brings, is the fact that other advanced programmers will accept it. For years, adoption of Flash Platform solutions was hindered because advanced programmers within existing organizations—particularly the Java, ColdFusion, and .NET guys—hated the Flash IDE. Nothing confuses a traditional programmer more than a timeline; it's like kryptonite to them.

This means that the Flash world, which has long suffered a shortage of advanced programmers, can now expect an influx of higher-level developers with more software development skills. If you are planning to staff up for a Flex project or are generally seeking Flex talent, you are no longer restricted to finding the most talented Flash ActionScript programmers. You can hire most any good web programmer, give him a copy of this book, and he's off!

And so, as Flex gains acceptance within the developer communities, the coding side of the Flash Platform is going to mature at a far more rapid rate than it has to date. And, as the visual and design experiences offered by the Flash authoring tool continue to wow and amaze, more and more creative types will be drawn to that tool, to blow out the possible experiences.

Summary

In this chapter, we dove right into the contributions of Flash technology to the amazing richness currently offered by the Web, and how Flex is adding to the sophistication and diversity of experiences enabled by Flash.

But, while it is easy for people like me to get carried away with the possibilities of Flash, and I have long been a fervent believer in the power of Flash Platform tools and what they have to contribute to the human experience of information, I recognize that they do not provide the proper solution to every problem. Indeed, you'll note I trace the origin of Web 2.0 to the Netflix ratings widget—a great example of Ajax.

In the next chapter, I will introduce you to the Rich Media Exchange (RMX), a social media network developed for the Adobe User Group communities, which is the subject of the case study for this book. Like the best of Web 2.0, the RMX integrates a variety of technologies, including Ajax, but the other authors and I make liberal use of Flex in the example application, and throughout the rest of this book, we will share the specific code, techniques, and lessons we learned in our development of this project.

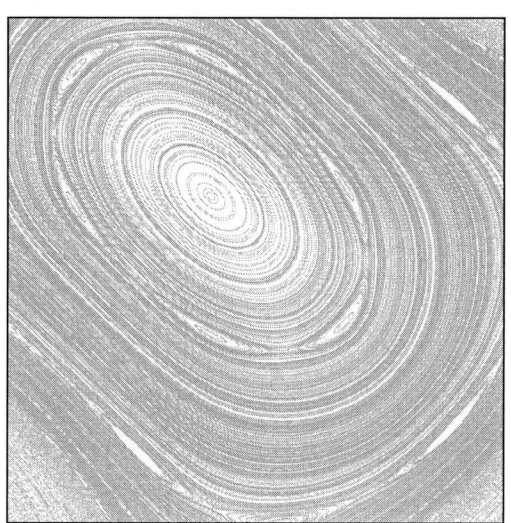

Chapter 2

DEFINING THE APPLICATION: INTRODUCING THE RMX

By R Blank

Social networking is the driving factor behind much investment and development in Web 2.0 applications. In the minds of many, Web 2.0 community is synonymous with MySpace or YouTube. But those are examples of communities emerging around the technologies: MySpace virtually owns generic social networking, and YouTube virtually owns generic video sharing. And that's how the Internet basically works for these types of businesses. You've heard it a million times before—there's only one Amazon, one eBay, one del.icio.us, one Blogger, and so forth. These are examples of companies having developed Internet-based communities basically from scratch, out of whole-cloth, fueled by innovative and well-timed use of unique technology. And they have each come to dominate their respective markets to the point where the #2 player in each space is not even playing the same game.

Of course, social networking did not start with Web 2.0, or even Web 1.0. Social networking has been a key attribute of humanity for all recordable history. And just like papyrus, Arabic numerals, the printing press, the telephone, the fax machine, and Web 1.0 before it, Web 2.0 is now providing a new set of tools to power these human networks.

So, while I am excited by the innovation represented by the Web 2.0 dot-coms, I am much more excited about what these Web 2.0 innovations mean for everyone else. Put another way, I don't think we should be as interested in building another YouTube, as much as we should be concerned with how to exploit the products and techniques innovated and marketed by YouTube (as well as MySpace, Netflix, Digg, and others) for the benefit of existing businesses, organizations, groups, and communities. There will likely be only one YouTube, but YouTube-like features will create tremendous value for countless organizations around the world.

In this chapter, I introduce the Rich Media Exchange (RMX), a social media network designed specifically for the Adobe User Group (AUG) community that is the subject of this book. The RMX is a case study in consciously applying and sculpting Web 2.0 innovations for the improvement and benefit of existing, terrestrial (or IRL, if you prefer) communities. Because applications only make sense in the context in which they are used, in order to understand how we built the RMX, it is important to describe what it is, how it emerged, and what purposes it specifically serves.

The amazing Adobe communities

I moved to Los Angeles in 2000 and became a freelancer in 2001. In any city, having a network of friends, colleagues, and associates is important; in Los Angeles, the most widely distributed metropolis in North America, it is vital. In part because of this, Los Angeles is home to many professional groups and societies, but as I struggled to attempt to build my career as a Flash developer, I lamented the lack of a community for what I did. Without a personal network, and with no directly relevant professional groups, I felt my career suffer.

Through the work I had done prior to becoming a freelancer, creating and marketing Flix and other tools with Wildform, I knew of the Macromedia User Group program—now the Adobe User Group, or AUG, program. Anyone familiar with the Adobe developer communities knows that many of the products in Adobe's line generate tremendous enthusiasm and excitement among the direct users of those tools, from Flash and ColdFusion to After Effects and Acrobat. This enthusiasm has led to the creation of hundreds of AUG communities around the world, formally recognized by Adobe.

AUGs can vary in size and activity from quite small and informal (five like-minded professionals meeting monthly), to much larger in membership and scope, like Flash in TO (FiTO), a large and relatively old Flash-based group in Toronto with regular meeting attendance north of 100. Whatever their size, most AUGs provide a crucial role in the Adobe world: they help developers learn, network, and find employment, they help employers find talent, and they help Adobe communicate directly with the most fervent users of their technology—a cycle that benefits developers, businesses, Adobe, and hundreds of millions of end users globally who are spending an increasing amount of their days experiencing content through Adobe-powered interfaces.

To find the AUG nearest you, visit www.adobe.com/go/usergroups.

I have long been a believer in the power of communities as a way to organize and channel the efforts of individuals to create resources that benefit large numbers of people. I knew that having an active group in Los Angeles would help my career, as well as those of my friends and colleagues, and could even serve as a force encouraging adoption of Flash, creating more work opportunities for developers. I believed that the lack of such a group contributed to the lack of focus and direction of Flash-related work in Los Angeles, the entertainment capital of the world, and the respect, or lack thereof, that we received as a regional industry. So, I guess more than anything, I felt the largest city in the United States just *needed* a Flash group.

I started the Los Angeles Flash User Group, LA Flash, in March 2003. Our early meetings averaged about 25 attendees and had a very personal feeling. Since then, benefiting from our location in a city with the resources of LA, we've grown to host three separate user groups, each meeting monthly (one meets online through Acrobat Connect), with over 3,000 registered members.

While many AUGs provide a major foundation in the establishment and support of local and regional developer networks, one drawback of AUGs is that, by definition, they meet at most 12 times a year. For the remaining 344 days in the year, the valuable platform that AUGs provide is largely dormant.

Beyond formal recognition and listing by Adobe, as well as sponsorships in the form of software and other raffle items, most AUGs operate with no real financial support or even revenue. Most AUGs are the result of the pro bono efforts of one or a few key motivated individuals. So little time or resources exist to invest in expanding the AUG platform; in the case of some AUGs, even hosting costs to maintain a basic web site with an accurate event calendar (a requirement of the AUG program) can be an issue. Some companies have provided free hosting for AUGs over the years, but not the actual web sites. Of course, each group maintains a site, but almost all are the result of the efforts of a motivated AUG member donating spare time. More frequently than not, the result is a minimally functional site, with a basic forum or mailing list.

For years at LA Flash, I experienced the same frustration. The design mission of the early LA Flash site was "make it as easy as possible for me to manage," so it was a simple HTML site that a couple others and I managed through Contribute. It served only to announce upcoming meetings and archive information about past meetings. It was, in a word, lame.

Eventually, we added a vBulletin installation, providing a community forum. Gradually, the traffic and activity on our site increased. It turned out that people in our community were just waiting for a way to network and communicate outside of our normal meetings. Over time, the forums—not our front page—became the default source of information, the place to check for all up-to-date information and what the rest of the community was up to.

The idea for the RMX is born

Then, in March 2006, Chris and Omar rebuilt the LA Flash site, providing a Drupal installation customized to the specific needs of our community, with an event calendar, blog, even a searchable index of our Acrobat Connect archives of our meetings. And suddenly we realized just how much our existing membership was waiting for a platform to express themselves more fluently online—to create a vibrant online, always-accessible component to our existing real-life community. After launching that site, Ed Sullivan, manager of the Adobe User Group program, told us, "You finally have a site as good as your group."

It quickly became apparent that a resource such as the web site we had just launched for our own group would add tremendous value to other AUGs around the world. When beginning to consider how to remedy this situation, and while meeting with other Adobe User Group managers at the annual Community Summit at Adobe in San Jose, it became very clear that most individual AUG members have no sense of the broader AUG network—a fact that limits the effect the AUGs can have and the power and value that the network brings to each of its members.

In this context, Shawn Pucknell (the founding manager of FiTO, and later FITC, one the largest and most respected Flash and rich media conferences) and I discussed how groups could benefit from an offering of community-centric web sites that would be designed to complement the needs of AUGs, and to cross-pollinate AUGs from around the world by linking members and information across the network of AUG sites. Thus, the idea for the Rich Media Exchange, or RMX, was born—an out-of-the-box community platform, built almost exclusively with Adobe technologies, with features aimed specifically at meeting the needs of AUGs, and with free hosting. The Rich Media Exchange would be a joint venture between the Rich Media Institute, the digital media training business I developed out of my work with LA Flash, and FITC, the digital media conference and event business Shawn developed out of his work with FiTO.

While working through plans to launch the Rich Media Exchange, Almer/Blank (my development agency) began work on a licensable video-sharing network, called FlexTube.tv. We realized that we should integrate those key FlexTube.tv features into the Rich Media Exchange.

Throughout a good chunk of time spanning 2006–2007, we worked on several revisions of the idea and then the actual software. This book is a study of many of the technical issues we encountered during our development of a social media network using Flex for much of the interface development, both of the public web site and the administration control panel required to manage the application.

Defining the goals and functionality

The first step of developing any application is to define the functional requirements. **Functional requirements** always begin with a goal or set of goals: what is this application actually supposed to accomplish?

Both Shawn and I have seen firsthand how energized developer communities can benefit entire regions, and the RMX is designed to facilitate that process and expand the reach of AUGs beyond the days they actually meet and the cities in which they meet. The Rich Media Exchange is an example of how this new generation of Web 2.0 community tools can add tremendous value to existing real-life communities of all types, and it is an example of Adobe developers using Adobe tools to create an Adobe-powered platform for the benefit of the Adobe communities.

The main goal of the RMX is to provide a powerful web-based community platform for the benefit of user groups, with two subgoals:

1. Enable user group members to communicate easily online.
2. Encourage cross-pollination between user groups around the world.

Of course, just as each type of community is unique and serves different users and purposes, each community will have to figure out how to harness these new features for its members. Determining the precise functionality required for your community will determine whether or not it is adopted by your members and how successfully they can express themselves online for the purposes of the community with those tools.

This is, of course, a vital part of any software development project—determining the actual needs of your users and ensuring the applications will be adopted. But, as the world of web-based applications really begins to increase in power, many are tempted to skip this process and copy what has been successful elsewhere, without considering the crucial aspect of how to customize what's been successful elsewhere.

To develop a useful and comprehensive set of functional requirements requires the input of people who deeply understand the target market and the ways in which the intended users will most frequently use the application. One of the main lessons I took from developing the IKEA PAX Wardrobe planner was the number of weeks that we spent in planning with sales floor staff, because they—more than I or the other designers and developers, more than IKEA management—understood exactly how the configuration system needed to function in order to be successful.

Fortunately, in this case, the developers—the AUG managers among them—were the target market. We were in a relatively unique position in application development that the developer is also the user. From our experiences with LA Flash and FiTO, we understood user groups to serve as a platform for three key services:

1. Education
2. Networking
3. Employment

So, the core features we planned for the RMX were designed to enable these same services.

Understanding the network

Before you dive into examining some of the major features of the RMX, you need to understand the two key factors that helped determine the basic architectural requirements of the application: it needed to be an independent application at an independent URL, and it had to have a flexible feature set. Let's examine these factors now.

Independent application at an independent URL

A key requirement of maintaining status as an AUG is that the AUG's web site be available at its own URL. This means that, from the beginning, the RMX had to be conceived as a community of independent web sites, rather than something more like MySpace, where all members and groups exist in the same application on the same domain.

Even though we understand the need and benefit of maintaining the independence of each user group web site, we also believed in one of our initial goals of facilitating cross-pollination across groups. So we needed to define a solution that balanced the needs of the independent operators and the network that integrates them. At the same time, we wanted to define a solution that would make it easy for individuals to join multiple AUGs. Los Angeles may be a bit unusual in that there are three Flash Platform–related user groups to choose from. But it is not at all unique in having multiple AUGs operating in the same city, so enabling members to join additional AUGs with ease would benefit both the members and the groups.

The two important elements of any social media network are the membership and the content they produce; the nature of content and membership on the RMX is each affected in different ways to support this balance between the member, group, and network.

Content on the RMX is generated on an individual site of the network, so a member of LA Flash sharing a video will do so through LAFlash.org. But Shawn might really like the content being generated at LA Flash and thus choose to syndicate it to his site for the benefit of his FiTO user group. At the same time, Adobe might have an important presentation or announcement that it wishes to share with the entire community, which would be shared across the entire network. Thus, content on the RMX needed to be syndicatable. The details of which users generate which types of content, and where that content is distributed, can be seen in Figure 2-1.

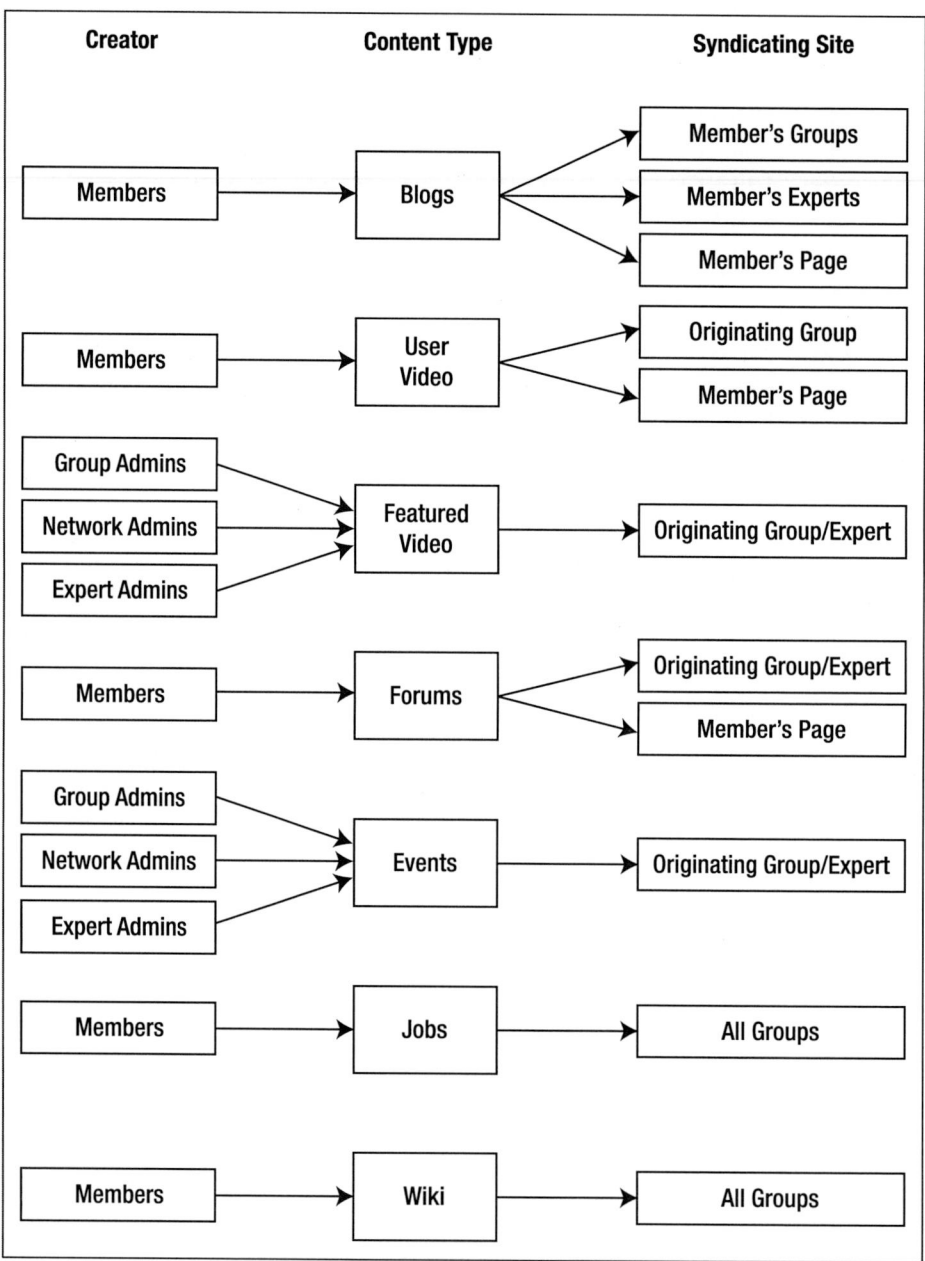

Figure 2-1. Content flow on the RMX from generation to distribution

To support access to the content and the groups that generate it, **membership** is, in essence, a subscription. When one joins an AUG on the RMX, one is actually joining the RMX and subscribing to that AUG. Subscription determines communication preferences (that is, which user groups have permission to contact a particular user via e-mail, and on which forums that user has permission to post), and custom content display (that is, which content a user sees when on the network). You can see an overview of network user permissions in Figure 2-2.

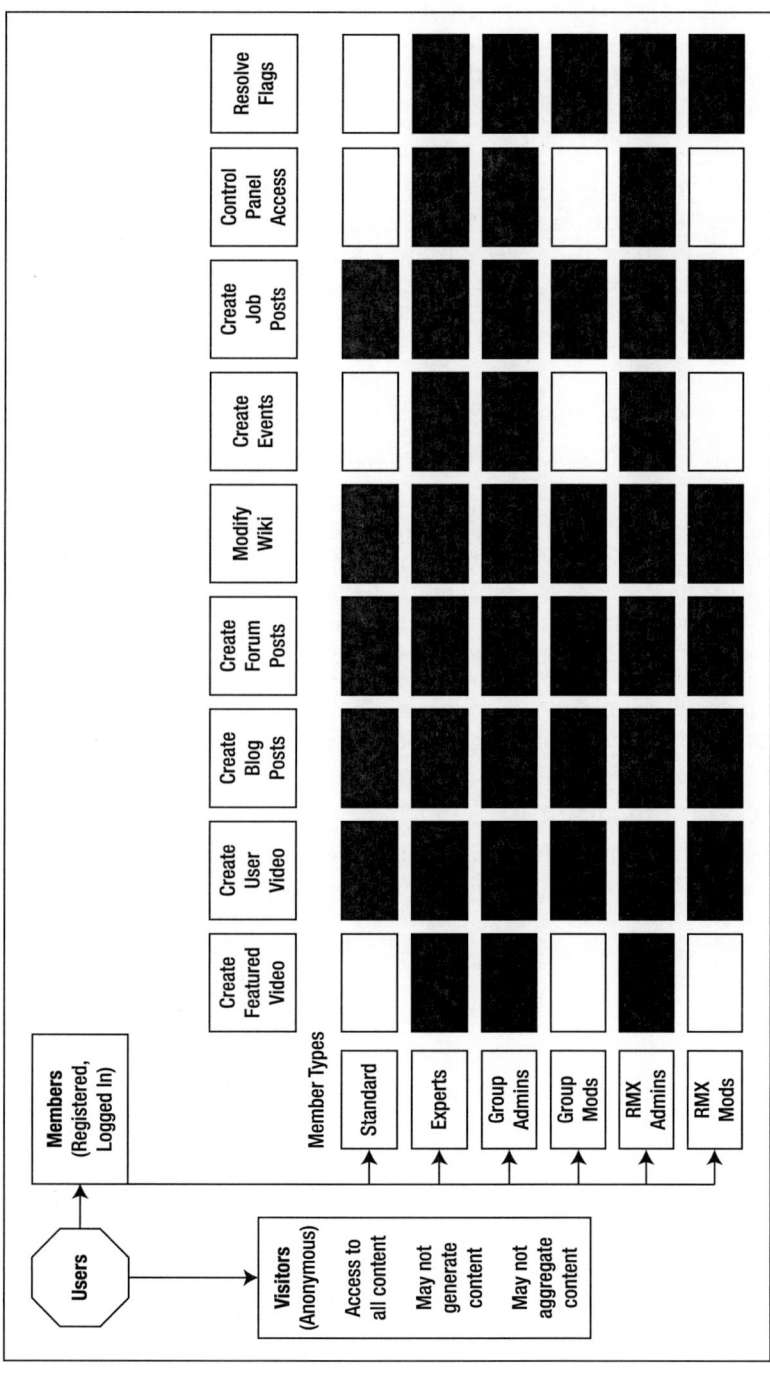

Figure 2-2. RMX users and their powers

Flexible feature set

The second factor with important ramifications on the structure of the RMX is that many of the larger and more successful AUGs do have some type of sponsorship to help offset the costs of hosting their web sites—for instance, a forum sponsorship that entitles the sponsor to place his logo on each forum page. So, to allow the manager of that group to join the RMX (for instance, to add video-sharing capabilities to the existing community forums web site), we needed to provide a way for that AUG to do so piecemeal—that is, to enable only those features the AUG desired and integrate the selected portions of the RMX into the AUG's existing web site.

So, as you examine the key features of the RMX in the upcoming text, keep in mind that **syndication** and **subscription** form the basic dynamic of the user experience of the Rich Media Exchange and provide the context for all features that are enabled on the network; and those features are enabled, by and large, on a case-by-case basis for each member group at its own URL.

Core features

Now let's look at the key features that make the RMX a killer Web 2.0 application for its market.

Event calendar

The main function of any AUG web site is to inform the community of upcoming events. So an event calendar is the most essential feature for the user groups. Since some AUGs also webcast their meetings using Acrobat Connect (and some meetings are held entirely online), the event calendar must have the ability to convey information for both physical and online events, as well as provide an optional RSVP system for both the actual and online meetings.

The event calendar should also include a convenient archiving system so that previous meetings, as well as the Connect archives, are automatically indexed and easily searchable.

Membership communication

Next to the ability to post upcoming event information is the ability to promote those events to membership. Sending e-mail to members is the most important function of a communications platform to a user group manager (UGM), and the RMX must make it easy to do so. At the same time, in order to comply with netiquette and antispam legislation, it is important to allow members to unsubscribe from such communications.

Forums

Forums are an essential component of online AUG communities, because they are the basic platform enabling members to easily communicate with each other. Forums enable the many-to-many communication that helps answer basic questions, helps people connect, and creates vibrant, interesting threads on random topics. As I mentioned, the vBulletin forums that we launched at LA Flash in 2004 contributed greatly to the growth and evolution of our group.

Forum topics are of two general types: technology-related and region-related. Before the RMX, LA Flash and FiTO hosted separate forums. While much of the content generated by each group would not be of interest to members of the other (for instance, upcoming LA events have little relevance to a Canadian), much of the content—especially posts and questions about Flash and ActionScript—is relevant to both groups. So, the forums are designed to be shared. For instance, when I create the LA

Flash group, I would want the LA Flash forums on the RMX to include the Flash and ActionScript help forums common to the network—the same ones to which FiTO's membership contributes. On the other hand, I might want an LA-based ColdFusion group to share the LA Flash events forum, since both groups are in the same region.

Blogs

Before YouTube came along, blogs were all the rage; the feature everyone expected of a sophisticated community was a blog. The main problem with blogs, of course, is that the vast majority of them die from inactivity.

Like forums, blogs allow members to easily communicate with others. Unlike forums, they do not facilitate the same easy back-and-forth—it's much more a unidirectional medium, even when comments are enabled on posts. Blogs are a place to spout off, be opinionated, be funny, contribute, and generate a long-term archive of content in a way that doesn't feel altogether appropriate for a forum. So, blogs are a feature that many AUGs want.

While there are those insane individuals who manage to maintain active blogs on their own, most of us who have something to say don't necessarily have *enough* to say to fill an entire blog; perhaps we can pull off an interesting post each week or each month. Taken individually, then, those blogs are not particularly interesting or of high value. But by aggregating them into larger communities, the aggregated blogs derive their significant value from the partial contributions of the individual members.

To improve the distribution of content across the network, we integrated a "blog this" function on most other content types. For instance, if I see a video, another blog post, an upcoming event, or a forum thread that particularly engages me, I may click blog this and generate a post on my personal blog, with a link to that content and my comments about it. In this way, the content on the network is more widely distributed, and indeed leads in turn to the generation of more content on the network.

On the RMX, LA Flash does not have a blog—the members of LA Flash have blogs. So, if I'm an infrequent blogger, and no one checks my blog, how would others on the RMX find my blog posts? This feeds into the next issue, front pages.

Front pages

Every web site needs a front page, of course, and the front page of an RMX partner group site should reflect the dynamic content-producing nature of the communities they serve and represent—that's what makes any social network exciting.

Front pages of communities need to update constantly, or else they appear stale. The front page of an RMX partner group is an opportunity to present the most important and highest quality information immediately to visitors, both regular members and anonymous guests. From my experience running LA Flash, I knew this consisted largely of two items: calendar events and blog posts. That is, our front page functions best and provides the highest-quality experience to our members when it delivers information on upcoming events and good blog posts from members of our community. So, admin-level users may promote any event to the front page and make it sticky (so it remains there until the stickiness is removed), and they may give certain of their member bloggers front page posting rights so they can contribute to the main community landing.

In addition, we provide gutters with the ability to link to RSS feeds so that the group front page may include more customized and frequently updated information—for instance, a list of the most recent forum posts or the MXNA feed (the legacy-named Macromedia XML News Aggregator).

Video network

Video sharing, a field now dominated almost exclusively by Flash Platform technologies, has become a vital feature of contemporary online communities. Providing a platform for this functionality was of high priority to us, and we accomplished it by integrating FlexTube.tv into the RMX. FlexTube.tv has accommodations for two types of video experiences: featured video and user video. The difference is more than semantic and reflects the variety of video experiences that Flash currently enables online.

Featured video is akin to the TV experience, with a playlist of content, each playing in order, and is designed for higher-quality content filtered through an editorial process. **User video** is the YouTube-style of video sharing, with each video residing on a unique URL, and search functionality to navigate the vast array of clips that are generated.

As partner admins may promote individual blog posts to the front page, so may admins promote particularly good user video to featured video. And, through syndication, RMX admins may push certain high-quality content out to the featured networks of member groups.

Jobs board

Working with Adobe technologies requires a set of specialized and increasingly valuable skills. Here in Los Angeles, as the amount of work done in Flash, and especially Flash video, has exploded, so has the traffic on our jobs board. Until LA Flash joined the RMX, the jobs board was just a forum on our site on which any member could post employment and contract opportunities for Flash designers and developers. Now, we had an opportunity to build a jobs board system from scratch to meet more of the specific needs of our communities.

The problem with trying to find Adobe talent on a general jobs board, like Monster, is the lack of specificity. Those of us in the industry know that a junior-level Flash animator is quite different from a senior-level Flash ActionScripter, but on no general-purpose jobs board is that a readily discernible fact; the two totally different talent prospects would be returned on a search for "Flash." Again, since we focused on a specific type of talent, we could customize the job postings to the specific needs of our industry.

In this case, that meant applying a much finer set of tags and modifiers to describe the work involved—for instance, choosing required product knowledge (such as "must know Flash and Photoshop") as well as specific functions and skill levels within those products (for instance, "production-level designer" or "coding and architecture").

The RMX jobs board was also designed in recognition of the fact that a huge amount of the work in our industry is conducted on a contract or freelance basis, so the board became equally valuable as a place to find employment and freelance opportunities. And, of course, as with any jobs board, we also needed to index opportunities by location, making it easy to find regionally relevant positions.

Social media functionality

Although it is not a stand-alone feature, the set of features that we will call "social media functionality" (mostly because I hate saying "Web 2.0 feature set") is an important consideration for information architecture. In this I include features like tagging, commenting, rating, sharing, and RSS feed generation—the features that make content searchable, that enable viewer participation in and feedback of the content, and that enable superior content to bubble up in the network.

Learning how to plan and develop these features is important because they are a basic expectation of any online community or social media application. On the RMX, they play a key role in fostering the intergroup content sharing described previously.

Tagging

Tagging is vital to all types of information—whether or not it is user generated, and whether or not it exists as part of a Web 2.0 community or a financial firm's internal databases. There are two general methods applied to describe, or tag, content: top-down and bottom-up.

Top-down tagging is otherwise known as **taxonomy**. This means that when you tag content, you are tagging the content with predefined tags that exist in the system. **Bottom-up tagging** is known as **folksonomy**, and it allows members of communities to create tags as they see fit.

There are also two times at which tags may be applied: at the moment of creation and on an ongoing basis. That is, I might tag a video with a certain keyword when I upload the video into the network. But then Omar might watch that video two days later and think of another keyword that should be applied to the content to improve its searchability and indexability in the system. For the lack of better terms, we call these **creator tagging** and **user tagging**.

Because tagging is a content-specific technique, and content on the RMX is of different types (for instance, a video is materially different from a job posting), we apply tagging in different ways to different types of content. For instance, jobs must be tagged from a predefined list—ensuring posts are indexed according to a rigid, established, and easily searchable set of tags—so we apply a network-wide jobs taxonomy to be used when creating and searching for job postings.

However, applying taxonomic standards to all content on the system would be far too constricting, as it would force all activity on the network to be indexed and searched on terms defined by the RMX. And, when users inevitably request the creation of new tags in the taxonomy, it would create additional work for the RMX admins. So, for content such as video and blog posts, we allow folksonomic naming, or tagging with any word you want.

Because of the amount of content moderation controls required to support it, we do not currently enable user tagging on the RMX, only creator tagging. But, because video is natively the least searchable of all current media types, we plan to support time-code-based user tagging of video in the near future.

Commenting

Commenting on content is important, because it ensures that any type of content, from a blog post to a shared video, does not exist in a purely one-to-many relationship; other members may participate in the content by commenting on it, thus generating further comments.

There are two types of comments, threaded and unthreaded. **Threaded comments** allow another member to reply to an individual comment in the comment chain, thus generating multiple threads of comments in the same comment chain. **Unthreaded comments** exist in a single-tier chronological list. While it may seem that threaded comments are superior, in fact both types have their advantages and disadvantages. Threaded comments are better at enabling conversations, a back and forth dialog within the comment chain. However, while threaded comments may allow blog readers to participate in a conversation more effectively than with unthreaded comments, others (myself included) often feel that threaded comments are harder to read and overall less enjoyable to participate in.

In my opinion, threaded comments are an attempt to squeeze forum-like functionality into a simple text posting feature, and if you want to enable a more fluid and fluent dialog, you do so through actual forums. This is why we have chosen not to enable threaded comments on the RMX.

Rating

Ratings are an immensely useful system for allowing the intelligence of the network to filter good content up and bad content down. As with taxonomic tagging, the system of ratings measurement is standard across the network.

Since all content is created by somebody, ratings also enable another important feature of Web 2.0 communities: reputation. Content ratings allow us to make certain judgments on the value, or "reputation," of the creator. It is actually quite difficult to plan precisely how you will harness the information generated by content rating, since you need an active network of content being rated to know what algorithms will create reputations that are valuable to the network.

In some communities, different content is rated differently. For instance, video may be rated on a scale of five stars, whereas threads may be rated on a Boolean system of recommended/unrecommended. In order to create a common and easily understood rating system on the RMX, we have applied the same Netflix-standardized five-star rating scale to all content, from posted video, to forum threads, to opinions of other members on the network.

Sharing

Sharing is actually quite a general term, which encompasses three separate functions: permalinking, embedding, and send-to-friend.

Permalinking is a method that ensures content generated on the network will be permanently available at a stable URL. Permalinking is the basis for all sharing, because users must rely on the content continuing to exist at a fixed location in order to be able to share that content with anyone else. Permalinking also ensures that content may be bookmarked by users and indexed by engines like Google. The storage and delivery of all information must take permalinking into account.

Embedding is really most relevant for video. Services like YouTube have made video embedding commonplace on the Internet. It entails the creation of a small, stand-alone player that may access your video content. The player is shared with an easily copyable <embed> tag, which references a specific video through permalinking so embedded players do not die. In addition to playing a shared video, the embedded player links to the content so viewers may learn more about it or participate in it through commenting, rating, or sending it to others.

Send-to-friend represents the ability to generate an e-mail to friends, not necessarily members of the same community, with a link to access specific content that is relevant to those friends. Other than specific validation techniques and the integration with an e-mail server, this really is no more complicated than a basic form, but is a key element in viral communication.

Flagging and moderation

Moderation is the process of approving or removing content and users from a network. It is, of course, a vital function for eliminating spam, and maintaining community focus and decency standards. On some sites, administrator moderation is required in order for generated content to be made public, as opposed to having your video or blog post published instantly. But sites that require initial moderator approval are very restricted in their growth, essentially discourage the creation of content, and often feel boring and stale in comparison to other sites with immediate posting.

The alternative to initial moderator approval is, as I mentioned, to make user-generated content public immediately. But how do you control the quality or decency of content that can be generated in massive amounts at any time of day?

Just like rating is a way to exploit the natural user interaction with content to help make it easier for other users to find better content, flagging is a way to exploit the user interaction with content to help moderators find the content and users that should be removed. In effect, you distribute the moderation function across your viewership: if a viewer finds anything to flag (mostly for reasons of spam, indecency, or copyright violation), he may do so immediately, triggering an e-mail to moderators and entering the content into the moderation queue in the control panel. Moderators can choose whether to respond to each flag or set a minimum number of flags (say five) that would trigger active moderation. Either way, flagging is a great way to maintain high-quality content while permitting the immediate gratification of instant content creation.

RSS feed generation

The RMX, like most contemporary online communities, is really just a content creation, management, and delivery system. Because of the nature of the Web, the content is most readily and commonly accessed through the web sites on the RMX. However, content is content, and experiencing it should not necessarily be limited to a web site. Many content-heavy web sites now make their content accessible through something called RSS.

RSS, which stands for Really Simple Syndication, is just a dynamically or periodically updated XML file of the content on your application. Because the XML file conforms to an existing RSS standard (there are actually a few, and it is possible to be compatible with all of them in the same feed), it can be consumed by a wide variety of RSS reading applications, including Firefox and Safari. Indeed, the practice known as podcasting involves a customized RSS feed that includes a link to an MP3 file that your podcasting playing software (such as iTunes) will automatically download. RSS is a **pull technology**, meaning updates to the feed aren't pushed to users; instead, the users' RSS reader will periodically ping the feed to see if there are updates.

Applying an RSS scheme to your application is actually quite simple. Every page on the RMX essentially represents a filtered search on the RMX content library—for instance, the LA Flash front page is just a query of the most recently updated events and promoted blog posts. Just as the results from that search can be rendered into a web page, so can they be rendered into an XML file. This feature is integrated into the Drupal content management system that we employed on the RMX.

RSS feeds are great for two reasons. First, they keep your members engaged in your community even when they are not actively logged on to the site. And second, they make any content on your site easily syndicatable to other portions of your site. For instance, if I want to include a list of the most recent forum posts on my front page, I can include an RSS reader module in my front page to consume that

RSS feed from my forums. Because so much of the information architecture of the Rich Media Exchange depends on syndication, RSS is a vital component of our application.

Advertising

To provide an application and service such as the RMX to AUGs and their members for no charge, we must have advertising to help support the network. The RMX is a desirable advertising platform precisely because it is so specialized—it represents an effective way to communicate to a very targeted market.

The RMX advertising system is network-wide; individual partner AUGs do not have control over the advertising on their sites, although there are accommodations for them to supplement their sites with additional advertising that they control. This means that we at the RMX control the campaigns that are distributed on the network.

Even though the RMX as a whole represents a niche target market, delivering all ad campaigns to all members across all groups, without regard to location or product focus, would be a massive lost opportunity. The advertising gains value to both the advertiser and the member viewing the ad, if the ad itself is relevant.

The way we determine relevance of advertising on the RMX is similar to how we index job opportunities: by product focus and region. On the jobs board, the information is tagged for on-demand searches; for instance, when I am ready, I will search the system for Flash coding jobs in Los Angeles. For the advertising system, that information exchange has to happen silently and invisibly. So, we tag each page on the network with information on the products covered by the group, the nature of the membership (for instance, in Los Angeles, much of our membership consists of freelancers), and of course, the zip code of the group's meeting location. In this way, we can sell much more targeted campaigns to sponsors and advertisers, and provide relevant sponsor-driven information to our membership.

The tools for the task

With the basic functional requirements in hand, I could move on to describing how we selected the key tools for developing and deploying the RMX. Before defining the tools, I should add one additional requirement to the set of functional requirements: use free options when possible. As a self-funded organization providing a free service, economics matter. And, fortunately, for many of the required components of an application like this—particularly on the server side—free options not only exist, but are also often robust and well-featured.

A word on GNU GPL

www.gnu.org/copyleft/gpl.html

As I walk you through the software we used in developing and deploying the RMX, you will note how many applications we employ that are free and open source. Almost all of these are released under the GNU General Public License (GPL), which basically means that it can be used for free for any purpose, as long as any enhancements and customizations you make are contributed back to the community. GNU is a nonprofit organization created in 1984 (GNU is a classic geek recursive acronym, Gnu is Not Unix) with the goal of developing an open source web-system alternative to Unix. Since then, the GPL licensing structure GNU developed has been applied to numerous technologies.

It is really difficult to overstate the significance the open source movement has had on the quality of the Internet; it really is remarkable how powerful and useful open source applications have become, with no licensing fees, and frequently massive community support and development.

Application platform

There are several important aspects to the operation of the RMX application platform, from the technologies used to build the application interfaces to the technologies providing the platform to run the application. Here is a broad overview of those we selected to power the RMX. While Flex is a core component of the application, and the central topic of this book, you will note how many other technologies are involved in delivering an application like this.

Flash and Ajax

Flash and Ajax provide the core interface technologies on the RMX. Every page on the network is generated using both technologies. As I underscored in Chapter 1, Flash and Ajax complement each other quite nicely in the Web 2.0 world, and established techniques exist for integrating them. As you proceed through this book and read about specific features, you will discover how these technologies cooperate to deliver tremendous experiences.

LAMP

`http://en.wikipedia.org/wiki/LAMP_(software_bundle)`

LAMP, sometimes known as the **LAMP stack**, is an acronym for Linux, Apache, MySQL, and PHP (sometimes LAMP is considered to include Perl and Python in addition to PHP, but not in the case of the RMX)—the most popular free software options that serve as the platform for the servers that deliver rich Internet applications. They are grouped together under the LAMP acronym because they are used so frequently in conjunction with each other, as they are free, open source, community supported, and powerful. Their popularity is fueled by the cost, the fact that the components are frequently bundled with Linux installations, and are also readily available on most web hosting companies. Because these are very common technologies, I will only address them briefly.

Linux

`www.linux.org`

Linux is the operating system running on the server. With a kernel originally developed by Linus Torvalds, Linux has been released under GNU GPL. Linux has emerged as the open source alternative to Unix that GNU originally envisioned, and while Linux has perhaps not (yet) seen the level of success on consumer desktops many once hoped for, it has become a very popular alternative to other server operating systems, including Windows and a variety of Unix flavors.

Apache

`http://httpd.apache.org/`

Apache is shorthand for the Apache HTTP Web Server, one of many projects hosted by the Apache organization and licensed under GNU GPL. Apache has been by far the most commonly used HTTP server (the software that delivers content over HTTP from your server to users' web browsers) for over 10 years.

MySQL

`www.mysql.com`

MySQL is the world's most popular open source database, and like Linux and Apache, it is available under GNU GPL. MySQL is popular because of its license, its power, and its ease of use.

PHP

`www.php.net`

PHP is an easy-to-use scripting language that can be easily inserted into HTML, which is readily understood by web browsers. It provides the middleware communication for communicating between the MySQL data source and the interfaces—essentially, it makes HTML dynamic. Like the other components of LAMP, PHP is open source but is issued under a different license, the PHP license (`www.php.net/license`).

FlexTube.tv

`www.almerblank.com`

Although FlexTube.tv is not an open source product, Almer/Blank developed and owns it, so usage of it is free for our purposes. And, for the moment at least, open source (or even just licensable) solutions to power video-sharing networks do not exist. FlexTube.tv was developed by Almer/Blank as a licensable product to power a variety of video-based applications. Initially released as a "private label YouTube" enabling organizations to launch their own custom-branded video-sharing networks, FlexTube.tv has been customized for a wide variety of purposes, from traditional video-sharing networks, to real estate classifieds and internal delivery of corporate training and communications. FlexTube.tv provides the core video-sharing capabilities of RMX, as well as much of the Flex-powered interfaces to administer FlexTube.tv and Drupal content through the RMX control panel.

Drupal

`www.drupal.org`

Drupal is an increasingly popular open source content publication and management system released under GNU GPL. Drupal 4.5 was the central aspect of the community-centric LAFlash.org launched in March 2006, described earlier. Now in version 5, Drupal is free and community supported, and its architecture has evolved to support the various data webs required to natively support the syndication and subscription needs of the RMX (the pace of innovation in Web 2.0 communication standards is evident in the fact that these advanced data-sharing models were not present in Drupal 4.5). We use Drupal to power the blogs, forums, and event calendars in the RMX. Drupal, along with the FlexTube.tv application, provides the core content and membership structures of the RMX.

Not only is Drupal powerful, but it is also an incredibly easy way for Flex developers, especially those who may not have the time or skills to build a complete Web 2.0 content management system, to build and maintain cool applications while focusing their efforts on interface development.

FFMPEG

http://ffmpeg.mplayerhq.hu

Any Flash video application needs a video encoder. Any application like the RMX, which wants to support user video sharing, needs an encoder running on the server, automatically converting source video into files playable by the Flash Player. For this task, we used FFMPEG.

As I mentioned in Chapter 1, there are effectively three separate video codecs in Flash: Sorenson Spark (Flash 7), On2 VP6 (Flash 8), and H.264 (Flash 9.0.6). FFMPEG is a collection of software libraries for transcoding media. FFMPEG is free software, and it can encode to Spark and to H.264. The only server-based video encoder that encodes to VP6 is the Flix Engine from On2 (the server version of the same Flix encoder you use on your desktop), which has an annual, per-server licensing cost of just under $4,000.

Since we are self-funded, and since the Flash Player now supports H.264, we made the decision to use FFMPEG from the start, at first supporting Flash 7 FLV output, and then migrating to H.264 output once we felt a sufficient number of viewers had the newest Flash Player.

OpenAds

www.openads.org

Formerly spread across three different projects, phpAdsNew, phpPgAds, and Max Media Manager, OpenAds represents a consolidation of the features of all three products in an open source ad campaign management and delivery solution that runs under Windows, Linux, and Mac server environments and is available under GNU GPL.

Banner advertising is obviously a vital component of so many web-based experiences and businesses. To deploy ads on a site that you control, there are three basic options:

1. Open an account with a firm like 24/7 or Accipiter or DoubleClick.
2. Consume Google AdWords.
3. DIY—do it yourself.

Option 1 can be quite expensive; you can figure on at least $1,000/month. And DoubleClick would require a lot more. Option 1 only begins to make sense when you have an established high level of traffic volume and advertising revenue. Option 2, on the other hand, is quite limiting. While AdWords is a great way to get some advertising up on your site (and theoretically make some money), you have no control over what ads are delivered (it's amazing how inappropriate some ads that match the keyword "Flash" and "Flasher" can be!). And, of course, while you can try to style the ads somewhat, they are boring, ugly, text-based content.

What if you want to deliver nice campaigns—actual banners, not JS-driving HTML inserts—and you don't want to pay $1,000/month for the privilege? Well, you would certainly not be the first, which is why a robust and well-featured open source ad solution exists, enabling us to manage our network-wide advertising needs on the RMX. Of course, utilizing OpenAds does not preclude also using AdWords, or any other ad network we choose.

EdgeCast

www.edgecast.com

While you can run a web application off almost any type of server hosting, to provide high-quality performance under stressful traffic levels to a geographically distributed audience requires use of a content distribution network, or CDN. CDNs host servers at multiple locations and replicate your content to various servers within the network. When a user visits the RMX, the CDN will determine which server is the most efficient to deliver the content, distributing and accelerating the delivery process. For the RMX, we selected EdgeCast, a newly launched CDN, as our host.

AMFPHP

www.amfphp.org

AMFPHP is an RPC toolkit for PHP—meaning it provides a connection between PHP and Flash, Flex, Ajax, and XML-RPC. AMFPHP was the first open source remoting gateway, with support for various database types including MySQL, MS SQL, Oracle, and others. On the RMX, AMFPHP provides a gateway for calling PHP methods as if they were local. Packaged with a service browser for easy testing of your services before implementation and a code generation template, AMFPHP is one of the more popular open source remoting solutions for integrating a Flex front end with a MySQL/PHP back end.

Design and development tools

Delivering the application and creating it are, of course, two entirely different things. Just as the type of work constructed for the Flash Platform is so varied, so are the development workflows across our industry. For the process of creating the RMX, we employed Adobe design and image processing tools, as well as Flex Builder. We have also identified some useful tools for working with Flex.

Adobe Illustrator, Fireworks, and Flash

All designs for the RMX were completed in Illustrator. For so many years, one of the most frustrating aspects of working with client-side designers was their insistence on using Photoshop to design Flash projects. Flash is vector based and Photoshop is raster based; certainly, Flash has raster capabilities, and Photoshop can support vectors, but they are fundamentally different tools for fundamentally different purposes.

Admittedly, this gap has closed significantly—first, with the amazing visual expression enhancements in Flash 8, such as blends and filters, enabling more "Photoshop-like" effects, and now even more so in Adobe Creative Suite 3 with the amazing cross-tool workflow improvements.

Still, the best tool for designing Flex skins is Illustrator, because you can design fluently in the vectors that Flex will natively understand. Once you are ready to attempt a Flex application that doesn't look like a Flex application, a good place to start is to download and dissect the source skins for the components that come with the Flex framework, and start messing around.

For those assets that needed to be produced as bitmaps, rather than vectors, we employed Fireworks to create PNGs from the design files, which can be easily embedded or loaded into Flex applications. Of course, it is worth mentioning that Flash (which is of course highly compatible with Flex) can also be a great design and production tool for Flex applications.

Adobe Flex Builder

Although the Flex framework is free, as well as the ability to compile it via the MXML Compiler (using the free command-line compiler, `mxmlc.exe`, on Windows), the Flex Builder IDE is a very powerful environment for developing Flex applications. Built on the Eclipse IDE engine, Flex not only leverages the powerful features of the Eclipse environment, but also offers a lot of new features that ease the process of developing Flex applications. The Eclipse IDE engine was the perfect choice for the Flex Builder IDE. Built by the open source community, Eclipse offers a highly extensible application IDE that, when combined with other Eclipse plug-ins, can really streamline your development workflow (as you will note when I discuss Subversion later in the chapter). From custom class introspection to the awesome WYSIWYG design mode, Flex Builder is a must for any serious Flex development.

Flex-Ajax Bridge

`http://labs.adobe.com/wiki/index.php/Flex-Ajax_Bridge`

The Flex-Ajax Bridge (FABridge) is a small, unobtrusive code library that you can insert into an Adobe Flex application, a Flex component, or even an empty SWF file to expose it to scripting in the browser. It is designed to make the integration between Flex and Ajax (which I keep saying is so great) much simpler, providing a direct channel for your Flash and JavaScript to communicate freely.

OmniGraffle Professional

`www.omnigroup.com/applications/omnigraffle/`

Development of the RMX began in 2006, long before the release of CS3, with its radical improvements in Fireworks wireframing. While many developers have taken to wireframing their Flex applications directly in Flex (a perfectly acceptable workflow if you are comfortable doing that), I don't feel that is sufficiently flexible to allow for really rapid design of page layout and functionality.

My tool of choice for this task is OmniGraffle Professional. OmniGraffle is a diagramming application for Macintosh that is amazingly easy to use and very flexible. It comes with a few dozen stencils, including the two I use most—Basic and Software GUI—and makes it quite easy to author your own stencils. With support for multiple master canvases, it is relatively easy to wireframe an entire project—even a large one—in a single file, and then export those screens in almost any format you wish (well, not MXML—yet!).

Firefox plug-ins

Among the many reasons so many developers prefer using Firefox as their default browser is Firefox's support for plug-ins. Many useful tools and applications have been written as Firefox plug-ins, including several specifically useful to Flex developers.

Live HTTP Headers

`http://addons.mozilla.org/firefox/3829/`

When working with remoting, sometimes you must know the values being sent to your remoting services. The Firefox plug-in Live HTTP Headers allows you to watch easily what is being sent from your browser to the servers running the application you're developing, greatly helping with the process of debugging remoting service calls.

Web Developer Toolbar

http://addons.mozilla.org/firefox/60/

The Web Developer Toolbar for Firefox comes with a lot of tools that help make a web developer's life a whole lot easier. With options to edit CSS in real time to resizing or disabling/enabling various features of your browser, it's like the Swiss Army knife of browser tools.

Charles Web Debugging Proxy

www.xk72.com/charles/

Charles is an amazing, lightweight, and cross-platform HTTP proxy and monitor that can sniff out all HTTP communication from your computer. It is available as a stand-alone tool and includes a plug-in for Firefox. With it, you can see the quantity, timing, and specific details of each request and response. It is an amazing tool when trying to see how your application is performing. It is, in a word, indispensable when debugging back-end powered Flash interfaces.

Project management tools

Project management is a vital aspect of any operation of any type. Of course, the less sophisticated and comprehensive the development process, the less sophisticated and powerful your project management process needs to be.

Although I have considered myself a Flash application developer for some time, at some point in 2006, as my firm grew into larger and larger Flex-based web applications, we noticed that we crossed a line from "interactive development" to "software development," and we had to radically improve our management systems in light of that.

I specifically mention this here because I believe this is a process of maturation that many more firms developing for the Flash Platform will have to endure over the next few years. So here I will share some of the key tools we use in our project management process, why we have selected those, and what specific purposes they fill.

MS Project and Project Insight

http://office.microsoft.com/project
www.projectinsight.net

Like most Adobe developers (and Mac-based ones at that), I have a healthy skepticism in general for Microsoft products. But the MBA and business owner in me also has an amazing amount of respect for their Office suite, especially Excel, Word, and Project—all revamped in 2007. And now with souped-up Intel dual-core Macs and Parallels (with coherence mode), running the Windows version of Office has become practical even for us Mac users and an integral part of our development process. The aspect of Office that is most significant for the purposes of this book is Project.

Project is an amazing project management tool that, despite the variety of uses to which it is applied, was designed specifically for software development. As with tools like Word and Excel, most people use about 10% of its amazing functionality, but even at that basic level, it becomes very easy to plan tasks, dependencies between tasks, assignments of tasks, and load balancing of work, given task assignments and the work calendar. It makes it much easier to plan projects, monitor their progress, and know when delays and budget breakers are occurring as soon as they occur.

Project is great for planning projects, which is done up-front. But I don't appreciate its group features, platform dependency, or cost structure to use it for team-wide ongoing project management. I prefer a project management system that exposes task assignments directly to developers in an easy to access and update format from any web browser. For this reason, at Almer/Blank, we use a web-based project management system to monitor and maintain projects once they have launched.

It is true that there are free, web-based project management systems, but we have come to realize that the required functionality of a good and usable project management system (as opposed to, for example, bug tracking, which I discuss immediately in the following section) requires us to use paid software. On this one, the free options just don't cut it. So, we use a web-based ASP, Project Insight, for ongoing project management. With an Ajax-powered interface, a feature set modeled after MS Project, and compatibility with the standard Project formats (as well as many other great features, including a versioned file repository for each project), Project Insight makes it simple to import the projects I plan in Project into a format that is easily accessible and updatable by all of my developers.

Mantis

www.mantisbt.org

While we use Project Insight for top-level task management, it isn't suited to micro-level task management—the type of issues common in testing and debugging phases. Fortunately, there are several open source tools that do this well, including Mantis and Bugzilla. At Almer/Blank, we use Mantis.

Authored in PHP, and fully compatible with a LAMP environment (although it works with other databases and operating systems), Mantis is free, open source, and available under GNU GPL (which is refreshing for a project management tool with real value).

We originally adopted Mantis to manage precisely the QA phase of development. But we found its architecture so flexible and the application so easy to use that we have adopted it for purposes throughout the project life cycle. As well, while at Almer/Blank we do not expose Project Insight to clients, we have found Mantis provides a terrific method for logging planning issues and decisions, and exposing appropriate aspects of the development process to the clients. And of course, by using Mantis so much throughout the project, we have a large, dynamic, and searchable archive of the progress and decisions made on a project.

Subversion

http://subversion.tigris.org
www.hosted-projects.com

One of the aspects of our industry that has always amazed me is how lax so many agencies and development firms are about version control. I have witnessed so many occasions when correct versions were overwritten or incorrect ones deployed—all of which could be easily avoided by adopting a proper version management system.

The heavier-duty coders out there are probably laughing in agreement; to them, version management has long been a part of their lives. But, as with so much else, those developing for the Flash Platform are growing and learning, and version management is becoming a higher priority in the industry.

For version management, we use Subversion (SVN), released under an Apache/BSD-style open source license (http://subversion.tigris.org/license-1.html). SVN was developed as an open source version control system for replacing the popular CVS. For any project being developed by a team, SVN is a must. Lost source code and sharing code base problems are a thing of the past.

And, as an example of the wide variety of benefits accompanying Adobe's decision to run Flex Builder in Eclipse, you can install Subclipse, the SVN plug-in for Eclipse, to integrate powerful version control right into your normal workflow, with no additional tools.

Our SVN is hosted and operated by Hosted Projects. Why did we choose a free, open source solution and then decide to pay someone to host it? It is certainly possible to operate your own SVN repository. But it also involves a lot of additional responsibility. We've worked with many other firms who operate their own SVN, and then spend tons of hours maintaining it, and often experience problems anyway. We chose Hosted Projects, since, like many people, we do not want the responsibility of managing our own SVN installation—we have other things to do, like building huge Flex applications!

Summary

In this chapter, I introduced the RMX, placing it in the increasingly popular context of Web 2.0 application development, and describing the core functionality and data structures that power this network of Adobe developers.

With that basis, I provided an overview of the key software we used in developing, managing, and deploying the RMX, many of which we will reference at different points in this book.

With the fundamental requirements in hand, along with knowledge of the tools we are going to use to complete this project, I will next show you how we began planning the development of the RMX.

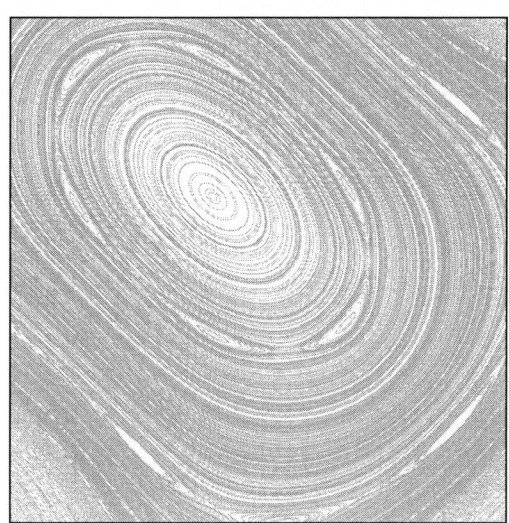

Chapter 3

PLANNING THE APPLICATION: BUILDING THE RMX

By R Blank

In this chapter, I describe the processing of planning development of the Rich Media Exchange. The goal here is twofold: first, to explore the process used for planning projects on the scope of the RMX, and then to explore some of the specific considerations we encountered in planning the RMX.

A note on complexity

Fred Brooks coined a law, known as **Brooks' law**, which reads "Oversimplifying outrageously . . . adding manpower to a late software project makes it later." Stated another way, "The bearing of a child takes nine months, no matter how many women are assigned." Although, to be fair, in some cases you can yield more than one child per woman per nine months.

Of course, this does not mean that it is optimal to assign fewer developers to a project. Rather, it is an indication of the complexity of software—developers, simply put, are not commodities. Software is of a degree of complexity that the time required to educate new development talent on the details of the application, the specification, and the existing design patterns comes at a cost so high as to create further delays instead of accelerating the completion.

For many years, while many viewed me as a "web designer" (ugh), I have considered myself to be an application developer. I have been working with Flash since 1999 and almost exclusively with the technology since 2001. In that time, I increasingly viewed the work that I did—whether it was a furniture planning system for IKEA, a medical device configuration tool for Medtronic, a video-based artificial cat to live on the Whiskas web site, or one of any number of other projects—as application development.

Of course, whether it was the client or the client's Java developers, few others outside the Flash world considered these activities as true application development. With Flex, an increasing number of individuals understand and accept that Flash is now the foundation for projects so complex and large in scope that it really is a software development platform. As the power of the Flash Platform continues to increase at a rocket pace, along with the number of uses to which the technology is applied, the scope of projects created with Flash-related technologies grows apace. And the work that I used to consider complex pales in the face of today's most dynamic applications, like the RMX.

This is not unique to Flash; the developer of Unreal Engine, a widely-used gaming engine, explains that his project is as complex as the operating systems of only a few years ago, and he expects to take four years to develop the next version. So, across a wide landscape, technologies have evolved to a point where their uses simply grow to exploit all the powers now available.

I mention this here because many ActionScripters are historically a unique breed. Many are self-taught, and ActionScript may well be their first language of any kind—although, again, this is less likely the definition of a Flex developer, unless the Flex developer has come from Flash. Indeed, many programmers in the Flash world may actually consider themselves designers who have picked up more code, although, admittedly, those are the least likely to dive into Flex. Even those on the higher-end of the Flash programming landscape, who may already be masters of other languages like Java and ColdFusion, are simply not used to projects of a scope like many of those now being pursued on the Flash Platform. Therefore, even if these ActionScripters consciously see themselves as software or application developers, most do not apply anything close to traditional software development models to their work. This includes coding architecture and techniques as well as project planning and management processes.

There isn't really any single feature in the RMX that's groundbreaking or patentable (at least, not yet). As I explained in Chapter 2, I feel the power of the RMX is its aggregation of a wide set of contemporary web application features and the customization of them for a specific market. When a good developer hears a client request a feature, more often than not, he will say, "Sure, I can do that." And that's likely true—the developer can do that. But, as the client continues to request additional features, the tendency of most developers is to examine them on an individual basis, divorced from the increasing mass of requirements. That is, each feature on its own is no problem. Taken together, however, not only do these features add up, but as they coexist in the same software, they have additional ramifications throughout the entire system. In other words, as the application grows, the addition of each new feature can have exponential ramifications in your development. And to create good software in a well-managed (and therefore hopefully relatively painless) process requires considering all of these features together.

Many talented Flash and ColdFusion developers whom I know personally have encountered this in their first Flex applications—they, in short, bit off far more than they could chew. And this is the sort of scenario that can create many stressful days and sleepless nights (or, knowing the work habits of developers, vice versa), and perhaps even jeopardize your business and livelihood.

Unfortunately, even adhering to strict software development practices is no guarantee of quality or even success. Indeed, one could argue quite convincingly about the staggering lack of standards and workmanship practices throughout much of the software industry, leading to a constant cycle of instability and upgrade patches, as well as an extraordinarily high degree of project failure. It is often cited that up to 80% of software development projects are considered failures, either because of failure to meet required deadlines or required specifications. Whether or not that statistic is actually true, it is certainly indicative of real trends: huge numbers of software projects are considered failures, even if they are completed and reach the market.

The pace of technological change and innovation, as well as the increasingly irrational timing demands of client-driven work, puts immense pressure on the code development process, meaning that there is never sufficient time to apply proper development or quality assurance methodologies. Still, these practices represent the accumulated knowledge of decades of experience, and as much as technology and timing allow, those at the higher end of the ActionScript food chain need to become more familiar with these existing models, as part of a continuing process of professionalism for our industry, in order to tackle the more ambitious projects that are possible with the power of ActionScript 3 and the workflow enabled by the Flex framework. One of the key concepts from software development that must increasingly be applied to Flash development is the idea of a phased release effort. Until now, most projects created in Flash were completed in relatively short order (the bulk falling anywhere from 1 to 16 weeks). This was due to many factors, from the scope of the applications completed in Flash, to the unappetizing thought of maintaining most Flash work over the long term. But, as we now enter the new Flex/AS3 world, as the scope of applications becomes more ambitious, and as the platform itself becomes more stable and conducive to long-term, team-based development efforts, many will find it helpful to consider releasing individual features, one at a time, on larger projects—that is, planning for a phased release schedule.

No matter what the size, scope, and nature of a project, detailed and high-quality documentation is key. The larger the project and the development team, the more important the documentation becomes. There is no single format to which software development documentation must adhere. The key metric by which success of documentation can be measured is its ability to communicate effectively all crucial details of the application functionality and presentation to all team members and project stakeholders.

The Rich Media Exchange is a large project, with a lot of moving parts. These were all lessons that we applied, as a team, to the development of the RMX. I'll walk you through a summary of the process we used when preparing for development of this large-scale application.

Stages of planning

Any development project, of any scope, represents a degree of risk. The actual amount of risk represented by any individual project is a function of a variety of factors, including the following:

- Scope and complexity of the work
- Nature of the individuals involved (developers, managers, and clients)
  - Their understanding of risk
  - Their ability to think comprehensively and make trade-offs
  - Their experience executing similar projects

- Amount of first-generation technology utilized in the project (First generation is essentially version 1 technology—the least proven, least adopted, and buggiest version of any technology, whether it is software like Flex or hardware like the iPhone.)
- Presence of hard (unmissable) vs. soft (flexible) deadlines and the costs of missing those deadlines

All projects, no matter how haphazardly handled, proceed through some type of planning process. The more comprehensive the planning process is, the more the actual risk exposure is known; and, of course, the less well planned a project is, the more likely surprises will appear (surprises being a definite bad thing in development). Before I address some of the issues specific to planning the RMX, I want to explain in general the nature of how we plan projects at Almer/Blank. I will walk through this process in four steps:

1. Defining the business requirements
2. Creating the wireframes
3. Authoring the project specification
4. Building the project plan

Now, let's take a look at the specifics of planning the RMX project.

Defining the business requirements

At Almer/Blank, projects begin with a document defining the business requirements of the project—in short, what the overall goals are. This should be expressed with as little mention of specific technologies as possible, because the actual technologies have no relevance at this point and will only serve to unnecessarily constrain development options—although you should be confident that you and your team will have sufficient skills to handle the possible technologies or begin locating freelance resources to fill any likely gaps. For client work, these requirements documents must be developed iteratively, in a back-and-forth dialog. The client conveys what he thinks he must have. The development agency must work in a dialog with the client to refine these indications.

It is really the development firm's responsibility to lead this process, while realizing that the client is the one who is actually most knowledgeable on how this product will be used and what the goals are. The result is, more often than not, better than either party could have independently envisioned at the start of the project. I often use the example of the IKEA PAX Wardrobe Planner, the planning of which involved active participation from IKEA sales floor staff. True, they had no concept of the technology we were employing (or even much of an idea how to use computers), but they knew precisely how they and their customers shop for wardrobes and provided very valuable feedback throughout the planning process.

Fortunately, in the case of the RMX, I was the head of the development agency, as well as the client, as well as a target user of the network. This scenario, while exceedingly rare, provides a tremendous amount of flexibility in the creation of the business requirements, as well as the wireframes and the functional specification that follow.

Business requirements documents can be of varying lengths, but they should cover the major requirements of the application that justify its development and cost. The document should be written in plain English so that most anyone would be able to understand its contents. The requirements should also state any important external deadlines, such as "Client needs Project X in stable beta no later than January 25 for an annual trade show."

In the case of the RMX, the business requirements document was quite simple, and much of its content was discussed in Chapter 2—that is, we wanted to create a social media network for the Adobe User Groups, but there were certain specific requirements (such as the event calendar) to make this usable for the target market.

Once all stakeholders have a good agreement on the goals of the project, it is time to proceed to the development of project planning documentation.

Creating the wireframes

I have split wireframes (or wires) and the project specification (or spec) into separate categories in this chapter for ease of description. However, it is important to understand that they are completed in an iterative fashion, and neither one is complete until both are complete.

Wireframes, along with other terms like **use cases**, can be quite intimidating if you don't yet know what they mean. Wireframes can take any number of forms and can be completed with any number of different tools, but at their simplest, they are black-line boxes on a page that indicate what content and functionality is required throughout the application. We currently use OmniGraffle Professional for wireframing, although Gliffy (at `http://gliffy.com`) is not only a free wireframing tool, but also a great example of a Flash Platform RIA. And Fireworks CS3 also has some great workflow for wireframing and styling Flex screens.

Indeed, while we did not use Fireworks CS3 for wireframing (or wiring) the RMX, Fireworks' new support for Flex application design is pretty significant and deserves a bit more discussion. Utilizing these new features, you can pretty easily plan your Flex wireframes and designs in Fireworks, and then export MXML directly from Fireworks for use in Flex.

> *For a great tutorial on utilizing Fireworks' MXML export functionality, check out Trevor McCauley's article "Exporting MXML and images from Fireworks CS3" at* `www.adobe.com/devnet/fireworks/articles/mxml_images_export.html`.

Fireworks CS3 includes a new feature called **rich symbols**, which are easily scaled, resized, and customized with JavaScript. Rich symbols are 9-slice enabled, meaning they resize inside your Fireworks document in the same way that Flex components do in the design view of Flex Builder. As with components in Flex, you can create your own rich symbols, but several are included with the base installation of Fireworks.

> *To learn how to build your own rich symbols as Flex components, check out Trevor McCauley's article "Creating rich symbols for MXML and Images export in Fireworks CS3" at* `www.adobe.com/devnet/fireworks/articles/rich_symbols_export.html`.

One set of preinstalled rich symbols is called **Flex components**. You can find these in the folder called Flex Components under the Common Library panel (select Window ➤ Common Libraries if the panel is not already visible) as you see in Figure 3-1.

As you can see, the components include the following:

- Accordion
- Button
- CheckBox
- ComboBox
- Cursor
- NumericStepper
- Panel

- PopUpButton
- RadioButton
- ScrollBar
- Tab
- TextArea
- TextInput
- ToolTip

Of these, the following are ignored on export to MXML, because there is no direct conversion available from Fireworks to Flex. They are used for decoration only.

- Cursor
- ScrollBar
- Tab
- ToolTip

You will note from the list of Flex components in Fireworks that there are two container components: Panel and Accordion. Container hierarchy structures in your MXML are determined purely through physical placement in Fireworks. If one component physically exists entirely within a container in Fireworks, it will be a child of that container in your XML; if your component is entirely outside or partially outside the container, it will not be a member of the container.

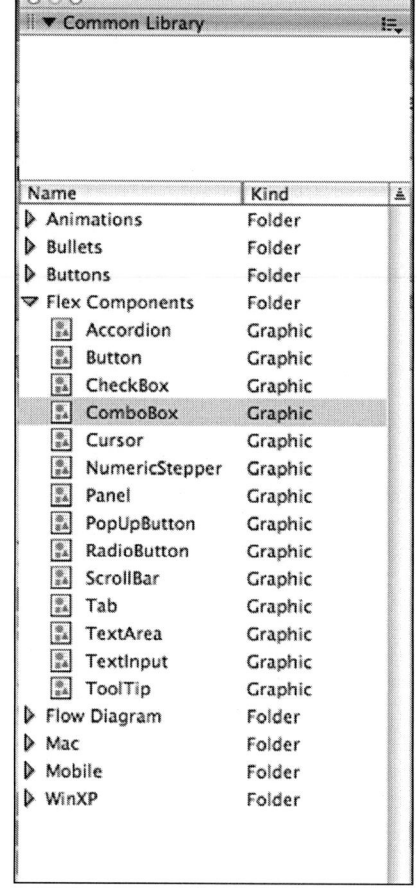

Figure 3-1. The Fireworks Common Library panel with the Flex Components folder expanded

There are a few other key limitations of these Fireworks features. First, skinning (as opposed to styling) is not supported. If you skin your Flex components in Fireworks, you will need to manually reapply the skin in Flex.

> For an example of how to port your Fireworks design skins to Flex, check out Peter Baird's article "Designing Flex applications with Fireworks CS3" at www.adobe.com/devnet/fireworks/articles/designing_flex_apps.html.

Second, all CSS is embedded in your MXML; if you want to externalize your CSS source, you must alter the MXML in Flex Builder (or your IDE of choice) after export. Finally, the supported properties are limited to text color, text disabled color, enabled, label, text rollover, and text selected (which you can see are configurable through the symbol properties when the component instance is selected in Fireworks, as shown in Figure 3-2), as well as x, y, width, height, alpha (where applicable), ID, and style name.

Despite these limitations, Adobe has created a workflow to facilitate the generation of styles in Fireworks for easy implementation in Flex. The Flex Style Explorer, available as a plug-in for Fireworks, makes it easy to generate Flex-compatible CSS through an attractive and easy-to-use GUI tool.

> *You can download the Flex Style Explorer component for Fireworks CS3 from* http://download. macromedia.com/pub/developer/flex_style_ explorer.zip.

Symbol Properties		
Name	**Value**	
State	Up	▼
color	ffffff	
disabledColor	AAB3B3	
enabled	true	▼
label	Button	
textRollOverColor	2B333C	
textSelectedColor	000000	
MXML	<mx:Button	

Figure 3-2. The Symbol Properties panel with a Flex component selected on the Fireworks document work area

Once you have downloaded the MXP component and installed it through the Adobe Extension Manager, you will see an option in the Fireworks window menu called FlexStyleExplorer. If you select it, you will see the Flex Style Explorer appear, as it does in Figure 3-3.

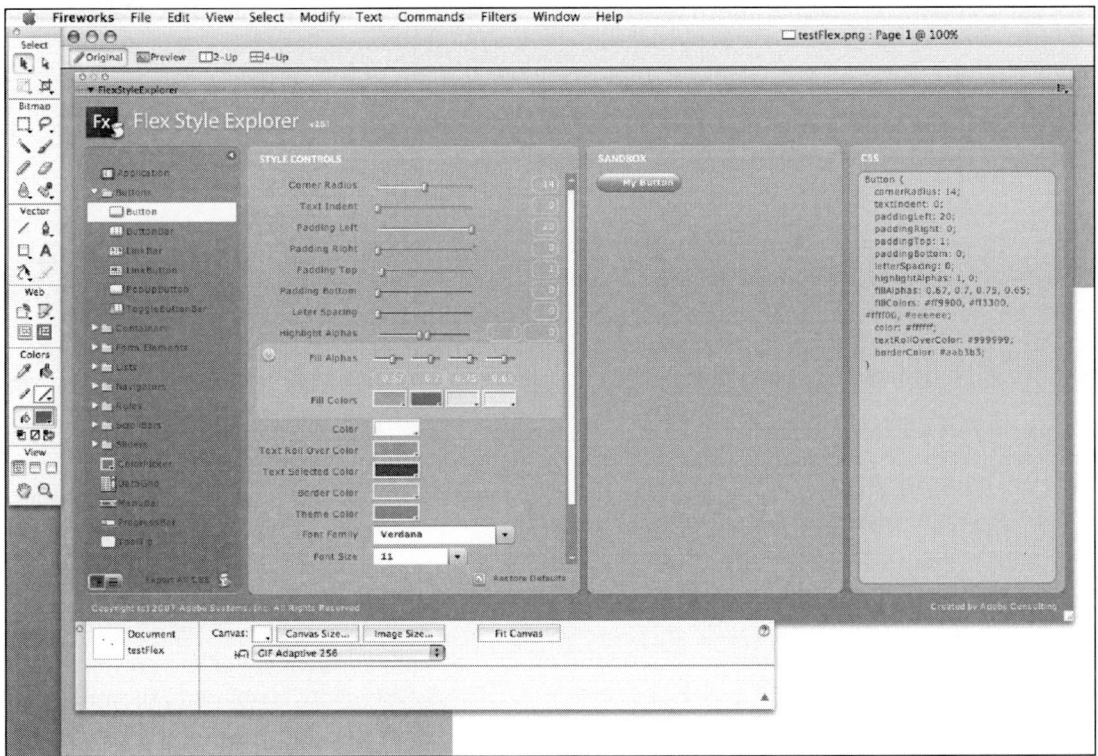

Figure 3-3. The Flex Style Explorer component in Fireworks

You can work with the Flex Style Explorer to generate a Cascading Style Sheet that matches your design, which you can have open at the same time. When you are ready, you can create your CSS and paste it into a new CSS file within your Flex project and apply it to your component (for more information on this, see Chapter 5).

Now, with Flex, many have taken to wireframing directly in Flex Builder, which brings the benefit of having interactive, clickable wireframes that can express the information flow in a way that is far more difficult with static pages. By interactive, I mean that everyone who views the wireframes can click around and see what interactions and functionality is planned, helping to reduce confusion as to the meaning of the wireframes and requiring fewer words in the documentation to express the requirements. Whether or not this makes sense for you depends both on your comfort level with Flex and the nature of the project. While I believe the best wireframers have some type of development background, at many larger firms wireframing is often completed by talent with little or no coding experience, so it may be best to adopt standards that can be completed without requiring code. As with everything in this chapter, you must customize the process to the skills and talents of your team.

Although I know how to code, I prefer wireframing in a traditional tool because of the overall flexibility it provides, as well as the ease and simplicity of creating, editing, and notating the wires, as well as the ease with which the wires may be inserted into the project documentation.

One of the skills that go into a good wireframer is an understanding of the nature of the base UI components—what a combo box is good for, why use radio buttons, and so on. Because Flex not only provides these components, but also makes it easy to create brand new ones and to create any number of different interactions (many of which would be impossible in other technologies such as Ajax), it helps to have some imagination and creativity to design the best UI for a given task. Flash technologies allow for such freedom and creativity, and not exploiting at least some of this flexibility leads to applications that are far more boring than they need to be. At the same time, it is important to understand that standards matter. Even if you wish to be imaginative in your design of an application, it is vital that you not require users to learn how to use your application. The application should have an interface that clearly represents its functionality off the bat.

In the world of application development, the wireframer wields tremendous power. Just as the designer plays an important role in graphical work, the wireframer of applications has complete control over how the application will appear and operate, and how people will use it. It is the job of the wireframer to translate the business requirements into an application that accomplishes the major goals while ensuring targeted users will know how to use it and be willing to do so.

The key skills required of wireframing include the following:

- Understanding the language of interactive applications, and especially being fluent in the existence and purpose of UI components
- Understanding how people comprehend and like to experience information
- Having a sense of the difficulty involved in production of different features

Of course, in order to begin wireframing, it is important to have an understanding of what technologies will be employed to create the project, but specifics such as "This will be Flash" and "This will be Ajax" are better left for the specification. This is actually something of a conflict: the wireframer must have a solid grasp of the capabilities of the technologies, but even if he knows how to work with those technologies, in most any larger development environment, it is unlikely that the same individual will both wireframe and develop—indeed, it is highly unlikely that only a single developer will be involved.

To help reduce the tension and confusion that can emerge in this period, at Almer/Blank the architect tasked with wireframing the application often reviews the wireframes in development with the developers who will likely be creating the actual code. Questions like "Is this possible?", "Is there a better way to do this?", and "What's actually involved in making this happen?" are asked. It really is amazing how changes that would appear as subtle or even meaningless to the client (such as changing one item from a ComboBox to a RadioButton group) can strongly influence the number of hours required to execute the development.

The wireframer has two goals that may appear in conflict but the balance of which helps increase the overall chances for project success. First, as I mentioned, the wireframer must accommodate the goals expressed in the business requirements document. Second, the wireframer must attempt to limit the scope of the work—that is, divorce himself from the desire to blow out the features. It is much easier to limit the scope of the project in this phase than in later phases. On this point, I've adopted one simple rule for version 1 projects: omit redundancy. While you may be tempted to create multiple ways, for example, to allow moderators to oversee video content on the network, it is only vital to have a single way. Creating redundancy in features can be quite useful from a usability perspective, but this is best left to subsequent versions of the project. It is also worth noting that attempting to wire as simple a process as possible benefits not only you, the developer, but also the end user, who has a lot less up-front learning to do in order to use your new application.

As technologies continue to improve, and the power to customize the precise user experience improves along with it, the characteristic "delight" can be found increasingly in those products and services humans consume. You may be unfamiliar with what I mean by delight in this context. I derive my usage of the term from the book *Blobjects & Beyond* by Steven Skov Holt and Mara Skov Holt (Chronicle Books, 2005), which describes the increasing importance of the human enjoyment that follows from the fluidity of the physical design of products. For instance, the click-wheel on an iPod is not only easy and functional, it is, in a very real sense, delightful to use; it almost makes you want to scroll through your 10,000-song library just for giggles. And Flash Platform technologies enable quite a wide array of delight, with drag-and-drop interactions providing an obvious example. While experience-centric Flash projects must always focus on delight (recall the Nike Air project referenced in Chapter 1), when engaging in the development of functionality-centric applications for Flash, delight should wait until version 2. The goal of version 1 of any software development project should be to establish the functional foundation—the basic architecture of the user experience and the data structures required to support that. As a case in point, I highlight the event calendar. The event calendar was originally specified to exist in multiple states, depending on what actually was selected. I realized that while this feature would likely make the event calendar more delightful to use, it would actually add nothing to the core functionality of the application, while it would require quite a few development hours. So, that has been held off until future releases. Only once the developers and the users are pleased with the functional foundation should the developers proceed to attempt to incorporate delight into the experience.

Once we had a solid version of the wireframes ready, we could proceed to authoring the project specification. The following describes this process and illustrates a few of the wireframes from the RMX and how we documented them.

Authoring the project specification

As I mentioned previously, at Almer/Blank, authoring the project specification occurs in tandem with the development of the wireframes. The primary goal of the project specification is to contextualize and explain the wireframes. As well, it must be clear from the spec how the business requirements are being met. Finally, it is important to explain additional concepts and structures required for the execution of the project (such as user levels and advertising requirements).

It is first important to understand that not every development agency maintains a project specification. Some maintain separate documents, such as a functional specification and a technical specification, with clear delineations between them. Some firms have an overall project spec, but call it something else, such as a project bible.

We begin a spec by inserting all wires into the document, dividing them up into sections, and then defining each screen. A screen definition consists of a few minimum requirements. First, we define the purpose of the screen, how it is accessed, and its place in the project (for instance, its location in a site map). At this point, both the architect and the client should be able to understand a fair amount about this screen. But, if you completed the screen definition at this point, you would be inviting two calamities:

- You would be assuming that your developers had an identical understanding of the screen as you did while wiring it.
- You would be inviting confusion down the line, as additional considerations popped up, items that you well may not have considered while wiring.

In order to prevent these occurrences, it is important to define use cases. A use case is defined as a single set of circumstances in which this screen is utilized. The "use cases" section of the screen definition consists of all likely individual use cases that the wireframer and architect can conceive. To reiterate, it is not important that your screen definition contain formal use cases; what is important is for all likely use cases to be handled and explained in the document. By convention, most place such indications in a formal "use cases" section. For instance, assume we are defining the Upload Video screen in the video-sharing portion of the RMX, as you see in Figure 3-4.

Only registered members who are logged in can upload video to the RMX. So, when considering user video uploads, there are two basic use cases:

- Non–logged-in (anonymous) user
- Logged-in (registered) user

In the case of the RMX, if a user who is not logged in clicks Upload to create video content on the network, that user is routed to a login screen that explains he must log in (or create an account) in order to upload video. That means a user who is not logged in will never see this screen, so this screen does not need to account for that use case—but the overall application does. Defining all these scenarios during planning means the messaging will be defined prior to development (rather than during testing), and the elegance with which the failures are handled is increased (because you can plan for it up-front).

When a user is logged in and links to this screen, there are several behavioral questions that arise:

- At what point is the Upload button enabled?
- Which fields are required?
- Are any characters illegal in any of the fields?

- What happens if the user selects a source video file with spaces or punctuation in the file name? (Hint: It should be stripped upon renaming when received by the server.)
- How do the Category and Subcategory ComboBoxes interact?
- What happens when the Upload button is clicked?

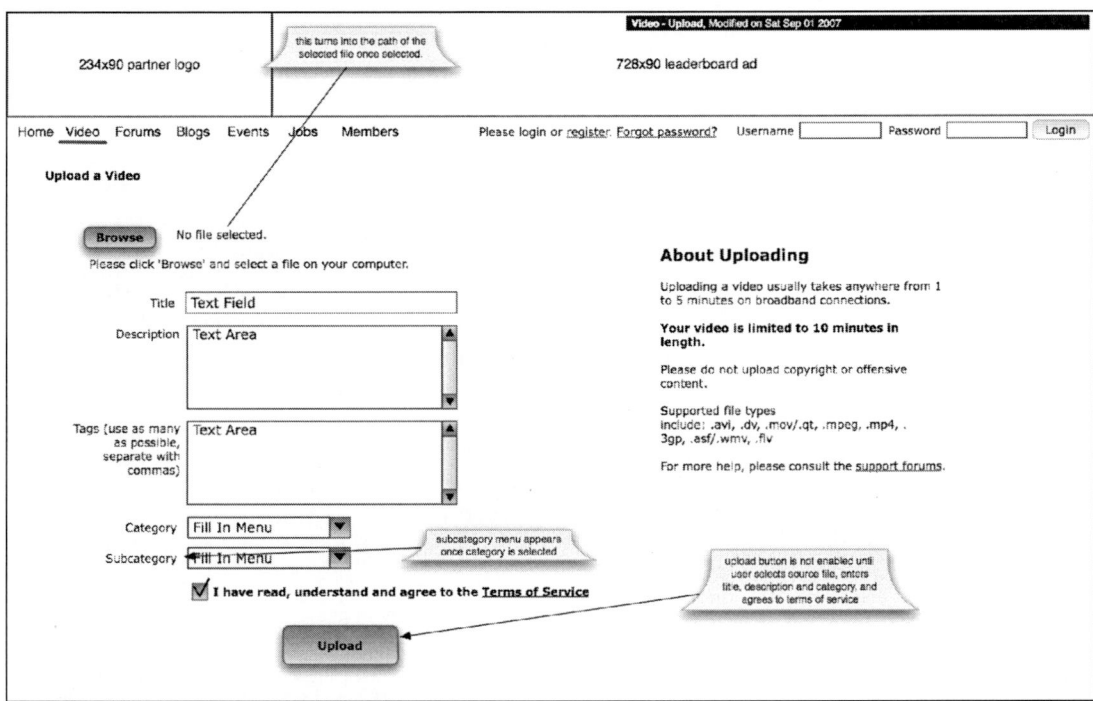

Figure 3-4. The wireframe for the Upload Video screen on the RMX

During the process of authoring the use cases, it may well be necessary to return to the wires for alterations and edits. This is why I stated that neither the wires nor the project specification are complete until both are.

When asked how detailed and comprehensive these use cases should be, I return to Abraham Lincoln's apocryphal response to the question "How tall should a man be?"—"Tall enough for his feet to reach the ground." Again, the point is to consider as many potential scenarios as possible during this planning stage, so that the screens and user experience may be altered now and not during development, and so the developer does not have to think in broad conceptual terms during the process of coding the screen and can instead focus on executing the specifically delineated requirements. The ultimate goal can be stated as follows: *reduce your risk by eliminating as many uncertainties as possible*, which is accomplished by thinking everything through and documenting those thoughts. And, I suppose if I were forced to define a goal for the ideal spec, it would be that anyone could pick it up and know how to build what has been defined.

Each aspect of the RMX that exists as a screen (for instance, all pages on the web site, but not the e-mail server) is wired. And, for those aspects of the application that do not easily conform to wireframes (for instance, the membership structures), we generate architectural diagrams. I earlier cited the example of user levels. By this example, I mean that each type of user that may exist in the application should be defined—as user types have a significant impact on the overall data structures in the project, as well as inform the nature and variety of required use cases. You can see a simplified version of the RMX user levels in Figure 3-5.

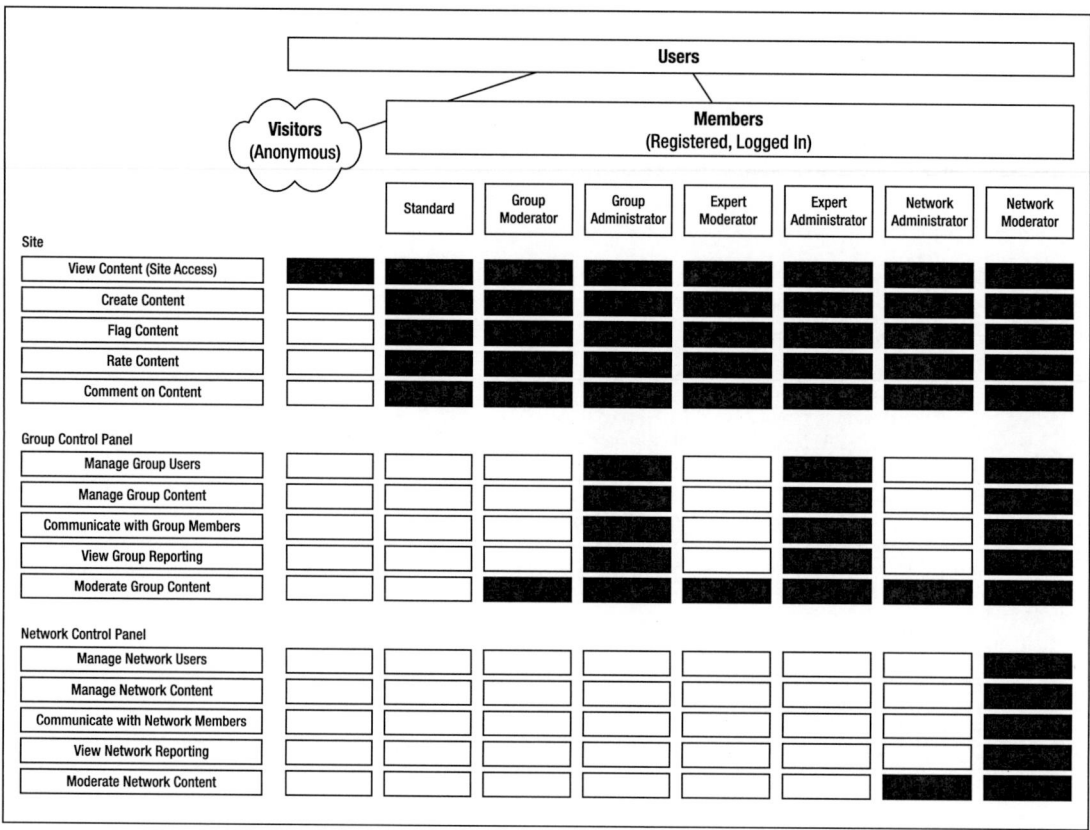

Figure 3-5. RMX user levels and general permissions

Even in this simple format, with highly generalized sets of functionality, a diagram such as this provides quite a useful reference during development, as it is like a CliffNotes version of the overall usage requirements of the application.

In our development, the functional specification serves as a repository of all key information. As I just explained, the core consists of the screen definitions and other main architecture and performance considerations, but encompasses much more. For instance, if the client has a specific branding to implement in the designs, the details of that branding (specific color codes, logos, and font faces) are all included in the spec.

Once the wireframing and specification processes are complete, we generate a printed version of the spec that all stakeholders (such as a representative from Almer/Blank and a representative from the client) must sign (called an **execution of the spec**), indicating the client's final approval. I cannot communicate sufficiently the importance of a final execution of this document; if change requests emerge during development, by referencing the spec it is possible to explain "But you approved X, and now you want Y," which gives you the power to reject or postpone the request, or accommodate it with corresponding changes in delivery time and development costs. Without a fixed project definition, you are inviting disputes and disagreements through the development phase.

The project specification is never "closed" until the project is actually released. That is, as the project moves into and through design and development, decisions will be reversed, new information added, and unforeseen situations will arise. The spec serves as a repository for each new decision that is made. For this reason, it is quite important to implement version control on your spec, even if it consists of a simple table at the start of the document, with version number, date, and change log, as you see in Figure 3-6. (You cannot simply rely on SVN for version control of the specification; the versioning must be clearly reflected in printed copies of the document.)

Tom FlexTube Implementation
Launch Specification

Version	Date	Author	Notes
1	2007-03-07	R Blank	Complete 1st draft of public website, control panel, users, and advertising. Back-end details to come.
2	2007-03-08	R Blank	Based on mantis updates from and conversation with Tom after version 1 of this document.
3	2007-03-13	R Blank	All sections Final, except for hardware details on back-end.
4	Saturday, March 17, 2007	R Blank	Including information for server-setup
5	Wednesday, March 21, 2007	R Blank	Final revisions from 3/19 + 3/20 talk with Tom
6	Thursday, March 22, 2007	R Blank	Final change from Tom re: required search fields
7	4/10/2007	R Blank	Change, post-execution, from mantis, re: • end-of-video behavior • front page • expired listing behavior (listing detail and shared player)
8	4/15/2007	R Blank	• Changed 'Agent' to 'Agent' throughout (pursuant to email request from Bryan) • Added proposed site content from Tom
9	5/2/2007	R Blank	• Videographer changed to videographer
10	5/3/2007	R Blank	• How to shoot a video content added

Figure 3-6. A sample version table from a living project specification

Building the project plan

Once the spec is complete, you can begin to map out the development. At Almer/Blank, the two deliverables of this phase are a project schedule and a project guide. The goal of this phase is, of course, to create a road map that gets the project to a stable completion, in a realistic schedule that will not kill you and your developers. It must include time for design, development, testing, and delivery.

Planning the plan

One key aspect of a good project plan is that it structures development in featured-based phases based around functionality, not grouping development by screen. The nature of the specification, based around defining the screens, leads you to consider functionality in the context of screens—to group together all functionality represented on a screen. However, a given screen might represent a tremendous number of functions, some of which might be required for a successful initial launch, and some of which may be delayed until after. And much of that functionality will be spread across many screens, not just one.

If you examine Figure 3-7, you see the wireframe for one state of the RMX video player.

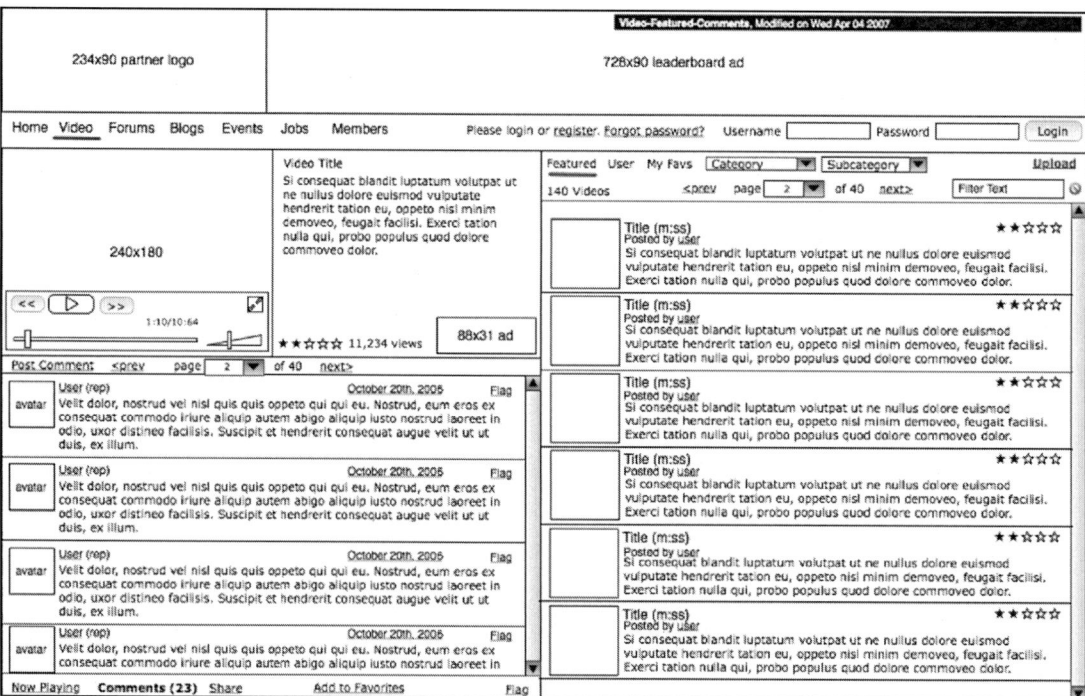

Figure 3-7. The View Comments state for a non–logged-in user of the RMX video player

On this single state of a single screen, you can see numerous features:

- Login (with links to register and to regenerate password)
- Banner advertising
- Watch video

- Control video playback
- Cycle videos in a playlist
- Playlist pagination
- Browse videos by category/subcategory
- Filter browse results
- Rate videos
- Comment on videos
- Flag comments on videos
- Pagination of comments
- Post comment
- Share (which requires permalinking schema)
- Add to favorites (which requires user preferences)
- Link to upload video

Of these, several are relevant to multiple screens:

- Login
- Banner advertising
- Content rating
- Content commenting
- Content flagging
- Content sharing
- Add to favorites

To attempt to build this one screen, then, would require spending time on a wide array of features and functions, some of which may need to altered or repurposed later on for implementations in other sections of the application. It is, in short, not a very efficient manner in which to group development efforts; therefore, we instead consider features one at a time, ordering by priority and complexity of development.

The order in which features are developed is informed by two key pieces of information:

- Which features are vital for launch
- Use-case scenarios

The temptation to build a sky-high specification is often present on the part of the client and the development agency; after all, everyone wants a great application, and it may indeed be practical to do so. One of the lessons from graduate school that has stuck with me is the success of Quicken. While Quicken is now the market king in personal and small-business financial management tools, it did not launch as that. In its initial version, all Quicken really did was make check writing easier by digitizing the process. That one feature was the hook—the function that gave it a market. From the point of securing the market, Intuit, the company that makes Quicken, could, step-by-step, blow out its offerings, creating what is now a massively powerful and comprehensive suite of financial management tools. Had Intuit attempted to launch with nearly as comprehensive a toolkit as it now has, it would have almost certainly failed.

With this in mind, while it is vital to allocate enough development time to your projects, it is often optimal to launch as early in the process as is feasible given the business requirements. In the case of projects for large businesses, it really helps to generate as much real-world user feedback as possible; it also helps the manager who approved the budget prove to his superiors that sufficient progress is being made. In the case of smaller firms or startups, for whom the project might represent their entire business platform, it is preferable to launch as early as possible in order to get their business operating. In the case of social networks of any type, it is often of strategic benefit to soft-launch as early as possible in order to begin generating content on the network—in effect, such applications only have value with content generated by their users. Delaying launch in order to complete the entire specification may make sense, but many times it does not.

So, once the project specification is complete, the stakeholders should sit down and decide which features are required for launch and which are not. In the case of the RMX video page referenced earlier in Figure 3-7, the ability to add to favorites, for example, is one that could wait until after launch, as are the requirements to display number of video or page views publicly (views are, by definition, never impressive at launch) or user reputations (which require a history of activity on the network to be of value). Similarly, paginating comments at launch is not as important, because you will be launching with no comments.

Revisiting the list of features represented in Figure 3-7, here are the features that we considered essential for launch:

- Login (with links to register and to regenerate password)
- Banner advertising
- Watch video
- Control video playback
- Cycle videos in a playlist
- Browse videos by category/subcategory
- Comment on videos
- Post comment
- Share (which requires permalinking schema)
- Link to upload video

Note this list is shorter. Taken across all screens in the application, this process can radically reduce time-to-launch.

With the knowledge of what is actually required for a preliminary launch, you then prioritize development with the use-case scenarios as guides. As an example, again based on the video page in Figure 3-7, in order to build the Video View screen, it is important to first build the Upload Video screen, which in turn requires user creation, user authentication, the FFMPEG implementation (to encode the video on the server), and the control panels to moderate and control users and video uploads. So, in that quick example, you get a sense of where in the overall development plan the video page falls (that is, what other features are required to be in place before this aspect of the application can function).

Creating the project guide

Having prioritized development by feature, we can now define precisely what functionality is required at each phase. This is vital in order to provide accurate estimates of development hours for each feature. For each feature built into the application, you should consider precisely what interfaces and services are required, which will in turn determine the database requirements.

As a simple example, examine the following four early phases common to many web application experiences, including the RMX:

- Member Creation
  - Screen: Site, Create Member
  - Database: Members
  - Service: Add Member
- View Members
  - Screen: Control Panel, Member Manager
  - Service: Read Member
- Edit Members
  - Screen: Site, Edit Member
  - Screen: Control Panel, Member Manager
  - Service: Update Member
  - Service: Delete Member
- Member Authentication
  - Screen: Site, Login
  - Screen: Site, Reset Password
  - Database: Passwords (encrypted)
  - Service: Authenticate Member
  - Screen: Control Panel, Member Manager
  - Service: Reset Password Member

The guide defines, in generally nontechnical terms, each aspect of the application that is touched by a phase. It should also include a brief description that explains the functional expectations represented by each line item. We do not need to create definitions in detail here, because we have already done so in the spec, in an easily referenced format. We simply need to refer to the relevant portions of the spec, and identify which aspects of that spec item should be completed in the given phase. For example, examine the line item "Screen: Control Panel, Member Manager." For convenience, I have included the relevant wireframe in Figure 3-8.

The definition for "Screen: Control Panel, Member Manager" could read as follows: "This refers to spec item 2.3.7, the Member Manager in the administrative control panel. In this phase, we only need the ability to view member records. We do not need the Revert, Save, Reset Password, Warn, or Ban buttons present or functional."

You should repeat this procedure for each deliverable in your project.

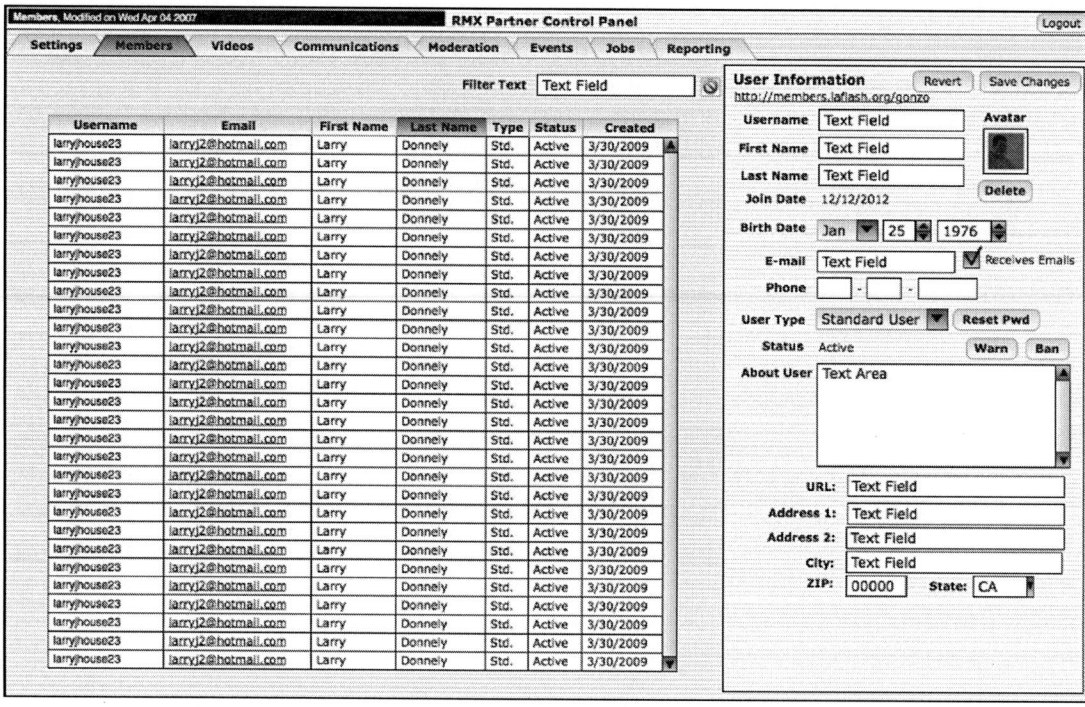

Figure 3-8. The Member Manager in the RMX control panel

Creating the project schedule

We have now produced a relatively detailed line-item schedule of deliverables. With this breakdown of our project in place, estimating hours per feature, and therefore delivery dates, is much easier.

The first step is to transfer each line item of the project guide into a task inside Microsoft Project (you may choose to use a different project management tool). Then we assign the right developers to the task, estimate the number of hours required for the task, and finally establish any task dependencies (which other tasks must be completed in order to begin this task). We also establish a start date and a working calendar for the project.

We use MS Project for three main reasons:

- It was designed to manage software development.
- It is a standard (meaning more people know how to use and understand it).
- It allows **leveling**: the power to balance resources across multiple tasks and projects, given the constraints of a work calendar and task dependencies.

The third item, leveling, is truly invaluable in an agency environment, where handling multiple projects in various stages of development is the norm. With the project calendar set, along with the hours and dependencies established for each task, we can level our project, which will calculate a realistic work schedule with start and end dates for each task and phase. If you have established your Project file inside a master project with shared resources (meaning the same developers are reused across multiple projects), you can level across the entire master project, meaning that you can relatively easily establish realistic deadlines for the new work, given the current workload.

When you develop inside a team environment, coordinating delivery of the various aspects that constitute a complete feature is a crucial factor in keeping the project on track and maximizing the efficiency of development hours.

Getting into development

With all the deliverables complete from the planning stages, we can formally begin development, which includes the design and development of the application, as well as the creation of more detailed technical documentation, and finishing with a testing phase. This section of the chapter is broken into five sections:

- Designs
- Technical specification
- Development
- Technical documentation
- Testing

Designs

For many projects, aspects of design will have begun along with the planning stages. The main goal of any design work completed in the planning stages is to establish overall branding, as well as look and feel. Some firms employ the use of **mood boards**, which represent the overall mood of the user experience—divorcing look and feel from the actual wireframes that could muddle decisions on the designs.

With the wireframes completed, the designer can begin implementing the look and feel across all required wireframes. Even though the designer might be able to begin work off of the raw wireframes, without documentation you will quickly find the designer making incorrect assumptions regarding the nature of the information and interactivity represented in the wireframes. Thus, in the long run, it is safer and a more efficient use of everyone's time if the design phase awaits the completion of the documentation.

While we address this at length further in the book (especially in Chapter 5), and Adobe even has an entire three-day course devoted to the subject, it is no secret that the most difficult aspect of working with Flex is getting it to look like something other than Flex—applying a real custom design. Unlike working with Flash, by default everything completed in a Flex project will have identical styling. And applying project-wide style sheets for a basic level of graphical customization is not difficult. Thus, it is important to consider whether or not your Flex application actually needs to be graphically designed. In the case of RMX, portions of the front-end application—such as the video-sharing network—were designed, indeed heavily so. However, the back-end administrative control panel application (accessible only to network administrators and moderators) was not, in any formal sense, designed, but instead had a style applied to it. This saved us significant design and development time and resources.

Technical specification

By this point in the process, you should have a pretty good understanding of the specific technologies that will be required to complete the application, many of which I addressed in Chapter 2. The architect can now sit down and plan all technical considerations, phase-by-phase in the project guide, including the following:

- How the various elements of the interfaces should be built
- How the database should be structured to accommodate all data requirements
- How the data services should be structured
- Additional server requirements

The technical specification provides a detailed outline for the developers as they approach and work through each task in the project guide. The technical specification, along with the project guide and specification, should ideally provide the developers everything they need to know to complete each assigned task.

Development

The rest of the book is about this single topic, so all that's important to note here is that by the time development begins, it is really vital that your developers have all the required assets and documentation, along with realistic assignments and deadlines, in order to make the most of their time. That's why the planning documentation is so vital.

Technical documentation

The documentation is actually only completed once development is completed. The goal of the technical documentation is to make the code base maintainable over time, by the developers who authored it and by others who may have to work on it at some point in the future.

Developers should document their code as they write it. This is different from commenting. Comments are quite a valuable tool to make code more readable, but documentation consists of standard elements explaining how to utilize the various classes and code. And, when you write your documentation properly, consider using one of the various tools available that will produce various outputs of the documentation in efficient formatting.

For instance, if you include the following multiline comment:

```
/*
    Function: Multiply

    Multiplies two integers.

    Parameters:

        x - The first integer.
        y - The second integer.

    Returns:
```

```
        The two integers multiplied together.

    See Also:

        <Divide>
*/
function Multiply (x:Number, y:Number):Number
{
return x * y;
};
```

you could automatically generate the documentation as shown in Figure 3-9.

And it would be organized inside the proper class, in an easily readable, searchable, and linkable HTML document.

> *One popular, open source documentation generator is Natural Docs, which I used to generate the output in Figure 3-9. Notes on formatting recommendations for Natural Docs may be found at* www.naturaldocs.org/documenting. html.

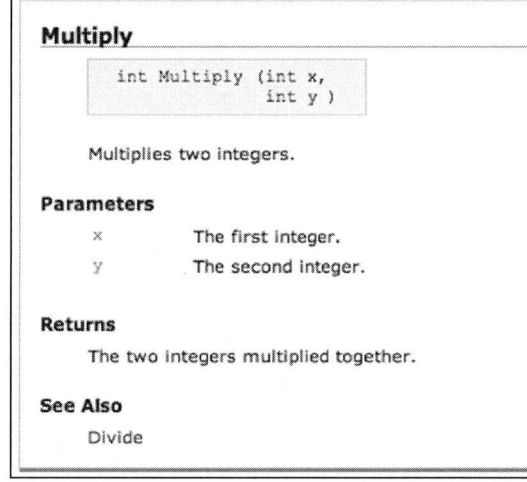

Figure 3-9. The sample output based on the preceding documentation

Unfortunately, documentation generators can only do so much. Your technical documentation should include other information such as server requirements and configuration, additional software utilized on the project, and how that software must be configured. In short, your technical documentation should contain anything *you* would want to have on hand if you took over an existing project.

Testing and release

The final stages of development include the process of validating the quality and performance of the application and launching it. These two stages, while often considered separately, are really part of one larger phase in which the application is made available to its intended users. As with all stages of development, the plan you follow to test and release your application should fit the scope and nature of the application.

Testing

Of course, developers perform a certain level of testing in the development process. Each time they compile to make sure what they built works, they are testing. However, developers focus on development—they do not focus on testing, nor should they. Of course, developers should endeavor to deliver high-quality code, but requiring them to validate each aspect of the application is an inefficient use of their time; it takes them away from development, and it distracts them when they return to coding. That's one main reason we consider testing separately from development.

Of course, as with development, the scope and importance of testing increases along with the size and complexity of your application. It is important, for the sake of realistic and reliable deadlines, to allocate sufficient time for testing, and for developers to address the bugs that testing reveals.

Testing generally falls into three broad types. **Quality Assurance** (QA) is an internal testing phase in which testers verify all use cases and identify bugs for repair. At the end of QA, the development agency says "This application is ready." The result of QA is a version of the application that is ready for limited release to users.

At this point, depending on the specific project (budget and timeline permitting), you might begin a **User Testing** (UT) phase, in which the application is released to a limited number of users. No matter how good your wireframing, information architecture, use-case analysis, and experience design is, users can't actually use the application until it's ready to be used. This means there are often ways in which the application can be altered to improve the user experience even when the application is complete. While UT may reveal some additional bugs, the focus of UT is not on bugs and stability, but instead on simplicity and ease of use. Does the application do what it needs to, and does it do it in a way that users understand? Sometimes, this involves signing up your friends or colleagues of your client. Sometimes, it involves bringing random users into a research facility to monitor the user interaction in detail in a tightly controlled environment, such as a lab.

While many of the ideas that are generated from UT are really valuable, only certain ones can be implemented in a short time span. So, you have to map out each suggested features, balance the value of the feature with the number of users for whom the feature adds value, and determine the amount of additional development the feature requires. Those features that cannot be incorporated into release often provide a good road map into the functionality of future releases.

The final stage of testing is called **User Acceptance Testing** (UAT), in which the client (or whoever has final say on approving the product) validates the product himself (not the developers, not the QA testers, and not the UT users), and when he is ready, signs off on the application. At that point, the testing process can be considered complete.

Use cases, which we documented in our specification to assist the developers building the application, are also important to the testers in QA and UAT phases. Testers are often unsophisticated users who are unfamiliar with the details of the application or the project. Nor is the intended behavior of an application always readily apparent; that is, it's not always clear what's a bug unless you know exactly what is supposed to happen. To ensure the testers know what to test, and do so comprehensively, you can give them the same use cases that you gave your developers. The use cases define exactly what the testers should validate and what is intended to happen. Use cases are not useful in UT, since the goal of UT is precisely to determine if the application is understandable and usable without documentation and assistance.

Release

Obviously, the goal of the testing phases is to have a releasable product. But, when developing any application of substantial scope, it is quite unlikely that the server on which you built the application is the same one on which it is being deployed. And, even if that is the case, if you are continuing development after a release (as is often the case) or just supporting the application without doing anything new, you will need access to a version of the application in a different location from the version that is currently live.

For these reasons, your release plan should incorporate a staged rollout across these various environments, and run inline with your testing phases. In the development of any application, it is useful to have at least three different environments in which the application runs:

- A development environment
- A staging environment
- A release (live) environment

Without at least three environments (and some shops can maintain six or more environments for an even more managed release path), managing the process of testing and releasing your software can become a real pain. The developers complete their work in the development environment. Once they believe a feature has been completed, it is pushed to staging. Once a sufficient number of features have been assembled into a sufficiently stable version of the application on the staging server, the decision maker may give the go-ahead to push it to the live environment. While the version on staging is being evaluated for public release on the live environment, the current live version remains stable, and the developers' progress is not interrupted, as they can keep working on the development environment.

If a user or tester finds a bug (what am I saying, "if"—I mean *when* a tester finds a bug), he reports it through Mantis, and the project manager determines whether it is real and reproducible (there are few greater sources of wasted time and frustration than routing incorrect or irreproducible bugs to developers), decides whether it should and can be addressed, and if so, routes it to the proper developer. Once the bug is quashed, the developer reposts to staging and passes the Mantis issue back to the reporter for validation. Once all requisite functionality of a phase works stably, the developer receives permission to push the phase to the release environment, where it becomes publicly accessible, and the Mantis issue is formally closed. Again, if you follow even this simple process reliably, you will maintain separate, usable environments for your application, saving you a tremendous amount of time and heartache from version conflicts and instability.

Just because a version is released doesn't mean it's universally and publicly available. Often, applications are released into a **public beta**, or a **soft launch**. In a public beta, users are invited to participate in a viral process (such as the way Gmail was launched). This helps control the rate of growth of the application, so that bugs and other needed improvements discovered in the course of the public beta may be addressed while the scale of the application is more manageable. As well, with any application like the RMX, which is heavily reliant on user-generated content, a public beta provides a very useful period in which the initial users can create enough content on the network to make it a valuable and attractive destination to others.

Because the iterative release of software has become so inexpensive and rapid (compared to only a few years ago, in which new CDs would have to be burned and boxes would have to be stuffed), public betas have become incredibly common. Indeed, the popular parody Web 2.0 Logo Creator (at http://h-master.net/web2.0/index.php) includes an option to automatically stamp a "beta tag" on your logo. Jokes aside, if your project can accommodate it, a public beta can be incredibly useful to incorporate in your release plan.

We included a public beta in the release plan for RMX. The RMX launched with LA Flash and Flash in TO as test groups. We backed up our original sites (powered by other forum technology), imported as much data as we could into the new RMX sites, and then began using the RMX. From there, we could work out any critical issues and start accepting real-world feedback. Once we were happy with the functionally and stability, we invited more groups into the fray.

Of course, development never stops on the RMX, and user feedback is often a critical factor in evaluating changes and new features. Like with many of today's RIAs, the functionality and appearance can constantly change.

Specific RMX planning considerations

In the previous sections, I discussed general practices for planning large projects of the scope of the RMX. In this section, I want to outline some of the considerations we approached specific to creating specs for and wiring the RMX.

General considerations

Let's start by covering some considerations that apply to the RMX in general, and not to any one specific part of the application.

Web page vs. application

Just because something runs in a web page does not mean it is a web page. It could well be an instance of an RIA running inside of a browser window. This difference is clearly more than semantic: it runs to the heart of the function of the application and the structure of the user experience.

Unfortunately, there are no clear lines between what distinguishes an application from a web page—and, of course, with advances including AIR and the Adobe Media Player, the landscape becomes even more varied.

There are two fundamental concepts of the user experience this decision directly influences: history integration (does the browser Back button work?) and bookmarking (can I bookmark the current URL to return to precisely where I am?). Permalinking, or direct linking (the ability to link to a specific page or state with a specific URL), which is a key attribute of contemporary Internet experiences, can be supported by both web pages and applications.

For years, one of the biggest complaints about projects completed entirely or largely in Flash was that these two characteristics were ignored. Developers constructed entire web sites in Flash, glossing over the fact that if the user hit the Back button, he may well leave the entire web site—at which time clicking Forward would return the user to the default front page of the site, whether or not that was the content the user was viewing when he clicked Back. Over the years, Flash has developed some inherent capabilities to handle these important functions, and beyond those built-in features, many developers created their own libraries or mechanisms to handle these requirements.

But, as Flash has improved its support for this type of usability, the uses to which Flash is applied have grown in complexity. Flash is now widely accepted as a formal application development platform. And applications do not conform to many of the traditional web usability guidelines (which is, in part, why there has in the past been such animosity toward Flash from the usability community). While there are different view states in Microsoft Word, is there a Back button? Of course not. The concept of **history** in an application is effectively replaced by that of **undo**, or the maintenance of a history of actions, rather than a history of view states. No one considers this a violation of usability, because it's an expectation of application performance.

Put the application in a web page, and suddenly the question is somewhat muddied. While the example of Word may be obvious, there are now versions of word processing and presentation creation tools created entirely in Flex, and with plans for AIR distribution.

> *For some great samples of what I'm talking about, you can check out the Buzzword word processor at* http://virtub.com/, *the YouTube Remixer (which utilizes Adobe Premiere Express) at* www.youtube.com/ytremixer_about, *or the Picnik online photo editor at* www.picnik.com/. *For a larger list of showcase Flex applications, you can visit* http://flex.org/showcase/.

While Flash is only one technology in the increasingly diverse and vibrant landscape of Internet-enabled development, it is the technology whose capabilities are most pressingly forcing these questions.

As the world for Flash and Ajax application development continues to expand, you will more frequently confront basic questions that boil down to whether you see the portion of your project as a web page or an application.

The central questions that underpin this decision include the following:

- How do you want users to consume the information?
- How do you want users to consume it today and in versions 2, 3, and 4?
- Will this preceding change?
- What type of experience are you trying to create?

The number of visual and usability considerations that accompany this decision are, of course, much larger than just "Back button vs. undo feature." For instance, web pages tend to rely on the browser scrollbar, and applications tend not to scroll or employ their own scrolling UI when necessary.

We view the RMX overall as a web-based application, consisting of many pages, some of which contain discrete applications and some of which contain more traditionally structured web sites. The entirety of the administrative control panel is a single application, with many different states encompassing a wide array of functionality and accessible from a single URL. While this type of application is perfectly suited for Flex development, this is even how HTML-based control panels, such as vBulletin's, tend to be structured.

The publicly available web sites of the RMX are a different matter. The two parts of the web site that exist almost entirely in HTML (like traditional web sites) are the blogs and the forums. We opted for this model for these sections of the RMX because they are text-heavy, and they are community experiences that people have come to expect delivered in an HTML web site. The point may come in the near future where we redevelop the blogs and forums using Flex, but that will depend on the feedback from our users over time.

The rest of the RMX site is a series of individual applications, including the video network, the jobs board, the membership directory, and the event calendar. The interfaces for these sections have been wired and designed to function as applications, and do not interact with browser history, although permalinks may be created to any individual piece of content that exists within these applications. So, you can send your friend a direct link to any video, job posting, member page, or event on the RMX network.

Searching and filtering

For information to be usable and valuable, it must also be accessible. Traditionally, in the world of projects for web distribution, search functionality has provided this accessibility. But in the world of RIAs, filtering takes on a new importance, often replacing and improving on the functionality offered by pure search.

At a purely technical level, the core difference between searching and filtering is that when you search, you reach out for results; Google is, of course, the perfect example of this. Alternatively, when you filter, you pare down existing results, just as when you filter your iTunes library (in the field labeled Search!). For this reason, filtering is instantaneous, while searching takes time; filtering does not generate any new results, while searching does.

Both have their place, and you will learn more about them in the context of the control panel and RMX sites next.

The nature of the network

The Rich Media Exchange exists as a network of independent group web sites. A **group** on the RMX is either an Adobe User Group or an industry expert with his own RMX web site; the core difference is that expert sites do not support user-generated video, or have a jobs board or a wiki. Members on the network, as explained earlier, effectively subscribe to different groups on the network. Since the network exists entirely of user-generated content, these relationships have broad implications across the entire RMX.

I briefly addressed the concept of user levels earlier. It's worth revisiting because of its effects on content distribution. In the RMX, there are standard members, group moderators, group admins, network moderators, and network admins. As you saw previously in Figure 3-5, different member types have different powers across the RMX, from viewing and creating content, to moderating and managing content. Group and expert admins may administer any of the content on their individual sites, as well as ban specific members from their sites, and network admins may manage all content and all members across the entire network. This is why there are four different views of the RMX control panel, reflecting different permissions levels and powers: one each for group and network moderators, and group and network admins.

The member level also determines the ability to create certain types of content. As you see in Figure 3-10, only admins may create featured video on the RMX, either by direct upload or by promoting specific user-generated videos. As well, only admins may post events. Beyond that, any member of any level (unless he is banned) may generate all other types of content on the network.

When a member generates content on the RMX, it can flow to various locations on the network, based on the subscriptions of the member. When I create a blog post, that post is syndicated to every group and expert site to which I belong across the network. It is also accessible through my personal RMX page.

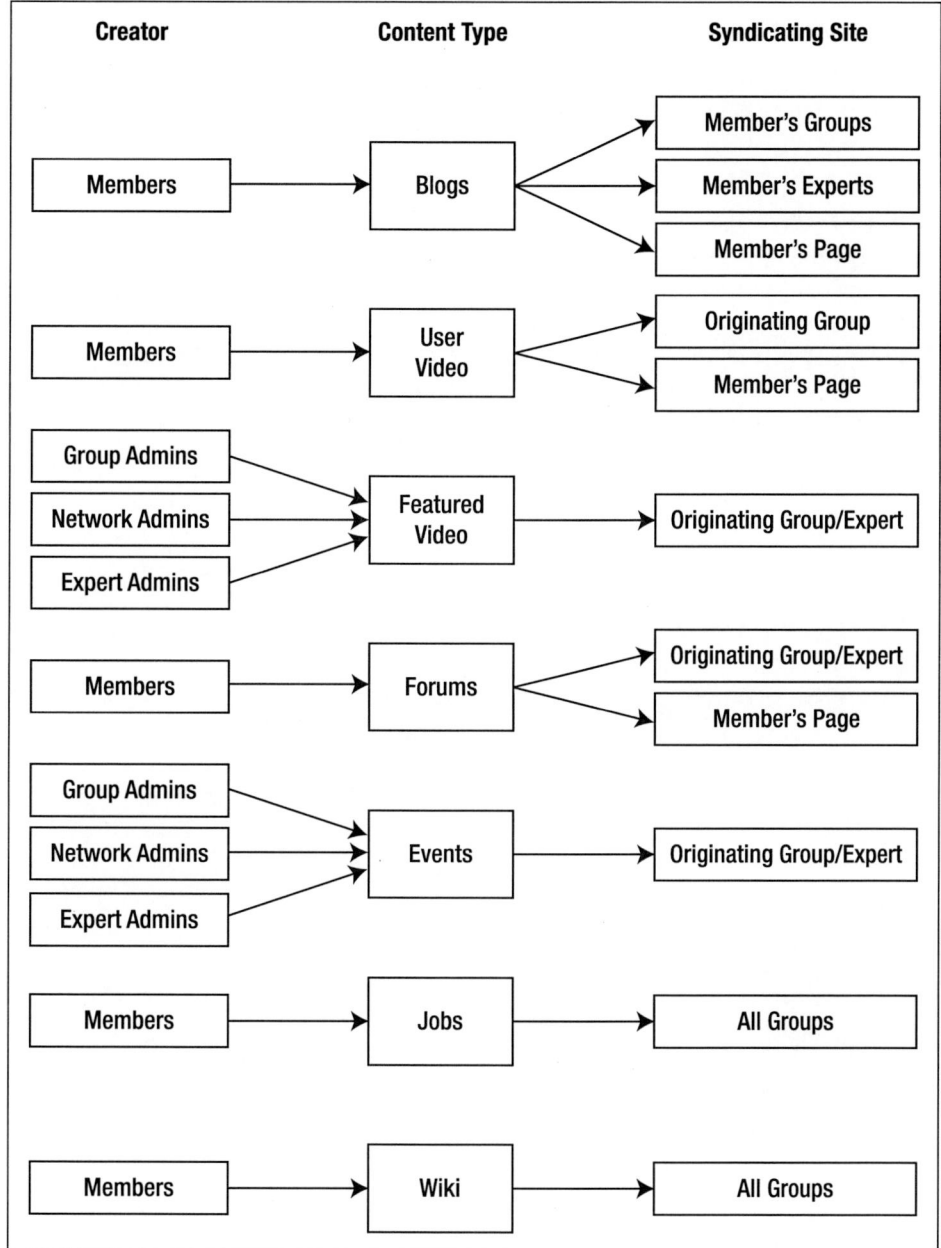

Figure 3-10. RMX content flow overview

When a member posts a job or edits the wiki, on the other hand, updates occur across all RMX sites. Specific consideration of the automatic syndication and distribution of content must be made on a case-by-case basis, given the nature of the content, the distributed network structure of the RMX, and the various relationships that exist on the network.

Central navigational elements

While there are many different interaction and UI elements across the RMX, I want to introduce some of the items and concepts that are central to presenting the RMX data and navigating around the experience.

The control panels

The control panels—the tools the RMX moderators and administrators use to control the content and activity on the network—are, of course, applications. We believe this is obvious not only to us, the developers, but also the consumers of the applications. Control panels, or dashboard applications in the parlance of Flex, are by definition applications. Indeed, they are arguably the ideal type of application for which Flex has been designed from the ground up to enable. Figure 3-11 includes a screenshot of one such panel: the Upload Moderation control panel on which moderators and admins can control which videos are allowed to be posted for the public.

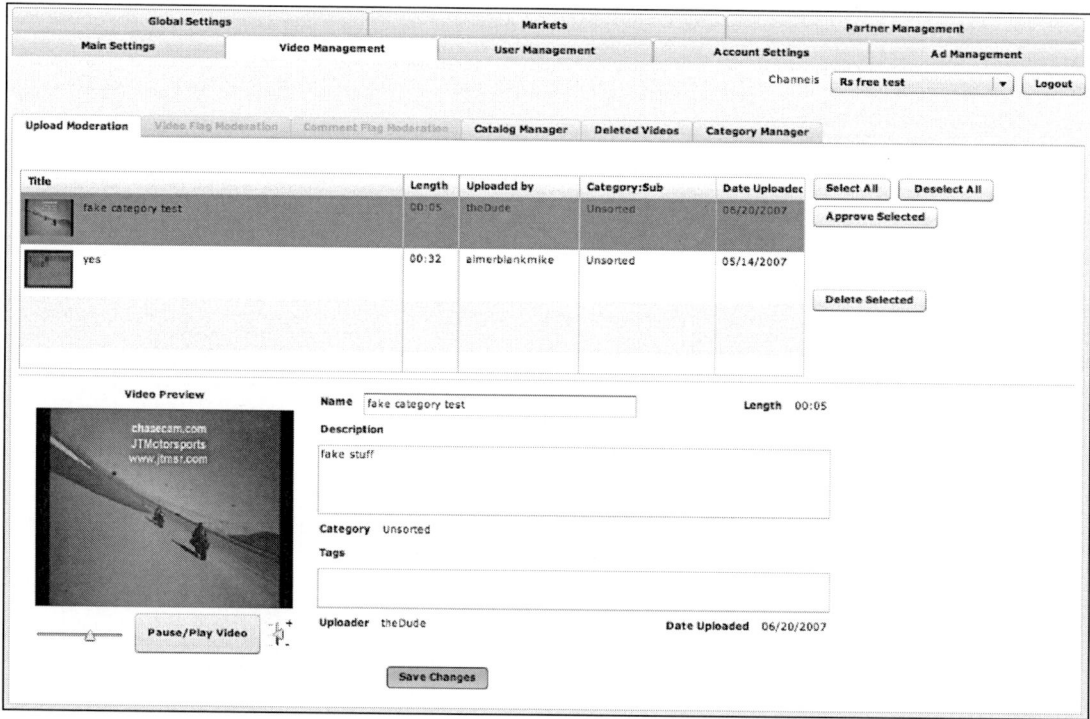

Figure 3-11. Version 1 of the Upload Moderation control panel

Let's examine some of the key features of this control panel, including saving data, tabbing between screens, and the key components used to display data within those screens.

Saving data

Whereas, for the most part, the RMX web site is about accessing information (and, because of RSS, is in effect only one of an infinite number of platforms in which the information may be consumed), the control panels are about both accessing and modifying information. Whenever data is modified, the changes must, of course, be saved.

It's odd—because again, in an application such as Microsoft Word, no one is surprised that they have to explicitly save their work. But because Flash applications derive more from the legacy of web experiences, this fact is not as obvious to users.

In an ideal world, all changes would be logged to the data server as soon as they were made. However, unless you need your application to be in continuous communication with your data server (a decision that brings very high levels of bandwidth and performance overhead), this is impractical.

In essence, what we are confronting is the difference between the view and the model. Because of how applications work, humans utilize views to alter the models. As soon as Joe User logs a change, he expects that change to be reflected in the model. But, because in many cases supporting that in a web-based application is untenable, we must pursue other options.

For this reason, some interactions, such as renaming categories or recategorizing videos, force dialog pop-ups that include explicit save and cancel functionality. Whenever an interaction is processed through a dialog box, the save functionality is obvious, inherent, and unescapable. However, executing the same feature without a dialog box will almost inevitably create for more refined user interactions.

As you can see in Figure 3-12, we disable the entire interface until getting a response from the server on the success of the data transaction to prevent the user from continuing to work with the data while its state is indeterminate.

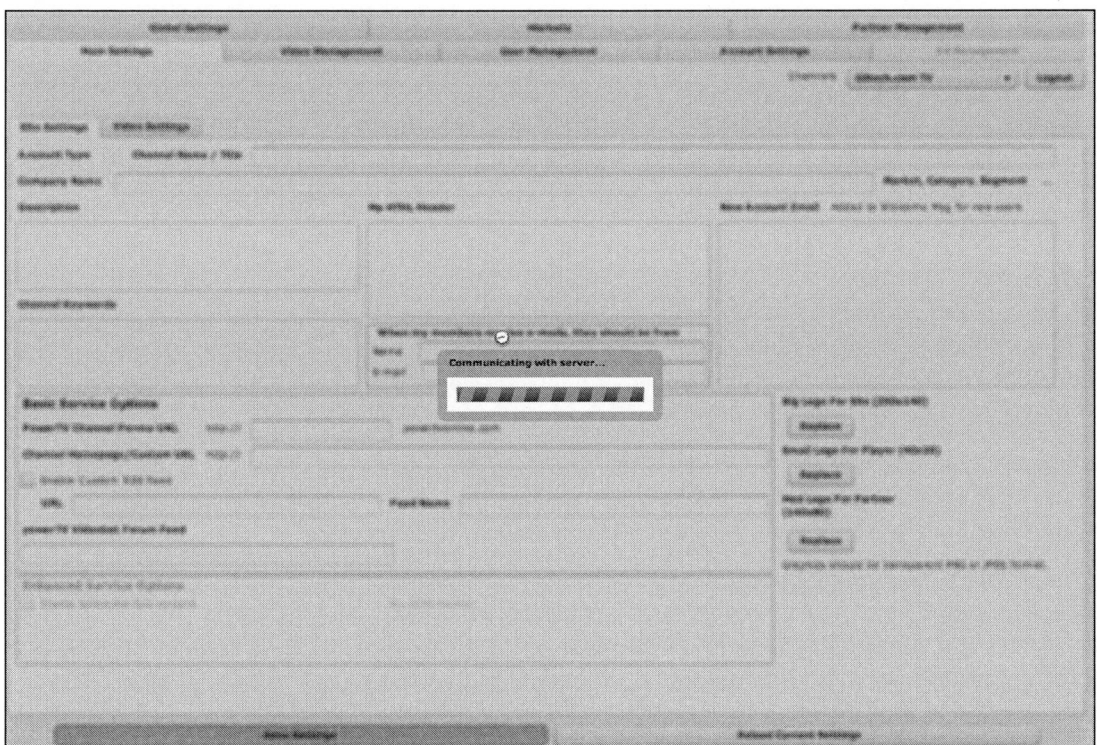

Figure 3-12. The RMX control panel while communicating with the server (such as saving changes)

As a result, virtually every page of the control panel contains Save Settings and Reload Current Settings buttons, the latter of which reverts the data to the state it was in on load. Indeed, in wiring the control panels, the question wasn't so much "Where do we need Save buttons?" as "Where can we omit the Save buttons?"

To simplify somewhat the confusion that could easily ensue from unlogged changes (the user expects data has been updated, when in fact it hasn't), I recommend utilizing a dialog box. For instance, if the data rendered in the view has been updated but not logged to the data server, you might consider popping up a message, just as you see when you close the Adobe Flash IDE without having saved your FLA: "There are unsaved changes. Are you sure you wish to leave this view without saving?"

Tabs

To segment the functionality of the control panels, we employ tabs. Tabs are a common method for creating an easy-to-use mechanism for rapid switching between various sets of functionality. Of course, tabs work best when the area available for displaying the tabs is sufficient to display the text in all the tabs. Once the information requirements force tabs to unreadable widths, they are no longer as practical. Of course, at that point, you could just create a second row of tabs, but you should be aware that the Flex TabNavigator component does not natively support multirow tabs.

The Flex TabNavigator natively supports browser history integration, which is appropriate given their function. Switching between tabs is a complete change of state. However, because of the nature of the RMX control panel and the desire not to make any individual section bookmarkable, we do not support the Back button in our control panel.

Because of some of the complexity in the required functionality of the control panels and the desire to keep the main navigation as simple as possible, in several areas of the control panels, we have implemented multiple tiers of tab navigation. For instance, there is a main Moderation tab, which in turn contains a second-tier tab navigator with Video Moderation, Comments Moderation, Profile Moderation, and Upload Moderation.

DataGrids

One vital aspect of Flex, and ActionScript 3–powered Flash applications in general, is that it can simply roar through data in a way that old-school Flash developers used to dream about. When combined with the E4X enhancements, meaning XML data no longer needs to be parsed, the overall performance of massive data sets is quite impressive.

I mention this here because the DataGrids in the RMX control panels are designed to accommodate massive reams of data. We have not incorporated pagination anywhere in the control panels precisely because we can rely on our DataGrids to handle many thousands of records.

One important question to consider whenever including DataGrids is how they are selectable. Depending on the function, some of the DataGrids in the RMX control panels have multiple row selections possible (for instance, if you wish to select several videos for rapid recategorization) and some enable only single selections (for instance, in the membership management panel, because of the interactions unique to that screen, only single rows may be selected).

It is also worth highlighting the importance of sorting and its inherent support in the Flex DataGrid components.

As well, when employing DataGrids, you have the option of making content directly editable in the DataGrids or having the DataGrids render data in an uneditable format. Almost all DataGrids in the RMX control panels render data such that it is uneditable.

Filters

Filters are the key mechanism behind making massive DataGrids usable. And again, with the performance improvements in ActionScript 3, as well as the inherent support in the Flex framework for filtering, inclusion of robust filtering is both easy and a no-brainer. Indeed, one of Almer/Blank's clients, Live Nation, contracted us to rebuild in Flex a content management system we'd initially built in Flash 8, precisely because of the filtering performance. Their acquisition of House of Blues, a chain of music venues and restaurants, forced our system to accommodate thousands of media records, whereas previously we'd handled only dozens.

Anywhere you see a DataGrid in the RMX, you see a filter field. And, per the Apple standard, there is always a Clear Filter button to the immediate right of the filter field. It is important to note that it is possible to have your filter mechanism filter by more information than is displayed in the DataGrid. For instance, in our membership management panel, we display only the base user information (name, e-mail, account ID, type, and status), but the filter mechanism can still scour the About Me field, even though that is not displayed in the DataGrid.

Trees

FlexTube.tv employs a category/subcategory system for the basic categorization of all video in the system. We use Tree components to handle the category/subcategory system in the control panel, making it easy to navigate through the various types of videos. They also make it relatively easy to select an entire category and to view all the videos in that category, as you can see in Figure 3-13, which displays the categories and subcategories of a test site on the RMX.

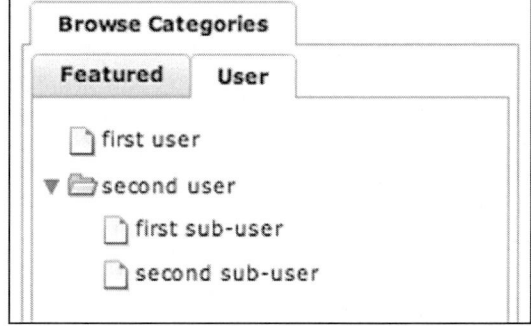

Figure 3-13. A sample of the tree from the control panel video category manager

Drag and Drop

One of the coolest interactions that Flex inherently supports is drag-and-drop capability. We utilize this to allow groups to establish the playlist that populates the featured player on their site front page. Drag-and-drop interactions are cool for three reasons:

- They are easy to understand and fun to use.
- In most cases they provide a more expeditious and click-free experience of whatever process they enable than an alternative mechanism.
- And, as I said, this interaction type is natively supported in Flex.

The site

The RMX control panel we just explored is an unskinned, relatively unstyled, raw Flex application. As such, it provides a "pure" example of the concepts highlighted previously—that is, the tab navigators look like tab navigators. As I begin the discussion of the RMX public web site, it is important to understand you are examining a relatively heavily skinned and styled implementation of Flex. As such, some of the mechanisms may be somewhat obscured.

Tabs

While the heavily skinned and styled RMX site navigation may not appear to have tabs, and while we may not actually consume the TabNavigator component, the main site navigation performs very much like tab navigation. Each button on the navigation links to a different section of the site. And, as most sections of the site are independent RIAs (again, with the current exceptions of blogs and forums), the main navigation is the only item of the site that consistently interacts with the browser history. That is, when you click from the video section to the event calendar, and then click around, those clicks within the event calendar do not interact with the browser history, but the click that switched you from the video section to the calendar does.

Pagination

In my mind, sites like Google have created what people now consider to be standard pagination navigation, as you see in Figure 3-14.

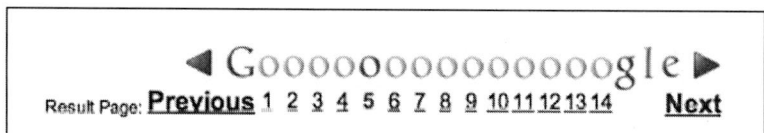

Figure 3-14. How Google handles pagination

While I understand this component is a de facto web standard, and when we discard web standards, we should do so with extreme care, this component has always bothered me for two main reasons. First, it is unclear in the widget how many pages are in the results, and second, it restricts the pages to which I can easily jump to those within close proximity of the page I'm currently viewing. I would like to know how many pages resulted from the search and like to have the ability to quickly access any individual one.

For this reason, throughout the RMX, we have implemented a different paging widget, shown in Figure 3-15 (both wired and designed), utilizing a ComboBox in place of a string of numbers linked to each results page.

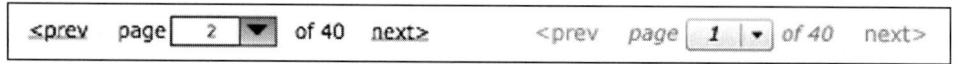

Figure 3-15. The RMX standard pagination widget, wired (left) and designed (right)

One immediate benefit from this design is space savings—Google is a sparse design with lots of vertical height in which to place elements. Much of the RMX is designed to fit within a single browser footprint to eliminate browser scrolling, so each pixel we can save is of great benefit to us. As well, this interface allows users to see how many pages are in the search and makes it easy to link to any single one.

Ratings

As described in Chapter 2, ratings are an important mechanism for allowing higher-quality content to bubble upward in the network, enabling easier access to a wider audience. Thanks to Netflix, the ratings widget, like the one you see in Figure 3-16, has become an easily understood UI component. This widget allows Netflix users to rate content on a scale of zero to five.

We employ this in various aspects of the RMX site, but most comprehensively in the video network, in which any video is easily ratable. Ratings widgets, such as the ones shown in Figure 3-17, appear throughout the video network.

The ratings widget has three states: noninteractive, ready for interactivity, and being interacted with. The noninteractive ratings widget is displayed, for example, to all anonymous (or non–logged-in) users on the RMX, since ratings require a member account in which to store the ratings.

In this state, the widget displays the average rating the content has received. In this respect, the behavior of ratings on RMX is different from on Netflix; if you browse the Netflix catalog without logging in, ratings are not presented in the interface, so there is no need for a noninteractive version of the widget. The noninteractive ratings widget has no need for an explicit zero setting, since no stars is the same as zero.

The interactive version of the ratings widget on the RMX, such as logged-in members see when viewing videos, displays the average rating of the content, just as the noninteractive version does. But members may rate the content through the widget by clicking the star that represents the rating—for example, clicking the fourth star assigns a rating of four stars, and clicking the zero icon sets a rating of zero. Once a member has rated a piece of content, the widget then displays that user's assigned rating for that piece of content. The user may change his rating by selecting a different star. For clarity, the average rating and the user's own rating are displayed using different colors.

Flagging

Just as any content on the network may be rated, it may also be flagged. Flagging marks the content for review, for whatever reason, for moderators. Moderators see the flag, review the content, and decide what to do. For simplicity of development and of user experience, we have employed a standard flagging widget. Wherever in the RMX the user sees the words "flag this," he may click to reveal a dialog box, as you see in Figure 3-18, that asks the user to specify the reason for the content flag. The user may either cancel out of the dialog or select a reason and process the flag. Once a piece of content is flagged, it is submitted to the content moderation queue in the administrative control panel.

Figure 3-16. The Netflix ratings widget in context

Figure 3-17. The three states of the RMX standard ratings widgets

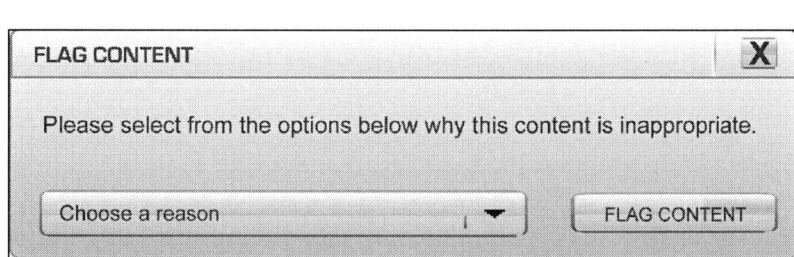

Figure 3-18. The RMX flag widget

Flagging content sends the content into the flagged content queue, which may be moderated through the RMX control panel. Moderators also receive e-mail notification when content has been flagged, which links them to the flagged content in the control panel.

Just as we attempted to simplify the process of flagging content in the site with a single flagging widget, so have we attempted to simplify resolving flags in the control panel. We utilize a widget, such as you see wired in Figure 3-19, on each of the Flag Moderation screens. This enables the moderator to rapidly remove the flag, delete the content, and possibly ban the creator of the content.

Figure 3-19. The flag resolution widget, seen in many locations within the RMX control panel

By developing standard widgets for the flagging of all content and the resolution of those flags, we have simplified the user experience of the RMX and made it easy to implement flagging functionality throughout the site.

Zip Codes

Information on the RMX is generated across the entire network, which spans most of an entire continent, even at launch, running from eastern Canada to the southwestern United States. Since, for example, each group site within the RMX shares the same jobs board, we employ a zip code lookup in the jobs board to facilitate local searches. The same technology is used elsewhere in the site, including in the advertising campaign management (so that ad campaigns may be targeted by zip code, among other factors). The ability to search within a radius of a zip code is a major factor in the usability of the jobs board and the value of the advertising network. And, as we implement zip code searching in more areas of the site, it will continue to increase the value of the RMX content catalog by making the content more meaningful.

There are many licensable products available to facilitate the development of zip code lookups. When searching for the solution that's right for your project, it is important to understand that different solutions provide different types of functionality. For instance, there are solutions that will identify the zip code of the visitor to your site by an IP-to-zip lookup. This is called **geotargeting**, and OpenAds natively supports the MaxMind GeoIP database (you can view details on the OpenAds geotargeting support at http://docs.openads.org/openads-2.0-guide/host-info-and-geotargeting.html and the MaxMind GeoIP solution at www.maxmind.com/app/ip-location). There are other zip code solutions that translate zip codes into the information about the zip code, such as town, county, state, area code, and time zone (like the Melissa Data zip code directory at www.melissadata.com/zd.html).

Neither of these solutions provides the functionality that we require on the RMX, and it is important to ensure the zip code solution you select has the power you need in your project. As mentioned previously, we require knowledge of all zip codes within a radius of a specified zip code. This is often referred to as a **zip code radius search**. We selected the ZIP Code Download solution, which supports an optional distance and radius lookup API. We spent about $150 for the data and services we needed. (For more information on this solution, please visit www.zipcodedownload.com/Products/Product/Z5Commercial/Standard/Overview/ and www.zipcodedownload.com/Products/Family/DistRad/.)

The way in which we expose this functionality to the user is through a slider-based component, as shown in Figure 3-20.

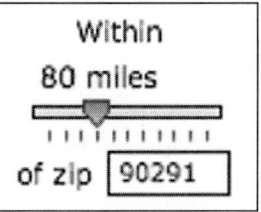

Figure 3-20. The zip code radius widget

Sliders are both intuitive and somewhat fun to use. Often they are used where they do not belong, however. For instance, just recently I took an online survey, and a slider was used to switch between three different options (positive, neutral, and negative) for each question asked. This was a really poor implementation of sliders. Users intuitively expect sliders to have many discrete possible values (like the volume control in iTunes), any of which may be selected by the positioning of the slider nub. In the example I just cited, a radio button mechanism would have been far more appropriate, since there were only three possible options; the slider was just the designer's idea of making the survey seem a bit cooler, but it resulted in a negative effect on the user experience.

In the RMX zip code widget, users enter a zip code (which will default to their own zip code if they are logged in) and then drag the slider nub to increase or decrease the size of the search radius. The minimum value (the far left) is 5 miles, and the maximum value (the far right) is Unlimited.

Search

If you examine version 1 of the RMX, you will notice that there is no button anywhere labeled "Search." Of course, I am certain that many usability experts will consider the lack of a site-wide search feature a sin. However, this was intentional for a few reasons. The primary reason is that, a general search feature seemed far too broad a functionality for a network of sites that include such a wide variety of content—videos (featured and user), event calendars, members, jobs, forum posts, and so on. We had originally wired a search function encompassing all the content on the network, but in reviewing the wires we decided it was too overwhelming, confusing, and not particularly useful.

For instance, let's say that my video is syndicated on the LA Flash and Flash in TO sites. How would I search for that video? Would all results appear on both LA Flash and Flash in TO? If I performed a general search on the RMX, and a video of mine was returned, would it link to the LA Flash video site, or the Flash in TO video site? Would it be different if I searched on LA Flash instead of across the entire network? And what compelling reason would there be to search through all content on the network? So, we have employed searching and filtering in various locations throughout the RMX (in particular, blogs and forums are searchable) but there is no site-wide general search.

I feel it is important to add that we are not wedded to this model in the long term. By the time RMX version 2 is released, we may feel that it is important to create a dedicated, network-wide search function. But this will depend on a variety of factors, including usage patterns of the network, the amount of data accessible on the network, and, of course, complaint e-mails. I am also not advocating this style of UI design as appropriate for everyone—I am instead explaining why we chose the functionality we did—and to reiterate how important it is to consider all these issues when planning a social media network, or perhaps more appropriately in the case of the RMX, a network of social networks.

While there is no site-wide or network-wide search function in RMX version 1, we do incorporate these features to different degrees in each section of the site. Let's examine just a few cases of how this functionality is handled on the RMX. For instance, we do include a Members link in the top navigation of each RMX group site. Clicking this link performs a search on all members of a particular group. Those results are sorted into pages of 20 members each, which in version 1 may be sorted alphabetically or chronologically by last login.

I wish to highlight that on the RMX we do not store the gender of our members, an intentional decision to prevent trolls searching for women on the network. This is a problem on sites like MySpace, which is why you find women on MySpace who list themselves as being 160 years old, just so that they are not returned in member searches. Added to that, we do not view gender as relevant to the purposes of what is, in essence, a professional network. This is also an issue you should consider on any similar type of social networking site.

In the RMX video network, we rely on classification by category/subcategory to generate sufficient organization for the content to be usefully accessible. We include filters here to improve the ability to target specific content within categories and subcategories by searching all text associated with a video (the title, description, and additional tags). Videos are listed 20 to a page. A true filter would only scan the text for the 20 videos currently displayed. In the case of the RMX video network, as you type a word in the filter, the results are updated in real time.

The jobs board, however, provides a different mechanism. Because job postings conform to a standard set of information, it is possible to create a very robust and detailed classification system for the content in that section of the site. By default, the jobs board displays jobs in reverse chronological order. To make it easier for job seekers to find the right jobs for themselves, we have included what we call filters, but they are really more appropriately called search filters. In the jobs board, a user may filter results by location, level of responsibility, required technologies, and zip code, among many other criteria. But clicking Apply Filters generates a new search—it does not simply filter the currently displayed results.

Planning parts of the RMX

While I've covered a broad range of issues involved in planning, wiring, and spec'ing the RMX, I would like to examine in a bit more depth the planning process for two sections of the application. As the events calendar and the jobs board are both parts of the RMX that have been built from scratch entirely in Flex, and because we write about how they were built in Chapters 13 and 14, let's take a moment to see how these operate. For each of these two features of the RMX, let's explore the goals of the feature (why we are building them and what constitutes success) and then how we translated the goals into wireframes to be placed into development. As well, we take a moment to explore the differences between the control panels for group and expert admins, and the network-wide control panel for RMX admins.

This section will cover the following topics:

- The RMX jobs board
- The RMX event calendar
- Planning different access levels for the RMX control panel

The jobs board

As a user group manager, I have personally noticed the value of maintaining a jobs board on the user group site. For years at LA Flash, the jobs board was nothing more than a forum on our boards. And still it attracted a large number of postings—growing from about one a week in 2003 to a dozen or more each week by the time we switched over to the RMX.

So, while maintaining a jobs board is not a requirement for running a user group, it is clearly of significant value both to the members of the user group communities and to employers in the regions in which the user groups operate. Therefore, we saw the inclusion of a jobs board in the RMX as an important feature for the success of the network.

In planning for this feature, the first goal was to create a system that was specific to the task. One of the reasons searching for these types of jobs is so frustrating in classifieds sites like Craigslist (one of the best existing sources for employment opportunities in Los Angeles) is that the work of those skilled in Adobe technologies is so specialized. How often have you seen job postings for "Flash guru" without knowing really what type of guru the employer is seeking? A skilled Flash animator is very different from a high-level ActionScripter—both are in-demand positions, and both would be returned for searches of "Flash" on any jobs site.

Instead of relying on an inappropriate information structure (as we had at LA Flash when we utilized forums for job postings) or the type of generic job posting criteria on sites like Craigslist, we decided to invest the time and effort to construct a basic jobs board that would provide a more efficient system for categorizing jobs—sculpting a jobs board specifically for Adobe designers and developers.

The goal of the jobs board is to provide an easily used and understood application for people to post employment opportunities and for the members of the RMX to sort through those opportunities in a manageable manner.

The first step in our planning was determining precisely what criteria would be most useful and relevant for jobs postings custom-tailored to the Adobe developer community. This information would allow us to plan both the interfaces of the jobs board as well as the database requirements to support the information requirements.

We determined the following pieces of information were vital to our vision:

- Title
- Description
- Date
- Location of posting (zip code)
- Location of work (onsite, offsite, onsite for meetings, doesn't matter)
- Level of involvement (employee, freelance)
- Source (employer or recruiter)
- Pay range
- Required technologies
- Role (e.g., print designer, web coder, video editing, project manager, etc.)
- Seniority

Associating these fields with each posting allows the user to search, for example, for all mid-level free-lance jobs, posted within the past 30 days, involving Flash and Photoshop, within 20 miles of his home, paying between $70–90/hr or a minimum of $80,000 annual salary. Alternatively, the user could search for all offsite full-time employment opportunities in Flex across the entire network that come directly from an employer, rather than through a recruiter. Basically, these fields enable most any type of search relevant to Adobe talent for the types of job opportunities they normally seek.

In terms of technologies required for the position, because the RMX is designed as a community for those skilled with Adobe technologies, we include a list of Adobe software packages. As well, because of the importance of open source technologies in the web development world and the fact that we view open source technologies as complementary to, not in competition with, Adobe technologies, we opted to include a second list of major open source technologies. We could add a lot more tools here from other manufacturers (like Electric Rain Swift 3D or Eyeblaster expandable ads, such as the ones I show you how to build in Chapter 11), but we opted to keep it simple for launch and cover the most relevant technologies. Over time, the list of technology tags will no doubt grow.

Only members may post jobs on the network to help reduce spam postings and to ensure we have the contact information of anyone who posts a job on the network.

In future versions of the RMX jobs board, the application process will be moderated by the network. That is, in version 2 of the jobs board, if I want to apply for a position, I will click Apply and the job poster will receive an e-mail indicating that I have responded to the post, including a link to my RMX member page. We realized that we did not need this full process in place for launch, and since it requires additional services and database development, we opted to remove this functionality from the launch spec. But we wanted to wire a process that would enable a seamless upgrade in function-ality at a later point in time. So, we have included an Apply button that, at launch, simply creates a new e-mail in your e-mail client, but in future versions the same button will do much more. If we had instead simply included the job poster's e-mail contact information, upgrading the functionality down the line would require altering the user interface.

In addition to viewing job postings, members should be able to forward relevant postings to their friends and colleagues, so we decided to include a way to trigger that "share" functionality. And, since job postings represent unmoderated user-generated content, we had to include the ability for mem-bers to flag questionable postings, sending them to moderators and admins for review.

The spec and wires

There are two sets of wires for the jobs board: one for the jobs board on the public site and one for moderating the jobs board content within the control panel.

Site interface

With the data requirements set, we could begin wiring the interfaces. We view the jobs board as an independent application within the RMX, so it is wired to create no browser scrolling, instead using scrollbars within the interface to handle all scrolling content. Results are returned 20 to a page, and the pagination is independent of the browser history. In Figure 3-21, you see the wire for the default state of the jobs board that any RMX user would see when clicking Jobs in the top navigation or when following a link to a specific job posting from a send-to-friend e-mail.

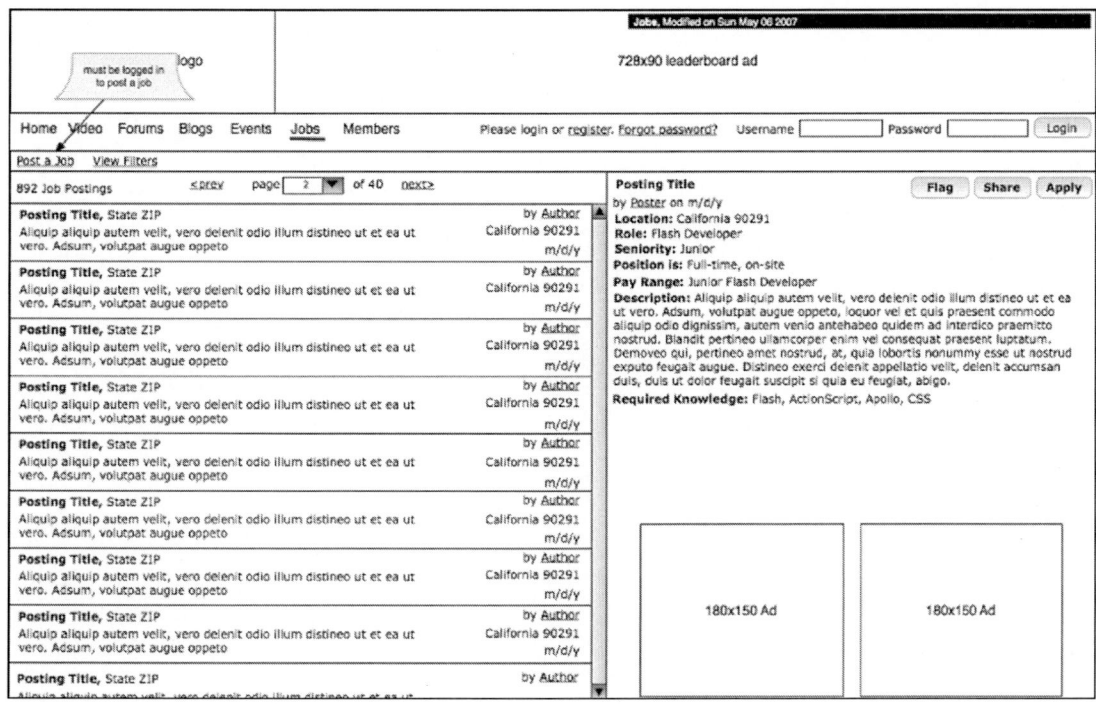

Figure 3-21. The default state of the RMX jobs board

The screen is broken into two main panels: a listing of jobs on the left and the detail of a selected job on the right. The default job listings include all job postings generated from the site on which the jobs are being viewed. The listing detail includes the ability to flag, share, or apply to the listing. Sharing the listing allows the user to send the posting to a friend's e-mail address, the state for which we diagrammed as shown in Figure 3-22. As I discussed in Chapter 2, sharing incorporates the ability to have a permalink to the content and to send that permalink through an automated e-mail to friends. Because this is a job posting, and not a video, there is no "embed" code.

Flagging the listing triggers the Flag Content dialog box (which you saw earlier in Figure 3-18), which submits the listing for review to the administrators and moderators on the site where the posting originated (remember, the site on which the listing is viewed may well be different from the site on which the user views the listing), as well as RMX network moderators and administrators.

From this default state, the user may customize his search by selecting View Filters, which switches the state of the application to the one you see wired in Figure 3-23.

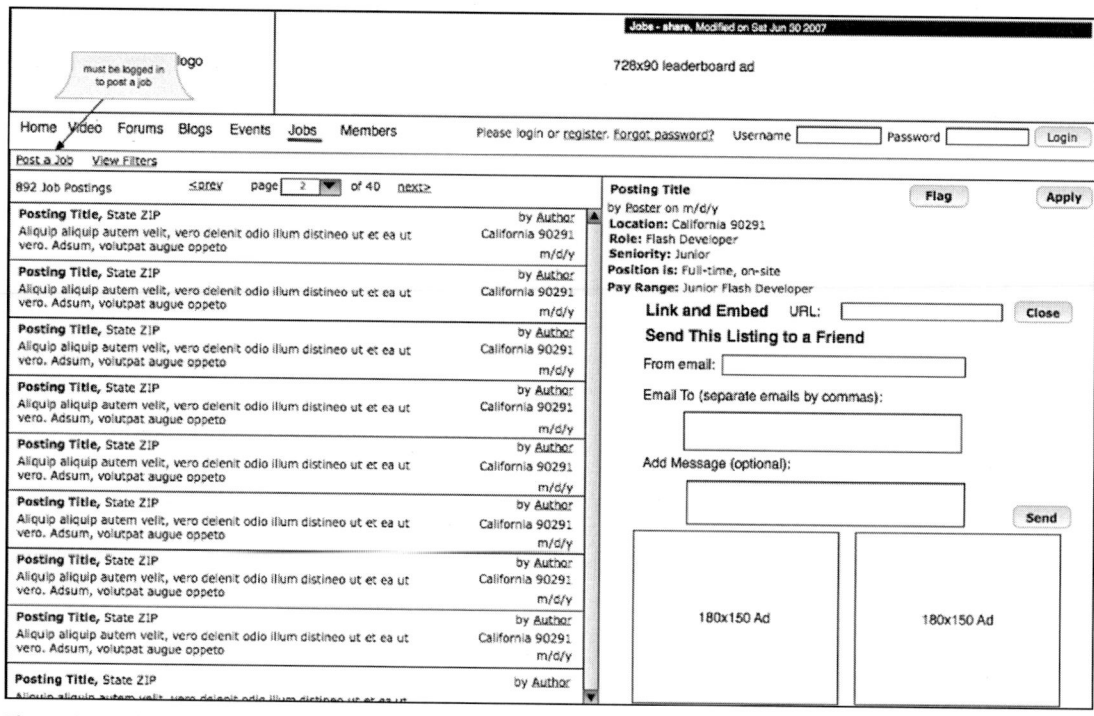

Figure 3-22. The wire for sharing an RMX job listing

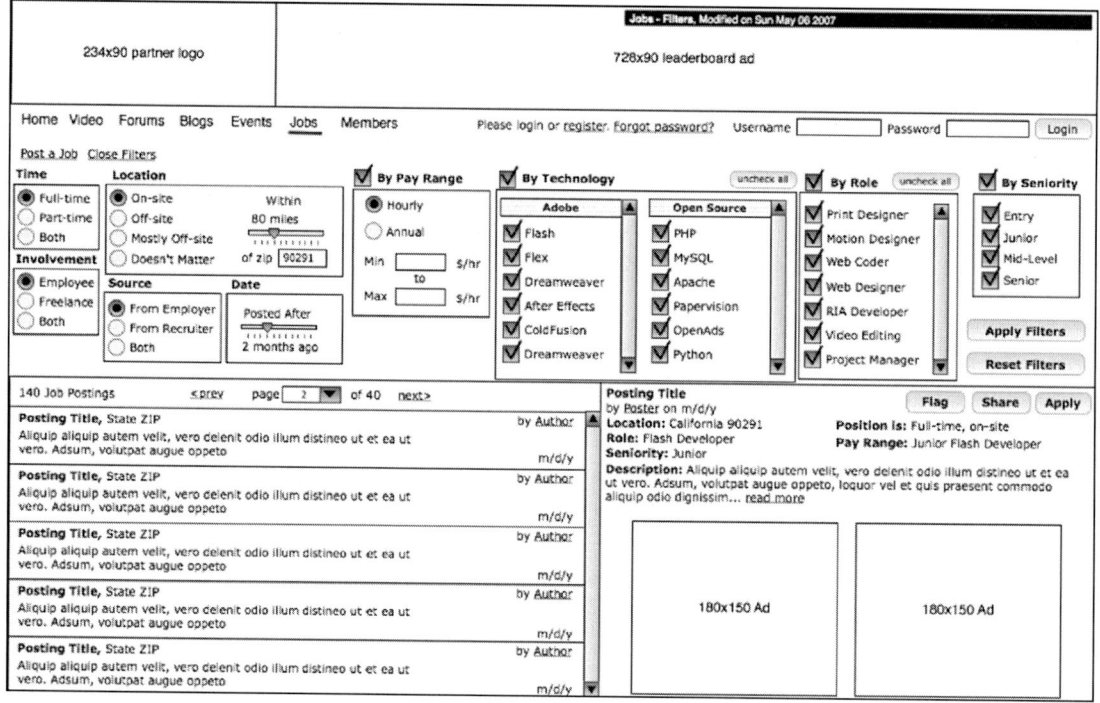

Figure 3-23. Viewing jobs filters

The search filters that are revealed in this state allow the user to specify in detail the nature of the job opportunities in which he is interested. We utilize radio buttons, check boxes, lists, text fields and sliders as appropriate to the nature of the specific information being filtered. Selecting Reset Filters returns all filters to the default state that generates the default search results in the initial state of the jobs application. Clicking Apply Filters generates a new job search based on the specified criteria. The user may also click Close Filters in order to return to the initial view of the screen, with more vertical space to display listings.

And at any time, a logged-in member may create a new listing on the network by clicking Post a Job, which brings the member to the screen that you see wired in Figure 3-24.

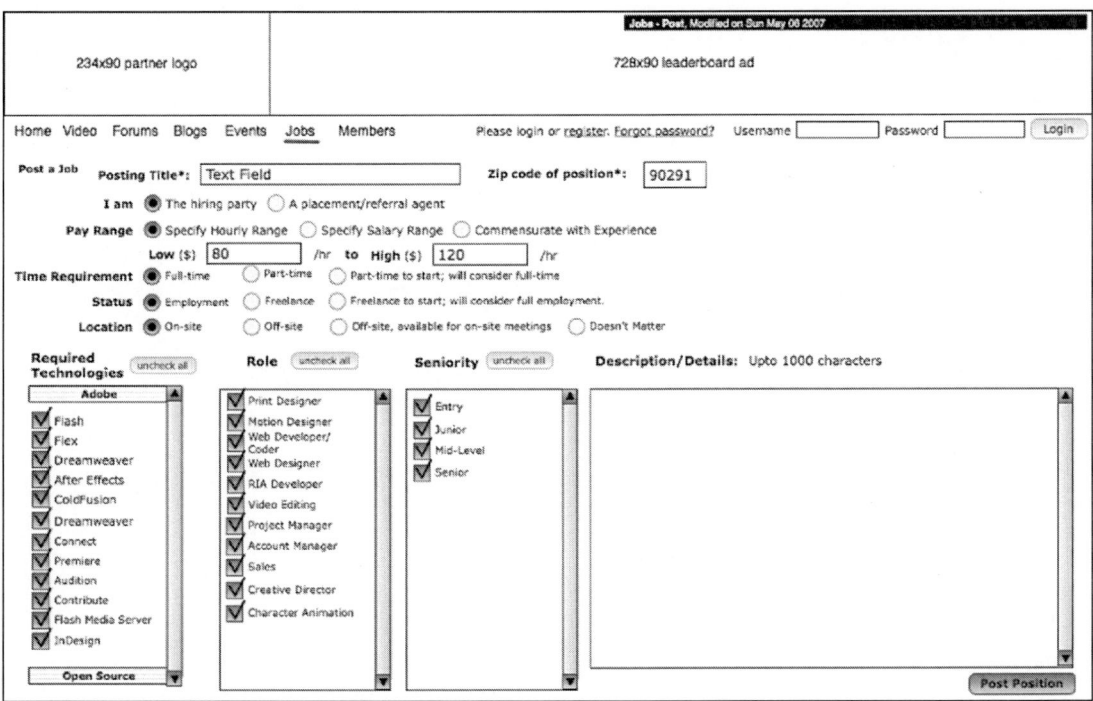

Figure 3-24. Posting a job on the RMX

On this screen, note the entry fields for each information type reviewed at the beginning of this section. Unlike the View Filters state of the jobs board, on this screen all fields are required. It is worth noting that this screen, like the screen on which users upload video to the network, includes no advertising. While advertising is a core business component for the free service the RMX provides, we view advertising as most appropriate in the content browsing portions of the RMX, and not in the context of content creation.

Control panel interface

All content generated on the network must be editable by administrators and moderators—this is a core requirement of any application with user-generated content catalogs. In general, this occurs in two places: in an interface that enables administrators to manage the content catalog and in an interface that allows moderators to review flagged content.

Because we were building the jobs application from the ground up as a Flex RIA, and the entire administrative control panel is a Flex RIA, we decided the most efficient way to develop the catalog manager was to port the jobs application in the RMX site into the control panel, so that we did not have to build a completely separate interface for the control panel. This meant we could reduce developer hours, centralize the code for the application, and make it easier to roll out new features in the future. You can see the result wired in Figure 3-25.

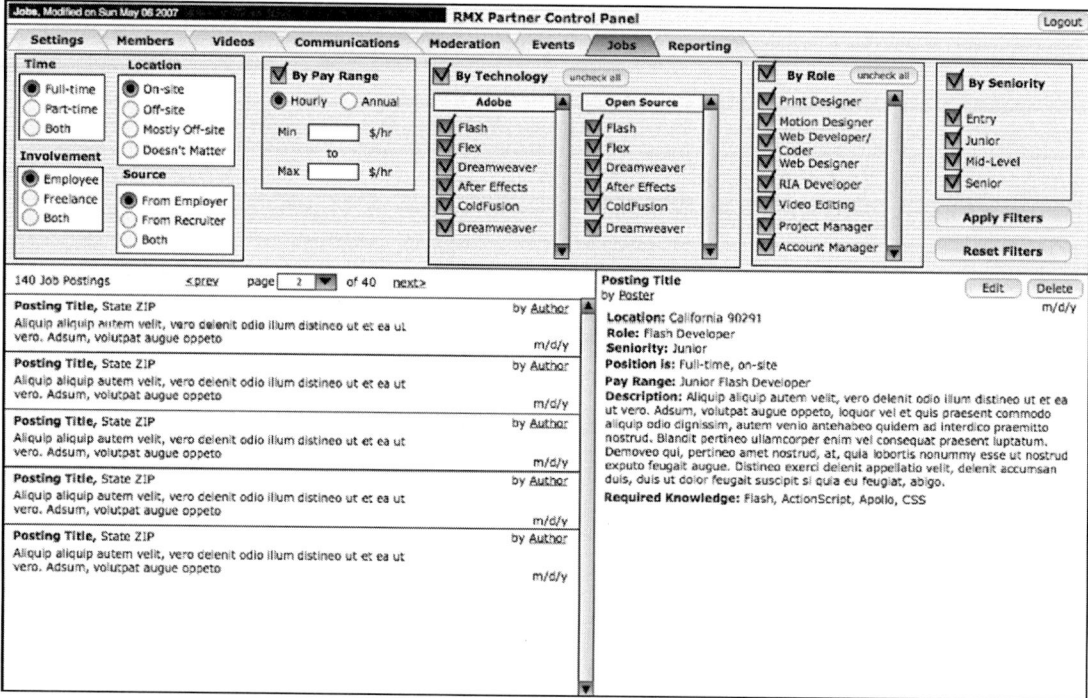

Figure 3-25. The administrative control panel for managing the catalog of job listings

This screen displays all the jobs created on that administrator's group site. So, as the administrator of LA Flash, I can modify or remove listings generated on my site, but I cannot view, modify, or delete the listings generated on another group's site, even though those listings will be displayed on my site.

This screen does have some differences from the public jobs board. First, the filters are always visible. As well, the Apply, Flag, and Share buttons are absent. And finally, note that Edit and Delete buttons are present. Deleting the listing deletes it from the entire network and is not undoable, so we present a confirmation dialog box prior to executing the order. Selecting Edit brings up the same screen as you saw earlier in Figure 3-24, the job posting screen, but inside the control panel. Again, this represents a way of reusing the existing code, almost wholesale, to complete an additional feature.

Reviewing flagged job listings occurs in a separate screen to enable moderator-level access, which you see wired in Figure 3-26.

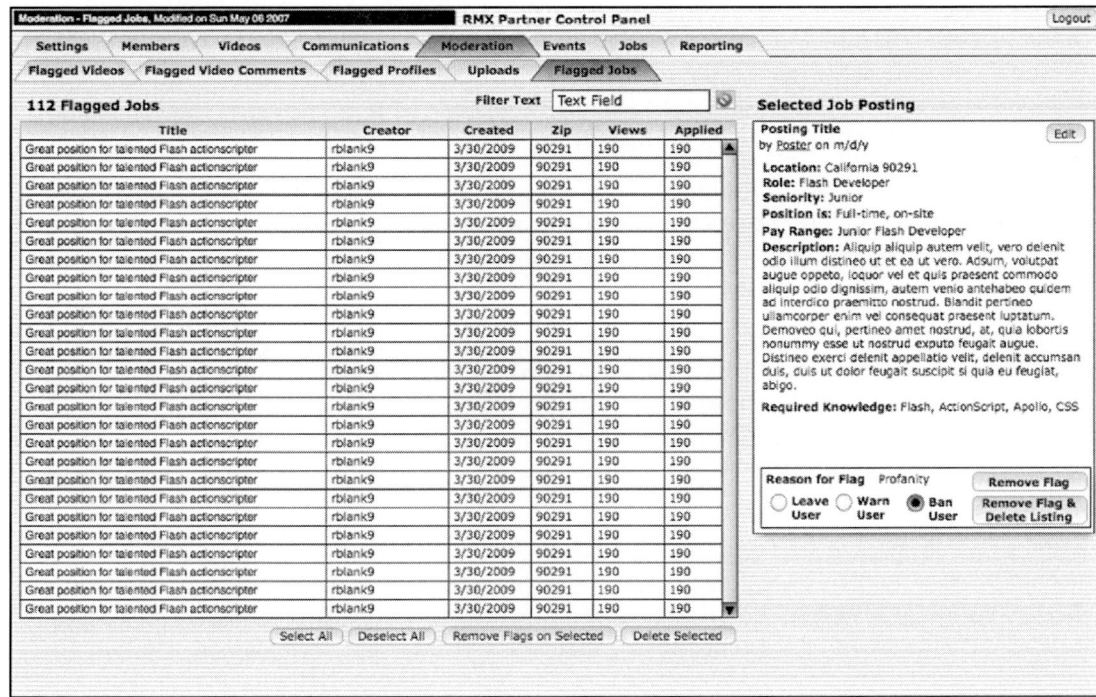

Figure 3-26. The Job Listings Flag Moderation screen

This screen shares many of the same elements and features as the other moderation panels, including flagged videos, flagged video comments, and flagged profiles. On this Flag Moderation screen, moderators may view all listings from their site that have been flagged. The DataGrid contains an entry for each flagged listing, with the title, creator, creation date, zip code, views, and number of times the Apply button was pressed. The DataGrid supports multiple row selection (an option in the Flex DataGrid component) for easy removal of flags on, or deletion of, multiple listings.

If a single row in the DataGrid is selected, the detail of that posting appears on the right, again with the Edit button present, functioning just as it does in Figure 3-25. The Delete button is not present because of the flag resolution widget, which is common to all Flag Moderation screens. The flag resolution widget displays the reason the flag was applied and enables the moderator to quickly either remove the flag or delete the flagged content, and, at the same time, optionally generate a warning e-mail to the member who posted the listing or ban him entirely. Unless done by a network administrator, banning only affects a member's status on a specific RMX site. So if I am banned on Flash in TO's site, I can still log in to LA Flash. In future versions, the flag resolution widget will likely include the information on the member who flagged the content, to identify whether this user is a profligate flagger, and options for warning or banning the flagger as well.

The event calendar

As the primary function of user groups is to hold meetings, an event calendar is a central function of this type of community site. Indeed, having an accurate list of upcoming events is a requirement of the Adobe User Group program. And a calendar is the best way to present this type of information.

Since an event calendar is part of the definition of a successful launch of the RMX, and since there are more events than just user group meetings that are of interest to user group members, we wanted to build a calendar system that could accommodate the variety of events of interest to this community. This includes training workshops, conferences, and Adobe-run presentations.

The event calendar is fundamentally different from the jobs board, not only in the information structures it supports, but also in how that information is generated. Content in the event calendar is not user generated; only administrators may create events in the calendar. So there is no interface to post events in the site, only in the control panels.

Of course, the calendar must display upcoming user group meetings. And since some user groups hold meetings virtually over Adobe Acrobat Connect, either to complement or to replace their real-life meetings, we included the ability to tag events with that information. Beyond user group meetings, there are other types of events we support. Events may also be tagged as Rich Media Institute training sessions, Adobe presentations (either road shows or Connect sessions), conferences, or the generic catchall "other."

Since groups will likely want to display their own events by default on their sites, there should be a mechanism to allow users to switch the view of the event calendar to restrict events to those of the group site they are on. The events should be easily browsable in a standard calendar-like interface. Event details should contain all the required information about the event, including the nature, location, description, and RSVP details. Users should be able to share events with a send-to-friend function. Finally, because users may be accessing the calendar from anywhere in the country, and people may tune into Connect sessions from many time zones away, it is important to place a time zone field in the calendar to enable the user to convert the local times of the event for the time zone of the viewer of the site.

Some user group meetings and events have RSVP requirements. At launch, the RMX event calendar allows the creator to specify whether or not an event requires an RSVP, and if it does, the address to which RSVPs should be sent. If a logged-in member clicks RSVP in the calendar, an e-mail is generated to the originator of the event with the information on the member who has RSVP'd. In future versions of the RMX, we plan to make the RSVP system more robust, with an expanded event management system, as I explain in Chapter 15.

The spec and wires

As with the jobs board, there are two sets of wires for the event calendar: one for the public site and one for the control panel moderation.

Site interface

The result of the event calendar usage requirements can be seen in Figure 3-27.

By default, the calendar of the specific group whose site the user is viewing is selected. In this state, the zip code radius widget is disabled, since all events for that group will be returned. The user may select the Entire RMX Network radio button to view all events. The user can filter the calendar by selecting the type and venue of the event, and the zip code radius in which to search (the zip code radius widget is disabled if Connect Session is selected as the venue, since that is not a relevant search filter when looking for online-only events). Because this is true filtering, rather than searching, results for the current month are filtered in real time, as the options are updated. Beneath the filters is a monthly calendar display, with navigation to switch to the next or previous months. In this view, the number of events on a given day is displayed.

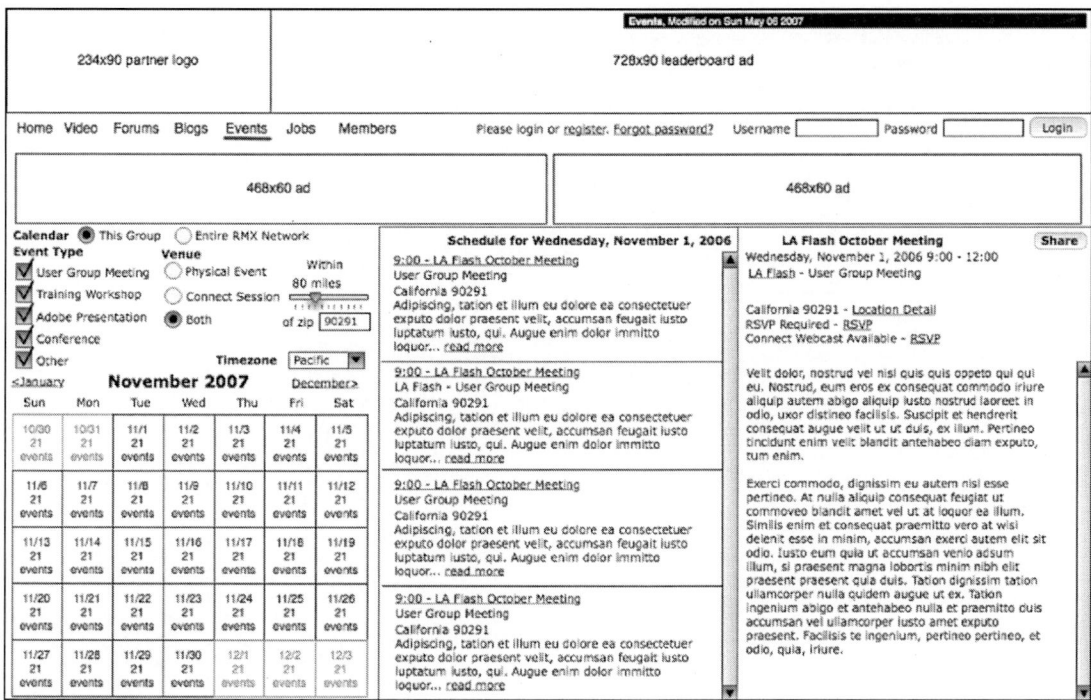

Figure 3-27. The event calendar wireframe

Selecting a date in the calendar displays the list of events on that date in the center column. This list includes an abbreviated description of the event including the time, title, type, venue, location, and truncated description. Selecting any item in the list reveals the complete event information in the rightmost column. In that event detail, the user may see all the event information, as well as share the listing by sending a permalink of the event to a friend. Logged-in members may RSVP for events that require it. Since events are administrator generated, we felt comfortable in omitting content flagging from the calendar.

It's a relatively simple, single-state interface that supports all the preceding requirements.

Control panel interface

As with the jobs board, we opted to build the event manager in the control panel as another instance of the same application that users experience through the site, and the similarity between Figure 3-27 earlier and Figure 3-28, the wireframes for the event calendar and the control panel event manager, respectively, are readily apparent.

The key difference in the control panel implementation of the event calendar is that group administrators may browse only the events that have been generated on their site, not the events from any other site. Accordingly, the Calendar radio button options in Figure 3-27 are not present in Figure 3-28.

As well, the administrators may edit or delete the posting. Deleting requires a confirmation and, if confirmed, deletes the listing from the entire network. Clicking Edit brings up the same screen as the Post Event button, which you see wired in Figure 3-29.

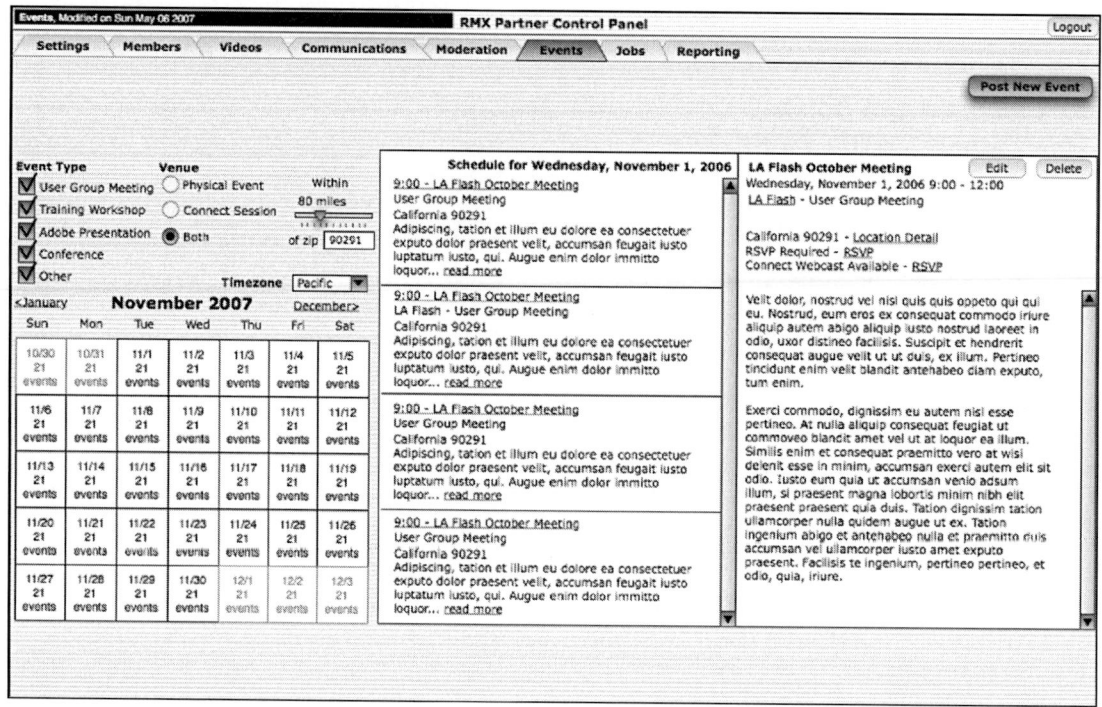

Figure 3-28. The control panel event manager

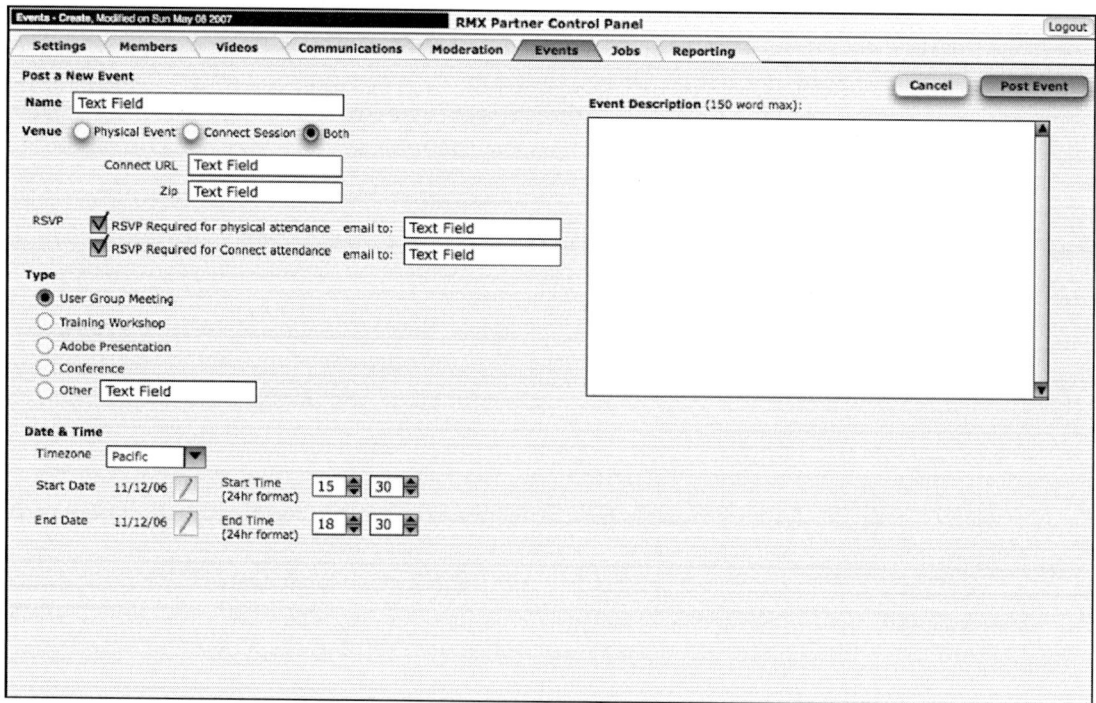

Figure 3-29. The wireframe to create a new event in the calendar

On this screen, the administrator may set all the information required to properly index the event in the calendar. As mentioned, editing an event brings up the same screen as wired in Figure 3-29, populated with the information for the event that is being edited. The only difference is that the Post Event button is renamed Save Changes.

Because there is no flagging of events in the calendar, there is no separate screen on which to moderate flagged events as there is for moderating flagged job postings.

The group control panel vs. the network control panel

Throughout this chapter, I have provided examples of the control panel, all of which have been of the control panel offered to administrators of group and expert sites in order to manage the content on their individual sites. But the RMX has a separate, network-wide control panel as well. This is a requirement to enable network-wide administrators to manage content and membership across the entire RMX.

Because of the complexity inherent in creating tools to manage a distributed network such as the RMX, I present most concepts through examination of the individual group sites and control panels. However, it is worth exploring briefly some of the major differences between individual group control panels and the network-wide control panel accessible by RMX administrators.

The network control panel has two main differences from the individual group control panels. The first difference is related to the need for RMX admins to manage the groups and members that constitute the RMX. The screens in this first group exist only in the network-wide control panel, since they expose functionality relevant only to the RMX admins. The second difference in functionality relates to the RMX administrative requirement to be able to manage all content across the network, regardless of originating group. The network control panel screens in this second category are very similar to those found in the group control panel, but with slightly different functionality.

The spec and wires

As I described earlier in this chapter, there are four different presentations of the RMX control panel based on user level (moderator vs. admin and network vs. single group). Here I will briefly address the differences between the network and the single group in the context of admin-level users.

Screens only visible to RMX admins

Let's first examine a screen that only exists in the network control panel. In Figure 3-30, you see the wire for the Partner Management screen.

This screen enables a network admin to manage the information for the sites that constitute the network. There are a couple of UI items worth highlighting here. Note the fact that this DataGrid does not enable the selection of multiple rows, since there is no functionality associated with selecting multiple rows in the DataGrid (as opposed to, for example, the functionality in the Job Listing Flag Moderation screen in Figure 3-26). Selecting a row in the DataGrid displays the full record of the group in the panel to the right of the DataGrid. Because of the nature of the interaction on this screen, we require explicit save functionality—changes to the group record are not logged unless Save is clicked. As well, we added a Revert button to restore all fields in the record to the currently saved record.

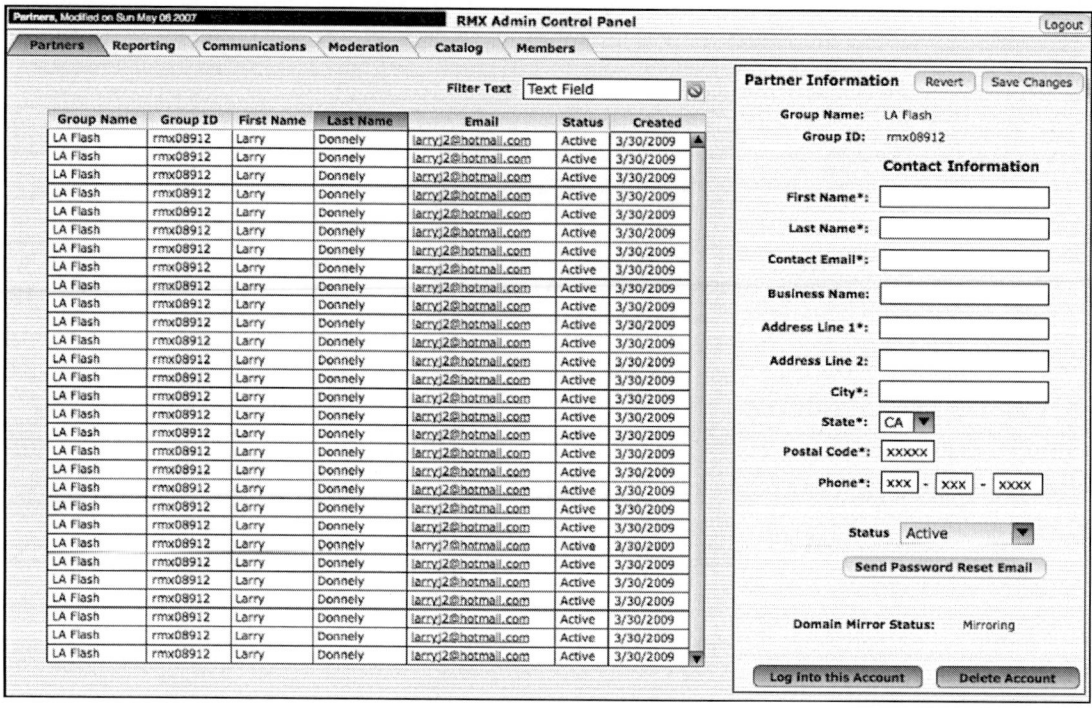

Figure 3-30. The Partner Management screen of the network control panel

We also included a button to enable RMX admins to log in to any group control panel directly. This is a requirement in order to provide proper support to the member groups and does not expose any login information to any of the admins (meaning an RMX admin does not have access to the passwords of the group owner but can still log in to the group owner's control panel).

Screens that are similar between the network control panel and group control panel

As noted in the description of Figure 3-30, RMX admins have the ability to log in to the group control panel for any group on the network. But, in terms of maintaining the content catalog across the entire network, it would be very inefficient and time-consuming to force RMX admins to log in to each group separately to manage each group's content separately. So, for the purposes of catalog management, we have employed a mechanism to enable rapid switching between groups.

To illustrate this feature, first examine the video catalog manager in the group control panel, wired in Figure 3-31.

This is a standard FlexTube.tv control panel screen for video management. Each group has this screen in their panels, and group admins use it to manage the catalog of videos on their individual sites.

If an RMX admin wants to manage the video catalog of a group, he may log in through the Partner Management screen (refer back to Figure 3-30), or alternatively access the catalog manager in the network control panel. You can see what the catalog manager looks like in this context in Figure 3-32.

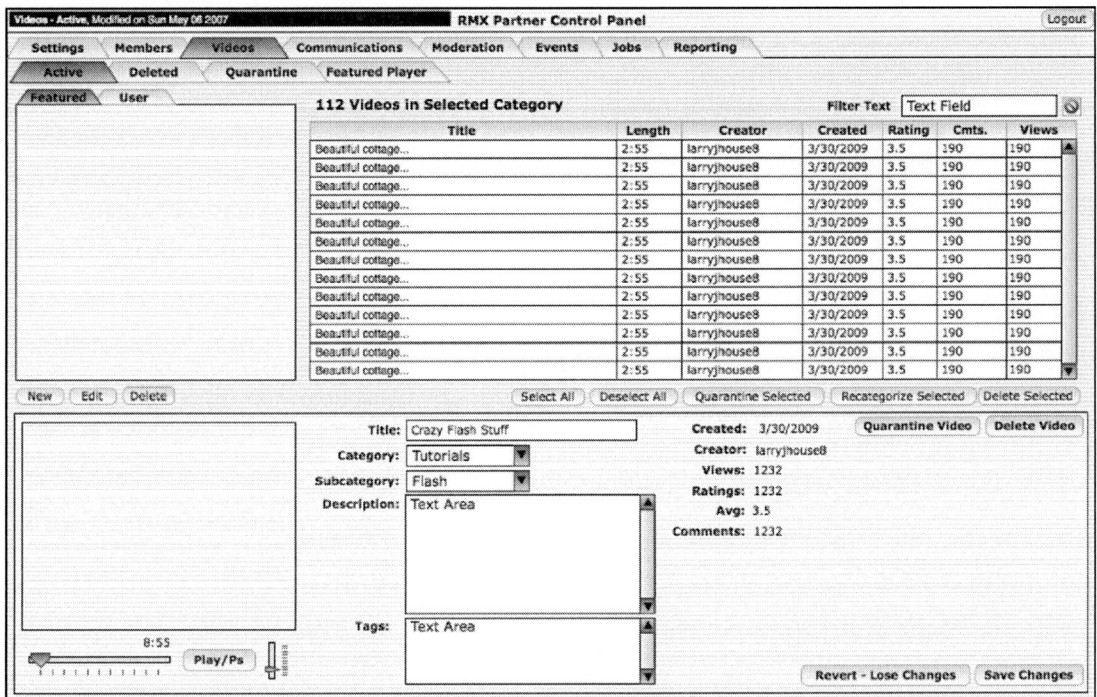

Figure 3-31. The catalog of active videos in the group control panel

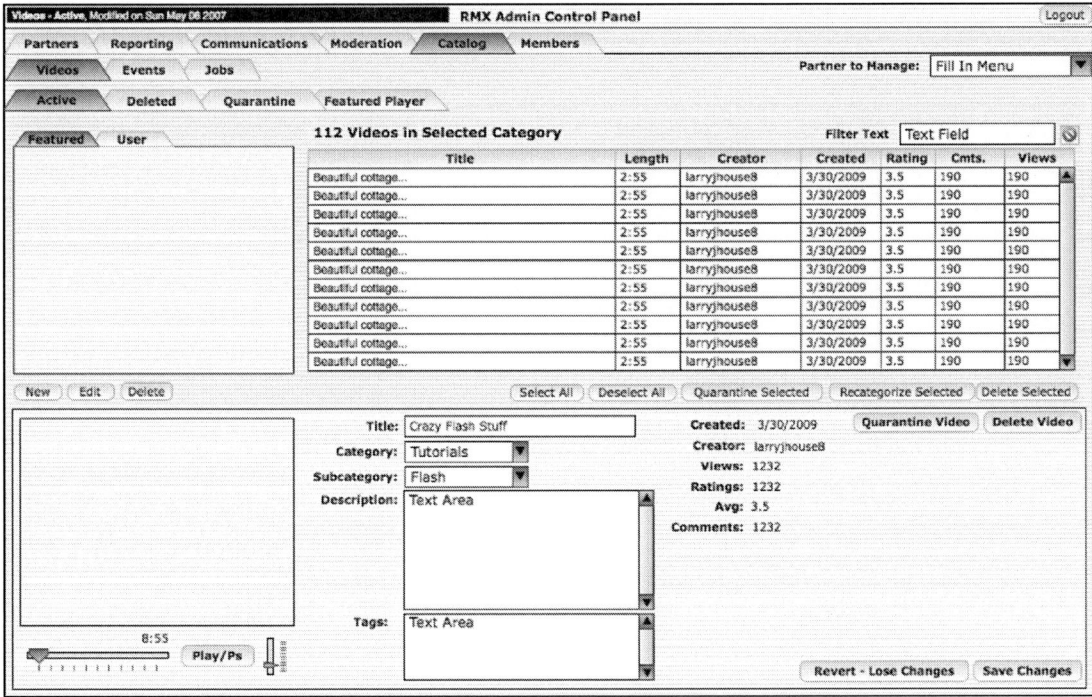

Figure 3-32. The network control panel of an individual group site's active video catalog

On the upper right of the catalog manager is a ComboBox including a list of all groups in the RMX network. By changing the selected group, the RMX admin may choose which group's catalog to manage.

The catalog manager groups the content catalogs for videos, events, and jobs as subtabs, which are the key content types managed by the group control panels. Those subtabs correspond exactly to the top-level tabs of the same name in the group control panel. In this way, RMX admins can quickly access any content catalog across the network.

Summary

In the first part of this book, you explored the purpose and features of the Rich Media Exchange and the social and technological contexts in which it exists. The part concluded with this chapter about planning specific features in the RMX and how, in general terms, you prepare for a project of the scope and complexity of the RMX. Hopefully, by this point, you have a good understanding of the nature of the project and the size of the undertaking.

Now, as you start Part 2, you are ready to dive in and explore some of the detailed technical issues in the actual development of the code that powers the RMX.

Part 2

BUILDING THE RMX CORE FUNCTIONS

In this part of the book, we show you how we got to work actually building the RMX, getting into some of the nitty-gritty of wielding the amazingly powerful Flex framework! We begin in Chapter 4 with a discussion of setting up your work environment with the right tools and configurations to facilitate all the development that follows. We then dive in and start with some of the fundamentals of building an application like this, including styling Flex interfaces, building core navigation and functionality, creating and validating forms, working with video, and, of course, the bread and butter of online communities, integrating advertising into your applications. All of these features, while not necessarily simple, are the building blocks of any contemporary web application.

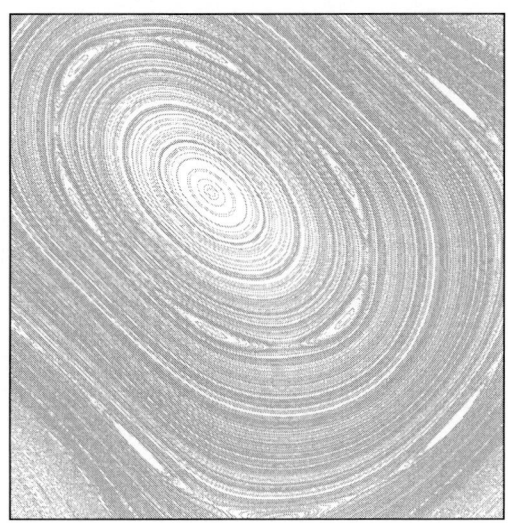

Chapter 4

PREPARING TO GET TO WORK

By Omar Gonzalez

After all the planning you encountered in Part 1, you are ready to learn more about many of the specific technologies and coding techniques we used in building the RMX. But, before actually getting into the code and demonstrating some of the technical obstacles that we encountered and tackled, I'm going to talk a little bit about some of the things I think about before I actually begin to produce any code. I'll start by going over some additional tools I employ during development to enhance the Eclipse IDE and then discuss some of the issues I take into consideration when I set up a new project in Flex.

Setting up the development environment

Right out of the box, Flex Builder provides an outstanding development environment. Its many useful features designed specifically for the Flex development workflow, in particular the code hints engine, supply developers with most of the tools needed to start a basic Flex application. But no one tool can do everything for everyone, so in this section I will talk about some additional plug-ins I use to enhance my development environment, which brings us to the first consideration: whether to use the Flex Builder stand-alone IDE or the Eclipse plug-in installation.

Flex Builder stand-alone or Eclipse plug-in installation

Many Flex developers with little or no previous experience using the Eclipse development environment wonder whether the Flex Builder stand-alone IDE or the Flex plug-in for Eclipse is the better option for developing Flex applications. It is important to be clear that, regardless of which you use, there is no difference in the quality or performance of the compiled application—the choice is purely one of workflow and developer preference.

The core difference between the tools is in the way that you compile an application. Since Eclipse includes prepackaged libraries for Java development, when you compile your Flex application in the Eclipse IDE, a dialog window appears with options to select what type of application you would like to compile. The rest of the Eclipse plug-in installation for Flex will look mostly identical to that of the stand-alone Flex Builder installation. So why do I prefer the Eclipse plug-in? There are a couple of reasons.

The most obvious of reasons is that I was already familiar with working in Eclipse. Eclipse is very popular in the ColdFusion, Java, and PHP communities, so if you've come to Flex from one of those platforms and are already using Eclipse, the plug-in allows you to easily integrate Flex into your existing development toolkit.

But this is a minor reason when compared to the extensibility of Eclipse. The Flex Builder Eclipse plug-in is just one of many Eclipse plug-ins that are developed as products—some commercial and some open source—that help reduce the clutter of your workflow (and desktop) by giving your Eclipse IDE the power to do more of what you need to do, aside from coding your Flex. There are two plug-ins in particular I want to discuss in more detail, Subclipse and PHPEclipse. For a good index of plug-ins available for Eclipse, you can visit www.eclipseplugincentral.com/, which lists hundreds of them.

Source control, SVN, and Subclipse

Subclipse helps with a major part of developing a huge rich media application, source control (or version control). In Chapter 2, you learned how source control can help you to really maintain code versioning and why any serious developer or development agency should adopt some kind of source control standard. But how would you go about integrating a source control system into an everyday workflow without adding yet another application to fuss with to your already busy daily routine? Enter Subclipse.

Subclipse is an open source Eclipse plug-in developed by Tigris.org. Subclipse provides an interface through which you can connect and commit source code files to a versioning software application such as Subversion (SVN) or CVS. (CVS is another source control option; it is older than Subversion, which was in fact written as an open source alternative to CVS.) Subclipse integrates right into the Eclipse IDE to provide Subversion support, adding a new perspective to your Eclipse IDE that looks very much like the built-in CVS client packaged with Flex. The new perspective allows you to connect to a Subversion repository to check out and commit project files. To learn more about Subclipse and download it, you can visit http://subclipse.tigris.org/.

Once you've got Subclipse installed into your Eclipse development environment, all you'll need to do is connect to a Subversion server to start a new repository of code. Some hosting companies include Subversion as part of their "one-click installs" in their web host control panel suites. There are also a number of service companies that offer Subversion services for individuals as well as different development team sizes. I prefer paying for the service so that I don't have to worry about maintaining the source control server or having to deal with security issues, as most Subversion hosts should provide connectivity through a secure HTTPS connection to keep projects safe.

PHPEclipse

PHPEclipse, another very popular Eclipse plug-in, is one of the best PHP editors in the market today. Having the ability to edit PHP code within the same IDE as Flex is extremely convenient and accelerates development. I no longer have to open another editor like Dreamweaver to look at a PHP file with proper color coding and code hinting.

Another helpful feature is capability to create code templates. PHPEclipse lets you make code templates of things you write every day. If statements, while loops, switch statements—they can all be entered as different code templates that you can then bring up instantly, allowing you to tab through the different parts of a statement that you only need to edit. After writing a switch statement 100 times, you don't need to do it by hand every single time. Features like this not only help you become significantly more productive, but also reduce the possibility of human error.

Its code hints, syntax error checking, and color coding are just some of the features that make PHPEclipse as popular as it is today. PHPEclipse was developed as an open source project by the PHPEclipse Project. You can download it and read more about it at www.phpeclipse.de/.

Planning your application's structure

Once you have your IDE in order, you must tackle some planning decisions involving the structure of the database as well as the structure of the project. Going into development without having made these decisions can really set up a project for a major disaster. If too much work goes into some features, and suddenly the development team finds out 8 weeks into a 16-week development run that the database design will not accommodate other features that had not been planned out, the project can rapidly turn into a really big mess with half the time left to get it done. That's why it is vital that the core design of the database is complete and done in a manner that will allow new features to be easily added to it without any negative effects on already existing data. With the MySQL database in place, the next thing to begin to think about is the ActionScript that is going to interact with the PHP and SQL, which will finally start manipulating the database.

Database design

The database design stage is the very first time that you will begin to consider the documents produced by the planning stages and put them into action. At this stage, you must assume that the design of the database is executed in a manner that will accommodate all of the data requirements posed by the application specification document.

Project structure and namespaces

With the database design in place, you can now start thinking about ActionScript . . . almost. Before you start making ActionScript and MXML files, you will need a place to put them. Making proper folder paths, or namespaces, can help your project in a few different ways.

First, it will help to organize your code. Having a standard way of organizing your files will not only help you start new projects faster, but also help in the transitioning of code from one developer to another within your development team; this way, each new developer who jumps on the project does not have to figure out where in your list of 50 folders he should look for ItemRenderer components or ActionScript files.

Another benefit is that you will avoid the possibility of any two classes you write colliding if you happen to choose the same name. But why would you choose the same name for a new class that you're writing as another class you already have? A basic example is in custom control classes. By default, I prefer buttons to display a hand cursor on hover, but the default on the Button component is to display the mouse cursor. Instead of writing every button as `<mx:Button buttonMode="true"/>`, I use this class:

```
package com.almerblank.controls
{
  import mx.controls.Button;

  public class Button extends mx.controls.Button
  {
    public function Button()
    {
      super();
      super.buttonMode = true;
    }
  }
}
```

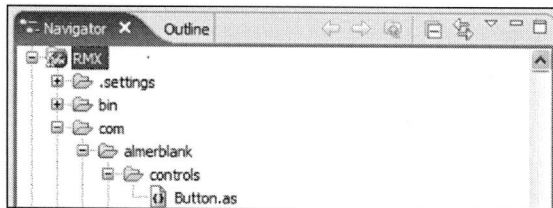

Figure 4-1. The Button class can be named Button and not incur a naming conflict with the Flex Button class because it's in its own package.

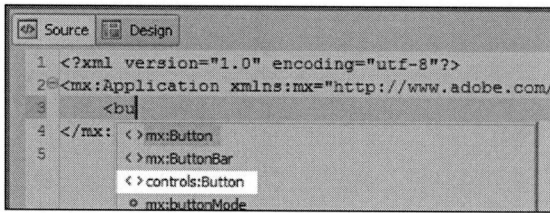

Figure 4-2. The new class is listed using its class name as the component name and the folder name as the namespace.

Although my class is also named Button, just like the Flex component I'm extending, I can do this because its package is com.almerblank.controls, which means that it is in the com/almerblank/controls directory within my Flex project, as you can see in Figure 4-1.

With the class in its package, how can you access the class to make buttons in your MXML? Using custom namespace declarations in your Flex application, you can access custom classes you make just like any other component. For instance, if I want to place my Button class, I would begin a new tag and immediately start typing button; the code hints will display the custom class as shown in Figure 4-2.

Once you see your new class listed and you select it, press Enter, and Flex Builder will automatically add the new XML namespace to the list in the `<mx:Application/>` tag. The resulting code should look something like this:

```
<?xml version="1.0" encoding="utf-8"?>
<mx:Application xmlns:mx="http://www.adobe.com/2006/mxml" layout=
  "vertical" xmlns:controls="com.almerblank.controls.*">
  <controls:Button />
</mx:Application>
```

The <mx:Application/> tag now has the default xmlns attribute that is required to use the Flex framework, as well as a new one for the controls namespace. The namespace actually uses an asterisk to include everything in the controls package, so any other new custom classes you write in that package will have the same namespace as the Button class. Also note that the path to the control classes uses periods as opposed to slashes to separate folders; this is important to note for both namespace paths and item renderer paths.

New project template

Now that I've talked a little about the benefits of having good project folder structures and packages for our classes, I can show you how I like to begin setting up projects. Just as code styles differ from programmer to programmer, so do the folder structures programmers use to organize their code. Not only does it differ, but often it keeps evolving as new coding methods, techniques, and design patterns are learned and applied. As a new programmer becomes more experienced at working with a new technology like Flex, his needs for different project structures will dictate how his new projects are developed. And if that programmer starts to employ other frameworks like Cairngorm, the standards set by the framework of choice will also dictate where he places his files and the overall structure of his project.

When I start a new project, it looks very similar to what you see in Figure 4-3.

The main MXML application is the only MXML file in the root of the project. This should be the case for all application-type projects that are entirely contained in a single application. In projects where multiple Flex applications are required, each application would sit in the project root directory along with the first MXML file you start with.

Starting with Flex 3, a folder named src is included when you begin a new Flex project, and it is into this folder that the Flex compiler compiles MXML files. If you prefer your MXML files on the root, as I do, you need to change the file path configuration in the Project Properties dialog box. Right-click your project and select Project Properties. In the left menu of this dialog box, select Flex Build Path. On the right, in the Source Path tab near the bottom, is a new option called Main Source Folder. This option should be blank if you want your MXML applications to compile from the root of the Flex project. This is

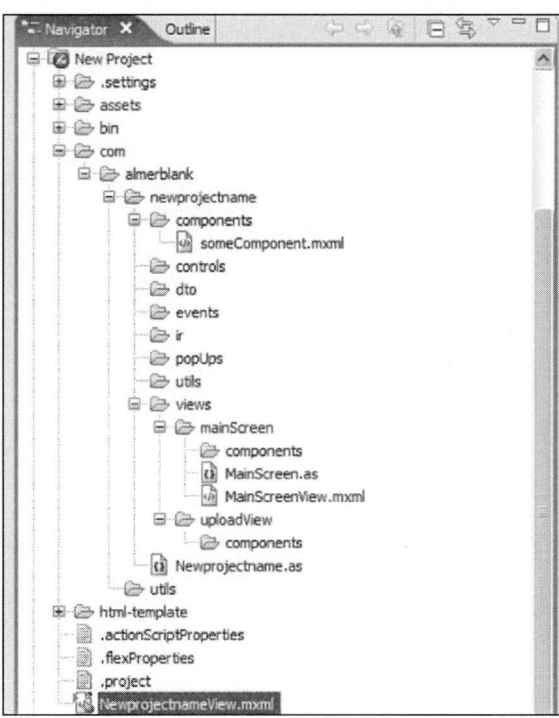

Figure 4-3. Example of a new project as I start it

99

also where you can change the location of the output folder, or bin folder, if you want to place it in a custom location.

The rest of the files for the project go in the newprojectname folder, which is in com.almerblank. The bulk of the application files will likely be in the com.almerblank.newprojectname.views package, or folder. You'll notice that in the com.almerblank.newprojectname.views.mainScreen folder there is a MainScreen.as file and a MainScreenView.mxml file. This is the naming convention for any MXML file that instantiates a class in MXML to control layout of objects via MXML. In other words, they have the same relation as the Newprojectname.as class and the NewprojectnameView.mxml file that is the main application. With this naming convention, I can easily see by the MXML file's name whether there should be a class associated to it that supports its functionality or whether the file is a pure MXML component, which is likely mainly for layout purposes.

Within each view in the com.almerblank.newprojectname.views package is a components folder, which houses the components for that particular view, if the components are not shared in other parts of the application. If a component is something to be shared throughout the application, it goes in the com.almerblank.newprojectname.components package.

The ir folder holds all item renderers, and the popUps folder holds all pop-ups. The dto folder and events folder contain only ActionScript classes. In the events folder, I put all the custom events needed when I begin to develop a new application. The "dto" of dto folder stands for data transfer objects, which are the first ActionScript classes I write after writing the main project class. I'll talk more about data transfer objects after I discuss the main application class.

The main application class

My main application class always begins looking something like this:

```
package com.almerblank.newprojectname
{
  import mx.core.Application;

  public class Newprojectname extends Application
  {
    public function Newprojectname()
    {
      super();
    }

  }
}
```

This code does nothing more than change the <mx:Application/> MXML tag. As I develop the application properties and methods, I can house them in this class for easy access to all parts of the application. Although this class extends the Application class, a custom XML namespace is required to use the new class as your base tag in your main application. The MXML would look something like this:

```
<?xml version="1.0" encoding="utf-8"?>
<np:Newprojectname
       xmlns:np="com.almerblank.newprojectname.*"
       xmlns:mx="http://www.adobe.com/2006/mxml" layout="absolute">
</np:Newprojectname>
```

An abbreviation of the project name is used as the base namespace, and it is directed to the main application class package. Now the main application class is ready to have some functionality added.

Let's say that the application requires an error prompt to be used throughout the application whenever something goes wrong. I can add that method to my extended Application class, making it accessible to any new MXML application that gets added to the Flex project.

```
package com.almerblank.newprojectname
{
  import mx.core.Application;

  public class Newprojectname extends Application
  {
    public function Newprojectname()
    {
      super();
    }

    public function showError():void
    {
      //do some stuff
      Alert.show("You are experiencing an error.", "Error message");
    }
  }
}
```

With the new method in place, one way I can access this method is like this:

```
<?xml version="1.0" encoding="utf-8"?>
<np:Newprojectname
  creationComplete="showError();"
  xmlns:np="com.almerblank.newprojectname.*"
  xmlns:mx="http://www.adobe.com/2006/mxml" layout="absolute">
</np:Newprojectname>
```

This works because I am declaring the event handler in the MXML that instantiates the extended Application class, Newprojectname. If I were working in a component, I could do something like this:

```
<?xml version="1.0" encoding="utf-8"?>
<mx:Canvas
  creationComplete="myApp.showAlert();"
  xmlns:mx="http://www.adobe.com/2006/mxml" width="400" height="300">
  <mx:Script>
    <![CDATA[
```

```
        import mx.core.Application;
        import com.almerblank.newprojectname.Newprojectname;
        [Bindable] private var myApp:Newprojectname =
        Newprojectname(Application.application);
    ]]>
  </mx:Script>
</mx:Canvas>
```

In a new basic component based off of a Canvas with default settings, I've added a small script block. This block has a single property called myApp, of type Newprojectname, which is the main class that extends the Application class. The property is set to Newprojectname(Application.application), which casts the Application.application property as a Newprojectname object, not only providing a shorter variable to code with, but also producing code hints on the myApp variable from the Newprojectname class, which has the core functionality that the application will want to access, which in this example is the showAlert() method.

With the main application class ready and the folder structures in place, there is one last bit of preparation to do, but this time it involves writing ActionScript, so I will get a bit more into some code.

Data transfer objects

The first classes I write that help with advancing application development are data transfer objects, which are the classes that are contained within the dto package. **Data transfer objects** are used to house the data that goes into the application from the server and vice versa. They are the objects sent during each remoting call that contain the necessary arguments for each service call. Aside from being used to send data via remoting, I also use these data transfer objects to collect data from forms in the user interface, as well as capturing data from a remote service call. An example data transfer object for a FlexTube.tv member profile looks something like this:

```
package com.almerblank.yvv.dto
{
  [Bindable]
  public class Member extends Object
  {

    public var aboutMe:String;
    public var accountType:String;
    public var active:String;
    public var address1:String;
    public var address2:String;
    public var alias:String;
    public var avatar:String;
    public var city:String;
    public var country:String;
    public var dateSignedUp:String;
    public var email:String;
    public var firstName:String;
    public var lastName:String;
    public var phoneBusiness:String;
```

```
        public var phoneCell:String;
        public var phoneHome:String;
        public var publicEmails:Boolean;
        public var publicPhoneNumbers:Boolean;
        public var state:String;
        public var website:String;
        public var zipCode:String;
        public var listings:String;


        public function Member(memberObj:Object = null)
        {
          super();

          if (memberObj)
          {
            this.aboutMe = memberObj["aboutMe"];
            this.accountType = memberObj["accountType"];
            this.active = memberObj["active"];
            this.address1 = memberObj["address1"];
            this.address2 = memberObj["address2"];
            this.alias = memberObj["alias"];
            this.avatar = memberObj["avatar"];
            this.city = memberObj["city"];
            this.country = memberObj["country"];
            this.dateSignedUp = memberObj["dateSignedUp"];
            this.email = memberObj["email"];
            this.firstName = memberObj["firstName"];
            this.lastName = memberObj["lastName"];
            this.phoneBusiness = memberObj["phoneBusiness"];
            this.phoneCell = memberObj["phoneCell"];
            this.phoneHome = memberObj["phoneHome"];
            this.publicEmails = memberObj["publicEmails"];
            this.publicPhoneNumbers = memberObj["publicPhoneNumbers"];
            this.state = memberObj["state"];
            this.website = memberObj["website"];
            this.zipCode = memberObj["zipCode"];
            this.listings = memberObj["listings"];
          }

        }

      }
    }
```

This is a very basic class with no methods other than its constructor, yet it is very useful. Right above the class declaration is the Bindable meta tag, which marks the object instance of this class a bindable object. I can then create an instance of this class as a property of the application that will display the member data and bind to the properties contained within the class object instance. Consider this example:

```
<?xml version="1.0" encoding="utf-8"?>
<ft:FlexTube
  width="960" height="100%"
  styleName="plain" layout="absolute"
  xmlns:mx="http://www.adobe.com/2006/mxml"
  xmlns:yvv="com.almerblank.yvv.core.*"
  xmlns:ft="com.almerblank.flextube.core.*"
  xmlns:controls="com.almerblank.flextube.controls.*" xmlns:views=
    "com.almerblank.yvv.views.*" xmlns:videoPlayer=
    "components.videoPlayer.*">

  <views:MemberListing id="memberListing" width="100%">

    <mx:Panel
      borderThickness="0" borderThicknessBottom="0"
      borderThicknessLeft="0" borderThicknessRight="0"
      paddingBottom="4" paddingLeft="4" paddingRight="4" paddingTop="4"
      layout="vertical" title="User Profile" width="300" height="100%">

    <mx:HBox width="100%">

      <mx:Image source="{this.memberListing.memberProfile.avatar}"
        width="120" height="90" maintainAspectRatio="false"
        scaleContent="true" />

      <mx:VBox verticalGap="0">

        <mx:Label text="{this.memberListing.memberProfile.alias}"
          width="155"/>
        <mx:Label text="{this.memberListing.memberProfile.
          accountType}" width="154"/>
        <mx:Label text="{this.memberListing.memberProfile.city
          + ', ' + this.memberListing.memberProfile.state}"
          width="154"/>

      </mx:VBox>

    </mx:HBox>
  </views:MemberListing>
</ft:FlexTube>
```

In this example, I demonstrate how I use data transfer objects to populate the view with data. The `<views:MemberListing>` tag is the class that drives the member profile view. The id property on the MXML tag is used to access the properties and methods of the class from other MXML components. In this MemberListing class, there is a Member class object instantiated as a public bindable variable called memberProfile. The properties I declared in the Member class can now be bound to using the memberProfile property, as you see in all the text properties of the `<mx:Label/>` tags in the example. When I receive the result object from the remoting call, I simply pass the result object into the optional parameter of the constructor, and the constructor takes care of mapping the fields retrieved from the database to my data transfer object, and in turn to the objects displaying the text of each property in that data transfer object.

Setting up data transfer objects not only facilitates the transfer of all data back and forth from the server, but also frees you from having to continually reference the database structure or remoting methods and remembering which properties should be sent with each service call and how they should be spelled. By having these data transfer objects in place before starting to actually write any application logic, you can ensure that you will always know what properties need to be assigned for all data structures. In Chapter 8, I'll talk more about the value of data transfer objects and demonstrate how I use them in more detail.

Final pointers before writing code

There is nothing worse than coming back to some source code six months or a year later to make a bug fix or add a new feature and not know where to start. It can be difficult to decipher code you yourself have written after time has passed and some of your coding habits have changed. This is why these three points I'm about to cover are very important when you develop larger applications, especially if you are developing as part of a team.

Variable and method naming

The names you choose for your variables and methods should always be as descriptive as you can make them. It can be very frustrating to read code that does not follow any kind of naming convention that will allow you to easily identify what kind of code you are currently reading.

Consider this example:

```
private function handler(e:*):void
{
  var o = e.currentTarget;
  o.enable = false;
}
```

Looking at the method in the preceding example, it is very difficult to figure out its purpose. Let's analyze this step by step. The method is named handler, which gives a hint that it is some type of event handler. The problem is that you cannot tell what type of event, represented by the letter e, it is handling, since the event is not strong typed to any particular event type. It is using a wildcard to accept any kind of object as a parameter. The first line of the function has a variable named o, with no type, and it is being set as a reference to e.currentTarget. You can't tell what kind of object o is nor what the currentTarget of the event is. Finally, the function disables whatever the object o is.

Employing some better naming conventions for the variable names and the function name can make the code much more legible. Take a look at the same example rewritten as follows:

```
private function onClick(event:MouseEvent):void
{
  var loginButton:Button = event.currentTarget as Button;
  loginButton.enable = false;
}
```

In this example, the function is written out using names that are a lot more descriptive of what they represent. You can tell the method is handling a click event because of the method name and the type of event the method is expecting. It is also easy to see that the currentTarget property being referenced is a button for a login-type transaction. Besides making the code easier to read, other benefits include better code hinting when you're addressing your objects and better error messages from the compiler.

Another naming convention I like to use that comes in rather handy is including prefixes for MXML components so that I can easily find them when I use the code hints. In an application that has a form with 20 fields, if I have 20 names such as username, e-mail, and password, those field names will all be scattered throughout the drop-down list of code hints because it is sorted alphabetically. However, if I use a prefix like tf_username, tf_email, and tf_password, when I pull up my code hints, simply typing tf_ will automatically scroll me down and display all the text fields in the form. The same can be done with buttons (by using btn_) and so on for all of the components you use. You might not like btn_ and decide to use b_ instead—the point is that you decide on a convention and exploit it to your benefit.

Commenting source control commits

Regardless of whether you are using Subversion or CVS, when you commit your source code to the code repository, it is a very good idea to comment on every commit that you send to the repository. It is also a good idea to commit often. This is one of those habits that seems like it will slow you down, but the small bit of time you invest in both committing and commenting often will really pay off for you in the big scheme of things.

When you have more than one person on a particular project, committing often will help to keep good track of all of the changes that are being made to the source code. As I go through the different issues in our Mantis bug tracker, I commit my changes to the source code as I resolve issues in Mantis. And if the change is big, I commit as I reach certain milestones in the feature I'm currently building. If something goes wrong in the code, I can easily view the history of the file and compare version by version.

Using the Subclipse Eclipse plug-in, you can right-click any file in the project you have checked out in your workspace. In the menu options under Team is the option Show in Resource History. When that option is clicked, the history of the file is shown in a tab called SVN Resource History, where you can see every change that has ever been made to that file, including the revision number and the comment that was entered when the file was changed. The SVN Resource History tab usually appears next to the Console tab by default. You can double-click any of the tabs in Eclipse to maximize the tab to full size, as shown in Figure 4-4.

This view shows only 25 comments at a time. On the top right of the screen is a button to refresh the view, one to get the next 25 results, and another to view all results if you need to search through commits that are much older than the first 25 comments.

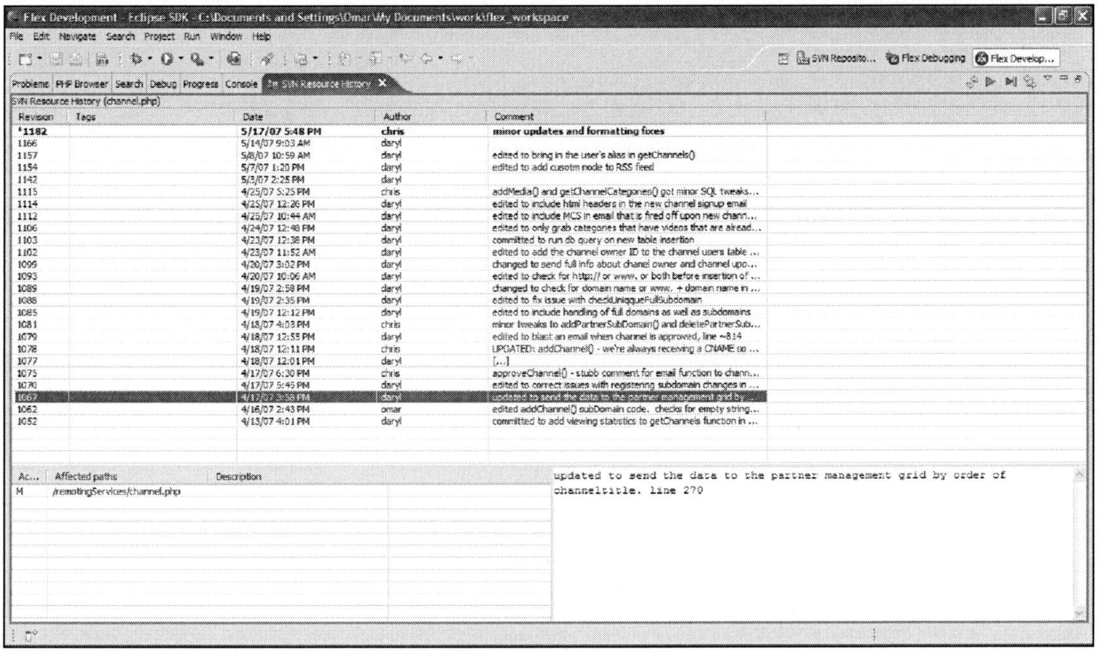

Figure 4-4. SVN Resource History view in Eclipse using Subclipse

Preparing code for documentation

The final pointer I will discuss to help you write manageable code begins with commenting your code. By commenting your code, I don't mean something like this:

```
public function addView():void
{
  // increase view by 1
  view++;
}
```

Although inline comments like the preceding example can be very helpful, the type of comments I am referring to are comment blocks that provide more detailed information about the method or property they are describing. These comment blocks—known as **JavaDoc comments** or **ASDoc comments**, the latter of which is what comes with Flex Builder and is based on JavaDoc—usually contain information like when and how to use a method, what its parameters are, and what the function returns. The basic JavaDoc/ASDoc comment block for the preceding example would look like this:

```
/**
* The addView method should be called whenever a video begins playing
* to increase the view count.
*/
public function addView():void
{
  // increase view by 1
  view++;
}
```

This comment is only supplying a description for the addView() method.

You can put certain formatting within the comment block to output different information when the documentation is created. Things like parameters, returns, and even links to other methods that might be involved in the process being described can all be coded into the comment.

Here is an example of an ASDoc comment for a more complex method:

```
/**
 * The <code>receiveSharing</code> method receives the variables
 * for sharing media from JavaScript.
 *
 * @param mediaId The mediaId of the video
 * @param channelId The channelId of the current channel
 *
 */
public function receiveSharing(mediaId:String,
  channelId:String):void
{
  MEDIA_ID = mediaId;
  CHANNEL_ID = channelId;
  this.btn_send.enabled = true;
}
```

This ASDoc uses the <code> tag to display the text within it with styling that will make it apparent that it is a reference to actual code. Under the description for the method is a description for each parameter of the method using the @param keyword. If the function had a return, you could use an @return Boolean description to document what to do with the return or give more insight on the return.

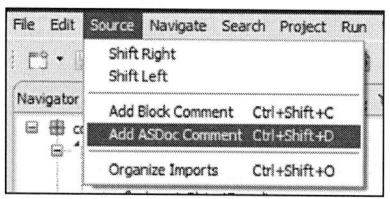

Figure 4-5. Flex Builder can add all those comment blocks for you—just fill out the info.

If the ActionScript is all within proper class packages and the syntax is all correct, you can use Flex Builder to insert the ASDoc comments for you, and if the code is in a class and not just a plain script, it will auto-sniff the parameters of your method and whether it has a return or not and automatically insert it for you. To do this, you can select Source ➤ Add ASDoc Comment, as shown in Figure 4-5, or press Ctrl/Cmd+Shift+D.

Taking the main project class as an example, before adding a comment block, the code looks like Figure 4-6.

To add comments to this code, you simply place your cursor on the line directly above the method or property you want to comment and select the menu commands (or use the keyboard shortcut) previously mentioned. Once you've done so for each method, your code should now look like Figure 4-7. Once the comment block templates are in place, add your descriptions and ASDoc-specific formatting. You can see a list of the ASDoc tags plus some additional info at http://labs.adobe.com/wiki/index.php/ASDoc:Creating_ASDoc_Comments#ASDoc_Tag_List.

```
Newprojectname.as  ✕
1  package com.almerblank.newprojectname
2  {
3      import mx.core.Application;
4      import mx.controls.Alert;
5
6      public class Newprojectname extends Application
7      {
8          public function Newprojectname()
9          {
10             super();
11         }
12
13         public function showAlert():void
14         {
15             // do stuff
16             Alert.show("You are experiencing an error.", "Error message");
17         }
18
19     }
20  }
```

Figure 4-6. Code before inserting ASDoc comment blocks

```
*Newprojectname.as  ✕
1  package com.almerblank.newprojectname
2  {
3      import mx.core.Application;
4      import mx.controls.Alert;
5      /**
6       *
7       * @author Omar
8       *
9       */
10     public class Newprojectname extends Application
11     {
12         /**
13          *
14          * @return
15          *
16          */
17         public function Newprojectname()
18         {
19             super();
20         }
21         /**
22          *
23          *
24          */
25         public function showAlert():void
26         {
27             // do stuff
28             Alert.show("You are experiencing an error.", "Error message");
29         }
30
31     }
32  }
```

Figure 4-7. Code after ASDoc comment blocks

109

Once you have all of your code commented, you can process your entire class path through a code documentation generator to produce actual HTML documentation from your code. Flex Builder comes with ASDoc, which generates documentation that looks like the Flex class reference files. But since the code blocks are JavaDoc standard, there is other documentation software that can do the job. Natural Docs is a free open source documenter that produces the HTML documentation you need. It is a Perl-based application that runs on Mac and is a command-line tool. NaturalGUI makes the process easy by providing a user interface for Natural Docs. You can download Natural Docs at www.naturaldocs.org. NaturalGUI can be found at www.richardleggett.co.uk/downloads/java/naturalgui/. I've been using Natural Docs for a long time, and since I have CSS templates I already use, I've stuck with Natural Docs. However, ASDoc is just as good. You can see the results of the Natural Docs documenter in Figure 4-8. Source code that is run through ASDoc will look exactly like the Flex Language Reference documentation files that come in the Flex Builder.

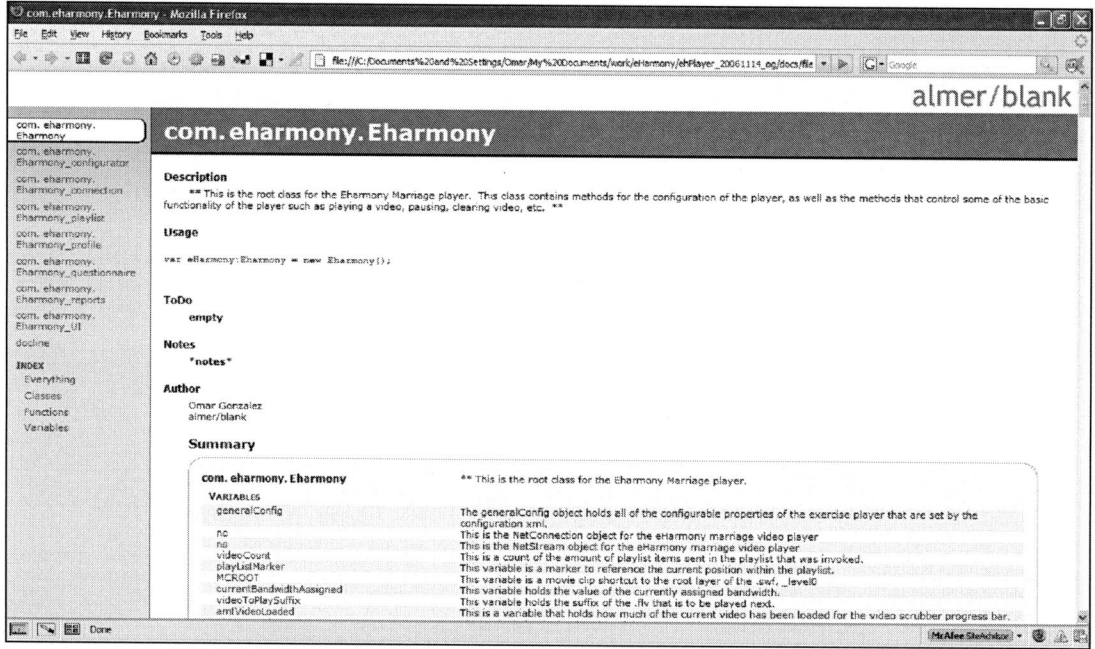

Figure 4-8. An example of Natural Docs documentation

Summary

In this chapter, I covered some of the things that should be considered when beginning a new project, from setting up your development environment, to planning the application's structure to have cleaner, more manageable code. These development tips, along with some of the tools covered in this chapter, really make a difference to help you concentrate on the things that really matter.

Although this might be all a little bit too overwhelming, if you aren't already practicing all of the methodologies in this chapter, the time that you invest in making these practices part of your everyday workflow can prove to be invaluable to you as you begin to reap the rewards of applying some, if not all, of the conventions and standards I've discussed here. Try adding comments to your existing projects using the Flex Builder IDE's ASDoc comment block feature and then run your source files through ASDoc or Natural Docs and see what kind of results you get. For source control, I recommend subscribing to a service like www.hosted-projects.com that provides hosting for you. I personally prefer the security of a managed solution that is going to do all of the backing up for me as well as provide any updates to Subversion.

Now, for the first stop in the development process, you're going to learn about some of the styling issues a Flex application like the RMX presents.

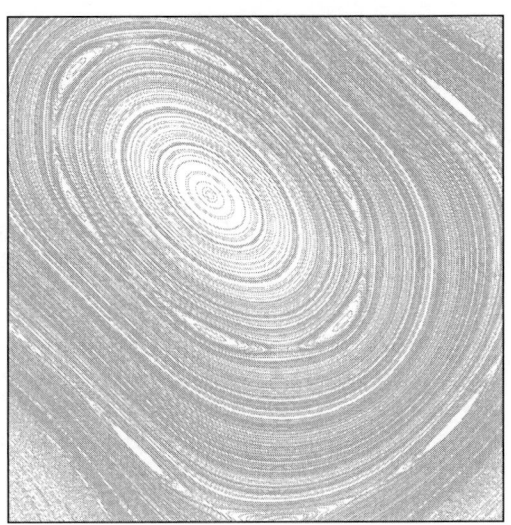

Chapter 5

STYLING FLEX

By Omar Gonzalez

CSS, or Cascading Style Sheets, was originally developed as a tool by Håkon Wium Lie and Bert Bos in 1998 to allow easy styling of markup on the Web. CSS, widely adopted throughout the world, is now an essential tool among web standards developers, who leverage the styling power of CSS in a wide variety of applications, from web sites to book publishing and now rich media applications. Since MXML is a markup language, CSS is also a natural choice for styling Flex applications, so Adobe has implemented the standards established in the CSS specification for the Flex framework.

In this chapter, you will learn the basics of CSS, why it's so popular, and why the technology is so well suited for its role of powering the styling of your Flex applications. In the past few years, the popularity of CSS has grown as an increasing number of web designers and developers have harnessed the power of this styling language. In addition to a comprehensive understanding of the basics of CSS and how the technology is implemented in Flex, you'll also learn how we exploited it for use in the RMX.

If you are interested in a more in-depth look at CSS and its methods or best practices, I recommend reading *Beginning CSS Web Development: From Novice to Professional* by Simon Collision (Apress, 2006) and *CSS Mastery: Advanced Web Standards Solutions* by Andy Budd et al. (friends of ED, 2006). Also, a great reference for anything CSS is A List Apart (www.alistapart.com).

The Flex implementation of CSS

Frameworks like Flex are designed to help standardize the workflow for developing RIAs. Accordingly, inclusion of CSS to aid in styling RIAs is complementary to the goals of the framework. By utilizing a powerful, widely known set of standards like CSS, Adobe makes it far easier for a wide variety of developers to transition into Flex and participate in the design of RIAs, and further streamlines the development workflow for such applications.

The implementation of CSS within the Flex framework is very similar to its traditional counterpart in XHTML. The fundamental difference is that the styles that you declare in an XHTML document are parsed by your web browser at runtime. In a Flex application, on the other hand, the styles that you declare are compiled into your SWF file or, since Flex Builder 2.0.1, you now have the option of compiling a CSS file as a SWF that your Flex application can load at runtime. Even though runtime CSS requires compiling a static SWF, the feature enables the easy customization and alternation of styles at application runtime, just as with traditional CSS in XHTML.

Many of the familiar attributes that CSS developers have come to know also exist in Flex. But there are also attributes that have been added to the Flex CSS specification that address components that are unique to the Flex framework. The Flex Language Reference documentation for each class has a complete list of style properties made available for that particular component. You should look at the style properties list of every new component you style so that you can see the unique style attributes for that component.

For a developer who already has had some experience with traditional CSS, transitioning into this implementation should not be overwhelming. And for a developer who has not had any experience styling using CSS, the relative simplicity of the standard means the learning curve should not be very steep.

CSS 101: A primer

Now that you know what the benefits of CSS are, let's see how it works. The first concept you must understand is the "cascading" part of CSS. CSS has an order in which it cascades from the top down, allowing the browser to make decisions on which styles override the properties set by styles that occur earlier in the cascade. For example, a blue font color applied to a <body> tag would cascade onto everything inside of the document body. However, if you then apply a red font color on a <p> tag that resides within the body, the color styling applied to the <p> tag overrides the blue color that cascaded from the body. You will see more examples as you learn about tag selectors.

So what does it all look like? Basic CSS declarations resemble basic ActionScript function declarations, without the parentheses. Not only do they resemble functions, but they also work similarly to functions in that they encapsulate a set of styling properties so that you may later easily and repeatedly apply those styles to any element. In HTML, a CSS declaration would look something like this:

```
<!DOCTYPE html PUBLIC "-//W3C//DTD XHTML 1.0 Transitional//EN" ➥
"http://www.w3.org/TR/xhtml1/DTD/xhtml1-transitional.dtd">
<html xmlns="http://www.w3.org/1999/xhtml">
<head>
<meta http-equiv="Content-Type" ➥
content="text/html; charset=iso-8859-1" />
```

```
<title>CSS 101 - A Primer</title>
<style type="text/css">
  .myFirstStyle
  {
    font-family: Arial, Helvetica, sans-serif;
    font-size: 20px;
    font-weight: bold;
  }
</style>
</head>
<body>
  <p class="myFirstStyle">Hello Friends of Ed!</p>
  CSS is neat!
</body>
</html>
```

The myFirstStyle class contains three basic CSS style properties: font-family, font-size, and font-weight. Since this is an XHTML example, the font-size style property is written using the px unit type (pixels, equivalent to points). In the Flex implementation of CSS, the unit type declaration is not needed and will cause an error when you attempt to compile (all font sizes in Flex are handled in pixels, so it is not necessary to use px). The font-weight CSS style property sets the text as bold and the font-family property declares Arial as the font of choice.

In a browser, the text within the <p> tag renders in Arial, at size 20, with a bold setting, as you see in Figure 5-1. However, the text outside the tag that reads "CSS is neat!" renders in plain Times New Roman.

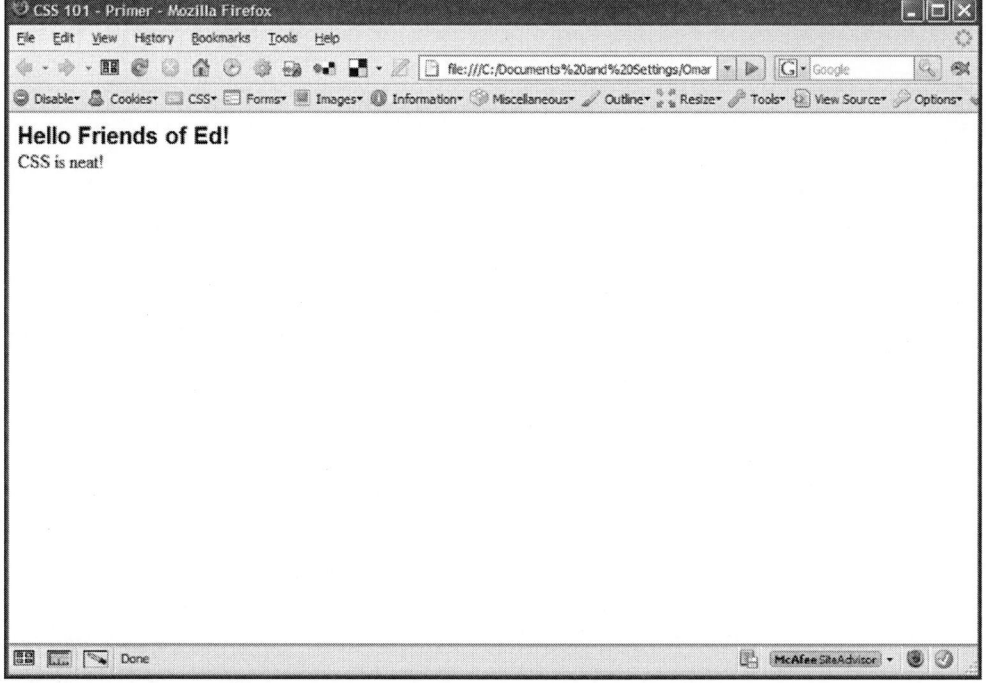

Figure 5-1. Notice the text outside the <div> tag is not styled by the CSS.

So what would an example like this look like in Flex? Well let's take a look! Using the same selector declaration, the Flex code appears as follows:

```
<?xml version="1.0" encoding="utf-8"?>
<mx:Application xmlns:mx="http://www.adobe.com/2006/mxml"
  layout="vertical">
  <mx:Style>
    .myFirstStyle
    {
      font-family: Arial;
      font-weight: bold;
      font-size: 20;
    }
  </mx:Style>
  <mx:Text styleName="myFirstStyle" text="Hello Friends of Ed!"/>
  <mx:Text text="CSS is neat!"/>
</mx:Application>
```

This sample code is a basic Flex application with two Text components. The first tag is the `<mx:Style>` tag, which is very much like the `<style>` tag in the XHTML code sample you saw earlier. The same three CSS style properties declared in the XHTML sample of the `myFirstClass` class selector are declared in the Flex example of the `myFirstStyle` class selector, the only difference being that the `font-size` property is not using a unit type of px, as noted earlier. In the XHTML sample, you saw first that the class selector was applied to the `<p>` tag by using the `class` attribute of the `<p>` tag. In Flex, the `styleName` attribute is used on the MXML component, in this case a Text component. When the code is compiled, the results appear as shown in Figure 5-2.

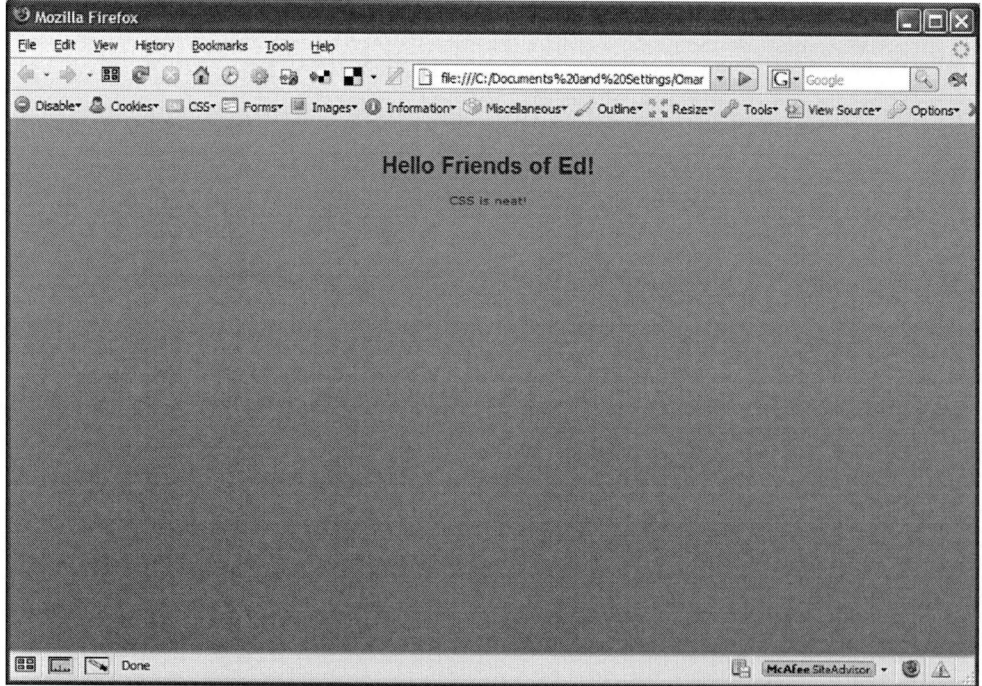

Figure 5-2. Here you can see how only the first Text component receives the styling.

This is just a very basic example of how CSS is used, but you can already start to note some differences in both how things are declared and how they are applied. For example, in XHTML, the CSS class declaration is applied by using the class attribute of a <p> tag, whereas in Flex, the styleName attribute of the Text component is used.

The differences that exist are trivial and do not affect any of the basic underlying principles of CSS. For example, one of the differences in Flex CSS is the ability to choose the syntax style in which you write your CSS attributes. You can write traditional hyphenated attributes like background-image, or you can use camel case–style syntax such as backgroundImage. However, when referring to styles through ActionScript, the attribute names *must* be written in camel case–style syntax.

Another key difference when working with CSS in Flex is how you declare font sizes. As you can see in the example using XHTML, the font-size CSS property is set by implicitly specifying that you are talking in pixels by using the px suffix. However, in Flex, the only unit of measurement used is the pixel, so there is no need to specify the font-size unit type.

Aside from font styles and colors, in XHTML, CSS also gives you the ability to control the dimensions of elements, such as setting widths and heights on <div> tags to achieve the layout that you are looking for. In Flex, you have many types of containers, but you cannot use CSS to set or affect their layout dimensions. Therefore, there is no CSS positioning in the Flex framework—a key difference between XHTML and Flex implementations of CSS. CSS in the Flex world serves only one purpose: styling. Layouts and positioning in Flex are handled by the different types of containers in the Flex framework, like HBoxes and VBoxes. Widths and heights in Flex are always set in either MXML tags or in ActionScript using the width or height properties. To use percentage-based sizing in ActionScript, you would use the percentWidth and percentHeight properties, setting them to an integer between 0 and 100 without the % (percent) character. In MXML, on the other hand, the % character is used in the width and height properties (e.g., width="100%") to specify percentage-based dimensions.

Tag selectors

Tag selectors function identically in Flex as they do in traditional XHTML CSS. A tag selector takes a group of CSS attributes and applies them to components of the same type after which it was named. Tag selectors are always a single word followed by a group of CSS attributes wrapped in curly braces, similar to the style used for the earlier Flex CSS example, except that tag selectors are capitalized and do not start with a period.

For example, if the CSS grouping is named Accordion, the grouping will style all <mx:Accordion/> instances in the application. With a single tag selector declaration, you can style or skin Flex components globally throughout your application just as you can style all paragraphs or headings with a <p> or <h1> tag selector declaration in traditional XHTML/CSS. Every instance of the declared tag (paragraph, header, Accordion, etc.) would be styled accordingly.

```
/* styles application with a gray background
 and size-12, black Arial text */
Application
{
  background-color: #dcdcdc;
  font-family: Arial;
  font-size: 12;
```

```
    color: #000000;
  }
  /* makes all text inputs bold, black, size-10 text */
  TextInput
  {
    font-size: 10;
    font-weight: bold;
    color: #ff0000;
  }
```

The Application tag selector is similar to styling a <body> tag in traditional CSS. By applying styles to the <mx:Application> tag, you are defining the general look of your entire application. Besides the usual background-color and color style properties you expect from CSS, you also get a style for Application called background-gradient-colors. This style, unique to Application, gives the ability to use a gradient as a background for the application without the need for an external image asset. Using the same example that earlier resulted in the output shown in Figure 5-2, I'll apply what I just discussed about the Application tag selector.

```
<?xml version="1.0" encoding="utf-8"?>
<mx:Application xmlns:mx=http://www.adobe.com/2006/mxml
  layout="vertical">
  <mx:Style>
    Application
    {
      background-gradient-colors: #cccccc, #000000;
      color: #ff0000;
    }
    .myFirstStyle
    {
      font-family: Arial;
      font-weight: bold;
      font-size: 20;
    }
  </mx:Style>
  <mx:Text styleName="myFirstStyle" text="Hello Friends of Ed!"/>
  <mx:Text text="CSS is neat!"/>
</mx:Application>
```

As you can see, all I've added to the code was an Application tag selector with two CSS properties: one that sets the background gradient colors and another that sets the color property to red. You can see the result in Figure 5-3.

Flex-specific tag selectors like Application and TextInput carry all of the basic inherited styles from a DisplayObject such as border, fontFamily, color, and so on. However, some of the components, like the Accordion or TabNavigator, have unique attributes that allow you to link to a class selector declaration that facilitates styling properties of said components, such as the headings of an Accordion panel or the tabs of a TabNavigator.

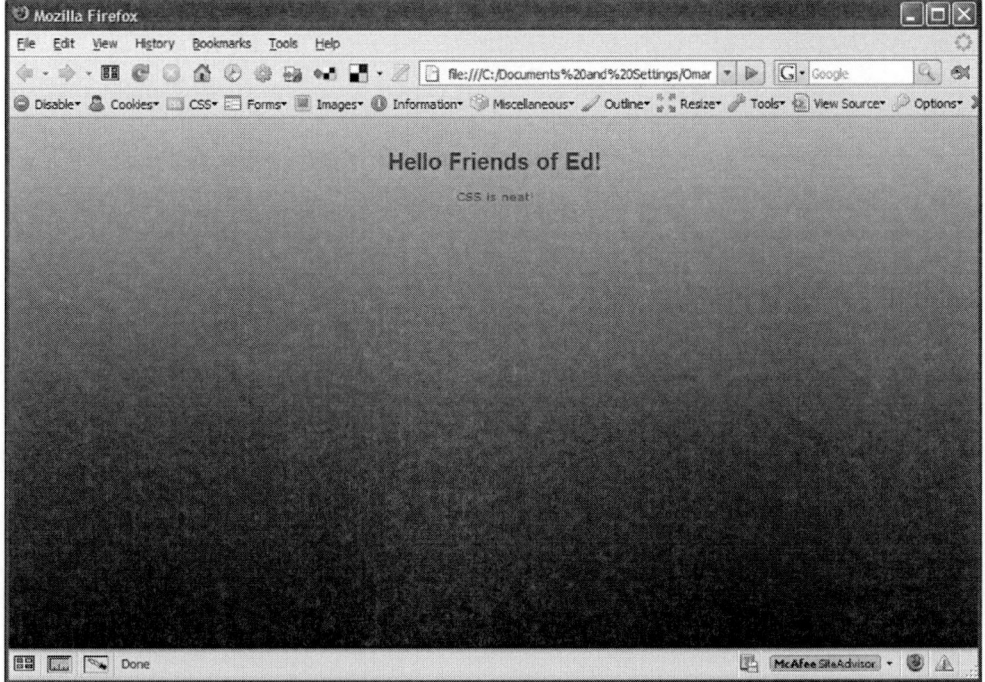

Figure 5-3. Notice that the text inputs have now inherited the color style from the Application selector.

The Flex Language Reference documents have a nice listing of all the inherited styles you can access for each component as well as the styles that are unique to a particular component that you want to style. It is possible to memorize them all, but I recommend becoming familiar with navigating the help and reference documents so that you may quickly find them when needed. I can never stress enough the importance of becoming familiar with those documents.

Class selectors

The implementation of class selectors in Flex is identical to that in XHTML. Class selectors are a group of CSS attributes with a unique arbitrary name. Unlike tag selectors, class selectors have two unique properties: they always start with a period, and they can be used multiple times on different components.

For example, if your application requires that some text inputs have red, bold, Times New Roman text, instead of using a tag selector and styling every text input with the bold, red text, you can use a class selector instead and simply apply it to the text inputs you wish to have the desired styling, just as you saw earlier in the CSS primer. This class selector declaration would look something like the following:

```
.redInputs
{
  fontFamily: Times;
  color: #ff0000;
  fontWeight: bold;
}
```

The redInputs class example would apply the bold, red, Times New Roman text to any component that has this class attached to it. In the MXML declaration of the component you want to style, you set the styleName property to the name of the CSS class you want it styled with. To apply the redInputs class to a text input, the MXML would look something like the following:

```
<?xml version="1.0" encoding="utf-8"?>
<mx:Application xmlns:mx=http://www.adobe.com/2006/mxml
  width="400" height="50">
  <Style>
    .redInputs
    {
      fontFamily: Times;
      color: #ff0000;
      fontWeight: bold;
    }
  </Style>
  <mx:TextInput id="myTextInput" styleName="redInputs">
    <mx:text>Hello world!</mx:text>
  </mx:TextInput>
</mx:Application>
```

This very basic application uses the redInputs style class to style the text in the TextInput component. This is just one way that you can use CSS in Flex. There are four different approaches to styling your Flex application: inline CSS, CSS in a <mx:Style/> tag, ActionScript-driven CSS, and runtime CSS. First, I will demonstrate the inline method.

Inline CSS styling

Inline CSS is the use of CSS attributes within your MXML code. All CSS style properties can be set just like the properties of any component, if they are available for the particular component. Just like you set the id property of components, you can set the fontFamily or color properties right in your MXML tag! However, as a rule of thumb, you should try to keep inline styles to a minimum. Attributes that affect layout like padding are fine to leave inline with the MXML. Your layout will not likely change much, so you won't be editing it as often as a style that affects your design implementation.

```
<mx:Text Area
  id="myTextArea"
  width="200"
  height="26"
  padding-left="8"
  padding-right="8"
  fontFamily="Arial"
  color="#ff0000"
/>
```

This allows you to easily change CSS properties like paddings in your design view when doing layout design. Although on the surface this may seem like a benefit, if you leave attributes like font color declarations and font sizes inline, in the long run the inline CSS can come back to haunt you. If the application you are building starts to get pretty big, managing your styles can become a nightmare pretty quickly if you need to make changes to the design. What if all of your styles were inline and you need to change all text inputs to have blue text instead of red text? You would have to find each instance of text input and change it from red to blue.

Instead, you can, and should, put them all in one central location: a script tag or an external CSS file. Just as with other code, editing styles in a central location makes development, maintenance, and transfer far, far easier.

The <mx:Style/> tag

The <mx:Style/> tag in MXML is very much like the <style /> tag in XHTML. There are two ways in which it can be used. The first is to write your class and tag declarations between the beginning <mx:Style> tag and ending </mx:Style> tags like this:

```
<mx:Style>
  Application
  {
    fontFamily: Arial;
    color: #999999;
  }

  .error
  {
    Color: #ff0000;
  }
</mx:Style>
```

The second is to use the source attribute to point it to a file path of a CSS file containing your CSS styles, which is actually like an HTML link tag: <link href="style.css"/>. The two files would be written as follows:

```
MXML
<mx:Style source="styles.css"/>

CSS File
  Application
  {
    fontFamily: Arial;
    color: #999999;
  }

  .error
  {
    Color: #ff0000;
  }
```

Using the <mx:Style/> tag is the preferred way of writing CSS styles for an application. Keeping your styling in external files will allow you to employ better information architectures that will enable you to keep your style code better organized. In smaller applications where there isn't the need to write many style declarations, a single organized CSS file can suffice to keep your code manageable. But, given the data, functionality, and performance requirements of contemporary applications, you will more than likely need to use a more sophisticated information architecture.

One basic way that you can organize your CSS code is in two external files. In the first file, tags.css, you can write all your tag selector declarations. In the second file, classes.css, you can organize your class selector declarations. This basic structure will keep your tag and class selectors isolated from one another and, in one easy step, make it a little easier to manage your CSS code.

Like the style declarations in your CSS, the <mx:Style/> tags in your MXML cascade from top to bottom in the order in which you wrote them. For this reason, when you use this basic way to manage your CSS, the tags.css Style tag is applied before the classes.css Style tag. With the following code, your tags.css file will apply your global tag selector declarations first, and only then will your class selector declarations be applied to the components that you've specified:

```
<Style source="tags.css"/>
<Style source="classes.css"/>
```

ActionScript-driven styling

Using the <mx:Style/> tag to attach a CSS style sheet to your application will take care of the vast majority of the needs required by a basic design implementation. Although it is possible to write the entirety of your styling using the ActionScript method setStyle, this is not recommended. Setting styles using the setStyle method is a drain on the viewer's CPU processing power and may negatively affect your application's performance, especially if too many ActionScript-based styling operations are executed while your application is initializing. However, there are still instances in which you will need to employ ActionScript code logic in order to address certain design requirements. For example, you might need to change the appearance of a button based on the current action it is performing, or you may need to change the border color of a container based on certain conditions. This kind of conditional styling is not possible with plain CSS in both XHTML and MXML. In XHTML, you use JavaScript and call it DHTML. In Flex, ActionScript drives any type of conditional styling that your application may need. With ActionScript, you can make decisions based off of certain events that happen in your application and apply style changes to provide a richer experience for the user. For example, you can change the background of a TextInput component to yellow when it receives focus. When it loses focus, ActionScript can change it back to white. As you can see, there are myriad possibilities.

The setStyle method

The setStyle method is the method you will use to interact with the style properties of all Flex components. The method expects two arguments, styleProp and newValue. The styleProp argument expects a string reference of the style you want to change, and the newValue argument expects an object that contains the new value for the style you want to change.

If you want to change the font color of a text field when you click a button, you would need to write some ActionScript that would respond to your click, like so:

```
<?xml version="1.0" encoding="utf-8"?>
<mx:Application xmlns:mx=http://www.adobe.com/2006/mxml
  width="300" height="20" creationComplete="init()">
  <Script>
  <![CDATA[
  private function init():void
  {
    this.myBtn.addEventListener(MouseEvent.CLICK, changeTextColor);
  }
  private function changeTextColor(event:MouseEvent):void
  {
    this.myTextInput.setStyle("color", 0xff0000);
  }
  ]]>
  </Script>
  <mx:TextInput id="myTextInput" text="Hello World!"/>
  <mx:Button id="myBtn" label="Change color"/>
</mx:Application>
```

This code assigns an event listener to the button you want to click to change the styling of the text input on the creationComplete event of the application. The event handler, changeTextColor, uses the setStyle method on the text input component and sets it to red.

When you use the setStyle method, all the style attribute string references that you pass as arguments must be formatted in the camel case style. If you attempt to use background-color instead of backgroundColor, the compiler will throw an error. Another thing to keep in mind is when setting color attributes, instead of using #ff0000, you must use proper hexadecimal number notation. The correct value would be the hexadecimal value 0xff0000, not the string #ff0000, which would also cause the compiler to return an error.

So, setting basic styles like color using the setStyle method as you just saw is pretty straightforward. But what if you want to use an image to skin the background of a button or container and then change it using the setStyle method depending on certain conditions? The newValue property only takes object references as a value, so a URL to an image would not load, resulting in an error.

The Embed metadata tag

In order to swap a background image using the setStyle method, you must first embed the image you wish to reference in ActionScript by using an Embed metadata tag. Unlike Flash, Flex does not have a project library where you can import imagery for your project and use it in your code by the assigned linkage ID or class name. Instead, in Flex you will use the Embed metadata tag to embed the image in the application and assign a variable to use as a reference.

You can use this method to change the background skin of a Flex Button component using the setStyle method and Embed metadata tags.

```
<?xml version="1.0" encoding="utf-8"?>
<mx:Application xmlns:mx=http://www.adobe.com/2006/mxml
  width="300" height="60" creationComplete="init()">
  <mx:Script>
```

```
<![CDATA[
[Embed(source="images/overskin.jpg")]
public var rolloverSkin:Class;

[Embed(source="images/upskin.jpg")]
public var rolloutSkin:Class;

private function init():void
{
  this.myButton.setStyle("overSkin", rolloverSkin);
  this.myButton.setStyle("upSkin", rolloutSkin);
  this.myButton.setStyle("downSkin", rolloutSkin);
}
]]>
</mx:Script>
<mx:Button id="myButton" label="My Button"/>
</mx:Application>
```

The Embed metadata tag begins and ends with brackets. Inside of it, you can use the Embed directive to supply a path to an image that you wish to embed into your application. This path is relative to the location of the MXML file from which the script is being compiled. The line following the Embed meta-data tag is a variable declaration that creates the variable, of type Class, to serve as the reference for the embedded image. By creating a variable reference for your image, Flex makes it quite easy to insert the image wherever it is required in your application, in this case applied to the upSkin, overSkin, and downSkin properties of the Button component.

This basic example demonstrates the use of the Embed metadata tag to switch skins in response to user rollover and rollout of a button. This method of embedding imagery and using a variable reference is very similar to how images are referenced from the Flash library using linkage identifiers, with the exception that there are no visual previews of the items you embed in Flex, nor does the Flex Builder compress the images you embed like the Flash library does when you compile a SWF in Flash (that is, you must apply explicit compression settings in a tool like Adobe Fireworks).

Asset libraries

At the end of the previous section I made a comparison between embedding image assets in Flex and building an asset library in Flash, where you assign linkage identifiers. In Flash, you can import image assets to your library and make them all accessible to your ActionScript code using linkage identifiers that Flash lets you assign to each asset in the library. This provides the ability to change the appearance of parts of the application through code very easily.

You can employ various techniques to bring Flash assets into Flex with ActionScript intact. Grant Skinner has a great article on one such technique on his blog at www.gskinner.com/blog/archives/2007/03/using_flash_sym.html. This article does a great job of covering that technique, so I'm not going to go into detail on it here. What I am going to cover, however, is making an ActionScript library of assets for use in your Flex projects. The end result of using this technique will essentially provide the same result as the technique described in Grant Skinner's article because the assets will be in the application, accessible through code. However, there are differences in how the assets are accessed and compiled. Using Flash to make the asset library requires that an asset SWF file be compiled. That asset SWF file then has to be loaded into a Flex application, and the assets accessed through the loaded file. Using the technique I'm about to cover, the assets are all accessed using an ActionScript class in your Flex project, so there is no need to compile another SWF file and load it, since the assets are embedded into the application through an asset library class. Another difference would be that the assets compiled in a Flash SWF file would be compressed by Flash. In Flex, you have to optimize your assets using Fireworks for the best quality and file size.

So how do you go about making an asset library class for Flex? It's quite simple actually. I usually keep assets in a folder that sits in the project namespace. For example, in the RMX project, the assets folder, or package, is com.rmx.assets. That folder contains all the image files and the asset library class. Using two images as an example, the class would look like this:

```
package com.rmx.assets
{
  [Bindable]
  public class AssetLib
  {
    [Embed(source='buttonUpSkin.png')]
    public static var buttonUpImage:Class;

    [Embed(source='buttonOverSkin.png')]
    public static var buttonOverImage:Class;
  }
}
```

This class is small and simple. Above the class declaration is the Bindable metadata tag. This marks the entire class as bindable, which gives us the ability to bind properties of objects to this class. Inside the class has two embedded images, using the Embed metadata tag technique covered earlier in this chapter. The key difference with this class is that the variables are now public static variables. This gives you the ability to access these assets from anywhere in the application without needing to initialize an instance of the AssetLib class over and over again. You can simply talk to the static properties of your asset class. The simplest way you can use these assets would be with MXML. Using an <mx:Button> tag, the code would look something like this:

```
<mx:Button upSkin='{AssetLib.buttonUpImage}'/>

<mx:Script>
  <![CDATA[
    import com.rmx.assets.AssetLib;
  ]]>
</mx:Script>
```

This is just one way that you can use the AssetLib class on a component. Another way assets can be applied to a component is by extending the component. For example, take a look at this class:

```
package com.rmx.controls
{
  import mx.controls.Button;
  import mx.events.FlexEvent;
  import com.rmx.assets.AssetLib;
```

```
public class SkinnedButton extends Button
{
  public function SkinnedButton()
  {
    super();
    super.addEventListener( FlexEvent.CREATION_COMPLETE, init );
  }

  private function init ( event:FlexEvent ):void
  {
    setStyle ( 'upSkin', AssetLib.buttonUpImage );
  }
}
}
```

This SkinnedButton class simply extends the Button class. In the SkinnedButton constructor, you can see an event handler assigned to its creationComplete event. When the SkinnedButton is done instantiating, the creationComplete event handler will apply the buttonImage asset from the AssetLib class to the upSkin property of the SkinnedButton. The SkinnedButton class can be used instead of the regular Button class anywhere. Using the new class would look something like this in MXML:

```
<controls:SkinnedButton/>
```

The button will appear with the buttonUpImage asset applied. This is a great technique when a custom styled component is used in multiple places of an application. As you see in the preceding MXML example, a class like this allows implementing styled buttons with a single tag. I'm sure you can think of other ways to exploit these techniques across your applications.

Component-unique properties

Certain components require the use of CSS properties that are unique to the styling needs of these components.

The first component that comes to mind that requires one of these component-unique properties is the Panel container component. The Panel component has a title you can set for the container. However, what if you want to have the title of your Panel be a blue font? Well, you can easily set the color style attribute to blue. But the problem with doing this is that not only will the title become blue, but so will the text in all other components in the Panel that display text. Unfortunately, the title property of the Panel does not accept HTML formatting, so using an HTML <font> tag is out of the question. This is where the titleStyleName property comes to play.

In order to properly style the title of the Panel component, you will need to first write a class selector declaration containing the style attributes that you would like applied to your Panel's title. Once you have your class written, you can set the titleStyleName property of the Panel you wish to style equal to the name of the class you just wrote. The following code sets a bold, blue, Arial font on a Panel component title:

```
<?xml version="1.0" encoding="utf-8"?>
<mx:Application xmlns:mx=http://www.adobe.com/2006/mxml
  layout="vertical">
  <mx:Style>
    Application
    {
      background-gradient-colors: #cccccc, #000000;
      color: #ff0000;
    }
    .myFirstStyle
    {
      font-family: Arial;
      font-weight: bold;
      font-size: 20;
    }
    .myTitleStyle
    {
      font-weight: bold;
      font-size: 16;
      color: #0000ff;
    }
  </mx:Style>
  <mx:Panel title="Main Panel" titleStyleName="myTitleStyle"
    width="100%" height="100%">
    <mx:Text styleName="myFirstStyle" text="Hello Friends of Ed!"/>
    <mx:Text text="CSS is neat!"/>
  </mx:Panel>
</mx:Application>
```

Using the code sample from the section "Tag selectors," you make two additions to the code. In the <mx:Style/> tag, add a new class selector declaration named myTitleStyle. This new CSS class sets the font to bold, size 16, blue text, using basic CSS font formatting style attributes.

The second addition to the code happens immediately after the </mx:Style> tag, where you begin to wrap the two Text components made earlier in a Panel component. The second part of this addition is the line before the </mx:Application> tag, where you finish wrapping the Text components by closing the <mx:Panel/> tag. In the <mx:Panel> opening tag, you apply the new CSS class using the new property you learned about, titleStyleName.

As you can see in Figure 5-4, when the example code is compiled, only the title of the Panel is rendered as blue, bold Arial. The Text component in the Panel retains its default styling.

The Accordion component has a unique attribute similar to that of the Panel component. In the same manner that you use the titleStyleName attribute to style the title of your Panel, the Accordion component has a headerStyleName attribute that you will use when you need to style the headers of each Accordion pane.

127

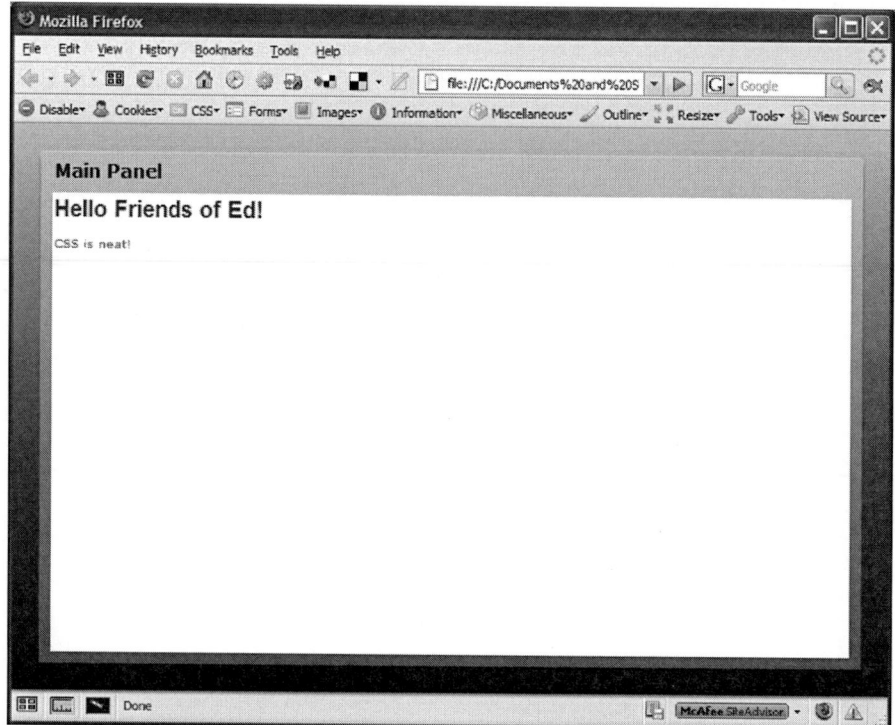

Figure 5-4. The Panel is styled according to the class style that was applied.

Unlike the `titleStyleName` attribute for the Panel component, the `headerStyleName` attribute will not allow you to use the `background-image` style attribute in order to set a custom background image. The headers of an Accordion behave as buttons. In order to style the Accordion headers with custom background imagery, the class you assign to the `headerStyleName` attribute must contain the style attributes used to style the different states of a button. The `upSkin`, `downSkin`, `overSkin`, `selectedUpSkin`, `selectedDownSkin`, and `selectedOverSkin` attributes provide several options for custom background imagery. The following code demonstrates how you can achieve this type of styling:

```
<?xml version="1.0" encoding="utf-8"?>
<mx:Application xmlns:mx=http://www.adobe.com/2006/mxml
  width="400" height="400">
  <Style>
    .myHeaderStyle
    {
      upSkin: Embed("images/upskin.jpg");
      downSkin: Embed("images/downskin.jpg");
      overSkin: Embed("images/overskin.jpg");
      selectedUpSkin: Embed("images/selectedupskin.jpg");
      selectedDownSkin: Embed("images/selecteddownskin.jpg");
      selectedOverSkin: Embed("images/selectedoverskin.jpg");
    }
  </Style>
  <mx:Accordion
```

```
            width="100%" height="100%"
            headerStyleName="myHeaderStyle">
            <mx:Canvas label="My First Pane">
              <mx:Text text="Hello world!" fontSize="16"/>
            </mx:Canvas>
            <mx:Canvas label="My Second Pane">
              <mx:Text text="Hello world!" fontSize="16"/>
            </mx:Canvas>
          </mx:Accordion>
        </mx:Application>
```

Scale 9 formatting feature

Scale 9 formatting for image embeds is supported in Flex 2. This formatting feature allows you to define a grid by dividing, or slicing, an image into nine different regions. Each region of the grid defines certain scaling behaviors for that particular region of the image, as shown in Figure 5-5. The positions of the grid lines can be calculated using any image-editing tool that will allow you to measure the areas that you want to define, or you can even eye it out until you get the desired effect. Fireworks CS3 includes a new feature that will allow you to determine the location of scale 9 grid lines in a visual environment similar to slices or guides.

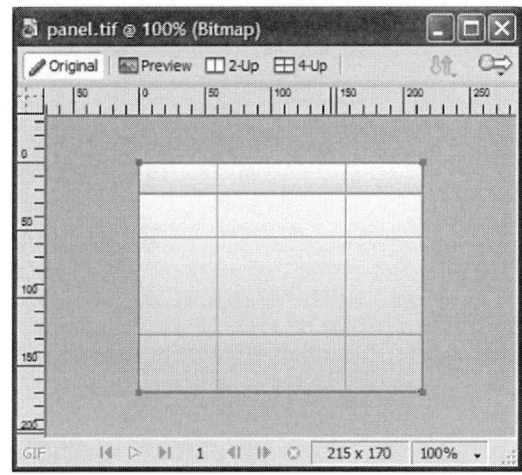

Figure 5-5. The scale 9 grid divides an image into nine separate regions.

The center region of the image retains regular scaling attributes. So as you scale your image, the center scales as it would without the scale 9 grid applied. The regions above and below the center region scale horizontally. The regions to the left and right of the center region scale vertically. Finally, the four corners do not scale at all. Using the grid, you could define the center region in a way that the rounded corners of this image would not be warped if scaled by using it on a Flex container that is a lot bigger than the image itself.

Panel components have some unique styling considerations as you've already learned from using the titleStyleName attribute. Another unique property of the Panel component is how it separates the styling of the inner content of the Panel and its title. In other words, if you want to apply the image from Figure 5-5 as styling for your Panel component, the image would have to be sliced in two sections, the header skin section and the section for the Panel content. I personally prefer to manage that image as a single asset by wrapping the Panel component in a Canvas and applying the asset as a background to the Canvas.

```
        <?xml version="1.0" encoding="utf-8"?>
        <mx:Application xmlns:mx=http://www.adobe.com/2006/mxml
          layout="vertical">
          <mx:Style>
            Application
```

```
      {
        background-gradient-colors: #cccccc, #000000;
        color: #ff0000;
      }
      .myFirstStyle
      {
        font-family: Arial;
        font-weight: bold;
        font-size: 20;
      }
      .myTitleStyle
      {
        font-weight: bold;
        font-size: 16;
        color: #0000ff;
      }
    </mx:Style>
    <mx:Script>
      <![CDATA[
        [Embed(source="images/panelBg.gif")]
        [Bindable]
        private var panelBg:Class;
      ]]>
    </mx:Script>
    <mx:Canvas backgroundImage="{panelBg}" backgroundSize="100%"
      width="100%" height="100%">
      <mx:Panel title="Main Panel" titleStyleName="myTitleStyle"
        width="100%" height="100%" backgroundAlpha="0"
        dropShadowEnabled="false" borderAlpha="0">
        <mx:Text styleName="myFirstStyle" text="Hello Friends of Ed!"/>
        <mx:Text text="CSS is neat!"/>
      </mx:Panel>
    </mx:Canvas>
  </mx:Application>
```

Taking the code modified in the titleStyleName example, you can make a few changes to implement the background image. First, you add an <mx:Script> tag and embed the background image using the same technique you learned in the section "The Embed metadata tag."

The second change is similar to what you did to wrap the Text components in the <mx:Panel/> tag, except this time the Panel component is being wrapped with a Canvas component, which is used to apply the background image. In the opening tag of the Canvas component, you include curly braces within quotes for the backgroundImage property to specify it is binding to an ActionScript variable, in this case panelBg, which is the reference to the embedded image. The backgroundSize property makes the image scale to the full size of the Canvas component, which is set to be 100% of the width and height allowed by the application.

The final change you must make is to the <mx:Panel/> tag, where you add three new properties. The backgroundAlpha property determines the opacity of the background for the content within the Panel component, and the borderAlpha property sets the opacity of the Panel component's borders, including the title area. These two are set to 0 in order to make the Panel component transparent, allowing the backgroundImage set on the Canvas component to show through. The final property you add is dropShadowEnabled, which is true by default, so you need to turn it off for this example by setting it to false. The remainder of the code is unchanged.

Using this technique, you can manage the asset as one. If you apply the image in Figure 5-5 to the Canvas that wraps the Panel in Figure 5-4, the corners of the image will warp, as you can see in Figure 5-6. The backgroundSize attribute is the key to making the image scale to the full size of the Canvas. Because the image does not have any scale 9 properties set in its Embed tag, the image becomes distorted. The image is embedded as in the previous example of the Embed metadata tag.

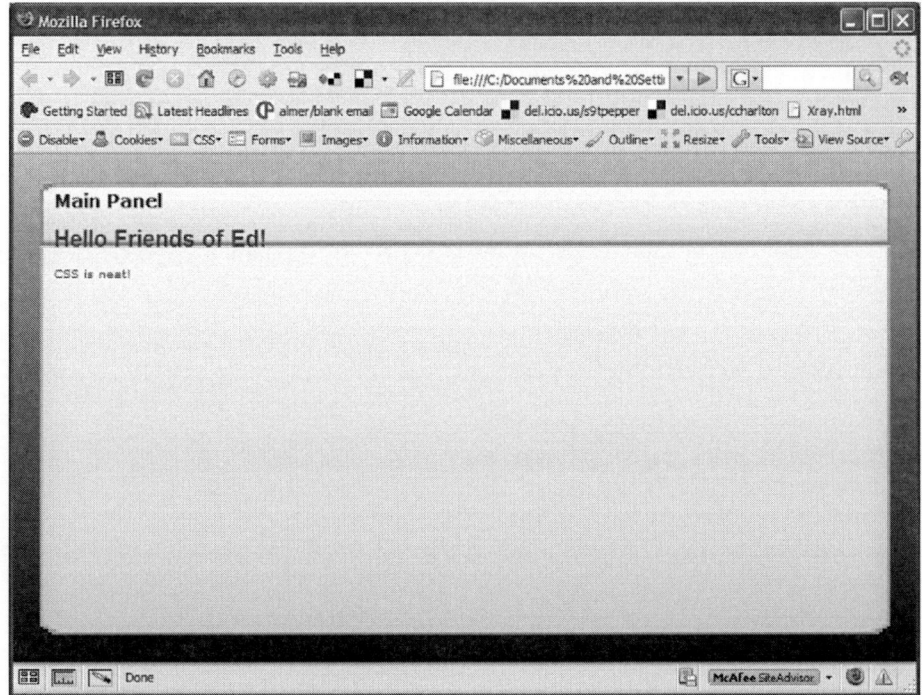

Figure 5-6. Notice the warping of the image.

Let's see how you can fix this with scale 9. Using the same code, add the scale 9 parameters to the Embed metadata tag to define the scalable areas. There are four parameters that you add to the Embed directive in order to apply scale 9: scaleGridTop, scaleGridBottom, scaleGridLeft, and scaleGridRight.

The scaleGridTop parameter defines the distance from the top of your image to make the topmost horizontal grid line. In this case, the value is set to 25, equal to the height of the header area of the image. This row will not scale vertically, so you must set the area of the image above the first grid line, or scaleGridTop, to 25.

The scaleGridBottom parameter defines the distance from the top of your image to make the bottommost horizontal grid line. If the image contained some kind of footer, this parameter should equal the height of the image minus the height of the footer area design. In the case of the Panel back-

131

ground for the RMX, scale 9 helps to maintain the rounded corners, so the value is set to 160 pixels from the top, allowing enough area at the bottom to not scale vertically, thus not warping the bottom rounded corners.

The scaleGridLeft parameter defines the distance from the left edge of your image to the leftmost vertical grid line. In the example, with the background applied to the Panel component, you set the value to 10, which is just wide enough to clear the end of the curves for the top-left and bottom-left rounded corners. This first column does not scale horizontally. More importantly, the top-left corner and bottom-left corner are now boxed in by the regions made from the first three grid lines. Since the rounded corners are now boxed in by the scale 9 corner sections, and the corner sections of a scale 9 grid don't scale, the rounded corners on the top left and bottom left will no longer be scaled when the Panel gets stretched to a size bigger than your original asset.

The grid is complete with the scaleGridRight parameter, which defines the distance from the left edge of your image to make the second of the two vertical grid lines. Since you only need 10 pixels to clear the curve of the rounded corners, the value is 203, which is 10 pixels less than the image width. This grid line completes the grid and boxes in the top-right and bottom-right corners in the nonscaled regions of the scale 9 grid.

These four parameters can be added to any image that you embed with ActionScript or any embedded SWF asset.

The following code also adjusts the font size for the header to 12 so that it will fit within the area for the header in the Panel graphic asset:

```
<?xml version="1.0" encoding="utf-8"?>
<mx:Application xmlns:mx=http://www.adobe.com/2006/mxml
  layout="vertical">
  <mx:Style>
    Application
    {
      background-gradient-colors: #cccccc, #000000;
      color: #ff0000;
    }
    .myFirstStyle
    {
      font-family: Arial;
      font-weight: bold;
      font-size: 20;
    }
    .myTitleStyle
    {
      font-weight: bold;
      font-size: 12;
      color: #0000ff;
    }
  </mx:Style>
  <mx:Script>
    <![CDATA[
      [Embed(source="images/panelBg.gif", scaleGridTop="25",
```

```
        scaleGridBottom="160", scaleGridLeft="10", scaleGridRight="203")]
        [Bindable]
        private var panelBg:Class;
      ]]>
    </mx:Script>
    <mx:Canvas backgroundImage={panelBg} backgroundSize="100%"
      width="100%" height="100%">
      <mx:Panel title="Main Panel" titleStyleName="myTitleStyle"
        width="100%" height="100%" backgroundAlpha="0"
        dropShadowEnabled="false" borderAlpha="0">
        <mx:Text styleName="myFirstStyle" text="Hello Friends of Ed!"/>
        <mx:Text text="CSS is neat!"/>
      </mx:Panel>
    </mx:Canvas>
</mx:Application>
```

The scale 9 grid applied produces what you see in Figure 5-7, with the header and corners of the image intact.

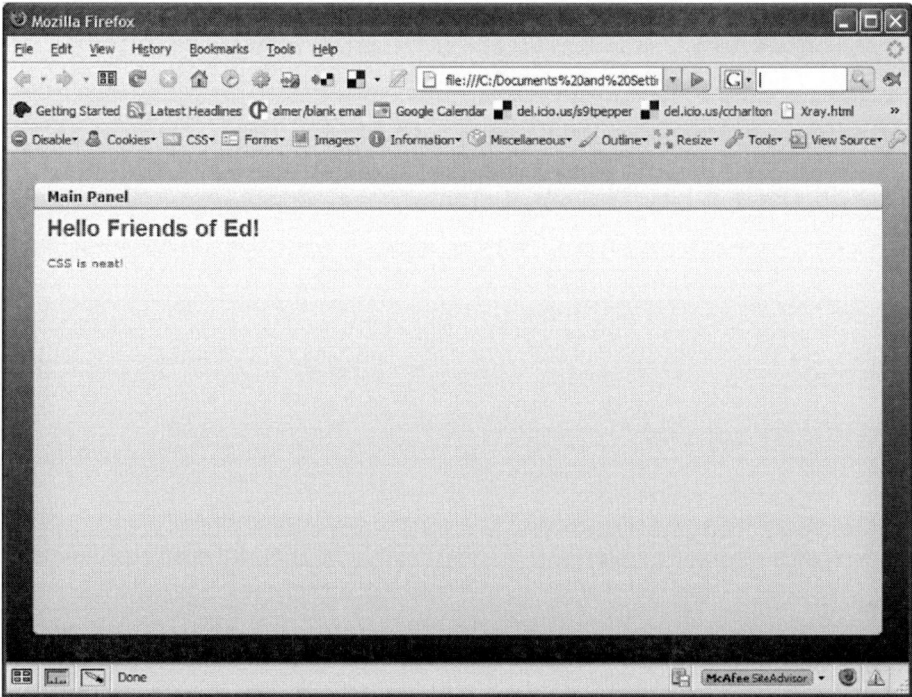

Figure 5-7. The image header is now intact. The Panel can be resized and the header stays the same height, corners are rounded, and everything else scales properly.

For this example, you've learned how to apply an image using scale 9 properties to define how it should scale when stretched to a Canvas component. However, the scale 9 feature can be used anywhere in any of the Flex components that allow skinning. For example, if you want to apply the same background we applied to a Button component, you would need to set the overSkin and upSkin CSS properties, which are accessible for the Button component from within your MXML and would apply the image using the scale 9 properties. Obviously, the asset is not meant to be used in a button, so the image will not look very attractive, but you could use the asset with its scale 9 properties if you desired.

Let's look back at the SkinnedButton class earlier in this chapter. If the button needed to be scaled, the asset applied would warp because it does not have a scale 9 grid applied to define its scaling behavior. Taking the SkinnedButton class to the next level, you can apply a scale 9 grid to the assets for the button. The changes would look like this:

```
package com.rmx.assets
{
  [Bindable]
  public class AssetLib
  {
    [Embed(source='buttonUpSkin.png', scaleGridTop='6',
    scaleGridLeft='6', scaleGridRight='16', scaleGridBottom='14')]
    public static var buttonUpImage:Class;

    [Embed(source='buttonOverSkin.png', scaleGridTop='6',
    scaleGridLeft='6', scaleGridRight='16', scaleGridBottom='14')]
    public static var buttonOverImage:Class;

    [Embed(source='buttonDownSkin.png', scaleGridTop='6',
    scaleGridLeft='6', scaleGridRight='16', scaleGridBottom='14')]
    public static var buttonDownImage:Class;
  }
}
```

The changes made to the class are minor: the scale 9 properties were added to the Embed tags, and one more Embed tag was added for a down skin. Now you can make these final changes to the SkinnedButton class:

```
package com.rmx.controls
{
  import mx.controls.Button;
  import mx.events.FlexEvent;
  import com.rmx.assets.AssetLib;

  public class SkinnedButton extends Button
  {
    public function SkinnedButton()
    {
      super();
      super.addEventListener( FlexEvent.CREATION_COMPLETE, init );
    }

    private function init ( event:FlexEvent ):void
    {
      setStyle ( 'upSkin', AssetLib.buttonUpImage );
```

```
            setStyle ( 'downSkin', AssetLib.buttonDownImage );
            setStyle ( 'overSkin', AssetLib.buttonOverImage );
        }
    }
}
```

The only lines added were two more setStyle method calls to apply the downSkin and overSkin properties. This class can now be used, and the up, over, and down states of the button will be skinned, with scale 9 properties to handle scaling.

Runtime CSS

Introduced in Flex 2.0.1, the runtime CSS features allows you to load your application styles from an external SWF source at runtime, instead of having the styles embedded into the application. This not only optimizes file size by externalizing CSS code, but it also gives you the ability to change the styling of an application without having to recompile the application itself.

There are three basic steps to loading your CSS style declarations at runtime. The first is to externalize all CSS declarations into a single CSS file, which is done simply by creating a new text file with a .css extension and pasting your CSS code into it. This will prepare the CSS for the second step and prepare the MXML for the third step.

The second step takes the CSS file and prepares it to load at runtime by compiling it into a SWF file. Simply right-click the CSS file in your Navigator panel of Flex Builder and check the option Compile CSS to SWF. Once you have that option checked, the next time you compile your application, the CSS will be compiled into an independent SWF file and placed in the project's bin folder. You can also press Cmd+B on a Mac or Ctrl+B on a Windows PC to compile the SWF. Once you see the SWF in your bin folder, you're ready for the third step. You can also uncheck the option to compile your CSS as a SWF, so that it doesn't slow down your application compiling. Of course, you'll need to turn this option back on and recompile the CSS SWF if you make any edits to your CSS styles.

In the third and final step to utilize the CSS SWF file, you employ the loadStyleDeclarations() method of the StyleManager class. In the following example, you load a SWF named styles.swf (containing your runtime CSS) in the same folder as your application.

Here's the MXML for this example:

```
<?xml version="1.0" encoding="utf-8"?>
<mx:Application creationComplete="init()"
  xmlns:mx="http://www.adobe.com/2006/mxml" layout="vertical">
  <mx:Script>
    <![CDATA[
      [Embed(source="images/panelBg.gif", scaleGridTop="25",
      scaleGridBottom="160", scaleGridLeft="10", scaleGridRight="203")]
      [Bindable]
      private var panelBg:Class;

      private function init():void
      {
```

```
            StyleManager.loadStyleDeclarations("styles.swf");
        }
    ]]>
  </mx:Script>
  <mx:Canvas backgroundImage={panelBg} backgroundSize="100%"
    width="100%" height="100%">
    <mx:Panel title="Main Panel" titleStyleName="myTitleStyle"
      width="100%" height="100%" backgroundAlpha="0"
      dropShadowEnabled="false" borderAlpha="0">
      <mx:Text styleName="myFirstStyle" text="Hello Friends of Ed!"/>
      <mx:Text text="CSS is neat!"/>
    </mx:Panel>
  </mx:Canvas>
</mx:Application>
```

And the CSS (styles.css):

```
/* CSS file */
Application
{
    background-gradient-colors: #cccccc, #000000;
    color: #ff0000;
}
.myFirstStyle
{
    font-family: Arial;
    font-weight: bold;
    font-size: 20;
}
.myTitleStyle
{
    font-weight: bold;
    font-size: 12;
    color: #0000ff;
}
```

The CSS has no changes, except for being put into a separate CSS file, which is simply a text file with a .css extension. The contents are identical to the contents within an <mx:Script/> tag.

The MXML has three changes. First, it no longer contains the <mx:Style/> tag with CSS, since you will load your styles at runtime. The CSS now exists only in the styles.css file compiled into a SWF.

The second change is on the <mx:Application/> tag, where you add an event handler for the creationComplete event. When the application finishes creating all its objects, the init() method will execute.

The third change is the init function declaration itself, where the StyleManager is used to load the CSS SWF once the application is done being created. The function contains one line, which executes a static method of the StyleManager class. StyleManager.loadStyleDeclarations() will load the compiled CSS SWF created by Flex Builder as described previously. The loadStyleDeclarations()

method expects a string parameter, which is a path to the CSS SWF that was created. Since the CSS SWF is in the same directory as the Flex SWF, the line reads StyleManager.loadStyleDeclarations ("styles.swf"). When you run the application, the results looks identical to Figure 5-7.

One of the differences in applying the styles at runtime as opposed to embedding them in the Flex SWF is the initial load is delayed by the initial download of the styles CSS SWF. On the other hand, the application initial download is faster, since it's not carrying the extra weight of styles and fonts if you've also embedded custom fonts. In an application like the RMX where there are multiple SWFs on a page, sharing the styles CSS SWF helps to trim down the size of the SWF files for faster downloads.

The Flex Style Explorer

On your quest to implement your design on your Flex application, one of the most helpful tools you can employ to facilitate your work is the Flex Style Explorer (see Figure 5-8). In its second incarnation, the Flex Style Explorer offers many features to help you achieve the look that you want. Built by Adobe Consulting, the Flex Style Explorer should be one of the first places you look to when you want to experiment with CSS.

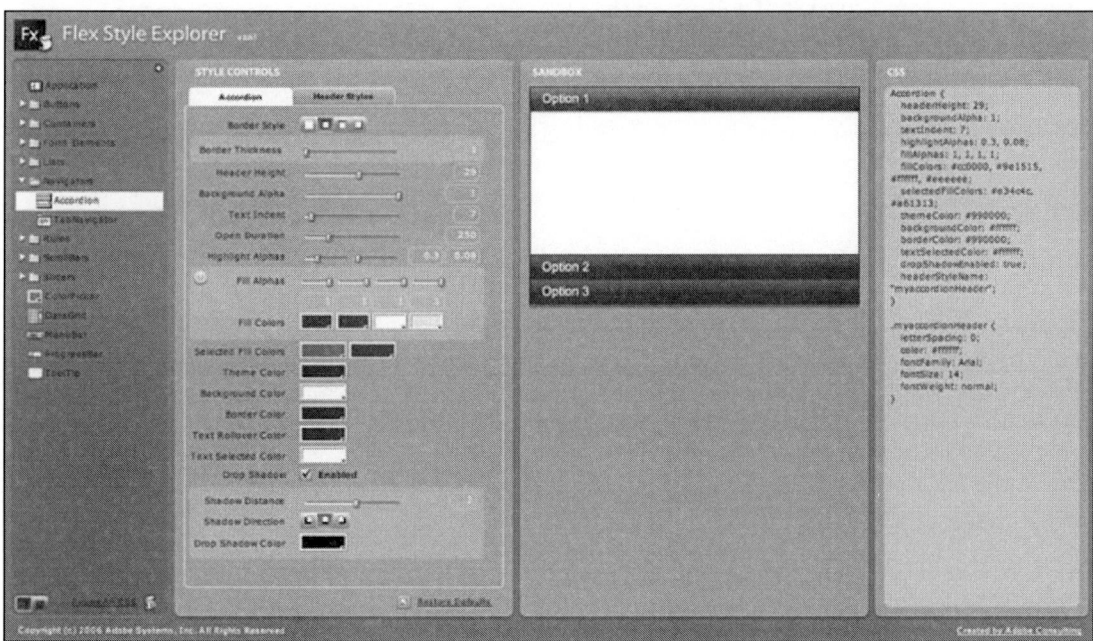

Figure 5-8. The new Flex Style Explorer

The application has four general areas, displayed in a four-column layout. From left to right, the first section is the component navigator. Here you can select the component you wish to experiment with from a tree view, which breaks the components down by type, a list view, or an icon view. Selecting one of the Flex components will change what is displayed by the two middle columns, the style controls and the sandbox; as you change the CSS properties of the component you select, the component will show a checkmark, indicating the styles have been modified from their default settings.

In the style controls area is a tab navigator with context-sensitive tabs that appear depending on which component you have selected. If you have a component with unique CSS properties, such as an Accordion component, the tab navigator will have an extra Header Styles tab, like you see in Figure 5-8. One of the neat features of the new Flex Style Explorer is what is known as **progressive disclosure of controls**. What this does is reveal CSS properties as they become available depending on other CSS properties being present. For example, there is no reason to display drop shadow colors and settings, if the Enabled check box next to Drop Shadows hasn't been checked. This helps to generate cleaner code as well as visualize CSS property dependencies.

The third column, which is the sandbox, simply serves as a preview of the CSS properties that are currently selected.

The last column displays the CSS as you customize your components, from which you can copy code. Or you can use a button at the bottom of the component navigator to export the CSS. Pressing this button copies the CSS to your clipboard, getting it ready to simply paste it into the file you wish to use it in. The application also includes an advanced color picker component and many new navigation improvements. The Flex Style Explorer is available at http://examples.adobe.com/flex2/consulting/styleexplorer/Flex2StyleExplorer.html. It can also be downloaded as an extension to Adobe Fireworks CS3 at http://download.macromedia.com/pub/developer/flex_style_explorer.zip. I recommend this tool, especially if you are just learning to work with CSS. The code generation by itself will help bring you up to speed on the basics of CSS. If you're already familiar with CSS, it will help you to explore different styles quickly, streamlining the design implementation workflow. And if you're interested in how it was built, you can view the source code by simply right-clicking the application and viewing the source! You can also download the source to run the Flex Style Explorer locally by clicking the Download Source link in the source viewer.

Styling considerations and the RMX

While developing the CSS for the RMX, I had to keep in mind that the spec of the application required the CSS to be written in a manner that could easily accommodate the Style Editor feature of the application. I had to ensure the application contained as little inline CSS as possible. Also, because the RMX contains both Flash and XHTML, I could fully exploit the benefits of delegating CSS styles between the application SWFs and the XHTML where the application was embedded, which allowed us to further optimize the file size of the Flex SWFs by loading some external assets for backgrounds using CSS's background-image property with XHTML.

One of the first advantages of this hybrid architecture is that it improved file-size optimization of the multiple SWF files that have to be delivered in the RMX. The backgrounds for each of the application's Flex modules were applied using CSS on the SWF's DIV container. This way the imagery did not have to be embedded into each SWF file, avoiding file bloat. The Flex modules have the backgroundAlpha attribute on the <mx:Application/> tag set to 0, and the embed code in the XHTML must have the wmode parameter set to transparent, allowing the DIV's background image to show through the Flex applications.

This same technique also simplified the styling of the application's module backgrounds. Instead of developing application logic to enable the upload of custom imagery for module backgrounds and then applying the images using the setStyle method, I only had to develop the upload module that would replace the image that the CSS loads into the DIV containers for the Flex modules. In doing so, I also avoided any performance drag that might result from importing and applying too many custom images through ActionScript.

By leaving the handling of the background imagery to XHTML and CSS, the Style Editor for the RMX only needs to handle the font sizes, colors, and overall theme color for the Flex application. This offers the ability to customize the look and feel of the RMX while keeping the process as simple and user friendly as possible.

RMX styling obstacles

As we implemented the RMX designs, most of the requirements were accomplished using CSS properties available in the framework. However, there were some cases in which the properties of a component did not behave in the exact way that we would have liked them to behave. These obstacles required a little bit of ActionScript and a little bit of creativity in order to achieve our goals.

Hand cursors on Accordion headers

A simple style request for our Accordion panels was the use of hand cursors on hover of the Accordion headers. By default, when you hover on an Accordion header, the cursor doesn't change from the regular arrow cursor, as you can see in Figure 5-9.

To achieve this on most components, you simply add the buttonMode attribute to the MXML declaration of the component you want a hand cursor to appear on and set the value to true. However, if you use the buttonMode attribute on the Accordion component, the hand cursor not only appears when you hover over the headers of your Accordion, but also appears anywhere within the contents of the panes of the Accordion.

Figure 5-9. The Accordion component uses the default mouse cursor on hover by default.

To properly get the hand cursor on hover of the Accordion header only, I used the technique illustrated here, which results in what you see in Figure 5-10:

```
<?xml version="1.0" encoding="utf-8"?>
<mx:Application
  creationComplete="init()"
  xmlns:mx="http://www.adobe.com/2006/mxml" width="400" height="400">
  <mx:Style>
    .myHeaderStyle
    {
      upSkin: Embed("images/upskin.jpg");
      downSkin: Embed("images/downskin.jpg");
      overSkin: Embed("images/overskin.jpg");
      selectedUpSkin: Embed("images/selectedupskin.jpg");
      selectedDownSkin: Embed("images/selecteddownskin.jpg");
      selectedOverSkin: Embed("images/selectedoverskin.jpg");
    }
  </mx:Style>
  <mx:Script>
    <![CDATA[
      import mx.controls.Button;

      private function init():void
      {
        var totalPanes:Array = this.myAccordion.getChildren();
        var header:Button;
        for (var i:uint; i < totalPanes.length; i++)
        {
          header = Button ( this.myAccordion.getHeaderAt(i) );
          header.buttonMode = true;
        }
      }
    ]]>
  </mx:Script>
  <mx:Accordion
    id="myAccordion"
    width="100%" height="100%"
    headerStyleName="myHeaderStyle">
    <mx:Canvas label="My First Pane">
      <mx:Text text="Hello world!" fontSize="16"/>
    </mx:Canvas>
    <mx:Canvas label="My Second Pane">
      <mx:Text text="Hello world!" fontSize="16"/>
    </mx:Canvas>
  </mx:Accordion>
</mx:Application>
```

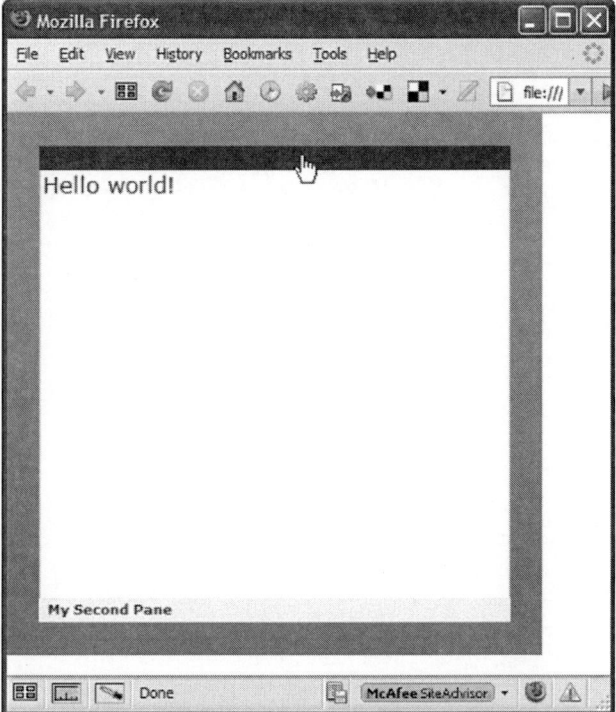

Figure 5-10. The headers of the Accordion trigger the hand cursor on hover with the described technique applied.

In this code example, the `creationComplete` event of the application invokes a script. This script uses the `getChildren()` method on the Accordion panel to get an array of the Accordion's panel headers. This array is then used to loop through each of the headers. In the loop, a variable of the type Button stores a reference to each header retrieved by using the `getHeaderAt()` method, using the `i` counter to step through each header. The return has to be cast as a Button to be stored in the Button variable. The last line uses the variable reference to set the `buttonMode` property to `true`. Compiling the sample results in a hand cursor appearing when a mouse is rolled over the panel headers.

Custom ItemRenderers with rollover skins

It is very common in contemporary applications to implement rollover states on parts of an application that invite user interaction. To display this type of visual feedback, the custom MXML ItemRenderer components that you will build in Flex Builder with MXML require that you employ a script to set some event listeners.

To view this example, start a new Flex application and place the application code (`main.mxml`) in the file. Then you will make a new MXML component in the root of the project for the ItemRenderer and name it myItemRenderer.mxml. That file would contain the ItemRenderer code (`myItemRenderer.mxml`) outlined in the following example. The example also requires that you use two image files, one named overskin.jpg and another named upskin.jpg. These would have to be in an images folder on the root of the application.

Following is the code for the application (main.mxml):

```
<?xml version="1.0" encoding="utf-8"?>
<mx:Application xmlns:mx=http://www.adobe.com/2006/mxml
  width="400" height="400">
  <mx:List itemRenderer="myItemRenderer" width="100%" height="100%">
    <mx:dataProvider>
      <mx:Array>
        <mx:Object>
          Label One
        </mx:Object>
        <mx:Object>
          Label One
        </mx:Object>
        <mx:Object>
          Label One
        </mx:Object>
      </mx:dataProvider>
    </mx:List>
</mx:Application>
```

And here now is the ItemRenderer (myItemRenderer.mxml):

```
<?xml version="1.0" encoding="utf-8"?>
<mx:Canvas
  creationComplete="init()"
  buttonMode="true"
  backgroundImage="{upskin}"
  xmlns:mx="http://www.adobe.com/2006/mxml" width="100%" height="100%">
  <mx:Script>
    <![CDATA[
      [Embed("images/overskin.jpg")]
      [Bindable]
      private var overskin:Class;
      [Embed("images/upskin.jpg")]
      [Bindable]
      private var upskin:Class;
      private function init():void
      {
        this.addEventListener(MouseEvent.ROLL_OVER, rollover);
        this.addEventListener(MouseEvent.ROLL_OUT, rollout);
      }
      private function rollover(event:MouseEvent):void
      {
        this.setStyle("backgroundImage", overskin);
      }
      private function rollout(event:MouseEvent):void
      {
```

```
            this.setStyle("backgroundImage", upskin);
         }
      ]]>
   </mx:Script>
   <mx:Text text="{data}"/>
</mx:Canvas>
```

Of the two files in this application, the main file is the application itself, which is main.mxml. The file is rather short, containing one actual List component in the application. The List component contains an inline data provider simply to populate the list with elements. The List component also has an itemRenderer property that links to the second file, an MXML ItemRenderer component.

The second file, myItemRenderer.mxml, is the MXML layout of the ItemRenderer component used in the list. The magic of the rollover states happens inside the ItemRenderer itself. In the first few lines of the <mx:Script/> tag are Embed metadata tags as demonstrated earlier in the chapter. The embedded images are used in the two background states of the ItemRenderer. Then on the creationComplete event of the ItemRenderer, the init function sets two event listeners on itself. In the rollover() and rollout() event handlers, the keyword this refers to the ItemRenderer itself. The event handlers use the setStyle method on this to swap to the correct background image for the current state of the ItemRenderer.

Summary

This chapter introduced you to the basic concepts of CSS and how they apply to the Flex framework. I covered different ways in which to implement CSS in Flex, and some of the considerations or problems you might encounter while implementing your application designs.

CSS is a huge topic, and even the subtopic of CSS in Flex could fill an entire book on its own. I've covered all the major points that should give you the foundation to accomplish most of the design challenges you might face. The important thing to remember is to become very familiar with navigating the Flex Language Reference documentation, which contains a complete list of the style properties available for each component that will come in handy when you style a component you haven't styled before, or if you simply need to look up the style properties available for a particular component.

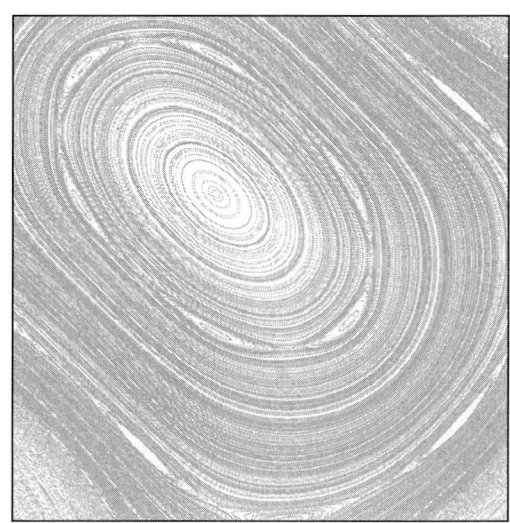

Chapter 6

COLLECTING AND WORKING WITH AGGREGATED CONTENT

by Chris Charlton

Most RIAs are complex—sometimes really complex. And in the context of a social media network, the ways in which you utilize content are a vital aspect of your application. The ability to generate, store, and access a wide variety of content types, from a large number of users, across a wide variety of platforms, is a requirement of any application in this space. As we all know, content is data, and managing that data properly is a fundamental requirement of any well-engineered application.

There are, of course, a huge number of topics that I could cover in this chapter. I've chosen to highlight a few of the key data features of the RMX—ones that would be applicable to many different applications—including how we handle data schemes for tagging, sharing, syndicating, and aggregating content from both external and internal sources. Those data sources, whether internal or external, can come from web services, XML, server scripts, relational databases, or any combination of these.

Data sources

In planning the RMX, we knew up front our most important data source would be our relational databases. We chose MySQL knowing it's an impressive work horse that powers the back end of many popular Web 2.0 sites like Digg, Flickr, YouTube, Wikimedia (Wikipedia), and the web pages for NASA, and it's the backbone of our content management framework, Drupal.

Databases

In an ideal scenario, there'd be a helpful, happy database administrator (DBA) who has the honor of overseeing database management full time. If there is no DBA, you should at least have someone in a data architect role to create a data model that is efficient and scalable, as oftentimes interface developers do not have either sufficient skills or sufficient grasp of the overall project requirements to execute this role properly. Instead, interface developers usually care more exclusively about how to interface with the data, rather than how to structure it. Usually developers interface with databases in the form of services or what's commonly known as an application program interface (API). However, in recent years, the term "API" has become easily synonymous with Web 2.0 as it should, since it promotes syndication by allowing interaction with content in any fashion. Any simple, well-documented set of services (or methods) is good enough to be considered your API, just don't tell the marketing team.

Your choice of database shouldn't have an impact on your overall database structure, but it will impact details of that schema, such as data and data types. Databases are usually interfaces with a database management system or DBMS. All DBMSs—MySQL, Microsoft SQL Server, SQLite, and so on—have standard and nonstandard features, usually to satisfy developer or enterprise requirements or performance boosts. Oftentimes though, following the simple route with your initial data design is best since that simple base can be built on top of. Don't waste time trying to gauge or answer questions of model complexity, just design. As a rule of thumb, keep all database designs simple; they'll grow before you know it. RMX started out simple.

MySQL

For the RMX, we knew we'd be running it on a LAMP (Linux, Apache, MySQL, and PHP) stack, MySQL being our database software, of course. MySQL hosting is available practically anywhere around the globe, and it's so good at its job that you can get good results from basic usage, and great results in terms of scalability. Those who get to expand their skill into the realm of higher relational database concepts and software functionality will agree that MySQL has web app written all over it.

MySQL is free, which makes it a potential winner for any project. The software itself runs databases and some tools to interact and administer databases. As for extensive tools for MySQL, we look to the large array of tools that third-party software makers develop. The MySQL group provides support services and has done so for years. Their recent addition of network tools and enterprise-level monitoring shows businesses that MySQL isn't just a cool database for web geeks but a serious contender in commercial and enterprise markets. But, we geeks can grin, since the "cool factor" does follow MySQL, powering the most popular Web 2.0 services and sites today.

MySQL itself has a really good set of features like query cache, custom functions, stored procedures, and triggers. While we don't cover these features in this book, you can easily find information on them in the many books on the market about MySQL, SQL, and relational databases. What we do cover can generally be applied to any database software you want to run; if we cover something that is MySQL specific, we will point it out.

> *Apress carries MySQL books for all levels, from beginner, to pro, to expert, even definitive guides. We suggest you check any or all MySQL titles out at* www.apress.com, *since we know your MySQL usage may become habitual.*

XML

XML is a great standard because it can be as loose or strict as we need it to be and it's cheap. Better than CSV and proprietary TXT files, XML files are solid data sources. Full document formats themselves are all XML. Some have been for a long time now, like Microsoft Office and the newly supported OpenDocument format. Since XML is the parent of all these formats, it's fitting that XML is also parent to every syndication format that exists on the Web today.

The Flex framework has really good XML support. Not just loading XML, but also chewing through XML with its E4X features, like XPath, that make working with XML a breeze. You can generate XML directly in ActionScript or with MXML. Most web languages or databases should have basic XML support, so applying XML throughout your application shouldn't be a problem.

XML structures and schemas

The **XML structure**, also known sometimes as a **schema**, is important. When you're designing your XML structure, start by just coming up with a simple idea of XML tags or groups of tags and their interrelationships. Always remember, don't overdo it with your schemas; they can and should remain simple.

XML web feeds

It was mentioned that XML is the parent of every syndication feed on the Internet. RSS seems to be winning popularity for web site syndication, especially for publishing frequently updated content, such as news headlines and blog entries. Adoption of web feeds like RSS made it possible for people to keep up to date with their favorite content by subscribing to it and being notified as new content becomes available. The software checks periodically, as often as people like—daily, monthly, or even hourly. Its popularity is new, but RSS itself is not. There are officially different versions of RSS, but RSS 2.0 is currently the best, as it allows custom XML extensions.

FeedBurner (www.feedburner.com) is one syndication company that uses XML extensions extensively. This company is famous for providing feed syndication stats, but the heart of its output relies on XML extensions, since it takes any feed you give it and dresses it up with fancy extensions from Yahoo (MRSS), Apple (iTunes), and dozens more. Since XML extensions are really easy to support and adopt, FeedBurner even allows anyone to submit an extension and instantly adds it to its service offerings.

ATOM, RDF, and OPML are other popular XML-based feeds. OPML complements RSS, while the others are alternatives to RSS. Offering these formats on your web site or application is not required but helps complement your syndication platform.

Sharing outside the network

There are a few ways that networks and services allow you to share content outside their domain—web links (permalinks), send-to-friend e-mails, and embed code. When you're planning to provide sharing features like these, each has their own set of rules.

Sharing permalinks

A URL is easy to pass around. It can be passed via instant messaging, e-mail, web sites, blog posts, and even verbally or in broadcast and print media. **Permalinks** provide unique URLs assigned to content for people to revisit and refer to that content as long as the content is available. The term comes from the phrase "permanent link." Permalinks are most commonly noticed on blogs, since they're a definitional requirement of blogs and a fundamental feature of the blogging community (in which bloggers often cross-link), and when you follow a link to a specific post, you are following a permalink. These permanent links work as unique keys. We use the unique keys to generate a permalink to serve the specified content.

The magic of permalinks is done on the server by Apache with what are known as **rewrite rules** using a module called mod_rewrite. We retain unique keys in a database for each piece of content and search against those, allowing us to offer short URLs that Apache internally rewrites or redirects to content. It's much easier to remember a shorter web link like http://videos.richmediax. com/abc123 versus http://videos.richmediax.com/?Population=25423642&category=Vegetation& content=abc123 or some other meaningless gibberish, which is the default behavior of many content management systems like Drupal. You can usually recognize a rewrite URL by its lack of query parameters. These types of links are also known as **clean URLs** or **search engine–friendly URLs**. Rewrite rules can be placed in a text file known as an **htaccess** file. Following is a sample of a mod_rewrite rule that takes a URL and checks it against a rewrite rule, redirecting the user's request when the rule is met.

```
Options +FollowSymLinks
RewriteEngine on
RewriteRule player/media/(.*)/embedded/(.*)/ ➡
player.swf?media=$1&embedded=$2 [R]
```

The preceding code must be saved in a .htaccess file in any folder on your server. The rule shown, RewriteRule player/media/(.*)/embedded/(.*)/ player.swf?media=$1&embedded=$2, has two parts. The first part, which I'll call the **rule** (or **test**), is player/media/(.*)/embedded/(.*), and it checks all URL requests sent to the server. It will notice any requests that follow that rule, which requires there be some value where each (.*) piece appears. The second part, which I'll call the **rewrite portion**, is player.swf?media=$1&embedded=$2. The $1 and $2 are numbered "tokens" that get populated or replaced by the characters that replace (.*) in the rule. If you're familiar with regular expressions, like in PHP or ActionScript 3, then Apache's usage of them for rewrite rules and tests should seem familiar.

Permalinks have been around longer than Web 2.0, so it shouldn't be hard to find out if your server has mod_rewrite capabilities to try out a couple of rules yourself. Since rewrite rules use regular expressions, that skill set is required to pull off more complex rewrite rules. Again, mod_rewrite is an Apache module, so if you plan to use Windows as your server platform, you'll have to get the IIS_rewrite engine.

> *Flash Player has support for regular expressions, meaning your Flash, Flex, or AIR applications all have this powerful yet complex language for searching, matching, filtering, replacing, or any other crazy rocket science we developers come up with.*

Sharing by e-mail

E-mail is the oldest form of web sharing. Much of the time, folks will pass a link in a digital or printed form, most commonly via e-mail. With e-mail communication, it is important to remember that there are two basic types of e-mail: HTML and text. Sending e-mail, we're able to send both HTML and text **bodies** in a single message. Also known as **MIME types**, these message bodies have a lot of freedom and a lot of restrictions. HTML e-mails cannot contain JavaScript, because this is a security concern. HTML e-mails can, however, have images and CSS styling embedded or linked externally. Embedded imagery and styling add a lot of file size, and the greater the file size, of course, the worse the user experience. By externalizing the images and CSS, we trim the size considerably while still offering a stylized experience should the user accept our HTML content.

Bringing things around, links in e-mails sent from your site, like a "send-to-friend" feature, should preferably consist of permalinks. First, this can reduce the fear that software or a service may force linefeeds in the middle of a URL. This would render the URL practically useless. Also, by utilizing your own permalinks in shared e-mails, users will end up becoming familiar with these link schemes and they'll promote them on their own.

Flex has no way to send e-mails without the help of a server component, like IMAP, POP, and so on. ActionScript 3 has the power to talk to these and many protocols, none of which are small feats, so you'll probably want to turn to a server-side scripting language like PHP. While PHP has a built-in `mail()` function that makes things easier, it does require a little attention to get good e-mails sent out easily. To cut out the headaches of dealing with MIME types from scratch, there is a free PHP class called eMail, which is available online at www.phpclasses.org/trackback/browse/package/1644.html. Here, you'll see how to use this PHP eMail class and call it from Flex using the RemoteObject tag:

1. After installing or uploading the eMail PHP class, you set up a function:

```
<?
include("class_mail.php");

// POST vars sent from Flex
if (isset($_POST) && ($_POST['emailTo'] && ➥
$_POST['emailFrom'] && ➥
$_POST['emailSubject'] && ➥
$_POST['emailMessage'])) ➥
{
sendEmail($_POST['emailTo'], $_POST['emailFrom'], ➥
$_POST['emailSubject'], $_POST['emailMessage']);
        return true;
} else {
        return false;
}

function sendEmail($to, $from, $subject, $message)
{
// Create a new eMail object
$email = new eMail("Flex PHP Mail Form", $from);

// Subject line
$email->subject($subject);

// To (address)
$email->to($to);
```

```
// HTML body message
$email->html($message);

// send e-mail
$email->send();
}
?>
```

2. Create the MXML form:

```
<?xml version="1.0" encoding="utf-8"?>
<mx:Application xmlns:mx="http://www.adobe.com/2006/mxml" ➡
layout="vertical">
   <mx:Script>
      <![CDATA[
         [Bindable]
         // Characters allowed by a legal e-mail address
         private var allowedEmailCharacters:String = ➡
"A-Za-z0-9\!\#\$\%\&\'\*\+\-\/\=\?\^\_\`\{\|\}\~\.";
         private var emailForm:EmailDTO = new EmailDTO;

         [Bindable]
         class EmailDTO
         {
            public var emailTo:String;
            public var emailFrom:String;
            public var emailSubject:String;
            public var emailMessage:String;

            public function EmailForm()
            {
            }
         }
      ]]>
   </mx:Script>
   <mx:HTTPService id="serviceSendEmail" showBusyCursor="true" ➡
resultFormat="text" concurrency="last" url="email.php" ➡
requestTimeout="60"/>

   <mx:Form id="frm_Email">
      <mx:FormHeading label="E-mail Form"/>
      <mx:FormItem label="To">
         <mx:TextArea id="emailTo" restrict= ➡
"{allowedEmailCharacters}" ➡
change="{emailForm.emailTo = this.emailFrom.text}"/>
      </mx:FormItem>
      <mx:FormItem label="From">
         <mx:TextInput maxChars="100" id="emailFrom" maxChars="319" ➡
restrict="{allowedEmailCharacters}" ➡
change="{emailForm.emailFrom = this.emailFrom.text}"/>
```

```
            </mx:FormItem>
            <mx:FormItem label="Subject">
                <mx:TextInput maxChars="100" id="emailSubject" ➡
change="{emailForm.emailSubject = this.emailSubject.text}"/>
            </mx:FormItem>
            <mx:FormItem label="Message">
                <mx:TextArea id="emailMessage" ➡
change="{emailForm.emailMessage = this.emailMessage.text}"/>
            </mx:FormItem>
            <mx:ApplicationControlBar width="100%">
                <mx:Button label="Clear"/>
                <mx:Spacer width="100%" height="100%"/>
                <mx:Button label="Send" ➡
click="{serviceSendEmail.send(emailForm);}"/>
            </mx:ApplicationControlBar>
        </mx:Form>
</mx:Application>
```

The form should like Figure 6-1 in design view.

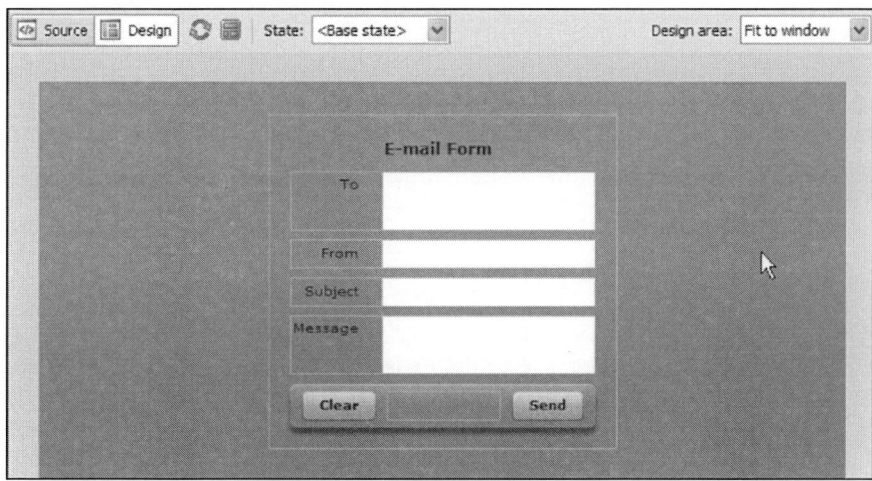

Figure 6-1. Flex form for the e-mail PHP script

You see the form is composed of mainly MXML with a dash of ActionScript. I'll explain the code briefly, but I don't want to give too much away since you'll be learning all about forms and validation in Chapter 8. We add an ActionScript variable, allowedEmailCharacters, which is a string filled with valid characters that we use as a whitelist in most of our form fields. This variable is bindable and is used as the value of the restrict attribute in many of the <mx:TextInput/> tags. The restrict attribute is very powerful, allowing only listed characters to be entered into a field while completely ignoring all other characters or keystrokes that a user may try to enter. Features like this are all covered in Chapter 8.

Each form field has a change attribute that assigns a value to the EmailDTO object as the user types or makes edits in the form field. Using a DTO simplifies integrating additional events and tasks a form may be expected to perform. This separation helps you when you want to add validators and then eventually hand off the form data.

The form in this exercise is designed to pass the form data off to a PHP page on the server. Time to test our form.

3. Upload files and test.

If all the files are uploaded, you can fill out the Flex form, and you should get an e-mail shortly after clicking the Send button, which should fire the send() method of your HTTPService. The following e-mail output is what we used for an early alpha of the RMX's e-mails.

> *Another industry professional like yourself felt you should see this RMX hosted video:*
>
> http://videos.richmediax.com/abc123
>
> *Please click or visit the link above to see the video that was recommended to you to watch.*
>
> *—RMX*
>
> *RichMediaX .com—turn-key community tools for Adobe & Open Source user groups worldwide.*

As you can see in the e-mail text, we use our permalink. You'll want to use your permalinks over and over, everywhere, like in e-mails and other sharing methods such as embed code, which you'll read about in the next section.

Sharing and embedding video

As soon as video on the Web became popular, there came the need to share these videos beyond just a standard link. And, thanks to applications like Adobe's Flash Player, people caught on to the fact that you could embed media into web pages and blog posts, resulting in today's Internet video boom. Now, video services allow users to take a single video and place it anywhere in their own web page or site by copying and pasting code provided by the video sharing service.

Embedding with JavaScript

JavaScript code to embed Flash video is usually very small. When using JavaScript for embed code, we pass around a <script> tag that points to an external JavaScript file that takes a few encapsulated arguments to know which video to return. For example:

```
<script type="text/javascript" src="http://www.embedmedia.com/➥
embedcode.js.php?w=100&h=100&media=976"></script>
```

As you can see in the src attribute of the <script> tag, the file embedcode.js.php has query parameters attached to its location. Using a query string, like ?w=100&h=100&media=976, allows us to pass any arguments or parameters we'd need to customize the embed code output. Taking a look at the code sample again, notice the width and height are w=100 and h=100 while media=976 is some ID or content key to the media the link is requesting. In the back end, this would parse and return a JavaScript line, `document.write(preparedEmbedCode);`, that contains the embed tags with parameters whose values are derived from the query string variables.

Embedding with XHTML

When it comes to passing around plain HTML or XHTML code, sometimes a simple `<embed>` tag suffices, but it's up to you and external sites if code should contain both an `<object>` and an `<embed>` tag. Regardless of the distribution method, each requires width and height attributes to be set. Leaving SWF dimensions out can lead to unexpected results.

You also need to point to the target SWF file in your embed code. The `<embed>` tag uses its `src` attribute for the SWF's location; the `<object>` tag uses the value attribute. You see both the `src` and dimensions set in the following embed code:

```
<embed id="rmxEmbeddedPlayer_976" width="640" height="480" ➥
title="RMX, centralizing cool videos" ➥
src="http:// videos.richmediax.com/player.swf" ➥
flashvars="media=976&embedded=true"/>
```

You'll notice there's a little more than just `width`, `height`, and `src`. There's a `title` attribute that provides users with an informative tooltip when they mouse over the embedded media. You add a unique `id` attribute by concatenating the media ID and giving it a value of `"rmxEmbeddedPlayer_976"`—named for its purpose and which media element it will render. This is to help you call each instance of the embedded video by this ID through external interfaces like JavaScript.

Looking at the rest of the embed code, you'll notice two more attributes with values; the `src`, which is the SWF location, and the `flashvars` attribute, which carries all the query parameters the application will need to run. While this works practically anywhere, some web sites may require external embedded media or services to only come from an approved source. Why? It's their business, it's their traffic, it's their house—so they want you to play nice, that's all. Too bad some don't play nice themselves.

For example, MySpace will add and change your embed codes by tweaking `<embed>` attributes and even adding some you didn't add: `allownetworking=internal`, `allowScriptAccess=never`, `enableJSURL=false`, `enableHREF=false`, and `saveEmbedTags=true`—all could cause your widget to be inoperable or just work incorrectly. You should log how each (target) site alters your embed code.

In addition, expected `FlashVars` could easily be targeted for removal within your embed code; this is something we have seen. One solution around this is concatenating `FlashVars` as query parameters in the `src` attribute like so:

```
<embed id="rmxEmbeddedPlayer_976" width="640" height="480" ➥
title="RMX, centralizing cool videos" ➥
src="http:// videos.richmediax.com/player.swf➥
?media=976&embedded=true"/>
```

Technically, there isn't a major difference between an embed code with `FlashVars` and one without (using the query parameters workaround). The `FlashVars` attribute arrived in the Flash world as a cleaner standard for passing in external values into embedded Flash elements on pages. Before `FlashVars`, everyone used the plain query strings method, but appending URL-encoded variables to SWF addresses basically prevents proper browser caching of SWFs, which is one reason `FlashVars` are considered superior. Also, query strings have some character limits, so moving to a valued attribute allows us to add as much data as we need, only resulting in a larger page size. We could also use HTML or PHP headers to prevent caching of the page and all elements in it; most may find this the cleanest solution.

Now, imagine you encounter a site that strips out all FlashVars and SWF query strings (removing everything that comes after the question mark in your src attribute URL). You'll need to hide the parameter values somehow. Try using the permalink mod_rewrite technique mentioned earlier. The following sample code is the third style of embed code, no FlashVars or query string values, using a mod_rewrite URL. This unique URL has both the server location and all the necessary arguments disguised as the SWF's location.

```
<embed id="rmxEmbeddedPlayer_976" width="640" height="480" ➡
title="RMX, centralizing cool videos" ➡
src="http://videos.richmediax.com/player/media/976/embedded"/>
```

As you can see, the embed code has the server URL, same as the other embed codes, but this time it's not pointing directly to a SWF. Instead you see a clean URL. Looking closer, you can see it says player/media/976/embedded, which Apache will internally rewrite or redirect to another location pointing to the real SWF like player.swf?media=976&embedded=true. Now that's a winner—this custom embed code can be embedded around the world reliably, today. I say "today" because at any time popular sites could create rules that remove your embed code if there's no file extension in the src attribute. If this is the case, to get around this, add a fake file name, like video.swf, at the end of the embed src URL, which technically doesn't exist and doesn't really affect the code much. Here's how the embed code would look changed to use the fake SWF in the src URL:

```
<embed id="rmxEmbeddedPlayer_976" width="640" height="480" ➡
title="RMX, centralizing cool videos" ➡
src="http://videos.richmediax.com/player/media/976/embeddedvideo.swf"/>
```

Using RSS

The syndicated web is very large and will only get more widespread. XML feeds, such as RSS and the like, all have one focus—to check for and fetch the latest relevant content. The content can be news on a web site, the latest blog posts, photo feeds, podcasts, or video feeds. Folks choose their own software to consume XML feeds, allowing the software to do all the grunt work of pinging web sites for updated content. I use the term "XML feed" because that's really what RSS is, but RSS is not alone. Other popular syndication formats are RDF and ATOM. Both are more robust and advanced than RSS, but RSS is the most popular since it's the type of feed many people have grown to recognize.

You'll learn how to generate a valid RSS feed, and extend the feed to use custom tags and popular media tags. First, I'll give you an overview of the basics of consuming a feed in the most-used browsers today. Syndicated content has a pseudo-standard icon that most browsers and applications have adopted (see Figure 6-2).

Figure 6-2. The most popular syndication or feed icon to date

The Mozilla Foundation was the first to popularize the icon in their web browsers. The icon then became a standard once it was offered as an open design freely to promote content syndication features in general, not just RSS. If you wish to adopt the icon, and I recommend you do, check out a web site called Feed Icons; this site not only offers information, but also has the icon in both vector and bitmap formats available free for download at www.feedicons.com (see Figure 6-3).

Figure 6-3. Feed Icons web site

Applications, like web browsers, typically use the feed icon to show which sites are notifying them there are feeds available for the URL you are visiting. Mozilla Firefox (see Figure 6-4) and Microsoft Internet Explorer (see Figure 6-5) use the standard feed icon. Apple Safari doesn't use the standard icon but their design isn't hard to miss (see Figure 6-4).

Figure 6-4. Mozilla Firefox and Apple Safari browsers and their XML/RSS feed icon

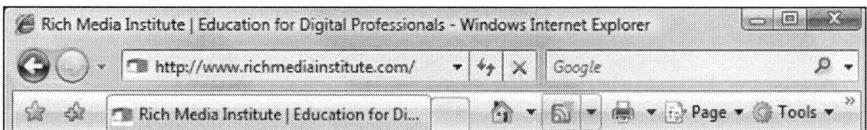

Figure 6-5. Microsoft Internet Explorer 7 on Microsoft Windows Vista uses the same icon to notify the page has an XML/RSS feed discovered.

Now let's look at a basic RSS feed, from the RMX, for the LA Flash user group:

```xml
<?xml version="1.0"?>
<rss version="2.0">
  <channel>
<title>LA Flash // Video Feed // RMX - ➡
  Rich Media Exchange</title>
<link>http://laflash.org/link>
<description>LA Flash, an authorized Adobe ➡
    User Group</description>
<language>en-us</language>
<pubDate>Thu, 14 June 2007 07:00:00 GMT</pubDate>
<lastBuildDate>Fri, 15 Jun 2007 07:00:00 GMT</lastBuildDate>
<generator>RMX - RichMediaX.com</generator>
<managingEditor>editor@laflash.richmediax.com</managingEditor>
<webMaster>webmaster@richmediax.com</webMaster>
    <item>
<title>Adobe AIR (Adobe Integrated Runtime)</title>
<link>http://laflash.org/news/2007/air.htm</link>
<description>Chris Charlton shows ➡
    off some Adobe AIR.</description>
<pubDate>Wed, 20 June  2007 11:39:21 GMT</pubDate>
<guid>http://laflash.richmediax.com/news/2007/air.htm</guid>
    </item>
    <item>
<title>Flex for Flash Designers</title>
<link>http://laflash.org/news/2007/➡
    flex_for _designers.htm</link>
<description>Flash production tips for Flex ➡
    Developers.</description>
<pubDate>Wed, 16 May 2007 10:30:00 GMT</pubDate>
<guid>http://laflash.org/news/2007/➡
    flex_for_flash_designers.htm</guid>
    </item>
    <item>
<title>AS3 for Beginners Nanocamp preview</title>
<link>http://laflash.org/news/2007/➡
    as3_begin_nanocamp_preview.htm</link>
<description>R Blank previews a Nanocamp, ➡
    AS3 for Beginners.</description>
<pubDate>Wed, 18 Apr  2007 10:39:21 GMT</pubDate>
<guid>http://laflash.org/news/2007/➡
    as3_begin_nanocamp_preview.htm</guid>
    </item>
  </channel>
</rss>
```

Some initial dissection of the feed shows the RSS standard root node, <rss version="2.0">, with a <channel> child node. The <channel> node carries children nodes that describe the feed's publisher and its syndicated content. Feed content is listed in the multiple <item> nodes that follow the channel's metadata. The nodes shown in the example feed are all the nodes you should start with. Additional nodes open feeds to software features and search-friendly syndication. Before covering <item> nodes, I'll run through the <channel> meta info for you:

- <title>: The title to display for the feed. Feed readers usually render this title in the list of feeds and sometimes near the top of a rendered feed.

- <link>: The corresponding URL for the channel, not the feed itself. Many feed readers use this URL to take you back to the web site of the feed publisher.

- <description>: A body of text providing a description of the feed itself or where it originated from.

- <language>: The language the feed is presented in. You cannot assume there's a default language, so it's best to make sure you include this node.

- <pubDate>: The publishing date of the feed. It's nice if you can use the original publishing date the feed first launched, but nobody will hate you if this isn't exact.

- <lastBuildDate>: The last build date is used by software to check if there's a published update to your feed since it was last checked.

- <generator>: The name of the service or software that generated the feed.

There are over a dozen nodes for a channel, but most are optional. There are nodes that pertain to tags or keywords, copyright, editor, even an image for the channel. Apple iTunes uses the channel image as the logo of the feed. If you care to review RSS's other channel nodes, you may do so at http://cyber.law.harvard.edu/rss/rss.html. Once you fill these nodes in with channel info, people and software will know who's responsible for the feed and apply your preferences. If you plan to publish content that may be explicit or mature, like foul language, violence, or nudity, you will want your feeds to adopt the rating system for the channel <rating> node. Now that you have channel info, it's time for the feed's content.

Remember, a feed's content is listed in the multiple <item> nodes that appear under the channel info. There's no limit to how many items can be listed in a feed. Honestly, the feed can be as long as you care to have it; the number of items depends on your feed's focus. Short feeds list around 10 to 20 items, while longer feeds can list hundreds of items. Only if you plan to use a feed as an archive would you use a lot of nodes, but RSS isn't exciting when listing stagnant content. As ActionScript developers, we really don't care about how large a feed is, since our E4X features are processed quickly on the client side.

You'll want to use RSS for new or updated content. Sites offer feeds for the latest content on their network or content in a category or tag. RMX uses RSS to list the latest content of an entire user group or any tag a user chooses. Items in a feed offer content meta info, like title and description, as well as tags for publish dates, keywords, and links to the content.

Take a look at this <item> node:

```
    <item>
<title>Adobe AIR (Adobe Integrated Runtime)</title>
<link>http://laflash.richmediax.com/news/2007/air.htm</link>
<description>Chris Charlton shows➡
 off some Adobe AIR.</description>
```

```
<pubDate>Wed, 20 June  2007 11:39:21 GMT</pubDate>
<guid>http://laflash.richmediax.com/news/2007/air.htm</guid>
    </item>
```

Similarly, in the `<channel>` node you see a `<title>` and `<description>` subelement for each `<item>`. The `<link>` subelement provides a URI to that piece of content. You will notice the `<guid>` node has the same value as the `<link>` node; this is for simplicity. The `<guid>` subelement requires a unique value for each unique piece of content, so instead of preparing complex code to handle that uniqueness, you reuse the content's link since those would be inherently unique. When it comes to filling out the `<guid>` and `<link>` tags, for each `<item>` node, you use your cool permalinks. The permalink values give you two benefits in your feed. One benefit is the links are short and will generally help keep RSS feeds slightly smaller, since long links would add more file size. Another benefit is that you help perpetuate the simple formatted URLs you hand out to users for sharing. You finish filling the `<item>` nodes with a properly formatted publish date, the `<pubDate>`, per item.

Attaching files to RSS feeds

Content doesn't have to be just text; you can use HTML or more XML to describe the content in a `<description>` subelement and attach files. Using an optional node for feed enclosures, these can be considered attachments, providing a link to a file or files. Enclosure-aware software sniffs for `<enclosure>` tags and downloads them as your preferences see fit. Feed enclosures are what gave podcasting its life, by linking to audio files people recorded. Take a look at the RSS feed example again, this time with feed enclosures:

```
    <item>
<title>Adobe AIR (Adobe Integrated Runtime)</title>
<link>http://laflash.org/news/2007/air.htm</link>
<description>Chris Charlton shows➡
   off some Adobe AIR.</description>
<pubDate>Wed, 20 June  2007 11:39:21 GMT</pubDate>
<guid>http://laflash.org/news/2007/air.htm</guid>
<enclosure url="http://richmediax.com/video/laflash/adobe_air.flv" ➡
length="6428422" type="video/x-flv" />
    </item>
    <item>
<title>Flex for Flash Designers</title>
<link>http://laflash.org/news/2007/➡
  flex_for_flash_designers.htm</link>
<description>Flash production tips for Flex ➡
  Developers.</description>
<pubDate>Wed, 16 May 2007 10:30:00 GMT</pubDate>
<guid>http://laflash.org/news/2007/➡
  flex_for_flash_designers.htm</guid>
<enclosure url="http://richmediax.com/audio/laflash/flexforflash.mp3" ➡
length="12216320" type="audio/mpeg" />
    </item>
    <item>
<title>AS3 for Beginners Nanocamp preview</title>
<link>http://laflash.org/news/2007/➡
  as3_begin_nanocamp_preview.htm</link>
```

```
<description>R Blank previews his latest Nanocamp, ➡
    AS3 for Beginners.</description>
<pubDate>Wed, 18 Apr  2007 10:39:21 GMT</pubDate>
<guid>http://laflash.org/news/2007/➡
    as3_begin_nanocamp_preview.htm</guid>
<enclosure url="http://richmediax.com/video/
    laflashs/as3_nanocamp.flv"
length="101010"➡
    type="video/x-flv" />
    </item>
```

You see the new <enclosure> tags have three attributes—url, length, and type. URLs point to the location of the enclosure, so they should be absolute paths, since people will be reading your feed on their computer, maybe even offline. length says how big the enclosure is in bytes, not time, and type gives the file or MIME type. FLV is pretty new for use in enclosures, so you'll want to know that you can use either of the MIME types in the preceding RSS snippet when referring to FLVs. You can essentially link to any kind of file, as there's no verification of any type; feed enclosures are just links to files, and the software is responsible for handling them. You can have multiple <enclosure> tags per item.

XML namespaces and extensions

Since RSS is XML, shouldn't you be able to make up your own tags and add them to the feed at will? Yes and no. XML is easy and RSS is XML, so yes, you're able to add tags but not without following a couple of important but easy rules. When adding custom tags to an existing XML structure, you need to make sure your tags don't conflict with tags that are already defined in the structure. Imagine you want to add a <name> tag, but is it for the name of the web site, the user, the publisher, or even the author? Even worse, what if someone else adds tags that are the same as yours, resulting in conflicts and validation errors? The right way to make sure your tags stay your own is by giving them what's known as an **XML namespace**. You declare your custom namespace in an xmlns attribute of the root node in your XML document. You're allowed to generate as many custom tags and attributes as you need with your namespace used as a prefix followed by a desired suffix, separated by a colon, like in these examples:

```
<?xml version="1.0"?>
<rootNode xmlns:rmx="http://richmediax.com" ➡
xmlns:myNamespace="http://someURL.com" ➡
xmlns:nameSpacePrefix="http://someOtherURL.com">
...
<nameSpacePrefix:suffix>...</nameSpacePrefix:suffix>
<myNamespace:myTag>...</myNamespace:myTag>
<rmx:name rmx:type="usergroup">...</rmx:name>
...
</rootNode>
```

This is the standard way for adding nodes, or groups of nodes, to existing XML structures. In a sense, you're extending the structure, that's why custom namespaces are sometimes known as XML extensions. Hundreds of XML extensions exist on the Web; anything to do with documents or media, it's out there. I'll show you how to extend this feed with a popular XML extension, Media RSS (MRSS), developed by Yahoo! and used by Adobe in their Adobe Media Player as well as other feed readers.

Now how would we get at these custom nodes through ActionScript? With E4X, of course, but we need to register the custom namespace so we can hit those nodes right. Here's some sample code:

```
var rmx:NameSpace = rssObject.namespace('rmx');
var rmxUserGroupNameFromFeed:String = rssObject.rmx::name.toString();
trace(rmxUserGroupNameFromFeed); ➡
// Outputs "LA AIR"
```

As you see, we created an ActionScript NameSpace object called rmx, reading from our loaded RSS feed (rssObject). We use the variable name rmx to keep it the same as our feed and keep it simple for our code too. Next, we access the nodes of the custom namespace similarly to how we access regular nodes.

> *Adobe released some free ActionScript 3 classes that parse XML feeds like RSS/ATOM/RDF, which were originally published on Adobe Labs (http://labs.adobe. com) and are now maintained over at Google Code (http://code.google.com). This class package is now part of a larger AS3 set called FlexLib. We recommend checking out the custom classes and components available at Google Code and at Adobe Exchange (www.adobe.com/exchange).*

For RMX, we knew we'd be publishing RSS feeds but needed some extra information embedded within the RSS feed <item> nodes, particularly geolocation and user group origin. Making up a custom namespace can be easy, since the URL doesn't have to exist to be valid, just as long as it's unique. Following is a sample of an RMX User Group video feed using our custom XML namespace and extension, rmx.

```
<?xml version="1.0"?>
<rss version="2.0" xmlns:rmx="http://richmediax.com">
  <channel>
<title>LA Flash // Video Feed // RMX - ➡
    Rich Media Exchange</title>
<link>http://laflash.richmediax.com</link>
<description>LA Flash, an authorized Adobe ➡
    User Group</description>
<language>en-us</language>
<pubDate>Thu, 14 June 2007 07:00:00 GMT</pubDate>
<lastBuildDate>Fri, 15 Jun 2007 09:00:00 GMT</lastBuildDate>
<generator>RMX - RichMediaX.com</generator>
<managingEditor>editor@laflash.richmediax.com</managingEditor>
<webMaster>webmaster@richmediax.com</webMaster>
<rmx:usergroup name="LA Flash">
<rmx:topics>
        <rmx:topic>Flash</rmx:topic>
        <rmx:topic>ActionScript</rmx:topic>
</rmx:topics>
<rmx:location>
<rmx:city>Los Angeles</rmx:city>
<rmx:state>CA</rmx:state>
<rmx:country>United States</rmx:country>
```

```
</rmx:location>
</rmx:usergroup>
    <item>
<title>Adobe AIR (Adobe Integrated Runtime)</title>
<link>http://laflash.richmediax.com/news/2007/air.htm</link>
<description>Chris Charlton shows ➡
    off some Adobe AIR.</description>
<rmx:tags>Flash, AIR, ActionScript, ActionScript 3, AS3</rmx:tags>
<pubDate>Wed, 20 June  2007 11:39:21 GMT</pubDate>
<guid>http://laflash.org/news/2007/air.htm</guid>
<enclosure url="http://richmediax.com/video/laflash/
    adobe_air.flv" ➡
length="6428422" type="video/x-flv" />
    </item>
    <item>
<title>Flex for Flash Designers</title>
<link>http://laflash.richmediax.com/news/2007/➡
    flex_for_flash.htm</link>
<description>Flash production tips for Flex ➡
    Developers.</description>
<rmx:tags>Flash, Flex, MXML, AS3, ActionScript, ➡
    Design</rmx:tags>
<pubDate>Wed, 16 May 2007 10:30:00 GMT</pubDate>
<guid>http://laflash.org /news/2007/➡
    flex_for_flash.htm</guid>
<enclosure url="http://richmediax.com/audio/laflash/
    flexforflash.mp3" ➡
length="12216320" type="audio/mpeg" />
    </item>
    <item>
<title>AS3 for Beginners Nanocamp preview</title>
<link>http://laflash.richmediax.com/news/2007/➡
    as3_begin_nanocamp.htm</link>
<description>R Blank previews AS3 for ➡
    Beginners.</description>
<rmx:tags>ActionScript 3, AS3, Flash CS3, ➡
    Flash 9</rmx:tags>
<pubDate>Wed, 18 Apr  2007 10:39:21 GMT</pubDate>
<guid>http://laflash.org/news/2007/➡
    as3_begin_nanocamp.htm</guid>
<enclosure url="http://richmediax.com/video/laflashs/➡
    as3_nanocamp.flv" ➡
length="101010" type="video/flv" />
    </item>
  </channel>
</rss>
```

The bold lines in the sample feed are custom tags that use our custom XML extension, or namespace. For example, <rmx:tags> is the custom element we use for content tags, which are totally valid.

161

MRSS and syndicating to the Adobe Media Player

Media RSS is a documented proposal by Yahoo! to help extend today's RSS to provide better publishing information embedded in RSS for media such as video, audio, or any file type for that matter. When using RSS's <enclosure> tag, you can assign one or more files to an <item> element, but it may only be one video format the feed can offer this way. For common formats, like JPEG, PNG, GIF, and MP3, this option seems perfectly fine for that scenario. What if you need to promote one feed that broadcasted all the common formats, and when you have video you want it to cater the format to the user's preference or whatever the supported software would automatically choose? Software would grab an FLV video, or iPod video, or PSP video, or even a QuickTime HD version of the video—I think you get the picture.

Yahoo! saw fit to include additional meta information like bit-rate choices, playback restrictions, content maturity ratings, and Creative Commons licensing. Here's an example from Yahoo! of a movie review feed, with a trailer, using a Creative Commons license:

```
<rss version="2.0" xmlns:media="http://search.yahoo.com/mrss"
xmlns:creativeCommons="http://backend.userland.com/➥
creativeCommonsRssModule">
<channel>
<title>My Movie Review Site</title>
<link>http://www.foo.com</link>
<description>I review movies.</description>
    <item>
        <title>Movie Title: Is this a good movie?</title>
        <link>http://www.foo.com/item1.htm</link>
        <media:content url="http://www.foo.com/trailer.mov"
        fileSize="12216320" type="video/quicktime" expression="sample"/>
        <creativeCommons:license>
        http://www.creativecommons.org/licenses/by-nc/1.0
        </creativeCommons:license>
        <media:rating>nonadult</media:rating>
    </item>
</channel>
</rss>
```

Adobe thought MRSS was a good extension to adopt in their new Adobe Media Player application (see Figure 6-6). Adobe Media Player supports RSS subscriptions with XML extensions, like MRSS, for content downloading, playback restrictions, custom branding options, and interactive advertisements over your content. MRSS information is available at http://search.yahoo.com/mrss.

Adobe Media Player, formerly code-named Philo, is a new application that has custom branding and advertising options for content publishers and supports subscribing to channels via RSS, similar to iTunes and other recent media players. To veteran podcast fans, this is no big deal, but Adobe's offering fills a void for users, since before they couldn't enjoy watching FLV and SWF files on their desktop easily. Adobe can do this now in a much more engaging way since they released AIR, allowing web developers to make desktop applications with Ajax and the Flash Platform.

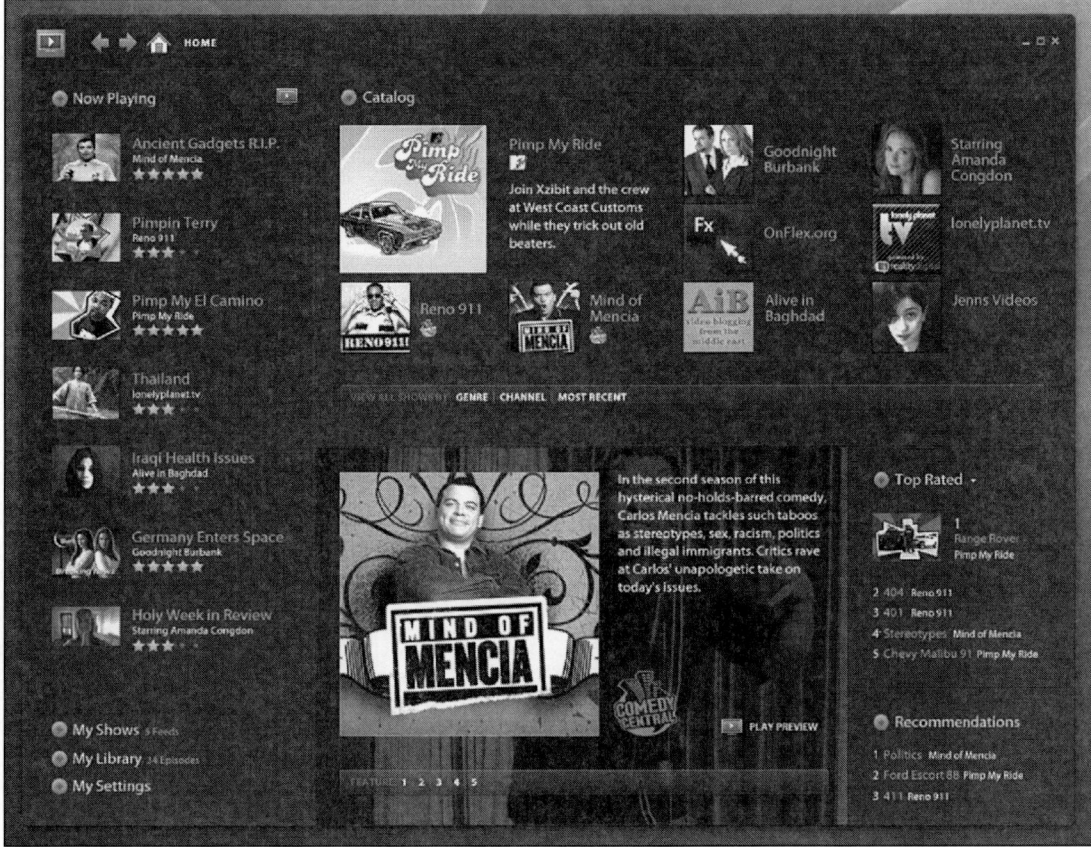

Figure 6-6. Adobe Media Player (alpha)

Summary

This chapter analyzed MySQL as a key data source (relational databases) and how you can render that data in basic and extended XML to generate core Web 2.0 functionality like podcasts. By providing members with ways to take or share content from the RMX network through permalinks, send-to-friend e-mails, and embed code, we provide the basic functionality users expect in contemporary social media networks.

In the next chapter, Hasan will explain how we built some of the key navigational items for the RMX.

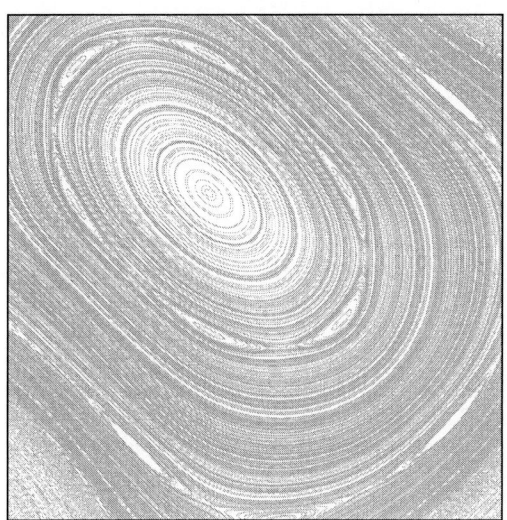

Chapter 7

SECONDARY NAVIGATION

By Hasan Otuome

Undertaking a project the size of the Rich Media Exchange (RMX) entailed some thought and planning as to how we would make all of this aggregated content available to end users. And, with something so massive, encompassing thousands and thousands of pieces of information and media, having search capabilities was a definite must. Thanks to some of the built-in goodness of the Flex framework, we were able to build this functionality in a relatively painless fashion.

In this chapter, I'll cover the concept of pagination, creating and managing searchable content, and history management, all in the context of the RMX.

Pagination

Pagination is defined as the act of or system of numbering pages. If you've surfed the Internet, there's no doubt you've run across this before. For example, think Google and its "Page 1 of 10" navigation. It's so prevalent nowadays that everyone has come to expect it whether consciously or not. And this feature is crucial when handling huge amounts of content in nonrefreshing RIAs. Although this is a feature of convenience that makes everything easier to read for the client, it also has definite performance benefits for the developer, like faster processing due to smaller query result sets per operation. Before looking at the Flex side of things, I want to show you the underlying technology that makes this all possible for the RMX.

Thanks to a built-in feature of the Structured Query Language (SQL), it's fairly easy to set this functionality up. SQL's LIMIT clause, added to a SQL SELECT statement, allows you to specify probably the two most important criteria for successful paging: where to start (aka **offset**) and how many items or rows to return (aka **page size**). Here's a sample query that makes use of the LIMIT clause:

```
SELECT * FROM videos ORDER BY id ASC LIMIT 0,10;
```

What this statement says is, "Select everything (*) from the videos table, order the results numerically by their id attribute, and return only the first ten videos." You could also write that same query leaving out the 0 (or offset) and still achieve the same results. Here's that query altered:

```
SELECT * FROM videos ORDER BY id ASC LIMIT 10;
```

This sounds great, but note that this only works for the first "page"—you'll soon understand why.

Consider this scenario. Suppose you have a product database filled with over 1,000 rows of products. Well, nobody would like to look at one page with 1,000+ items on it because it would mean scrolling for a couple of hours to make it from the top to the bottom. Seriously though, that would be no fun at all. Since this is a products database, it's eventually going to be available to other eyes than yours, so here's a good situation to make use of pagination.

Instead of forcing 1,000 products on the user at once, you can break up the information into more digestible chunks, or **pages**. First, you need to figure out how many products you want on a page, and this will constitute your page size.

> This can also be a variable size that you might let the end users adjust to their tastes.

Once you've come up with a page size, you need to determine where your starting point will be for each page, and this point then becomes your offset. So, say you've determined your page size to be 20 products per page. Logically, your starting point for page 2 would be product #21 or row #21. You already know how to return the first page of results using a query like the following:

```
SELECT * FROM products LIMIT 20;
```

Well, to return the second page, you determine the offset value for page 2 is 21, and you just need to modify the original query as follows:

```
SELECT * FROM products LIMIT 21, 20;
```

Continue modifying your offset by 20 all the way to 981, and you've easily given end users the means to consume all 1,000 products should they so choose in groups of 20, without a lot of effort and using just the LIMIT clause. If you still don't believe in the power of LIMIT, let's see how you feel after we build a pseudo product browser using nothing more than Flex, PHP, and MySQL. I like this trio because Flex rocks, and PHP and MySQL are open source and, most importantly, cross-platform.

> Although PHP and MySQL are important to the product browser and to the RMX, delving too deeply into them is outside of the scope of this book. For more details on PHP and MySQL, check out www.php.net and www.mysql.com, and pick up a good book on PHP, such as PHP Solutions: Dynamic Web Design Made Easy by David Powers (friends of ED, 2006).

Creating the database

Building the pseudo product browser is relatively simple as long as you plan effectively. The first thing you need is the product database that you'll be working against. I've taken the liberty of creating a sample products table that you can import into your MySQL setup. You'll find `products.sql` in the code download for this chapter, available through the Source Code/Downloads page on the Apress web site (`www.apress.com`). Once you've gotten that file, load up your favorite MySQL administration tool and import the file into your database. Since this has proven to be a confusing task to some, I'll walk you through the process of getting this data into MySQL using phpMyAdmin (`www.phpmyadmin.net`). First, create a database to hold the data as shown in Figure 7-1.

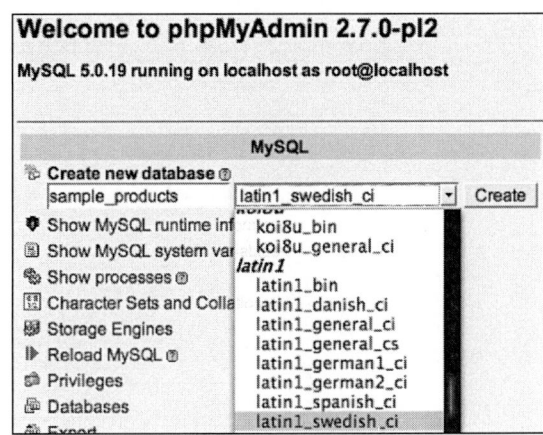

Figure 7-1. Creating a database in phpMyAdmin

After you've created the database, you basically have two options to get `products.sql` into the database: SQL querying or importing the file. The one you choose should be the one you're most comfortable with, but I'll cover them both. SQL querying is just what it sounds like—using SQL queries to perform operations on a database. In phpMyAdmin, ensure the `sample_products` database is selected. Now, select the SQL tab from the navigation bar, and you'll be presented with the screen shown in Figure 7-2.

From here you can open up `products.sql`, copy and paste the contents of that file into the query text box, and click Go to create the products table filled with some sample data. Figure 7-3 shows the results of a successful operation.

As an alternative to performing SQL queries, you could also use phpMyAdmin's Import feature, which basically reads `products.sql` and performs the preceding operation for you. To utilize this feature, click the Import tab, and click the Browse button to locate the `products.sql` file on your hard drive. After you've located the file, click Go to import the data into the database. Figures 7-4 and 7-5 illustrate this process.

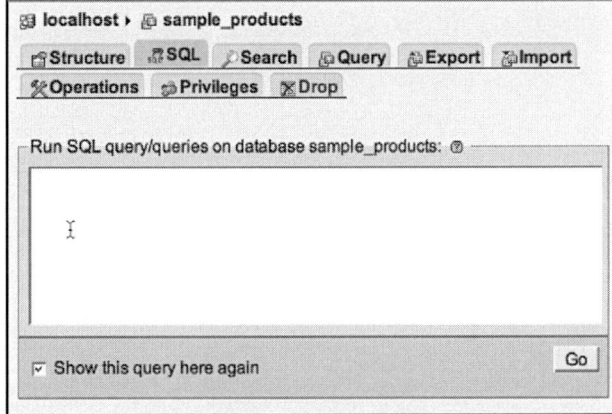

Figure 7-2. phpMyAdmin's SQL query utility

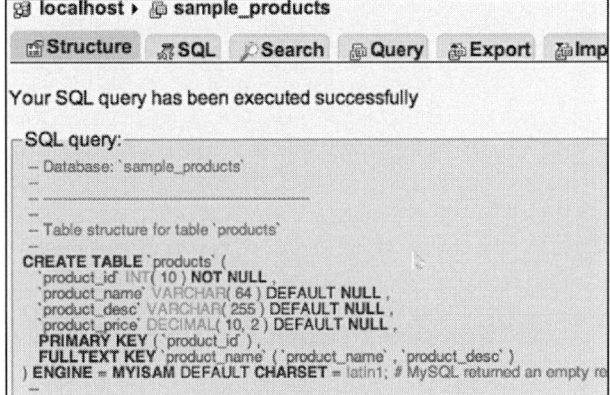

Figure 7-3. phpMyAdmin's SQL query results

167

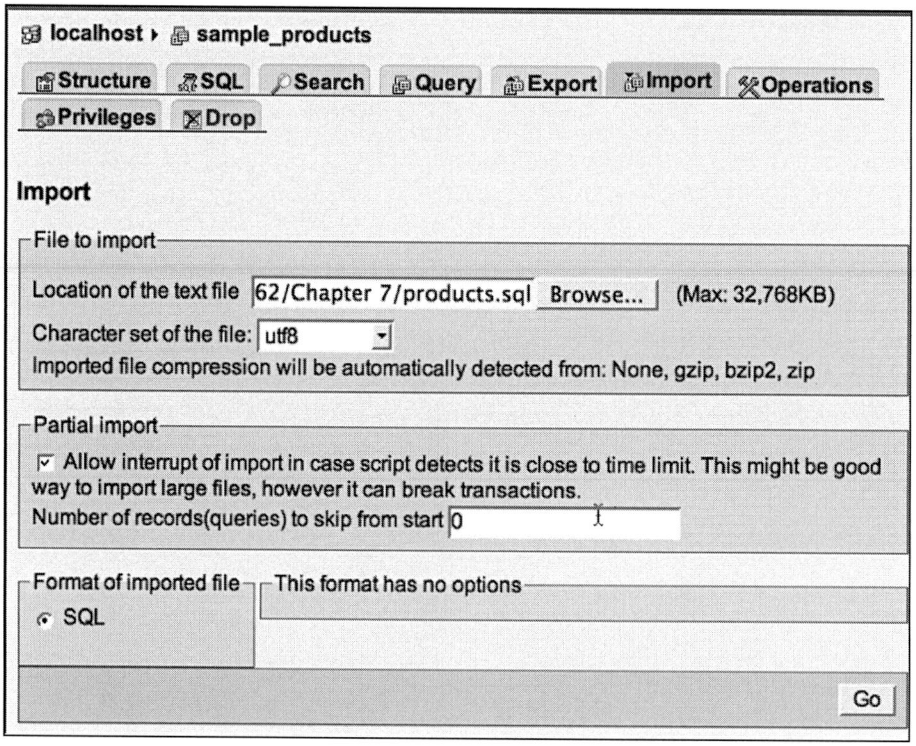

Figure 7-4. Selecting a SQL file to import

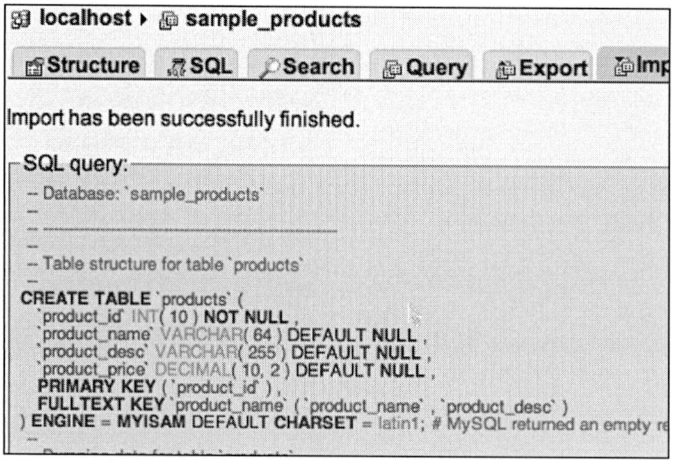

Figure 7-5. Results of a successful import operation

Building the Products class

Now that you've got the products table, it's time to create the PHP class that will allow you to browse the products in paged sets. For this example, you'll be making use of AMFPHP, which is a Remote Procedure Call (RPC) toolkit for PHP that allows seamless communication among PHP and Flex and other technologies. If you don't already have it installed, take a moment to grab the latest version from the AMFPHP web site (www.amfphp.org). Installation is fairly straightforward: unzip the download and copy the amfphp folder to the root of your web server. Once you have AMFPHP installed, browse to the services directory located in the root of your amfphp folder; this is where you will create the PHP class file. So, open up your favorite PHP editor, create a new file, save it as Products.php in the services directory, and add the following code:

```php
<?php
require_once 'Data.php';
?>
```

The first thing you want to do after adding your opening and closing PHP tags is to take care of all external file dependencies. For this example, you'll only need one file for this, and that's Data.php. What is this file, you ask? It contains database access information that could be included in the actual class file, but it's best practice not to; should your application grow to numerous class files, each containing data connection code, and the connection info were to change, you would have to update all those files versus just updating one.

Here's a template that you can use for your Data.php file:

```php
<?php
# for use with amfphp and other PHP class files

class Data {
  public function Data(){}

  public function connect(){
    define("DB_HOST","localhost");
    define("DB_USER","your_mysql_username");
    define("DB_PASS","your_mysql_password");
    define("DB_CONN","sample_products");

    $dbc = mysql_connect(DB_HOST,DB_USER,DB_PASS);
    mysql_select_db(DB_CONN);

    return $dbc;
  }
}
?>
```

> *This code is based on PHP 5. To use it with previous versions of PHP, simply delete all instances of the* public *keyword.*

As you can see, this class has an empty constructor function and one public method, connect(). The connect() method is what takes care of establishing a connection to your MySQL database and returns that connection to you so you can communicate with the database in your other classes. Save this file in the same location as Products.php, and then switch back to Products.php to continue building the class.

Now that you have your required external files taken care of, the next thing to do is add your class declaration to Products.php like so:

```php
<?php
require_once 'Data.php';

class Products{

}
?>
```

Before you build the constructor function, you first need to declare some variables that will be used throughout the class: dbc, offset, pagesize. Your code should now be updated to the following:

```php
<?php
require_once 'Data.php';

class Products{
  var $dbc;
  var $offset = 0;
  var $pagesize = 5;
}
?>
```

$dbc will hold the database connection returned by the Data class, while $offset and $pagesize will allow you to dynamically set the offset and page size to use in the LIMIT clause of the SQL query you'll write shortly. With variable declarations and definitions taken care of, you can build your constructor function. For AMFPHP version 1.25, you are required to have a constructor function that defines a variable named methodTable, which is basically a descriptive listing of all the publicly accessible methods for the class. Following is the constructor function for the Products class (shown in bold)—add this to your code now:

```php
<?php
require_once 'Data.php';

class Products{
  var $dbc;
  var $offset = 0;
  var $pagesize = 5;

  function Products(){
    $this->methodTable = array(
        'browse' => array(
            'access' => 'remote',
            'description' => 'for browsing available products'
        )
    );
    $this->dbc = Data::connect();
  }
}
?>
```

It's very important that you follow the preceding syntax for defining the methodTable variable, or your class will not work in AMFPHP version 1.25 (the methodTable requirement has been removed in AMFPHP version 1.9).

Now, all that is left for you to finish your Products class is to create the method that you listed in the methodTable array, browse(), which will allow a user to browse the products database in a paged fashion. Add a function block to the Products class for the browse() method so that your updated Products class now looks like the following:

```php
<?php
require_once 'Data.php';

class Products{
  var $dbc;
  var $offset = 0;
  var $pagesize = 5;

  function Products(){
    $this->methodTable = array(
        'browse' => array(
            'access' => 'remote',
            'description' => 'for browsing available products'
        )
    );
    $this->dbc = Data::connect();
  }

  function browse($arr){

  }
}
?>
```

As you can see, the browse() method takes one argument. The type of the argument is an array, and it will contain the value for your offset variable. The following bold line added to the method illustrates how the argument will be processed:

```php
<?php
require_once 'Data.php';

class Products{
  var $dbc;
  var $offset = 0;
  var $pagesize = 5;

  function Products(){
    $this->methodTable = array(
        'browse' => array(
            'access' => 'remote',
            'description' => 'for browsing available products'
```

```
        )
      );
      $this->dbc = Data::connect();
    }

  function browse($arr){
      $this->offset = ($arr[0] > 0) ? $arr[0] : $this->offset;
    }
  }
?>
```

Here you use shorthand syntax for an if...else conditional statement. I use this syntax often to conserve space when performing simple comparisons. With this one line, you are saying that if the value of element 0 of the array is greater than 0, make that value the new value for the offset variable; otherwise, use the initial value set for offset. You can just as easily set the offset equal to $arr[0], but I wanted to show you this approach to demonstrate if...else shorthand, which you will see again shortly in the Flex code.

After setting the offset, you need to retrieve the total number of products in the database and store that information in a variable that you can pass back to Flex. This variable becomes important for both information display and application control (whether to display previous and next buttons). Add these three lines to the browse() method just below the previous line:

```
$get_count = mysql_query("SELECT product_id FROM products");
$count = mysql_num_rows($get_count);
$total_products = array(array('totalProducts'=>$count, 'offset'=>➥
      $this->offset, 'pageSize'=>$this->pagesize));
```

The first line runs a query against the database to retrieve all the products, the second line counts the number of rows returned by that query, and the third line (which appears here as two lines due to space constraints) creates an array of an array that contains keys and values for count, offset, and page size. This array will be appended onto the end of the results fetched by your paging query that you're about to add to the method. Add the following line below the definition for $total_products:

```
$query = "SELECT * FROM products ORDER BY product_id ASC LIMIT ➥
      {$this->offset}, {$this->pagesize}";
```

You see that this is just like the hard-coded LIMIT clause from before, with the only difference being the use of variables for offset and page size. The only thing left to do is run the query and package the results for the return trip to Flex. Adding the following code beneath $query will accomplish just that:

```
$products = mysql_query($query);

if($products){
  while($row = mysql_fetch_object($products)){
    $results[] = $row;
  }
  $return = array_merge($results, $total_products);
} else {
  $return = array('DEBUG_OUTPUT', mysql_error());
```

```
        }

    return $return;
```

The results of the query will be stored in the $products variable. From there, you check that a result was returned. If a result was returned, you use a while loop to loop through the results, set $row equal to the currently iterated row, and push that row onto the end of an array called $results[]. Once the loop has completed, you want to create an aggregate array comprised of the $results you just compiled and the $total_products array you created earlier. If a result was not returned, you want to gracefully let someone know why it failed. Finally, you want to return whatever the value of $return is after all that processing. Here's the complete code for Products.php:

```php
<?php
require_once 'Data.php';

class Products{
    var $dbc;
    var $offset = 0;
    var $pagesize = 5;
    var $total_products;

    function Products(){
        $this->methodTable = array(
            'browse' => array(
                'access' => 'remote',
                'description' => 'for browsing available products'
            )
        );
        $this->dbc = Data::connect();
    }

    function browse($arr){
        $this->offset = ($arr[0] > 0) ? $arr[0] : $this->offset;

        $get_count = mysql_query("SELECT product_id FROM products");
        $count = mysql_num_rows($get_count);
        $total_products = array(array('totalProducts'=>$count, ➥
                'offset'=>$this->offset, 'pageSize'=>$this->pagesize));

        $query = "SELECT * FROM products ORDER BY product_id ASC LIMIT ➥
                {$this->offset}, {$this->pagesize}";
        $products = mysql_query($query);

        if($products){
            while($row = mysql_fetch_object($products)){
                $results[] = $row;
            }
            $return = array_merge($results, $total_products);
        } else {
```

```
        $return = array('DEBUG_OUTPUT', mysql_error());
    }

    return $return;
    }
}
?>
```

You should now be able to open up the AMFPHP service browser, navigate to the Products class, and use the browse() method to page through the products. Unfortunately, the service browser wasn't designed to be a public page that you'd want to share with visitors. Let's examine how to consume this data easily using the Flex framework.

Building a Flex interface for Products.php

Open Flex Builder and create a new Flex project entitled Chapter7_Exercise1. After you've finish setting up your project, the first thing you want to do is to add your visual elements or controls to the stage. These elements are displayed in the Components panel located in the lower-left corner of the Flex Builder IDE. Right now you only need a DataGrid control and two Button controls, so go ahead and drag those out onto the stage. Don't worry about the exact layout at this point, because that will be easy to finalize once the application works as expected. Once you've got your controls added to the stage, you need to give them unique IDs and wire them to communicate with the code you'll be writing shortly.

Select the DataGrid control and look to the sidebar on the right. There you will see a panel labeled Flex Properties (as shown in Figure 7-6). Here is where you can set the ID for the control and set its data provider or the source where the information will come from. If you take a look at Figure 7-6, you can see the naming conventions I used for both. Notice the curly braces ({ }) surrounding the name of the data provider for dgProducts. This tells the Flex compiler that you want to create a binding between the DataGrid and the data source. What this means is that if changes are made to the data source, those changes should be broadcast to all interested parties bound to said data source. In other words, bindings let you copy the value of one property to another at runtime. Setting up the buttons is very similar except they don't have a data provider property. The buttons instead have a click property, On click in the Flex Properties panel, which is what you will assign your navigation actions to. Figures 7-7 and 7-8 depict the Flex Properties panel settings for both buttons.

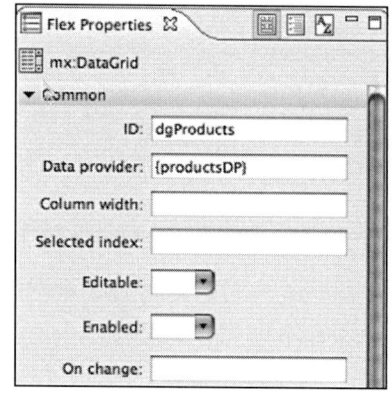

Figure 7-6. DataGrid setup

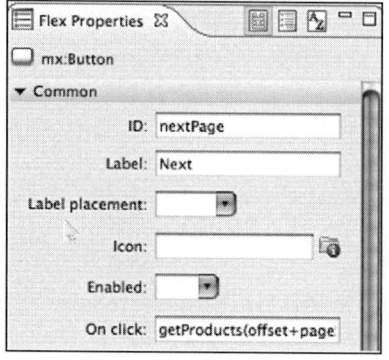

Figure 7-7. Next button setup

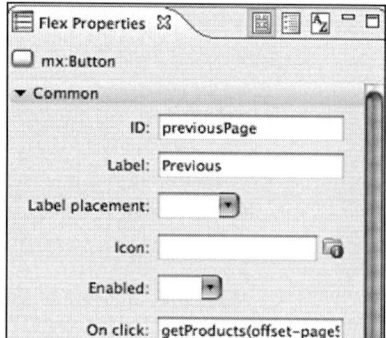

Figure 7-8. Previous button setup

Don't worry about not being able to read the entire On click values right now because you will deal with that in a moment when you switch to code view. With your basic layout complete, you can now switch over to code view because this is where you'll be for the remainder of this project.

Look at Figure 7-9, which depicts the MXML markup for the DataGrid control you just added to the stage in design view. Here you see the two properties that you set in design view and descriptors for each column of the DataGrid. You can set many options on a DataGrid column, but the ones that you will focus on for this example are headerText, dataField, and width. headerText is simply the name that you want displayed over each column. The standard practice is to use names relevant to the data the column will hold, and that's why I chose the names you see in Figure 7-9. dataField refers to the actual item of the data provider that a column should be tied to. Looking back at the PHP class you created earlier, you know that the browse() method will return an object with the following fields: product_id, product_name, product_desc, and product_price. So these are the fields that you want to display in the DataGrid. As far as width is concerned, it appears here merely to tweak the DataGrid layout and can be finalized during the final stages of development.

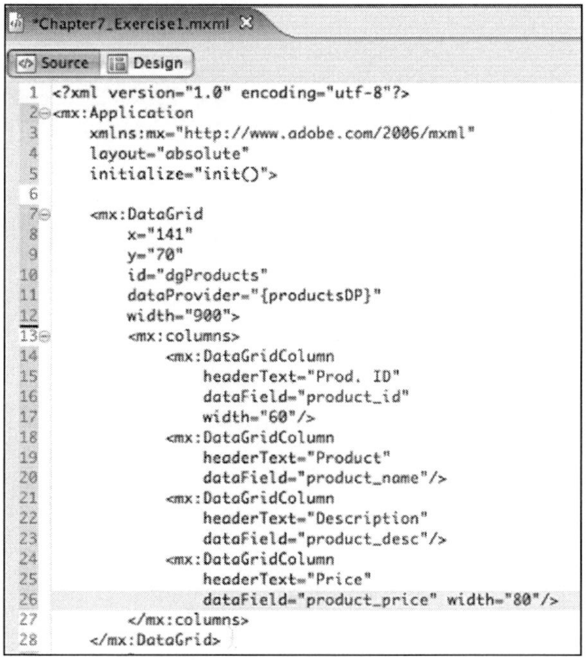

```
*Chapter7_Exercise1.mxml

<> Source   Design

 1  <?xml version="1.0" encoding="utf-8"?>
 2  <mx:Application
 3      xmlns:mx="http://www.adobe.com/2006/mxml"
 4      layout="absolute"
 5      initialize="init()">
 6
 7      <mx:DataGrid
 8          x="141"
 9          y="70"
10          id="dgProducts"
11          dataProvider="{productsDP}"
12          width="900">
13          <mx:columns>
14              <mx:DataGridColumn
15                  headerText="Prod. ID"
16                  dataField="product_id"
17                  width="60"/>
18              <mx:DataGridColumn
19                  headerText="Product"
20                  dataField="product_name"/>
21              <mx:DataGridColumn
22                  headerText="Description"
23                  dataField="product_desc"/>
24              <mx:DataGridColumn
25                  headerText="Price"
26                  dataField="product_price" width="80"/>
27          </mx:columns>
28      </mx:DataGrid>
```

Figure 7-9. DataGrid in code view

Now, let's look at the MXML markup for the buttons (see Figure 7-10). Here you can see the complete value for each button's click property. Each button click will fire a method that you'll soon write called getProducts(), and at that point I'll discuss the argument passed to the method. Another important property of each button for this project is visible. As you can see in the illustration, that property for both buttons will be bound to two Boolean variables that you'll later program the application to set for you, and these variables will control whether to display the previous and next buttons.

Next stop, the Script block. The variable definitions and method creations are all that stand between you and a finished application. So, start off by inserting an <mx:Script> block between the opening

<mx:Application> tag and the opening <mx:DataGrid> tag. Once you've completed that process, your code should now look like that in Figure 7-11.

```
29⊖      <mx:Button
30           x="141"
31           y="244"
32           id="previousPage"
33           label="Previous"
34           visible="{previousVisible}"
35           click="getProducts(offset-pageSize)"/>
36⊖      <mx:Button
37           x="{dgProducts.width-2}"
38           y="244"
39           id="nextPage"
40           label="Next"
41           visible="{nextVisible}"
42           click="getProducts(offset+pageSize)"/>
43
44  </mx:Application>
45
```

Figure 7-10. Buttons in code view

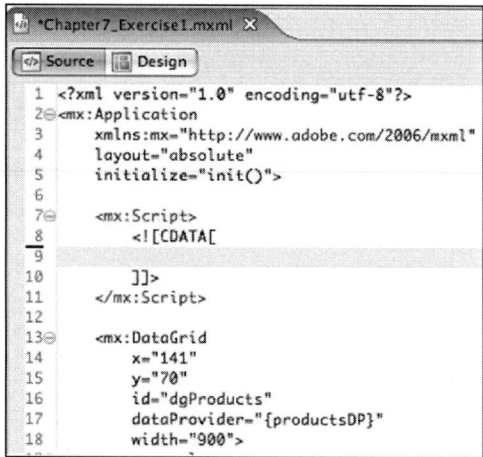

Figure 7-11. Inserting an <mx:Script> block

Time to import your classes

Before you start building the methods, it's always good practice to import all the necessary classes that you need for a particular project first. That way you minimize workflow interruptions due to the Flex compiler complaining about a class you left out. For this project, you'll be making use of five different classes:

- Alert
- ArrayCollection
- ObjectUtil
- CursorManager
- ServiceUtility

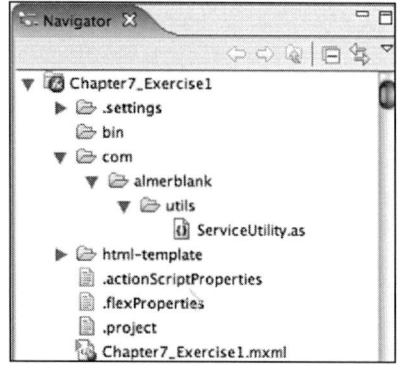

Figure 7-12. Adding the almerblank class package to your project

The first four classes are part of the Flex framework, while ServiceUtility is a custom class that I conceived to simplify working with AMF remoting. It's just a Singleton that encapsulates all the functionality required to communicate back and forth with any remoting service. In the downloads for this chapter, you'll find a folder named com, which contains ServiceUtility. Copy this folder and paste it into your Flex project by selecting the project name in the Navigator panel and selecting Paste. Once you've done that, your Navigator panel should look like Figure 7-12.

> *If you are unfamiliar with Singletons, they are classes designed using the Singleton design pattern, which is used to restrict instantiation of a class to one object. Using this pattern, you only have to worry about managing that one instance. This is yet another convenience when dealing with larger projects, so I personally employ it as much as possible.*

With that important step done, add the following import statements (shown in bold) to the <mx:Script> block you just added:

```
<mx:Script>
  <![CDATA[
    import mx.controls.Alert;
    mx.collections.ArrayCollection;
    import mx.utils.ObjectUtil;
    import mx.managers.CursorManager;
    import com.almerblank.utils.ServiceUtility;
  ]]>
</mx:Script>
```

Including these statements will not only ensure that you don't get any funky compile-time errors, but also ensure that you have access to those ultra-helpful code hints that can be your best friend when developing large projects. With the import statements taken care of, it's always a good idea to declare the variables that you will be using next. For this project, you'll be making use of seven variables and two constants. Add the following lines to your <mx:Script> block:

```
private var amfphp:ServiceUtility = ServiceUtility.getInstance();
private const GATEWAY:String ➥
  = 'http://www.yoursite.com/amfphp/gateway.php';
private const POLICY:String ➥
  = 'http://www.yoursite.com/amfphp/crossdomain.xml';

[Bindable] private var productsDP:ArrayCollection;
[Bindable] private var offset:uint = 0;
[Bindable] private var pageSize:uint;
[Bindable] private var totalProducts:uint;

[Bindable] private var previousVisible:Boolean = false;
[Bindable] private var nextVisible:Boolean = true;
```

The first variable, amfphp, will serve as your instance of the ServiceUtility class. GATEWAY and POLICY are constants used in conjunction with the ServiceUtility class, and I'll touch on them more in a minute. productsDP is an ArrayCollection where you will store the data that is returned by the service. The metadata tag [Bindable] is what tells Flex that a variable, or class for that matter, should be made available for binding operations. offset, pageSize, and totalProducts will all be placeholders for the values of the properties sharing the same name that you are returning from the getProducts() service you wrote earlier. previousVisible and nextVisible are those Booleans that I talked about earlier that will be bound to the previous and next buttons' visible properties to toggle their respective visibilities.

Having completed the variable declarations section, you can now start creating the actual methods that will make this Flex application tick. The first method you should code is the private function init(). If you look at Figure 7-11 again, you will see that init() is the value for the application's initialize property. In this context, initialize is an event, so think of init() as the event handler. Here's the code for the init() method—add this beneath the last [Bindable] variable:

```
private function init():void{
    amfphp.init(GATEWAY, false, null);
    getProducts(offset);
}
```

With this code, you are simply calling the init() method of the ServiceUtility class, passing it the arguments that it expects, and making an initial call to the getProducts() method that you will soon create. Calling that method after the application initializes will ensure that you don't have an empty DataGrid. If you're wondering about the decision to use the private keyword, it is purely a matter of preference. The more I code, the more I like labeling variables and functions private if they don't need to be accessed from outside of the class. It just feels cleaner to me to mark something public only when necessary. And, since all interactions will only take place in this main application file, everything will be private. On that note, here's the code for the getProducts() method—add this beneath the init() method:

```
private function getProducts(startID:uint):void{
    amfphp.call('com.almerblank.ISBN8962.Ch7.Products.browse', ➥
        resultHandler, faultHandler, startID);
    CursorManager.setBusyCursor();
}
```

The getProducts() method will be responsible for handling the outgoing communication to your service. This is accomplished by using the call() method of the ServiceUtility class, which expects four arguments: the service to call, the result handler for successful remoting, a fault handler for remoting failures, and a rest array for any parameters that you wish to pass along with your service call. For organization purposes, I chose to place my service inside of a package inside of the services folder of my AMFPHP installation, hence the com.almerblank.ISBN8962.Ch7 notation before the class name, Products, and the method name, browse(). A **package** is simply a hierarchy of folders that helps you to keep your code well organized and free from conflicts. If you were to browse for the Products class in your services directory using Explorer or Finder, its physical location would be represented as *your_amfphp_install_location*/services/com/almerblank/ISBN8962/Ch7/. resultHandler() and faultHandler() are two methods that you will soon write. resultHandler() will take care of populating all of your variables, thereby bringing the application to life, while faultHandler() will provide the application user with a description of why things didn't work should the remote operation fail. startID is the offset variable that the AMFPHP service needs passed to it to perform the paging functionality. The last line calls the CursorManager's setBusyCursor() method, which will display a clock animation while the remote operation is processing. This is a very nice element to have so that end users always have a sense of what's going on with your application.

Handling navigation

Before creating the aforementioned service handlers, you should take a moment to code the method that will handle the navigation buttons' visibility, setButtonVisibility(). The code for this method is as follows—add this below the getProducts() method:

```
private function setButtonVisibility():void{
  previousVisible = (offset > 0) ? true : false;
  nextVisible = (totalProducts > offset + pageSize) ? true : false;
}
```

Here you are setting previousVisible to true if the current offset value is greater than 0. If it equals 0, you are on page 1 and won't need a previous button, so it remains false. Likewise, nextVisible is set to true if the value of totalProducts is greater than the sum of the current value for offset plus the value for pageSize. If it equals that sum, you are on the last page of results and therefore don't need a next button. This is pretty standard logic, and setButtonVisibility() will be called into action after every successful remoting operation, as you'll soon see in the code that follows for the resultHandler() method. This should be added below the setButtonVisibility() method:

```
private function resultHandler(result:Array):void{
  try {
    productsDP = new ArrayCollection(result);
    pageSize = productsDP.getItemAt(5).pageSize;
    offset = productsDP.getItemAt(5).offset;
    totalProducts = productsDP.getItemAt(5).totalProducts;
    setButtonVisibility();
  } catch(error:*) {
    trace('get products error: '+error.message);
  } finally {
    CursorManager.removeBusyCursor();
  }
}
```

Processing the results

Remember that you've coded the browse() method of your service to return an array, hence the reason resultHandler() is expecting that array argument to be passed to it. With the array successfully returned, you want to process the result, but it's a good idea to encapsulate that processing inside of a try...catch block first. What try...catch basically does is it tries to perform whatever actions you want to take, but if an error occurs that could cause the Flash Player to halt operations, it catches that error for you before operations are halted and lets you deal with the error in a more user-friendly manner, by either suppressing the error completely or allowing you to display a friendly message to the user concerning the error. The finally clause is used when you want a certain action performed regardless of whether the try was successful or an error was caught.

So, the first thing you want to try to do is define your productsDP variable by creating an ArrayCollection of the result array. If you don't already know, an ArrayCollection, new to ActionScript 3, is simply a wrapper for a source array, in this case result. It allows you to manipulate the data without affecting the underlying source array. And, once the ArrayCollection has been set, you can use the ArrayCollection.getItemAt(itemIndex) method to access the objects contained in the result. Since you know that the offset, pageSize, and totalProducts variables will always be the last values of the result array, because you programmed it that way, you can consistently access the object containing those values at index 5 of the 0-based indices. After setting the values of those variables, all that is left is to make a call to the setButtonVisibility() method you just created. If an error is caught, you can suppress it. I chose to just trace out the error message so I can at least see what might have happened. Finally, you want to call the CursorManager's removeBusyCursor()

method to indicate to the user that remote operations are complete. With that, the resultHandler() method is complete, and you can move on to the faultHandler() method, which is far less intensive. Here's the code for faultHandler()—add this before the closing </mx:Script> tag:

```
private function faultHandler(fault:Object):void{
  Alert.show(fault.description, 'Service Error:');
}
```

AMFPHP returns an object when a remote operation fails. It's filled with all sorts of goodies, but the one you're most interested in is the description property because you will display the value of this property to the user in the event that the remote operation fails. And, with that, the code for this application is complete. Following is the complete <mx:Script> block:

```
<mx:Script>
  <![CDATA[
    import mx.controls.Alert;
    import mx.collections.ArrayCollection;
    import mx.utils.ObjectUtil;
    import mx.managers.CursorManager;
    import com.almerblank.utils.ServiceUtility;

    private var amfphp:ServiceUtility = ServiceUtility.getInstance();
    private const GATEWAY:String = 'http://amfphp:8888/gateway.php';
    private const POLICY:String = 'http://amfphp:8888/crossdomain.xml';

    [Bindable] private var productsDP:ArrayCollection;
    [Bindable] private var offset:uint = 0;
    [Bindable] private var pageSize:uint;
    [Bindable] private var totalProducts:uint;

    [Bindable] private var previousVisible:Boolean = false;
    [Bindable] private var nextVisible:Boolean = true;

    private function init():void{
      amfphp.init(GATEWAY, false, null);
      getProducts(offset);
    }

    private function getProducts(startID:uint):void{
      amfphp.call('com.almerblank.ISBN8962.Ch7.Products.browse', ➥
          resultHandler, faultHandler, startID);
      CursorManager.setBusyCursor();
    }

    private function resultHandler(result:Array):void{
      try {
        productsDP = new ArrayCollection(result);
        pageSize = productsDP.getItemAt(5).pageSize;
        offset = productsDP.getItemAt(5).offset;
        totalProducts = productsDP.getItemAt(5).totalProducts;
```

```
        setButtonVisibility();
      } catch(error:*) {
        trace('get products error: '+error.message);
      } finally {
        CursorManager.removeBusyCursor();
      }
    }

    private function faultHandler(fault:Object):void{
      Alert.show(fault.description, 'Service Error:');
    }

    private function setButtonVisibility():void{
      previousVisible = (offset > 0) ? true : false;
      nextVisible = (totalProducts > offset + pageSize) ? true : false;
    }
  ]]>
</mx:Script>
```

If your MySQL database and AMFPHP are set up correctly, you should be able to run the application (see Figure 7-13) and browse through the products. The next section looks at extending this application by adding a few bells and whistles including a product search feature.

Figure 7-13. Running the application

Search integration

In its simplest form, search integration in a Flex-powered application can be achieved by first creating a server-side database table that stores the keywords or tags for the associated content; you then need to provide a search field into which end users can type keywords and phrases to receive some kind of information back concerning matches between their text input and the stored keywords. With the RMX, we chose to return links to other Flex pages or views that contained or referenced the input text.

Before we started coding, we first had to answer an all-important question: how much search functionality was right for the project? This was important because we didn't want to get too "Flex happy," thereby making the app harder to use with no apparent benefit. On the other hand, we also didn't want to skimp on this feature because that would only render the RMX's growing library of content inaccessible.

> *Use MyISAM for the engine type when creating full-text-searchable tables, because you can't create full text indices on InnoDB tables.*

Performing a search using SQL is relatively simple. You're already familiar with SELECT. The only thing different is that you will now make use of a more advanced WHERE clause that includes the MATCH and AGAINST arguments. In case you're unfamiliar with these arguments, MATCH specifies what column or columns to search against, while AGAINST specifies the keyword to search for. Here's a simple query search for products with "Star Wars" as keywords:

```
SELECT * FROM products WHERE MATCH(product_name, product_desc) ➡
        AGAINST ("Star Wars");
```

You can also refactor that query to look for all *Star Wars*–related products by modifying your AGAINST argument like so:

```
SELECT * FROM products WHERE MATCH(product_name, product_desc)➡
    AGAINST ("Star Wars" with query expansion);
```

So what does with query expansion do exactly? Well, it tells MySQL to go over the index twice. On the first pass, it will find all records with the searched keyword and then build a set of keywords that appear together with the search string, thereby creating an expanded set of keywords. On the second pass, it searches for that expanded set of keywords. This will ensure that all relevant records are returned. This useful feature leads to the topic of **weighting**. In MySQL searches such as this one, MySQL weighs the words according to their frequency, and if the keyword appears too often, the weight for that particular product becomes 0, making it nonrelevant.

You will now add a search() method to the Products class that will be used to successfully search the products table. Go ahead and open Products.php in your favorite text editor. Once you have it open, create a new line after the definition for the browse() method in your methodTable, and then add the bold code shown here so that your methodTable now looks like the following:

```php
<?php
require_once 'Data.php';

class Products{
  var $dbc;
  var $offset = 0;
  var $pagesize = 5;

  function Products(){
    $this->methodTable = array(
        'browse' => array(
            'access' => 'remote',
            'description' => 'for browsing available products'
        ),
        'search' => array(
            'access' => 'remote',
            'description' => 'for searching products based on keywords'
        ),
        );
      $this->dbc = Data::connect();
  }
```

Now that you've added this code to the methodTable, you can create the actual method. The search() method will be very similar to the browse() method except for the number of arguments required and the use of the WHERE clause discussed earlier. Here's the code that comprises the search() method—add this beneath the browse() method:

```
function search($arr){
  $keywords = $arr[0];
  $offset = $arr[1];
  $this->offset = ($arr[1] > 0) ? $arr[1] : $this->offset;

  $get_count = mysql_query("SELECT product_id FROM products
                    WHERE MATCH (product_name, product_desc)➡
                      AGAINST ('$keywords')");
  $count = mysql_num_rows($get_count);
  $total_products = array(array('totalProducts'=>$count, ➡
          'offset'=>$this->offset,'pageSize'=>$this->pagesize));

  $search = "SELECT * FROM products
                    WHERE MATCH (product_name, product_desc)
                      AGAINST ('$keywords') ORDER BY product_id ASC
                        LIMIT {$this->offset}, {$this->pagesize}";

  $products = mysql_query($search);

  if($products){
    while($row = mysql_fetch_object($products)){
        $results[] = $row;
    }
    $return = array_merge($results, $total_products);
  } else {
    $return = array('DEBUG_OUTPUT', mysql_error());
  }

  return $return;
}
```

So let's examine how this differs from the browse() method. Here you are passing in the keywords first, followed by the offset. Like before, you want to get the count of all the products in the database, but here you want to specify that the total is the sum of only the products that match the supplied keywords. Your search query will pull everything from the database where the product name or description matches the supplied keywords; to enable paging, you limit the returned results just like you did for the browse() method. When the results are returned, you want them packaged up the same way as before. You should now have a working search service. If you run the service from AMFPHP's built-in service browser (http://your_amfphp_install_location/browser/), you should get results similar to Figures 7-14 and 7-15.

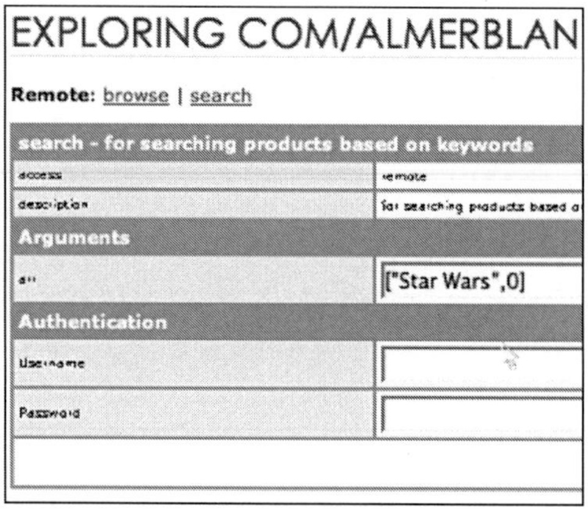

EXPLORING COM/ALMERBLANK/ISBN8962/

Results | Trace headers | Arguments | Stats

array		
0	array	
	product_id	11
	product_name	Star Wars Saga DVD
	product_desc	the only place to get the entire epic digitally remastered and on one DVD
	product_price	89.99
1	array	
	product_id	2
	product_name	Star Wars Collector Mug
	product_desc	a long time ago, in a galaxy far, far away some people set their sights on the stars...
	product_price	199.99
2	array	
	totalProducts	2
	offset	0
	pageSize	5

EXPLORING COM/ALMERBLAN

Remote: browse | search

search - for searching products based on keywords	
access	remote
description	for searching products based o
Arguments	
arr	["Star Wars",0]
Authentication	
Username	
Password	

Figure 7-14. Using the search service

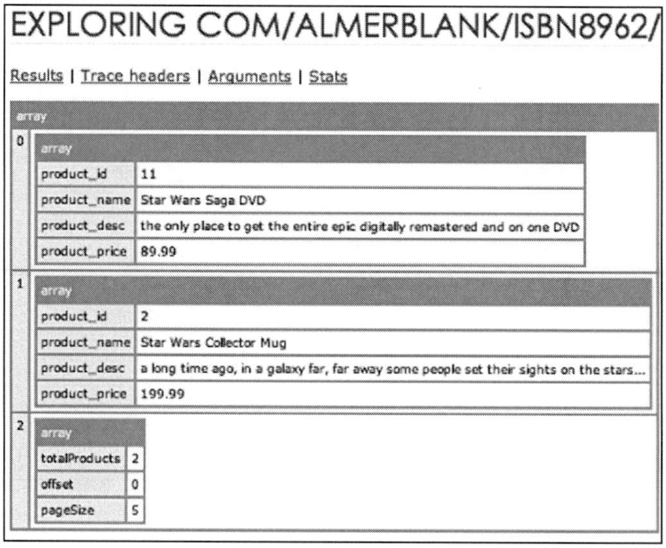

Figure 7-15. Results of the search service

Upgrading the Flex application

Now that you know the service is working, you can move on to rewiring your Flex app to use your new service. For this, you're going to create a clone of Chapter7_Exercise1, so open up Flex Builder and create a new Flex project using the same process as you did for the last project and entitle it Chapter7_Exercise2. There will be two enhancements to this version of the application. The first will be the addition of a form that will allow users to enter keywords to search the database for. The second will be a page indicator in the form of *x–y* of *z*. Once you have your application file open, copy the finished code from the previous exercise and paste it into this file.

> *This brings up a good point: always reuse code whenever possible. And, since this project is very similar to the last, it's a prime candidate for this methodology.*

Just like before, you want to add your interface elements to the stage before adding any more code. The simplest of the two enhancements is the page indicator. It will be nothing more than a Text component bound to a variable that will be set based on the current results. Ensure you're in code view, and then insert the following code between the MXML markup for the two navigation buttons:

```
<mx:Text x="500" y="244" text="{pageText}" color="0xffffff"/>
```

Modularization

With one of the design enhancements completed, you could switch to design view and drag out a TextInput component and a Button component and be done with the visualization, but this seems like an excellent opportunity to implement **modularization**. In this context, the goal is to group similar application elements into their own component file. One benefit is that any interactions necessary with these elements is confined to this component file, making debugging a little easier if something should go wrong. It also keeps your main application file lean and mean while promoting reusability. Before creating the search component, you need to add the folder structure to the project first.

Next, you want to create a new MXML component and place it inside the components folder. Although you could also create the component in the application root, if you are going to modularize your application into different pieces, it's also best to organize those pieces in their own space, so to speak. Right-click the components folder and select New ➤ MXML Component. Specify the values shown in Figure 7-16 for Filename and Based on.

Once Flex finishes creating the component, it's time to start adding the visual elements. This component will be visual-only—its functionality will be coded in the main application. In your choice of either design view or code view, add a TextInput component and a Button component. Once you have added those components, switch to code view and ensure both of these components have the same attributes as the following code:

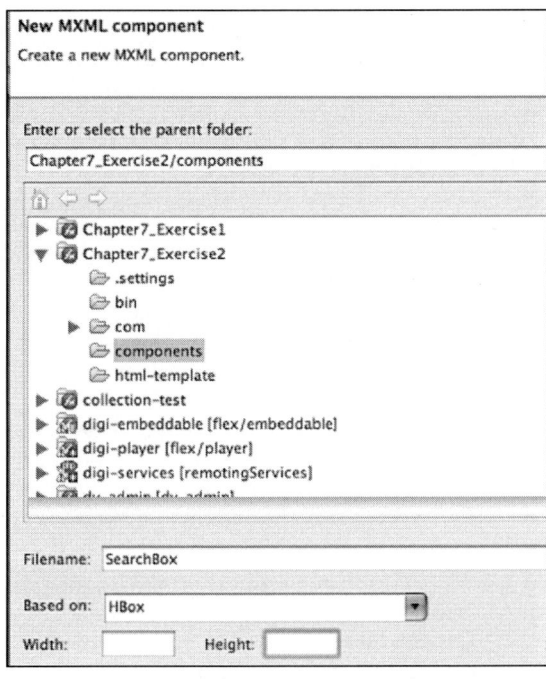

Figure 7-16. Naming the new component

```xml
<?xml version="1.0" encoding="utf-8"?>
<mx:HBox xmlns:mx="http://www.adobe.com/2006/mxml">
  <mx:TextInput id="keywords"/>
  <mx:Button
      id="searchButton"
      label="Search"
      click="parentApplication.searchClickHandler(event)"/>
</mx:HBox>
```

After you have saved your work, you can close your SearchBox component and jump back over to the main application to integrate it. Before you can add SearchBox to your application, you first need to create a **namespace**, which is basically a mapping that tells the compiler where your component class files are located. To do so, add xmlns:components="components.*" beneath the default namespace definition, as shown in Figure 7-17.

After adding the namespace, you can add the MXML markup for the SearchBox component by inserting the following code between the closing </mx:Script> tag and the opening <mx:DataGrid> tag:

Figure 7-17. Creating the components namespace

```
<components:SearchBox id="searchBox" x="{dgProducts.width-100}" ➥
        top="40"/>
```

185

The curly brace notation for the *x*-coordinate ensures that SearchBox will be neatly aligned to the right edge of the DataGrid. With all the visual elements in place, you can now modify the code in the <mx:Script> block to accommodate these changes.

Enhancing the code

First, you want to add any new variables that the enhancements will require. What variables do you need? Well, you'll need a variable to hold the contents of the TextInput component inside SearchBox. You'll also need two variables to hold the low and high limits for the current page. And finally, you'll need the pageText variable, which is to be bound to the text property of the page indicator component. So insert the following code at the end of your variable declarations section at the top of the <mx:Script> block:

```
[Bindable] private var keywords:String = '';

[Bindable] private var lowLimit:uint;
[Bindable] private var highLimit:uint;

[Bindable] private var pageText:String;
```

This will take care of all the variable declarations for this project. The next thing you can do is to create the searchClickHandler() method that you assigned for the Button inside of the SearchBox component. This method will allow you to access the current keywords input by the user, call the required services, and modify the Button's label based on the current state of the component. Here's the code that comprises searchClickHandler()—add this beneath the setButtonVisibility() method:

```
public function searchClickHandler(event:MouseEvent):void{
  var button:Button = event.target as Button;
  var widget:Object = button.parentDocument;
  if(button.label == 'Search'){
    keywords = widget.keywords.text;
    if(keywords != ''){
      searchProducts(0);
      button.label = 'Cancel';
      widget.keywords.enabled = false;
    } else {
      Alert.show('Please enter something to search for.', ➥
          'Search Error:');
    }
  } else {
    keywords = '';
    widget.keywords.text = '';
    getProducts(0);
    button.label = 'Search';
    widget.keywords.enabled = true;
  }
}
```

Here you create local variables for both the Button as well as the SearchBox component itself so that you can easily communicate with the component. Next, you use conditional logic to determine the current label of the clicked button. If it's "Search," you want to grab the text from the TextInput and store that in the keywords variable, and then you want to do a quick integrity check to ensure that keywords is not empty. If it's not, you want to call the searchProducts() method, which you'll soon write, change the Button's label to "Cancel," and disable the TextInput to prevent unexpected behavior; otherwise, you want to notify the user that your application doesn't like performing empty searches. Now, on the other hand, if the Button's label is "Cancel," you want to clear both the keywords variable and the TextInput's text value. Additionally, you want to call the original product browse() method getProducts(). And finally, you want to change the Button's label to "Search" again and reenable the TextInput for user interaction.

That was the most intensive part of the application enhancements—the remaining methods are essentially clones of other methods you've already created. The first of the clones is the searchProducts() method. It is very similar to getProducts() except for the actual service called, the result handler, and the passing of an additional argument. Insert the following code for the searchProducts() method into your <mx:Script> block:

```
private function searchProducts(startID:uint):void{
  amfphp.call('com.almerblank.ISBN8962.Ch7.Products.search', ➥
      searchResultHandler, faultHandler, keywords, startID);
  CursorManager.setBusyCursor();
}
```

The searchResultHandler() method is even more similar to its counterpart, resultHandler(). The only difference besides the name of the method is the addition of a call to a soon-to-be-created method, setPageText(), and the language of the trace for trapped errors. Add the following code immediately below the searchProducts() method:

```
private function searchResultHandler(result:Array):void{
  try {
    productsDP = new ArrayCollection(result);
    var total:uint = productsDP.length - 1;
    pageSize = productsDP.getItemAt(total).pageSize;
    offset = productsDP.getItemAt(total).offset;
    totalProducts = productsDP.getItemAt(total).totalProducts;
    setPageText();
    setButtonVisibility();
    trace('offset = '+offset+'\npageSize = ➥
        '+pageSize+'\ntotalProducts = '+totalProducts);
  } catch(error:*) {
    trace('search products error: '+error.message);
  } finally {
    CursorManager.removeBusyCursor();
  }
}
```

The setPageText() method also needs to be added to resultHandler() since it needs to determine the text for the page indicator component regardless of the service used. The method is pretty straightforward. It sets the values of the lowLimit, highLimit, and pageText variables, nothing more, nothing less. Insert the following code for setPageText() into your <mx:Script> block:

```
private function setPageText():void{
    lowLimit = offset+1;
    highLimit = (totalProducts > 5) ? lowLimit+4 : totalProducts;
    pageText = 'Displaying items '+lowLimit+' - '+highLimit+' ➡
            of '+totalProducts;
}
```

Let's briefly examine this method. lowLimit is derived by adding a value of 1 to the current offset value. This is done because the offset index is a 0-based index, and while that's fine for computer programming, it would be pretty weird reading something like "Displaying items 0–4 of 20." highLimit is obtained by first checking to see whether the value for totalProducts is greater than 5. If it is, highLimit should be set to the value for lowLimit plus 4, since the index is 0-based and the page size is five products per page. With those two variables defined, the value for pageText should be obvious, since it just creates a variable text phrase based on those previously derived values.

The last of the new methods for this project is fetchPage(). Its sole purpose is to be a traffic controller to the navigation buttons. It will first check to see whether the value for the keywords variable is an empty string or not. If it's not, the searchProducts() method should be called; but if it is, the getProducts() method should be called. Insert the following code at the bottom of your <mx:Script> block:

```
private function fetchPage(startID:uint):void{
    if(keywords != ''){
        searchProducts(startID);
    } else {
        getProducts(startID);
    }
}
```

That completes the application enhancements. All that's left to do is to update the navigation buttons to call this latest method instead of getProducts() and pass the same arguments as before. Figure 7-18 shows the updated click properties for both buttons.

Although this is not the only way to search-enable a Flex application, you now have an application that successfully allows you to both browse and search a product catalog. In the next section, I'll show you options for enabling history management in the application.

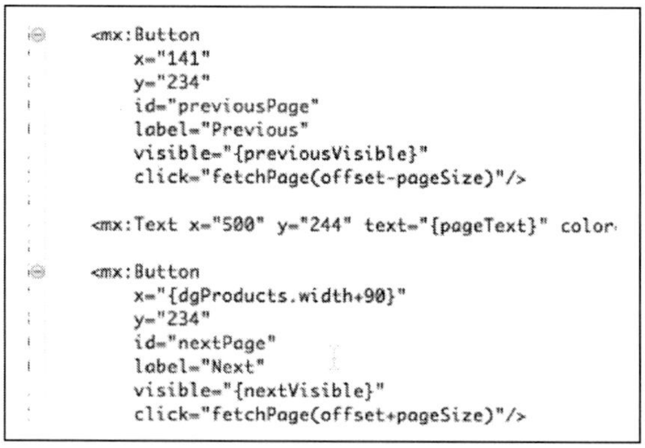

```
<mx:Button
    x="141"
    y="234"
    id="previousPage"
    label="Previous"
    visible="{previousVisible}"
    click="fetchPage(offset-pageSize)"/>

<mx:Text x="500" y="244" text="{pageText}" color

<mx:Button
    x="{dgProducts.width+90}"
    y="234"
    id="nextPage"
    label="Next"
    visible="{nextVisible}"
    click="fetchPage(offset+pageSize)"/>
```

Figure 7-18: Updating the navigation buttons

History management

What is history management? Flex's HistoryManager lets users navigate through a Flex application by using the web browser's back and forward navigation commands. For example, a user could make use of a TabNavigator component to navigate through various views of an application. Since the TabNavigator component is history management–enabled, the user could use the web browser's Back button to traverse back through those views and eventually return the application to its initial state. In other words, it allows you to keep track of where you are in an application; however, it doesn't provide undo/redo functionality (that is, it doesn't "remember" what you have done along the way).

History management is made possible in Flex applications by implementing a set of files that are referenced in the application's wrapper. **Wrapper** in this context collectively refers to the HTML page that houses the Flex SWF file and the JavaScript file that embeds that SWF into the HTML page. Flex Builder's default wrapper comes prewired to support history management, but if you're compiling via the command line or are implementing a custom wrapper, you will have to wire the wrapper to include this support. Fear not though. Some wrapper templates are included with your Flex Builder installation. You can find the following wrapper template directories in your `/flex_builder_install_path/Flex SDK 2/resources/html-templates` directory:

- `/client-side-detection-with-history`
- `/express-installation-with-history`
- `/no-player-detection-with-history`

When creating a customized wrapper with history management support, remember to keep your JavaScript separate from the HTML page. When you put the JavaScript inside the HTML, you ensure that you will invoke the wrath of the great and powerful Internet Explorer Eolas patent god (http://en.wikipedia.org/wiki/Eolas#Browser_changes). Other than that, it's not difficult to enable history management in your custom wrapper. Here's a list of what's typically required:

- *your_wrapper*.html
- *your_flex_app*.swf
- history.js
- history.htm
- history.swf

The last three files on the list can be obtained from the `templates` directory I mentioned earlier, or if you're using Flex Builder, they are added to the `html-template` folder of your Flex project automatically. And, the good thing is that you don't have to modify them when using a custom wrapper; you just ensure your wrapper references them. For `history.js`, use a `<script/>` tag in your HTML page's `<body>` to reference the file. For `history.htm`, use an `<iframe/>` tag placed at the bottom of the HTML page just before the closing `</body>` tag to reference it. Additionally, the name of the `iframe` element must be set to `_history`, and the width of the element must be set to a minimum of 22 to ensure smooth sailing with Internet Explorer. I'll discuss in a moment how Flex interacts with these files to provide this functionality, but first, here are code examples of the required tags for your custom wrapper:

```
<script language="JavaScript" type=➡
"text/javascript" src="history.js">➡
    </script>
<iframe name="_history" src="history.htm" frameborder="0" ➡
    scrolling="no" width="22" height="0"></iframe>
```

History management is enabled by default for the Accordion and TabNavigator containers but disabled in the ViewStack container. To toggle this feature on or off for one of these controls, set the container's historyManagementEnabled property to true or false, respectively. Now, this doesn't mean that other elements in your Flex app are left out—quite the contrary. To enable custom history management for other objects in an application, you'll need to do the following:

1. Implement the IHistoryManagerClient interface (mx.managers.IHistoryManagerClient).
2. Register the component with the HistoryManager's register() method.
3. Save the component's state when its state changes.
4. Implement the interface's saveState() and loadState() methods.

So, say for example you have created a component, YourComponent.mxml, with several view states, and you want to enable history management for the component. Here's some example code on how to make that happen:

```xml
<!-- YourComponent.mxml -->
<?xml version="1.0" encoding="utf-8"?>
<mx:Canvas
  xmlns:mx="http://www.adobe.com/2006/mxml"
  implements="mx.managers.IHistoryManagerClient"
  creationComplete="initComp()"
  currentStateChange="viewChanged()">

  <mx:Script>
   <![CDATA[
    import mx.managers.HistoryManager;
    import mx.states.States;

    private function initComp():void{
      HistoryManager.register(this);
    }

    private function viewChanged():void{
      HistoryManager.save();
    }

    public function saveState():Object{
      return {currentState: currentState};
    }

    public function loadState(state:Object):void{
      var newState:State = state ? state.currentState : '';
      if(newState != currentState) currentState = newState;
    }
   ]]>
  </mx:Script>

  <mx:states>
    <mx:State name="Welcome">
      <mx:RemoveChild target="{button}"/>
      <mx:AddChild>
```

```
            <mx:Text text="Welcome to my site!!"/>
        </mx:AddChild>
    </mx:State>
</mx:states>

<mx:Button id="button" label="Enter Here" ➥
        click="this.currentState='Welcome'"/>

</mx:Canvas>
```

This effectively registers YourComponent with the HistoryManager class and satisfies the other requirements for enabling history management for custom components. But, how does HistoryManager integrate with the web browser? First, it uses navigateToURL() to invisibly load your <iframe> into the current browser window. Next, it encodes your Flex application's navigation states into the iframe's URL query parameters. From here, history.swf, which lives inside history.htm, decodes those parameters and sends the navigation state back to the HistoryManager class. This sequence is illustrated in Figure 7-19.

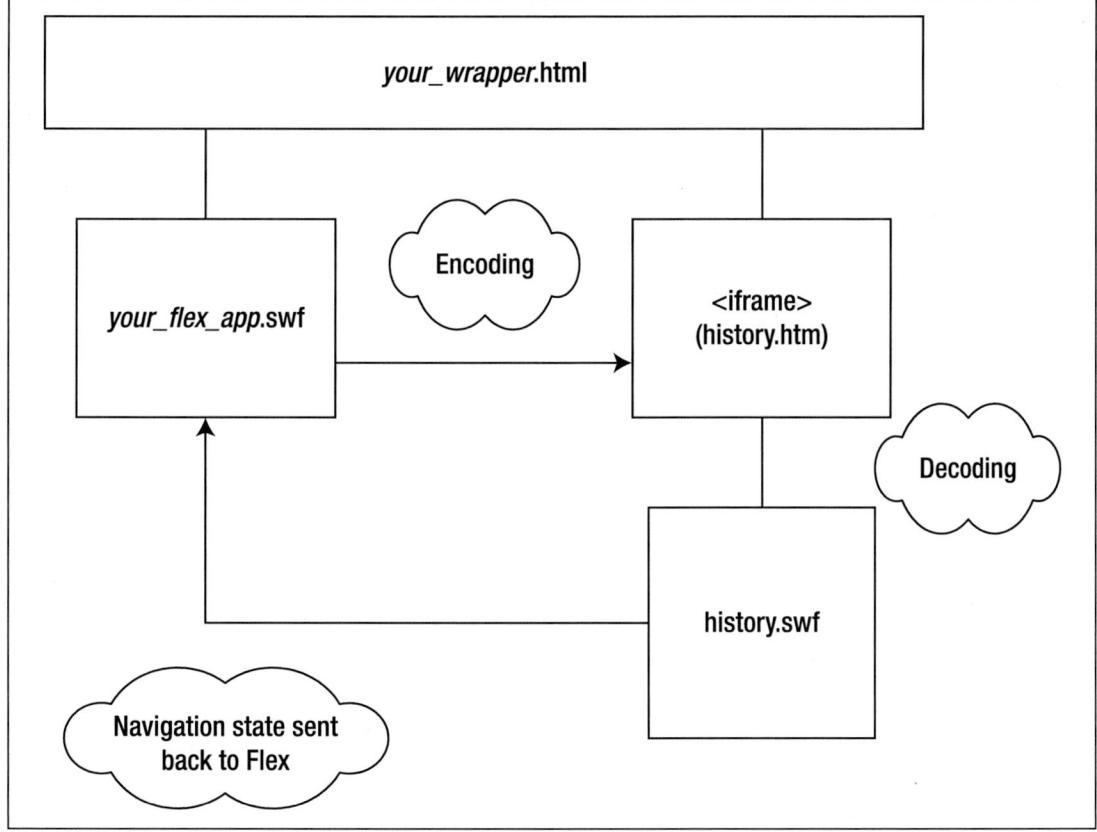

Figure 7-19. HistoryManager flowchart

That's just a basic overview of what happens behind the scenes. But, rather than delve too deeply into custom history management theory, I'll show you how you can further enhance the previous exercises to include basic history management.

So, create a new project the same way you did in the "Search integration" section and name it Chapter7_Exercise3. This project will start as a clone of Chapter7_Exercise2, so copy the contents of the Chapter7_Exercise2 application file and paste it into Chapter7_Exercise3 once Flex Builder finishes creating your application file. Also, remember to copy over the com and components folders to the new project as well. The following list details the enhancements to be made in this project:

- Adding a header to the main view
- Creating a component to display detailed product information
- Adding a ViewStack container to house both the main view and detail view
- Enabling history management on the ViewStack

The header that you're going to add to the application will be comprised of a Label and Text component. The Label will serve as the view's title, while the Text will serve as instructions to the end user on how to view more information about a particular product. Insert the following code just above your SearchBox component:

```
<mx:Label x="141" fontSize="18" fontWeight="bold" ➡
        text="Product Catalog" top="30"/>
<mx:Text x="141" text="Select a product to view more details" ➡
        top="50"/>
```

The next step is to build a product details component that can display extended information about a selected product as well as give the option to purchase the product. Follow the same steps to create this component as you did in the "Search integration" section for the SearchBox component, but name it ProductDetails. Once the component file has been created, add the following code to the file:

```
<!-- ProductDetails.mxml -->
<?xml version="1.0" encoding="utf-8"?>
<mx:Canvas xmlns:mx="http://www.adobe.com/2006/mxml">
  <mx:Form id="productInfoForm">
    <mx:FormHeading label="Product Details" fontSize="18" ➡
          fontWeight="bold"/>
    <mx:FormItem id="productImage">
      <mx:Image ➡
            source="{parentApplication.selectedProduct.product_img}"/>
    </mx:FormItem>
    <mx:FormItem id="productID" label="SKU#">
      <mx:Text text="{parentApplication.selectedProduct.product_id}"/>
    </mx:FormItem>
    <mx:FormItem id="productName" label="Name:">
      <mx:Text ➡
            text="{parentApplication.selectedProduct.product_name}"/>
    </mx:FormItem>
    <mx:FormItem id="productDesc" label="Desc:">
      <mx:Text ➡
```

```
                text="{parentApplication.selectedProduct.product_desc}"/>
        </mx:FormItem>
        <mx:FormItem id="productCost" label="Price:">
          <mx:Text ➥
                text="${parentApplication.selectedProduct.product_price}"/>
        </mx:FormItem>
        <mx:FormItem id="productRating" label="Rating:">
          <mx:Text text=➥
                "{parentApplication.selectedProduct.product_rating} stars"/>
        </mx:FormItem>
      </mx:Form>
      <mx:ApplicationControlBar x="60" y="{productInfoForm.height}">
        <mx:Button label="Back"➥
                click="parentApplication.productViews.selectedIndex=0"/>
        <mx:Button label="Purchase"/>
      </mx:ApplicationControlBar>
    </mx:Canvas>
```

In addition to the fields displayed in the DataGrid, the ProductDetails component will also display a thumbnail for the product, as well as the average rating for the product. This component also provides the means for the user to navigate back to the catalog browser. Purchasing ability will be added at a later time.

This component also makes reference to a property of the parent application named selectedProduct, but this variable has yet to be defined. Switch back to the main application and add a new, bindable public variable named selectedProduct of type Object to the end of your variable declarations section. While you're there, import the ListEvent class found in the mx.events package. This class will allow you to capture and process the user selections as you see fit. How exactly will that happen? By assigning a new method, fetchProductDetails(), to the DataGrid's itemClick event property, you'll be able to learn which product the user clicked and initialize ProductDetails with that data. Figure 7-20 shows the opening tag for the DataGrid with the itemClick property added.

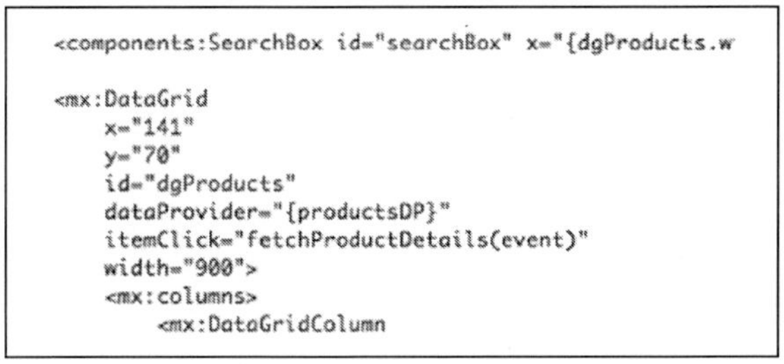

```
<components:SearchBox id="searchBox" x="{dgProducts.w

<mx:DataGrid
    x="141"
    y="70"
    id="dgProducts"
    dataProvider="{productsDP}"
    itemClick="fetchProductDetails(event)"
    width="900">
    <mx:columns>
        <mx:DataGridColumn
```

Figure 7-20. Assigning an event handler for the DataGrid's itemClick event

The code for fetchProductDetails() is relatively simple in that it takes the currently selected DataGrid item, which is of type Object, and assigns it to the selectedProduct you just created. The selectedProduct object is in turn bound to the various form items of your ProductDetails component. This method also switches the selectedIndex of the ViewStack to the index occupied by your component. Insert the code for this method at the end of your <mx:Script> block in your main application file:

```
private function fetchProductDetails(event:ListEvent):void{
  selectedProduct = event.target.selectedItem;
  productViews.selectedIndex = 1;
}
```

The only thing left to do now is set the `historyManagementEnabled` property of your ViewStack to true in order to use the web browser's navigation buttons with your application. Save your work and run the application.

> *When developing with Flex's* `HistoryManager`, *you'll get sandbox errors when trying to use this feature locally. To avoid this setback, either publish the app to your local web server or mess around with your security sandbox settings.*

Summary

In this chapter, I covered some of the development features and concepts that are important to a Flex developer in architecting usable applications. I showed you what pagination is, when it's needed and when it's not, and how to employ this technique in a Flex application tied to a PHP/MySQL back end. I also touched on search integration. You learned one method of search-enabling a Flex app and how to determine what amount of search functionality is right for a project. Additionally, I talked about history management and how this built-in feature of Flex's can help to alleviate some of the complaints about multimedia applications and browser navigation integration. You'll learn even more about history management, search functionality, and pagination as you explore additional features of the Flex framework throughout the remainder of the book. In the next chapter, you will be able to apply these concepts and techniques as you learn a little about how we syndicate, aggregate, and access the RMX's content.

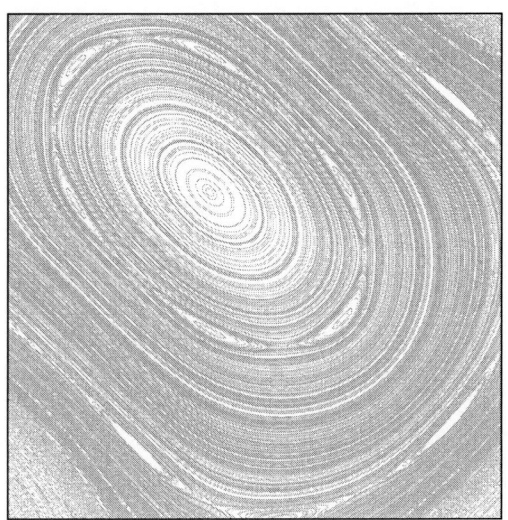

Chapter 8

FORMS AND VALIDATION

By Omar Gonzalez

Forms and validation are areas in which Flex natively excels compared to other technologies like HTML, which have provided a more traditional and common way of handling input from users (and generally require a page refresh—ugh!).

In this chapter, I will talk about how I handle the forms for the RMX while exploiting the great features that Flex offers. You will also learn about Flex validators by extending a validator to customize it. So let's get started!

Data transfer objects

By the time I start thinking of building a form, I usually have finished writing all the basic data transfer objects, or DTOs. Still, there will be times that I need a new DTO that I had not planned for, and so before I start a new form, I analyze whether I need to produce any new DTOs.

Why use DTOs?

I use DTOs in my coding for a couple of reasons. When I'm in the middle of coding a Flex form in ActionScript, the last thing I want to do is distract myself by having to open a PHP file to reference what data object structure is expected by the remote service call. By setting up the properties of the object in a DTO class, I no longer need to worry about having to remember the structure of the object because it will all be built into the class and will come up in the Flex Builder code hints.

I also use DTOs to bind display objects to the properties in those DTOs. This way I can use the DTOs to send data to the display when I get a return from a remoting call. I'll talk more about using DTOs throughout this chapter. First, I talk about setting up the DTOs for the RMX application in this chapter.

Setting up a DTO

The examples in this chapter are based on the RMX form for member registration. With that in mind, the DTO I set up first is the Member.as DTO. The structure of the DTO class for a member is based on the object that the PHP remoting method is expecting. The PHP method would start something like this:

```
class Members
{
  var $username;
  var $password;
  var $email;

  function addMember($memberInfo)
  {
    $this->username = $memberInfo["username"];
    $this->username = $memberInfo["username"];
    $this->username = $memberInfo["username"];
    ...
  }
}
```

The PHP method accepts a single object as an argument. I use this setup because it makes it easier to add additional properties to the method's single argument object as needed, as opposed to modifying the method definition each time. It also helps keep code better organized.

In the first lines of the method, the member information is stored in the class variables; these property names are the names that will be used in the DTO. With that in mind, the DTO would look like this:

```
package com.almerblank.rmx.dto
{
  [Bindable]
  public class Member extends Object
  {

    public var username:String;
    public var password:String;
    public var address1:String;
    public var address2:String;
    public var city:String;
    public var state:String;
    public var zip:String;
    public var email:String;
```

```
      public function Member()
      {
        super();
      }
    }
  }
```

All the DTOs for the application go in the dto folder. The class is simply a basic class that extends an Object with one public property for each piece of data that you are sending to the remote PHP method. For this Member DTO, I have set up basic user information for the example in this chapter. Although the Object class is the default package, I like to specify it anyway in my written code simply because I prefer my code to be as detailed and clear as possible.

The properties of a DTO are usually all public since they are meant to store data that should be available for transferring easily throughout the application, which also allows the properties to be used for binding. By using the Bindable metadata tag, the properties can be used as bindable variables to display data when it is returned from a remote method. I'll expand more on this as I cover setting up a form.

Setting up a form

Unlike the <form> tag in XHTML, the Flex <mx:Form/> tag is not required to process data in input fields. This tag is still useful in Flex, though, because it helps to lay out a form easily with the <mx:FormHeading/> and <mx:FormItem/> tags. Along with the layout capabilities are other properties I will go over throughout this section. It is still possible to process a form without the use of these form-specific tags; however, the use of these tags helps with traditional form layouts.

The <mx:Form/> tag

With a DTO ready for the member registration form, I can start the application. In the rmx folder, I have a forms folder to keep all the forms used in the RMX. To start a new class here, I right-click the folder and choose New ➤ ActionScript Class.

The New ActionScript Class dialog box through which the class is created will appear. This is a really nice feature because it not only writes the class out for you, but also gives you all the options you would need when creating a new class like public and internal modifiers, superclass explorer, and others. It also helps reduce the possibility of human error when writing out long folder paths for packages or constructor names. With the options filled out properly, the dialog box should look like what you see in Figure 8-1.

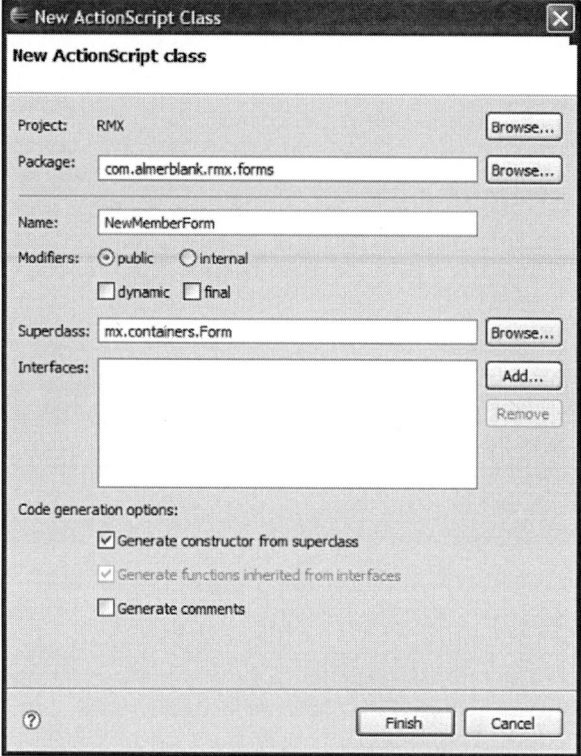

Figure 8-1. The dialog box for creating a new ActionScript class, ready to create the NewMemberForm class

Clicking Finish creates the ActionScript file and writes the class for you, including imports and the options you chose for the class. The output for this example looks like this:

```
package com.almerblank.rmx.forms
{
  import mx.containers.Form;

  public class NewMemberForm extends Form
  {
    public function NewMemberForm()
    {
      super();
    }

  }
}
```

Now I can use this class to start the layout of the form. In the MemberRegistration application, I can simply open a tag and begin to type the class name NewMemberForm. The class will appear in the code hints, and I can select it from the drop-down list to start the form, as you can see in Figures 8-2 and 8-3.

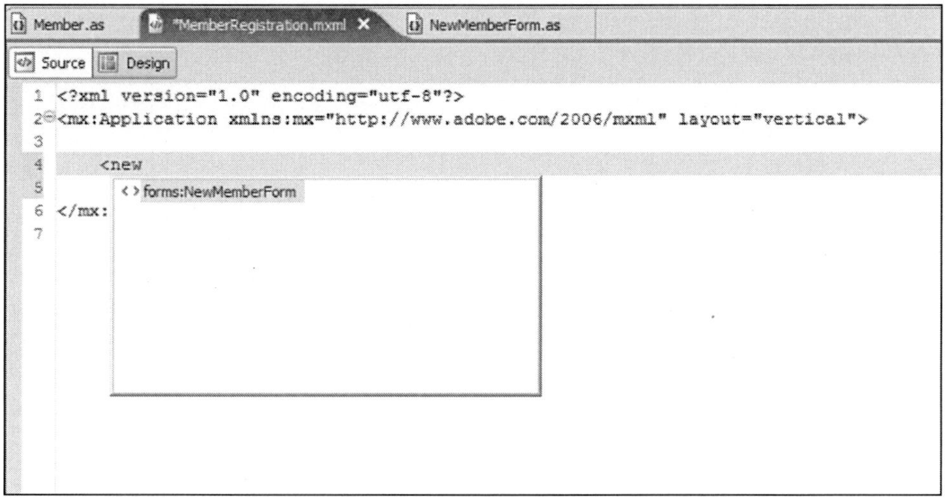

Figure 8-2. The code hints in Flex Builder bring up custom classes to use easily in MXML.

Figure 8-3. Flex Builder makes the xml namespace for you—forms is the package and NewMemberForm is the class.

After selecting my class from the drop-down list, Flex Builder adds the xml namespace for the package that contains the form class and starts the tag for me. For now, the class simply acts as a normal form, but this is all I need it to do while I set up the layout of the form.

The <mx:FormHeading/> tag

The first form-specific tag I'm going to talk about is the <mx:FormHeading/> tag. This creates a simple component meant to be used to give a form a heading. It only requires one property, the label property, to display text as a heading in the form. You can then apply any styling you wish to all form headings in CSS using the <mx:FormHeading/> tag, as an example of how you might work with this tag.

After I add a form heading of Member Registration with the <mx:FormHeading/> tag to the form being built, the MXML now looks like this:

```
<?xml version="1.0" encoding="utf-8"?>
<mx:Application
  width="560" height="300"
  xmlns:mx="http://www.adobe.com/2006/mxml" layout="vertical"
  xmlns:forms="com.almerblank.rmx.forms.*">

  <forms:NewMemberForm
    width="100%" height="100%">

    <mx:FormHeading label="Member Registration"/>

  </forms:NewMemberForm>

</mx:Application>
```

The form now has a form heading of Member Registration. I also make slight modifications to the previous example of the code by giving the <mx:Application/> tag dimensions, as well as the NewMemberForm. Compiled, the form so far looks like Figure 8-4.

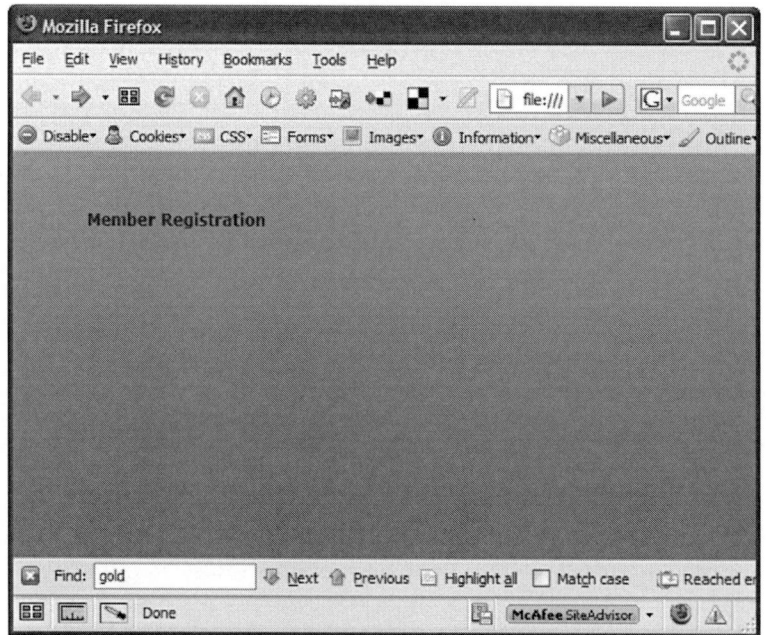

Figure 8-4. The default look of the <mx:FormHeading/> tag

The form is ready for the fields it is going to submit. Next, I'll talk about the <mx:FormItem/> tag.

The <mx:FormItem/> tag

The <mx:FormItem/> tag is the main tag used to house the different elements of the form. It is the container for each TextInput or TextArea component of the form. The main property of the <mx:FormItem/> tag is the label property, which places a label for the contents of the <mx:FormItem/>.

Another property that really comes in handy is the required property. This property inserts a red asterisk by default, indicating a field is required. If I add username and password fields to the form, as required, the MXML code would look like this:

```
<?xml version="1.0" encoding="utf-8"?>
<mx:Application
  width="560" height="300"
  xmlns:mx="http://www.adobe.com/2006/mxml" layout="vertical"
  xmlns:forms="com.almerblank.rmx.forms.*">

  <forms:NewMemberForm
    width="100%" height="100%">

    <mx:FormHeading label="Member Registration"/>

    <mx:FormItem label="Username:" required="true">
      <mx:TextInput id="tf_username"/>
    </mx:FormItem>
    <mx:FormItem label="Password:" required="true">
      <mx:TextInput id="tf_password"/>
    </mx:FormItem>

  </forms:NewMemberForm>

</mx:Application>
```

The <mx:FormItem/> tags will stack one on top of the other as if they were in a VBox container. Because the <mx:FormItem/> tags are within the <mx:Form/> tag, the FormItems take on dynamic width attributes that adjust the width of all the label displays of the form, making the labels all the same in relation to the widest label. The labels also become right-aligned, including space for the required asterisk, as you can see in Figure 8-5.

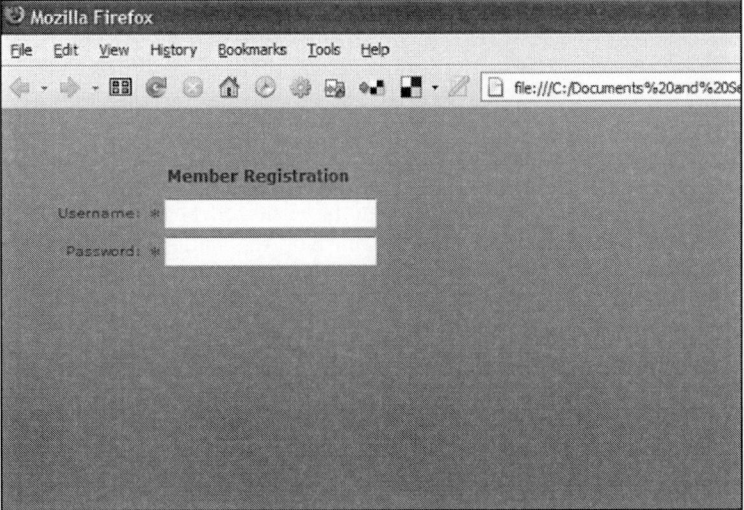

Figure 8-5. <mx:FormItem/> tags inside a form make laying out a form easy.

In the same fashion, I add the rest of the basic fields for a member registration. In addition, I add a Button component, also in a <mx:FormItem/> tag. With the rest of the fields in place, the MXML now looks like this:

```
<?xml version="1.0" encoding="utf-8"?>
<mx:Application
  width="560" height="300"
  xmlns:mx="http://www.adobe.com/2006/mxml" layout="vertical"
  xmlns:forms="com.almerblank.rmx.forms.*">

  <forms:NewMemberForm
    width="100%" height="100%">

    <mx:FormHeading label="Member Registration"/>

    <mx:FormItem label="Username:" required="true">
      <mx:TextInput id="tf_username"/>
    </mx:FormItem>
    <mx:FormItem label="Password:" required="true">
      <mx:TextInput id="tf_password"/>
    </mx:FormItem>
    <mx:FormItem label="Confirm Password:" required="true">
      <mx:TextInput id="tf_confirmPassword"/>
    </mx:FormItem>
    <mx:FormItem label="Email:" required="true">
      <mx:TextInput id="tf_email"/>
    </mx:FormItem>
    <mx:FormItem label="Confirm Email:" required="true">
      <mx:TextInput id="tf_confirmEmail"/>
    </mx:FormItem>
    <mx:FormItem>
      <mx:Button id="btn_submit" label="Sign up"/>
    </mx:FormItem>

  </forms:NewMemberForm>

</mx:Application>
```

For a basic member registration, I will add an Email field and Confirm Password and Confirm Email fields. I'll talk more about confirming the values later in the section "Validating user input." For now, the form is set up to have its functionality fleshed out. Here I include the id properties to the text components that will be gathering data. Compiled, the form appears as shown in Figure 8-6.

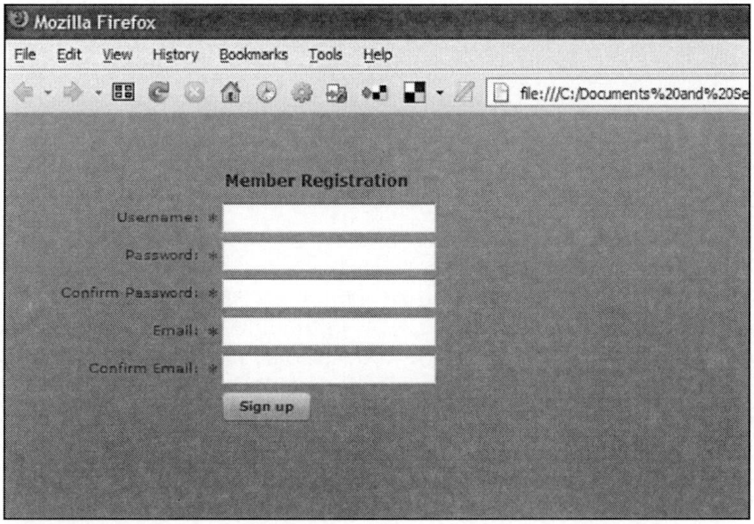

Figure 8-6. The completed form layout

Now that the layout is complete, the next step is to make this form collect user input as data. In the next section, I show you how to do just that.

Handling user input

To make this form work, a few things are needed. First, the form needs to have a place to store data. Then the data can be stored. But the form should first make sure the data being collected is complete and correct. Once the data is ready, a submit button should send the form data to the server to be processed and respond to the server's response. I will use the Flex validators to validate data on the client side and explore other features to help with data validation. First, let's take a look at collecting data.

Collecting the user input

The first step in processing the form is to collect the data in it. Before that happens, the code needs a couple of changes. First, I add an instance of the DTO I made at the beginning of the chapter to store the data in the NewMemberForm class:

```
package com.almerblank.rmx.forms
{
  import mx.containers.Form;
  import com.almerblank.rmx.dto.Member;

  public class NewMemberForm extends Form
  {
    [Bindable]
    public var memberInfo:Member = new Member();
```

```
      public function NewMemberForm()
      {
        super();
      }

    }
  }
```

An instance of the Member DTO is added as memberInfo. I also make the property bindable, so I can bind the text fields to the object's properties. Now there is a place to store the data. To update the object, I use the change event of the text fields, right in the MXML. With all the fields connected to their respective properties in the DTO object, the MXML should now look like this:

```
<mx:Application
  width="560" height="300"
  xmlns:mx="http://www.adobe.com/2006/mxml" layout="vertical"
  xmlns:forms="com.almerblank.rmx.forms.*">

  <forms:NewMemberForm id="newMemberForm"
    width="100%" height="100%">

    <mx:FormHeading label="Member Registration"/>

    <mx:FormItem label="Username:" required="true">
      <mx:TextInput id="tf_username"➥
change="this.newMemberForm.memberInfo.username =➥
 this.tf_username.text"/>
    </mx:FormItem>
    <mx:FormItem label="Password:" required="true">
      <mx:TextInput id="tf_password"➥
change="this.newMemberForm.memberInfo.password =➥
 this.tf_password.text"/>
    </mx:FormItem>
    <mx:FormItem label="Confirm Password:" required="true">
      <mx:TextInput id="tf_confirmPassword"/>
    </mx:FormItem>
    <mx:FormItem label="Email:" required="true">
      <mx:TextInput id="tf_email"➥
change="this.newMemberForm.memberInfo.email =➥
 this.tf_email.text"/>
    </mx:FormItem>
    <mx:FormItem label="Confirm Email:" required="true">
      <mx:TextInput id="tf_confirmEmail"/>
    </mx:FormItem>
    <mx:FormItem>
      <mx:Button id="btn_submit" label="Sign up"/>
    </mx:FormItem>

  </forms:NewMemberForm>
</mx:Application>
```

First change is to the NewMemberForm opening tag, where I add an id value. Giving the tag an id lets me talk to the properties of the class from the scope of the other objects within the main application. Then, in the change event of the Username, Password, and Email fields, the relevant property is set to the field's text property. This is all that needs to happen to have the object updated every time a user inputs a value. If you were to compile this application now, you would see nothing has changed. But the values typed in the three fields would be properly updated as they are being typed. If you were to enter a password, you would notice that it is visible. To change this and hide the password, I simply add the displayAsPassword property to the Password and Confirm Password fields. The MXML should look like this now:

```
...
    </mx:FormItem>
    <mx:FormItem label="Password:" required="true">
      <mx:TextInput id="tf_password" displayAsPassword="true"➥
change="this.newMemberForm.memberInfo.password =➥
this.tf_password.text"/>
    </mx:FormItem>
    <mx:FormItem label="Confirm Password:" required="true">
      <mx:TextInput id="tf_confirmPassword" displayAsPassword="true"/>
    </mx:FormItem>
    <mx:FormItem label="Email:" required="true">
```

After these changes, anything typed into the Password and Confirm Password fields is now hidden from view. I placed the displayAsPassword properties after the id property only because of personal preference. I like to read the identifiers first, but the placement of properties in an MXML tag is completely up to you. By default, Flex uses asterisks to hide password characters, as shown in Figure 8-7.

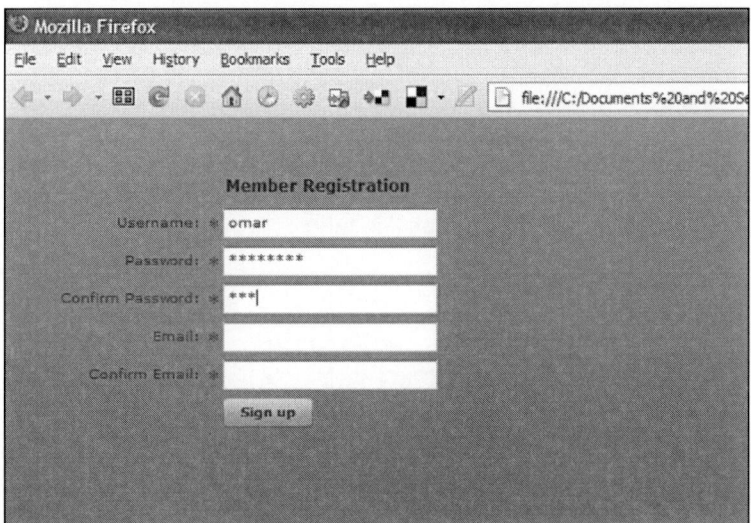

Figure 8-7. The password is hidden by asterisks as it is typed when displayAsPassword is set to true.

Validating user input

The form is now gathering the data it needs to send to the server, but the Confirm Password and Confirm Email fields don't do anything, and I don't necessarily need to input an e-mail address in the Email or Confirm Email fields. In this section, I show you how I handle the data validation on all the Flex forms on the RMX. Using the Flex built-in validation classes, I show how to validate the data as it gets entered and on form submission.

The validators array

To make the validation of the fields easy on submission, the Validator class (which is the parent class of all the built-in validators) provides a method to fire multiple validators. To do this, an array of all the validators of the form is required. While there are several ways to harness the validator events, in this case I preferred to make an array in the MXML, which I can then access from within the class. I set up the array in the MXML like this:

```
<?xml version="1.0" encoding="utf-8"?>
<mx:Application
  width="560" height="300"
  xmlns:mx="http://www.adobe.com/2006/mxml" layout="vertical"
  xmlns:forms="com.almerblank.rmx.forms.*">

  <mx:Array id="formValidators">

  </mx:Array>

  <forms:NewMemberForm id="newMemberForm"
    width="100%" height="100%">

    ...
</mx:Application>
```

The array must be right under the Application tag, so that the validators compile correctly. To reference the array of validators from the form class, I add a bindable public property that can be used to reference the array. The class change should look like this:

```
package com.almerblank.rmx.forms
{
  import mx.containers.Form;
  import com.almerblank.rmx.dto.Member;

  public class NewMemberForm extends Form
  {
    [Bindable]
    public var memberInfo:Member = new Member();

    [Bindable]
    public var validators:Array;
```

```
        public function NewMemberForm()
        {
          super();
        }

    }
}
```

Now in the MXML, I bind the array to the form property like this:

```
<?xml version="1.0" encoding="utf-8"?>
<mx:Application
  width="560" height="300"
  xmlns:mx="http://www.adobe.com/2006/mxml" layout="vertical"
  xmlns:forms="com.almerblank.rmx.forms.*">

  <mx:Array id="formValidators">

  </mx:Array>

  <forms:NewMemberForm id="newMemberForm"➥
  validators="{this.formValidators}"
    width="100%" height="100%">
```

The validators array is built and bound to the validators property of the array. Now it's time to build the validators.

Using the Validator classes

Both the Username and Password fields require a StringValidator to effectively validate the input. I start by validating the username. In the formValidators array, I make the first validator for the Username field:

```
<?xml version="1.0" encoding="utf-8"?>
<mx:Application
  width="560" height="300"
  xmlns:mx="http://www.adobe.com/2006/mxml" layout="vertical"
  xmlns:forms="com.almerblank.rmx.forms.*">

  <mx:Array id="formValidators">
    <mx:StringValidator
      source="{this.tf_username}"
      property="text"
      trigger="{this.tf_username}"
      triggerEvent="change"
      listener="{this.tf_username}"
      required="true"
      requiredFieldError="The user name field is required, please
enter a user name."
      minLength="6"
```

```
            maxLength="20"
            tooLongError="The user name you entered is too long, please
            make your user name between 6 and 20 characters."
            tooShortError="The user name you entered is too short, please
            make your user name between 6 and 20 characters."
            />
        </mx:Array>

        <forms:NewMemberForm id="newMemberForm"➥
    validators="{this.formValidators}"
        width="100%" height="100%">
```

The first seven properties are used in most of the validators. From top to bottom, this is what they do:

- source: The property that is bound to the text component being validated.
- property: The property of the text component linked to the source that should be validated, most commonly the text property. Must be set if the source is set.
- trigger: The text field that triggers the validation; usually the same as source.
- triggerEvent: The event on the text field that triggers the validation. I like to use change so that the validators trigger as the user types. Other events you can use to trigger the validator are valueCommit and focusOut.
- listener: The text component that will display a red border and the error message if the text in the text component is invalid. This value also is usually the same as source.
- required: A Boolean flag used to designate the field as required, meaning it must meet all validation requirements.
- requiredError: The property that sets the error to be displayed if the validation is not valid.
- minLength: The minimum length allowed for a valid entry.
- maxLength: The maximum length allowed for a valid entry.
- tooShortError: The property that sets the error to be displayed if the string is too short.
- tooLongError: The property that sets the error to be displayed if the string is too long.

The last four properties are only found on a StringValidator. Each validator contains unique properties relevant to the data that they validate. The Flex Language Reference documents do a good job of outlining all the properties and what they are used for.

I also need a StringValidator for the password:

```
<?xml version="1.0" encoding="utf-8"?>
<mx:Application
  width="560" height="300"
  xmlns:mx="http://www.adobe.com/2006/mxml" layout="vertical"
  xmlns:forms="com.almerblank.rmx.forms.*">

  <mx:Array id="formValidators">
    <mx:StringValidator
      source="{this.tf_username}"
```

```
            property="text"
            trigger="{this.tf_username}"
            triggerEvent="change"
            listener="{this.tf_username}"
            required="true"
            requiredFieldError="The user name field is required, please
            enter a user name."
            minLength="6"
            maxLength="20"
            tooLongError="The user name you entered is too long, please
            make your user name between 6 and 20 characters."
            tooShortError="The user name you entered is too short, please
            make your user name between 6 and 20 characters."
            />
        <mx:StringValidator
            source="{this.tf_password}"
            property="text"
            trigger="{this.tf_password}"
            triggerEvent="change"
            listener="{this.tf_password}"
            required="true"
            requiredFieldError="The password field is required, please
            enter a password."
            minLength="6"
            maxLength="20"
            tooLongError="The password you entered is too long, please ➡
    make your password is between 4 and 20 characters."
            tooShortError="The password you entered is too short, please ➡
    make your password is between 4 and 20 characters."
            />
    </mx:Array>
    ...
```

The properties are exactly the same as for the username validator, except the error messages are tailored to the Password field, and the Text component it's bound to is of course the Password field. To validate the Email field, the StringValidator does not provide the validation I need. Next, I demonstrate the similarities of working with another type of validator class, as well as use the unique properties of the validator.

The EmailValidator

This validator is perfect for the Email field. Although it can't specifically say whether the e-mail address is actually valid and can receive e-mail, it does provide the necessary logic to ensure the format of the string data matches that of an e-mail. Under the two string validators, I add the EmailValidator:

```
        ...
        make your user name between 6 and 20 characters."
          tooShortError="The user name you entered is too short, please
          make your user name between 6 and 20 characters."
          />
```

```
      <mx:StringValidator
        source="{this.tf_password}"
        property="text"
        trigger="{this.tf_password}"
        triggerEvent="change"
        listener="{this.tf_password}"
        required="true"
        requiredFieldError="The password field is required, please
        enter a password."
        minLength="6"
        maxLength="20"
        tooLongError="The password you entered is too long, please
        make your password is between 4 and 20 characters."
        tooShortError="The password you entered is too short, please
        make your password is between 4 and 20 characters."
        />
      <mx:EmailValidator
        source="{this.tf_email}"
        property="text"
        trigger="{this.tf_email}"
        triggerEvent="change"
        listener="{this.tf_email}"
        required="true"
        requiredFieldError="The email field is required, please fill
        out your email."
        invalidCharError="Your email has an invalid character."
        invalidDomainError="Your email address has an invalid domain."
        invalidIPDomainError="Your address has an invalid IP domain."
        invalidPeriodsInDomainError="There are invalid periods in
        your email domain."
        missingAtSignError="Your email is missing an @ sign."
        missingPeriodInDomainError="Your email domain is
        missing a period."
        missingUsernameError="Your email is missing a user name."
        tooManyAtSignsError="Your email has too many @
        signs, please reduce to one @ sign."
        />
    </mx:Array>

  <forms:NewMemberForm id="newMemberForm"➥
  validators="{this.formValidators}"
    width="100%" height="100%">
  ...
```

As you can see in the code, the first seven properties are identical to those of the StringValidator, but after the common properties are eight different custom error messages that can be set for all of the different types of errors the validator can detect. All of these properties have default values, but they're available to set with more human-readable error messages that can provide more insight into what is wrong with a particular entry.

More validation

Flex comes with a variety of validators. Phone numbers, credit cards, numbers—they all have validators to make validating data easier. There is also a regular expression validator available for those times when the built-in validators aren't enough. On top of all these, there are two very handy properties that I use on all the forms I code. The `restrict` property and the `maxChars` property of Text components help to provide the first level of validation very effectively.

The restrict property

The `restrict` property works on both the TextInput and TextArea components. The default value for this property is `null`. Either a `null` value or an empty string will have no effect on the components. When used with a string, the Text component will restrict the characters allowed to be entered in the component to either the specific characters typed or the range of characters entered. You can enter ranges of characters by using a hyphen in a regular expression type notation. Entering a string like A-Za-z0-9 would allow all uppercase characters, all lowercase characters, and all numbers. This is because the string does not start with a ^ character, so it initially disallows all characters and then permits the ones specified in the string. If the string started with the ^ character, it would allow all characters to start and disallow each character that came after. If the `restrict` property was assigned a string like ^0-9, the components would allow all characters, and then disallow all digits from 0 through 9. Finally, because characters like ^ and - have special meanings when the string is interpreted, if you wanted to allow the - character as one of the characters that can be entered into the text component, you would have to escape the character. This means that you have to use a \ character before it, telling the parser to ignore this character as an operative. So I could change the first example to something like A-Za-z0-9\-.

> *If you want to allow a space, you can escape the space in the same way that you escape a hyphen, by putting a \ before the space.*

For the username and password, I don't want to allow any punctuation or spaces. I simply want alphanumeric characters. So I make the following changes to the form:

```
...
  </mx:Array>

  <forms:NewMemberForm id="newMemberForm"➡
validators="{this.formValidators}"
    width="100%" height="100%">


    <mx:FormHeading label="Member Registration"/>

    <mx:FormItem label="Username:" required="true">
       <mx:TextInput id="tf_username"➡
change="this.newMemberForm.memberInfo.username =➡
this.tf_username.text" restrict="A-Za-z0-9"/>
    </mx:FormItem>
    <mx:FormItem label="Password:" required="true">
```

```
            <mx:TextInput id="tf_password" displayAsPassword="true"➥
        change="this.newMemberForm.memberInfo.password =➥
        this.tf_password.text" restrict="A-Za-z0-9"/>
          </mx:FormItem>
          <mx:FormItem label="Confirm Password:" required="true">
            <mx:TextInput id="tf_confirmPassword" displayAsPassword="true"➥
        restrict="A-Za-z0-9"/>
          </mx:FormItem>
          <mx:FormItem label="Email:" required="true">
            <mx:TextInput id="tf_email"➥
        change="this.newMemberForm.memberInfo.email = this.tf_email.text"/>
          </mx:FormItem>
          <mx:FormItem label="Confirm Email:" required="true">
            <mx:TextInput id="tf_confirmEmail"/>
          </mx:FormItem>
          <mx:FormItem>
            <mx:Button id="btn_submit" label="Sign up"/>
          </mx:FormItem>

        </forms:NewMemberForm>

      </mx:Application>
```

When the application is compiled, the text fields now only accept alphanumeric characters, no spaces, and no punctuation. This property really helps to ensure that you are receiving exactly the data that the application requires.

The maxChars property

Another property that is effective in ensuring clean and proper data is the maxChars property. It simply limits the number of characters allowed in a text component. Although the StringValidators have a maxLength property, it's still good to include the maxChars property to not allow too many characters to ever be present.

After setting the property on the form, the form now looks like this:

```
        <forms:NewMemberForm id="newMemberForm"➥
        validators="{this.formValidators}"
          width="100%" height="100%">


          <mx:FormHeading label="Member Registration"/>

          <mx:FormItem label="Username:" required="true">
            <mx:TextInput id="tf_username"➥
        change="this.newMemberForm.memberInfo.username =➥
        this.tf_username.text" restrict="A-Za-z0-9" maxChars="20"/>
          </mx:FormItem>
          <mx:FormItem label="Password:" required="true">
            <mx:TextInput id="tf_password" displayAsPassword="true"➥
```

```
       change="this.newMemberForm.memberInfo.password =➥
       this.tf_password.text" restrict="A-Za-z0-9" maxChars="20"/>
          </mx:FormItem>
          <mx:FormItem label="Confirm Password:" required="true">
            <mx:TextInput id="tf_confirmPassword" displayAsPassword="true"➥
       restrict="A-Za-z0-9" maxChars="20"/>
          </mx:FormItem>
          <mx:FormItem label="Email:" required="true">
            <mx:TextInput id="tf_email"➥
       change="this.newMemberForm.memberInfo.email =➥
       this.tf_email.text" maxChars="319"/>
          </mx:FormItem>
          <mx:FormItem label="Confirm Email:" required="true">
            <mx:TextInput id="tf_confirmEmail" maxChars="319"/>
          </mx:FormItem>
          <mx:FormItem>
            <mx:Button id="btn_submit" label="Sign up"/>
          </mx:FormItem>

       </forms:NewMemberForm>

     </mx:Application>
```

The Username and Password fields will now make sure the lengths of the strings are a maximum of 20 characters. Together with the string validators, you can be sure that the lengths will not exceed the max allowed. The Email field is set to 319 because that is the maximum number of characters possible for any e-mail address. The username may only be 64 characters long, including the "@" sign, which makes 63 available to choose as a username for the e-mail account. The remaining 255 characters are for the rest of the e-mail address.

Confirming the password and e-mail address

Flex natively comes with a variety of validators to validate form data. The list includes the following:

- CreditCardValidator
- CurrencyValidator
- DateValidator
- EmailValidator
- NumberValidator
- PhoneNumberValidator
- RegExpValidator
- SocialSecurityValidator
- StringValidator
- ZipCodeValidator

Not included in this list is a way to validate and confirm that one field is equal to another. To accomplish that task, I could write some sort of if statement that would check that both the Confirm Password and Confirm Email fields are equal to their counterparts and bring up an alert dialog box if they are not equal. The problem here is that the values would not be validated until an event triggered the event handler to run that comparison.

In order to handle the validation of the Confirm Password and Confirm Email fields more effectively, I wrote a custom validator class. The sole purpose of the class is to make sure that the field it is assigned to equals the contents of another Text component to qualify as valid. This class makes validating the data while the user inputs the confirmation password or e-mail easy. It also helps to easily include these fields when the form gets validated on clicking the submit button, which I will show you how to code in the next section.

First I want to show the class code and then explain how I have extended an existing validator to make this new validator. The class looks like this:

```
package com.almerblank.libs.flex.validators
{
    import mx.validators.StringValidator;
    import mx.validators.ValidationResult;
    import mx.core.UIComponent;

public class ConfirmTextFieldValidator extends StringValidator
{
  [Bindable]
  public var confirmAgainst:UIComponent;
  public var validateProperty:String;
  public var fieldsDontMatchError:String = "The fields do not match,
  please make sure both fields match";

  public function ConfirmTextFieldValidator()
  {
    super();
  }

  override protected function doValidation(value:Object):Array
  {
    var result:Array = super.doValidation(value);
    var r:ValidationResult;

    if (result.length == 0)
    {

      if (value != confirmAgainst[validateProperty])
      {
        r = new ValidationResult(true);
        r.errorMessage = fieldsDontMatchError;
        result.push(r);
      }
      else if (value == confirmAgainst[validateProperty])
```

```
            {
                // do nothing, value is valid
            }
            else
            {
                r = new ValidationResult(true);
                r.errorMessage = fieldsDontMatchError;
                result.push(r);
            }
        }

        return result;
    }

  }
}
```

This class extends the StringValidator class so that all of the properties and methods available to a StringValidator are available to the ConfirmTextFieldValidator, which would also be validating a string value. In the constructor, all that is needed is a call to the super(), which starts the StringValidator instance as a normal StringValidator.

The class, however, has two new properties. The validateProperty is the property to use on the component you're checking against. The confirmAgainst property is a reference to the text component that the confirmation field should equal. The type is set to UIComponent so that it can accept either a TextInput component or a TextArea component. The other new property is fieldsDontMatchError, which has a default value of "The fields do not match, please make sure both fields match". This property is also public so that it can be customized for the field it's confirming.

The next piece of code is the part that actually adds the logic to confirm the field against another field. To accomplish this, I use the override keyword, which requires that I follow the exact signature of the method I want to override in the superclass. In the superclass, the doValidation() method accepts a data object, which gets processed to make sure it meets all the requirements to validate. If the value does not validate, the method returns an array of ValidationResult objects, each containing details of what it found wrong. On the first line, I make a call to the super.doValidation() method and pass the data object to validate it, and I store the result in a function variable named result.

The first thing that is checked is the length of the result variable. If the result is not equal to 0, the application skips the code and simply returns the result of the super.doValidation method and moves on. If the result is equal to 0, meaning the super.doValidation method did not find any errors, the application proceeds to check the Text component values. First is the if statement, which checks whether the value of the confirmation Text component is not equal to the text property of the confirmAgainst Text component reference. If they're not equal, a new ValidationResult object is instantiated, and the errorMessage property is set equal to the fieldsDontMatchError value, so it appears as the tooltip text on the Text component when it shows up as invalid. Then the ValidationResult object gets added to the result array returned by the super.doValidation() method.

The next section of the if statement checks for the values that are equal to each other, which would satisfy the conditions for a valid entry. In this case, the statement does not perform any additional logic because no errors are found.

Finally, if any other condition not specified happens, it returns an error, same as when the fields do not match. This section of the if statement should never really be reached, but I include it just in case.

To use this validator in MXML like the Flex validators, simply start a new tag and begin the class name once you have added the class in the proper folder in your project. With the properties set, the MXML should look something like this:

```xml
<?xml version="1.0" encoding="utf-8"?>
<mx:Application
  width="560" height="300"
  xmlns:mx="http://www.adobe.com/2006/mxml" layout="vertical"
  xmlns:forms="com.almerblank.rmx.forms.*"
    xmlns:validators="com.almerblank.libs.flex.validators.*">

  <mx:Array id="formValidators">
    <mx:StringValidator
      source="{this.tf_username}"
      property="text"
      trigger="{this.tf_username}"
      triggerEvent="change"
      listener="{this.tf_username}"
      required="true"
      requiredFieldError="The user name field is required, please
      enter a user name."
      minLength="6"
      maxLength="20"
      tooLongError="The user name you entered is too long, please
      make your user name between 6 and 20 characters."
      tooShortError="The user name you entered is too short, please
      make your user name between 6 and 20 characters."
      />
    <mx:StringValidator
      source="{this.tf_password}"
      property="text"
      trigger="{this.tf_password}"
      triggerEvent="change"
      listener="{this.tf_password}"
      required="true"
      requiredFieldError="The password field is required, please
      enter a password."
      minLength="6"
      maxLength="20"
      tooLongError="The password you entered is too long, please
      make your password is between 4 and 20 characters."
      tooShortError="The password you entered is too short, please
      make your password is between 4 and 20 characters."
```

```
    />
<mx:EmailValidator
  source="{this.tf_email}"
  property="text"
  trigger="{this.tf_email}"
  triggerEvent="change"
  listener="{this.tf_email}"
  required="true"
  requiredFieldError="The email field is required, please fill
  out your email."
  invalidCharError="Your email has an invalid character."
  invalidDomainError="Your email address has an invalid domain."
  invalidIPDomainError="Your address has an invalid IP domain."
  invalidPeriodsInDomainError="There are invalid periods in
  your email domain."
  missingAtSignError="Your email is missing an @ sign."
  missingPeriodInDomainError="Your domain is missing a period."
  missingUsernameError="Your email is missing a user name."
  tooManyAtSignsError="Your email has too many @ signs,
  please reduce to one @ sign."
  />
<validators:ConfirmTextFieldValidator
  source="{this.tf_confirmPassword}"
  property="text"
  trigger="{this.tf_confirmPassword}"
  triggerEvent="change"
  listener="{this.tf_confirmPassword}"
  required="true"
  requiredFieldError="The confirm password field is
  required, please confirm your password."
  confirmAgainst="{this.tf_password}"
  validateProperty="text"
  fieldsDontMatchError="The passwords do not match, please
  make sure that both of your passwords are the same."
  />
<validators:ConfirmTextFieldValidator
  source="{this.tf_confirmEmail}"
  property="text"
  trigger="{this.tf_confirmEmail}"
  triggerEvent="change"
  listener="{this.tf_confirmEmail}"
  required="true"
  requiredFieldError="The confirm email field is required,
  please confirm your email."
  confirmAgainst="{this.tf_email}"
  validateProperty="text"
  fieldsDontMatchError="The emails do not match, please make
  sure that both of your emails are the same."
  />
```

219

```
            </mx:Array>

            <forms:NewMemberForm id="newMemberForm"➡
         validators="{this.formValidators}"
            width="100%" height="100%">


            <mx:FormHeading label="Member Registration"/>

            <mx:FormItem label="Username:" required="true">
              <mx:TextInput id="tf_username"➡
         change="this.newMemberForm.memberInfo.username =➡
         this.tf_username.text" restrict="A-Za-z0-9" maxChars="20"/>
            </mx:FormItem>
            <mx:FormItem label="Password:" required="true">
              <mx:TextInput id="tf_password" displayAsPassword="true"➡
         change="this.newMemberForm.memberInfo.password =➡
         this.tf_password.text" restrict="A-Za-z0-9" maxChars="20"/>
            </mx:FormItem>
            <mx:FormItem label="Confirm Password:" required="true">
              <mx:TextInput id="tf_confirmPassword" displayAsPassword="true"➡
         restrict="A-Za-z0-9" maxChars="20"/>
            </mx:FormItem>
            <mx:FormItem label="Email:" required="true">
              <mx:TextInput id="tf_email"➡
         change="this.newMemberForm.memberInfo.email = this.tf_email.text"➡
         maxChars="319"/>
            </mx:FormItem>
            <mx:FormItem label="Confirm Email:" required="true">
              <mx:TextInput id="tf_confirmEmail" maxChars="319"/>
            </mx:FormItem>
            <mx:FormItem>
              <mx:Button id="btn_submit" label="Sign up"/>
            </mx:FormItem>

          </forms:NewMemberForm>

        </mx:Application>
```

Except for the tag namespace, the ConfirmTextFieldValidators look almost identical to Flex validators. Two new properties appear after the first seven common to most validators; these are responsible for assigning a field to validate against and an error to display if the fields do not match. When the
application is compiled now, the confirmation fields will glow red and display the custom error on
hover while you type until the text component contains the same value as the field it is assigned to
confirm.

Now all the code is in place to make sure that any input that users are making gets stored and validated, presenting users with uniform errors for all text fields when they do not meet necessary
requirements. Next, let's take a look at handling the form submission.

Submitting the form

With all the validators in place, the form is ready to take user input. What the current code doesn't provide is a way to make sure that all the validators come back as valid when a user attempts to submit the form. In this section, I talk about handling this, and I also talk about how I manage all the different remoting calls of an application.

Validating the form on submission

In order to validate the form on submission, I demonstrate using another validator. The Validator class, which is the parent of all validators, provides a public static method named validateAll(), which accepts an array of validators. The method takes the array and executes each of the validators, storing all of the returned errors in an array that it returns. In the NewMemberForm class, I add a new method as follows:

```
package com.almerblank.rmx.forms
{
  import mx.containers.Form;
  import com.almerblank.rmx.dto.Member;
  import mx.validators.Validator;
  import mx.controls.Alert;

  public class NewMemberForm extends Form
  {
    [Bindable]
    public var memberInfo:Member = new Member();

    [Bindable]
    public var validators:Array;

    public function NewMemberForm()
    {
      super();
    }

    public function validateForm():void
    {
      var validationResults:Array;
      validationResults = Validator.validateAll(this.validators);

      if (validationResults.length == 0)
      {
        // form is valid
      }
      else
      {
        Alert.show("The form still contains invalid fields, ➥
        please fill out the form completely and make sure ➥
        none of the fields glow red.", "Invalid Fields");
```

```
          }
        }

      }
    }
```

The new method, validateForm(), takes the public property validators, which is bound to the array of validators in the application and runs it through the validateAll() method of the Validator class. The result is stored in a validationResults function variable. Next, the method checks whether the length of the results is 0; if so, the form is valid, and I can add the code to handle a valid form within the if statement. Otherwise, the length would be greater than 0, indicating the presence of errors. In this case, an alert dialog box is displayed informing the user that there are invalid fields in the form. To call this method in the MXML, I can simply do this:

```
        ...
          </mx:FormItem>
          <mx:FormItem label="Confirm Email:" required="true">
            <mx:TextInput id="tf_confirmEmail" maxChars="319"/>
          </mx:FormItem>
          <mx:FormItem>
            <mx:Button id="btn_submit" label="Sign up"➥
      click="this.newMemberForm.validateForm()"/>
          </mx:FormItem>

      </forms:NewMemberForm>

    </mx:Application>
```

Near the bottom of the code I add a click event to the submit button. Here it executes the new validateForm() method just added to the NewMemberForm class. This form is now ready to be sent off to the server.

Managing remoting calls

In most of today's rich media applications, the list of calls to the server can start to get pretty long. Later down the road, the need to change the name of a remote call or path to a remote call can be pretty daunting if the developer has not looked at the code in a very long time. Global searches in Eclipse are fine and help to get this kind of job done, but properly preparing for this in advance can make the job even easier.

To manage remoting calls in projects I code, I write a gateway class to centralize all the service calls, making it easier to edit and call different remote methods. A sample class would look something like this:

```
      package com.almerblank.rmx.utils
      {
        import flash.net.Responder;
        import mx.managers.CursorManager;
```

```
public class RMXGateway
{
  // service calls
  public static const ADD_NEW_MEMBER:String = "Members.addMember";
  public static const DELETE_MEMBER:String = "Members.deleteMember";

  // gateway url
  private static const _gatewayURL:String =➡
"http://www.yoururl.com/amfphp/gateway.php";

  // gateway variables
  private static var _gateway:RemotingConnection;
  private static var _onSuccess:Function;
  private static var _onFault:Function;

  /**
   * The constructor, should not be used to instantiate a variable
   * as this class is not meant to be instantiated.
   *
   * @return
   *
   */
  public function RMXGateway() {}

  /**
   * The <code>call()</code> method is used to make a remoting call.
   *
   * @param command String path to the remote method being called.
   * @param success Function that is called on a successful
   * communication with the server.
   * @param fault Function that is called when the server
   * returns an error.
   * @param data Data object sent to the remote method
   * @param showBusyCursor Defaults to true to handle the busy
   * cursor while communicating with the server. Set to false if you
   * do not want a busy cursor.
   *
   */
  public static function call(command:String, success:Function, ➡
fault:Function, data:* = null, showBusyCursor:Boolean = true):void
  {
    _gateway = new RemotingConnection(_gatewayURL);

    _onSuccess = success;
    _onFault = fault;


    var __responder:Responder = new Responder(onSuccess, onFault);
```

```
            if (data)
            {
              _gateway.call(command, __responder, data);
            }
            else
            {
              _gateway.call(command, __responder);
            }

            if (showBusyCursor)
            {
              CursorManager.setBusyCursor();
            }


          }

          /**
           * Private method that handles firing the function that was
           * specified in the call method and removes the busy cursor.
           *
           * @param result
           *
           */
          private static function onSuccess(result:*):void
          {
            _onSuccess(result);

            CursorManager.removeBusyCursor();
          }
          /**
           * Private method that handles firing the fault function that was
           * specified in the call method and removes the busy cursor.
           *
           * @param fault
           *
           */
          private static function onFault(fault:Object):void
          {
            _onFault(fault);

            CursorManager.removeBusyCursor();
          }



        }
      }
```

```
import flash.net.NetConnection;
import flash.net.ObjectEncoding;

class RemotingConnection extends NetConnection {

  public function RemotingConnection(sURL:String)
  {
    objectEncoding = ObjectEncoding.AMF0;
    if(sURL){
      connect(sURL);
    }
  }

  public function AppendToGatewayUrl(s:String):void{
    //
  }
}
```

This class has public static constants, one for each remoting call that exists in the application. The class is set up with static methods, allowing me to call remoting calls from anywhere in the application without having to instantiate a new object. The class also handles the busy cursor management for me, so that I don't have to write that extra code each time. To use this method, I place the call to the ADD_NEW_MEMBER remoting call in the successful if conditional. The code would look like this:

```
package com.almerblank.rmx.forms
{
  import mx.containers.Form;
  import com.almerblank.rmx.dto.Member;
  import mx.validators.Validator;
  import mx.controls.Alert;
  import com.almerblank.rmx.utils.RMXGateway;

  public class NewMemberForm extends Form
  {
    [Bindable]
    public var memberInfo:Member = new Member();

    [Bindable]
    public var validators:Array;

    public function NewMemberForm()
    {
      super();
    }

    public function validateForm():void
    {
      var validationResults:Array;
      validationResults = Validator.validateAll(validators);
```

```
        if (validationResults.length == 0)
        {
          // form is valid
          RMXGateway.call(RMXGateway.ADD_NEW_MEMBER, onSuccess,➥
onFault, this.memberInfo);
        }
        else
        {
          Alert.show("The form still contains invalid fields, please ➥
          fill out the form completely and make sure none of the ➥
          fields glow red.", "Invalid Fields");
        }
      }

    }
  }
```

The one line I added is using the static call method of the RMXGateway class. The first parameter is the remote method to call, which I access using the public static constants I set up. Next are the onSuccess event handler and the onFault event handler. As the code stands, the application will not compile. The onSuccess and onFault methods need to be declared and handled. However, the remoting call is ready, and the DTO object with all the data is being sent off. Whether you're using a JSP, PHP, or ASP page, the concepts are the same; only the server-side pages and returns will differ.

Forms, PHP, and security

The validation techniques covered for Flex provide a great first line of defense on the client side, ensuring user input is both a valid entry and a valid type the form is expecting. Even with your nice validation done on the client side, you still need to always validate on the server side. In the case of the RMX, the server language is PHP. This section, written by Chris Charlton, covers some security fundamentals to implement when accepting user-generated content.

Security: Being careful with user-supplied content

Trust no one. Trust nothing. This is the serious tone you should respect when dealing with user-generated content. Be cautious with any input freedom you provide any set of users. Being wary of what's submitted keeps you sharp to analyze and scrutinize areas that could be used to hurt or break your application, by mistake or on purpose. Additionally, everyone wants their applications to soar without any friction, but to be honest, the number one area applications experience bumps is around features that allow or deal with user input or generated content. The honest answer is, "Just don't do it." Here, I cover scenarios of accepting user input and ways you can deal with these demands.

The Flash Platform and frameworks like Flex offer great development features that are much safer than standard JavaScript because they go beyond restricted input and simple masking techniques found in most DHTML/Ajax applications. Additionally, JavaScript can be disabled, leaving only your server-side validation as your sole defense, but with a SWF that wouldn't be the case.

The PHP Security Consortium is a great resource for methods and information on all security concerns PHP web apps should deal with. You can visit the PHP Security Consortium at www.phpsec.org. I'd recommend reading all their published articles and their library of publicly available articles. There is even a free tool available on their web site, PhpSecInfo, that outputs security reports and information about your PHP environment and offers suggestions for improvement.

Accepting text and dealing with form data

All applications accept user input generally through forms. No matter the technology, accepting plain text has tons of security concerns, including, but not limited to, SQL injections, database hacks, cross-site scripting (XSS), or at least malformed form data that may result in orphaned (bunk) records. Allowing users markup of any kind, like HTML, CSS, or, even scarier, JavaScript, is treading into deep shark-infested waters. Those seemingly harmless languages can hurt your design, functionality, and even possibly upset advertisers. How? If your users were allowed to add any CSS code freely, folks would learn how to hide all the advertising throughout the application that you may require on free memberships. Obviously, this would destroy all advertising revenue.

Before allowing users to submit fancy markup, you must take care of good old plain text. Not an exciting subject on the surface, but I assure you this is the most dangerous stuff around. So what's the danger? I mentioned things like SQL injections, database hacks, and orphaned or malformed data. These are all very real issues with every web application, public or not. Since RMX is an RIA, you use the Flex framework's form validation features to reduce most, if not all, improper data. Still, you should take no chances; your application tier (PHP) and database (MySQL) layers should each have their own logic for checking what gets posted from your Flex forms.

Accepting user-generated HTML

Allowing HTML can be dangerous if you blindly permit any HTML tag to get saved and parsed through to your presentation layer. It may be true that most social networking sites allow custom HTML to be pasted into member profiles, but that doesn't mean that they let every HTML tag pass untouched.

PHP provides a strip_tags() function that disallows all HTML tags from a string variable. This function strips both HTML tags and PHP code. Now what if you don't want to strip every tag—you want to allow a list of accepted tags? The strip_tags() function has an optional argument that allows you to define an array of allowed HTML tags. Here's an example:

```php
<?php
$allowed_tags = array('a', 'strong', 'em');
$text = '<p>Paragraph one.</p><br/><p>Paragraph <em>two</em>.</p>';
echo strip_tags($text, $allowed_tags);

// Outputs:
// Paragraph one.Paragraph <em>two</em>.
?>
```

Notice the <em> tag in the preceding example. The $allowed_tags array contains the list of HTML tags allowed. There are a lot of HTML tags to remember, so I've categorized the most common tags into groups.

- **Formatting**: This refers to markup used to beautify bodies of text, like `<b>`, `<strong>`, `<i>`, `<em>`, `<br>`, `<q>`, and `<del>`. These tags are generally harmless if you've accounted for them in your CSS ahead of time.

  If you only wish to support or allow XHTML versus HTML, you'll have to run some conversion of tags like the `<b>` tag into their XHTML equivalent, which in this case would be the `<strong>` tag.

- **Structure**: These are tags that help define content structure, like `<h1>`, `<h2>`, `<h3>`, `<h4>`, `<h5>`, `<h6>`, `<p>`, `<abbr>`, `<acronym>`, `<address>`, `<blockquote>`, `<ol>`, `<ul>`, `<li>`, `<dl>`, `<dd>`, and `<dt>`.

- **Layout**: These are tags that can be used to control or modify layout, like `<span>` and `<div>`.

- **Redundant**: Since user-generated HTML content will be parsed inside your `<body>` tag, it'd be no use and harmful for your site to end up with more than one `<body>` tag. You need to be sure these tags (`<head>`, `<body>`, `<html>`, `<link>`, `<meta>`, and the like) are not coming in with the user's content.

- **Script, frame, and style tags**: These are tags that allow additional code or languages embedded to run when a page loads and are therefore extremely dangerous. Suspect tags are `<script>`, `<style>`, `<iframe>`, `<frame>`, `<noscript>`, `<applet>`, `<embed>`, and `<object>`.

This is nowhere near an exhaustive list, but it does cover many of the common tags that can be responsible for causing damage to your site. The official HTML and XHTML specifications are available at the web site of the W3C (www.w3.org), also known as the World Wide Web Consortium. For some, these documents may be boring and too technical for their needs, so another recommendation for quick references of HTML and XHTML is a web site called W3Schools, which can be found at www.w3schools.com.

To be honest, the best and safest solution is to not accept any HTML code, but commercial demands may require you to allow some markup to give users a degree of personalization. Compile a whitelist of tags that will be allowed across your entire application or site. Limits like this need to be documented so every team member, and clients themselves, know what restrictions will always apply when adding object properties and input elements. Too bad this is only half the problem when allowing markup.

Unfortunately, strip_tags() does not modify tag attributes. Tag attributes should be taken as seriously as tags themselves. Any attribute could be exploited. An `<a>` tag's href attribute could activate some scary JavaScript or a link that's not acceptable under your terms-of-use policy. What's worse is that even if you managed to filter href attributes, someone could use an onmouseover attribute that you let get by to run some hidden malicious code. The last thing you want to find is users hiding code that would allow them to siphon cookies from other users, enabling the hacker to log in to the site disguised as another user. A good solution would be hunting down some reliable regular expressions. Or check out a PHP Extension and Application Repository (PEAR) class called HTML_Safe (available online at http://pear.php.net/package/HTML_Safe), which does a good job at cleaning up tags, links, and tag attributes of your choice.

If you have any plans for accepting JavaScript or similar code from users, you multiply your headaches of safely accepting and rendering user content. Most advertisements use JavaScript in their ad code, and you can't trust any code from users. People can use JavaScript for malicious attacks on you and your users, and that would suck. You also can't be sure that everyone's JavaScript code works as intended. Any snippet of copied JavaScript could potentially break the rendering or other scripts of your pages. Not good for you, and not good for your users. If your application doesn't need to accept JavaScript code, don't let it. Starting with plain text or only HTML is more than enough for many users.

Accepting user-generated CSS

Cascading Style Sheets, or CSS, is a W3C recommended standard that helps reduce markup by taking care of all the formatting, styling, and layout for documents. Here, I'll touch on the main aspects of CSS you need to watch out for when securing your application. Since CSS is popular, you can surf the Web on your own to find more detailed discussion on how CSS can compromise your design or security.

The first two questionable CSS properties are display and visibility: both can be used against any area of the page and easily hide required branding and advertisements. Something like this should be a violation of your usage policies, since it's affecting the application in an unintended way and hurts advertisement campaigns.

Here's a usable CSS style declaration that won't fix or prevent anything, but each line should give you some insight into how that style property would hurt your application or site.

```
.fakeEvilStyle, #header, #ads, .ad, #footer, body, #content:before,
#content:after, #content:hover
{
    /* your page will be hidden entirely */
    display: none; visibility: hidden;
    /* your page can be rendered offstage */
    top: -1000; left: -1000;
    /* can add unexpected content to the page */
    content: string('hacked by CSSx0r');
    /* masks your entire site to a 1px by 1px. */
    clip: rect(0px,0px,1px,1px);
    /* fake (invisible) image used for some bad reason */
    backround-image: url('http://site.com/tracking/you_with/fake.jpg');
}

.lessHarmfulStyles, #content, h1, h2, h3, h4, h5, h6, p
{
    /* All harmless but when used together they're suspicious */

    width: 0; /* no width is not what you intended I'm sure */
    height: 0; /* no height is not what you intended either */
    overflow: hidden; /* mixing false width/height makes it suspect */
    z-index: -100; /* moves elements to the "back of the canvas" */
}
```

Again, you should think how each line of the preceding code sample would affect your site if a proficient user has the chance to override your style sheets. As mentioned earlier, just not accepting the input is always the safest move, but you're going to hear it from someone upstairs that his teenage kid can't tweak his profile like on some other site. The only real way to get around this is to take a smarter approach than just looking for style properties. You need to ensure your application forces your own CSS declarations over any set by users while tossing out everything people try to slip by.

A good recommendation for this server magic is CSS Parser, a small PHP class that is available freely at www.phpclasses.org/cssparser. PEAR fans can use a package called HTML_CSS, available at http://pear.php.net/package/HTML_CSS. Both provide methods for handling style sheet declarations and can parse strings and CSS documents to inspect any CSS selector and property. For CSS cleanup jobs, I use classes like CSS Parser to make sure advertisements and their <div> tags don't get altered with "harmless" CSS.

First, imagine your pages have <div> tags wrapped around each advertisement with their class="advertisement" applied. You'll use the CSS Parser class to read your official styles and inspect all user input to make sure users aren't sneaking anything in that could hurt your ads. The following code loads the CSS Parser class, loads your CSS documents, and then prunes unwanted user-generated content:

```php
<?php
include("classes/cssparser.php");

// CSS declarations and properties we're protecting against.
$styles_CSS_should_not_override = array("html", "body",➡
"#nav", ".advertisement");
$bad_CSS_properties = array("display", "visible", "clip",➡
"content", "backround-image");

$css = new cssparser();

// Grab input from the user or database
$css->ParseStr($user_inputted_data);

// Check against each style we defined in an array
foreach ($styles_CSS_should_not_override as $style)
{
    // Subcheck against each property we defined in array
        foreach ($bad_CSS_properties as $property)
            {
            If ($css->Get($style,$property) != "")
            {
            echo("Caught the user using: ".$style. " : ".$property);
            }
        }
}
?>
```

Now this code is pretty small, but it packs a punch. You see the code will go through each CSS style you don't want to get changed by the user in any way and echo onscreen a message if the user did try to sneak in some CSS styles that you've learned aren't so welcomed anymore. This type of whitelist is a prudent approach to any user-generated content you plan to render, no matter the input or format.

As you saw through the HTML and CSS examples, users can affect areas of your site, whether they intended to or not.

Summary

In this chapter, I covered what is necessary to build and process a form using Flex. I discussed setting up a basic form layout, using DTOs with the form, capturing the data, validating the data, and submitting the data. I also talked a bit about creating your own validators and managing your remoting calls. Finally, Chris talked about important security concerns with common CSS, and you saw how any innocent markup language could be a potential hazard for your app—meaning your front end and back end both need to carry checkpoints and scrub data clean before accepting it into your database.

The next chapter will walk you through the development of a user communications panel in Flex.

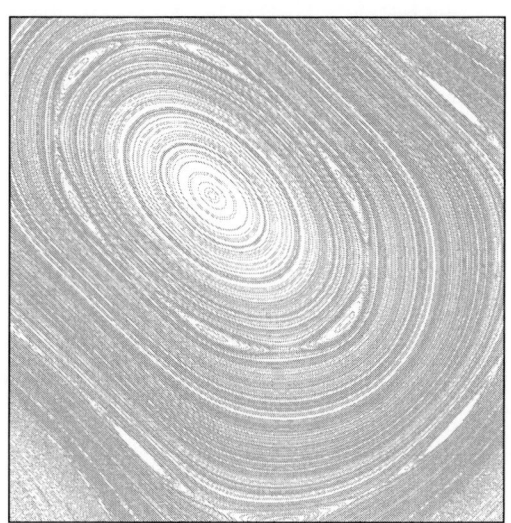

Chapter 9

USER COMMUNICATIONS

By Hasan Otuome

For a massive project like the RMX, you need a system in place that allows RMX system administrators and individual group administrators (partners) to easily communicate with registered users. In this chapter, you'll learn some of the ways we enabled this ability in the RMX using the techniques and methodologies described in earlier chapters.

Building the communications control panel

One of the requirements of the RMX was the ability to create and edit various "Network" e-mail templates to be used by the RMX administrators and partners to communicate with RMX members. We chose to use the Flex framework to build out this feature, as we had previously used it on other client projects with great success. In fact, this feature is merely one of the modules, or screens, comprising the Flex control panel that we built for the RMX.

Once I received the wireframes (wires) for the admin and partner control panels, I had to examine the screens for both to get an idea of what functionality was expected and what controls or components would be required. And, since wires are essentially developer guides, having them available takes a considerable amount of time off of the development process. Figures 9-1 through 9-5 illustrate the various screens required for the communications modules.

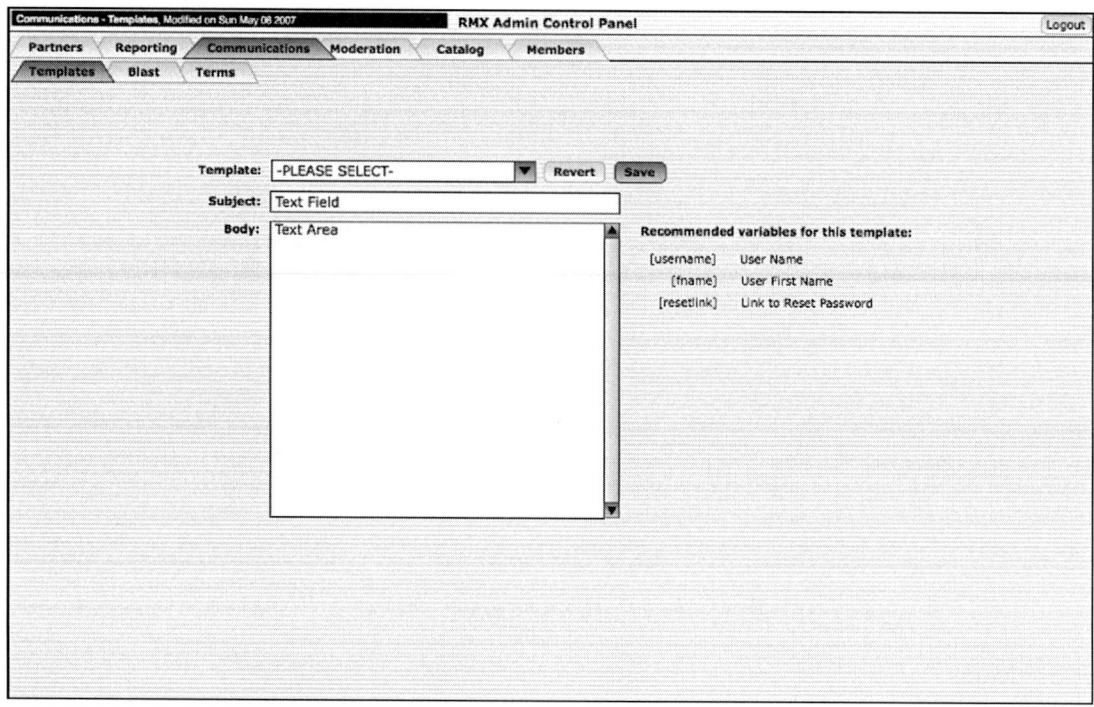

Figure 9-1. Admin e-mail templates screen

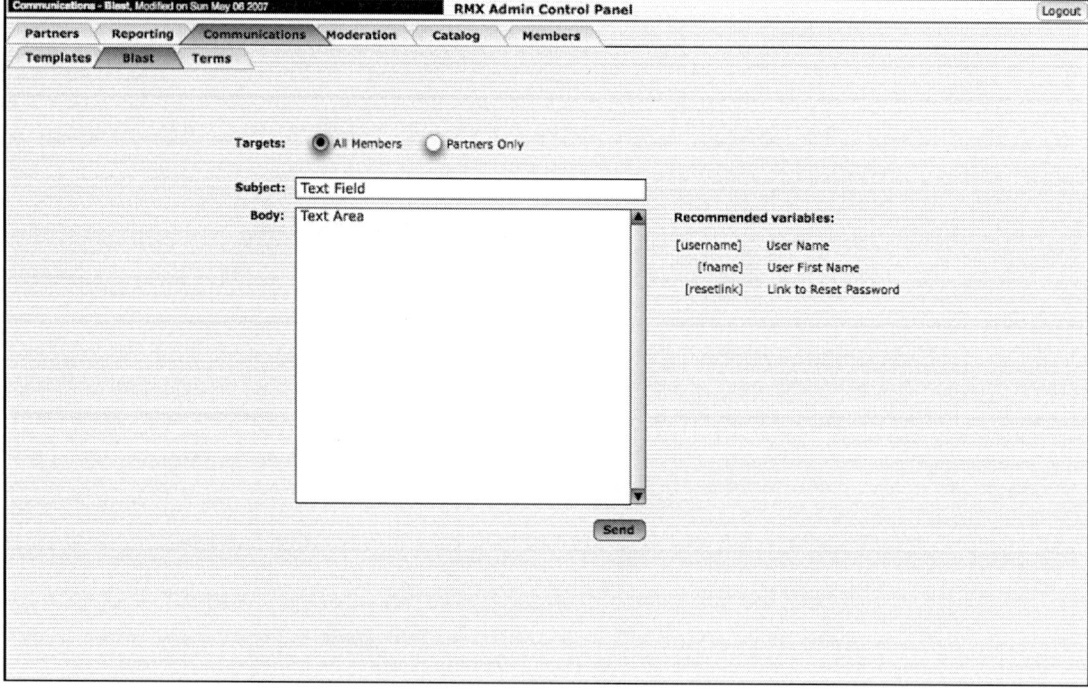

Figure 9-2. Admin e-mail blast screen

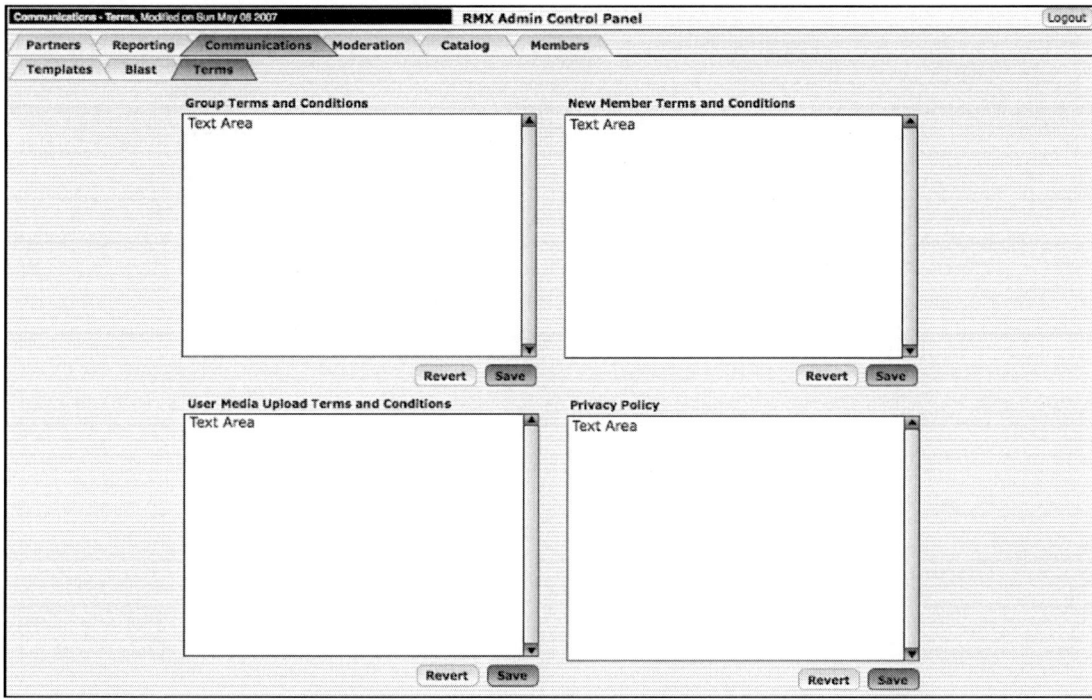

Figure 9-3. Admin policies templates screen

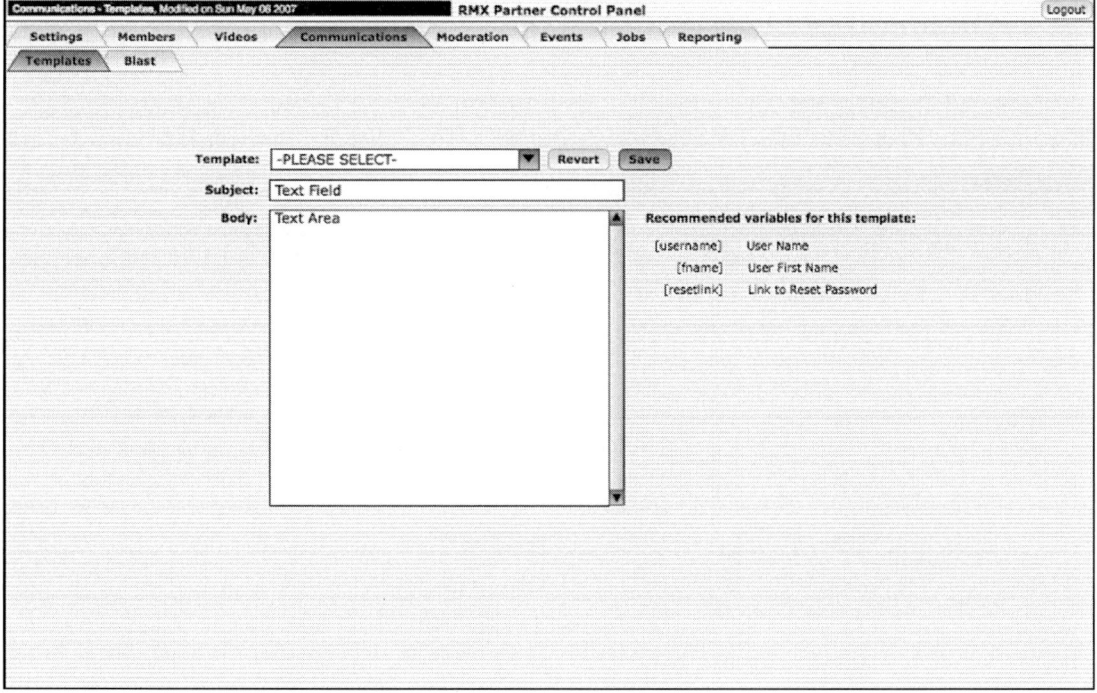

Figure 9-4. Partner e-mail templates screen

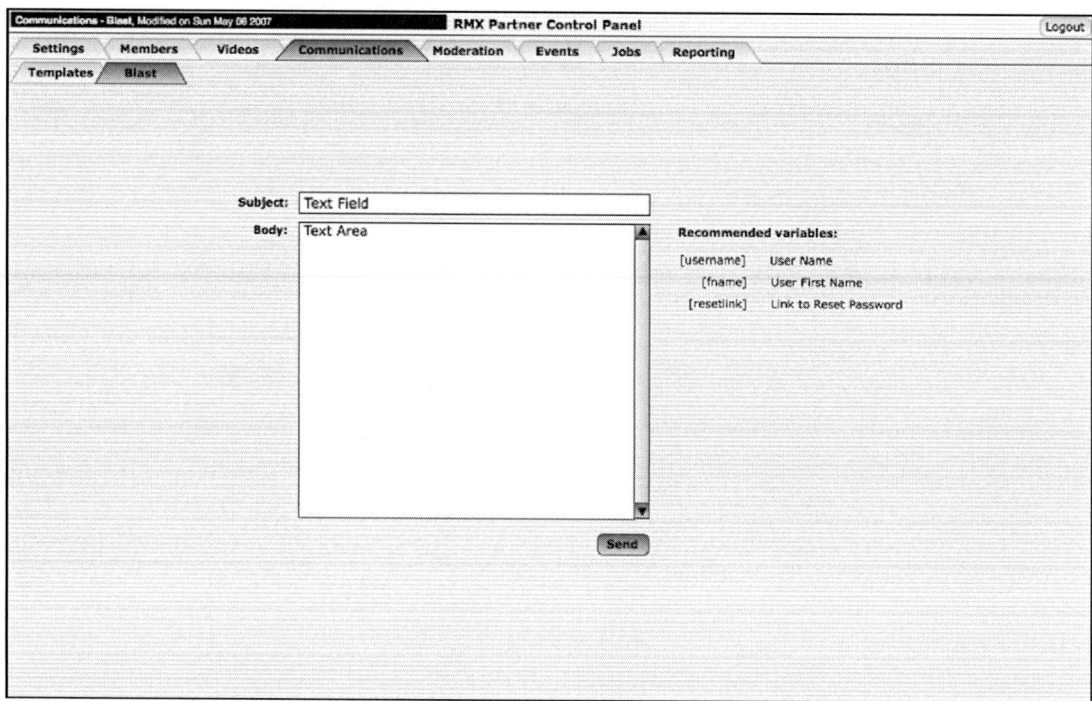

Figure 9-5. Partner e-mail blast screen

In the beginning there was ActionScript

Armed with these screens, I could then open up Flex and start setting up the actual modules. Before I actually started designing and coding though, I took some time to set up my development environment with the core classes that I like to use. My application skeletons always include a series of Singleton classes that allow me to manage an application's functionality much more easily than without.

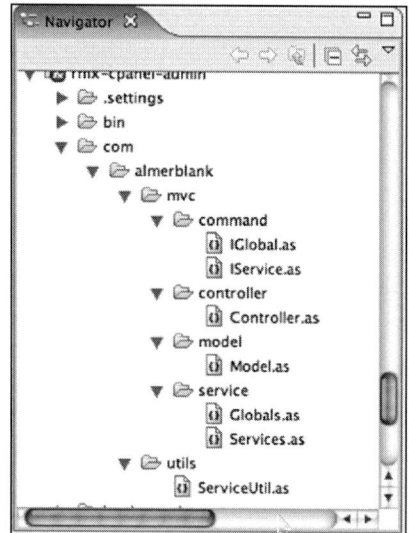

Figure 9-6. Custom application skeleton

Singleton classes, in this context, refers to ActionScript classes that are coded using the Singleton design pattern, which as I mentioned in Chapter 7 is used to restrict instantiation of a class to one object. This is accomplished via a class method, usually getInstance(), that creates a new instance of the class if one does not exist. If an instance already exists, it simply returns a reference to that class. This approach is very useful when you need only one instance of a class to coordinate actions across an entire system or application.

By having a set of templates already prepared, I save myself a considerable amount of time by not having to type the code for these from scratch on every project. Figure 9-6 shows a listing of the classes I include at the start of a project.

Overview of the ServiceUtil class

As you can see, the com.almerblank.mvc package is the most extensive because this is where the majority of the heavy lifting takes place. It represents my modified version of the Model-View-Controller (MVC) concept. Before I describe the classes in this package, I'd like to take a moment to describe the ServiceUtil class. At Almer/Blank, we do a lot of remoting with AMFPHP (www.amf-php.org). In the early stages, we had to ensure we always had the proper dependencies (ActionScript files) included and had to do a bunch of new Gateway() and new Responder() definitions throughout the application. Enter ServiceUtil. I created this class to simplify remoting by minimizing my code investments to only two method calls. Here's the code for the ServiceUtil class:

```
package com.almerblank.utils{
  import flash.net.Responder;
  import flash.system.Security;

  public class ServiceUtil{
    private static var _instance:ServiceUtil;

    public var gatewayURL:String;
    private var _gateway:RemotingConnection;
    private var _response:Responder;

    public function ServiceUtil(enforcer:SingletonEnforcer){}

    public static function getInstance():ServiceUtil{
      if(ServiceUtil._instance == null){
        ServiceUtil._instance = new ServiceUtil(new SingletonEnforcer);
      }
      return ServiceUtil._instance;
    }

    //set your gateway URL
    public function init(url:String,security:Boolean,policy:String):➥
      void{
      if(security){
        flash.system.Security.loadPolicyFile(policy);
      }
      gatewayURL = url;
    }

    //call your AMFPHP service
    public function call(service:String, resultHandler:Function,➥
         faultHandler:Function,... params):void{
      _response = new Responder(resultHandler, faultHandler);
      _gateway = new RemotingConnection(gatewayURL);
      _gateway.call(service, _response, params);
    }
  }
}
/**
```

```
    * Helper class for remoting
    */
   import flash.net.NetConnection;
   import flash.net.ObjectEncoding;
   class RemotingConnection extends NetConnection{
     public function RemotingConnection(sURL:String){
       objectEncoding = ObjectEncoding.AMF0;
       if(sURL){
         connect(sURL);
       }
     }

     public function AppendToGatewayUrl(s:String):void{
       //
     }
   }
   class SingletonEnforcer{}
```

Using this approach, I only have to worry about one public variable, gatewayURL, and two public methods, init() and call(). You'll see exactly how this is implemented shortly. Now, let's continue our exploration by examining the interfaces.

ActionScript interfaces

If you are unfamiliar with ActionScript interfaces, they are classes that declare all the public methods that a particular class must define. A class that *implements* an interface must include the methods that are declared in the interface. Think of an interface as a set of rules that the implementing class must follow. This strict adherence helps to ensure the implementing class does what it's supposed to do.

The use of interfaces also has other benefits as well. First, you can document interfaces so that they are also included in any API documentation that you or your team utilizes. Second, the use of an interface will cause the compiler to check whether or not the implementing class actually defines the required methods. This is crucial on any large project, as you may inadvertently forget to code a method or code a method's signature improperly and without an interface; the compiler may not complain, but if it does, the complaint may be a vague one, which inhibits an easy solution. With an interface, the compiler will tell you exactly what you did wrong. And interfaces are not just limited to methods, because you can include variables as well.

Here's the code for the IGlobal interface:

```
   package com.almerblank.mvc.command{
     public interface IGlobal{
       function init():void;
     }
   }
```

Both the IGlobal and IService interfaces each have only one method in the beginning of any project, init(). You'll learn more about what init() actually does as we explore the Controller class.

Class exploration

The following sections explore various ActionScript classes that I used for the communications control panel.

The Controller class

The Controller class is the "traffic controller" for the application. It receives requests from throughout the application and passes those requests on to the appropriate classes for processing. Here's the initial code for the Controller class:

```
package com.almerblank.mvc.controller{
  import com.almerblank.mvc.model.Model;
  import com.almerblank.mvc.service.Globals;
  import com.almerblank.mvc.service.Services;

  import mx.core.Application;
  import mx.core.IUID;
  import mx.events.*
  import mx.utils.*;
  import mx.managers.*;
  import mx.validators.*;
  import mx.controls.*;
  import mx.containers.TitleWindow;
  import mx.collections.ArrayCollection;
  import flash.system.*;
  import flash.events.*;
  import flash.net.*;

  [Bindable]
  public class Controller extends EventDispatcher{
    private static var _instance:Controller;

    private var _model:Model = Model.getInstance();
    private var _globals:Globals = Globals.getInstance();
    private var _svc:Services = Services.getInstance();

    private var _app:Object;

    public function Controller(enforcer:SingletonEnforcer){}

    public static function getInstance():Controller{
      if(Controller._instance == null){
        Controller._instance = ➡
        new Controller(new SingletonEnforcer());
      }
      return Controller._instance;
    }
```

```
      public function initApp():void{
        _globals.init();
        _svc.init();
      }
    }
  }
class SingletonEnforcer{}
```

In the early stages, Controller starts off with just initApp(). This is where any application initialization takes place. First, the init() methods of all the Singletons used in the application are called. From there, the sky's the limit. So, if a login needs to be processed or a LocalSharedObject (LSO) needs to be checked at startup, this is the place to do it. Figure 9-7 shows how this method gets called.

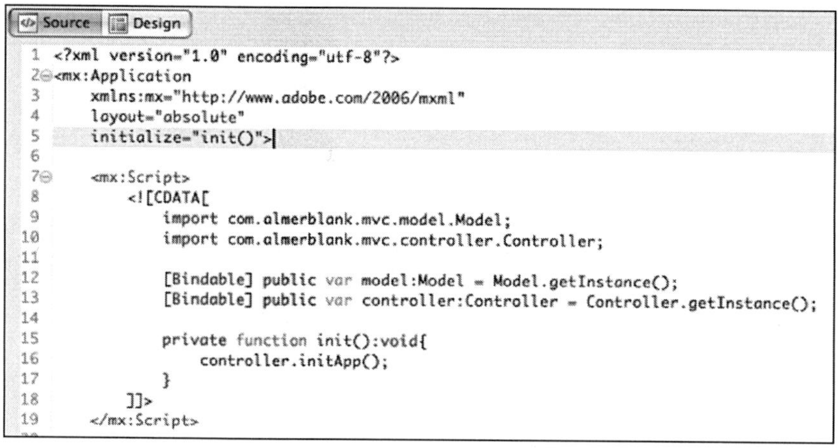

Figure 9-7. Application initialization

The Model class

The Model class is like a dictionary of all application variables or properties. Think of it as a data transfer object (DTO) or value object (VO). It acts as a storehouse for application properties, allowing them to easily be retrieved from a central location. In other words, you define it once and use it anywhere. Here's the initial code for the Model class:

```
package com.almerblank.mvc.model{
  import mx.utils.ObjectProxy;
  import mx.collections.ArrayCollection;
  import mx.containers.TitleWindow;

  [Bindable]
  public class Model{
    private static var _instance:Model;

    public function Model(enforcer:SingletonEnforcer){}
```

```
    public static function getInstance():Model{
     if(Model._instance == null){
      Model._instance = new Model(new SingletonEnforcer());
     }
     return Model._instance;
    }
   }
  }
class SingletonEnforcer{}
```

If you place all your application variables in the variable declarations section, you can then access them using the variable defined in Figure 9-7 like so: model.someVariable. The use of this class can definitely help make your application more modular and scalable.

The Globals class

The Globals class is where I house functionality that may not need to be modularized any further. For example, if a particular functionality requires only two methods such as login() and logout(), I will include those methods in Globals rather than creating a separate Login class. In other words, I keep my "top-level" methods in this class. Here's the initial code for Globals:

```
package com.almerblank.mvc.service{
   import com.almerblank.mvc.command.IGlobal;
   import com.almerblank.mvc.model.Model;
   import com.almerblank.mvc.controller.Controller;

   import mx.core.Application;
   import mx.collections.*;
   import mx.events.*;
   import mx.managers.*;
   import mx.controls.*;
   import mx.containers.*;
   import mx.utils.*;
   import mx.containers.TitleWindow;
   import flash.events.*;
   import flash.net.*;
   import flash.display.*;

   [Bindable]
   public class Globals extends EventDispatcher implements IGlobal{
     private static var _instance:Globals;

     private var _model:Model;
     private var _controller:Controller;
     private var _app:Object;

     public function Globals(enforcer:SingletonEnforcer){}
```

```
public static function getInstance():Globals{
  if(Globals._instance == null){
    Globals._instance = new Globals(new SingletonEnforcer());
  }
  return Globals._instance;
}

public function init():void{
  _model = Model.getInstance();
  _controller = Controller.getInstance();
  _app = Application.application;
}
  }
}
class SingletonEnforcer{}
```

Now, let's explore the init() method. All it does is ensure that I have access to the Singletons that I'll need to work with, as well as giving me access to the Application object. Although you can probably implement this differently, I've found that this is the least error-prone implementation that suits my development needs.

The Services class

The Services class is where all of the AMFPHP communication methods are housed. Any service calls that need to be made or service returns that need to be processed are handled here. I usually set it up so that the class is only accessed through Controller; sometimes in the early stages of development, however, I'll allow direct access to quickly build a working demo, and then lock it down once the groundwork is in place. Here's the initial code for Services:

```
package com.almerblank.mvc.service{
  import mx.core.*;
  import mx.events.*;
  import mx.managers.*;
  import mx.controls.*;
  import mx.utils.*;
  import mx.containers.TitleWindow;
  import flash.events.EventDispatcher;
  import com.almerblank.mvc.command.IService;
  import com.almerblank.mvc.model.Model;
  import com.almerblank.mvc.controller.Controller;
  import com.almerblank.utils.ServiceUtil;

  [Bindable]
  public class Services extends EventDispatcher implements IService{
    private static var _instance:Services;
```

```
          private var _model:Model;
          private var _controller:Controller;
          private var _amfphp:ServiceUtil;

          public function Services(enforcer:SingletonEnforcer){}

          public static function getInstance():Services{
            if(Services._instance == null){
              Services._instance = new Services(new SingletonEnforcer());
            }
            return Services._instance;
          }

          public function init():void{
            _model = Model.getInstance();
            _controller = Controller.getInstance();
            _amfphp = ServiceUtil.getInstance();

            _app = Application.application;

            try {
              //any initial calls here...
            } catch(error:*) {
              trace('service init error: '+error.message);
            }
          }

          private function faultHandler(fault:Object):void{
            Alert.show(fault.description, 'Service Error:');
            CursorManager.removeBusyCursor();
          }
        }
      }
      class SingletonEnforcer{}
```

Any other classes added to the com.almerblank.mvc.service package will be specific to the application, such as the Communications class that the Communications management screen uses. Once I've gotten those class templates in place, I stop with class creation and set up the design elements before beginning creation of any specific classes.

MXML development

You've already seen part of the main MXML file in Figure 9-7, which showcased the script block that sets everything in motion. Now, it's time to start creating the various screens specified in the wires. I use the wire shown earlier in Figure 9-1 to outline in my mind what Flex components to use. Figure 9-8 shows what this outline would look like if I chose to physically diagram it.

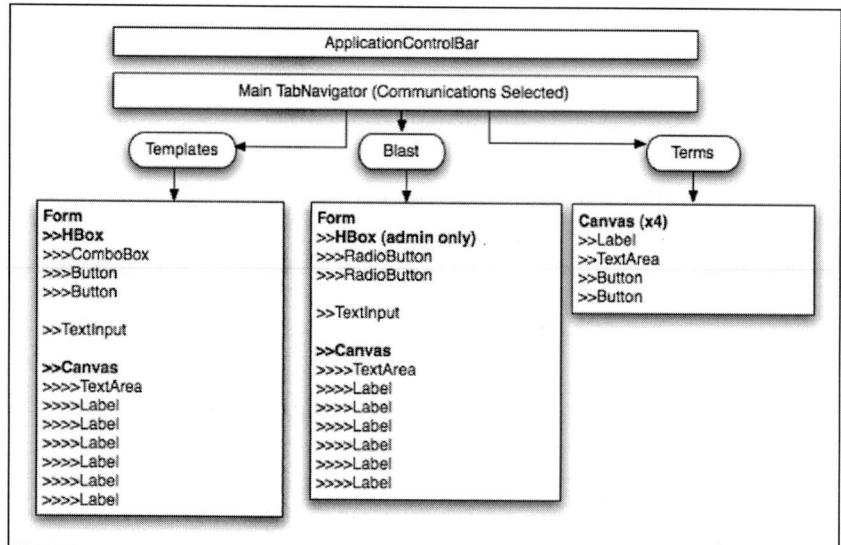

Figure 9-8. Mental MXML layout diagram

At the very top of Figure 9-1 is the title of the application and an access control button for logging in and out of the application. That combination is also present on all the other screens, so I place this combo in an ApplicationControlBar component. The main navigation in this wire is represented as a set of tabs, which screams for the TabNavigator component, as does the subnavigation of that screen. After reaching this point, I examine each subview and try to determine the optimal way to lay them out. Once I've got the mental picture illustrated by Figure 9-8 in my head, I start implementing the layout. Figures 9-9 and 9-10 show the design and code views in the early stages of the app.

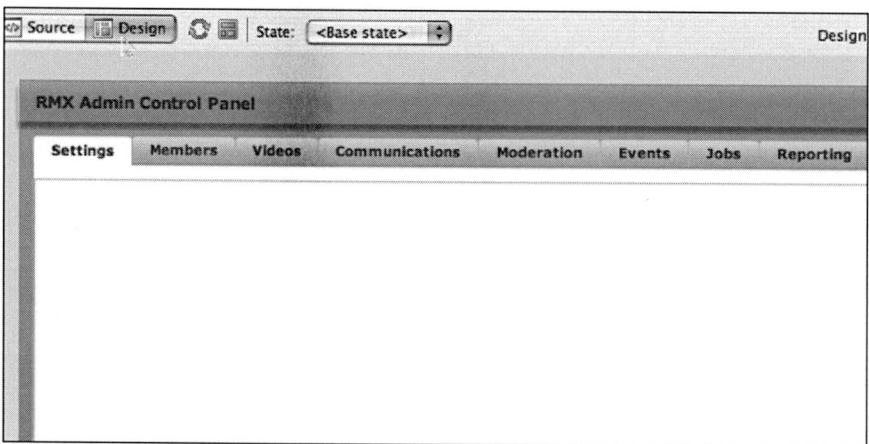

Figure 9-9. Early design view of my app

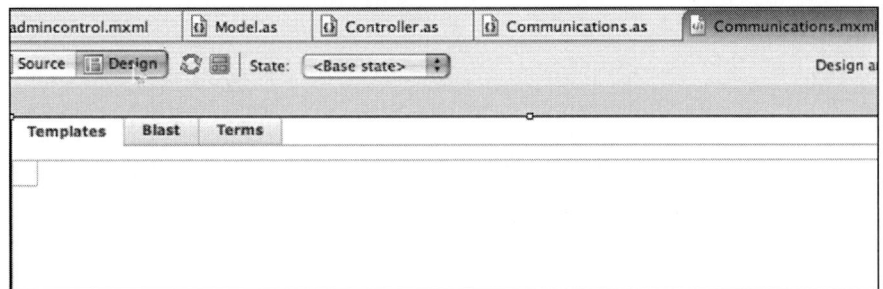

```
</> Source    Design
21  <mx:ApplicationControlBar id="controlBar" dock="true" width="100%" paddingBottom="0" p
22      <mx:Label left="10" top="10" text="RMX Admin Control Panel" fontSize="12" fontWeig
23      <mx:Spacer width="100%" height="100%"/>
24      <mx:HBox visible="false">
25          <mx:Label id="lblUser" text="Username:"/>
26          <mx:TextInput height="18" id="username" fontSize="9"/>
27          <mx:Label id="lblPass" text="Password:"/>
28          <mx:TextInput height="18" id="password" displayAsPassword="true" fontSize="9"/
29          <mx:VBox>
30              <mx:Button height="18" id="btnStatus" label="Login"/>
31              <mx:Spacer height="1"/>
32          </mx:VBox>
33      </mx:HBox>
34  </mx:ApplicationControlBar>
35  <mx:TabNavigator x="10" y="10" width="100%" height="100%">
36      <mx:Canvas label="Settings" width="100%" height="100%">
37      </mx:Canvas>
38      <mx:Canvas label="Members" width="100%" height="100%">
39      </mx:Canvas>
40      <mx:Canvas label="Videos" width="100%" height="100%">
41      </mx:Canvas>
42      <mx:Canvas label="Communications" width="100%" height="100%">
43      </mx:Canvas>
44      <mx:Canvas label="Moderation" width="100%" height="100%">
45      </mx:Canvas>
46      <mx:Canvas label="Events" width="100%" height="100%">
47      </mx:Canvas>
48      <mx:Canvas label="Jobs" width="100%" height="100%">
49      </mx:Canvas>
50      <mx:Canvas label="Reporting" width="100%" height="100%">
51      </mx:Canvas>
52  </mx:TabNavigator>
```

Figure 9-10. Early code view of my app

Time to organize

Having the core MXML in place, I can now start building the various modules required for the Communications screen. Before doing so, I create two new folders; views and components, to better organize my forthcoming creations. The views folder holds all the modules that make up the content of the main TabNavigator. Instead of putting all that code in the main MXML file, I can break it down into smaller chunks to make it easier to read and thus easier to maintain as it grows. Figures 9-11 through 9-13 show the Communications view and how it's implemented in the main MXML file.

Figure 9-11. Communications screen (design view)

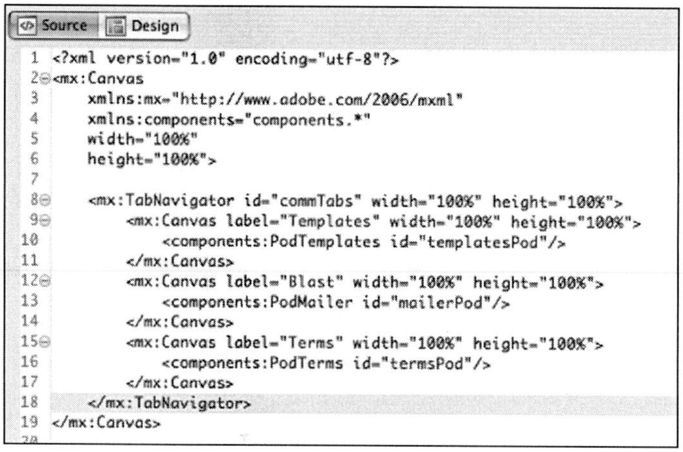

```
 1  <?xml version="1.0" encoding="utf-8"?>
 2  <mx:Canvas
 3      xmlns:mx="http://www.adobe.com/2006/mxml"
 4      xmlns:components="components.*"
 5      width="100%"
 6      height="100%">
 7
 8      <mx:TabNavigator id="commTabs" width="100%" height="100%">
 9          <mx:Canvas label="Templates" width="100%" height="100%">
10              <components:PodTemplates id="templatesPod"/>
11          </mx:Canvas>
12          <mx:Canvas label="Blast" width="100%" height="100%">
13              <components:PodMailer id="mailerPod"/>
14          </mx:Canvas>
15          <mx:Canvas label="Terms" width="100%" height="100%">
16              <components:PodTerms id="termsPod"/>
17          </mx:Canvas>
18      </mx:TabNavigator>
19  </mx:Canvas>
```

Figure 9-12. Communications screen (code view)

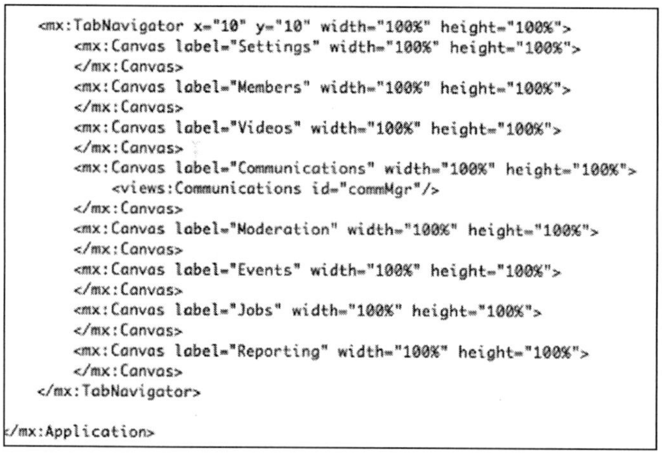

```
<mx:TabNavigator x="10" y="10" width="100%" height="100%">
    <mx:Canvas label="Settings" width="100%" height="100%">
    </mx:Canvas>
    <mx:Canvas label="Members" width="100%" height="100%">
    </mx:Canvas>
    <mx:Canvas label="Videos" width="100%" height="100%">
    </mx:Canvas>
    <mx:Canvas label="Communications" width="100%" height="100%">
        <views:Communications id="commMgr"/>
    </mx:Canvas>
    <mx:Canvas label="Moderation" width="100%" height="100%">
    </mx:Canvas>
    <mx:Canvas label="Events" width="100%" height="100%">
    </mx:Canvas>
    <mx:Canvas label="Jobs" width="100%" height="100%">
    </mx:Canvas>
    <mx:Canvas label="Reporting" width="100%" height="100%">
    </mx:Canvas>
</mx:TabNavigator>

</mx:Application>
```

Figure 9-13. Communications incorporated into the main MXML

Layout design

With the foundation laid, all that's left to do is build out the components required for the Communications screen: PodTemplates, PodMailer, and PodTerms. Reexamining my mental diagram, I see that it would be a lot better to use a "fluid" layout to build these components vs. using a bunch of containers within containers. When you do the latter, you unnecessarily add weight to your app, since each one of those container classes has to be compiled. To achieve my fluid layout, I mentally group related components and use data binding to "snap" them together. The following code from PodTemplates.mxml illustrates this approach:

```
<?xml version="1.0" encoding="utf-8"?>
<mx:Canvas
  xmlns:mx="http://www.adobe.com/2006/mxml">

  <mx:Label
    id="lblTemplates"
```

```
      x="10"
      y="10"
      text="Templates: "
      fontWeight="bold"/>
<mx:ComboBox
    id="selectedTemplate"
    x="{lblTemplates.x+lblTemplates.width+4}"
    y="10"
    width="300"/>
<mx:Button
    id="btnRevertTemplate"
    x="{selectedTemplate.x+selectedTemplate.width+4}"
    y="10"
    label="Revert"/>
<mx:Button
    id="btnSaveTemplate"
    x="{btnRevertTemplate.x+btnRevertTemplate.width+2}"
    y="10"
    label="Save"/>

<mx:Label
    id="lblSubject"
    x="10"
    y="{selectedTemplate.y+selectedTemplate.height+8}"
    text="Subject: "
    fontWeight="bold"/>
<mx:TextInput
    id="templateSubject"
    x="{selectedTemplate.x}"
    y="{selectedTemplate.y+selectedTemplate.height+8}"
    width="400"/>

<mx:Label
    id="lblBody"
    x="10"
    y="{templateSubject.y+templateSubject.height+8}"
    text="Body: "
    fontWeight="bold"/>
<mx:TextArea
    id="templateBody"
    width="400"
    height="300"
    x="{templateSubject.x}"
    y="{templateSubject.y+templateSubject.height+8}"/>

<mx:Text
    id="txtVariables"
    x="{templateBody.x+templateBody.width+50}"
    y="{templateBody.y}"
```

```
            text=" Acceptable variables for this template"
            fontWeight="bold"/>
        <mx:List
            id="templateVariables"
            x="{templateBody.x+templateBody.width+50}"
            y="{txtVariables.y+txtVariables.height+4}"/>

    </mx:Canvas>
```

This approach really works well and only takes a little thought and planning to replicate for other layouts, whether similar or not. There is, however, one downside to this: you can't preview your layouts in design view. Other than that, it's pretty easy to implement. Figures 9-14 through 9-16 show the finished screens after using this layout approach.

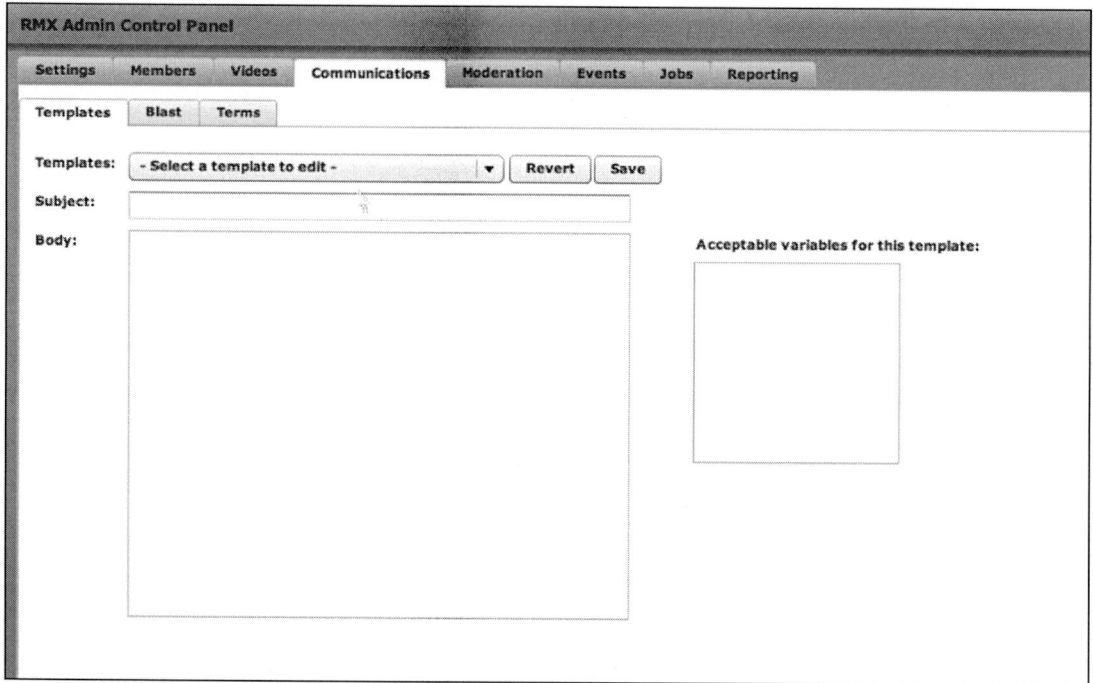

Figure 9-14. Admin e-mail templates screen

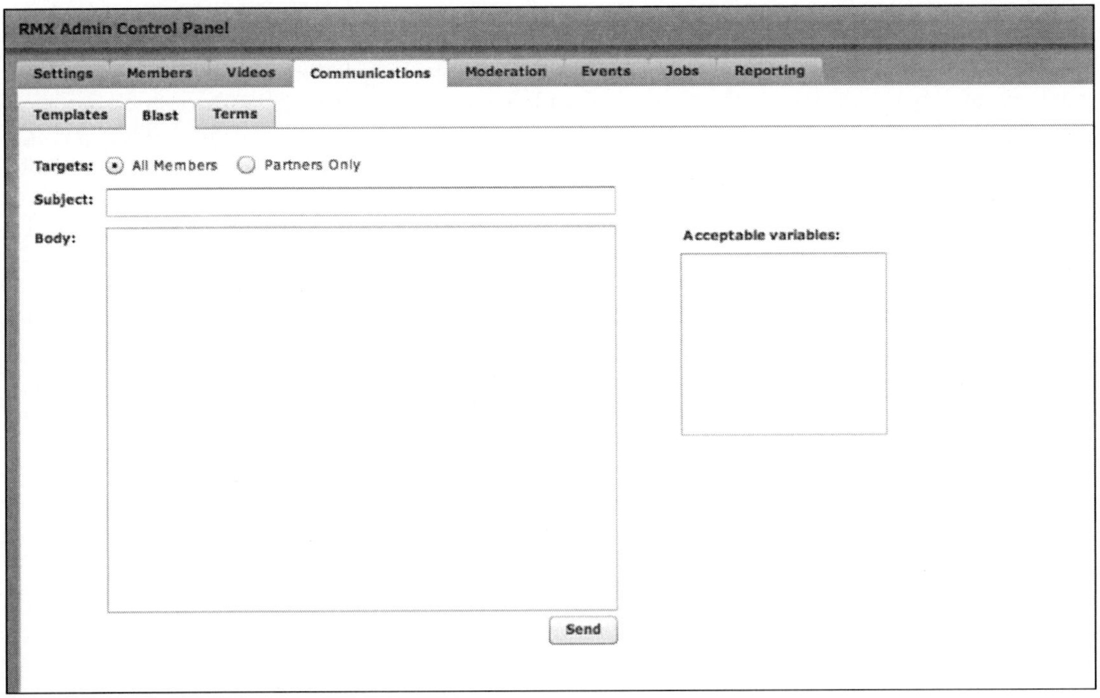

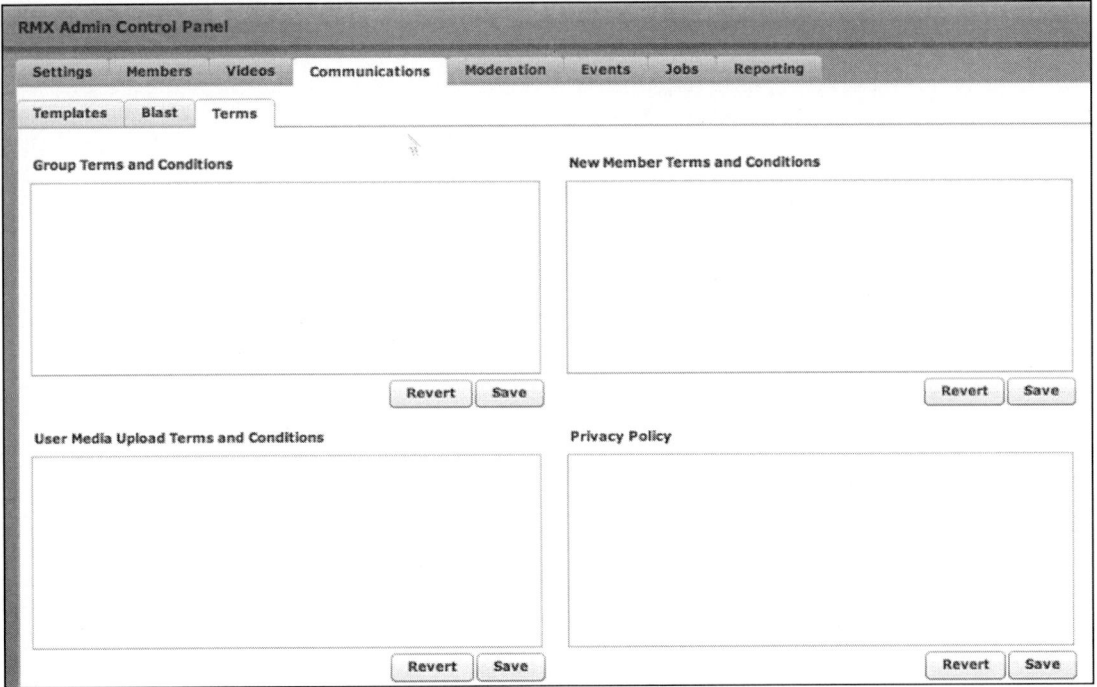

Figure 9-15. Admin e-mail blast screen

Figure 9-16. Admin terms screen

Incorporating the data

With the basic layout complete, I usually start bringing the data model into the picture. I consider what kinds of data I need to bring in and build off of that. For the Communications screen, I need two data sets, one for the e-mail templates and one for the policies. So, I add two ArrayCollections, templateDP and termsDP, to the Model class for just that purpose. Now, I start thinking in terms of everything the first subview needs to make it tick. While still in the Model class, I add two more variables, templateObj of type Object and template of type ObjectProxy. templateObj represents a dummy object that I like to use when dealing with data-bound forms in Flex. It consists of a set of keys with empty values that I use in a form-reset operation to bring the form back to its default empty state. I'll show you how shortly. template is the object to which the form is actually tied. I chose to use ObjectProxy because, when developing this system, I found that for members of the Model class this was the easiest way for me to maintain my data bindings, since Flex complains about binding to a plain Object's properties. Speaking of bindings, it's time to start binding the template to the proper controls in PodTemplate. Here's the updated code for PodTemplates.mxml with the additions in bold:

```
<?xml version="1.0" encoding="utf-8"?>
<mx:Canvas
  xmlns:mx="http://www.adobe.com/2006/mxml">
  <!-- template selection -->
  <mx:Label
    id="lblTemplates"
    x="10"
    y="10"
    text="Templates: "
    fontWeight="bold"/>
  <mx:ComboBox
    id="selectedTemplate"
    x="{lblTemplates.x+lblTemplates.width+4}"
    y="10"
    width="300"
    dataProvider="{parentApplication.model.templateDP}"
    labelField="templateName"
    change="parentApplication.controller.loadTemplate(event)"
    prompt="- Select a template to edit -" />
  <mx:Button
    id="btnRevertTemplate"
    x="{selectedTemplate.x+selectedTemplate.width+4}"
    y="10"
    label="Revert"
    click="parentApplication.controller.cancelEmailChanges(event)" />
  <mx:Button
    id="btnSaveTemplate"
    x="{btnRevertTemplate.x+btnRevertTemplate.width+2}"
    y="10"
    label="Save"
    click="parentApplication.controller.saveEmailChanges()" />

  <!-- template subject -->
  <mx:Label
```

```
        id="lblSubject"
        x="10"
        y="{selectedTemplate.y+selectedTemplate.height+8}"
        text="Subject: "
        fontWeight="bold"/>
    <mx:TextInput
        id="templateSubject"
        x="{selectedTemplate.x}"
        y="{selectedTemplate.y+selectedTemplate.height+8}"
        width="400"
        text="{parentApplication.model.template.templateSubject}"
        focusOut="parentApplication.controller.➡
updateTemplateSubject(event)" />

    <!-- template body -->
    <mx:Label
        id="lblBody"
        x="10"
        y="{templateSubject.y+templateSubject.height+8}"
        text="Body: "
        fontWeight="bold"/>
    <mx:TextArea
        id="templateBody"
        width="400"
        height="300"
        x="{templateSubject.x}"
        y="{templateSubject.y+templateSubject.height+8}"
        text="{parentApplication.model.template.templateBody}"
        focusOut="parentApplication.controller.➡
updateTemplateBody(event)" />

    <!-- template variables -->
    <mx:Text
        id="txtVariables"
        x="{templateBody.x+templateBody.width+50}"
        y="{templateBody.y}"
        text="Acceptable variables for this template"
        fontWeight="bold"/>
    <mx:List
        id="templateVariables"
        x="{templateBody.x+templateBody.width+50}"
        y="{txtVariables.y+txtVariables.height+4}"
        borderStyle="none"
        dataProvider="{parentApplication.model.template. ➡
templateVariables}"  />
```

In these updates, I'm binding the text properties of the TextInput and TextArea components, as well as the dataProvider properties of the ComboBox and List components, to the appropriate properties of the template ObjectProxy, and I've set what action I'd like to take place when a user updates part of the template, as well as what happens when a user clicks the Revert or Save buttons. Now that I have a sense of how I want the data model to be tied to the design and what path I want the top-level interactions to follow, I can move on to adding these methods to the Controller class.

Remember, the Controller class is nothing more than a traffic controller, basically receiving events and passing them on to the appropriate service class. Here are the additions for the Communications class:

```
///////////////////////// communication methods \\\\\\\\\\\\\\\\\\\\\\\\\\\
public function getTemplates():void{ _svc.getTemplates(); }
public function loadTemplate(event:Event):void➡
{ _comm.loadTemplate(event); }
public function reloadTemplate(id:uint):void➡
{ _comm.reloadTemplate(id); }
public function updateTemplateSubject(event:FocusEvent):void➡
{ _comm.updateTemplateSubject(event); }
public function updateTemplateBody(event:FocusEvent):void➡
{ _comm.updateTemplateBody(event); }
public function saveEmailChanges():void{ _comm.saveEmailChanges(); }
public function cancelEmailChanges(event:MouseEvent):void➡
{ _comm.cancelEmailChanges(event); }
public function blastNetwork():void{ _comm.blastNetwork(); }
public function getPolicies():void{ _svc.getPolicies(); }
public function updatePolicy(event:FocusEvent):void➡
{ _comm.updatePolicy(event); }
public function savePolicyChanges(event:MouseEvent):void➡
{ _comm.savePolicyChanges(event); }
public function cancelPolicyChanges(event:MouseEvent):void➡
{ _comm.cancelPolicyChanges(event); }
```

As I said previously, Controller receives an action request, such as getTemplates(), and directs that request to the appropriate service class, in this case Services.getInstance().getTemplates(). I pre-fer fleshing Controller out using this shorthand notation because it more closely resembles the structure of an ActionScript interface, and I can then just copy and paste these methods into the appropriate interfaces. This gives me a greater degree of organization and control while still maintaining a measure of sanity. And, since I know that I need to build Communications before Services, Communications is my next stop on the ActionScript express.

Building the Communications class

Between Controller and ICommunication, I have a very clear picture of what methods I need to build into Communications. Now, I have to think about exactly how these methods need to work. On the surface, I want and need them to do what their names indicate. Keeping this in mind helps me stay focused as I'm usually coding three-to-four files at once. Here's my first pass on the template-related methods in Communications.as:

```
///////////////////////// email template methods \\\\\\\\\\\\\\\\\\\\\\\\\\\
public function loadTemplate(event:Event):void{
  _selectedIndex = event.target.selectedIndex;
  if(_templateEdited == false){
```

```
      _view = event.target.parentDocument;
      var id:uint = event.target.selectedIndex;
      var tmpObj:Object = _model.templateDP.getItemAt(id);
      _originalTemplate = _model.templateDP.getItemAt(id);
      _model.template = new ObjectProxy(tmpObj);
   } else {
      Alert.show('You have unsaved changes. Do you wish to save your➡
changes?', 'WARNING:', 3, null, _editCloseHandler);
   }
}

private function _editCloseHandler(event:CloseEvent):void{
   switch(event.detail){
      case 1:
         saveEmailChanges();
         break;
      case 2:
         var id:uint = _model.template.emailTemplateId-1;
         _svc.reloadTemplate(_selectedIndex);
         _templateEdited = false;
         _continueTemplateLoad();
         break;
   }
}

private function _continueTemplateLoad():void{
   var tmpObj:Object = _model.templateDP.getItemAt(_selectedIndex);
   _model.template = new ObjectProxy(tmpObj);
}

public function updateTemplateSubject(event:FocusEvent):void{
   _model.template.templateSubject = event.target.text;
   if(_templateEdited == false){
      _templateEdited = true;
   }
}

public function updateTemplateBody(event:FocusEvent):void{
   _model.template.templateBody = event.target.text;
   if(_templateEdited == false){
      _templateEdited = true;
   }
}

public function saveEmailChanges():void{
   if(_model.template.emailTemplateId == 0){
      Alert.show('You must first select a template to edit before ➡
performing this operation.', 'User Error:');
   } else {
```

```
        _svc.editTemplate(_model.template);
      _templateEdited = false;
    }
  }

  public function cancelEmailChanges(event:MouseEvent):void{
    if(_model.template.emailTemplateId == 0){
      Alert.show('You must first select a template to edit before ➡
performing this operation.', 'User Error:');
    } else {
      var id:uint = _model.template.emailTemplateId-1;
      _svc.reloadTemplate(id);
      _templateEdited = false;
    }
  }

  public function reloadTemplate(id:uint):void{
    var tmpObj:Object = _model.templateDP.getItemAt(_selectedIndex);
    _model.template = new ObjectProxy(tmpObj);
    _app.commMgr.templatesPod.selectedTemplate.selectedIndex = ➡
      _selectedIndex;
  }
```

Let's start with loadTemplate(). This method is called every time the user makes a selection on the ComboBox. I store the selectedIndex property of the ComboBox so that it can be easily referenced from the other methods. After that, I check for whether the template has been edited with _templateEdited. If it hasn't, I want to continue with the template loading; otherwise, I want to alert the user that he has unsaved changes that will be lost if he continues on without saving first. This interaction is where _editCloseHandler() and _continueTemplateLoad() come into play. With updateTemplateSubject() and updateTemplateBody(), I want to set the appropriate property of the template ObjectProxy equal to the text that's currently entered in the related text components and then ensure that _templateEdited gets updated correctly. For saveEmailChanges() and cancelEmailChanges(), I want to first check whether or not the user has selected a template to edit. If the form is still in the default state, I want to notify the user that no action will be taken while the form is in this state. If a template has been selected, I either want to edit the template, saveEmailChanges(), or reload the template, cancelEmailChanges(). Finally, reloadTemplate() works in conjunction with both saveEmailChanges() and cancelEmailChanges() and is the last stop in a cancel or edit operation. With Communications now in good shape, I can move on to my final destination before compilation, Services.

Building the Services class

I use the same process as before, using Controller, IService, and now Communications as my guide as to what to add to Services. After completing that review, I know that all I initially need are service calls to retrieve all the templates and to send an edited template back to the server. Here's my first pass at the required code:

```
  public function getTemplates():void{
    amfphp.call(_commService+'.getTemplates', _getTemplatesHandler, ➡
faultHandler);
```

```
      CursorManager.setBusyCursor();
  }

  private function _getTemplatesHandler(result:Array):void{
    if(result[0] == 'DEBUG_OUTPUT'){
      trace(result.toString());
      CursorManager.removeBusyCursor();
    } else {
      var templates:Array = result.filter(_truncTemplates);
      _controller.setAC('templateDP', ➡
_controller.makeArrayCollection(templates));
      CursorManager.removeBusyCursor();
    }
  }

  private function ➡
_truncTemplates(element:*, index:int, arr:Array):Boolean{
    return element.templateName != 'TOTAL FAILURE!';
  }

  public function editTemplate(obj:ObjectProxy):void{
    var tmpObj:Object = _controller.convertObjProxy(obj);
    _amfphp.call(_commService+'.editTemplate', _editTemplateHandler, ➡
_faultHandler, tmpObj);
    CursorManager.setBusyCursor();
  }

  private function _editTemplateHandler(result:Array):void{
    if(result[0] == 'DEBUG_OUTPUT'){
      trace(result.toString());
      CursorManager.removeBusyCursor();
    } else {
      var templates:Array = result.filter(_truncTemplates);
      _controller.setAC('templateDP', ➡
_controller.makeArrayCollection(templates));
      _controller.reloadTemplate(_templateID);
      CursorManager.removeBusyCursor();
      Alert.show('Changes saved successfully.', 'STATUS: Success');
    }
  }

  public function reloadTemplate(id:uint):void{
    _templateID = id;
    _amfphp.call(_commService+'.getTemplates', _reloadTemplateHandler,➡
_faultHandler);
    CursorManager.setBusyCursor();
  }
```

```
private function _reloadTemplateHandler(result:Array):void{
  if(result[0] == 'DEBUG_OUTPUT'){
    trace(result.toString());
    CursorManager.removeBusyCursor();
  } else {
    var templates:Array = result.filter(_truncTemplates);
    _controller.setAC('templateDP', ➥
_controller.makeArrayCollection(templates));
    _controller.reloadTemplate(_templateID);
    CursorManager.removeBusyCursor();
  }
}
```

As you can see, the public methods are very straightforward. All they really do is call the specified AMFPHP service, pass along any additional parameters as required, and signal the user that something is happening with CursorManager.setBusyCursor(). It's the result handlers that really determine what will be experienced via the interface when using the app. If the e-mail templates can successfully be retrieved, _getTemplatesHandler() will populate templateDP with that data, but not before stripping out the noneditable template for a total system failure. _editTemplateHandler() is very similar in how it operates, only adding an alert prompt notifying the user that his edit was successful and also reloading the edited template. Finally, _reloadTemplateHandler() is exactly like _editTemplateHandler() except for the lack of an alert prompt to the user. All that's left to do now is flesh out the Blast and Terms subviews using the same process that I did for the Templates subview.

The MXML and ActionScript required for the Blast and Terms subviews is so similar to the code implemented for the Templates subview that elaboration of it here would just be redundant. However, I will take a moment to discuss how to integrate this portion of the Flex app with a simple but robust PHP e-mail system on the back end.

Extending to the inbox

The RMX admin control panel provides both network and group admin users the ability to send both plain text and HTML e-mails to the entire network via the Blast subview. When an admin user presses the Send button, his message is packaged in an Object containing the subject, message, and intended audience and is then sent via AMFPHP to the server, where the real magic happens. Here's the code that processes that object:

```
function blastNetwork($arr){
  foreach($arr[0] as $key=>$value){
    $$key = $value;
  }

  if($blastAudience == ''){
    $return = array('Error, message not sent.', 'STATUS: Failure');
  } else {
    if($blastAudience == 'All Members'){
      $return = $this->sendMail($blastSubject, $blastBody, true);
```

```
      } else {
        $return = $this->sendMail($blastSubject, $blastBody, false);
      }
    }
  return $return;
}


//helper function for blastNetwork
function sendMail($subject, $message, $toAllMembers){
  set_time_limit(0);

  if($toAllMembers){
    $query = "SELECT * FROM tbl_members";
    $return = array('Message sent to all members successfully.', ➥
'STATUS: Success');
  } else {
    $query = "SELECT * FROM tbl_partners";
    $return = array('Message sent to all partners successfully.', ➥
'STATUS: Success');
  }
  $result = mysql_query($query);

  while($network=mysql_fetch_assoc($result)){
    $mail = new Email(RMX_ADMIN, RMX_ADMIN_EMAIL);
    $mail->subject($subject);
    $mail->to($network['email']);
    $mail->text($message);
    $mail->send();
  }

  return $return;
}
```

The first method, blastNetwork(), processes the object sent in from Flex using a for...each loop. After that, it's time to see to whom the message needs to be sent. In either case, I pass the subject and message on to the private sendMail() method along with a Boolean to indicate whether to blast members or partners. Once the torch is passed to sendMail(), I set the script timeout limit, and then I grab the proper data based on the message audience. After that step, I run the proper query, and then use a while loop to step through the result set and send out the message. To actually send the message, I will integrate Daniel Käfer's eMail class (www.danielkaefer.de). This nifty little class takes care of properly constructing a multipart e-mail in the MIME format, allowing me to send text and HTML messages by simply setting the $text and $html variables of the eMail class. Once the messages have been sent, the proper response will be returned to Flex and displayed to the user. Having implemented that part of the communications system, it's now time to compile the Flex app. Figures 9-17 through 9-19 illustrate the compiled result of the first passes on the Communications screens.

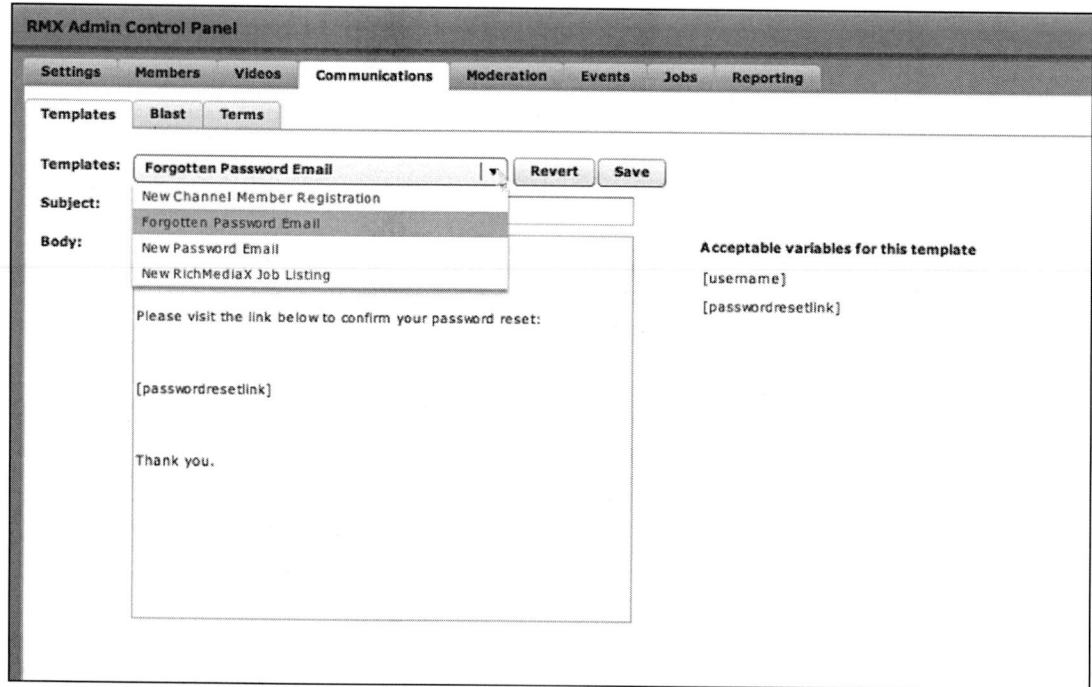

Figure 9-17. Templates subview, first draft

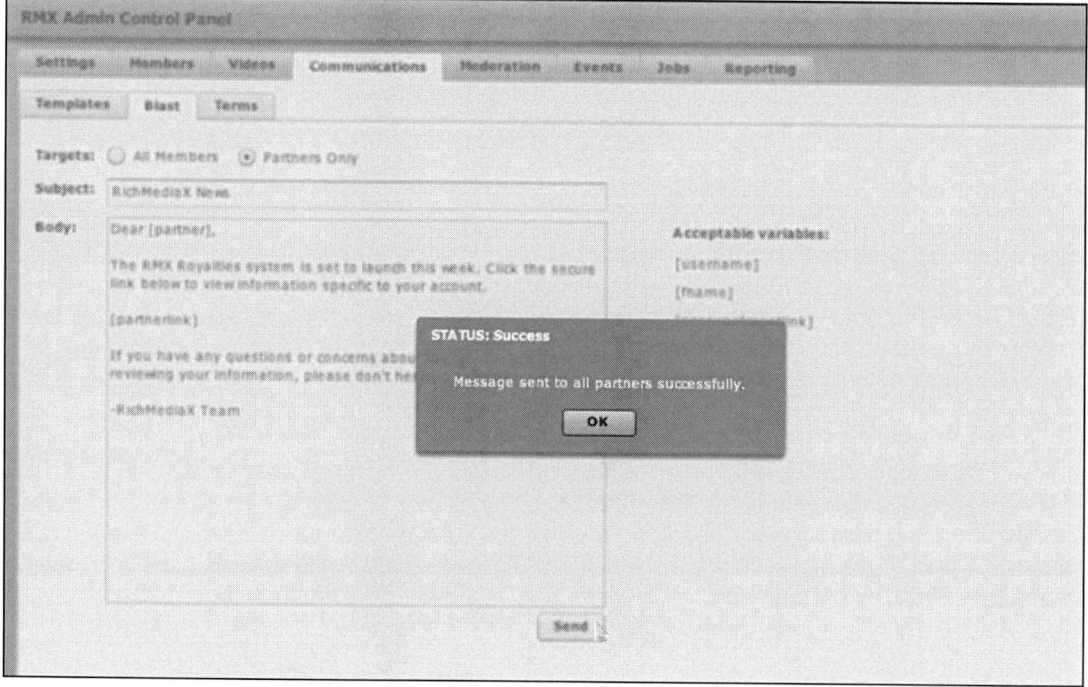

Figure 9-18. Blast subview, first draft

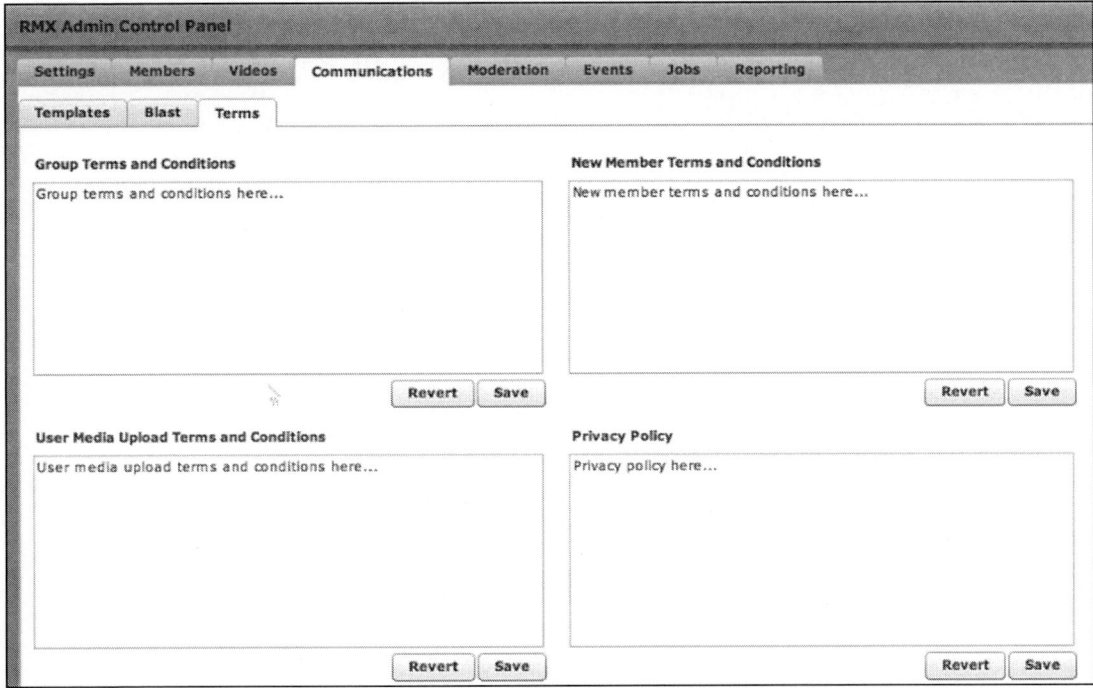

Figure 9-19. Terms subview, first draft

Now the Communications interface is successfully wired to both the Flex code and the PHP back-end code via remoting. This milestone constitutes a solid code foundation that I can branch out from and refactor in a nondestructive manner. This workflow can be followed for the other management screens as well. Once the entire app is complete, usability enhancements can easily be added, as well as custom styling that will really bring the app to life. The lessons that you learned in Chapter 5 on Flex styling definitely become applicable at this point. But for now, take a moment to catch your breath and regroup before forging on, because you deserve it.

Summary

In this chapter, you learned about the process that I used to meet the user communications system requirements for the RMX. You saw one approach to constructing the actual MXML layout by using data binding. You also explored my simplified version of the Model-View-Controller design pattern and how using such a process can help to increase your productivity. Finally, I showed you the fruits of all that labor by bringing those wireframes to life with the help of the Flex framework and PHP. In the chapter that follows, you'll learn about how we work with video in the RMX.

Chapter 10

WORKING WITH VIDEO

By Omar Gonzalez

In this chapter, I will attempt to give you a thorough understanding of the video display object of the Flex framework, with some specific insight into a few of the key video playback features in the RMX, including playlists and UI considerations for instream advertising. First, R Blank will start off with a brief word on some core video compression concepts that are important to understand—even for coders—in the preparation and delivery of Flash video.

Video boot camp

Although this chapter is about working with Flash video, as opposed to creating Flash video, in this section, I want to cover some of the basic issues in the preparation of video in Flash, before Omar discusses how to load and display the video files.

Compressing video is much like compressing flat images to bitmap formats like JPG. The compressor examines the source media, breaks it into separate blocks of pixels, and seeks redundancies it can exploit to represent those blocks with less data. This is how a 20MB PSD can be prepared into a 78KB JPG file for placement in a web site. Of course, with video, you have an additional dimension of data. Just as JPG compression seeks these shortcuts in two dimensions of visual data, or within a frame, video compression analyzes and processes three dimensions of color pixels, within a frame and between frames—both intraframe and interframe compression. So, when compressing video as opposed to still imagery, you have some additional settings available to you.

It's also worth noting, if you are relatively new to video, that video encoding is more an art than a science. There is never a single set of encoding settings that will objectively work for your video. It depends both on the characteristics of your source file (both the nature of the content as well as the technical settings of the digital media file) and your eye. It is a process of trial and retrial until you are happy with the results. Of course, the more you know about what settings you have at your disposal, the more tools you have in this process. As video compression technologies improve in quality, and the pipes you use to distribute compressed video grow, the less you must compress your media, and the less this matters.

Key video compression concepts

Video compression formats, including FLV, and the formats that support H.264 (such as MP4, MOV, and 3GP) share many concepts with other compressed video formats. These concepts include

- Codec
- Bitrate
- Framerate
- Keyframe frequency
- Constant vs. variable bitrate

Let's tackle these one at a time.

Codec

Derived as an abbreviation of COder-DECoder, a **codec** is the toolkit that is used to compress your source video, and to understand and view it in the player. Flash Player 9 has two video codecs: Sorenson Spark and On2 VP6. Spark was introduced in Flash Player 6 (although until Flash 7 the Flash Media Server was required), and VP6 was added to Flash Player 8. The first versions of Flash Player 9 included no new codecs, but with the release of version 9.0.6, Flash Player now also supports H.264 video. So that little magic software we call Flash Player now supports three codecs.

Spark is lower quality, but encodes faster and requires less processing power to play back. VP6 is much higher quality and has support for transparency, but takes longer to encode and requires a faster processor for proper playback. H.264 encodes quickly and has good quality at all bandwidth and qualities, from mobile-quality 3GP files to high-definition QuickTime MOVs, but has only been available in the player for a short time—it won't be until late 2008 when you can assume the vast majority of users will be able to view those videos.

For audio tracks, Flash 7 and Flash 8 video use the MP3 format—unless you are, for example, recording the user's microphone through a Flex application to a Flash Media Server (FMS) or Red5 server, in which case Flash will encode the audio using the closed Nellymoser codec. With support for H.264 video, Flash Player now also supports AAC audio, the standard codec used for audio tracks in H.264-encoded video files.

Bitrate

Bitrate, sometimes called **data rate**, is the key metric for all compressed media. It is measured in the number of bits per second that are encoded into the media file (8 bits = 1 byte). Most contemporary media, particularly in the online world, is measured in kilobits per second, or kbps, such as the 128kbps audio files you purchase from the iTunes store. Other types of media, such as DVD, are measured in megabits per second, or mbps.

The higher the bitrate, the better your media will look, and the bigger your total file size will be. This is a key note about bitrates: it is the single encoding setting that determines the total file size of the encoded media file. All other encoding settings represent trade-offs within the number of bits that you allocate when you specify the bitrate. The total size of your media file can be calculated as bitrate * length. When your video also includes an audio track, it is important to remember that the total bitrate of your encoded media will include the video bitrate and the audio bitrate. So, for example, if you encode your video to 400kbps and your audio to 96kbps, your total bitrate is 496kbps. If your video is 5 minutes long, your total file size will be just over 18MB, as you see in Figure 10-1.

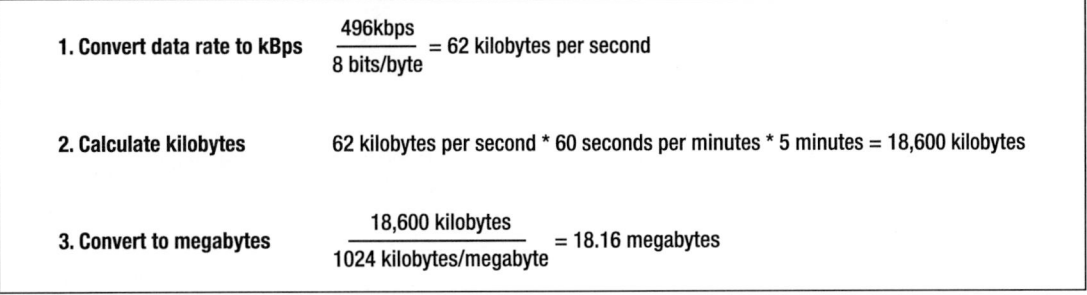

1. Convert data rate to kBps $\dfrac{496\text{kbps}}{8 \text{ bits/byte}}$ = 62 kilobytes per second

2. Calculate kilobytes 62 kilobytes per second * 60 seconds per minutes * 5 minutes = 18,600 kilobytes

3. Convert to megabytes $\dfrac{18{,}600 \text{ kilobytes}}{1024 \text{ kilobytes/megabyte}}$ = 18.16 megabytes

Figure 10-1. Calculating total file size from bitrate and length

Framerate

Framerate is a concept that is familiar to many in the Flash world, as framerate has long been a key document setting of Flash development files. Framerate is measured in the number of frames per second, or fps. Film, for example, is 24fps, and the standard for NTSC video is 29.97fps. The higher the framerate, the more fluid the sense of motion. But, for a given bitrate, higher framerates mean that fewer bits are available to each frame—so the motion might be better, but the average image quality will be lower. A setting of 10fps is considered the minimum for convincing motion. Since source video is almost never greater than 30fps (or 60fps interlaced), an output of 30fps is the maximum you should apply for most encoded video.

In general, when transcoding video, it is optimal to maintain the original framerate or to encode to a framerate that is a factor of the original framerate—for instance, if your source is 30fps, it is optimal to encode to 10-, 15-, or 30fps.

Unlike the framerate of your Flash SWF, which represents the maximum framerate at which your SWF will play back, the framerate of your video is a guaranteed fixed setting. And if the person viewing your video does not have a processor powerful enough to view your video properly, frames will be dropped in order to ensure the video will continue to play back at its intended speed.

As well, it is important to understand that the framerate of your FLVs is entirely independent of the framerate of the Flash application that loads and displays those FLVs. SWF video players of 60fps or 10fps can play back 30fps FLVs without any trouble or speed issues.

Keyframe frequency

One of the results of interframe compression is that only some frames are complete frames, or **keyframes**. Keyframes are akin to a JPG version of the frame from the source file. But most frames in your compressed video file are not keyframes—they actually include only partial information about the frame, representing the parts of the image that have changed since the previous keyframe. This is the key manner in which video compression can create files so much smaller than the source file.

At higher keyframe frequencies, fewer keyframes are encoded into the video. As well, since keyframes represent complete image information, keyframes consume more bits than non-keyframes; so, for a specific bitrate, the more keyframes in your video, the lower the average image quality of your video.

The right number depends on the content you are encoding. If your video does not change much, you don't need many keyframes. This is often referred to as **talking-head video**, since in an interview, for example, when you see talking heads, not much of the image changes over time. If your video represents a lot of activity and motion, for instance, if it is footage of a NASCAR race, you will want more keyframes.

Most video encoders have an automatic setting for keyframe placement; as you can see in Figure 10-2, there is a combo box labeled Key frame placement, which defaults to Automatic, in the lower right of the Video settings panel of the Flash CS3 Video Encoder.

In Flash video, you can only seek to keyframes. So if you want your video to be easily scrubbed with a progress/seek bar, you will want a lower keyframe frequency, resulting in more keyframes in the encoded media file.

Constant vs. variable bitrate

The bitrate is a main determinant of the quality of your encoded video file—the more bits you have at your disposal, the better in general your video will look. But, just as with JPG, some types of imagery require fewer bits to look good, while other types of imagery require more bits to look decent. Since JPG was optimized for photographic-style imagery, generally flat blocks of color (for instance, a white wall) require many more bits to avoid the type of visual artifacts typical of poor image compression (blocky, splotchy, and pixilated images).

The same is true for video. Unfortunately, not all video files are of the same type of imagery. For instance, footage of a sports event could include motion-heavy coverage of the event as well as talking-head footage of the announcers. So, wouldn't it be nice if you could allocate more bits to the part of your video that needs it, at the expense of the portions of your video that don't?

That's what **variable bitrate encoding** is for. The Adobe Flash CS3 Video Encoder only encodes with a **constant bitrate**, or CBR, meaning each second of video has the same number of bits as each other second of video in your file. But, if you use a tool like On2 Flix or Sorenson Squeeze, you can specify variable bitrate, or VBR, encoding. In almost all cases, encoding with VBR will produce a better-quality encoding.

Figure 10-2. The Flash CS3 Video Encoder Video settings panel

This also brings up the topic of 1-pass and 2-pass encoding. In 1-pass encoding, the encoder reads through the source video one time and produces the compressed video as it reads the source. In 2-pass encoding, the encoder will run through your source video twice—a preliminary pass analyzes all the content of your video, and a second pass actually encodes the video, given the information it acquired in the first pass. VBR encoding requires 2-pass encoding, so it always takes much longer than 1-pass CBR encoding.

Cue points

In addition to streaming video and audio, Flash video also streams **cue points**—or customizable bits of information tied to specific timecodes in your FLV. One common use for this would be to create a closed-captioning system in your video player. Since cue points can consist of most any type of information, they also have many other potential uses. For example, you could utilize cue points to integrate hotspots into your FLVs. All you need is a metadata event handler to process the cue points as they are received on the NetStream.

Cue points may be inserted into your FLV through your video encoder, as you see in Figure 10-3, in the Cue Points settings panel of the Adobe Flash CS3 Video Encoder.

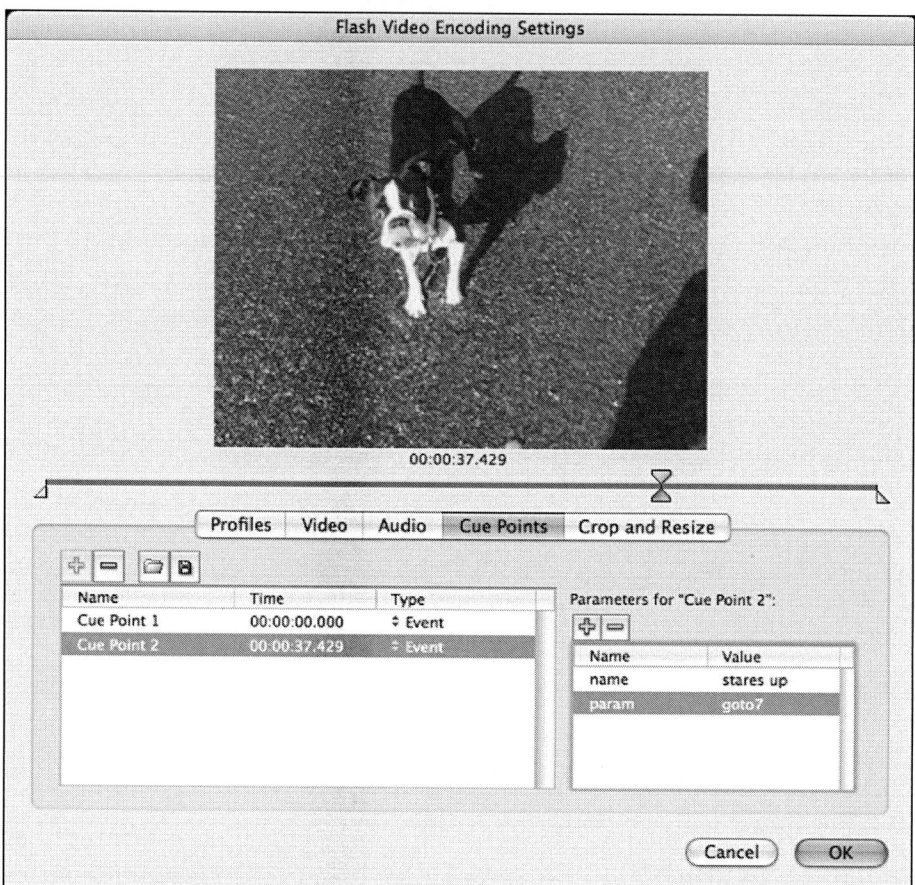

Figure 10-3. The Cue Points settings panel in the Adobe Flash CS3 Video Encoder

New in the Flash CS3 Video Encoder is the ability to easily import and export cue points from this settings panel in an easily-understood XML format. Setting cue points in the encoder means the data is effectively baked into your FLV.

If you want to add cue points to an FLV that was encoded without them, you may choose to process the FLV using Burak's Captionate, a Windows-based tool that allows you to bake cue points into already encoded FLVs. For more information on this tool, you may visit http://buraks.com/captionate/.

If your FLV does not have cue points, or you want to easily apply the same set of cue points to any FLV your player loads, you may assign cue points in ActionScript without affecting the data in the FLV itself. For more information on how to do this, you may view the Flex LiveDocs entry at http://livedocs.adobe.com/flex/201/html/controls_059_20.html.

Delivering Flash video

While FLV files are not directly viewable in the Flash Player, you can quickly and easily build applications to run in the Flash Player that will load and play back FLVs. This can be done without any special additional software.

When you load your FLVs like this, you are playing back your FLVs progressively. Many people mistakenly believe that Flash is a streaming format; it is instead a progressive format—though the concepts are similar and often confused.

From a usability perspective, streaming video differs from progressive video in one key aspect—the ability to seek. In progressively delivered media, including SWFs, the content that is downloaded may be accessed as the rest of the content is delivered. In a streaming format, the user may seek to any portion of the media and effectively jump right to it, no matter how much has already been delivered to the viewer. For example, if you are delivering a video progressively, if the viewer wishes to view minute 10 of the video, he must wait for all of minutes 1 through 10 to download. If the video is streamed, however, the viewer may jump immediately to minute 10.

Beyond this capability to seek, streaming your Flash video brings additional technical benefits. First and foremost, it is very difficult to "steal" streamed FLVs. If you deliver your FLVs progressively, they are cached on the viewer's machine and may be easily copied. Streamed FLVs never reside on the viewer's machine, and access to them is obscured by the streaming server. For this reason alone, many major entertainment brands have opted to stream their FLV video. More recently, Adobe has beefed up the content access protection features available in the Flash Media Server. For more information on this, you may read Chris Hock's DEVNET article at www.adobe.com/devnet/flashcom/articles/digital_media_protection.html.

When you stream your FLVs, you may also exploit the capability to dynamically detect the viewer's bitrate. If the viewer is accessing the video on a slower connection, you can deliver a lower bitrate version of the media; similarly, viewers on faster connections may view the higher-quality version. It is important to note that neither FMS nor Red5 will dynamically reencode your video for the different bitrates—you must instead prepare different media files for the different bitrates you wish to support and then route the viewer to the correct version of the media file.

Streaming also brings additional delivery costs. First, there is the cost of the Flash Media Server, but in addition to that, since the bandwidth over which streaming media is delivered must be more reliable, streaming bandwidth incurs premium pricing. So many firms forgo streaming in favor of the less expensive progressive delivery. And almost each and every video-sharing network you have seen online delivers their FLVs progressively for the same reason.

Next, Omar will go over playing back video in Flex.

VideoDisplay component

In order to play back FLV media files, Flex provides the VideoDisplay component. Unlike the FLVPlayback component in Flash CS3, this component provides only the video display area, without any prebuilt user interface elements. To build a video player user interface in Flex, you need to harness the events dispatched by the VideoDisplay component. The VideoDisplay component comes with several events and properties that enable you to code custom functionality for the video player, as I'll demonstrate in this section.

Overview of basic properties/events

The VideoDisplay component has many events and properties that you will become familiar with as the chapter goes on, but the first of the properties I want to introduce you to is the source property. This is the property you use every time you want to load a new video to play. The string path to the FLV and the name of the file to play back must both be provided to the source property as one string. If the video is in the same directory as the SWF, the property should simply be set to the file name.

By default, the autoPlay property is set to true. This means that the instant the source property is set, the VideoDisplay component will begin to download, and when half a second of video has loaded (the default setting of the bufferTime property), Flash will begin playing back the video. This will also trigger the first event, the ready event, which signifies that the bufferTime has been met on load and is dispatched once per loaded video. So let's start looking at some code.

Playing a single static video

Now that I've covered the basic properties of the VideoDisplay component, I will go over getting the video to play. Using only the source property to play back a video that is in the same directory as the application SWF, the code would look as follows:

```
<?xml version="1.0" encoding="utf-8"?>
<mx:Application
  width="600" height="600"
  xmlns:mx="http://www.adobe.com/2006/mxml"
  layout="absolute">

  <mx:VideoDisplay source="video.flv" width="100%" height="100%"/>

</mx:Application>
```

This represents a basic Flex application set at a width and height of 600, with a sole component instance of a video display whose source is set to video.flv. The <mx:VideoDisplay/> is set to scale to 100%. The VideoDisplay component has a black background, as you can see in Figure 10-4. Also, notice that once the video starts to play, black bars appear above and below the video. This occurs because the maintainAspectRatio property's default value is true.

To debug or run the SWF, you will need to place the video.flv file in the bin folder. Since the SWF is output to that folder, when the file is opened in the browser, the browser will look for the FLV in the same directory.

If the maintainAspectRatio property is set to false, the video fills the display area, stretching the video out of proportion as you can see in Figure 10-5.

Figure 10-4. The property maintainAspectRatio causes the video to scale and keep proportion, resulting in the black strips.

Figure 10-5. With maintainAspectRation set to false, the video now fills the display component.

To achieve the outcome you see in Figure 10-5, I update the VideoDisplay instance with the maintainAspectRatio parameter set to false:

```
<mx:VideoDisplay source="video.flv" width="100%" height="100%"
    maintainAspectRatio="false" />
```

So with a few lines of MXML, the application is playing back an FLV file, and I've covered how to control the aspect ratio of video when it's played back—all without writing a single line of ActionScript! That, however, won't be the case when I get into handling some of the component events and build a user interface for the video player.

Adding a time played/total time display

Before I start to add an interface to the video player, I put the VideoDisplay component in a container. For this example, I use a Panel component to lay out the video player. The code changes look like this:

```
<?xml version="1.0" encoding="utf-8"?>
<mx:Application
  width="600" height="600"
  xmlns:mx="http://www.adobe.com/2006/mxml"
  layout="absolute">
  <mx:Panel title="Video Player" top="10" bottom="10"
    left="10" right="10">
    <mx:VideoDisplay source="video.flv" width="100%"
      maintainAspectRatio="false" height="100%" autoPlay="true"/>
    <mx:ControlBar>
      <mx:HBox width="100%">
        <mx:Spacer width="100%"/>
        <mx:Label id="tf_playtimeDisplay"/>
      </mx:HBox>
    </mx:ControlBar>
  </mx:Panel>
</mx:Application>
```

The first thing I add is a Panel component that wraps the VideoDisplay component I already have. The Panel component has a title, and I've set the top, bottom, left, and right properties to 10, making the Panel component fill the entire application, leaving a space of 10 pixels from the outer edges.

I also add another container component beneath the video display. The ControlBar component gives the Panel component an area below the panel's content that provides space for me to add controls for my player. To start, I place a Label component in an HBox in the control bar, where I will display the playback progress of the video. The spacer pushes the time display to the far right; compiled, it looks like Figure 10-6. There is no time display in the figure because the Label component does not have a default value set to its text property, and there isn't any video updating the text yet.

Figure 10-6. The thick area at the bottom of the panel is the control bar, where the UI elements will be.

Now that I have a place to display the time, I set up an external ActionScript file named videoPlayer.as (I'll run through its content in a moment), which I place in the same directory as the MXML file in the project folder. This is where all the event handlers for the video player will be declared. The MXML code should now look like this:

```
<?xml version="1.0" encoding="utf-8"?>
<mx:Application creationComplete="init()"
  width="600" height="600"
  xmlns:mx="http://www.adobe.com/2006/mxml"
  layout="absolute">
  <mx:Script source="videoPlayer.as"/>
  <mx:Panel title="Video Player" top="10" bottom="10"
    left="10" right="10">
    <mx:VideoDisplay source="video.flv" width="100%"
      maintainAspectRatio="false" height="100%" autoPlay="true"/>
    <mx:ControlBar>
      <mx:HBox width="100%">
        <mx:Spacer width="100%"/>
        <mx:Label id="tf_playtimeDisplay"/>
      </mx:HBox>
    </mx:ControlBar>
  </mx:Panel>
</mx:Application>
```

The only line added in the MXML file is the <mx:Script/> tag. I also add a call to the init() method in the creationComplete event of the application. In the videoPlayer.as file, I add two event listeners to the VideoDisplay component and declare the event handlers for the events. The ActionScript looks like this:

```
// ActionScript file videoPlayer.as

import mx.events.VideoEvent;
import mx.formatters.DateFormatter;

private var videoLength:String;
private var start:Date;
private var timeDisplayFormatter:DateFormatter;

/*
* Handles the creationComplete event. The
* <code>start</code> Date object is used to
* calculate playback time using the <code> timeDisplayFormatter</code>
* DateFormatter object.
*/
private function init():void
{
  start = new Date("1/1/2000");
  timeDisplayFormatter  = new DateFormatter();
  this.myVideoDisplay.addEventListener(VideoEvent.READY, videoReady);
  this.myVideoDisplay.addEventListener(VideoEvent.PLAYHEAD_UPDATE,
  updateTimeDisplay);
}
/*
* Handles the videoReady event. Takes totalTime from the
* VideoDisplay to calculate the end time based on the
* time in the <code>start</code> Date object.
*/
private function videoReady(event:VideoEvent):void
{
  // to add hours to the display use military time format,
  // use "J:NN:SS" or "JJ:NN:SS",
  timeDisplayFormatter.formatString = "NN:SS";
  var totalTime:Date = new Date ( start.getTime() +
      (this.myVideoDisplay.totalTime * 1000) );
  this.videoLength = timeDisplayFormatter.format(totalTime);
}
/*
* Handles the playheadUpdate event, updating the display.
*/
private function updateTimeDisplay(event:VideoEvent):void
{
  timeDisplayFormatter.formatString = "N:SS";
  var currentTime:Date = new Date ( start.getTime() +
```

```
            (event.playheadTime * 1000) );
        tf_playtimeDisplay.text = timeDisplayFormatter.format(currentTime)
          + "/" + this.videoLength;
    }
```

In the init() method, the first two lines declare a Date object and a DateFormatter object that will be used to determine the current and total play times of the VideoDisplay. The start variable, a Date object, is instantiated using the date January 1, 2000. It does not matter what date string is entered, as it serves as only a point of reference from which to measure time against. What is important is not providing a specific time, just a date. This defaults the Date object to January 1, 2000, 12:00:00 a.m. Using the DateFormatter object, I can get a 24-hour string for the time display, resulting in 00:00:00 when formatted.

The first event listener I add is for the ready event of the VideoDisplay component. As I went over earlier, this event is dispatched once, when the video is loaded and ready to play back. I use this event to calculate the total video length with the VideoEvent.READY event handler, videoReady(). In the event handler, I first set the formatString property of the DateFormatter object, timeDisplayFormatter. The string "NN:SS" will give a format of minutes and seconds with leading zeros when values are less than 10. The formatting characters are defined by the DateFormatter class. To get a full list of the formatting possibilities, look up the Flex Language Reference document for the DateFormatter class. The complete list of formatting characters is well explained there.

The next line declares a Date object, totalTime, which will perform the calculation of how long the video is. To retrieve the length of the video, I use the start Date object to measure against. Using the getTime() method of the Date object, I get a millisecond representation of the start Date object. Then I add the totalTime property of the VideoDisplay component; because totalTime returns the length of the video in seconds, I need to multiply by 1000, as the start Date object value returned by getTime() is in milliseconds. This adds the total time in milliseconds to the start date time, which is 0:00:00, or 12:00:00 a.m. Using the format() method of the DateFormatter object, timeDisplayFormatter, I get a formatted string of the total video length. Finally, I store a reference of the formatted string in the videoLength variable to use later when I update the user interface display.

The second event handler is for the playheadUpdate event of the VideoDisplay component. This is the event used to update the user interface display. By default, the VideoDisplay component's playheadUpdateInterval value is set to 250 milliseconds, which is usually sufficient for a proper updating of the display. The updateTimeDisplay event handler calculates the current play time of the VideoDisplay component and updates the display. In this method, I again use the timeDisplayFormatter DateFormatter object; however, this time I change the formatString. The same DateFormatter object is deliberately reused for application memory optimization. The string "N:SS" will return a format of minutes and seconds, using single digits when the minutes value is less than 10. The next line uses the exact same technique used in the videoReady event handler to calculate the current play time of the VideoDisplay component. The difference in the updateTimeDisplay event handler is that instead of multiplying 1000 by the VideoDisplay component's totalTime, the playheadTime property of the VideoEvent.PLAYHEAD_UPDATE event is used instead. In the last line, I use the DateFormatter object on the currentTime Date object to get a formatted string of the current play time just like in the first event handler. The string is concatenated with a slash and the videoLength variable stored by the videoReady event handler. The complete string is set to the text property of the tf_timeDisplay component, which is the Label component in the user interface that displays the video's current and total play times. Looking at Figure 10-7, you can see the two different format results.

Figure 10-7. Notice the two different formats, resulting from the two formatStrings of the DateFormatter.

Adding video controls

Now that I've gone over how to play a video and get a timer display, I will cover how to go about adding controls to the VideoDisplay component. In this section, you'll see how to use the playing property of the VideoDisplay component to create a Pause/Play button, as well as a Stop button and volume control.

Pause/Play button

Before adding any code to create the pause/play functionality, I prepare the MXML by adding a Button component to use as the Pause/Play toggle button. In the control bar area of the Video Player panel, I add a button.

```
...
    <mx:ControlBar>
      <mx:HBox width="100%">
        <mx:Button label="Pause/Play" id="btn_playToggle"/>
        <mx:Spacer width="100%"/>
        <mx:Label id="tf_playtimeDisplay"/>
      </mx:HBox>
    </mx:ControlBar>
...
```

Continuing with the same code, the only line I add is the Button component with the label of Pause/Play and an ID of btn_playToggle. It is placed right above the Spacer component, so that it appears on the far-left edge of the control bar area. This is the button that will be used to toggle video playback. Next, I add the event handler that will handle the code to toggle playback. In the init() method, I add one line to attach the event listener, and I also add the event handler definition. That code looks like this:

```
// ActionScript file videoPlayer.as
...
private function init():void
{
  start = new Date("1/1/2000");
  timeDisplayFormatter  = new DateFormatter();

  this.myVideoDisplay.addEventListener(VideoEvent.READY, videoReady);
  this.myVideoDisplay.addEventListener(VideoEvent.PLAYHEAD_UPDATE,
    updateTimeDisplay);
  btn_playToggle.addEventListener(MouseEvent.CLICK, togglePlayback);
}
...
/*
* Toggles the video playback.
*/
private function togglePlayback(event:MouseEvent):void
{
  if (this.myVideoDisplay.playing)
  {
    this.myVideoDisplay.pause();
  }
  else if (this.myVideoDisplay.source)
  {
    this.myVideoDisplay.play();
  }
}
```

In the ActionScript side of things, I first add an event listener to the VideoDisplay component in the init() method for mouse click events. The togglePlayback event handler is assigned to the event, and at the bottom of the previous code I declare the event handler. In the event handler, there is an if statement that uses the playing property of the VideoDisplay component, which returns as true when a video is currently playing back, and executes the pause() method of the VideoDisplay component if the video is playing. In the else clause, if the VideoDisplay component has a source, the method executes the play() method. The video player now appears as in Figure 10-8, and the Pause/Play button is fully functional.

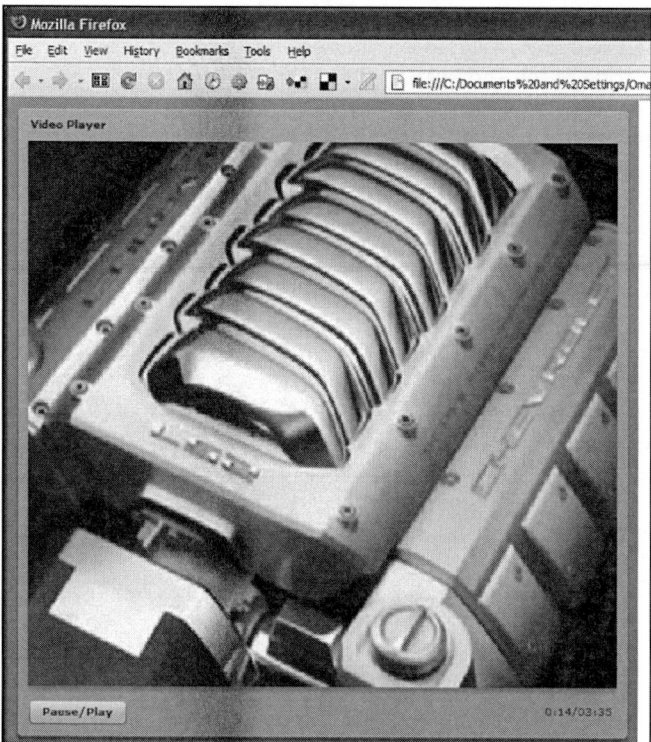

Figure 10-8. The Pause/Play button added to the control bar

Stop button

The Stop button is implemented very much in the same manner that the Pause/Play button was in the previous section. Like the first button, I first prepare the MXML layout. The Stop button is between the Pause/Play button and the spacer so that it appears immediately to the right of the Pause/Play button. The code looks as follows:

```
...
    <mx:ControlBar>
      <mx:HBox width="100%">
        <mx:Button label="Pause/Play" id="btn_playToggle"/>
        <mx:Button label="Stop" id="btn_stop"/>
        <mx:Spacer width="100%"/>
        <mx:Label id="tf_playtimeDisplay"/>
      </mx:HBox>
    </mx:ControlBar>
...
```

The Button component I add is directly under the Play/Pause button. Again, like the previous example, I add an event listener and declare the event handler. The ActionScript looks like this:

```
...
private function init():void
{
  start = new Date("1/1/2000");
  timeDisplayFormatter  = new DateFormatter();

  this.myVideoDisplay.addEventListener(VideoEvent.READY, videoReady);
  this.myVideoDisplay.addEventListener(VideoEvent.PLAYHEAD_UPDATE,
    updateTimeDisplay);
  btn_playToggle.addEventListener(MouseEvent.CLICK, togglePlayback);
  btn_stop.addEventListener(MouseEvent.CLICK, stopPlayback);
}
...
private function stopPlayback(event:MouseEvent):void
{
  this.myVideoDisplay.stop();
}
```

After adding the stopPlayback event listener to the VideoDisplay component in the init() method, the event handler is declared at the bottom of the function list. In the event handler, I call the stop() method of the VideoDisplay component, stopping the playback of the video. By default, with the stop() method, if the autoRewind property of the VideoDisplay component is set to true, the VideoDisplay will automatically rewind to the beginning of the video; by using the pause() method, I can subsequently continue playback from the same position in the video with the play() method. If the autoRewind property is set to false, the stop() method has the same behavior as the pause() method. The Stop button appears as shown in Figure 10-9.

Volume control

With the playback controls in place, I will now talk about adding a control for the VideoDisplay volume. To do this, I use a VSlider component and some binding in MXML to get the volume slider working. In the control bar area, before the closing tag

Figure 10-9. The Stop button appears immediately to the right of the Pause/Play button because of the Spacer component.

of the component, I add the vertical slider component so that it appears on the far right. With the rest of the properties written out, the MXML code looks like this:

277

```
    ...
        <mx:VideoDisplay volume="{volumeSlider.value}" id="myVideoDisplay"
          source="09Camaro.flv" width="100%" maintainAspectRatio="false"
          height="100%" autoPlay="true"/>
        <mx:ControlBar>
          <mx:HBox width="100%">
            <mx:Button label="Pause/Play" id="btn_playToggle"/>
            <mx:Button label="Stop" id="btn_stop"/>
            <mx:Spacer width="100%"/>
            <mx:Label id="tf_playtimeDisplay"/>
            <mx:VSlider id="volumeSlider" liveDragging="true" value=".75"
              minimum="0" maximum="1" height="34"/>
          </mx:HBox>
        </mx:ControlBar>
      ...
```

One newly added component and one MXML attribute on the VideoDisplay component, and the volume control is functional. These are the types of things that a great framework like Flex makes quick and easy to handle. So let me explain what is going on here.

The VideoDisplay component handles volume on a scale from 0 to 1. The volume property is a bindable property. This allows me to bind other bindable variables to it, so that when the variable it is referencing is updated, it too is automatically updated. Using the curly braces in the volume property, I bind the volume property of the VideoDisplay component to the value property of the volumeSlider, which is the vertical slider component I've added in the control bar area.

In order to get the slider to return valid volume values to the VideoDisplay component, I set the minimum and maximum properties of the VSlider component between 0 and 1. I also set the value property to .75, which sets the default volume of the VideoDisplay component to 75% volume. By default, the liveDragging property of the VSlider component is set to false; this means that when you drag the slider thumb bar across the slider, the value does not get updated until you release the thumb bar. By setting the liveDragging property to true, the VSlider component updates its value property as you drag, in turn updating the VideoDisplay volume property because they are bound. Finally, I set the height to 34 pixels so that it fits better within the control bar area. The end result looks like Figure 10-10.

Figure 10-10. The VSlider component, at the far right, controls the volume of the VideoDisplay component via a binding.

Additional functionality

With the basic controls of the video player written, there is still functionality that can be developed out of this same VideoDisplay component. In this section, I will handle some more events to create a video download progress bar, a playback progress bar, and a video scrubber bar. Then I will show how these same Flex components were used together to build the same functionality in the video player for the RMX while making it appear to be a single slider component.

Download progress bar

To display the progress of the video download, I add a ProgressBar component within the Panel component that is holding the VideoDisplay component. Since it really only takes one line of ActionScript to get the VideoDisplay component to update the progress bar, I set an event handler in the MXML. The code changes look as follows:

```xml
<?xml version="1.0" encoding="utf-8"?>
<mx:Application
  creationComplete="init()"
  width="600" height="600"
  xmlns:mx="http://www.adobe.com/2006/mxml"
  layout="absolute">
  <mx:Script source="videoPlayer.as"/>
  <mx:Panel title="Video Player" top="10" bottom="10" left="10"
    right="10" layout="vertical" verticalGap="0">
    <mx:VideoDisplay
    progress="this.downloadProgress.setProgress(event.bytesLoaded,
    event.bytesTotal)" volume="{this.volumeSlider.value}"
    id="myVideoDisplay" source="video.flv" width="100%"
    maintainAspectRatio="false" height="100%" autoPlay="true"/>
    <mx:ProgressBar id="downloadProgress" width="100%" label=""
      height="10" trackHeight="10" minimum="0" maximum="100"
      mode="manual"/>
    <mx:ControlBar>
      ...
```

I'll start by explaining the layout changes. On the Panel component, I set the layout property to vertical, so that the ProgressBar component stacks under the VideoDisplay component. I also set the verticalGap property to 0, so that there isn't any spacing between the display and the progress bar.

Next, I add the ProgressBar component, downloadProgress, directly under the VideoDisplay component. I set the trackHeight CSS property to 10 to match the overall height of the component. The label property is set to an empty string because I have chosen not to use a label for this example. If you wish to use a label, the height of the ProgressBar component must be larger than the trackHeight, so that there is space to display the label. The minimum and maximum properties are set to 0 and 100, respectively. Finally, the mode property is set to manual, so that the progress event of the VideoDisplay component can update the progress.

The last step is the ActionScript that updates the ProgressBar component. In the VideoDisplay component, I add the progress event handler, which uses the setProgress() method of the ProgressBar component to update the download progress. The first parameter is the current value, and the second parameter is the total value. The VideoEvent carries this information in the bytesLoaded and bytesTotal properties of the video progress event. When the code is compiled, the progress bar appears as shown in Figure 10-11.

Figure 10-11. The progress bar appears right under the display.

Playback progress bar

With the video download progress bar in place, the next bit of information to be displayed in the user interface is the current playback position. To display the position of the VideoDisplay component, I'll use an HSlider component. If you simply want to show the progress of playback, a ProgressBar component would work just as well. However, I choose an HSlider component for this example because I want to add a scrubber, and I'll use the same HSlider for that task as well.

For this example, I place the HSlider component inside the Panel component, directly under the download progress bar, along with a couple of bindings to bring this component to life. The MXML addition looks like this:

```
...
    <mx:ProgressBar id="downloadProgress" width="100%" label=""
      height="10" trackHeight="10" minimum="0" maximum="100"
      mode="manual"/>
    <mx:HSlider id="playbackProgress" width="100%" height="10"
      minimum="0" maximum="{this.myVideoDisplay.totalTime}"
      value="{this.myVideoDisplay.playheadTime}"/>
    <mx:ControlBar>
...
```

If I were to recompile the video player, it would now display the playback progress using the HSlider component I just added. So what's going on in this component? The first three properties are basic properties, id, and dimension properties width and height. The other three are what make the component display the playback progress of the VideoDisplay component.

First, the minimum and maximum properties of the HSlider must be set so that it knows what the range is that it will be sliding through. minimum is hard-coded to 0, since that's the beginning of all videos. The maximum property uses a bind to set the maximum to the totalTime property of the VideoDisplay component.

Now that the slider has its properties set to slide through the length of the video, the value property of the HSlider component brings the display to life. This is accomplished by using a binding to bind the value property of the HSlider to the playheadTime property of the VideoDisplay component. Because the slider's range is 0 to the VideoDisplay component's totalTime, setting the value of the HSlider using the playheadTime property puts the HSlider thumb bar in the exact value of where the video playhead is at. The end result is what you see in Figure 10-12. The beauty of using binding this way is that I don't have to worry about the properties I'm binding being available to the component. Because all of the components are instantiated in MXML, all the properties are available to be bound to. If the components were created dynamically, I would have to wait until the creationComplete event of each component was dispatched before I can bind to its properties, or I could use other events such as applicationComplete or videoReady.

Figure 10-12. The playback progress is being displayed by the HSlider component added under the progress bar.

Video scrubber

The playback progress bar is the base for the video scrubber. By adding a few properties and event handlers, I can scrub the video using the thumb bar of the HSlider component. First, I add some properties in the MXML to scrub using the thumb bar of the HSlider:

```
...
<mx:HSlider
thumbPress="if ( myVideoDisplay.playing ) {
this.myVideoDisplay.pause(); }"
thumbDrag="this.seekTo = this.playbackProgress.value;?
thumbRelease="this.myVideoDisplay.playheadTime = this.seekTo;
this.myVideoDisplay.play();"
liveDragging="true"
```

```
        id="playbackProgress" width="100%" height="10" minimum="0"
        maximum="{this.myVideoDisplay.totalTime}"
        value="{this.myVideoDisplay.playheadTime}"/>
    <mx:ControlBar>
...
```

In the HSlider component, I insert a carriage return to create a new line for the new code; the new code is still within the same HSlider. The first property is actually an event, thumbPress. The code within the quotes is executed in the event handler for thumbPress; since it is only one line, I include the ActionScript inline. The if statement checks whether the video display is playing; if so, it pauses the playback so that updates to the HSlider value stop, allowing the viewer to drag the thumb bar. Of course, for code cleanliness and portability, I'd normally want all of these handlers in a class, but for the purposes of this example, I include many of these one-line event handlers inline.

When the thumb bar gets dragged, the thumbDrag event is dispatched, and that is what is declared next. In the thumbDrag event handler code, I keep track of where the thumb bar was dragged by setting a new variable I declare in the ActionScript file called seekTo. This is the variable used to actually make the VideoDisplay component seek. The change to the ActionScript should look like this:

```
// ActionScript file videoPlayer.as

import mx.events.VideoEvent;
import mx.formatters.DateFormatter;
import flash.events.MouseEvent;

private var seekTo:Number;
private var videoLength:String;
private var start:Date;
private var timeDisplayFormatter:DateFormatter;

...
```

The only change to the ActionScript file is the declaration of the seekTo variable. The third MXML property I add is for the thumbRelease event. In the event handler code for the thumbRelease event, there are two ActionScript statements. The first one is the one that actually makes the VideoDisplay seek by setting the playheadTime property of the VideoDisplay component to the value of the seekTo variable.

The fourth property is a property of the VideoDisplay component. By default, the liveDragging property is set to false, which means that the value of the HSlider component does not get updated until the thumb bar is released, which would only dispatch the change event once, not updating the seekTo variable. By setting the liveDragging property to true, the value property of the HSlider is updated as the thumb bar gets dragged. When the thumb bar is released, the seekTo variable has the value of the last position that was dragged to. When the code is compiled, the video is now seekable.

Even though the video is seekable, what happens if the track is clicked? That scenario has not been handled yet, so the thumb bar quickly bounces back to the updated playhead position. To handle this scenario, I use the clickTarget property of the change SliderEvent in the MXML code. The change looks like this:

```
...
    <mx:ProgressBar id="downloadProgress" width="100%" label="
    " height="10"    trackHeight="10" minimum="0" maximum="100"
     mode="manual"/>
    <mx:HSlider
    change="if (event.clickTarget=='track') {
    this.myVideoDisplay.playheadTime = event.value; }"
    thumbPress="if(myVideoDisplay.playing){
    this.myVideoDisplay.pause();}"
    thumbDrag="this.seekTo=this.playbackProgress.value"
    thumbRelease="this.myVideoDisplay.playheadTime =
    this.seekTo; this.myVideoDisplay.play();"
    liveDragging="true"
      id="playbackProgress" width="100%" height="10" minimum="0"
    maximum="{this.myVideoDisplay.totalTime}"
    value="{this.myVideoDisplay.playheadTime}"/>
    <mx:ControlBar>
...
```

In the HSlider component, I drop a new line to enter the change event. In the event handler code, the if statement checks the clickTarget property to see whether it is equal to the string "track". If it is, I set the playheadTime property of the VideoDisplay component to the value property of the event. When I compile, the track now seeks the video at the point where I click.

Up until this point, the examples I've shown have catered to delivering video using progressive downloading. The reason I bring this up in this section of the chapter is that if the connection currently being used were to a streaming server, like Flash Media Server or Red5, the video scrubber as is would be perfect, since I'd be able to scrub to any position in the video, and the stream would take care of feeding the proper position in the video. However, if the video uses a progressive connection, like the vast majority of Flash video players on the Internet, I would not be able to scrub to a position past what is currently downloaded for that particular video. Next, I will show you how I restrict scrubbing past what is downloaded in the video player of the RMX.

Restricting the scrubber for progressive video players

In order to restrict scrubbing past what is currently downloaded, I make a couple of adjustments to the maximum value of the HSlider component, as well as adjust the total width of the HSlider component—the goal being that the thumb bar stays in the same position, but the width of the HSlider increases as the download nears completion. In order to make these calculations, I need to capture and store the value of the video file size, which the VideoDisplay component strips from the video metadata for me and makes available through properties of the VideoDisplay. To prepare for this, I declare a new variable in the ActionScript file called videoFileTotalBytes. The simple change looks like this:

```
// ActionScript file videoPlayer.as

import mx.events.VideoEvent;
import mx.formatters.DateFormatter;
import flash.events.MouseEvent;
```

```
private var seekTo:Number;
private var videoFileTotalBytes:Number;
private var videoLength:String;
private var start:Date;
private var timeDisplayFormatter:DateFormatter;
...
```

With that variable declared, I capture the file size in the progress event. In the VideoDisplay component, in the MXML file, I add the following change:

```
...
<mx:VideoDisplay
progress="this.downloadProgress.setProgress( event.bytesLoaded,
event.bytesTotal ); this.videoFileTotalBytes = event.bytesTotal;"
volume="{this.volumeSlider.value}" id="myVideoDisplay"
source="video.flv" width="100%" maintainAspectRatio="false"
height="100%" autoPlay="true"/>
...
```

With the file size now stored, I can make the adjustments to the HSlider to prevent the scrubbing. Those changes look like this:

```
...
<mx:HSlider
change="if (event.clickTarget=='track') {
this.myVideoDisplay.playheadTime = event.value; }"
thumbPress="if(myVideoDisplay.playing){
this.myVideoDisplay.pause();}"
thumbDrag="this.seekTo=this.playbackProgress.value"
thumbRelease="this.myVideoDisplay.playheadTime =
this.seekTo; this.myVideoDisplay.play();"
liveDragging="true"
id="playbackProgress"
width="{ (downloadProgress.value / videoFileTotalBytes ) *
downloadProgress.width}" height="10" minimum="0"
maximum="{ myVideoDisplay.totalTime *
( downloadProgress.value / videoFileTotalBytes ) }"
value="{this.myVideoDisplay.playheadTime}"/>
...
```

So I make two adjustments here. First, in the maximum property, I adjust the totalTime by the percentage of the video that has been downloaded, by dividing the product of the totalTime of the VideoDisplay component and the value of the ProgressBar component by the videoFileTotalBytes variable I stored. This adjusts the maximum value to be the same as the available seconds to play back.

The second adjustment needed is to the width of the HSlider, so that the thumb bar is in the correct position in relation to the width of the HSlider, even before it reaches 100% width. I accomplish this by setting the width of the HSlider to the width of the ProgressBar, multiplied by the value of the ProgressBar divided by the videoFileTotalBytes variable. If you run this example, the HSlider now adjusts its width as more of the video becomes available, in effect restricting the area you can scrub. Keeping these calculations for width and maximum in the MXML makes it simple to keep those values updated using bindings, while at the same time keeping the binding dynamic in the sense that it is not coming from a single property, which makes it more difficult to bind using ActionScript and the BindingUtils class.

The RMX video player controls

Although the video player for the RMX looks different from the one I've built in the examples of this chapter, I used all of these same coding techniques. So how did I make the video download progress bar, playback progress bar, and scrubber appear as though they were one custom-built component? I put together the RMX video player control bar using the same components I used in the previous examples, but with some small yet significant layout tweaks and CSS. First, let's take a look at the layout changes.

I begin by setting up the ProgressBar component and the HSlider component to appear to look as one. I will accomplish this by wrapping the two in a Canvas container. By placing the ProgressBar first in the <mx:Canvas/> tag, the HSlider will be layered on top of the ProgressBar. The MXML looks like this:

```
...
<mx:Canvas width="100%">
<mx:ProgressBar id="downloadProgress" width="100%" label=""
  height="10" trackHeight="10" minimum="0" maximum="100"
  mode="manual"/>
<mx:HSlider
  change="if (event.clickTarget=='track') {
  this.myVideoDisplay.playheadTime = event.value; }"
  thumbPress="if(myVideoDisplay.playing){
  this.myVideoDisplay.pause();}"
  thumbDrag="this.seekTo=this.playbackProgress.value"
  thumbRelease="this.myVideoDisplay.playheadTime =
  this.seekTo; this.myVideoDisplay.play();" liveDragging="true"
  id="playbackProgress"
  width="{(downloadProgress.value/videoFileTotalBytes)*
  downloadProgress.width}" height="10"
  minimum="0" maximum="{myVideoDisplay.totalTime *
  (downloadProgress.value/videoFileTotalBytes)}"
  value="{this.myVideoDisplay.playheadTime}"/>
</mx:Canvas>
...
```

By wrapping the ProgressBar and HSlider with a Canvas that is 100% wide, the HSlider now appears to be on top of the ProgressBar, as you can see in Figure 10-13.

Figure 10-13. The HSlider is now on top of the ProgressBar, because it's wrapped in a Canvas.

With the HSlider now on top of the ProgressBar, it almost appears as though it were one component. However, because you can see the track of the HSlider component, it is still clear there are two overlaid components. To get rid of the track of the HSlider, I use CSS and an invisible image. Using Fireworks, I create a 1✕1 invisible PNG file (an empty 1✕1 PNG file exported with transparency on) and put it in my images folder in my Flex project. I embed the image as the trackSkin. The MXML looks like this:

```
...
    <mx:HSlider
      trackSkin="@Embed(source='images/inv.png')"
...
```

The inv.png file is embedded using the Embed directive, and when I compile the component, looks as if it were just one, as you can see in Figure 10-14.

The only difference between this example and the RMX is that the video player for the RMX also has a skin applied to the thumb bar, using the thumbDownSkin, thumbOverSkin, and thumbUpSkin properties of the HSlider component. I can assign images to those properties using the Embed directive like the example in the video player, or I can embed it in the ActionScript and bind a reference to the class variable, as demonstrated in Chapter 5.

Figure 10-14. The thumb bar of the HSlider now appears as if its track were the ProgressBar, making it appear as if it were a single component.

Playlists

Now that I have all the controls for my video player, the next step is to add a playlist. Obviously, there are many different ways to load a playlist into a Flex application, and I cannot cover them all, and in any case, that is not the purpose of this section. The purpose is to show how to handle the VideoDisplay component events so that I can play continuously off of any playlist. For the example, I've chosen to load an XML file, which is one of the most common formats to consume data in. Whether you're working with an XML object, array object, or plain object, the fundamentals are the same.

I've prepared a simple XML file to serve as the playlist. The playlist.xml file looks like this:

```
<playlist>
  <video title="First Video" file="video.flv"/>
  <video title="Second Video" file="video.flv"/>
  <video title="Third Video" file="video.flv"/>
</playlist>
```

The first edit to the existing code will be to remove the source property from the VideoDisplay component. I will be setting the source property using ActionScript after I've loaded the playlist, so I simply delete the source attribute from the VideoDisplay component.

Now that the video player is ready for dynamic video loading, I load the playlist XML file, playlist.xml, using the HTTPService class. I load the XML in the init() method by calling the new loadPlaylist() method. The result event handler for the playlist loading will play the first video. The ActionScript file now looks like this:

```
// ActionScript file videoPlayer.as

import mx.events.VideoEvent;
import mx.formatters.DateFormatter;
import flash.events.MouseEvent;
import mx.rpc.http.mxml.HTTPService;
import mx.rpc.events.ResultEvent;
import mx.rpc.events.FaultEvent;

private var videoLength:String;
private var start:Date;
private var timeDisplayFormatter:DateFormatter;
private var seekTo:Number;

private var playlist:XMLList;
private var playlistCursor:uint;

[Bindable]
private var videoFileTotalBytes:Number;



private function init():void
{
  start = new Date("1/1/2000");
  timeDisplayFormatter  = new DateFormatter();

  myVideoDisplay.addEventListener(VideoEvent.READY, videoReady);
  myVideoDisplay.addEventListener(VideoEvent.PLAYHEAD_UPDATE,
      updateTimeDisplay);
  btn_playToggle.addEventListener(MouseEvent.CLICK, togglePlayback);
  btn_stop.addEventListener(MouseEvent.CLICK, stopPlayback);

  loadPlaylist();
}

private function loadPlaylist():void
{
  playlistCursor = 0;
  var playlistService:HTTPService = new HTTPService();
  playlistService.url = "playlist.xml";
  playlistService.resultFormat = "xml";
  playlistService.showBusyCursor = true;
```

```
    playlistService.addEventListener(ResultEvent.RESULT,
      onPlaylistResult);
    playlistService.addEventListener(FaultEvent.FAULT,
      onFault);
    playlistService.send();
}

private function onPlaylistResult(event:ResultEvent):void
{
    var resultXML:XML = new XML(event.result);
    playlist = new XMLList(resultXML.video);
    playVideo();
}

private function playVideo():void
{
    this.myVideoDisplay.source = this.playlist[playlistCursor].@file;
}

private function onFault(event:FaultEvent):void
{
    trace(event.fault);
}

    ...
```

I'll begin my explanation of the new ActionScript I add by describing the imports and declared variables. The HTTPService, ResultEvent, and FaultEvent classes are used for the loading of the playlist XML file. I also declare a variable named playlist, of type XMLList. I'll use this array to go through the playlist. The playlistCursor variable will be used to store the current position in the playlist that the video player is playing back.

The next change is in the init() method. At the end I add a call to a new method called loadPlaylist(). This method is where I load the XML file using the HTTPService class. Let's go through this method line by line.

In the first line, I initiate the playlistCursor to 0 so that I can play the first video after the playlist has loaded. In the next line, I declare a function variable, playlistService, as an HTTPService object. Then, I assign three properties of the HTTPService object. The first is the url property, which is a string path and file name to the XML file I want to load. Since the playlist.xml file is in the same directory, I just enter the name of the file, "playlist.xml". The second property is the resultFormat, where I specify that I want XML as the result. The third property, showBusyCursor, is set to true, so that the service call displays a busy clock cursor while it loads the XML file. Once the basic properties for the HTTPService are set, there are two event listeners I add to the HTTPService object. One is for the ResultEvent of the HTTPService object, and the second is for the FaultEvent. For the result event, I assign the onPlaylistResult event handler, and for the fault event, I assign the onFault event handler. Hopefully, the fault event handler will not fire, but if it does, a trace will be received by the console, alerting it to what the fault was. In the case of a successful load, the onPlaylistResult() event handler is fired.

Figure 10-15. The first video plays back as usual.

In the first line of the onPlaylistResult() method, I declare a function variable named resultXML, of type XML object. The XML object is initiated using the result property of the ResultEvent to start the XML object. In the second line, I initiate the playlist XMLList object, using the resultXML variable, which is equal to the root node of the playlist.xml file, <playlist/>. By sending resultXML.video as the constructor argument for the XMLList object, an array is created with all of the video nodes to play back. The last line is a call to another new method called playVideo(). In the playVideo() method, I have a single line where I set the source of the VideoDisplay object using the playlist XMLList that was created. Using the playlistCursor, I access the first element in the array, and I use E4X to access the file attribute of the XML node. Once the source is set, the VideoDisplay automatically plays the video once the video is ready for playback. If I compile the example, the video plays as usual, first loading the XML and then assigning the source, as you see in Figure 10-15.

Now that I have the first video playing, I need to get the video to play the next video once the current video is done playing. For this, I will handle another event of the VideoDisplay component. The changes now look like this:

```
// ActionScript file videoPlayer.as
...
private function init():void
{
  start = new Date("1/1/2000");
  timeDisplayFormatter  = new DateFormatter();

  myVideoDisplay.addEventListener(VideoEvent.READY, videoReady);
  myVideoDisplay.addEventListener(VideoEvent.PLAYHEAD_UPDATE,
      updateTimeDisplay);
  myVideoDisplay.addEventListener(VideoEvent.COMPLETE, videoComplete);

  btn_playToggle.addEventListener(MouseEvent.CLICK, togglePlayback);
  btn_stop.addEventListener(MouseEvent.CLICK, stopPlayback);

  loadPlaylist();
}

...
```

```
private function videoComplete(event:VideoEvent):void
{
  if (this.playlistCursor < this.playlist.length() - 1)
  {
    this.myVideoDisplay.playheadTime = 0;
    this.playlistCursor++;
    this.playVideo();
  }
}
```

There are two basic changes I make to the ActionScript. First, in the init() method, I add a new event listener for the video complete event of the VideoDisplay component. To handle this event, I assign the videoComplete event handler. In the event handler, an if statement checks whether the playlistCursor is less than the length of the playlist, less one because the cursor is a zero-based index. If the condition is true, I reset the playheadTime of the VideoDisplay component to 0, increment the playlistCursor by 1, and call the playVideo method once again to play the next video. When the new code is compiled, the video player now loads the next video in the XML file when the video has completed playing.

Adding playlist control buttons

Before adding the ActionScript to power the Next and Prev buttons, I must prepare the layout of the buttons. In the control bar, I add the two buttons with spacers on the left and right of them so they appear in the center of the empty area between the timer display and the buttons. The MXML now looks like this:

```
...
    <mx:ControlBar>
      <mx:HBox width="100%">
        <mx:Button label="Pause/Play" id="btn_playToggle"/>
        <mx:Button label="Stop" id="btn_stop"/>
        <mx:Spacer width="100%"/>
        <mx:Button id="btn_previous" label="Prev"/>
        <mx:Button id="btn_next" label="Next"/>
        <mx:Spacer width="100%"/>
        <mx:Label id="tf_playtimeDisplay"/>
        <mx:VSlider id="volumeSlider" liveDragging="true" value=".75"
          minimum="0" maximum="1" height="34"/>
      </mx:HBox>
    </mx:ControlBar>
  </mx:Panel>
</mx:Application>
```

The MXML changes are within the ControlBar component. To handle the functionality of the Next and Prev buttons, I declare a new event handler. The ActionScript looks like this:

```
// ActionScript file videoPlayer.as
...
private function init():void
{
```

```
        start = new Date("1/1/2000");
        timeDisplayFormatter  = new DateFormatter();

        myVideoDisplay.addEventListener(VideoEvent.READY, videoReady);
        myVideoDisplay.addEventListener(VideoEvent.PLAYHEAD_UPDATE,
          updateTimeDisplay);
        myVideoDisplay.addEventListener(VideoEvent.COMPLETE,
          videoComplete);

        btn_next.addEventListener(MouseEvent.CLICK,
          playlistControlsHandler);
        btn_previous.addEventListener(MouseEvent.CLICK,
          playlistControlsHandler);

        btn_playToggle.addEventListener(MouseEvent.CLICK,
          togglePlayback);
        btn_stop.addEventListener(MouseEvent.CLICK,
          stopPlayback);

        loadPlaylist();
    }

    ...

    private function playlistControlsHandler(event:MouseEvent):void
    {
      switch (event.currentTarget.label)
      {
        case 'Next':
          if (playlistCursor <playlist.length() - 1)
          {
            if (myVideoDisplay.playing) {myVideoDisplay.pause(); }
            myVideoDisplay.playheadTime = 0;
            playlistCursor++;
            playVideo();
          }
          break;
        case 'Prev':
          if (playlistCursor - 1 >= 0)
          {
            if (myVideoDisplay.playing) {myVideoDisplay.pause(); }
            myVideoDisplay.playheadTime = 0;
            playlistCursor--;
            playVideo();
          }
          break;
        default :
          break;
      }
    }
```

The changes to the ActionScript include the addition of two event listener assignments in the `init()` method and a new method for navigating through the playlist. First, in the `init()` method, I add the same event handler for both the Next and Prev buttons. At the bottom of the ActionScript, I declare the `playlistControlsHandler()` method, which is fired every time a user presses either the Next or Prev buttons.

In the `playlistControlsHandler()` method, there is a `switch` statement to check the label of the Button control that fired the handler. If the Next button is pressed, the code proceeds to an `if` statement to check whether the cursor is less than the length of the playlist (again, less one because of the zero-based index). If the condition is true, the code in the `if` statement prepares the video player to play the next video. To begin the process of loading a new video, the code checks whether the player is currently playing a video, in which case the `pause()` method is triggered. Next, I reset the `playheadTime` to 0 so the next video starts at the beginning, and then increment the playlist cursor by one. Finally, I call the `playVideo()` method to play the next video.

In the case for the Prev button label, the `if` statement checks whether decrementing the `playlistCursor` by one is equal or greater than zero; if so, the cursor is still within range of the playlist. When the condition is met, the first line again checks whether the video display is currently playing a video, and if so pauses the display. Then the `playheadTime` is set back to 0 so the next video to play starts from the beginning. Next the playlist cursor is decremented by one, and finally the selected video is played. If I compile the code, the video player now has the Prev and Next buttons, which can be used to navigate the loaded playlist. You can see the controls in Figure 10-16.

Figure 10-16. The Prev and Next buttons appear in the center because of the spacers on the left and right of the two buttons.

Restricting playlist controls during ad playback

Playing back ads can be handled in many different ways, depending on the ad service and delivery method of the ads. The one thing that all these methods share in common is the fact that the video controls should not be available during the playback of a paid advertisement. For this example, assume that the video ads are received in the same call as the playlist. To differentiate a regular video from an advertisement, I make a change to the `playlist.xml` file that gets loaded. In each of the video nodes, I add a type attribute, which will be equal to "ad" whenever a video is designated as an advertisement. The changes to the XML look like this:

```
<playlist>
  <video title="First Video" file="video.flv" type="video"/>
  <video title="Second Video" file="xvideo.flv" type="ad"/>
  <video title="Third Video" file="_video.flv" type="video"/>
</playlist>
```

With these changes to the XML, I can now tell the difference between a regular video and an advertisement. Now I need to make the changes to the ActionScript so that the video player recognizes this difference.

To make the video player recognize and disable the user interface, I need to create a method to toggle the availability of the video controls, and I need to fire this method somewhere. The new method will be fired every time a new video is played, so I will expand on the playVideo() method. In that method, I will fire the toggleVideoControls() method. The ActionScript should now look like this:

```
// ActionScript file videoPlayer.as

...

private function playVideo():void
{
  if (this.playlist[playlistCursor].@type == 'ad')
  {
    this.toggleVideoControls(false);
  }
  else
  {
    this.toggleVideoControls(true);
  }
  this.myVideoDisplay.source = this.playlist[playlistCursor].@file;
}

...

private function toggleVideoControls(enable:Boolean):void
{
  this.btn_playToggle.enabled = enable;
  this.btn_next.enabled = enable;
  this.btn_previous.enabled = enable;
  this.btn_stop.enabled = enable;
  this.playbackProgress.enabled = enable;
}
```

At the bottom of the ActionScript file, I declare a new function that will enable and disable the user interface. The method accepts a Boolean argument, which is used to set all the user interface elements to either enabled or disabled. Then, in the playVideo() method, I add a new if statement, which checks the type attribute of each video node. If the type attribute is equal to "ad", the toggleVideoControls() method is fired with a false as the argument, disabling all controls. Otherwise, it enables the controls. In Figure 10-17, you can see the controls disabled after the video player has recognized the second video as an advertisement.

Figure 10-17. All controls except the volume slider have been disabled, because this video is designated as an "ad" by the type attribute in the playlist.xml.

Limitations of the VideoDisplay class

For the majority of video projects where a progressive download system will be used, the VideoDisplay class is more than adequate enough to handle the job of delivering video. However, because the VideoDisplay component encapsulates the NetConnection and NetStream objects within the class, those objects are not available to customize the handling of the events that they provide. Aside from this barrier, it also makes it not possible to add new callbacks on the client property of those objects, something that some content distribution networks (CDNs) require in order to make a successful connection to their Flash Media Servers.

To add to these limitations, I also encountered a very rare circumstance where the VideoEvent.COMPLETE event would not dispatch at the end of a video clip. This very rare occurrence would actually halt the entire playback of a playlist, because the playlist relies on that event being dispatched to move on to the next video. A client for whom we implemented a video encoder was having issues reported where the playlist was completely stopping at the end of a specific video. Upon further investigation, I discovered that the actual length of the video was 3 milliseconds shorter than the length being reported by the VideoDisplay component. This was in effect causing the player to reach the end of the video, but it would not register the actual end of the video, which would cause the event to never be dispatched.

To get around all of these hurdles, I wrote a new class called VideoBitmapDisplay, which very closely emulates the events and properties provided by the VideoDisplay class—the benefit, of course, being that I now have complete control over the NetConnection and NetStream objects, I can write and refine my own end-of-video detection code, and I can modify the class for any specific FMS requirements.

Aside from being able to customize the handling of the NetStream and NetConnection objects, I added a new bindable property to the class called bitmapData. Like the name suggests, it provides a bitmapData object of the video stream being played back. I've used this object to bind it to a Bitmap object, and then set that to the source of an Image object so that I can easily add effect filters to the video or do any number of bitmapData transformations to create video with weird effects and such. I won't go over the use of the class, as it is used exactly like the VideoDisplay class described in this chapter, with the addition of the bitmapData property. Feel free to use and modify it as you please! I currently have this working in a couple of projects, but if you decide to use it, you still must make sure that you test it thoroughly to assure that it meets the needs of your project. You can get creative with it! Head on over to the friends of ED Downloads page (www.friendsofed.com/downloads.html) for the source code to the VideoBitmapDisplay class.

Summary

In this chapter, I aimed to provide a look into the types of coding techniques we used on the RMX to execute the precise video playback requirements of the project. As well, I attempted to do so with as little ActionScript as possible, highlighting ways the native characteristics of the framework can be exploited to achieve much of the required behavior. I also covered some of the limitations of the VideoDisplay component and provided a class for you to play with. R covered the ins and outs of encoding video and preparing it for delivery. With the topics covered in this chapter, you should now be ready to build your own video players with all of the expected functionality of a standard Flash video player. Additionally, I included a class I built to customize the handling of the NetStream and NetConnection objects and added a bitmapData property to play with the video image and get creative with. Now, you're ready to dive into the world of online advertising.

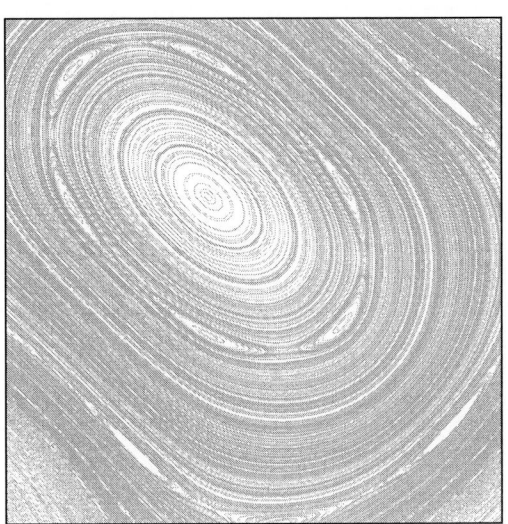

Chapter 11

ADVERTISING AND FLEX

By R Blank

Advertising is a vital aspect of many Internet-based projects, and the RMX is no different. In this chapter, I will discuss some of the options available for banner and instream (or video) advertising, explain the problems with using most mainstream solutions inside of Flash-based applications, and show how we solved these issues for our project—utilizing open source technologies.

Why advertising matters

The RMX is free. Free to members and visitors, that is. In reality, the RMX—and any web-based application like it—costs real money, even when not accounting for our own time spent developing and maintaining the application, and especially when dealing with bandwidth- and storage-hogging video. But we, the owners, incur those costs and do not pass them on directly to our community.

One of the ways we try to make back some of that cost, as with most any widely trafficked site, is through advertising.

Although in the early days of the Internet, advertising failed to produce on the promises and expectations of many businesses and analysts, today advertising can make you a decent amount of money. This is especially true when the community consists of a highly specific and desirable market demographic—in this case, the Adobe user communities.

The mechanics of online advertising are quite simple but also quite powerful and varied. Someone wants to show an ad, so they buy space. Unlike television advertising, where space is based on channel, time, and geography, online advertising can be based on a much more complex set of variables—all entirely transparent to the user. You can deliver ads based on the content of a page (for instance, an ad for guitars along with a blog post review of a new Ovation). You can deliver ads based on the previous browsing history of the user (for instance, showing certain ads only to more frequent visitors or to members who have previously posted job opportunities on the jobs board). Or you can deliver ads based on reverse IP lookup (to get the geographical location of the visitor based on his IP address) or gender (based on a user profile the user has filled out). Or you can use a combination of all of these factors, and many more.

The goal is to deliver the most relevant ad that you can to that viewer at that point in time. This brings the most value not only to the advertiser, but also to the viewer. That is, consumers derive real value, and sometimes enjoyment, from exposure to more-relevant marketing messaging. And advertisers can get much more detailed information about the track record and success of individual ads and advertising campaigns—indeed, advertisers expect detailed metrics on their advertising. Any advertising management system or network will offer this type of data; it's one of the key reasons to use such a system instead of just building your own from scratch. Because, after all, all you're doing is loading media into a web page, and we all know a thousand ways to do that.

You can either consume ads from an existing third-party advertising network or sell your own ads. Using an existing network, while much easier, is frequently less lucrative and can provide less-relevant messaging to your visitors. One of the simplest options is Google AdSense (www.google.com/adsense), which is free to implement and use. Google gives you some code to insert in your site, and based on the words that Google sniffs in the pages in which that code is embedded, Google AdSense delivers contextually relevant advertising. If users click those ads, you get some money.

If you want to sell your own ads, you need an ad management system. It will help you manage advertising campaigns (with options like expiration dates and impression throttling, which ensures ads are only shown a certain number of times) and provide you the tracking metrics your advertisers will require. Many solutions are available on the market, from open source (read: free) to full custom ad networks (read: definitely *not* free).

To open source or not to open source?

As with most any similar decision, the verdict comes down to this: do you have money to spend, and are the open source alternatives usable? In the case of advertising on the RMX, the answers were "Not really, no" and "Yes." The paid ad management systems like Accipiter, 24/7, and DoubleClick (now owned by Google) provide tremendous functionality and performance. At the same time, they can cost a lot of money, anywhere from $1,000–10,000 a month and much more depending on your traffic.

So, for this reason, we chose one of the preeminent open source advertising campaign managers, OpenAds (www.openads.com). OpenAds (formerly known as phpAdsNew) is a pretty powerful and functional open source ad management system, well supported by its community with frequent updates.

I'll get into how we actually work with OpenAds in one moment. But first, I want to touch on a couple of additional aspects of online advertising that are very relevant for Flex and Flash developers to understand and consider when planning applications.

Flash and ads: Play nice, kids!

We all know that Flash has become an incredibly popular format for delivering online advertising. The ads can be incredibly cool and engaging, even at really small file sizes. Of course, you can also have video and audio seamlessly integrated with the advertising experience, with no additional plug-ins. Your ad can even be dynamic, pulling from an RSS feed, for example. And, with options like Eyeblaster (www.eyeblaster.com) and PointRoll (www.pointroll.com), you can have user-initiated expandable ads. These expandable ads, always constructed and delivered with Flash, actually grow out of the standard banner area on user interaction (say, a click) to reveal a much larger canvas with all the functionality that Flash has to offer, including interactivity, animations, and even inline video. Expandables are really micro-sites or mini-applications that allow the viewer to participate with the brand and message in a meaningful and enjoyable way, without ever leaving the page he is viewing. This experience-rich type of advertising exploits the tremendous power of Flash, and a lot of Flash developers make a good living building these ads.

But, just because Flash is a great option for developing ads, it doesn't mean actually consuming ads in Flash is just as easy and popular. In fact, at Almer/Blank, we've had to chop up many an otherwise beautiful Flex and Flash application, just to make space for the frames and layers to hold the ads.

Why? Because almost every ad on the Internet is invoked with JavaScript or PHP. When you sign up for Google AdSense, you get JavaScript to paste into your pages. When you install and use OpenAds, you get JavaScript code to insert into your pages. This code is called an **invocation code** since the code loads, or invokes, an ad. And, while Flash can communicate with JavaScript and PHP, Flash can't directly load and interpret JavaScript or PHP, so you cannot have your advertising invocation codes in your Flash application.

Why not just utilize DIV layers to place the ads above the Flash? Unfortunately, that solution is unreliable cross-browser/cross-platform, since in some browsers, Flash will always render on top of all other content, regardless of depth.

In fact, the only really robust out-of-the-box option for Flex and Flash developers to integrate seamless ads into any application or web site is DART Motif Flash-in-Flash from DoubleClick (www.doubleclick.com/us/products/dart_motif_for_flash_in_flash/). But DoubleClick is the most expensive of the paid options, so it's totally out of consideration for all but the largest Internet presences.

So, as I said, at Almer/Blank we've had to chop some client applications that would have been perfectly delivered as single SWFs into as many as eight or nine SWFs in a page, just to support the ads.

What about instream ads?

Instream ads are video ads. They are often referred to as preroll and postroll ads (depending on whether they precede or follow the main video content). Any site planning distribution of significant amounts of video—especially Flash video—will want to consider delivering instream advertising.

And while all of the major ad management networks (such as the ones I mentioned previously) offer instream management and delivery, the problem with instream advertising is that the options for delivery management are far fewer than for banners. Google (at least at the time of writing—it's bound to change in the near future) does not offer a free instream advertising network the way it does with text banners with AdSense. You can get third-party instream advertising with a solution like

Brightcove's, but then you must use its player or API and host and deliver your content through that company. And OpenAds doesn't natively support the delivery of instream ads.

Our solution

When we started building the RMX, we had complete control of how the advertising would operate, so we decided to find a way around these two challenges. That is, we wanted to use the free and relatively powerful OpenAds, but we also wanted the flexibility to deliver ads to any part of the RMX, whether the specific RMX interface consuming the ads was built as HTML or Flash, and we wanted the same system that ran our banner delivery to also power our instream advertising.

So Daryl Bowden, one of our developers at Almer/Blank, came up with a solution to deliver ads (banner or FLV) from OpenAds into Flex and Flash applications. I want to share this with you in this chapter because, again, OpenAds is a pretty good and totally free solution, and this technique allows any Flex developer to offer a robust advertising solution along with his applications, pretty much out of the box for no cost. What's more, the same logic I'm about to explain can be used with most any ad management system that does not natively support delivery to Flash! (But you will have to modify the JavaScript and ActionScript for each case, because each system's code is different and utilizes somewhat different data, structure, and logic.)

So, first I'll show you how to set up OpenAds so that you have an ad management and delivery system in place, and then I'll demonstrate how to get into Flex to consume those ads. Let's dive into the details!

Setting up OpenAds

Before you get to the fancy code that powers our solution, you have to get set up to deliver the ads for this walkthrough. To that end, you need to have an environment that will support an OpenAds installation. Basically, you need a server that has PHP version 4.4.2 or higher installed, as well as MySQL, preferably version 3.23.2 or higher.

> For a more in-depth list of requirements, you may visit http://docs.openads.org/openads-2.0-guide/system-requirements.html.

Now that you have an adequate setup, you will need to point your favorite browser to www.openads.org. When you get there, you will be greeted with a link on the right side of the page inviting you to download the latest stable version of OpenAds (which, at the time of writing, is 2.0.11-pr1, as you see in Figure 11-1). Go ahead and click that link, and your download will begin immediately. Many people have reported that the Max Media Manager (the newest development version at the time of writing) works incredibly well; however, I prefer to stick with the sure bet.

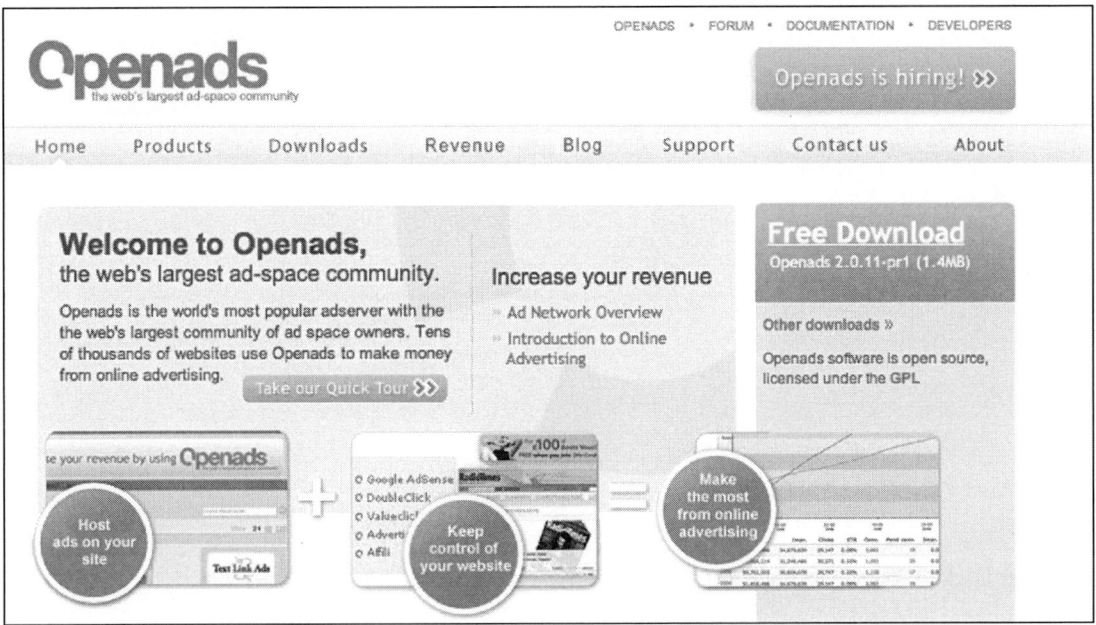

Figure 11-1. The OpenAds home page

Once the download has completed, you will need to extract the files onto your desktop. Then, open your FTP client and connect with your server. On your server, you will need to create a new directory to house your files; for this example, name it /adserver, which will be located at the web root. Once you have created this directory, copy all of the contents of the folder you downloaded into it. Now that the files are on your box, go to the /adserver folder on whichever domain you are using (such as www.richmediax.com/adserver) and you will see that OpenAds does all the hard work for you.

With your folder installed, you need to set up your MySQL database. If you have access to a web host control panel such as phpMyAdmin or Plesk, this will be a five-second job; if not, you'll need to use the command line. If you have trouble with this, you can find plenty of help at www.mysql.com.

Once you have completed installing OpenAds, it's time to get familiar with how it works. Almost anyone reading this book will find the administrative control panel easy to use; however, for less-tech-savvy folks, it can be a little difficult to get a grasp of exactly how it works. In either case, as with most open source applications, there is a huge user base out there just ready to answer your questions and give you whatever advice you may need.

> *You can find the OpenAds forums at* http://forum.openads.org/. *This is a great source for anything you might need relating to OpenAds.*

To get into the guts of the application, simply point your browser once again to the adserver folder on your development domain, and you'll see the login screen pictured in Figure 11-2.

Figure 11-2. The login screen you should see after a successful installation of OpenAds

Once logged in, you will be taken to the Inventory screen (see Figure 11-3), which is the main screen for OpenAds and one that you will visit often. To get started, you first need to create a new advertiser. To do this, simply click the Add new advertiser link.

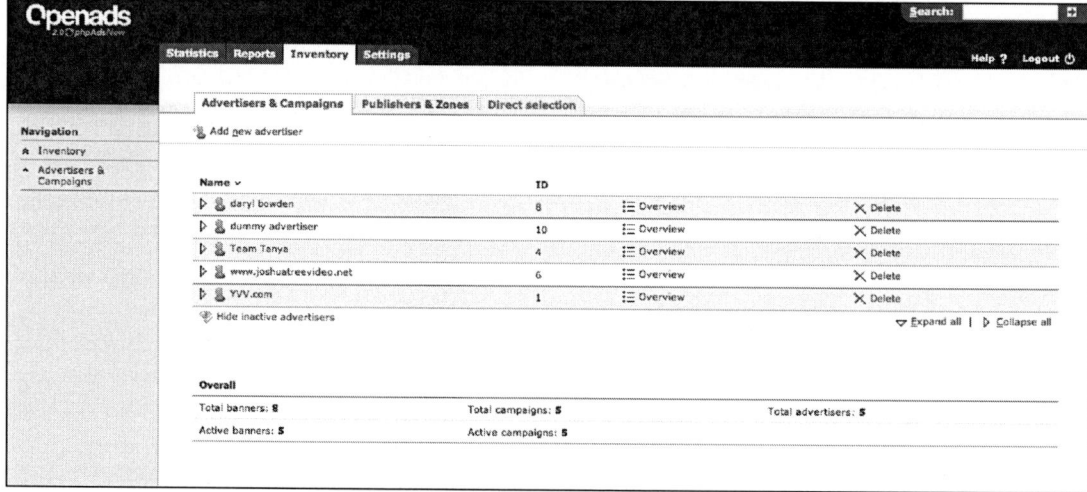

Figure 11-3. The OpenAds Inventory screen

On the Add new advertiser screen shown in Figure 11-4, you will assign your advertiser properties. You'll also notice that this advertiser can have its own login, which can be helpful if you would like your advertisers to access and modify their accounts directly.

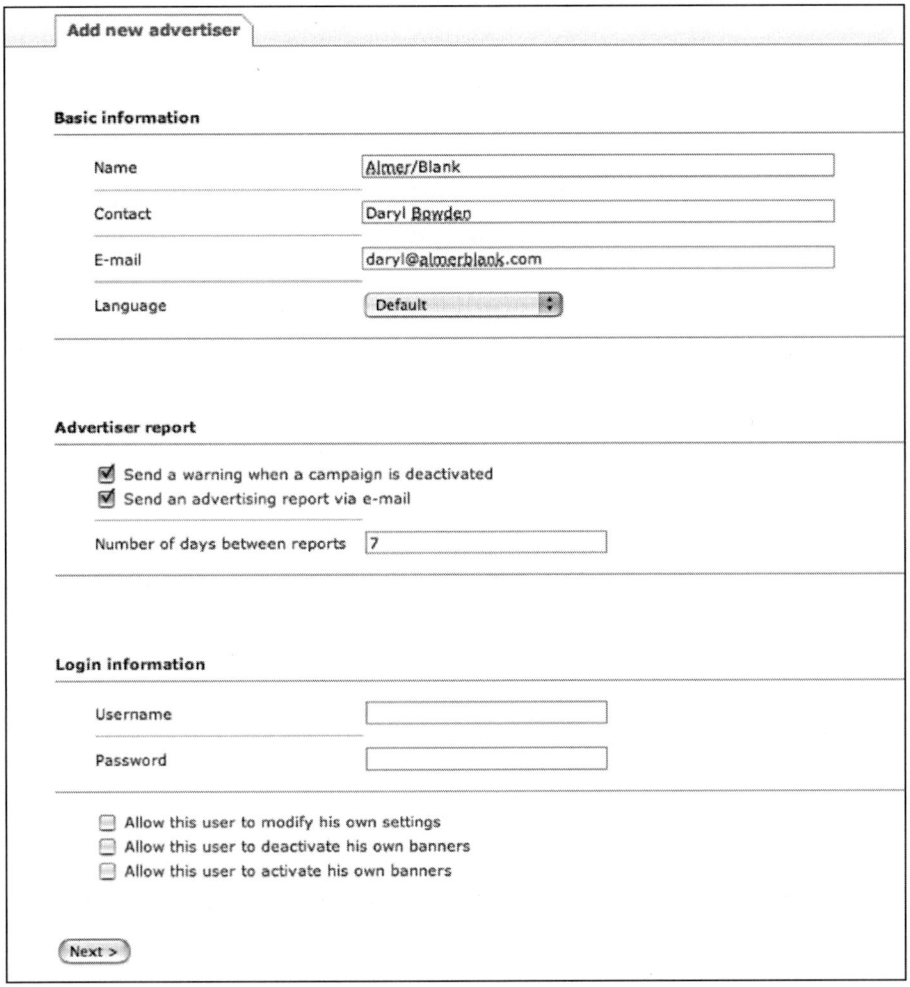

Figure 11-4. The Add new advertiser screen lets you specify properties for an advertiser.

Once you have filled in the requisite information, press the Next button to proceed to the next screen (see Figure 11-5), which will allow you to create a campaign.

A **campaign** includes a set of different ads along with the logic to deliver those ads, including start and end dates, maximum impressions, and priority. This page allows you to set up the start and end dates for the campaign (if there are any), as well as allows you to monitor the activity for this account (this page is also visible after the account has been created).

Once you're done here, click Save Changes, and then click the tab labeled Banner overview. Here you will stock your campaign with all the banners you need to get going.

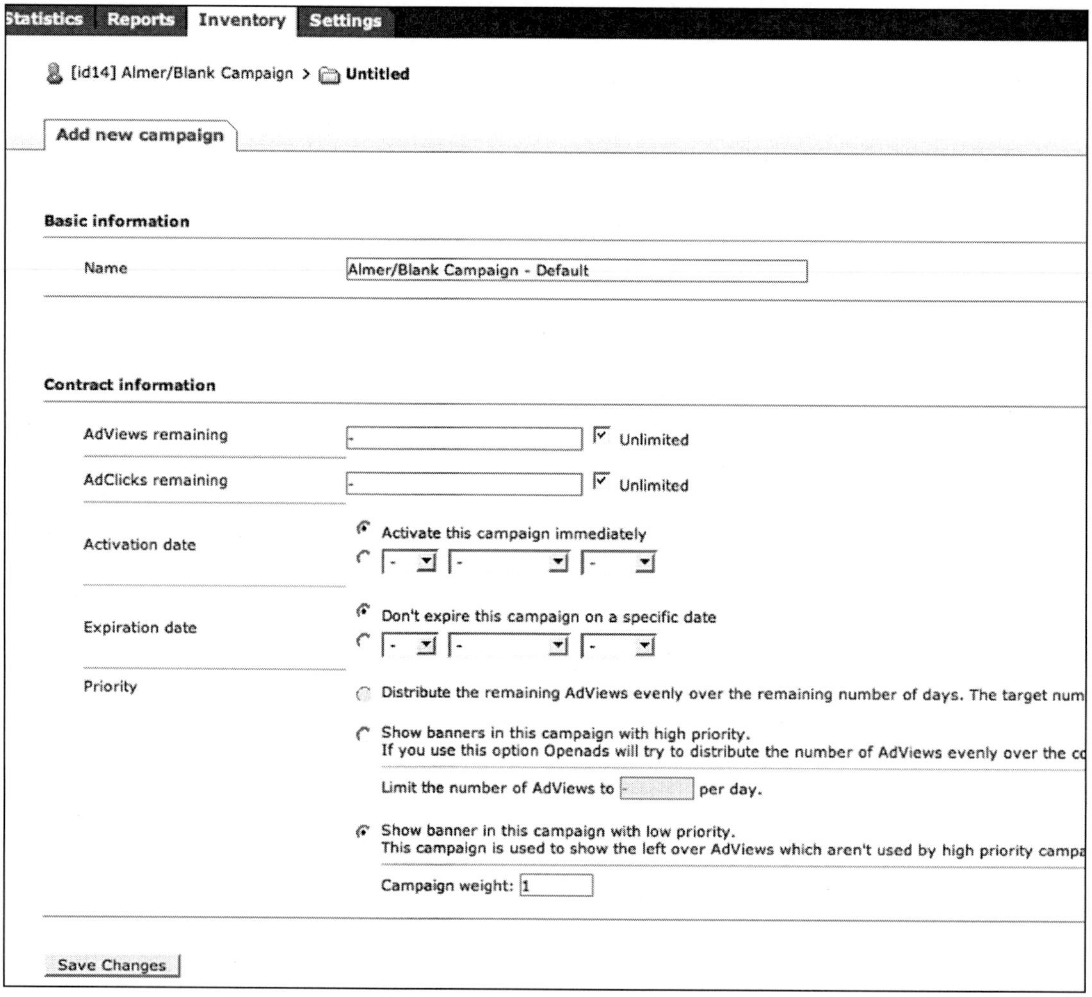

Figure 11-5. You can create a campaign and set its properties on this screen.

From the banner overview page, simply click Add new banner to take you to the Add new banner screen (pictured in Figure 11-6), and you can start uploading your banners. As you upload each banner, you can enter the destination URL (which specifies the page the user will be taken to when he clicks the banner) as well as the target (the browser target, just as in the navigateToURL ActionScript method: either _top, _self, or _blank depending on the browser window in which you want the destination URL to launch). When you upload a banner, remember to give the banner a clear description, as this will make it easier to differentiate later on when you may have hundreds of banners in your database. Continue to upload banners until you have uploaded all the banners you would like to include for this campaign.

That's all you need to do within OpenAds for now, so next you can dig into the Flex side of this solution.

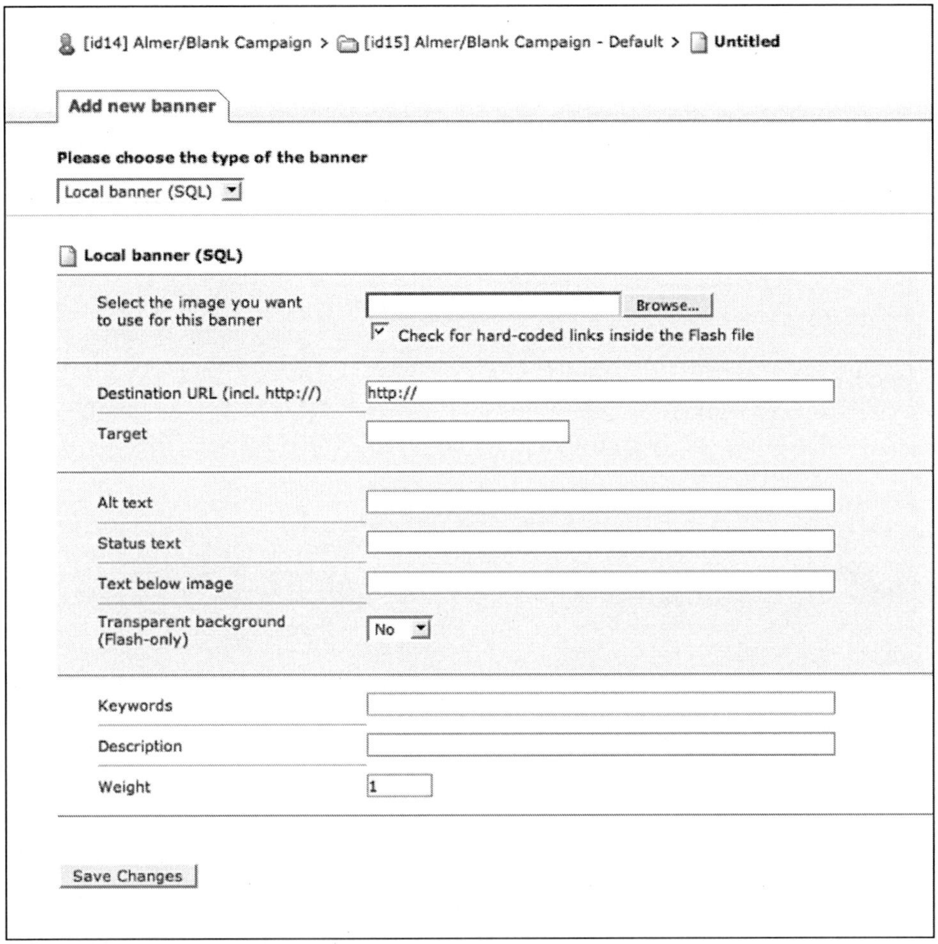

Figure 11-6. The Add new banner screen

Consuming OpenAds in Flex

As cool as this solution is, the Flex side of the equation is really rather simple. You need a little bit of ActionScript, one line of MXML, and you're done.

To get started, create a new Flex project. In your application file (I've called mine openAds.mxml), begin with the ExternalInterface class. This class enables your SWF to talk to its wrapper so that it can call a JavaScript function located on the HTML page in which your SWF is embedded. Not only that, but it also allows you to return data back to the SWF to be further manipulated by your Flex code. In fact, this class also works the other way around: you can also use it to call Flex functions from within the JavaScript.

I will show you all the Flex code involved and then go through it step by step with you.

```
<?xml version="1.0" encoding="utf-8"?>
<mx:Application xmlns:mx="http://www.adobe.com/2006/mxml"
layout="absolute" creationComplete="callWrapperBanner()">
<mx:Script>
  <![CDATA[
  import flash.net.navigateToURL;
  import mx.controls.Alert;
  import mx.collections.XMLListCollection;
  import flash.external.*;

  [Bindable]
  public var adReturn:*;
  public var javascriptReturn:XML;

  [Bindable]
  public var imageSource:String;
  [Bindable]
  public var imageClick:String;

  public function callWrapperBanner():void
  {
    //check to see if external interface is available
    if(ExternalInterface.available)
    {
      //callOpenAds is the name of the JS function
      //contained in the wrapper
      var wrapperFunction:String = "callOpenAds";
      //make the call to the wrapper and the JS function
      adReturn = ExternalInterface.call(wrapperFunction);
    } else{
      Alert.show("Failed to initiate external connection");
    }
    //convert HTML to XML
    var img:String = "<root>"+adReturn+"</root>";
    //correct malformed HTML that comes back from OpenAds
    img = img.replace("></A", "/></A");
    img = img.replace("></DIV", "/></DIV");
    //create new XML object and use that object to
    //parse out the tags you need
    javascriptReturn = new XML(img);
    imageClick = javascriptReturn.A.@href.toString();
    imageSource= javascriptReturn.A.IMG.@src.toString();
    //add event listener so that click-through and link still works
    // the way the user expects
    adImage.addEventListener(MouseEvent.CLICK, adClick);
    adImage.buttonMode = true;
  }
```

```
    private function adClick(event:MouseEvent):void
    {
      //set variable to contain destination path for ad
      var ur:URLRequest = new URLRequest(imageClick);
      //send user to link on click
      navigateToURL(ur);
}]]>
</mx:Script>

<!-- Set source to the bindable variable imageSource which
contains the img src of the return from the JS -->

<mx:Image source="{imageSource}" id="adImage" />
</mx:Application>
```

To begin, you declare a few variables. First, you declare two strings, imageSource and imageClick, and both must be declared as [Bindable] since you will use these as the data source for both your Image component and your click event. The other two variables are adReturn, which will hold the return value from the JavaScript function in the HTML, and javascriptReturn, the variable you will convert to XML. javascriptReturn does not need to be bindable, as you will not be using it outside of this function.

You'll note that this file only contains two functions: one to call the ad and another to enable the click. The main function, callWrapperbanner(), uses the ExternalInterface class that I referred to at the start of this section. To set this up, you first set up a conditional statement to ensure that the ExternalInterface is available (meaning that JavaScript is enabled in the viewer's browser). Assuming this tests true (meaning JavaScript is available, which it will be about 96% of the time), you can proceed. If JavaScript is unavailable, this solution won't work—but in those cases, you wouldn't have been able to load ads into the web page anyway, regardless of whether the interface is Flash or HTML, since the ad can never be invoked by the invocation code.

Knowing that JavaScript is available, you assign your variable wrapperFunction the string "callOpenAds". The naming of your variable is a very important step. The name that you give this variable needs to be the same as the JavaScript function you are going to create on your wrapper page; otherwise, the communication won't work, and your ads will not render correctly. When done, your conditional should look like this:

```
    //check to see if external interface is available
    If (ExternalInterface.available)
    {
      //callOpenAds is the name of the JS function
      //contained in the wrapper
      var wrapperFunction:String = "callOpenAds";
      //make the call to the wrapper and the JS function
      adReturn = ExternalInterface.call(wrapperFunction);
    } else{
      Alert.show("Failed to initiate external connection");
    }
```

Next, you parse through the information that is returned to you from the wrapper and contained in the variable adReturn. You will prepend it with <root>, append it with </root>, and store it in the local variable img, typed as a string. This will convert the HTML that was returned into valid XML, so that your Flex code can access the relevant information.

This is where you run into the biggest issue with the OpenAds delivery system. The HTML it uses for displaying images is malformed (shh . . . don't tell anyone); the <img> tag in the OpenAds-generated HTML does not include a proper closure, and therefore it cannot be recognized as XML by Flex without some modification. Fortunately, this failure (or "feature," I suppose) is a consistent one, so to remedy this, we use the replace() method, which allows us to parse through a string and replace a specified substring with another string value. When calling replace(), you pass the substring you wish to replace as the first parameter and the string to insert in its place as the second parameter. By looking through the returned information, you'll see that the <img> tag should be closed right before the <a> tag closes. Here, you can see the method with the proper syntax, as used in this example:

```
img = img.replace("></A", "/></A");
```

Now that you have corrected the form of your return, you can treat it as XML and parse through it. Take the javascriptReturn variable that you declared earlier and set it as a new XML object with the local variable img as the source. Now that you've converted the return value into valid XML, you can grab the hyperlink from the <a> tag in the return. To do this, assign your imageClick variable the value of the link, like so:

```
javascriptReturn = new XML(img);
imageClick = javascriptReturn.A.@href.toString();
```

Here you grab the href attribute of the <a> node from our XML. Appending the call to toString() converts the data to a string value so that you may use it as the destination for a navigateToURL call. Next, you'll perform the same operation on the source attribute of the <img> tag to grab the media source, like this:

```
imageSource= javascriptReturn.A.IMG.@src.toString();
```

Once you have the source for the banner, you'll hop out of the ActionScript and into your MXML, which consists of only one line:

```
<mx:Image source="{imageSource}" id="adImage" />
```

This is simply an <mx:Image/> tag, with an id of "adImage" and the source set to the bindable value of the imageSource variable. And now you've displayed your ad! And, if this were an instream ad, rather than a banner, your one line of code would look almost identical:

```
<mx:VideoDisplay source="{imageSource}" id="adImage" />
```

Next, you need to set up the click event that will allow the image to act as a user expects a banner to act. To do that, you'll jump back into the callWrapperBanner() function and append these few lines at the end:

```
adImage.addEventListener(MouseEvent.CLICK, adClick);
adImage.buttonMode = true;
```

The first line simply adds an event listener to your image. When the image experiences a click event, it will fire the adClick() function. So, next you'll write that callback function. Like all of the Flex code so far in this chapter, adClick() is a very simple function consisting of only two lines:

```
private function adClick(event:MouseEvent):void
{
  //set variable to contain destination path for ad
  var ur:URLRequest = new URLRequest(imageClick);
  //send user to link on click
  navigateToURL(ur);
}
```

The first line within the function creates a new URLRequest object using the imageClick variable as the source. The next line simply redirects the user to the destination when the event is fired.

Finally, I would like to point out one very important line of code to you. In the opening <mx:Application> tag, you'll see a creationComplete event that calls the main function callWrappperBanner().

```
<mx:Application xmlns:mx="http://www.adobe.com/2006/mxml"
layout="absolute" creationComplete="callWrapperBanner()">
```

Now you can compile your Flex application, since you have finished your Flex work (I told you the code was going to be easy); so to finish the job, you'll move on to the very minimal JavaScript this project requires.

To keep things easy, you're going to use the default HTML page that Flex creates when you compile your SWF. You can use any HTML editor to edit the file (I generally prefer to stay within the Eclipse environment, so I use the JSEclipse editor, which can be downloaded and installed from www. eclipse.org).

The first task for the JavaScript is to grab your invocation code—the code that returns the banners to you from OpenAds. To grab this code, you'll log back in to the OpenAds installation and click the Inventory link in the left sidebar. On the Inventory screen, click the Direct selection tab. Once you've gotten to the Direct selection screen (pictured in Figure 11-7), you will see a drop-down menu with a default state of Local Mode. Click that drop-down menu and select Remote Invocation for JavaScript. Then select the campaign you created from the Campaign drop-down menu. Once you have selected everything, click the Generate button at the bottom of the page (the button will be labeled Refresh once you've generated the code the first time). Now, you will see that the Banner selection box is populated with the invocation code. You'll grab that code by selecting it and copying it to your clipboard.

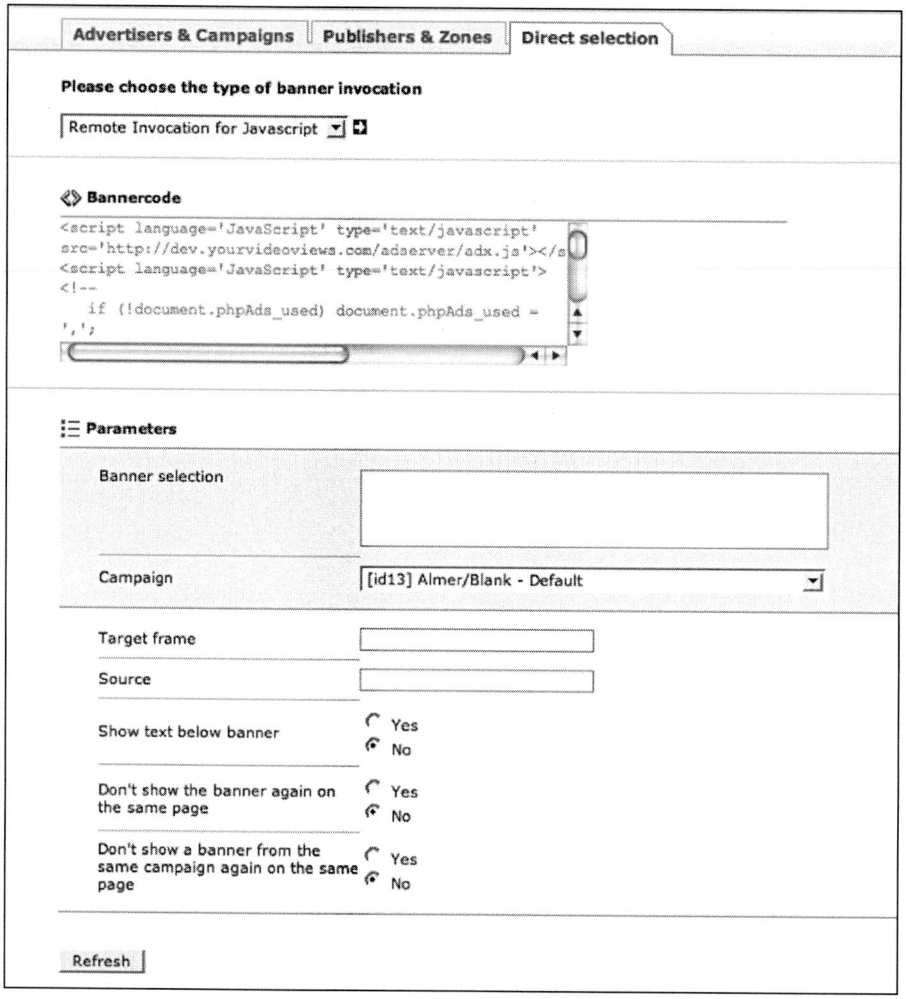

Figure 11-7. The Direct selection tab in OpenAds, from where you can grab your ad invocation code

Once you have copied the code, open up the default HTML file that Flex created for you. In this file, you will create a new DIV within the body of your document and paste the invocation code into it.

```
<div id="advertise" style="display:none; visibility: hidden;">
<script language='JavaScript' type='text/javascript'
src='http://dev.yourvideoviews.com/adserver/adx.js'></script>
<script language='JavaScript' type='text/javascript'>
<!--
   if (!document.phpAds_used) document.phpAds_used = ',';
   phpAds_random = new String (Math.random()); phpAds_random =
   phpAds_random.substring(2,11);
   document.write ("<" + "script language='JavaScript'
type='text/javascript' src='");
   document.write ("http://www.fakeserver.com/adserver/adjs.php?n=" +
   phpAds_random);
```

```
document.write ("&amp;clientid=7");
document.write ("&amp;exclude=" + document.phpAds_used);
if (document.referrer)
document.write ("&amp;referer=" + escape(document.referrer));
document.write ("'><" + "/script>");
//-->
</script><noscript>
<a href='http://www.fakeserver.com/adserver/adclick.php?n=a45038aa'
target='_blank'>
<img src='http://www.fakeserver.com/adserver/adview.php?clientid=7&amp
;n=a45038aa' border='0' alt=''></a></noscript>
</div>
```

The only modification you need to make beyond pasting the code into your new DIV is that to assign the DIV an id of "advertise"—this id is very important to keep track of, as you will shortly reference this DIV layer by its id in your code.

Now that you have created your DIV and pasted in the invocation code, you will open a new JavaScript script block in the head of the page. In this block, you'll define one function, callOpenAds()—this should sound familiar from the ActionScript you programmed just earlier. This function body consists of only two lines:

```
<script language='JavaScript' type='text/javascript'>
<!--
function callOpenAds()
{
  var temp = advertise.innerHTML;
  return temp;
}
//-->
</script>
```

The first line utilizes a built-in JavaScript property, which will grab all of the HTML from inside the DIV that you just created. This is why it was so important to name your DIV—each HTML element in a document has an innerHTML property, which may be accessed by JavaScript to grab the contents from the element (in this case the DIV) and return it to your local variable, temp. In the next line, you return temp back to your Flex application.

Once these lines have been added to your default HTML page, you are done; simply upload the contents of your bin folder to your test site and browse to your HTML page. You'll see your ad appear on the page inside of your Flex SWF. If you go ahead and click it, you'll be transported to whatever site you set the target to during your campaign setup.

Voilà! You can now sell and deliver ads however you want!

Really, how powerful is this solution?

No doubt, this solution is simple. At least, the required ActionScript and JavaScript code is pretty low level. But that doesn't mean it isn't powerful. As I indicated earlier in the chapter, this technique can be used with almost any ad management system that does not natively support Flash. I used OpenAds in this example because it's a free and easy-to-use solution that you can utilize in your projects. But, if a client wants to support standard or instream ads inside a Flash application off of an existing ad management system, in most cases, all you'll have to modify from this solution is how you parse the returned data. However, you must check with the terms of service of the ad management system to ensure your utilization of their system is permitted. (Click fraud is a very serious consideration in online advertising, so some networks are more restrictive than others in how they allow you to utilize their services; indeed, that might be one more reason to consider OpenAds.)

Now, I say this will work with "almost" any system, because it doesn't work with all; in fact, it doesn't work with Google AdSense, which, of course, is a major network. That's because this solution allows you to use application-native invocation codes written in JavaScript or PHP to *invoke* an ad. But this solution still relies on the ad that is returned from the invocation to itself be in a format that Flash can understand—which includes SWF, FLV, and H.264 video; JPG, PNG, and GIF (nonanimated); and the limited subset of HTML that Flash TextFields can interpret. Google AdSense returns HTML that cannot be understood by Flash, and therefore Google AdSense cannot render in the Flash Player.

Beyond the banner

I already illustrated how this solution works not only for banners, but also for pre- and postroll instream ads. But, by adding your own code logic to supplement what you've done here, you can support most any type of advertising model.

An **overlay** ad is an ad that superimposes some other media, usually a video, without pausing or otherwise affecting the main content. Overlays often include some transparency (whether it's SWF, PNG, or GIF), and if they are Flash ads, they can also include interactivity. Since you can build your own Flash overlays, you can even have an overlay interact with the video player; for example, you could integrate interactivity into the overlays, and if the user does interact with the ad, pause the video playback. And like the expandable ads I mentioned previously, overlays can also grow over the content they superimpose. Since overlays cover other content, they are less likely to be ignored by viewers.

As an example, let's say you wanted to load an overlay ad on top of a video starting from when the viewer is 30 seconds into the video and display it for 30 seconds. First, you could create a new campaign in OpenAds to manage your overlays (separately from your prerolls, for example), and then upload some custom SWF content to serve as the overlay media. You'd have to paste the invocation code for the new campaign into your HTML, as you did for your banners and instream ads earlier in the chapter.

Then, you would add some additional logic to your Flex application so it would know when to call an overlay. For instance, you could create a Timer object to call a function that pings the current timecode of the video being played back. When the viewer is at 30 seconds, the function would call an ad from the overlay campaign, as you did with your banner earlier, and display it in an Image component. The Timer callback can then hide the ad after it's been displayed for 30 seconds.

Using the same type of logic, you can also support interstitials. **Interstitial advertising** is advertising that occurs in the middle of some other content, again usually video. Just as a preroll ad plays before your main video content and a postroll plays after, an interstitial plays at a certain point during the video, pausing the video while it is visible. For example, you could interrupt a three-minute video after two-and-a-half minutes and display an ad (generally of any type supported by Flash—though they tend not to be as interactive as overlays or expandables). This would work just as I explained for overlays, except your Timer would pause and hide the video to display the interstitial, and then show and resume the video when it hides the ad.

Advertising in AIR

You might be wondering if any of this applies to Flex application development for AIR. Well, the good news is, yes it does. But, because of the power of AIR, you don't even need it.

AIR includes a web browser with JavaScript support. So AIR applications can run HTML and JavaScript as well as Flash. In fact, the root of your application can be HTML or it can be Flash. Therefore, very similarly to embedding Flex-generated SWFs into a web page, you can embed your Flex-generated application inside an HTML page and export that as an AIR application. That HTML shell can include the JavaScript and DIV layers you used in the web-based example, and the Flex-generated application can call the JavaScript in the same way. You can even build in some additional support if the user of the AIR application is offline while running the application; for example, you can pull from some locally stored ads, precached on the user's machine, or display some other preset content (such as animated logos or "Did you know?" help content to assist the user with the application).

However, recall the discussion much earlier in the chapter on why I've needed to chop up Flex applications in the past to display ads. When Flash content runs on the Web, it can only interpret a very small subset of HTML, and you can only display that content in TextFields—it can't load HTML content into a frame within the Flash application itself. Well, with AIR, you can create frames for HTML content within your Flex application; so you can have a display area the size and location of your advertising that displays HTML content which includes the logic to load and display ads. Your Flex application can then communicate via the ExternalInterface with a JavaScript function that would trigger the display and refresh of those ads, without going through all the bother of having Flex parse the results, display the ad, and manage the clicks. You can even support Google AdSense this way!

Summary

I started this chapter discussing some of the core considerations of delivering ads in your Internet applications. I then covered a specific technique to bring ads—both banners and instream—into your Flex applications with some really simple code and some free software. I really love techniques that are both simple and powerful. And just to reiterate, this same logic can be applied to ads delivered from any ad management system that doesn't natively support Flash Player delivery.

Continuing with our utilization of powerful, community-supported open source solutions, in the next chapter Hasan is going to introduce you to the basics of working with Drupal, an open source content management system, showing you how to build a blog in minutes. After that, just as I demonstrated in this chapter how to harness OpenAds for Flex, Hasan and Omar will show you how to build Flex applications off of a Drupal-powered CMS.

Part 3

BUILDING OUT NEW FEATURES

In Part 2, we got up and running, covering many key elements and considerations required for executing large-scale Flex applications. In the next four chapters, we begin putting those together to build some specific applications, including our blog, jobs board, and event calendar. Then, in Chapter 15, R will place these applications in context by explaining some of our thinking about future additions to the RMX.

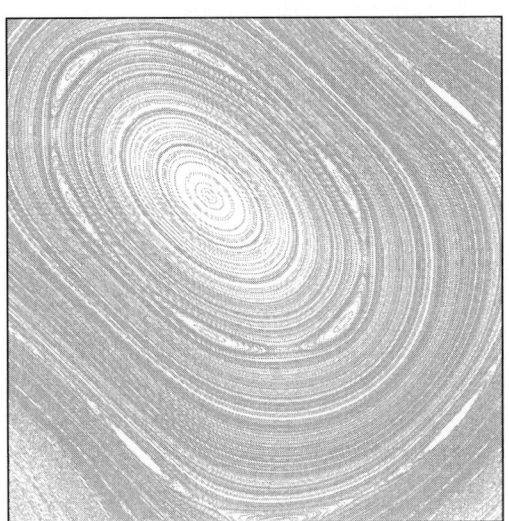

Chapter 12

BUILDING THE BLOG

By Hasan Otuome

The purpose of the RMX is not just to provide aggregated content, but also to build a diverse online social network. You need to ensure that you provide your members with the right content creation and distribution tools, designed in the right ways for their needs and enjoyment to allow the network to grow. In this chapter and the chapters that follow, you'll see the four ways we allow RMX members to network and communicate with each other, starting with blogs.

Even though the RMX blogs are not Flex applications, I wanted to include coverage of them here as a means of introducing you to Drupal, because the chapters that follow discuss building customized Flex interfaces powered by Drupal modules. Working with content management systems like the increasingly popular Drupal is a vital aspect of building many types of contemporary community applications, and Flex developers more and more require familiarity with these systems for front-end integration. Blogs are a great way to start working with Drupal, since blogs are included in the base Drupal installation.

A blog?

A blog, short for weblog, can provide news or commentary on a particular subject like politics, sports, technology, and so forth. And many blogs function more like personal diaries. Most blogs are text based, but with the daily advances in web development, it's not uncommon to find blogs focused on photographs (photoblog), videos (vlog), or audio broadcasts (podcast).

Blogs can have single authors or multiple authors. In addition, most blogs have support for comments. The support for comments is key in the ability to generate a community around a blog, and indeed blogs without comments feel very different from blogs with comments.

While the term "blog" dates back to 1999, and "weblog" to 1997, blogging can be traced to some of the earliest stages of the Internet. In fact, the first blog was probably born out of a Usenet newsgroup. Brian E. Redman created and managed the mod.ber newsgroup, where he and some friends would post summaries of interesting postings and threads that took place elsewhere on the Web. These posts would often include links to other interesting places on the Internet. This gave birth to the online diary, where people kept chronological accounts of their personal lives. The online diary, in turn, gave birth to the modern blog.

Today, blogs are used in various ways, such as to share ideas, gain new clients, or even enrich one's life with new friendships. Some companies even pay people to blog so they can advertise their company's products or services. You can share dialog or spontaneously debate with an ever-increasing freedom of expression. Through blogs, you can often discover people's underlying attitudes and wisdom. You can help people adapt their views or acquire new knowledge and skills. Or, you can just spread new social messages to a global audience.

At their start, blogs were manually updated elements of a web site. This was a definite pain, I'm sure. But, through the evolution of blog production and maintenance tools, the publishing process became more appealing to the growing yet less technical Internet population. Now, blogging is as easy as installing WordPress or MovableType onto your web server or using a service like Blogger or LiveJournal. As a Flex/Flash developer, you may one day be called on to build custom front ends to these popular tools. For the RMX's blog feature, we chose to use the built-in features of the open source Drupal content management system (CMS), available at www.drupal.org.

Introducing the RMX blog

For the RMX, we chose Drupal because it has built-in support for a variety of web applications including large community-driven sites. Because of the production deadline, it proved more feasible for us to work with the highly extensible Drupal as opposed to creating a blog completely in Flex. Now, that's not to say that you can't create a blog in Flex. My personal site (hasan.otuome.com) is a Flex application that features both a journal and vlog. While possible to imitate those results with the RMX, it was better to work with Drupal since it already had modules available to help us meet the following usage-flow requirements:

- A registered member has his own blog.
- A member's posts are automatically syndicated to the blogs of the groups to which the member belongs (e.g., I'm a member of the LA Flash and Flash in TO groups, so all my posts will be syndicated to those groups).
- Group admins can promote selected posts to the posts aggregated on the group's front page.

Armed with this information, we set out to build the blog infrastructure with the understanding that "if you build it, they will come." So, here I'll walk you through the steps necessary to get something like this up and running.

Installing Drupal

To install Drupal, follow these steps:

1. You can download the latest release from the Drupal site at http://ftp.osuosl.org/pub/drupal/files/projects/drupal-5.1.tar.gz. Before downloading though, make sure your development and/or production server meets the following requirements:

   - **Web server**: Apache (recommended)
   - **Scripting**: PHP 5 (for Drupal versions 5 and later)
   - **Database server**: MySQL 4.1 or 5.0 (recommended)

2. After downloading, you have two options: unzip the package locally or upload the package to your web server and unzip it remotely.

   > *If you choose the second option, keep in mind that you'll need Secure Shell (SSH) access to perform the decompression. Since most web hosting companies don't enable that kind of access by default, the remainder of this discussion will focus on developing locally and then transferring the finished version the old-fashioned way, folder by folder and file by file.*

3. Unzip the Drupal package to your desktop, and you'll end up with a drupal-5.1 folder. When developing locally, I usually copy the contents of this folder into the domain (or folder) of the client project I'm working on. I use MAMP (www.living-e.com), a prepackaged Apache, MySQL, and PHP setup for Mac OSX, so for me that location would be /Applications/MAMP/htdocs/site_to_install_drupal_into.

4. Once you've completed that step, you can open your web browser and surf to http://localhost/drupal_site/install.php to complete the installation. After the file has loaded, you should see a message similar to the one displayed in Figure 12-1.

This error message just means that you need to apply chmod to the security settings for that particular file. chmod is a Unix command that changes permissions of a given file or files according to the mode setting. By default, the security setting is 644, but it needs to be 777 to complete installation successfully. For more on chmod, do a Google search on "chmod," and you'll get a wealth of information on the subject.

5. To change the security setting for this file, you can either use the command line or use an FTP client to get into that directory and change the setting using your FTP tool's permissions management options. Of the two, the latter is the easier to perform. Figures 12-2 and 12-3 illustrate this operation using Transmit (www.panic.com/transmit).

Figure 12-1. Drupal installation snag

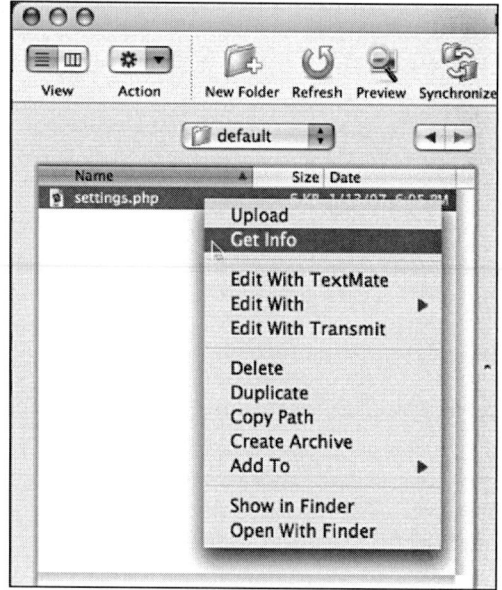

Figure 12-2. Using Transmit to access the Drupal installation

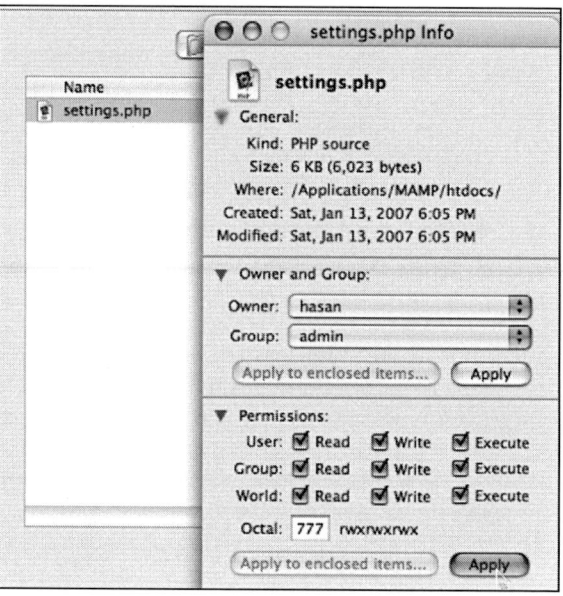

Figure 12-3. Change (chmod) the write permissions for settings.php

6. Once you've completed this change, the install link should now allow you access to the configuration screen illustrated in Figure 12-4. Input the necessary information on this screen and click Save configuration to get a screen similar to the one in Figure 12-5.

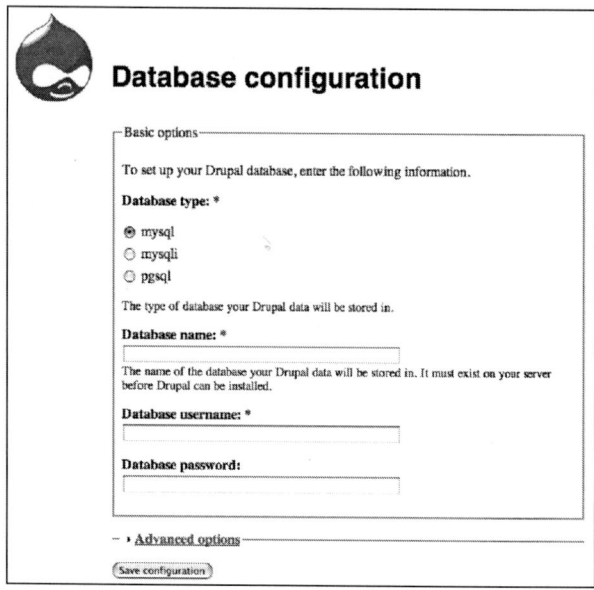

Figure 12-4. Drupal database setup

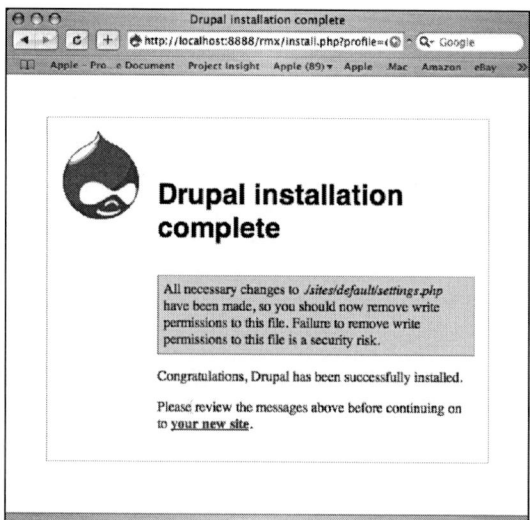

Figure 12-5. Drupal installation complete

7. Follow the same process as before to revert the permissions on settings.php back to the default 644, and you're now ready to start administering your new site.

8. Click the new site link after you've changed the permissions, and you'll come to the default installation page. Here is where you create the super user or admin account. Click the create the first account link shown in Figure 12-6 to start the process.

Figure 12-6. Preparing to administer the installation

9. To create your account, specify a username and e-mail address, and click the Create new account button, as shown in Figure 12-7.

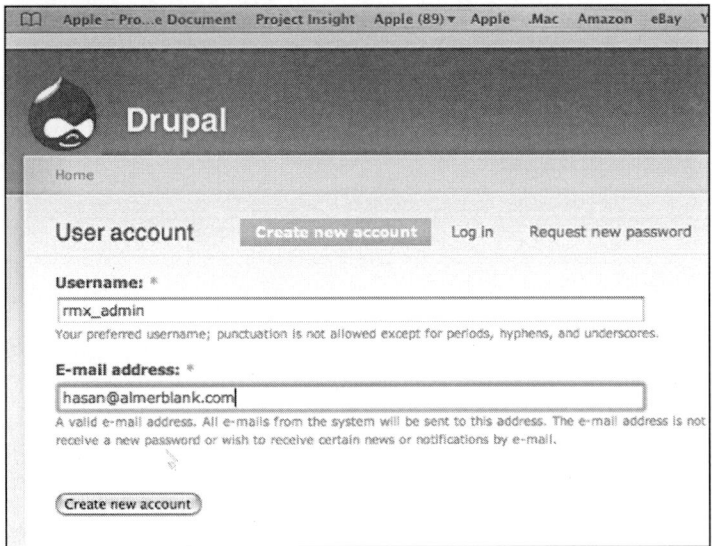

Figure 12-7. Creating the first account

10. On the screen that appears (see Figure 12-8), change the default password. After that click Create new account, and you'll see the screen shown in Figure 12-9.

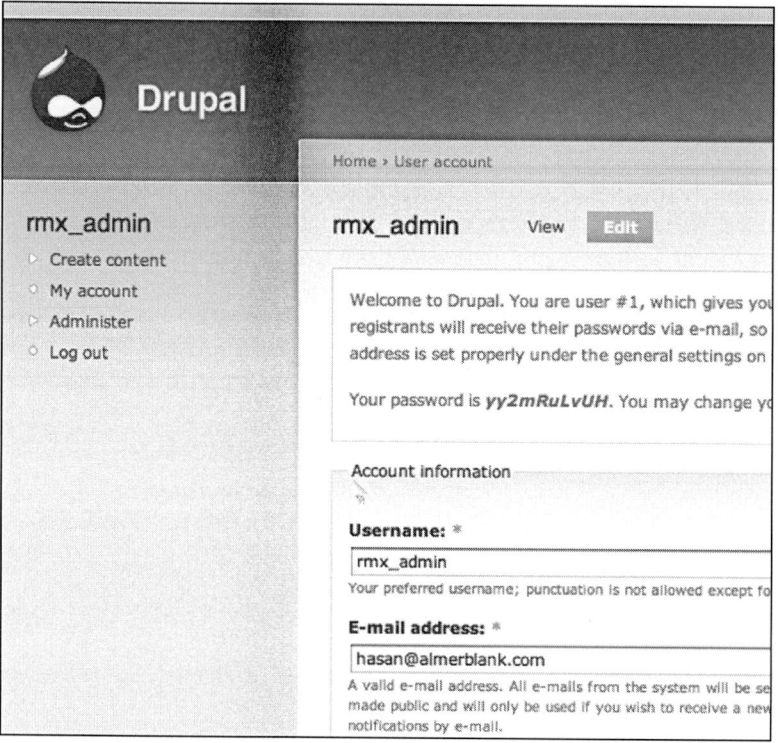

Figure 12-8. Changing the default password

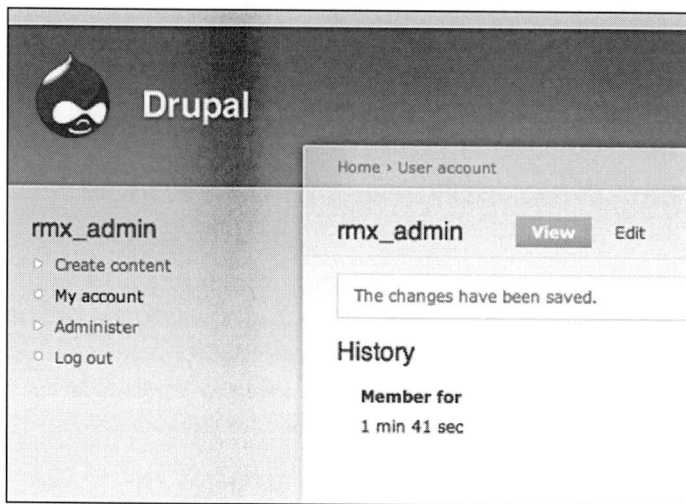

Figure 12-9. Account created and edited successfully

11. After you've successfully created the super user, click the Administer link to finish the last installation steps. If your setup meets the recommended requirements, you should only have two issues that need to be resolved now: cron settings and the permissions on the files directory. Figures 12-10 and 12-11 illustrate the messages that Drupal gives you concerning these issues.

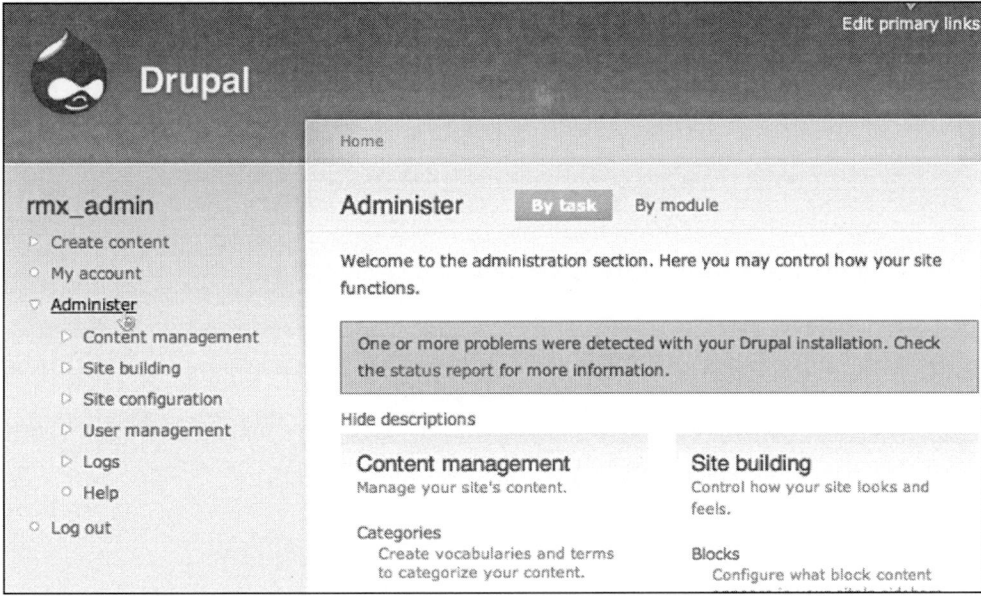

Figure 12-10. Administering Drupal

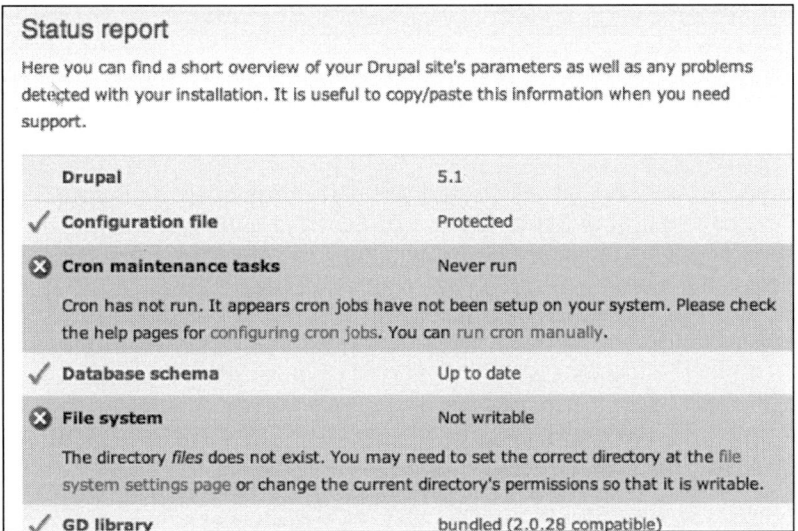

Figure 12-11. Drupal installation problems

> *Cron is a time-based scheduling service found on NIX operating systems (Unix, etc.). A configuration file called* crontab *fuels cron and indicates shell commands to run at specific intervals.*

12. You can run cron manually from the status report page for now without messing anything up. For files, you'll have to create the directory in the root of your Drupal installation and then use chmod to change the permissions on that directory to 777. Once you've done that, reload the current page, and you should see something similar to what's displayed in Figure 12-12.

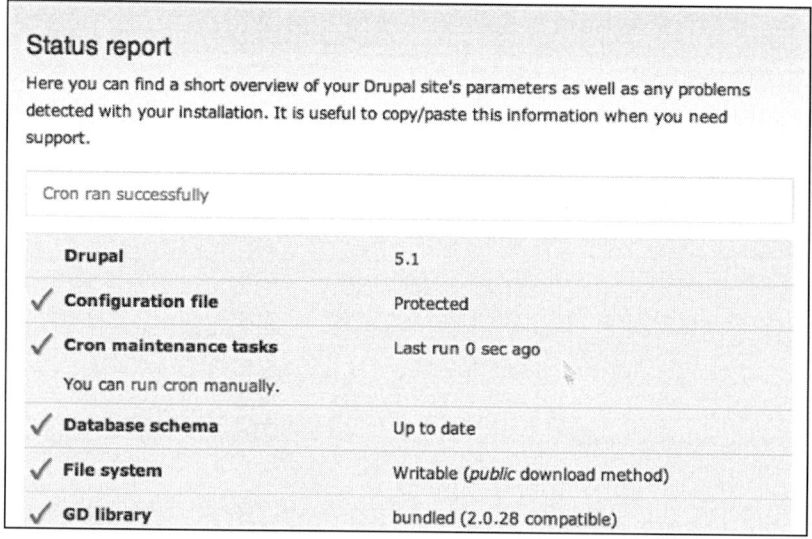

Figure 12-12. Problems solved

Building the blog

At this point, surfing to your site root will bring up the default front page. This page will display as the home page for your site until you've created some content and promoted it to the front page. You're almost ready to start building the blog, but first you need to administer a few things and make sure everything is decent and in order.

Before getting into these tasks, you first must understand some important Drupal concepts as they relate to building a site. The following is a list of the core elements of a Drupal site and their functions:

- **Blocks**: The content that appears in the sidebars, header, footer, and so forth
- **Menus**: Site navigation, primary links, and secondary links
- **Modules**: Add-ons that enhance your site (PayPal, Google, etc.)
- **Themes**: Templates that control the look and feel of the site

Now, what you want to be concerned with first is ensuring that the necessary modules are enabled to allow blogging.

13. Click the Administer link to go back to the administration page illustrated in Figure 12-10.

14. Look under the Site building section for the Modules subsection. Click Modules to navigate to the module management page where you can enable or disable all of your installed modules.

15. The modules that are of interest to you right now are Aggregator, Blog, and Blog API. Enable these modules by clicking the check box next to each module's name and then click Save configuration. Figure 12-13 shows these modules properly enabled.

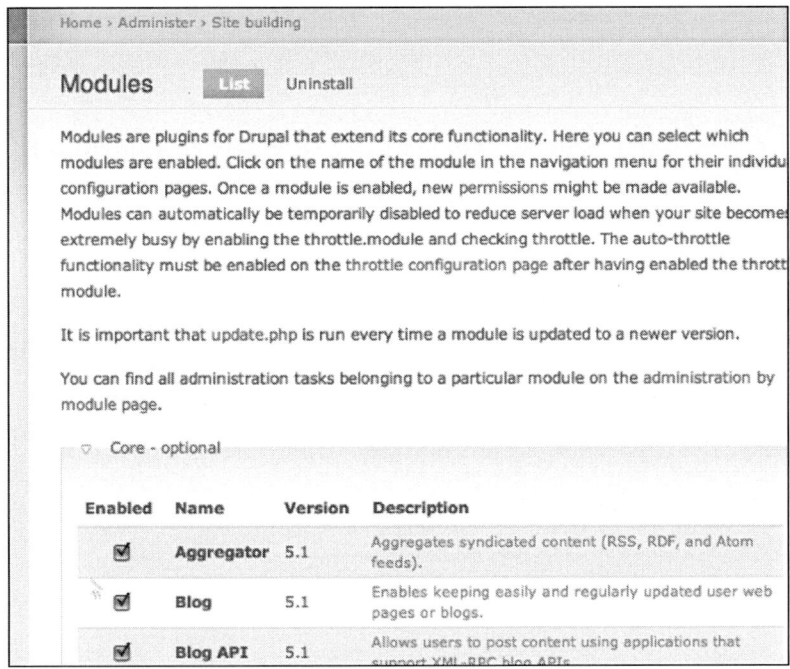

Figure 12-13. Enabling the Aggregator, Blog, and Blog API modules

Now you are ready to build out the blog, but first let's spend a moment reviewing these modules you just enabled.

The Aggregator module

The Aggregator module is a powerful one that gathers fresh content from Drupal sites and blogs around the Web and makes it available from your site. It allows users to view this content either in the main display or the source view (RSS). It provides the administrator the ability to add, edit, and delete feeds plus select how frequently each individual feed is checked for updated content. You can tag individual feeds with categories, offering selective grouping of some feeds in separate displays. It relies on cron to perform its update checks.

Administration of the module is pretty straightforward. Follow these steps:

1. You want to first set up your list of feeds by navigating to Administer ➤ News aggregator as shown in Figure 12-14.

2. Add a new feed by clicking Add Feed. Figure 12-15 shows the input required to set up a new feed to LAFlash.org, for example.

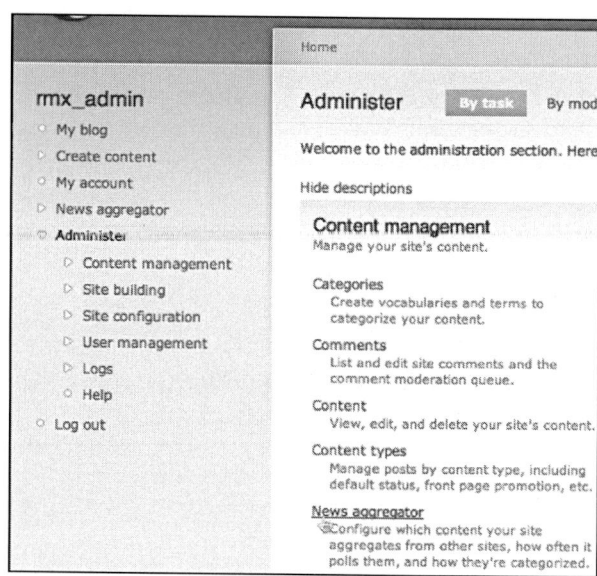

Figure 12-14. Administering the news aggregator

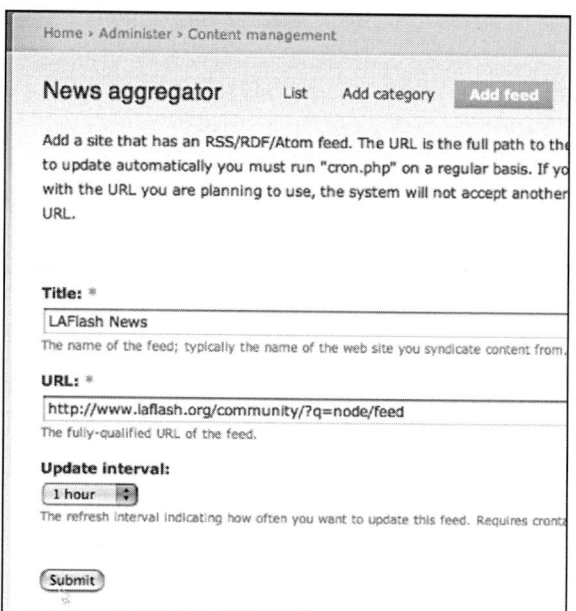

Figure 12-15. Adding a new feed

3. After you've added your feed, add a category to group that feed with similar feeds by specifying a title and description, and click the Submit button. Figure 12-16 illustrates this process.

Figure 12-16. Adding a feed category

> *You could have also added the category before adding the feed with the same result in the end. Adding the category first gives you the option of assigning a feed to that category during feed creation.*

4. Once you've finished adding all your feeds and categories, it's time to return to the Status page (Administer ➤ Status). Here you want to run your cron job manually to fetch the content. Figure 12-17 shows the results of the cron operation.

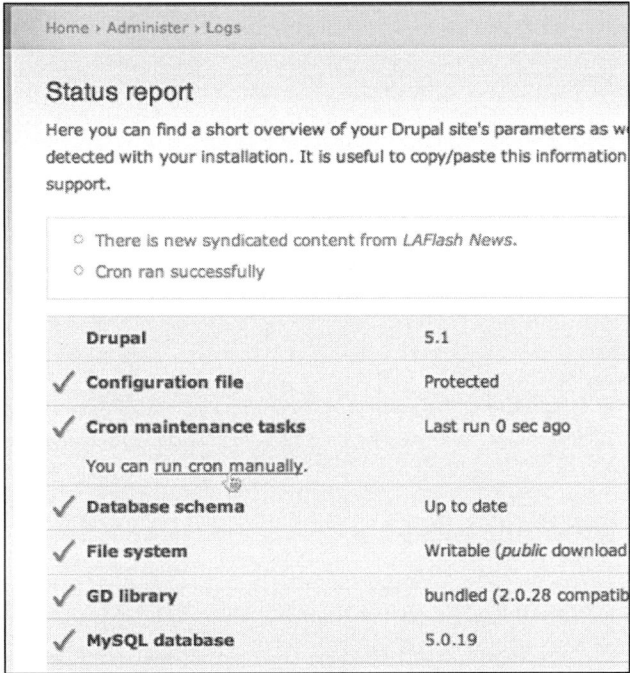

Figure 12-17. Running cron to populate the aggregator

Now you have syndicated content on your Drupal site. All that's left to do is tidy up a bit. You want to enable Clean URLs to do away with the ?q= in the site's URLs and replace it with more human-friendly text. You also want to set the aggregator as the front page.

5. On the Clean URLs screen (see Figure 12-18), click Run the clean URL test. If the test is successful, as indicated by the message shown in Figure 12-19, go ahead and select Enabled and click Save Configuration.

6. Now set your aggregator to be your front page as shown in Figure 12-20.

> *To enable clean URLs to work properly, you'll need the .htaccess file that's included in the Drupal installation. If the file is not visible, you can temporarily enable visibility and copy the .htaccess file to the root of your local or remote Drupal site.*

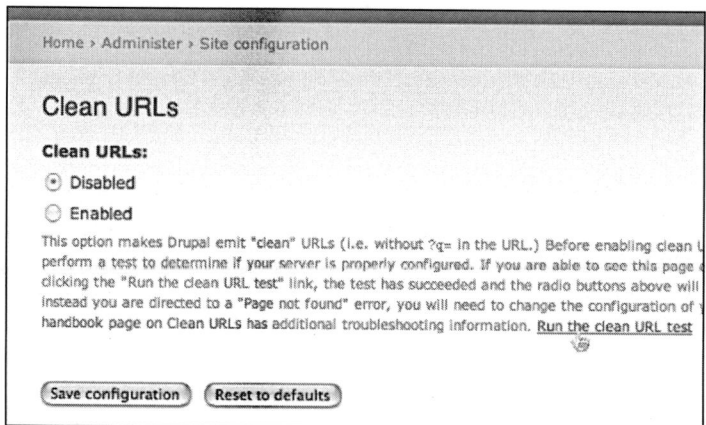

Figure 12-18. Testing for clean URL capabilities

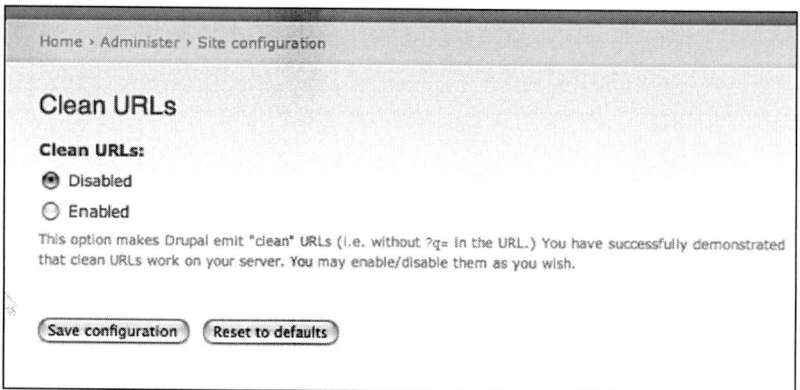

Figure 12-19. Successful results for the clean URL test

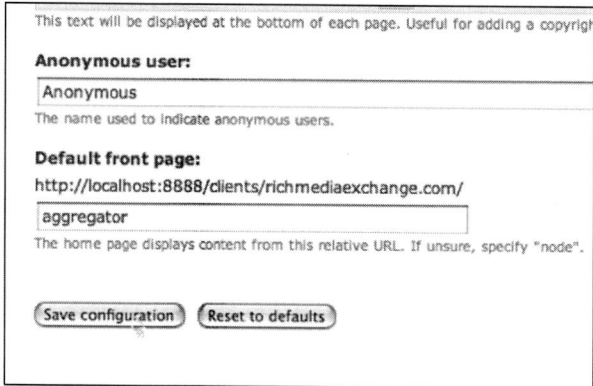

Figure 12-20. Making the aggregator the front page

Once you've completed all these steps, surf to your home page, and you should see news items similar to those in Figure 12-21.

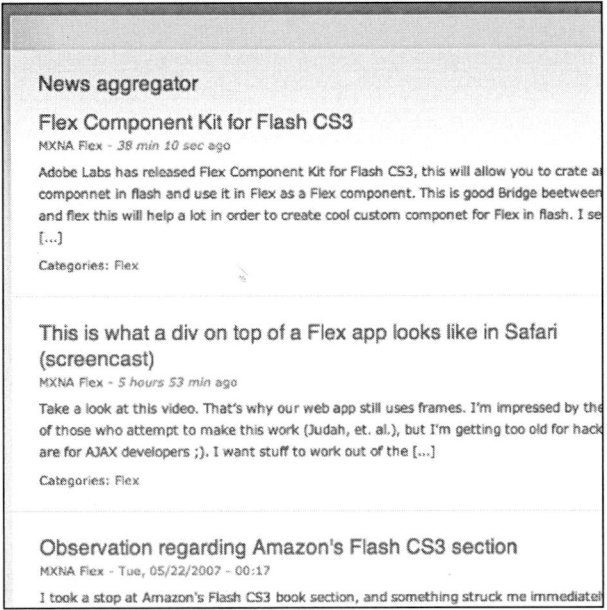

Figure 12-21. The new home page

One thing I did forget to mention is that by default the Aggregator module retains 16 weeks' worth of content per feed, which may be more than you desire. Who wants 1,000+ news items on their home page? That's some serious indigestion! To modify this default behavior, go to Administer ➤ News aggregator ➤ Settings and change the Discard news items older than value to something more to your liking, similar to Figure 12-22. Finally, you can have your categories appear in your sidebar by enabling them in the Blocks administration section (Administer ➤ Blocks) as shown in Figure 12-23.

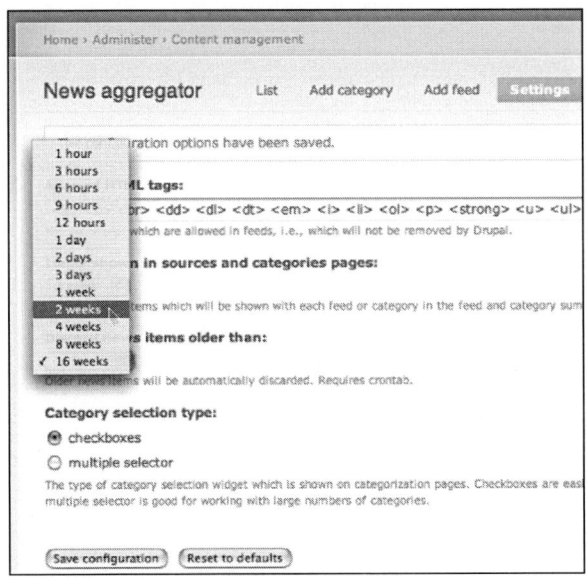

Figure 12-22. Adjusting the aggregator's pruning setting

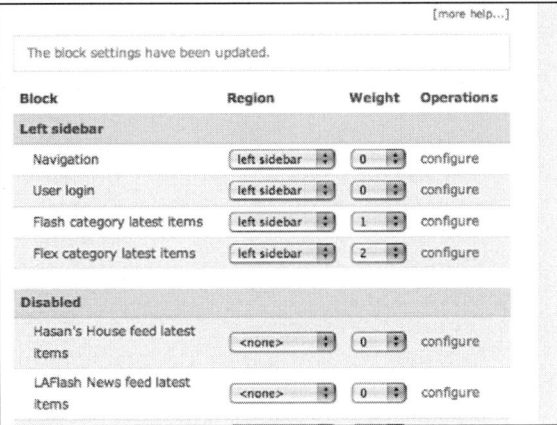

Figure 12-23. Enabling the category blocks

The Blog module

The Blog module is even more straightforward than the Aggregator module. Once it's enabled, you simply go to Create content ➤ Blog entry to start posting. And the cool part is that you don't have to do anything special to enable this feature for other site members. Each member can create and manage his own blog. If you want to include a particular member's postings on the front-page aggregator, grab his RSS feed link from his blog page. Look for the orange feed icon at the bottom of the page, copy that link, use it to create a new feed like you did in the previous section on aggregation, and voilà!

The Blog API module

The Blog API module enables blogging on a Drupal site using external tools like the Blogger API, MovableType API, MarsEdit (Mac), or Microsoft Word 2007 (Windows). It basically provides you the freedom to use the blogging tools you're already comfortable with while using Drupal as the blogging server. As an administrator, you can determine which content types can be posted via these external applications. Figure 12-24 shows some of choices based on the modules you have installed and enabled.

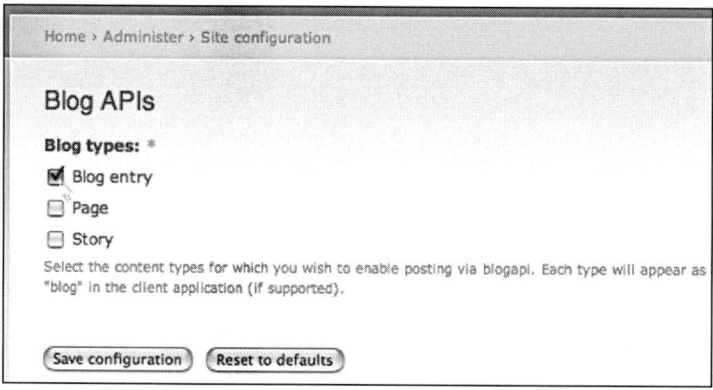

Figure 12-24. Configuring the Blog API module

Customizing the look and feel of Drupal

Naturally, when using a prepackaged solution such as Drupal, you save a lot of time by not having to develop the core functionality of a rather common feature like a blog. However, using these types of solutions presents other obstacles to conquer that a developer would not experience if the application was built from the ground up. One of the best examples of these challenges is customizing the appearance of Drupal (which is not a challenge you have to worry about in the next three chapters, as we'll be demonstrating how to build those custom interfaces in Flex, rather than customizing Drupal's display). Here, I want to give you a jump start on learning how to work with these themes.

Drupal comes prepackaged with a small variety of themes that can be applied to a Drupal installation to change its appearance. Many more themes are listed in the downloads section of the Drupal site (http://drupal.org/project/Themes). Before downloading a theme, make sure that your Drupal installation version is supported by the theme, and download the appropriate one. Also, if the theme lists a template engine requirement, you will have to update your Drupal installation to include the template engine as well. After downloading the theme, and template engine if necessary, it is ready to be installed.

Before starting, make sure to read the ReadMe.txt file that comes with the theme to make sure the theme does not require any special installation instructions other than the usual steps involved in adding a new theme to a Drupal installation. For the purpose of this explanation, and because the RMX Drupal installation is version 5+, I will assume you have downloaded version 5 or later. The instructions for version 4 and older differ in the location of where the files should be placed. Assuming that the readme file did not include any special instructions, uncompress the contents of the downloaded theme. In the Drupal installation directory add a path, /sites/all/themes/, where the theme files will go in a new folder, something like /sites/all/themes/downloadedThemeName.

If the new theme requires a template engine to be installed, uncompress the downloaded template engine files. Starting again from the Drupal installation directory is themes/engines; here you will upload the downloaded template engine files to themes/engines/downloadedEngineThemeName. Once you've uploaded all files to their locations, click Administer, and then click Themes to enable the new theme. Drupal will auto-detect the new file and display it as an option.

These themes, as nice as they may be, will not suffice for an installation that requires extensive design implementation. To implement a design of high complexity, the base theme should provide the ability to organize the Drupal blocks in a type of column layout or whatever specific design elements that are required by the design. Then you can simply add another style sheet in the theme directory, and Drupal will offer the new style sheet as an option of the theme on which you are basing your theme. To begin writing the custom CSS to apply a custom design, open the site in Firefox. Using the Web Developer Toolbar, click the Information menu and choose Display Id & Class Details, as shown in Figure 12-25.

Figure 12-25. How to display class and ID info with Web Developer Toolbar in Firefox

This tool will allow you to see the names of all the classes that affect the different elements on the page, as shown in Figure 12-26. You can use this to begin to identify the different classes and start implementing your custom design.

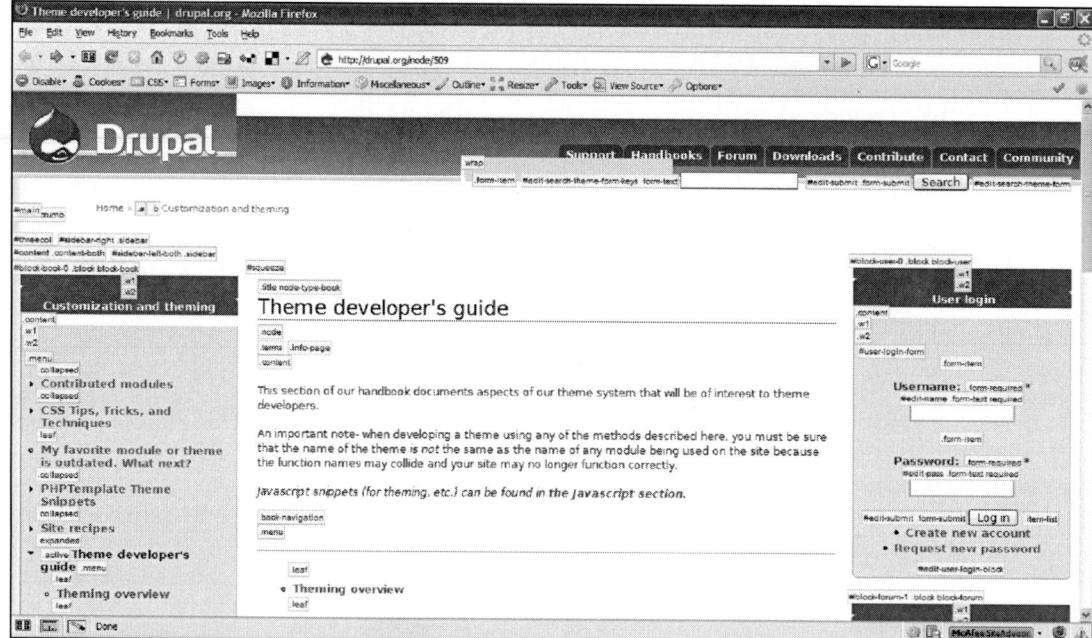

Figure 12-26. Displaying the class names and ID names of all block-level elements

Theme development for Drupal is another topic that merits its own book. Here, I am simply trying to get you on the right path to developing your own custom themes. Aside from what I have already mentioned, you also have the option of developing your own theme engine, which requires writing PHP code and possibly JavaScript, aside from the CSS to implement the styling. For a more complete overview and guide to developing custom Drupal themes, check out the Drupal Theme developer's guide at http://drupal.org/node/509.

Summary

In this chapter, you learned what a blog is, its origins, and the role it plays in Internet communications. From there, you learned how to use the Drupal CMS to set up a site that includes news aggregation and blogging capabilities similar to the methods we've implemented in the RMX.

In the chapter that follows, you'll see how we built the RMX jobs board.

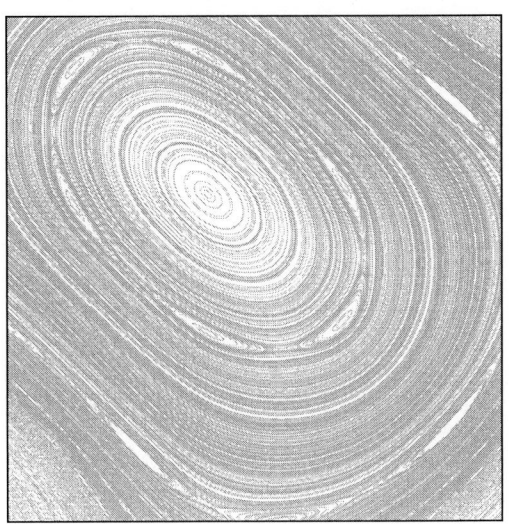

Chapter 13

BUILDING THE JOBS BOARD

By Omar Gonzalez

In this chapter, I am going to cover the building of the jobs board for the RMX, starting with setting up the Drupal side and then shifting quickly to building the Flex interface. I will discuss retrieving records from a Drupal data source and displaying those records in a Flex-powered interface, and end with reviewing how I built the view filters in the Flex interface. You've already explored some of these concepts, so now it's time to put them to practical use. But first, Chris Charlton is going to cover content management and our overall use of Drupal.

Content management

To handle the tons of content being populated by hundreds of user groups worldwide, we need what's known as a **content management system** (CMS). A database is required for scalable content management systems, and MySQL is more than up for that task, so knowing what database software will house our data, the only choice left is deciding on the actual CMS.

As Hasan discussed in Chapter 12, we selected Drupal as our CMS. Flex and Drupal share a lot in common; they're both open source frameworks and have very modular ways of working with data and objects. If one thing can be guaranteed in this book, if you spend enough time with either of these frameworks, you'll get hooked.

So what power does this CMS provide? First, all the CRUD is handled for us—create, read, update, delete—allowing us to concentrate on application logic, as opposed to writing create, read, update, and delete code from scratch. Since entering and retrieving data for us will be handled by Drupal, we only need to concern ourselves with how we're to get that data from Drupal to Flex and back again. This turns out to be easy, using an approach that might be new to you: Flash Remoting. If you've never heard of Flash Remoting, don't be intimidated; it's just another component we're adding to the mix. Adobe has a protocol for Flash and Flex, the Action Messaging Format (AMF), that allows the transparent transfer of data and objects to or from Flash/Flex. The most popular remoting gateways for PHP are WebORB and AMFPHP.

In case you are unfamiliar with AMF gateways, I'll briefly define them here. Usually our front ends need to communicate to a server or script somehow. These AMF gateways allow our server scripts to be called or accessed directly in our Flex, almost as if they're ActionScript methods themselves. There are many tutorials on this topic floating on the Web dedicated to AMFPHP if you feel like getting your hands dirty. If you are already familiar with remoting gateways, when it comes to integration with Drupal, previous AMF experience helps, but you really won't have to get your hands dirty here. All this is new territory, so details matter, but you may be surprised how far Drupal will get you.

Drupal modules

Once you have Drupal installed (as Hasan covered in Chapter 12), you can begin extending it, customizing it to your needs. We mentioned earlier that Drupal was a modular framework, and nothing says it more than the hundreds of modules available for download on Drupal's web site. There's everything from dumb clocks to sophisticated modules that even require other modules be preinstalled for them to work.

You should understand that Drupal itself has a core with a set of built-in modules that not only control Drupal, but also allow you to make more modules and even interface with other installed modules. The most important module is the Node API. Drupal calls practically everything a node. Imagine a content node as a basic object, and a complex content node extended from that basic node. Each node has a title, body text, and an originating author. Anything above that is dealt with in a custom content node. Our content management framework allows us to do things like make new nodes and custom content types without any hand coding, so I won't go into detail here about how to create these types manually. If you are interested in a detailed look at the inner workings of Drupal, check out *Pro Drupal Development* by John K. VanDyk and Matt Westgate (Apress, 2007) and *Building Online Communities with Drupal, phpBB, and WordPress* by Robert T. Douglass, Mike Little, and Jared W. Smith (Apress, 2005).

The RMX runs off dozens of modules (see Figure 13-1), not so much as to offer dozens of features, but because some modules work together, and as we mentioned earlier, some modules require other modules in order to run properly. The two modules required for connecting a Flex front end to a Drupal back end are the Services module and the AMFPHP module. Another module that's key is the Views module, which isn't for counting page views but for generating views more common to what database people build. All those modules are available on Drupal's web site at no charge.

Modules, which are just PHP files with a .module file extension, are really simple to install. Just upload the module file to your Drupal's sites/all/modules/ directory, and then activate it in the user access administration area. We'll be using all three modules I've just mentioned (AMFPHP, Services, and Views) for this chapter and the next, so you may want to install them to follow along.

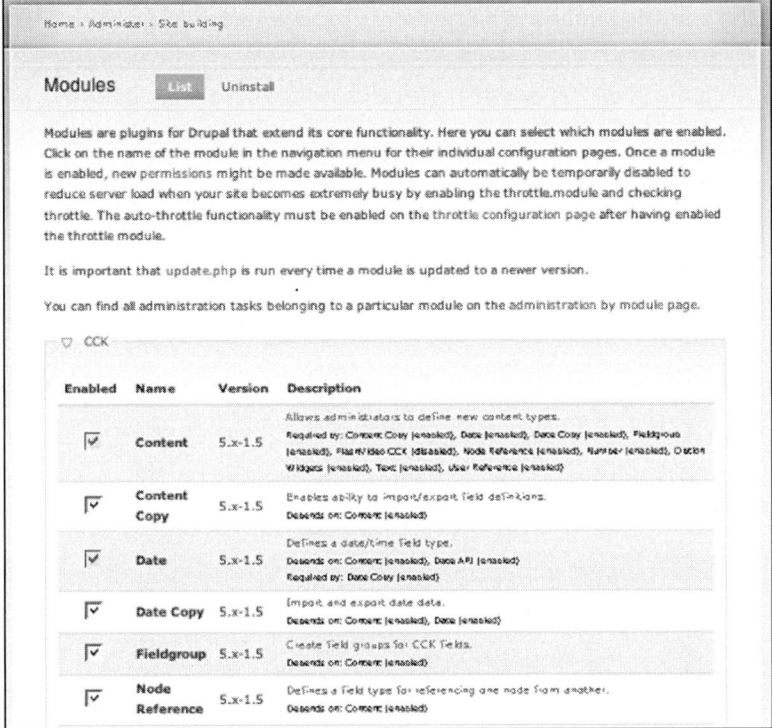

Figure 13-1. Drupal modules page

Once you have your modules uploaded, you need to configure a couple of additional settings within Drupal. One key setting is to enable clean URLs; this option activates Apache's mod_rewrite to clean up the URLs our application generates. Also, Drupal has user access rights that always need to be set for every module you install. Make sure user access is turned on for both the Services module and the Views module. You should then see both modules listed in the administration page. Now that you're set up, it's time to generate some Views and access them through the Services module.

Generating services and Views

Once the modules have been uploaded and installed properly, you can start to generate Views. The term "Views" can mean many things to different developers; as I mentioned previously, database developers may be familiar with these types of Views. A View is an outlook on a set of data. Normally, retrieval of data returns a simple set, like a list of users. Additional database code is required to join or filter data from more than one database table, and this is where Views come in handy. A prepared View can bring back not only a list of users, but also login stats, multiple permissions, and anything else an application would need when retrieving a list of users. Another way to look at Views is that they're almost like superqueries since they can call subqueries internally and even alter or format the data before it is returned.

Some neat people released the Views module for Drupal to help everyone generate Views in a web form (see Figure 13-2) and reduce hand coding. If you don't plan to add any custom content types above what the core offers—blog posts, forums, pages—you won't need to generate Views much or even at all. Since we're using custom content types, we definitely need to generate some Views for the RMX Drupal implementation. Browse to the Views module in the Administration area of Drupal.

You might have caught the point earlier that the Views module isn't required for Flex and Drupal communication, but trust me when I say it's insanely handy. I'll stick to my promise and not get your hands dirty. The Views we have built require no SQL or PHP coding.

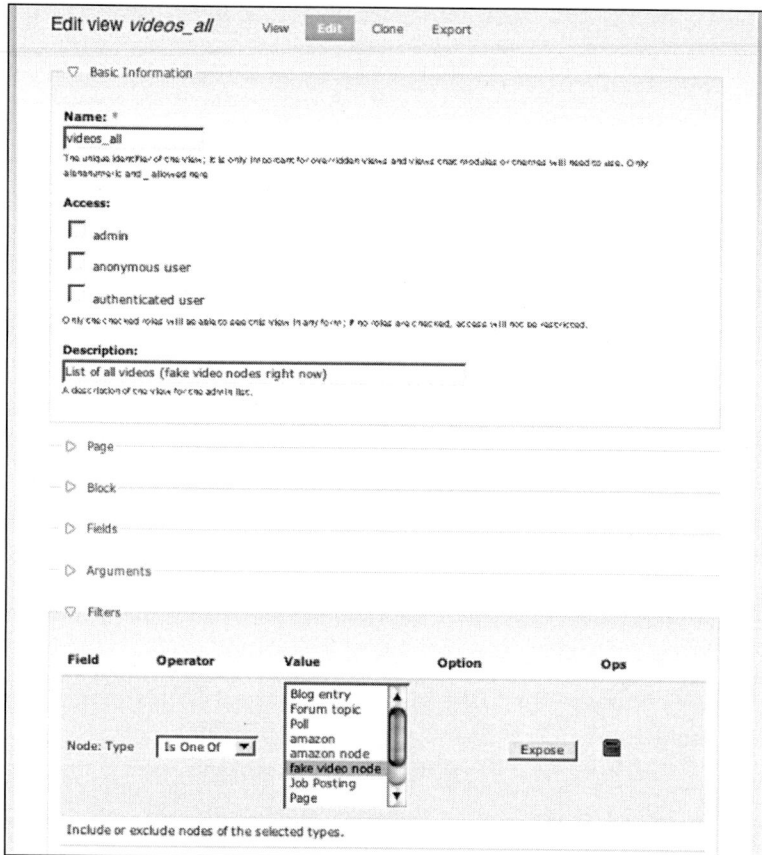

Figure 13-2. Drupal Views start page

Generating Views in Drupal

At first glance, the long form for creating or editing a View can be either quite intimidating or appetizing. There are many sections to the form, mostly optional, and to complete a View you only need to fill out the Fields, Arguments, Filters, and Sort Criteria sections. Depending on your needs, you may not even need to edit all those sections, and the form tries to be informative, so give each section a read to determine whether it is required for your needs.

The top of the Views form asks for a human-readable and machine-readable name for the View to be created. The machine-readable name is necessary for the testing and ActionScript code in this example, so be sure to specify one if you are following along.

Be sure to add content for whatever node type you'll be retrieving from the View; otherwise, you'll have no fun testing the service and not see any data come back. If Drupal is still too new for you, add content through the Create content menu in your Navigation menu block. Once you're done making a View, it's time to test it through the Services module.

Religious coders may wonder why we used the Views module, as opposed to coding the PHP and SQL by hand. Well, when working with Drupal's framework, which is technically a content management framework (CMF), we want to use portions of the framework that work best for us, and when retrieving data, a View is the quickest maintainable solution. So, unless you planned to get thoroughly schooled in Drupal standards and programming methods, you'd spend at least a good couple of days just reading and learning the terminology. We're here to get you up and running today. So, yes, you can code all this out, but when there's a good tool for you to use instead, why not use it?

Calling Views through the Services module

I know you're excited to get your Views module running in your interface, but you need to test the Views through the Services module first. The Services module is the gateway; you can use it to send messages between PHP and Flex in ActionScript-ready formats. Remember, behind the services curtain is AMFPHP providing the remoting gateway, so you'll first test to ensure the AMFPHP is set up correctly (see Figure 13-3). When you browse to the Services module's screen, you'll see a list of servers (see Figure 13-4); click the AMFPHP - /services/amfphp link to test your gateway. If this fails, you must resolve the issue before proceeding. Make sure all the AMFPHP files are uploaded and that the proper Drupal modules are installed and activated. Your user account should also have permissions to access the Drupal modules installed.

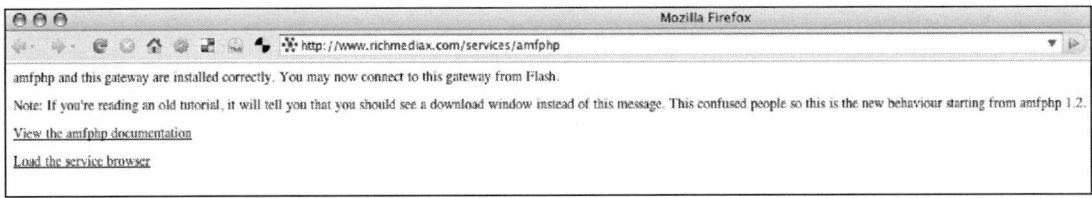

Figure 13-3. AMFPHP gateway test

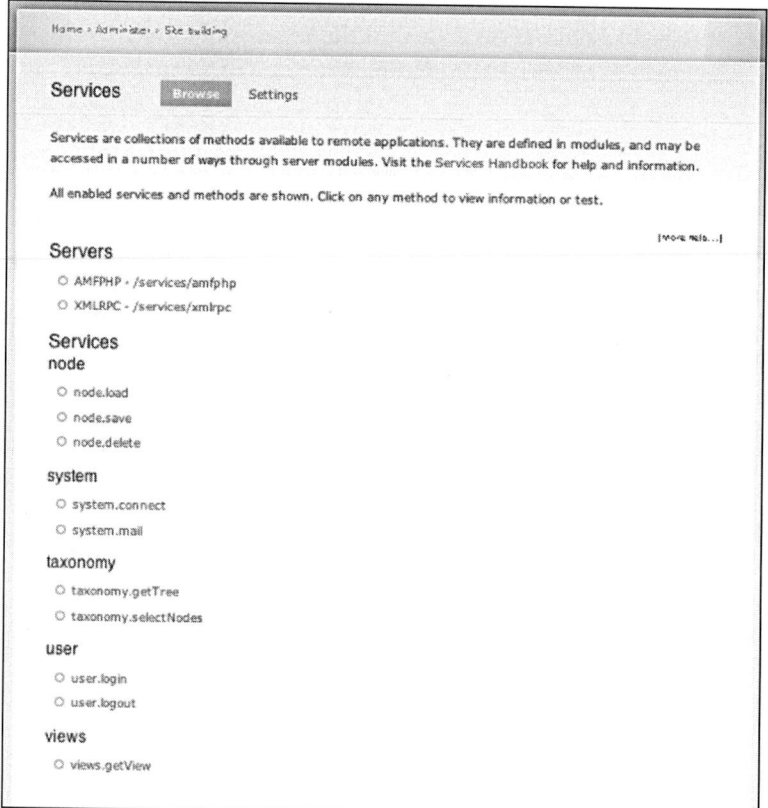

Figure 13-4. Drupal Services start page

Under the list of servers you should notice a few lists of services for node, system, taxonomy, user, and Views. Obviously, you'll be using the Views service for that new View you made earlier. Click views.getView (see Figure 13-4) and enter your machine-readable name for your custom View in the view_name field of the service testing form. To start, you only need to enter the View name (see Figure 13-5) and click the Call method button. You should then see some data or a data structure come back. Remember, you need to add some content before you head over to Flex, so if you haven't done that yet, please do so now. Take a screenshot or make a list of the data structure that is returned: these are the fields to which you'll be mapping bindings and code.

When you're satisfied with your View being returned through the services test form, it's time to bust out your front end in Flex.

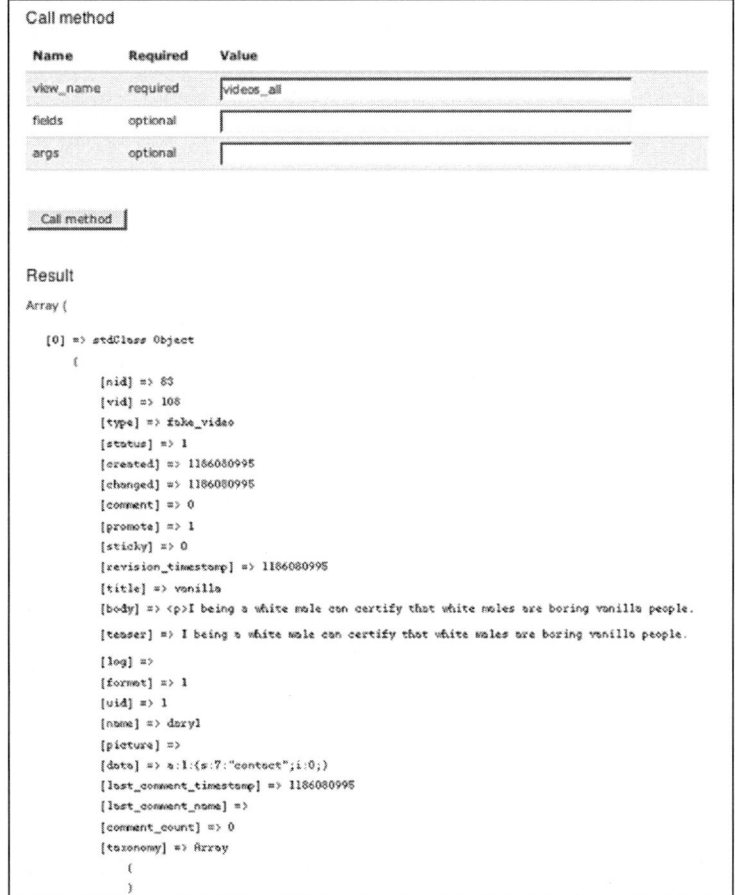

Figure 13-5. Services result showing data structure returned from a View

Learning more about the Drupal Services module

Technically, you can roll any CMF/CMS with AMFPHP or similar, but we've chosen Drupal. Drupal has many handbooks available on its web site, and each module tries to document as much as it can, but remember, the modules are mostly free, so they're all being developed in people's spare time. Luckily, there are a few tutorials and video recordings of how to install Drupal and modules, and even some basics of working with the Services module.

Even with these helpful videos, it's important not to get frustrated when you can't find information or are stuck—you're not alone. The entire array of wiring an AMF gateway into Drupal is new, so there aren't really any bugs that will hold you up, but the limited documentation can create hurdles. The Services and AMFPHP modules are currently handled by one person, and hopefully this won't be the case moving forward. And now let's get back to Omar to build the Flex interface to bring our information to life.

Preparing to start the jobs board

As I underscored in Chapter 4, the first place I start coding any application is by examining what kinds of data the application will handle, and then map out all the data transfer objects (DTOs) I will need in development. For this particular application, the jobs board, I only need a Job DTO to get information for a particular job from one part of the application to another. However, because the objects being received from Drupal are not objects we formatted ourselves for easy transfer, and because the Drupal objects are big, we need a more robust DTO than the basic DTO I covered earlier in the book.

Advanced DTOs

In my first example, of a DTO in Chapter 4, the data object handled by the DTO was rather simple. The object held one property only. In the case of the data objects returned from Drupal to the jobs board application, I first have to parse the data, assigning values within the DTO, to facilitate my work transferring the data.

To begin to understand the need for the extra parsing, you must first look at the data object I am receiving from Drupal. This is what one record return would look like for a sample job entry:

```
Drupal return = (Array)#0
  [0] (Object)#1
     body = "<div class="wiki-content"><p>Lorem ipsum dolor sit amet.
Ut purus neque, viverra a, interdum dignissim, nonummy
Sed a massa a augue eleifend vulputate. Vivamus tortor quam, eleifend
</p><p>Donec lacinia blandit urna. Phasellus sed purus. Donec laoreet
Vestibulum aliquet lorem ac arcu. Donec imperdiet metus sed nunc Sed
non elit non elit aliquet viverra. CSS Nunc ultrices sodales dui.
</p><p>Suspendisse leo eros, laoreet condimentum, accumsan elementum.
Vestibulum volutpat arcu ut quam. Praesent leo ipsum, sodales a, nulla.
Sed lacinia varius libero. Vivamus tortor felis, rhoncus eget.
</p></div>"
     body_value = "Lorem ipsum dolor sit amet, consectetuer adipiscing.
neque, viverra a, interdum dignissim, nonummy Flash eget, nisi. Sed
eleifend vulputate. Vivamus tortor quam, eleifend et, laoreet faucibus,
pede. Vestibulum risus. Nam pede. Praesent ac libero. Proin arcu. "
     changed = "1184881339"
     comment = "2"
     comment_count = "0"
     created = "1184881274"
     data = "a:1:{s:7:"contact";i:0;}"
     field_employment_status = (Array)#2
       [0] (Object)#3
         value = "Full-time"
     field_job_role = (Array)#4
       [0] (Object)#5
         value = "Web Developer/Coder"
       [1] (Object)#6
         value = "RIA Developer"
       [2] (Object)#7
         value = "Video Editor"
```

```
    [3] (Object)#8
      value = "Project Manager"
  field_location = (Array)#9
    [0] (Object)#10
      value = "On-site"
  field_location_zip = (Array)#11
    [0] (Object)#12
      value = "90909"
  field_pay_range_max = (Array)#13
    [0] (Object)#14
      value = "200"
  field_pay_range_min = (Array)#15
    [0] (Object)#16
      value = "100"
  field_payment_contract = (Array)#17
    [0] (Object)#18
      value = "Hourly"
  field_seniority = (Array)#19
    [0] (Object)#20
      value = "Mid-Level"
  field_source = (Array)#21
    [0] (Object)#22
      value = "From Employer"
  files = (Array)#23
  format = "1"
  last_comment_name = (null)
  last_comment_timestamp = "1184881274"
  log = ""
  name = "daryl"
  nid = "40"
  picture = ""
  promote = "0"
  revision_timestamp = "1184881339"
  status = "1"
  sticky = "0"
  taxonomy = (Object)#24
    1 = (Object)#25
      description = "Adobe Flash is a super awesome way to make cool
things even cooler"
      name = "Flash"
      tid = "1"
      vid = "2"
      weight = "-10"
    10 = (Object)#26
      description = ""
      name = "MXML"
      tid = "10"
      vid = "3"
      weight = "0"
    11 = (Object)#27
```

```
          description = ""
          name = "AS3"
          tid = "11"
          vid = "3"
          weight = "0"
      12 = (Object)#28
          description = ""
          name = "CFML"
          tid = "12"
          vid = "3"
          weight = "0"
      2 = (Object)#29
          description = "Flex Builder, Flex Framework, MXML"
          name = "Flex"
          tid = "2"
          vid = "2"
          weight = "-9"
      3 = (Object)#30
          description = ""
          name = "Dreamweaver"
          tid = "3"
          vid = "2"
          weight = "-7"
      4 = (Object)#31
          description = "Adobe Integrated Runtime"
          name = "Adobe Integrated Runtime (AIR)"
          tid = "4"
          vid = "2"
          weight = "-8"
    teaser = "Lorem ipsum dolor sit amet, consectetuer adipiscing elit.
viverra a, interdum dignissim, nonummy Flash eget, nisi. Sed a massa
vulputate. Vivamus tortor quam, eleifend et, laoreet faucibus, euismod.
Vestibulum risus. Nam pede. Praesent ac libero. Proin arcu. Morbi
lacus. Nullam vulputate, augue suscipit mollis pellentesque, ligula
pharetra commodo arcu dolor et ante. Duis a eros et magna congue."
    title = "the newest job I swear"
    type = "job"
    userid = "1"
    vid = "65"
```

The record object is pretty long, and the application does not need every bit of data to display the job details required by the specification for the jobs board (which R discussed in Chapter 3). For example, the job details have a required knowledge field, and the values for that display are contained within the taxonomy array in the data object returned by Drupal. The completed Job.as DTO looks like this:

```
package com.almerblank.rmx.flex.dto
{
  [Bindable]
  public class Job extends Object
  {
```

```
      public var title:String;
      public var description:String;
      public var postedBy:String;
      public var positionIs:String;
      public var jobLocation:String;
      public var requiredKnowledge:String;
      public var jobRoles:String;
      public var seniority:String;
      public var payrange:String;
      public var minimumPay:Number;
      public var maximumPay:Number;
      public var location:String;
      public var jobSource:String;
      public var paymentContract:String;

      public function Job(newJob:Object = null)
      {
        super();
        if (newJob)
        {
          parseObject(newJob);
        }
      }

      private function parseObject(newInfo:Object):void
      {
        title = newInfo.title;
        description = newInfo.body;
        postedBy = newInfo.name;
        jobLocation = newInfo.field_location_zip[0].value;
        seniority = newInfo.field_seniority[0].value;
        payrange = newInfo.field_pay_range_min[0].value + ' - ' +
  newInfo.field_pay_range_max[0].value;
        minimumPay = newInfo.field_pay_range_min[0].value;
        maximumPay = newInfo.field_pay_range_max[0].value;
        location = newInfo.field_location[0].value;
        jobSource = newInfo.field_source[0].value;
        paymentContract = newInfo.field_payment_contract[0].value;

        var tag:Object;
        var tags:Array = new Array();
        for each (tag in newInfo.taxonomy)
        {
          if (tag)
          {
            tags.push(tag.name);
          }
        }
        requiredKnowledge = tags.toString();
```

```
        var role:Object;
        var roles:Array = new Array();
        for each (role in newInfo.field_job_role)
        {
          if (role)
          {
            roles.push(role.value);
          }
        }
        jobRoles = roles.toString();

        var positionType:Object;
        var positions:Array = new Array();
        for each (positionType in newInfo.field_employment_status)
        {
          positions.push(positionType.value);
        }
        positionIs = positions.toString();

      }
    }
  }
```

In this example, the code that assigns values to the DTO's properties is in its own method called parseObject, which is mainly to keep the code cleaner and organized. The first few lines of the method look very similar to the ones in Chapter 4, except that in this example I use dot notation instead of bracket notation to gain access to the properties I want from the Drupal return. Some properties like payRange concatenate two of the properties from the Drupal record object, which is another example of some of the custom logic written to get the data transferred to the display formatted the way the application requires it in order to be viewed on the display according to the spec documents.

Right after the first block of code, there are three for each loops that populate some of the DTO's properties. These loops are necessary because the information is returned by Drupal in an array object. So, for example, the first for each loop cycles through the members of the taxonomy array returned from Drupal. From this array object, the display only needs the name property, so that is what gets stored.

Setting up custom events

To have the application react to certain user inputs, you use events like a mouse click or a rollover. Not only do they let you know that something has happened, but they also carry information that is relevant to what just occurred within the application. In the case of the jobs browser, the List component that displays each job dispatches an itemClick event. Although this event notifies the application that something has been clicked in the jobs list, the native event does not contain very useful information, such as the details of which event has been clicked. This means I need to gain access to it either through a property on the event or directly through the application.

With a custom event, it is possible to add a property of the event that holds the information or object you need access to. In the example of the jobs browser, the job itself would be included. To do this, a new class must be written that extends the Event class. This new class, which extends Event, can have all the custom properties necessary for a particular event in the application. Going back to the jobs board, the custom event class looks like this:

```
package com.almerblank.rmx.flex.events
{
  import flash.events.Event;
  import com.almerblank.rmx.flex.dto.Job;

  [Event(name="jobSelected",
type="com.almerblank.rmx.flex.events.JobsBoardEvent")]
  public class JobsBoardEvent extends Event
  {
    public static const JOB_SELECTED:String = "jobSelected";

    public var job:Job;

    public function JobsBoardEvent(type:String, bubbles:Boolean=false,
                                   cancelable:Boolean=false)
    {
      super(type, bubbles, cancelable);
    }

  }
}
```

The class is very small, but extremely handy. The first line, just before the class declaration but inside the package, is the event metadata. This metadata is there for the Flex compiler so that it can recognize the events as MXML tag attributes from within an MXML file. It should be above the class so it is bound to the class, and not to a particular member of the class.

The next line is a static constant, which is what should be used as the type parameter when creating a new JobsBoardEvent. The third line in the class is the job custom property of Job type, which is the DTO for the jobs board. This property will be used to transfer data from the jobs list to the rest of the application.

From the base class for the item renderer of the jobs list, which you can see in Figure 13-6, I assign a mouse click event on the root container of the item renderer. In this event handler method, jobSelected(), I dispatch the custom event that carries the job DTO in it. This code in the item renderer looks as follows:

```
...
    private function jobSelected(event:MouseEvent):void
    {
      var e:JobsBoardEvent = new JobsBoardEvent(
JobsBoardEvent.JOB_SELECTED, true);
      e.job = job;
      dispatchEvent(e);
    }
    ...
```

The jobSelected method is an event handler for the mouse click event on the item renderer's base container. In it, a variable e has been initialized, which is my custom event object. As the first argument, I use the JOB_SELECTED constant to determine the event type, and then send true in the second argument, which determines whether the event bubbles or not. I want to listen for this event on the base class of the JobsBoard application, so I set this to true so that it bubbles up. If it were omitted, the event would not be heard by the base class of the application. It would only be heard locally on the item renderer object.

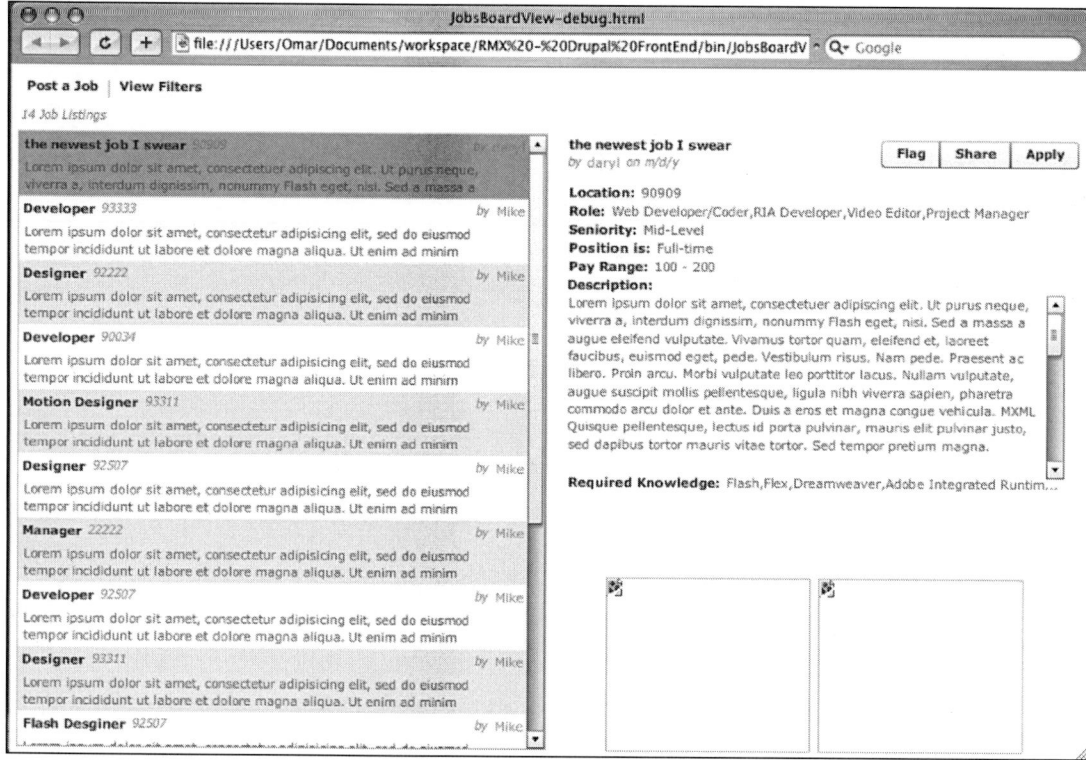

Figure 13-6. The jobs browser for the RMX jobs board

Connecting to the Drupal services

The next bit of code to cover is how the Flex front end connects to the AMFPHP Drupal services. The setup needed for interfacing with the Drupal services requires a few variables in the way that the RemoteObject is set up, so I encapsulated that functionality into a Services class that would be easy to use and easy to maintain.

The next challenge I faced was writing this with minimal documentation. The Flex language documents do not provide examples for using the RemoteObject class in ActionScript, and I could not find many examples online, so I had to go through a bit of trial and error to write this class.

The class looks something like this:

```
package com.almerblank.rmx.flex.network
{
  import mx.rpc.remoting.mxml.RemoteObject;
  import mx.rpc.events.FaultEvent;
  import mx.rpc.events.ResultEvent;
  import mx.rpc.remoting.Operation;
  /**
   * The Services class is a static class used to call all services.
   *
   * @author OmarG
   *
   */
  public class Services
  {
    // jobs board services
    public static const GET_JOBS:String = "view_jobs_all";
    public static const GET_EVENTS:String = "event_date_cc";


    // Service properties
    /**
     * The serviceProperties object holds all the properties
     * for each remote method.
     */
    public static const serviceProperties:Object = {
    "view_jobs_all" : {'module': 'views', 'method':"getView",
'view':'view_jobs_all','fields':null },
    "event_date_cc" : {'module': 'views', 'method':"getView",
'view':'event_date_cc',
'fields':null }
        };


    private static var _remoteObj:RemoteObject;
    private static var _showBusyCursor:Boolean = true;

    /**
     *
     * @param methodName - the service being called
     * @param result - the result handler
     * @param fault - the fault handler
     * @param arguments - used to pass information to Drupal to process
     * @param showBusyCursor - set to false to manage cursor yourself.
     *
     */
    public static function call(methodName:String, result:Function,
                                    fault:Function,
```

```
                              arguments:Array = null,
                              showBusyCursor:Boolean = true):void
    {

        if (!showBusyCursor)
        {
          _showBusyCursor = false;
        }


        startRemoteObject();

        _remoteObj.addEventListener(FaultEvent.FAULT, fault);
        _remoteObj.source = serviceProperties[methodName]['module'];


        var op:Operation = new Operation(_remoteObj);
        op.name = serviceProperties[methodName]['method'];

        var svc:Operation = _remoteObj.getOperation(
serviceProperties[methodName]['method'])
as Operation;
        svc.addEventListener(ResultEvent.RESULT, result);

        // send service code for getView method.
        // wrapped in if statement to accomodate for
        // possibility that the parameters sent in svc.send() method
        // might change in order.
        if (serviceProperties[methodName]['method'] == 'getView')
        {
          if (serviceProperties[methodName]['fields'] && arguments)
          {
            svc.send(serviceProperties[methodName]['view'],
                    serviceProperties[methodName]['fields'], arguments);
          }
          else if (serviceProperties[methodName]['fields'])
          {
            svc.send(serviceProperties[methodName]['view'],
                    serviceProperties[methodName]['fields']);
          }
          else
          {
            svc.send(serviceProperties[methodName]['view']);
          }
        }

    }
```

```
/**
 * Starts a new remote object
 * @private
 */
private static function startRemoteObject():void
{
  _remoteObj = new RemoteObject();
  _remoteObj.destination = 'amfphp';
  _remoteObj.concurrency = 'last';
  _remoteObj.requestTimeout = 60;

  if (_showBusyCursor)
  {
    _remoteObj.showBusyCursor = true;
  }
}

  }
}
```

There are only two calls within this example of the Services class: one for retrieving a jobs list and one for retrieving events. Dissecting this one piece at a time, let's start with the two constants at the top of the class. These two constants are used to choose which service call in the class you want to access, either Services.GET_JOBS or Services.GET_EVENTS. These constants work together with the serviceProperties private object, which contains all of the variables needed to make a successful Drupal AMFPHP service call to the Services module.

To actually call a service, I use the only public method in the class, call(), which is actually a public static method. I made the class based on a static method so that it is easily invoked from anywhere in the application code without first instantiating the class, and I do not need multiple object instances of this functionality for the application. This makes the class more convenient and flexible. The call method expects five arguments, two of which are optional. The first argument is the methodName I want to call, which I use the predefined constants for. The second and third arguments are the result and fault handlers, in that order. The fourth argument defaults to null, which is for any additional arguments that I want to send to the service. The last argument, showBusyCursor, defaults to true so that it handles the turning on and off of the busy cursor while the call is being made.

Within the call method is where the guts of the class exist. The first thing I do is make sure that the showBusyCursor hasn't been set to false. After that simple check, there is a call to the startRemoteObject() method. This method sets up a basic remote object and assigns the correct values to the properties that don't change when you call different remote methods. After that is done, the next two lines set up the first two dynamic properties that change on the RemoteObject instance. The fault event handler passed in to the call method is assigned to the remote object, and the source attribute is retrieved from the serviceProperties object, using the static const as the array index to grab the values appropriate for the call.

The next bit is what I couldn't find any documentation for, and that is how the <mx:method/> tags get interpreted into ActionScript. The <mx:method/> tags are turned into instances of the Operation class. On the first line, I start a new Operation instance, and pass in the RemoteObject instance so that it starts the Operation instance. On the next line I point the name property to the method to execute from the serviceProperties object. Once that is done, in order to execute the operation, I use the getOperation method on the RemoteObject instance. With another function variable called svc, I retrieve the Operation instance with the getOperation method using the name I assigned to it after instantiation. On the svc reference, I add the result event handler that was passed into the call() method of the Services class, which executes whatever logic I need after I get the results from the service call.

Finally, the last if statement checks which method is being called, and changes the arguments accordingly. To accommodate for that possibility, the if statement makes sure certain conditions are met to make the appropriate call, using the svc.send() method. This small and handy class saves me time when I need to call a service, and centralizes all code dealing with service calls to this one class.

The RMX base class

In Chapter 4, I talked about extending the <mx:Application/> tag in order to add the functionality to your application within that class. For this project, there is more than one application, so the class cannot be shared by all the RMX applications. However, there are still things that the applications share, so for this type of project setup, I use an RMX class that extends the Application class. This class includes things like service fault handlers, and it looks something like this:

```
package com.almerblank.rmx.flex
{
  import mx.core.Application;
  import mx.utils.ObjectUtil;
  /**
   * The <code>RMX()</code> class is the base that contains
   * functionality common to all of
   * the RMX. This class gets extended to make
   * applications such as the jobs board.
   *
   * @author Omar Gonzalez
   *
   */
  public class RMX extends Application
  {

    /**
     * @constructor
     */
    public function RMX()
    {
      super();
    }

    /**
     * The <code>svcFault(fault)</code> method handles all
     * service call errors and
     * displays a human readable error display and an
```

```
   * option to see the technical error
   * details.
   *
   * @param fault Fault object from server response.
   *
   */
  public function svcFault(fault:Object):void
  {
    trace('onFault()');
    trace('ObjectUtil.toString(fault) ='+ObjectUtil.toString(fault));
  }


 }
}
```

I can include other content shared by the multiple applications in the RMX. For example, this could be CSS classes and overall application properties like width and height. When I begin work on a new application, such as the jobs board, the application class can extend RMX.as.

Setting up the jobs browser

To start the jobs board, I add a new package within the views package. Inside it is a components package, which holds all of the components that make up the jobs board. The project folder structure looks like what you see in Figure 13-7.

Most of the components are simply made up of MXML layouts for the different parts of the jobs board. The job post has two files, JobPost.as, which is the base class for JobPostView.mxml, and JobRenderer.as, which is the base class for JobRendererView.mxml. The main application file is in the root, named JobsBoardView.mxml. This MXML file, shown here, initializes the JobsBoard.as class and holds the base functionality of the jobs board application.

```
JobsBoardView.mxml
<?xml version="1.0" encoding="utf-8"?>
<rmx:JobsBoard
  layout="vertical" verticalGap="0"
  styleName="plain"
  paddingBottom="6" paddingLeft="6" paddingRight="6" paddingTop="6"
  width="960" height="600"
  xmlns:mx="http://www.adobe.com/2006/mxml"
  xmlns:rmx="com.almerblank.rmx.flex.views.frontend.jobsboard.*"
  xmlns:components=
"com.almerblank.rmx.flex.views.frontend.jobsboard.components.*"
  xmlns:controls="com.almerblank.flex.controls.*">
  <rmx:states>
    <mx:State id="filterState" name="filterState">
      <mx:AddChild relativeTo="{jobsBrowser}" position="before">
        <components:JobFilters id="jobFilters"
creationPolicy="all" height="1"/>
```

```
            </mx:AddChild>
        </mx:State>
    </rmx:states>
    <rmx:transitions>
        <mx:Transition id="toFiltersTransition" fromState="*"
toState="filterState">
            <mx:Sequence id="tf" targets="{[jobsBrowser, jobFilters]}">
                <mx:AddChildAction/>
                <mx:Resize duration="600" target="{jobFilters}"
heightFrom="1" heightTo="200"
                        startDelay="100" easingFunction="{easeOut}"/>
            </mx:Sequence>
        </mx:Transition>
        <mx:Transition id="toNormalTransition"
fromState="filterState" toState="*">
            <mx:Sequence id="tn" targets="{[jobsBrowser, jobFilters]}">
                <mx:Resize duration="600" target="{jobFilters}"
heightFrom="200" heightTo="1"
                        easingFunction="{easeOut}"/>
                <mx:RemoveChildAction/>
            </mx:Sequence>
        </mx:Transition>
    </rmx:transitions>

    <mx:WipeUp id="hideViewWipe"/>
    <mx:WipeDown id="showViewWipe"/>

    <mx:Style source="com/almerblank/rmx/flex/css/rmx.css"/>

    <!-- these tags instantiate the objects in the JobsBoard tag/class,
making them and their children/properties accessible from the
class code. -->
    <components:Controls id="controls"/>
    <mx:ViewStack id="vs_jobsBoardViews" width="100%" height="100%">
        <mx:VBox width="100%" height="100%" hideEffect="{hideViewWipe}"
                showEffect="{showViewWipe}">
            <components:JobsBrowser id="jobsBrowser"/>
        </mx:VBox>
        <components:JobPostView id="jobPostView"
                                hideEffect="{hideViewWipe}"
                                showEffect="{showViewWipe}"/>
    </mx:ViewStack>
</rmx:JobsBoard>
```

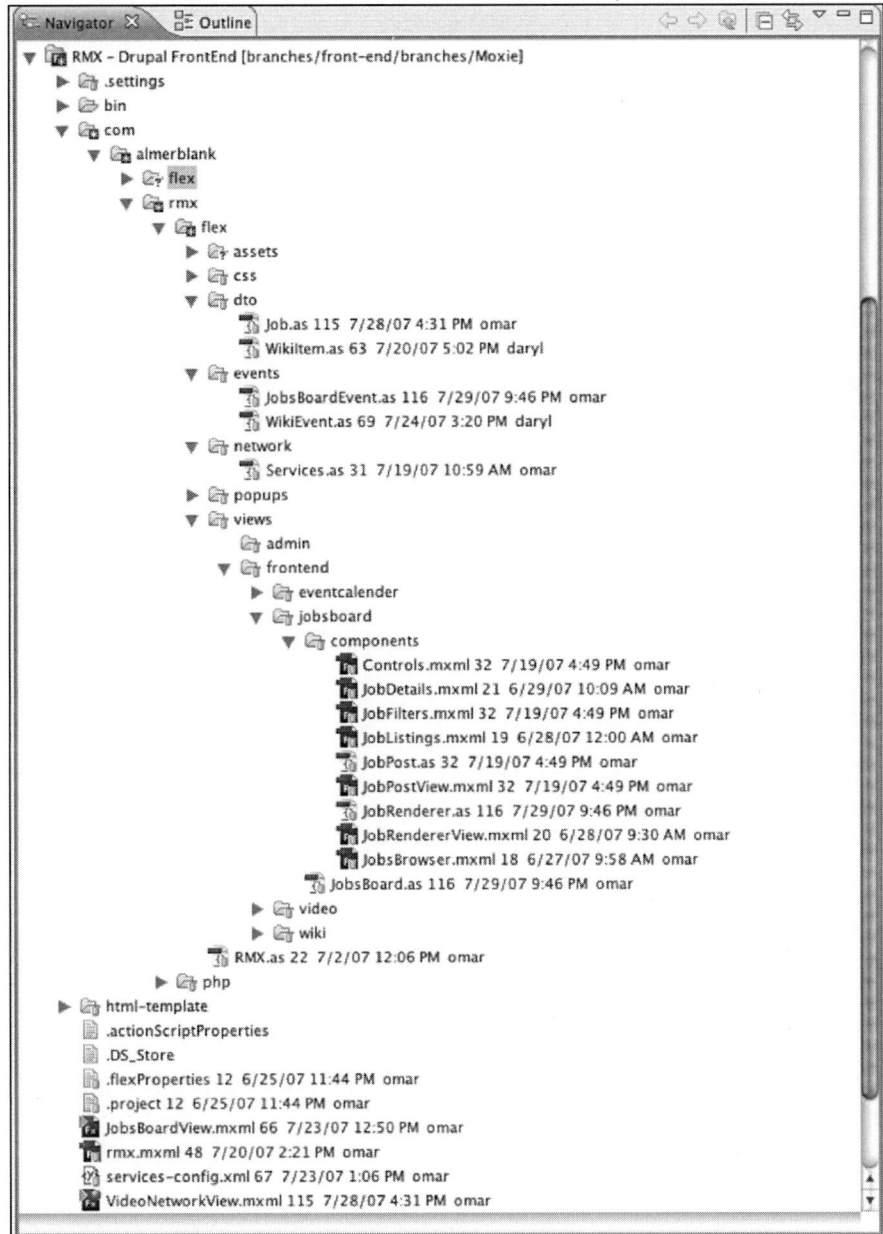

Figure 13-7. The project folder structure for the jobs board

The majority of the code in this MXML file is mainly for the state change when the filters come in and the transitions are used between the filtered View and the nonfiltered View. The core of the application, which starts after the comment under the `<mx:Style/>` tag, is really two base tags. One is a controls component that has the menu for the application, `Controls.mxml`, and the other is a ViewStack, which holds the JobsBrowser component and the JobPost component. Since this section is about the jobs browser, let's explore the JobsBrowser component.

```
JobsBrowser.mxml
<?xml version="1.0" encoding="utf-8"?>
<mx:HBox
        horizontalGap="0"
        xmlns:mx="http://www.adobe.com/2006/mxml" width="100%"
height="100%"
        xmlns:components=
"com.almerblank.rmx.flex.views.frontend.jobsboard.components.*">
        <components:JobListings id-"jobListings"/>
        <components:JobDetails id="jobDetails"/>
</mx:HBox>
```

This component file is small, containing only two tags. Since it's an HBox, on the left is the JobListings component, and on the right the JobDetails component, which is what you saw in Figure 13-6 earlier. Let's take a look at the JobListings component, since this is the first place something happens. As soon as the application loads, the jobs are listed in this component. This component doesn't have any base class with functionality in it, as you may have guessed because the name does not end with the word "View"; it is simply a layout MXML file. The file looks like this:

```
<?xml version="1.0" encoding="utf-8"?>
<mx:VBox
   verticalGap="0"
   xmlns:mx="http://www.adobe.com/2006/mxml"
   width="100%" height="100%">
   <mx:Label id="tf_listingsCount" styleName="miscInfo"
text="0 Job Listings" height="22"/>
   <mx:List id="lt_jobsList"
      alternatingItemColors="[#E8EEF1, #FFFFFF]"
      rowHeight="56"
      width="100%" height="100%"
      itemRenderer=
"com.almerblank.rmx.flex.views.frontend.jobsboard.components.
JobRendererView"/>
</mx:VBox>
```

This is another small component with two tags in it. The base tag is `<mx:VBox/>`, and the first thing from the top down is the Label component that handles displaying the total number of jobs listed in the system. The second tag is for a List component that actually lists the jobs. Attached to the List via the `itemRenderer` attribute is the JobRendererView.mxml file.

Calling the jobs service

Since these components are all MXML layouts, how is the application started? Let's take a look at the JobsBoard.as class. This class is a bit long, so I'll start by discussing a little bit of it at a time.

```
package com.almerblank.rmx.flex.views.frontend.jobsboard
{
  import com.almerblank.flex.controls.Button;
  import com.almerblank.rmx.flex.RMX;
  import com.almerblank.rmx.flex.dto.Job;
```

```
import com.almerblank.rmx.flex.views.frontend.jobsboard.
                         components.Controls;
import com.almerblank.rmx.flex.views.frontend.jobsboard.
                         components.JobsBrowser;
import flash.events.MouseEvent;
import mx.collections.ArrayCollection;
import mx.events.FlexEvent;
import com.almerblank.rmx.flex.network.Services;
import mx.utils.ObjectUtil;
import mx.rpc.events.ResultEvent;
import mx.utils.ArrayUtil;
import com.almerblank.rmx.flex.events.JobsBoardEvent;
import com.almerblank.rmx.flex.views.frontend.jobsboard.
                         components.JobFilters;
import com.almerblank.flex.controls.CheckBox;
import mx.core.Application;
import mx.events.ItemClickEvent;
import mx.effects.easing.Quadratic;
import mx.containers.ViewStack;
import com.almerblank.fl.utils.abcmenu.ABCMenu;
/**
 * The JobsBoard class is the base for the jobs board
 * application for the RMX.  This class is instantiated
 * in the application file for the jobs board, RMXJobsBoard.mxml.
 *
 * @author Omar Gonzalez
 *
 */
public class JobsBoard extends RMX
{
  /**
   * The JobsBrowser object gets instantiated in MXML, this object
   * does not need instantiation within this class.
   */
  [Bindable] public var jobsBrowser:JobsBrowser;
  /**
   * The Controls object gets instantiated in MXML, this object
   * does not need instantiation within this class.
   */
  public var controls:Controls;
  [Bindable] public var jobFilters:JobFilters;
  [Bindable] public var vs_jobsBoardViews:ViewStack;
  [Bindable] public var jobDetails:Job = new Job();

  /**
  * @private
  */
  private var _jobsDP:ArrayCollection;
```

```
[Bindable]
public var adobeTechnologiesDP:Array;
[Bindable]
public var openSourceTechnologiesDP:Array;
[Bindable]
public var rolesProviderDP:Array;
[Bindable] public var easeOut:Function = Quadratic.easeOut;

private var _filters:JobFilters;
private var _lastControlsDP:Array;

/**
 * @constructor
 */
public function JobsBoard()
{
  super();

  addEventListener(FlexEvent.CREATION_COMPLETE,
          jobsBoardComplete);
  addEventListener(JobsBoardEvent.JOB_SELECTED,
          showJobDetails);

}
  ...
```

At the top public variables are declared with the same name as the id values that the MXML tags of their object type have in JobsBoardView.mxml. For example, the <mx:JobsBrowser/> tag has an id of jobsBrowser, so there is a public variable in this class called jobsBrowser, which gives me access and code hinting into that instance of <mx:JobsBrowser/>. There are also a few other properties that are used throughout the application, like data providers for job type combo boxes and such. Right now the first area of interest is the class constructor, which is what gets the ball rolling, so to speak. After the super() call, which gets the super class started, I add two event listeners. One is for the custom event that is being dispatched by the item renderer, which I talked about briefly earlier in this chapter, and the other event listener is for the creationComplete event on the JobsBoard class. The event handler for creationComplete, jobsBoardComplete, is where I start the application. That method looks like this:

```
/**
 * The <code>jobsBoardComplete(event)</code> method handles
 * the creationComplete event of the application,
 * setting up the initial state of the application.
 *
 * @param event Flex creationComplete event.
 *
 */
private function jobsBoardComplete(event:FlexEvent):void
{
  controls.addEventListener(ItemClickEvent.ITEM_CLICK,
          buttonClickHandler);
```

```
    contextMenu = ABCMenu.getInstance();

    makeDataProviders();
    getJobs();
}
```

The first line here adds the event handler for the menu at the top of the jobs board. The second line is a custom contextual menu class that gives the ability to right-click and go forward or back. The makeDataProviders() method basically makes an array of technologies for the jobs view. The last line is where I make my call to the Drupal services. This is what a service call looks like using the custom class from earlier in the chapter:

```
/**
 * The <code>getJobs()</code> method retrieves all jobs from the
 * RMX server and sends to the display.
 */
private function getJobs():void
{
    Services.call(Services.GET_JOBS, onResult, svcFault);
}
```

The call consists of one line, and doesn't require any imports since the call() method is static. The call gets the result and fault methods, and the class takes care of the rest.

Setting up the list view

When the service call receives the result from the server without any errors, the onResult() method handles the result. The onResult() event handler must expect a single argument of ResultEvent type; the method for the RMX looks as follows:

```
private function onResult( event:ResultEvent ):void
{
    jobsDP = new ArrayCollection(
            ArrayUtil.toArray( event.result ) );
}
```

As you can see, it's another one-line method to handle the Drupal return. The result property on the event is an object, so using the ArrayUtil class, I make an array of it that goes into an ArrayCollection to be shown in the list view. The jobsDP, however, is a setter, so there is more code than meets the eye. The jobsDP setter looks like this:

```
/**
 * The jobsDP setter sets the data provider for the jobs list.
 *
 * @param jobs The ArrayCollection of jobs to set
 * the data provider to.
 *
 */
public function set jobsDP(jobs:ArrayCollection):void
{
```

```
        _jobsDP = jobs;
        jobsBrowser.jobListings.lt_jobsList.dataProvider = _jobsDP;
        _jobsDP.refresh();

        jobsBrowser.jobListings.tf_listingsCount.text =
            jobsDP.length.toString() + ' Job Listings';
    }
```

This setter basically takes care of two things. First, it makes sure that every time the jobsDP is set, the List component is properly updated by manually calling the refresh() method. The second thing it takes care of is updating the Label component above the list, which displays how many jobs are currently listed.

The itemRenderer is attached to the List component in the MXML, like this:

```
<mx:List id="lt_jobsList"
    alternatingItemColors="[#E8EEF1, #FFFFFF]"
    rowHeight="56"
    width="100%" height="100%"
    itemRenderer="com.almerblank.rmx.flex.views.frontend.
            jobsboard.components.JobRendererView"/>
</mx:VBox>
```

In the JobRendererView component is the MXML layout for what is seen for every job listing rendered. This MXML file has a base class that handles some of its functionality. The JobRendererView.mxml file looks like this:

```
<?xml version="1.0" encoding="utf-8"?>
<JobRenderer
  width="100%" height="56"
  xmlns="com.almerblank.rmx.flex.views.frontend.jobsboard.components.*"
  xmlns:mx="http://www.adobe.com/2006/mxml">

  <mx:VBox verticalGap="0"
    top="0" right="0" bottom="0" left="0">

    <mx:HBox horizontalGap="0" width="100%">

      <mx:Label id="tf_title" text="{job.title}" styleName="title"
            enabled="false"
            disabledColor="{tf_title.getStyle('color')}"/>
      <mx:Label id="tf_stateZip" text="{job.jobLocation}"
            styleName="miscInfo"
            enabled="false"
            disabledColor="{tf_stateZip.getStyle('color')}"/>
      <mx:Spacer width="100%"/>
      <mx:Label id="tf_by" text="by" styleName="miscInfo"
            enabled="false"
            disabledColor="{tf_by.getStyle('color')}"/>
```

```
    <mx:Label id="tf_author" text="{job.postedBy}" styleName="link"
              enabled="false"
              disabledColor="{tf_author.getStyle('color')}"/>

  </mx:HBox>

  <mx:HBox horizontalGap="0" width="100%">

    <mx:Text id="tf_description" htmlText="{job.description}"
             width="100%" height="100%"
             selectable="false" enabled="false"
             disabledColor="{tf_description.getStyle('color')}"/>
    <mx:VBox verticalGap="0">

      <mx:Label id="tf_secondState" enabled="false"
                disabledColor="{tf_secondState.getStyle('color')}"/>
      <mx:Label id="tf_date" enabled="false"
                disabledColor="{tf_date.getStyle('color')}"/>

    </mx:VBox>

  </mx:HBox>

</mx:VBox>

</JobRenderer>
```

This is basically a layout like any other. The Text and Label components have their text and htmlText properties bound to a job property, which exists in the JobRenderer class. Let's take a look at that class:

```
package com.almerblank.rmx.flex.views.frontend.jobsboard.components
{
  import mx.containers.Canvas;
  import mx.controls.Label;
  import mx.controls.Text;
  import mx.events.FlexEvent;
  import com.almerblank.rmx.flex.dto.Job;
  import mx.utils.ObjectUtil;
  import flash.events.MouseEvent;
  import com.almerblank.rmx.flex.events.JobsBoardEvent;

  [Bindable]
  public class JobRenderer extends Canvas
  {
    // mxml instantiated objects
    public var tf_title:Label;
    public var tf_stateZip:Label;
    public var tf_author:Label;
```

```
        public var tf_secondState:Label;
        public var tf_date:Label;
        public var tf_description:Text;

        public var job:Job;


        public function JobRenderer()
        {
          super();
          super.horizontalScrollPolicy = 'off';
          super.verticalScrollPolicy = 'off';
          super.buttonMode = true;

          addEventListener(FlexEvent.CREATION_COMPLETE, rendererComplete);
          if (data)
          {
            job = new Job(data);
          }
          else
          {
            job = new Job();
          }
        }

        private function rendererComplete(event:FlexEvent):void
        {
          if (data)
          {
            job = new Job(data);
          }

          addEventListener(FlexEvent.DATA_CHANGE, jobChanged);
          addEventListener(MouseEvent.CLICK, jobSelected);
        }

        private function jobSelected(event:MouseEvent):void
        {
          var e:JobsBoardEvent = new JobsBoardEvent(
                      JobsBoardEvent.JOB_SELECTED, true);
          e.job = job;
          dispatchEvent(e);
        }

        private function jobChanged(event:FlexEvent):void
        {
          if (data)
          {
```

```
      job = new Job(data);
    }
  }


  }
}
```

This is the class that contains the custom event from earlier in this chapter. The JobRenderer class has a job property that is basically a DTO containing the data for the item renderer, just like the data property. The difference is that the DTO has my data already formatted the way I want it, so I can bind that data directly to the text components. The creation complete event handler adds two event listeners, the mouse click, which dispatches my custom event when a job is selected, and another listener for the dataChanged event. The data change event handler handles reformatting the data object that the item renderer gets.

Handling the details pane

So now that you took a look at the browser, I can show you what happens after the user selects a job. Knowing that the application is dispatching a custom event when a user clicks a job item, the first place to look is where the event handler is being assigned for that event.

In the constructor for the JobsBoard class, an event listener is added for the jobSelected event; the showJobDetails event handler is assigned to this task. This event handler looks as follows:

```
private function showJobDetails(event:JobsBoardEvent):void
{
  jobDetails = event.job;
  if (!jobsBrowser.jobDetails.vs_jobDetails.visible)
  {
    jobsBrowser.jobDetails.vs_jobDetails.visible = true;
  }
}
```

This is another small event handler, but there are no tricky setters here. The jobDetails property is a bindable property that the JobDetails component's Text components are bound to. Whenever a job gets selected, the event handler catches the event and assigns the job in the event to the jobDetails property, effectively updating the details display. The MXML for the details looks something like this:

```
<?xml version="1.0" encoding="utf-8"?>
<mx:Canvas
  xmlns:mx="http://www.adobe.com/2006/mxml"
  width="100%" height="100%"
  xmlns:controls="com.almerblank.flex.controls.*"
        verticalScrollPolicy="off">

  <mx:Dissolve id="fadeOut" alphaFrom="1" alphaTo="0" duration="500"
               easingFunction="{mx.effects.easing.Quadratic.easeOut}"/>
  <mx:Dissolve id="fadeIn" alphaFrom="0" alphaTo="1" duration="1500"
               easingFunction="{mx.effects.easing.Quadratic.easeOut}"/>
```

```
<mx:VBox y="22" verticalGap="0" width="100%" height="100%">
  <mx:ViewStack id="vs_jobDetails" width="100%"
        creationPolicy="all" visible="false">
    <mx:VBox verticalGap="-4" width="100%" showEffect="{fadeIn}"
      paddingBottom="0" paddingLeft="16" paddingRight="16"
        paddingTop="0">
      <mx:Label id="tf_title" text="{jobsBoard.jobDetails.title}"
        styleName="title"/>
      <mx:HBox width="100%" horizontalGap="0">
        <mx:Label text="by" styleName="miscInfo"/>
        <mx:Label text="{jobsBoard.jobDetails.postedBy}"
          styleName="link"/>
        <mx:Label text="on" styleName="miscInfo"/>
        <mx:Label text="m/d/y" styleName="miscInfo"/>
      </mx:HBox>
      <mx:HBox width="100%" horizontalGap="0" paddingTop="10">
        <mx:Label text="Location:" styleName="title"/>
        <mx:Label text="{jobsBoard.jobDetails.jobLocation}"/>
      </mx:HBox>
      <mx:HBox width="100%" horizontalGap="0">
        <mx:Label text="Role:" styleName="title"/>
        <mx:Label text="{jobsBoard.jobDetails.jobRoles}"
          width="400"/>
      </mx:HBox>

      ...etc...

    </mx:VBox>
  </mx:ViewStack>
  <mx:Spacer height="100%"/>
  <mx:HBox id="ads" horizontalAlign="center" width="100%">
    <mx:Image width="180" height="150" />
    <mx:Image width="180" height="150" />
  </mx:HBox>
</mx:VBox>
<controls:ButtonBar dataProvider="['Flag','Share','Apply']" top="26"
        right="4" visible="{vs_jobDetails.visible}"/>
<mx:Script>
  <![CDATA[
    import mx.effects.easing.Linear;
    import com.almerblank.rmx.flex.views.frontend.
        jobsboard.JobsBoard;
    import mx.core.Application;
    [Bindable]
    private var jobsBoard:JobsBoard =
        JobsBoard(Application.application);
  ]]>
</mx:Script>
</mx:Canvas>
```

At the bottom of the component is a small Script block, which is used to basically start a private variable of type JobsBoard, to which I assign the Application.application property type cast as JobsBoard. This gives me the ability to bind to the jobDetails property on the JobsBoard class, bringing the details pane to life.

The jobs filters

One of the neat features of the RMX's jobs board is the ability to filter jobs quickly and easily on the client side in real time. To provide this feature, the application exploits the abilities of the filterFunction property that is built into the Collection classes, ArrayCollection and XMLListCollection. But to get to the filters, I must first reveal them. At the top of the RMX jobs board is the small menu, which first displays Post a Job and View Filters, which is the Controls component. Once the user clicks View Filters, the application goes into a new state, bringing in the filters. The current View animates, resizing to reveal the filters for the jobs, as you see in Figure 13-8.

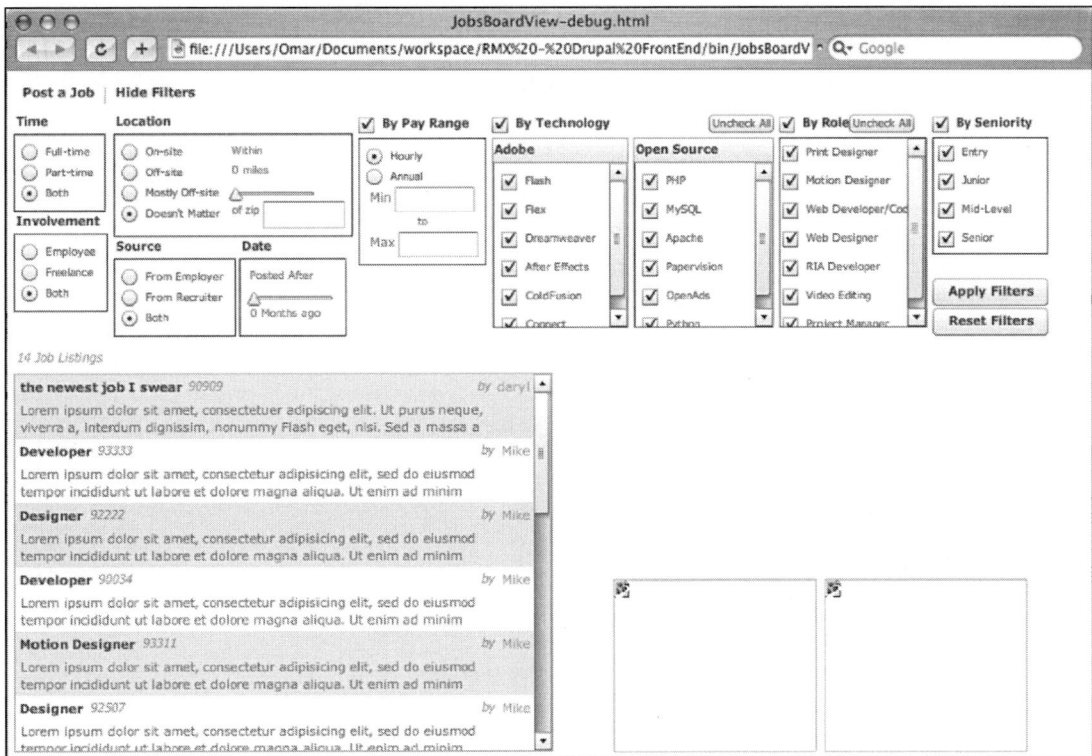

Figure 13-8. The jobs filters after being revealed

The JobFilters.mxml file has the layout for the whole filter section. It does not have a base class for functionality, so the MXML is pure layout.

To make these filters work, I apply a click event handler to the Apply Filters button. The click handler calls the applyFilters method on the JobsBoard main class, passing a reference to this, giving the listener function direct reference to the selected filters. The applyFilters method looks like this:

```
public function applyFilters(filters:JobFilters):void
{
  _filters = filters;
  _jobsDP.filterFunction = filterJobs;
  _jobsDP.refresh();

// using dp setter to set dp and update display on refresh
    jobsDP = _jobsDP;
    jobsBrowser.jobDetails.vs_jobDetails.visible = false;
}
```

This method first stores a reference to the filters component, for the actual `filterFunction` to access, which I set on the following line. Once the `filterFunction` is applied, I call the `refresh()` method to make sure the display is updated. I then use the `jobsDP` setter to update the display count, and hide any details that were currently being viewed, since the list is changing.

The bulk of the work is actually done by the `filterJobs` method, which is the `filterFunction` for the `_jobsDP` ArrayCollection. This is the longest method in the application, and it looks like this:

```
private function filterJobs(data:Object):Boolean
{
  var returnThisJob:Boolean = false;
  var thisJob:Job = new Job(data);

  // job time filter
  if ( _filters.timeGroup.selectedValue == "Both" )
  {
    returnThisJob = true;
  }
  else if ( thisJob.positionIs.search(
        _filters.timeGroup.selectedValue ) > -1 )
  {
    returnThisJob = true;
  }
  else if ( thisJob.positionIs.search(
        _ _filters.timeGroup.selectedValue == -1 ) )
  {
    return false;
  } else return false; // end job time filter

  ... ( doing the same for each group of filter options ) ...

  // by seniority filter
  if ( _filters.cx_bySeniority.selected )
  {
    var seniorities:Array = _filters.seniorities.getChildren();
    var seniority:CheckBox;
    var jobQualifies:uint;
```

```
    for each ( seniority in seniorities )
    {
      if ( seniority.selected )
      {
        if ( thisJob.seniority.search( seniority.label ) > -1 )
        {
          jobQualifies++;
        }
      }
    }

    if ( jobQualifies )
    {
      returnThisJob = true;
    } else return false;

  } // end by seniority filter


  return returnThisJob;
  }
}
```

This filter function basically goes section by section, first checking whether the user actually wanted to filter for the values within that subsection of filters. If the main check box is checked, it then goes into the individual choices and performs searches to determine whether the item should be returned to the display or not. In the case that any of the chosen filters fail, the function gets stopped by a false return, removing the item from the visual display.

Summary

There are myriad possibilities when combining Flex and Drupal. These two open source framework technologies provide platforms for creating a great foundation for Rich Internet Applications. Both are extensible, benefit from large user communities, and are widely adopted by Fortune 500 companies worldwide.

Using the methods discussed in this chapter to create views in Flex from Drupal, combined with the methods discussed in the following chapters, will provide you with the ability to create your own combination of these technologies to power your next-generation RIA.

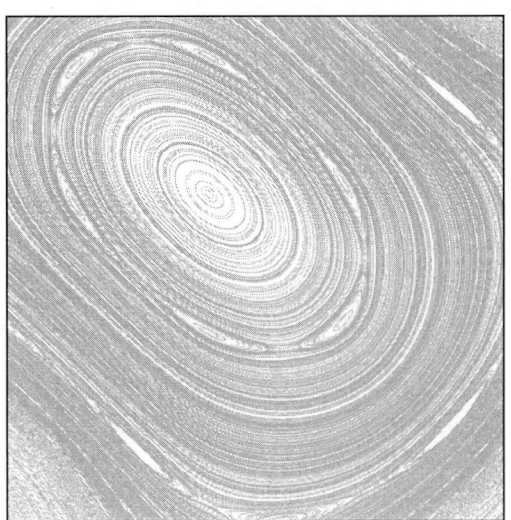

Chapter 14

BUILDING THE EVENT CALENDAR

By Hasan Otuome

In this chapter, I'll cover dating (Web 2.0 style), the RMX event calendar, and back-end integration.

Dating (Web 2.0 style)

As we've stated many times, many sites today are not just static web sites but online social networks where people from all over the world can connect with one another to share ideas and information. These sites, when successful, benefit from the same magic that happens whenever people get together at home, or meet at the movies or the beach. Some people are able to find love, while others enjoy the ease of recording a guitar solo to a studio on the other side of the country via the Internet. There are a variety of ways that people are using the Internet to connect to each other, and in the case of the RMX, we wanted to connect users through a combination of physical (live) and online events via our event calendar.

Examining the RMX calendar

With the event calendar, we sought to create a viable mechanism that takes advantage of the power of the Flex framework to enable administrators to push event content to the user and for the user to consume that content. And, since the RMX is comprised of a "trusted" network of friends, associates, and peers all interested in the same things, this would make the RMX event calendar a truly beneficial online interactive resource for that community by making it easy to explore local and remote areas, communicate, coordinate, cooperate, and make decisions together, all without the constraints of space.

Research has found that providing localized event information is of great value to online users. A Jupiter Research survey found that Internet users from ages 18–54 spend 60% of their online time viewing local content (Jupiter/Ipsos-Insight, individual user survey, "US Online Activities By Age, 2003," June 2003). So, it's extremely cool to have such a strong group of content partners in the RMX and to provide those partners a centralized place to aggregate information about some of the best technology events in the world. Before we move into the technical aspects of this mechanism, I want to spend some time touching on the different elements required to form this complete system. The following is a list of top-level functionality we were after with the event calendar:

- Viewing
- Filtering
- Sharing
- Creating
- Updating
- Deleting

We felt that all these elements were definitely crucial for us to develop a viable system, and within each of these we uncover the true power of the system.

Viewing events

One of the purposes of the event calendar is to be a good online resource to find, learn about, update, and add events of interest to Flash, Flex, and/or AIR developers. These events can be either live or local events, online webcasts, or a combination of the two. Through the RMX interface, we connect its users with the plethora of events offered by the RMX content partners. From a technical standpoint, we opted for providing this functionality through a combination of a 30-day calendar view, daily events list, event details, and event filtering. It's the filtering that really drives the view, so let's look at the concepts behind the filtering of events.

Filtering events

The main display components for RMX event listings are a 30-day calendar and a chronological list. A user can select a date on the calendar and view a chronological listing of events for that date. And, with our event filters, we allow users to further refine the view to browse a variety of events that are specific to a certain category, location, and time zone. Figure 14-1 shows a diagram of the user interaction flow with regards to filtering, while Figure 14-2 shows the wireframe of the widget that controls that filtering.

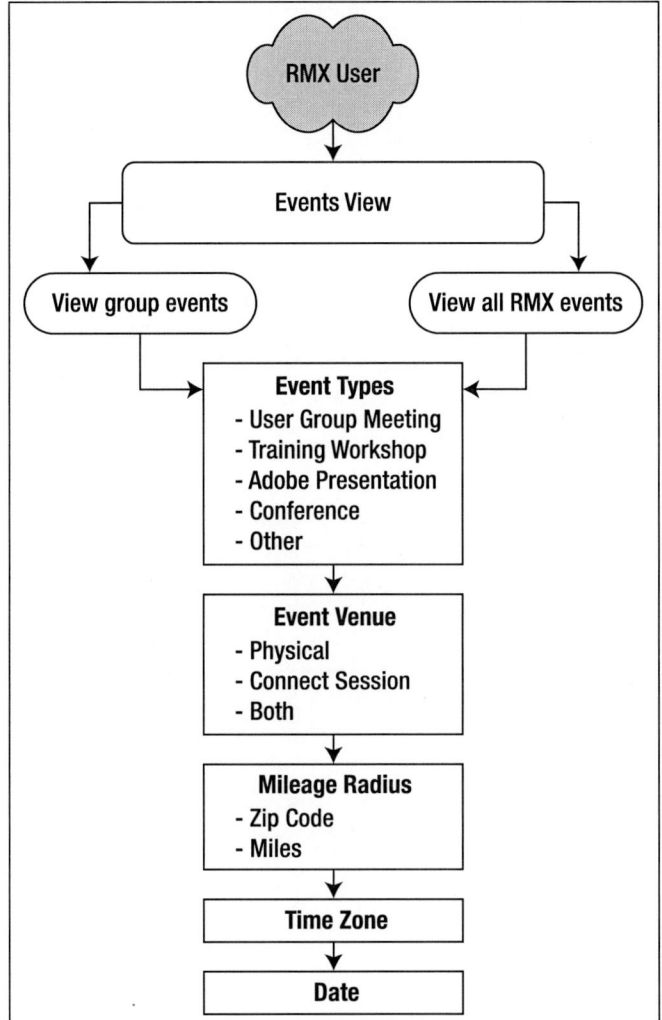

Figure 14-1. Diagram of user filtering for the Events view

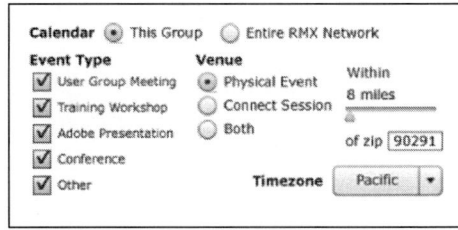

Figure 14-2. Filtering widget wireframe

So, how would you think about this in terms of programming? One way is to think about it in natural language terms. For example, the viewing of events is fundamentally a request for data. The filters help to shape what the data returned from that request will look like or be composed of. In this context, a user possibly wants to find events that meet one or more of the following criteria:

- Belong to a certain group
- Are user group meetings, training workshops, Adobe presentations, conferences, etc.
- Are physical events, webcasts, or both
- Are within *x* number of miles of the zip code of the specified group
- Are located in a specified time zone
- Occur on the selected date

If the user wants to see events that span the entire RMX network, the first criteria can be omitted. Through the aid of the diagrams, wireframes, and natural language outline, you end up with a pretty clear picture of how you can provide this level of functionality to the user using the tools at your disposal. Add that with the technical implementation details that were discussed in Chapter 13, and you have everything necessary to build out this feature custom tailored for events.

Sharing events

For the initial release of the RMX, we chose to offer basic functionality for the sharing of events. Each event listed in the directory features an option that allows a user to send an e-mail to a friend letting him know about the event or import the event to the user's personal calendar like iCal. The next phase could possibly include such features as a user-based ratings system that includes both user ratings and comments.

Creating events

For event creation, the goal was to allow user group managers to easily post new events to the community. This is something that Flex is really good at, as you'll discover shortly. RMX administrators would need the ability to create both general events that aren't tied to a specific user group and events specific to a selected user group. Figure 14-3 shows the wireframe for this feature.

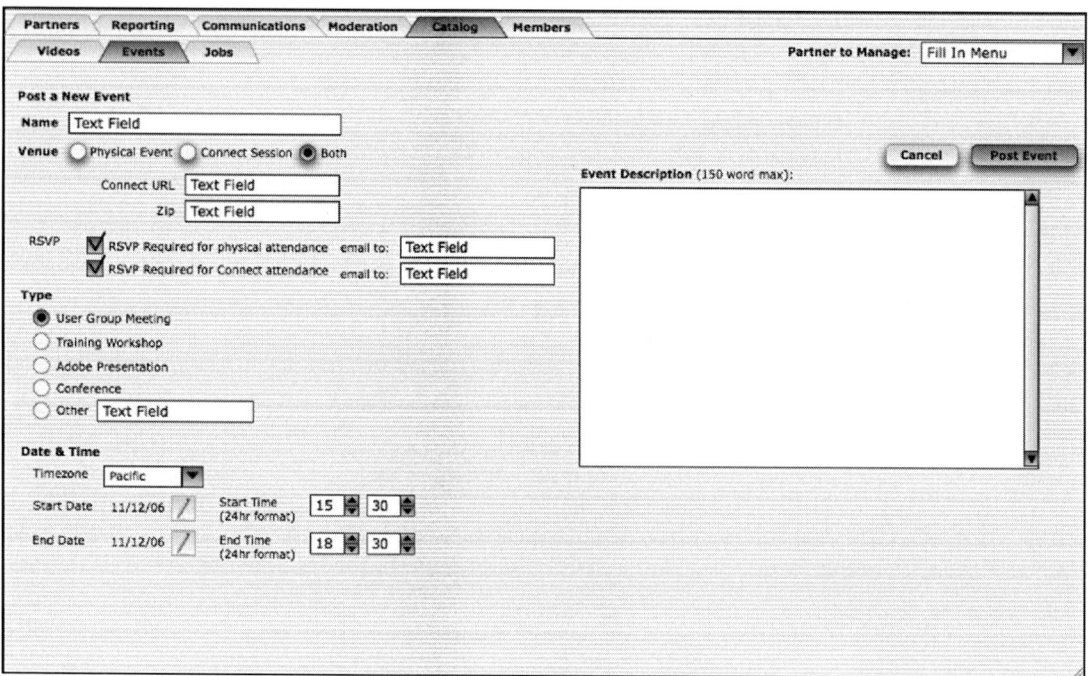

Figure 14-3. Event creator wireframe

Updating events

The technical aspect of the data update mechanism was not hard at all as you'll soon see. The only major goal we had for this component was ensuring that group-level administrators have the ability to update events they own while RMX-level administrators have the ability to update any event listed in the network.

Deleting events

Whether there were mistakes in input, an event was canceled, or the data becomes outdated and it's no longer desirable to maintain it in the system, this feature is necessary for ensuring accurate and meaningful data to the user. The same goals that applied to updating also applied to this feature as far as the initial launch was concerned.

Building the interface

Since it's not discussed in any of the other chapters, let's talk about the user interface for event creation. The interface itself is an MXML file called EventsCreate.mxml. It's pure MXML in that there are no script blocks in that file. All of the scripting that needs to take place is handled in the base class for the component, Events.as. Here's the MXML that comprises the event creation form:

```
<?xml version="1.0" encoding="utf-8"?>
<Events
  xmlns="com.almerblank.rmx.flex.views.admin.components.*"
  xmlns:ab="com.almerblank.flex.controls.*"
  xmlns:mx="http://www.adobe.com/2006/mxml">

  <!-- data model for timezone combo box -->
  <mx:Model id="tz" source="timezones.xml"/>
  <mx:ArrayCollection id="timezones" source="{tz.zone}"/>

  <mx:Label
    x="10" y="10"
    text="Post a New Event"
    fontSize="14"
    fontWeight="bold"/>
  <mx:Form id="frmNewEvent" x="10" y="36">
    <mx:FormItem label="Name" labelWidth="40">
      <mx:TextInput
        id="tf_eventName"
        text="{rmxEvent.eventName}"
        change="rmxEvent.eventName=tf_eventName.text"/>
    </mx:FormItem>
    <mx:FormItem label="Venue" labelWidth="40">
      <mx:HBox>
        <mx:RadioButtonGroup
          id="rbg_eventVenue"
          change="updateVenue(event)"/>
        <mx:RadioButton
```

```
          label="Physical Event"
          value="Physical Event"
          groupName="rbg_eventVenue"
          selected="true"/>
        <mx:RadioButton
          label="Connect Session"
          value="Connect Session"
          groupName="rbg_eventVenue"/>
        <mx:RadioButton
          label="Both"
          value="Both"
          groupName="rbg_eventVenue"/>
      </mx:HBox>
  </mx:FormItem>
  <mx:FormItem>
    <mx:VBox>
      <mx:FormItem id="connectUrlBox" label="Connect URL">
        <mx:TextInput
          id="tf_connectUrl"
          change="rmxEvent.eventUrl=tf_connectUrl.text"
          enabled="{connectEnabled}"/>
      </mx:FormItem>
      <mx:FormItem
        id="zipBox"
        label="Zip"
        textAlign="right"
        labelWidth="76">
        <mx:TextInput
          id="tf_zip"
          textAlign="left"
          change="rmxEvent.eventZip=uint(Number(tf_zip.text))"
          enabled="{zipEnabled}"/>
      </mx:FormItem>
    </mx:VBox>
  </mx:FormItem>
  <mx:FormItem label="RSVP" id="ckg_RSVP" labelWidth="40">
    <mx:HBox>
      <mx:CheckBox
        id="ck_rsvpPhysical"
        label="RSVP Required for physical attendance"
        selected="{rmxEvent.rsvpPhysical}"
        change="rmxEvent.rsvpPhysical=ck_rsvpPhysical.selected"/>
      <mx:Label text="email to:"/>
      <mx:TextInput
        id="tf_rsvpEmail1"
        text="{rmxEvent.rsvpPhysicalEmail}"
        change="rmxEvent.rsvpPhysicalEmail=tf_rsvpEmail1.text"
        enabled="{ck_rsvpPhysical.selected}"/>
    </mx:HBox>
```

```
        <mx:HBox>
          <mx:CheckBox
            id="ck_rsvpConnect"
            label="RSVP Required for Connect attendance"
            selected="{rmxEvent.rsvpConnect}"
            change="rmxEvent.rsvpConnect=ck_rsvpConnect.selected"/>
          <mx:Label text="email to:"/>
          <mx:TextInput
            id="tf_rsvpEmail2"
            text="{rmxEvent.rsvpConnectEmail}"
            change="rmxEvent.rsvpConnectEmail=tf_rsvpEmail2.text"
            enabled="{ck_rsvpConnect.selected}"/>
        </mx:HBox>
      </mx:FormItem>
      <mx:Label text="Type" fontWeight="bold"/>
      <mx:RadioButtonGroup
        id="rbg_Type"
        change="rmxEvent.eventType=String(rbg_Type.selection.value)"/>
      <mx:RadioButton
        label="User Group Meeting"
        value="User Group Meeting"
        groupName="rbg_Type"
        selected="true"/>
      <mx:RadioButton
        label="Training Workshop"
        value="Training Workshop"
        groupName="rbg_Type"/>
      <mx:RadioButton
        label="Adobe Presentation"
        value="Adobe Presentation"
        groupName="rbg_Type"/>
      <mx:RadioButton
        label="Conference"
        value="Conference"
        groupName="rbg_Type"/>
      <mx:HBox>
        <mx:RadioButton
          id="rb_Other"
          label="Other"
          value="Other"
          groupName="rbg_Type"/>
        <mx:TextInput
          id="tf_otherType"
          text="{rmxEvent.otherType}"
          enabled="{rb_Other.selected}"/>
      </mx:HBox>
      <mx:Label text="Date &amp; Time" fontWeight="bold"/>
      <mx:FormItem label="Timezone">
        <ab:ComboBox
```

```
                id="cmb_timezone"
                dataProvider="{timezones}"
                prompt="- Please select -"
                change="rmxEvent.timezone=cmb_timezone.selectedItem.data"/>
         </mx:FormItem>
         <mx:FormItem label="Start Date">
           <mx:HBox>
             <mx:DateField
               id="df_startDate"
               text="{rmxEvent.startDate}"
               change="rmxEvent.startDate=df_startDate.text"/>
             <mx:Text htmlText="Start Time&lt;br/&gt;(24hr format)"/>
             <mx:NumericStepper
               id="ns_startHour"
               minimum="0" maximum="23"
               value="{rmxEvent.startHour}"
               stepSize="1"
               change="rmxEvent.startHour=ns_startHour.value"/>
             <ab:ComboBox
               id="cmb_startMinute"
               dataProvider="{minutes}"
               selectedIndex="0"
               change="rmxEvent.startMinute=
                   cmb_startMinute.selectedItem.data"/>➥
           </mx:HBox>
         </mx:FormItem>
         <mx:FormItem label="End Date">
           <mx:HBox>
             <mx:DateField
               id="df_endDate"
               text="{rmxEvent.endDate}"
               change="rmxEvent.endDate=df_endDate.text"/>
             <mx:Text htmlText="End Time&lt;br/&gt;(24hr format)"/>
             <mx:NumericStepper
               id="ns_endHour"
               minimum="0" maximum="23"
               value="{rmxEvent.endHour}"
               stepSize="1"
               change="rmxEvent.endHour=ns_endHour.value"/>
             <ab:ComboBox
               id="cmb_endMinute"
               selectedIndex="0"
               dataProvider="{minutes}"
               change="rmxEvent.endMinute=cmb_endMinute.selectedItem.data"/>
           </mx:HBox>
         </mx:FormItem>
      </mx:Form>
      <mx:VBox x="{frmNewEvent.width+20}" y="66">
        <mx:HBox>
```

```
    <mx:Spacer width="{ta_eventDesc.width-170}"/>
    <mx:Button height="16" label="Cancel"
          click="cancelEventAction()"/>➡
    <mx:Button height="16" label="Post Event" click="createEvent()"/>
  </mx:HBox>
  <mx:HBox horizontalGap="0">
    <mx:Label text="Event Description:"/>
    <mx:Label text="150 word max (appx. 1100 characters)"/>
  </mx:HBox>
  <mx:TextArea
    id="ta_eventDesc"
    width="325" height="335"
    text="{rmxEvent.eventDesc}"
    maxChars="1097"
    change="rmxEvent.eventDesc=ta_eventDesc.text;
          totalChars=ta_eventDesc.text.length"/>➡
  <mx:HBox>
    <mx:Spacer width="184"/>
    <mx:Label text="Total Characters:"/>
    <mx:Label text="{totalChars}"/>
  </mx:HBox>
</mx:VBox>
<mx:HBox x="{frmNewEvent.width+90}" y="10">
  <mx:Label text="Partner to Manager:" fontWeight="bold"/>
  <ab:ComboBox
    id="cmb_groups"
    dataProvider="{app.model.groupsDP}"
    change="rmxEvent.eventGroupId=cmb_groups.selectedItem.data"/>
</mx:HBox>
</Events>
```

There is nothing fancy here as far as the MXML is concerned, other than my use of ASCII syntax in the Start Time and End Time labels. It would be nice to use <br/> tags instead, but the Flex compiler needs them represented in ASCII format in order to compile the application. Other than that, I'm using the same technique mentioned in Chapter 13 where this component's base class is a custom class that extends one of the built-in container component classes. It's inside this custom class that the variable rmxEvent is declared and defined, and it's also where all the methods necessary for the use of the form are housed. Notice the first namespace declaration, xmlns="com.almerblank.rmx.flex.views. admin.components.*"; this is where this component's base class, Events.as, can be found.

I'll show you that class next, but I want to take a minute to talk about how we're getting the form data from the form. Let's use the component cmb_groups at the bottom of the previous code for an example. I'm setting an action to take anytime that component fires its built-in CHANGE event. In this case, I want to set the eventGroupId property of the rmxEvent object equal to the data property of the cmb_groups component's currently selected item. As you can see from the previous code, I use the same technique for all the other components except for rbg_eventVenue, where I call the updateVenue() method because I need to take additional actions based on the user's selection. That method, along with cancelEventAction() and createEvent(), are all contained in the base class, so let's look at that now.

```
package com.almerblank.rmx.flex.views.admin.components
{
  import flash.events.*;

  import mx.collections.ArrayCollection;
  import mx.core.Application;
  import mx.containers.*;
  import mx.controls.*;
  import mx.events.*;
  import mx.effects.easing.Quadratic;
  import mx.formatters.DateFormatter;

  import com.almerblank.rmx.flex.dto.RmxEvent;
  import com.almerblank.rmx.flex.events.EventsEvent;

  import com.almerblank.fl.utils.logging.Logger;
  import com.almerblank.flex.containers.TitledList;

  [Bindable]
  public class Events extends Canvas
  {
    public var app:admincontrol;

    public var rmxEvent:RmxEvent;

    public var currentDate:Date;
    public var currentDateStr:String;

    public var minutes:ArrayCollection;

    private var dateFormatter:DateFormatter;

    //references to the components contained in the MXML file
    public var rbg_eventVenue:RadioButtonGroup;
    public var tf_connectUrl:TextInput;
    public var tf_zip:TextInput;
    public var rbg_Type:RadioButtonGroup;
    public var cmb_timezone:ComboBox;
    public var cmb_startMinute:ComboBox;
    public var cmb_endMinute:ComboBox;
    public var ns_startHour:NumericStepper;
    public var ns_endHour:NumericStepper;

    public var eventsDetail:EventsDetail;
    public var showEvent:Boolean=false;

    public var connectEnabled:Boolean = false;
    public var zipEnabled:Boolean = true;
```

```
public var detailsWidget:Object;
public var rsvpWidget:Object;

private var _eventId:uint;

public var buttonBarDP:Object = ['Edit', 'Delete', 'Hide'];
public var rsvpButtonBarDP:Object = ['Cancel', 'RSVP'];

public var totalChars:Number = 0;

//constructor function
public function Events()
{
  super();
  app = admincontrol(Application.application);
  app.addEventListener(EventsEvent.EVENT_SERVICED, _viewEvents);
  app.addEventListener(EventsEvent.CLEAR_EVENT,
      _clearEventDetails);➡
  rmxEvent = new RmxEvent();
  minutes = app.model.minuteOptions;
}

//create a new event
public function createEvent():void
{
  rmxEvent.eventVenue = (rmxEvent.eventVenue == null)
        ? 'Physical Event' : rmxEvent.eventVenue;➡
  rmxEvent.eventType = (rmxEvent.eventType == null)
        ? 'User Group Meeting' : rmxEvent.eventType;➡
  rmxEvent.startMinute = (rmxEvent.startMinute == null)
        ? '00' : rmxEvent.startMinute;➡
  rmxEvent.endMinute = (rmxEvent.endMinute == null)
        ? '00' : rmxEvent.endMinute;➡
  rmxEvent.startTime = String(rmxEvent.startHour)
      + ':' + rmxEvent.startMinute;➡
  rmxEvent.endTime = String(rmxEvent.endHour)
      + ':' + rmxEvent.endMinute;➡
  app.service.createEvent(rmxEvent);
}

//handle form abandonment
public function cancelEventAction():void
{
  rmxEvent = new RmxEvent();
  rbg_eventVenue.selectedValue = 'Physical Event';
  rbg_Type.selectedValue = 'User Group Meeting';
  cmb_timezone.selectedIndex = -1;
  cmb_startMinute.selectedIndex = 0;
  cmb_endMinute.selectedIndex = 0;
```

```
      parentDocument.currentState = '';
      app.eventsMgr.viewEvents.eventsList.
        eventsList.tileList.selectedIndex = -1➥
}

//perform additional steps based on user's venue selection
public function updateVenue(event:Event):void
{
  var venue:String = String(event.target.selection.value);
  rmxEvent.eventVenue = venue;
  switch(venue)
  {
    case 'Physical Event':
      tf_connectUrl.enabled = false;
      tf_zip.enabled = true;
      break;
    case 'Connect Session':
      tf_connectUrl.enabled = true;
      tf_zip.enabled = false;
      break;
    case 'Both':
      tf_connectUrl.enabled = true;
      tf_zip.enabled = true;
      break;
  }
}

//reset the form every time a new event is created
private function _clearEventDetails(event:EventsEvent):void
{
  rmxEvent = new RmxEvent(null);
  Logger.log(rmxEvent);
  if(detailsWidget != null)
  {
    detailsWidget.visible = false;
  }
  else
  {
    showEvent = false;
  }
  totalChars = 0;
}

//return to the event browser
private function _viewEvents(events:EventsEvent):void
{
  app.eventsMgr.currentState = '';
  app.eventsMgr.viewEvents.eventsList.
    eventsList.tileList.selectedIndex = -1➥
```

```
            }
        }
    }
```

First thing that I do is to import any classes or packages that I need from the Flex framework. After that, I import any of the custom classes that I need. RmxEvent is the data transfer object (DTO), EventsEvent is the custom event class, Logger is a custom class we use at Almer/Blank internally for allowing runtime debugging both locally and remotely, and finally TitledList is a custom container that's actually used in the EventsView component, which is part of the events browser mechanism.

The next important section is the variable declarations section where I include, among other things, references to the components contained in the MXML file. The other variables important to event creation are app, rmxEvent, minutes, connectEnabled, zipEnabled, and totalChars. The app variable is my shortcut to the main MXML file. As detailed in Chapter 13, this gives me code hinting and error checking as I work out my custom visions, and that's seriously cool. rmxEvent is the object that you saw referenced in the form and it's of type RmxEvent, so that variable lets us access the DTO and update its properties without a whole lot of effort. I'll show you the DTO shortly, but once again, this is a timesaving concept. Speaking of time, the minutes variable is the dataProvider for the ComboBox components cmb_startMinute and cmb_endMinute. The totalChars variable is the numeric display attached to the TextArea component, ta_eventDesc, which indicates how many characters have been typed in the text field. That takes care of the variables section, so let's step into the guts of the class.

This class extends Canvas, so the first thing we do in the constructor is call the constructor of the super class so that we have access to all its public properties and methods. After that, we define app as an instance of Application.application type-cast to admincontrol, which is the name of the main MXML file. That step is what gives us the code hints and error checking. Next, we add a couple of event listeners to app for the EVENT_SERVICED and CLEAR_EVENT events. EVENT_SERVICED is dispatched after a successful remoting call, in this instance creating an event, while the Post Event button found on the events browser page dispatches CLEAR_EVENT when it's clicked. Its purpose is to ensure that the form is reset every time a new event is to be created.

The methods for handling event creation are quite simple actually. In the first four lines of createEvent(), we first check to see if those properties of the DTO still have their default values of null. If they do, then that means that no user selection was made (the user chose to stick with the default component selections). If that's the case, we need to update those properties of the DTO. After that's done, we need to create the values for the startTime and endTime properties of the DTO, which are a combination of the values of the startHour, startMinute, endHour, and endMinute DTO properties. Once all of that's complete, we can call the remote service createEvent(), passing our DTO as the only argument.

The cancelEventAction() method is similar to createEvent(), only here we want to empty the DTO, set the radio button groups, check boxes, and combo boxes back to their default values, and we want to return the user to the events browser. The updateVenue() method is called when a user changes the selection for the Venue radio button group. In this method, we just need to enable or disable the Connect URL and Zip fields based on the user's venue selection and then update the eventVenue property of the DTO with that selection. The _clearEventDetails() method is the event handler for that CLEAR_EVENT mentioned earlier. It does all the work as far as resetting the DTO. The conditional statement only has relevance to the events detail component. The _viewEvents() method is the event handler for the EVENT_SERVICED event that was mentioned earlier, and it's responsible for returning the user to the events browser after a successful event posting. That covers all of the mechanics behind the event creation form, so let's look at the DTO to see how the object that we're sending to the server is actually constructed.

Have data, will travel

In my humble opinion, data transfer objects are the coolest thing since sliced bread when it comes to data exchange in the Flex universe. They just make your development life a lot easier when utilized properly. Our DTO for the events section of the RMX is very similar to the one described in Chapter 13 for jobs. Here's the code for it:

```
package com.almerblank.rmx.flex.dto
{
  import mx.utils.ObjectUtil;
  import com.almerblank.fl.utils.logging.Logger;

  [Bindable]
  public class RmxEvent extends Object
  {
    //default data properties
    public var eventId:uint;
    public var eventVenue:String = 'Physical Event';
    public var eventName:String;
    public var rsvpPhysical:Boolean = false;
    public var rsvpPhysicalEmail:String;
    public var rsvpConnect:Boolean = false;
    public var rsvpConnectEmail:String;
    public var eventType:String = 'User Group Meeting';
    public var timezone:String;
    public var startDate:String = '';
    public var endDate:String = '';
    public var startTime:String;
    public var endTime:String;
    public var eventDesc:String;
    public var eventGroupId:uint;
    public var eventZip:uint;
    public var eventUrl:String;
    public var eventGroupName:String;
    public var eventLocation:String;

    //custom external property (php only!!!)

    //custom internal properties (flex only!!!)
    public var startHour:Number = 15;
    public var startMinute:String;
    public var endHour:Number = 17;
    public var endMinute:String;
    public var otherType:String;
```

```
public function RmxEvent(newInfo:Object=null)
{
  super();
  if(newInfo) _parseObject(newInfo);
}

private function _parseObject(newInfo:Object):void
{
  try
  {
    for(var i:String in newInfo)
    {
      if(this.hasOwnProperty(i)) this[i] = newInfo[i];
    }

    //process our internal vars
    var eventStartTime:Array = startTime.split(':');
    startHour = eventStartTime[0];
    startMinute = eventStartTime[1];

    var eventEndTime:Array = endTime.split(':');
    endHour = eventEndTime[0];
    endMinute = eventEndTime[1];

    Logger.log('new event data = ' +
      ObjectUtil.toString(this), this);➥
  }
  catch(error:*)
  {
    Logger.log(ObjectUtil.toString(error), this);
  }
}


}
```

When declaring DTO properties, I always organize them into categories so that I have a better under-standing of their purposes. Here there are three main categories: default, PHP-only, and Flex-only. The default properties are ones that exist in the database. These are the ones that will be returned by a SQL query. The PHP-only variables can be anything that you might want to use once the data makes it to the server but that you don't necessarily need or want to include in your database updates. The internal variables are those that derive their value from one or more of the default values. For exam-ple, in this DTO I set the values for endHour and endMinute after splitting endTime into an array. So, for incoming or outgoing data operations, you'll always have nice little code hints that tell you what's available to be read (viewing) or modified (creating/updating).

Back-end integration

As you've probably seen for yourself in the previous chapter, interfacing with Drupal is very cool. It definitely saved us a bunch of time from developing a complete back-end system from scratch. Out of the box, and with minimal tweaking, we were able to build a system to satisfy the seemingly insatiable appetite of the RMX for complex data. In Chapter 13, you discovered how to set up your development and production environments for Flex/Drupal integration, as well as how to pull in the job listings for viewing via the jobs browser. Here, we'll explore how the events created via the Flex form are dissected on the Drupal side.

We took some time and effort to configure the service returns and server-side object parsing so that they didn't add any additional overhead to the Flex code. In other words, I get to receive my data and send my DTO in the formats described earlier, and in the case of a create or update event, that DTO is parsed on the server and mapped to the proper fields for insertion into the Drupal database. In this way, I don't have to know how Drupal labels these various pieces of data. As a Flex developer, this is heaven, because Drupal does underscores and all-lowercase for your custom field names when you create custom nodes, and that's no fun to read or work with especially when you have a lot of data to process.

Now, since we've covered custom module creation in the previous chapter, I'll just focus on the service method of the custom events module that lets us write new data to the database, events.create. We need to do the same things for this method as we did for the jobs view: we need to define the method in the "method table" and create the callback for the method. Here's the code needed for the method definition:

```
array
(
  '#method'=>'events.create',
  '#callback'=>'events_service_create',
  '#return'=>'struct',
  '#args'=>array
  (
    array
    (
      '#name'=>'event',
      '#type'=>'struct',
      '#description'=>t('An event object to send to the service.
          Include "type" for creation.'),➥
    )
  ),
  '#help'=>t('Creates a new event.')
),
```

Here we define the method as events.create and then we define the callback method, or the method that's going to do all the real work, as events_service_create. We set the return type to struct, but when the data comes back to Flex, it's going to be an array of objects. You might want to think of it this way at all times, because unless you're from a Java or C background, you might not have ever heard of structs before. And, in case you haven't heard of this term before, a struct is just a data type that has one or more members, each of which can have different types, for example, "Object." After setting the return type, we define what kind of argument we expect passed in to the method. And finally, we define the help text that's displayed in the Drupal service browser.

Our callback method is constructed very similarly to how we'd perform this kind of operation in a traditional AMFPHP install. The major difference is we have to rely on Drupal "hooks" to ensure operational success. These are basically intrinsic API methods that let you "hook" your custom code into the Drupal core. Let's look at the code for events_service_create:

```
function events_service_create($arr)
{
  foreach($arr[0] as $key=>$value)
  {
    $$key = $value;
  }

  node_validate($arr);
  if($errors = form_get_errors())
  {
    return services_error(implode("\n", $errors));
  }
  $node = node_submit($arr);

  //some default values you may want to populate
  $node->uid = 1;
  $node->type = 'rmx_event';
  $node->title = $eventName;
  $node->body = $eventDesc;
  $node->created = time();
  $node->teaser = $node->body;

  //fill in the values necessary for Drupal's event module
  $node->event_start = strtotime($startDate);
  $node->event_end = strtotime($endDate);
  $node->timezone = 487;

  //fill your custom fields
  $node->field_rsvpphysical_value = $rsvpPhysical;
  $node->field_rsvpphysicalemail_value = $rsvpPhysicalEmail;
  $node->field_rsvpconnect_value = $rsvpConnect;
  $node->field_rsvpconnectemail_value = $rsvpConnectEmail;
  $node->field_eventtype_value = $eventType;
  $node->field_timezone_value = $timezone;
  $node->field_starttime_value = date('H:i', $node->event_start);
  $node->field_endtime_value = date('H:i', $node->event_end);
  $node->field_eventgroupid_value = $eventGroupId;
  $node->field_eventzip_value = $eventZip;
  $node->field_eventurl_value = $eventUrl;
  $node->field_eventvenue_value = $eventVenue;

  node_save($node);
```

```
//populate your auxillary table
$result = db_query("INSERT INTO {content_type_rmx_event}
(vid, nid, field_rsvpphysical_value, field_rsvpphysicalemail_value,
field_rsvpconnect_value, field_rsvpconnectemail_value,
    field_eventtype_value,➡
field_timezone_value, field_starttime_value, field_endtime_value,
field_eventgroupid_value, field_eventzip_value, field_eventurl_value,
field_eventvenue_value)
VALUES (%d, %d, '%s', '%s', '%s', '%s', '%s', '%s', '%s', '%s',
'%s', '%s', '%s')", $node->vid, $node->nid,
    $node->field_rsvpphysical_value,➡
$node->field_rsvpphysicalemail_value, $node->field_rsvpconnect_value,
$node->field_rsvpconnectemail_value, $node->field_eventtype_value,
$node->field_timezone_value, $node->field_starttime_value,
$node->field_endtime_value, $node->field_eventgroupid_value,
$node->field_eventzip_value, $node->field_eventurl_value,
$node->field_eventvenue_value);

$count = db_affected_rows();
if($count > 0)
{
  $success = true;
}
else
{
  $success = false;
}

return $success;
}
```

First, we run a for...each loop to gain knowledge of the argument passed in. After we gain access to our key/value pairs, we use the Drupal core to first validate our proposed node, and then we use the submit method to "prep" the object with all of the default attributes that Drupal expects of any node type. Those values are the ones listed under the comment suggesting you populate the default values yourself instead of relying on Drupal to recognize your custom content for you.

After the default node values are set, you can set the values that the Drupal event module needs to expose your custom event to the rest of the system (RSS, iCal, etc.). Once you've done that, you've taken care of the core definitions, so it's time to tend to your custom fields. As with the jobs node from Chapter 13, we set up the custom node rmx_event using the Content Creation Kit (CCK) module to have all of the custom fields listed under the "custom fields" comment. The _value appended to the end is how Drupal maps field names to field values because they are stored in different tables in the Drupal database.

With all of our properties set with values, it's time to make another Drupal API call. This time, we call node_save() and we pass the $node that we just created as the argument. Unless there's an error, Drupal will return here after it finishes saving the node—but wait, there's a catch. The node_save() method doesn't seem to do anything with those custom fields we added to the node. The reason for this is that node_save() is a low-level method, and at that level, Drupal is only concerned with Drupal and not with our custom data. So, we have to add our custom values to our custom table the old fashioned way. We use Drupal's SQL syntax to perform an INSERT operation on the content_type_rmx_event table, which holds all the values for our custom fields for the rmx_event node type. After running the insert, we want to count the number of rows affected by that operation. The result should be 1, in which case we return a value of true to the Flex application; otherwise, we return false.

Is this the only way creating a custom event can be handled? Of course not, but it is one method that has been proven to work. This could be further enhanced by incorporating taxonomy and user ratings into the picture, but that is a subject best left for the Drupal version of the book. After all of that hard work, we can use something like the interface in Figure 14-4 to add RMX events to the Drupal database, and that my friends makes all the effort worth it.

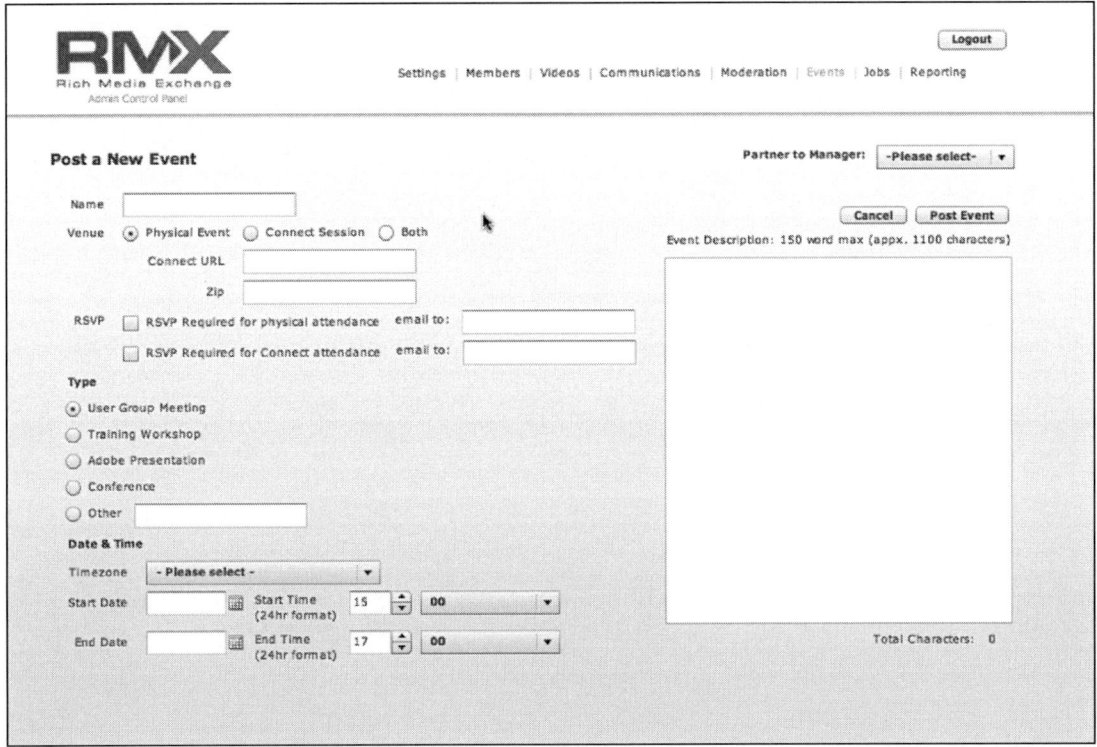

Figure 14-4. Events creation interface

Summary

In this chapter, I covered the benefits that online networks provide as well as how the RMX sought to provide some of those benefits through a highly specialized Flex application within an even larger ecosystem. I discussed the goals we sought to achieve, how that translates to technical development in the Flex universe, and how to take that translation and turn it into a living, breathing machine by attaching the Flex interface to a feature-rich Drupal system on the back end. In the next chapter, you'll see how we plan to take this concept of community even further with ideas for the future.

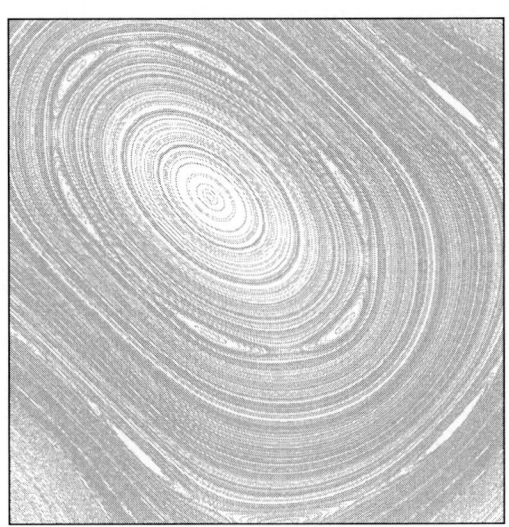

Chapter 15

IDEAS FOR THE FUTURE: EXTENDING THE RMX

By R Blank

In this book, we describe a lot of what has gone into version 1 of the RMX. In this chapter, I want to outline just a few of the ideas that we'd like to pursue after launch to provide some insight into our longer-term vision for the application and the direction in which it is headed, and to perhaps give you some ideas about features you'd like to build into your own Flex applications. I've broken these features into five different buckets: data, advertising, money, UG-specific features, and distribution options.

Much of this chapter is conceptual, defining ways in which the other authors and I will seek to expand the scope and value of the RMX as a platform. However, this also gives me an excuse to dive into Adobe's Flash-Flex Integration Kit.

But, before getting into the specifics, let's take a moment to consider how to think about feature road maps.

The future

I have a vision . . . it is the distant future . . . the nature of the Internet has completely shifted from what we know today . . . the year is . . . 2009.

True, that's a joke (you can tell by how funny it is), but at the same time, the pace of technological innovation—particularly in the user experience of Internet applications—is mind-spinning. In all aspects of work and life, you have to think ahead—as a developer of contemporary RIAs, thinking ahead involves a remarkably short evaluation horizon. The landscape of possible features is always growing, and your users expect a continuous evolution of the experience; otherwise, your site will grow stale, and quickly (a few sites, like Craigslist, are the rare exceptions that prove this rule).

As I explained in Chapter 3, the launch version of the RMX represents less than half of the feature set we really wanted to include. So, even before we launched the RMX, we had a pretty large set of features planned in our road map, some of which I highlight in this chapter. And I'm sure that the members of the RMX will continue to contribute a wealth of suggestions for additional features and functionality.

At the same time, the Flash Platform landscape is evolving at a dramatic pace. Not only is the Flash Player becoming increasingly robust and functional, but the recent additions of Flex 3, AIR, and AMP, as well as the new support for full-screen HD H.264 video, dramatically enlarge the scope of potential features.

In other words, our road map for the RMX certainly does not suffer from a lack of ideas or opportunities. And man, if we had 100 developers to throw full time at the RMX, we'd pursue each and every one of them. But, of course, we don't. Which means that we must pick and choose the features we want to add in a careful and considered manner. We must balance the value of each feature with the effort required to bring it to life.

The best way to start a plan like this is to think about what it is you already have in place, and how you create more value for your application, your members, and yourself by exploiting that existing content and feature set with additional features. Again, the Netflix ratings widget I cited in Chapter 1 is a great example—Netflix didn't have to add any servers or build a new database. Instead, it added one new, small component to the web site and instantly impacted the user experience in a noticeably positive way. Many of the ideas in this chapter are based around this concept of employing minimal resources to exploit existing content and infrastructure to increase the value of the RMX user experience.

At the same time, we cannot ignore the opportunities represented by the ever-expanding powers of the Flash Platform. So, as we plan features that create value by exploiting our existing network, content, and users, we are also considering how we can forge new creations utilizing the new tools and features from Adobe. However, be forewarned. The option of working with new tools is often sexy and alluring to developers like you and me, but at the same time, adopting beta or first-version software always carries risk, and it will almost always take you longer than you expect. You must learn how to use these tools as a professional, and you must also learn the limitations and bugs from direct experience. And if the new tool you are using is one that requires a new player for the user (for example, Flash Player 9.0.6 for Flex 3 and AIR 1), you must also consider how many (or how few) people will have the necessary tools to experience your project. Adobe projects are based on historical trends that it takes approximately 12 months for a new Flash Player to reach 90% distribution. And no one can really predict how quickly AIR will penetrate desktops.

With that in mind, let's examine some of our ideas from both buckets. Some of the ideas in this chapter represent the low-hanging fruit—features that don't actually require any new technology or inventions, but instead just require some focus and developer hours to execute. Others reflect our thinking about how to approach some of the brand-new opportunities that are being forged by Adobe's recent technology releases.

Data

As you've read many times in this book, the core of any application like the RMX is the data. And while we're doing a lot with data in version 1, there's a lot more that we'd like to do in the future.

Audio-to-text

As Google proves, searching text is pretty easy. Searching other forms of media, especially video and audio, is much harder, first because the data does not exist as text, and second because these media types include an additional dimension: time. That is, it's not enough to know that a video contains a discussion of, for example, Boston Terriers, but for the search to have real relevance, you must also know where in that video that relevant information is addressed.

While there are many imaginative ways in which to make video more searchable, simply converting the audio track of a video to a text transcript is a low-hanging fruit. While it won't be easy, it is certainly possible to convert all clearly spoken audio content into text—which is easily searchable—tagged with timecodes, so it would be easy to jump to the right portions of the video based on the specific search parameters.

Creating text transcripts of audio yields four main benefits:

- Searchability
- Advertising relevance
- Translation
- Closed captioning (or subtitles)

The first of these, searchability, is obvious. With a text transcript of media files, users can search beyond the basic title, description, and tags associated with a video, and instead search exactly what's said in the video.

On the second point of advertising relevance, the same traits of a transcript that make video more searchable also enable vastly improved advertising relevance. Again, when your advertising engine can analyze more detailed and accurate information about the media displayed in a web page, you can deliver much more relevant advertising. Relevance in advertising means two things: you get more money from advertisers, and your users will be more interested in the advertising messages they see in your site—both of which are definite pluses.

Another benefit of creating a transcript of the audio is the ability to then translate that information into other languages. You likely already know of services like Google's Language Tools (www.google.com/language_tools) that allow you to translate the contents of most web pages into a wide variety of languages. Suddenly, your video-sharing site, which may have started as language specific, can have value to an international audience by converting the audio to a transcript and then translating that transcript.

> *To learn more about Adobe's current initiatives in the realm of multilingual localization, visit the Labs site for the Adobe Language Pack,* http://labs.adobe.com/wiki/index.php/Language_Pack, *currently available for Catalan.*

The translations can be searchable in the user's native language, and you can also add closed captioning in the selected language. Which brings us to the fourth point, closed captioning.

Closed captioning in Flash

As I described in Chapter 10, FLVs stream not only video and audio, but also metadata, and you can assign specific timecodes to that metadata, generating cue point events inside Flash when your FLV plays back. But wait, there's more. Not only does FLV support metadata in cue points, but Flash also has native support for closed captioning. Since we'll already be generating the transcript, it makes sense to display the transcript of the video as closed captioning. And, in fact, Flash CS3 includes a brand-new component to make implementation of closed captioning incredibly easy—the FLVPlaybackCaptioning component.

Now, I know what you're saying: "UGH, Flash! This is a Flex book, for crying out loud!" Well, hold your horses. As I explained in Chapter 1, Flash is Flash is Flash. We use Flex because it makes Flash Platform application development so much easier. But, there are certain things Flash does really well—some things it does far better than Flex, and other things, like timeline animations, are basically impossible in Flex.

Which is why Adobe created the Flash-Flex Integration Kit. What happens when you have a Flash animation that you want to include in your Flex application? The Flash-Flex Integration Kit allows you to create Flex components out of any Flash movie clip.

While the kit was designed primarily to facilitate integration of Flash-designed skins and animations into Flex, you can also use it to exploit the FLVPlaybackCaptioning component in Flash CS3 by packaging it into a Flex component. Of course, you could write your own closed-captioning system in Flex, but since it comes with Flash, why bother?

First, let's take a look at this component. You can find the LiveDocs entry at http://livedocs.adobe.com/flash/9.0/ActionScriptLangRefV3/fl/video/FLVPlaybackCaptioning.html.

The FLVPlaybackCaptioning component is actually quite simple. Drop it on your stage, and point it to an FLVPlayback component (which will be playing your video) and a source XML file with your captions. The component expects an XML source file that supports a subset of the Timed Text Tags XML specification. Flash's implementation of Timed Text Tags is defined on LiveDocs: http://livedocs.adobe.com/flash/9.0/ActionScriptLangRefV3/TimedTextTags.html and http://livedocs.adobe.com/flash/9.0/main/wwhelp/wwhimpl/common/html/wwhelp.htm?context=LiveDocs_Parts&file=00000611.html.

For this example, you will see how to utilize a caption XML file (from a transcript of an excerpt from President Kennedy's speech at Rice University about his vision for sending man to the moon) that looks like this:

```
<?xml version="1.0" encoding="UTF-8"?>
<tt xml:lang="en" xmlns="http://www.w3.org/2006/04/ttaf1">
  <body>
    <div xml:lang="en">
      <p begin="00:00:00.00" dur="00:00:03.50">But if I were to say, my
fellow citizens,</p>
        <p begin="00:00:03.50" dur="00:00:02.43">that we shall send to the
```

```
moon,</p>
        <p begin="00:00:05.93" dur="00:00:06.17">240,000 miles away from
the control station in Houston,</p>
        <p begin="00:00:12.10" dur="00:00:06.26">a giant rocket more than
300 feet tall, the length of this football field,</p>
        <p begin="00:00:18.36" dur="00:00:05.64">made of new metal alloys,
some of which have not yet been invented,</p>
        <p begin="00:00:24.00" dur="00:00:06.60">capable of standing heat
and stresses several times more than have ever been experienced,</p>
        <p begin="00:00:30.60" dur="00:00:04.13">fitted together with a
precision better than the finest watch,</p>
        <p begin="00:00:34.73" dur="00:00:07.83">carrying all the equipment
needed for propulsion, guidance, control, communications, food and
survival,</p>
        <p begin="00:00:42.56" dur="00:00:01.84">on an untried mission,</p>
        <p begin="00:00:44.40" dur="00:00:02.73">to an unknown celestial
body,</p>
        <p begin="00:00:47.13" dur="00:00:02.97">and then return it safely
to earth,</p>
        <p begin="00:00:50.10" dur="00:00:05.56">reentering the atmosphere
at speeds of over 25,000 miles per hour,</p>
        <p begin="00:00:55.66" dur="00:00:03.47">causing heat about half
that of the temperature of the sun</p>
        <p begin="00:00:59.13" dur="00:00:02.30">- almost as hot as it is
here today -</p>
        <p begin="00:01:01.43" dur="00:00:04.03">and do all this, and do it
right,</p>
        <p begin="00:01:05.46" dur="00:00:03.60">and do it first before
this decade is out,</p>
        <p begin="00:01:09.06" dur="00:00:03.04">then we must be bold.</p>
        </div>
      </body>
    </tt>
```

You'll note that for each <p> node, you need to include begin and dur attributes specifying the time-codes for the start and length for that individual line of text. You could also use end in place of dur to specify the end timecode, instead of the duration. If you specify neither end nor dur, the next caption will replace the current one.

The FLVPlaybackCaptioning component parses the Timed Text Tags XML file, converting the <p> nodes into cue points based on the begin timecode. ActionScript names these points beginning with the prefix fl.video.caption2.0.

I should note the spec for a Flash closed-captioning file also includes accommodations for styling your captions, which I am not utilizing in this example. The specification also allows for multiple languages (to bring back in the point about translation earlier). For more information on multilingual closed captioning, visit www.adobe.com/livedocs/flash/9.0/main/00000608.html#wp130224.

To get this to work in Flash is, again, really easy. I'll describe it quickly because this functionality will serve as the base for the Flash-generated Flex component.

First, save an ActionScript 3 FLA file to a folder. This folder should also include the XML file defined previously (which you'll name kennedyCaptions.xml) and the FLV (which is named kennedy2.flv). Now, add an FLVPlayback component to the stage from your Components panel (Window ➤ Components), and name the instance vid in the Properties panel. Also in the Properties panel, you can set the width and height of the component instance to 320 pixels wide and 240 pixels tall. In the Component Inspector, set the source to kennedy2.flv and the skin to SkinUnderPlayStopSeekCaptionVol.swf (you must also make sure this skin SWF is in the same folder as your FLA and other files), as you see in Figure 15-1 (I'm including this skin in this example because it is one of the skins that has an integrated button to enable and disable the captions).

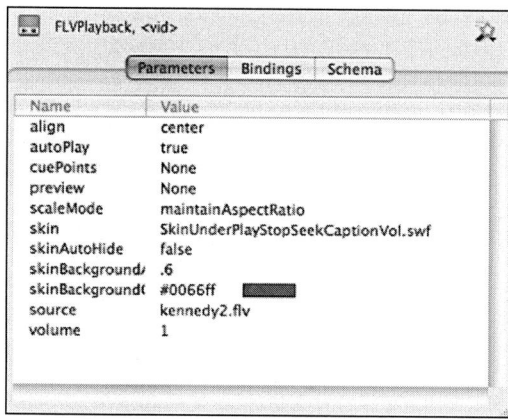

Figure 15-1. The Component Inspector with the proper source and skin set for the instance of the FLVPlayback component

Next, drag an FLVPlaybackCaptioning component to your stage and name the instance cap. In the Component Inspector, set the flvPlaybackName to vid and the source to kennedyCaptions.xml, as you see in Figure 15-2.

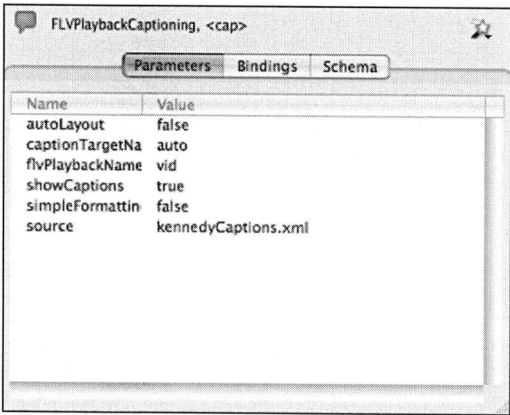

Figure 15-2. The Component Inspector with the proper XML source and associated FLVPlayback component instance set for the instance of the FLVPlaybackCaptioning component

Now, your stage should look something like what you see in Figure 15-3.

Figure 15-3. The stage with instances of both the FLVPlayback and FLVPlaybackCaptioning components

If you compile your movie by selecting Control ➤ Test Movie, you will see your movie play back the video and display captions automatically, as shown in Figure 15-4.

This is incredibly easy and really remarkable. Of course, you could utilize the styling specification of the captioning file to customize the display of your captions. You can also set the captionTargetName parameter of the FLVPlaybackCaptioning component to any TextField instance, which you format and position however you like. But, for the purposes of this example, just keep the default style for your captions, which renders the captions toward the bottom of the video display within your FLVPlayback component instance.

Now, taking the same concept, I'll show you how to make a Flex component from the amazingly convenient FLVPlaybackCaptioning component in Flash. Although everything I am about to show could be coded in a keyframe on the timeline, to make it more palatable to Flex developers, I am externalizing almost all the code in a custom package.

Figure 15-4. The SWF playing back with the specified video and captions displayed

397

Creating a Flex component in Flash

Before you begin, you should install the Flex Component Kit, which you can download from the Flash-Flex Integration Kit site at http://labs.adobe.com/wiki/index.php/Flex_Component_Kit. The kit consists of an MXP file (MXP being the format for Adobe extensions), which can be installed into Flash CS3 through the Adobe Extension Manager. Simply double-click the MXP file, and the Extension Manager should launch and automatically install and enable the Flex component, as you see in Figure 15-5.

Figure 15-5. The Adobe Extension Manager with the Flex component installed and enabled (checked)

You will then need to restart Flash if it is open.

Building the component

You'll start by creating a new ActionScript 3 FLA and save it to CaptionComponent.fla. Next, add the FLVPlayback and FLVPlaybackCaptioning components directly to your FLA library. You can drag them directly from the Components panel to your FLA library so that they aren't added to your stage (import statements alone do not actually force Flash to include the components—they must be explicitly added to your library).

Next, in the Library panel menu, select New Symbol, as you see in Figure 15-6.

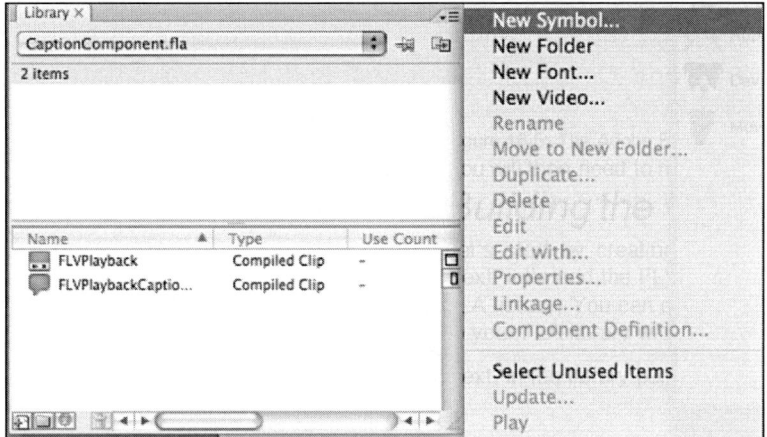

Figure 15-6. The New Symbol option in the Library panel menu

In the dialog box that appears, select Movie clip for type, and enter the name RCaption as you see in Figure 15-7 (the name of this symbol will be the name of the component in Flex).

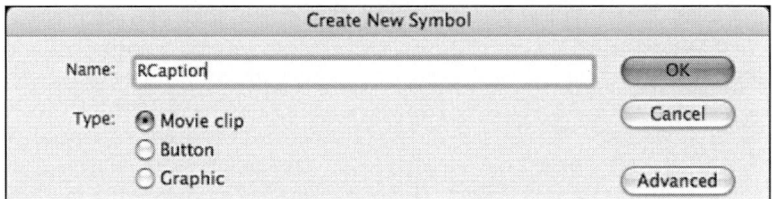

Figure 15-7. The Create New Symbol dialog box with your settings

Click OK. Now back to a text-based coding environment. Whew.

Create a new AS file in the same folder as your FLA, and name it RCaptionDO.as.

Add the following code to the RCaptioDO.as file:

```
package
{
  import flash.display.Sprite;
  import fl.video.FLVPlaybackCaptioning;
  import fl.video.FLVPlayback;

  public class RCaptionDO extends Sprite
  {

    var cap:FLVPlaybackCaptioning;
    var vid:FLVPlayback;

    function RCaptionDO()
    {
      cap = new FLVPlaybackCaptioning();
```

```
            vid = new FLVPlayback();
            cap.flvPlayback = vid;
            addChild(vid);
            addChild(cap);
        }

        public function setupVideo(capSkin:String,capVidWidth:Number,
                                   capVidHeight:Number,capSource:String,
                                   flvSource:String):void
        {
            vid.skin = capSkin;
            vid.setSize(capVidWidth,capVidHeight);
            cap.source = capSource;
            vid.play(flvSource);
        }
    }
}
```

This class must be a display object container in order to display other display objects, but you don't need to consume all the resources of a movie clip, which is why it extends the Sprite class. Next, you import the FLVPlayback and FLVPlaybackCaptioning classes so that you can create and control instances of those components within this class. Again, I want to remind you that you had to add these components to your library so that they will export properly with your SWF.

Within the class RCaptionDO, you see the code that essentially mimics what you did without code in the Flash IDE earlier when you created the simple closed-captioning video player. You have also created a setupVideo function that allows this to take in parameters to define the video source, caption XML file, and dimensions of your component. You create your cap instance of the FLVPlaybackCaptioning component and the vid instance of the FLVPlayback component, and attach both to the display list. And voilà: your custom captioning display class, wrapping the existing components, is ready.

The final step before you can prepare your component is to instantiate the RCaptionDO class from the RCaption movie clip. In your Flash library, double-click RCaption to edit that symbol. Then, on frame 1 (it should be your only frame) of the empty timeline, add the following code:

```
var rCap:RCaptionDO = new RCaptionDO();
addChild(rCap);
function getCap():RCaptionDO
{
    return rCap;
}
```

This code creates an instance of the RCaptionDO class, called rCap, and adds it to the stage (because the instance of the RCaptionDO class is instantiated on the stage, you can effectively attach the vid and cap instances to the display list as you did in the RCaptionDO class). You also create a function called getCap that will return the RCaptionDO instance—you will use this function to kick off your component in Flex.

Now you are ready to create the component. In your library, select (single-click) the RCaption movie clip. Then, in your menu, select Commands ➤ Make Flex Component (this option only exists if your Flex component is installed and enabled, as you took care of earlier), like you see in Figure 15-8.

Figure 15-8. The Make Flex Component menu option

If your FLA frame rate is not set to 24fps (frames per second), the default Flex frame rate (which it wouldn't be if you left it at the default Flash frame rate of 12fps), you will now see a dialog box like the one in Figure 15-9, prompting you to approve the change to 24fps. If you do see this dialog box, click OK. Fortunately this will have little effect on our component since all code and object instances occur on a single frame.

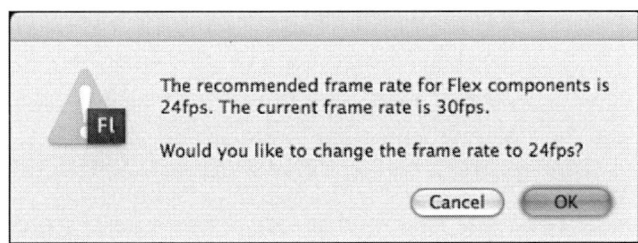

Figure 15-9. You should change your frame rate to 24 if you haven't already

The first time you compile this component, in the Flash Output panel, you should see messaging similar to this:

```
Command made the following changes to the FLA:
    Turned on Permit Debugging
    Turned on Export SWC
    Set frame rate to 24
    Imported UIMovieClip component to library
Component "RCaption" is ready to be used in Flex.
```

It is worth noting that fifth line, "Imported UIMovieClip component to library". The UIMovieClip class is not natively part of Flash, but it is required to make this component accessible to Flex. An instance of the UIMovieClip component has been added to your FLA library, as you see in Figure 15-10.

If you check the linkage on your RCaption movie clip (by right-clicking RCaption in the library and selecting Linkage), you will see that RCaption now inherits from mx.flash. UIMovieClip, rather than flash.display.MovieClip, as you see in Figure 15-11.

All that remains is to actually publish your FLA, which you can do by selecting File ➤ Publish. Now you will see CaptionComponent.swc has been created in the same folder

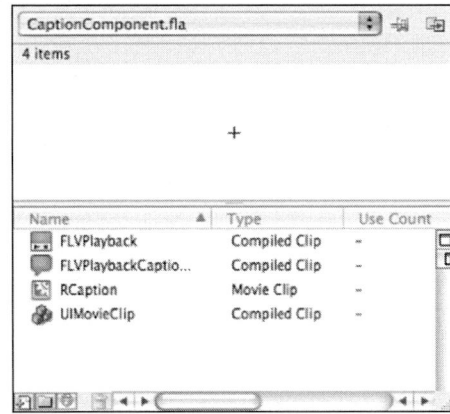

Figure 15-10. Your FLA library after creating the Flex component

as your CaptionComponent.fla (please note that while the class name I will refer to in Flex is RCaption, after the movie clip you exported as your component, the SWC is named after the FLA document). So, now you're ready to begin using your brand-new component in Flex.

Using your Flash-generated SWC in Flex

Start by creating a new basic Flex project to work in and call it Captions. Now, to add the SWC to the project, modify the Library paths by selecting Project ➤ Properties. In the left column, you will want to select Flex Build Path, and in the right panel, select the Library path tab. The default state of this panel should look something like Figure 15-12.

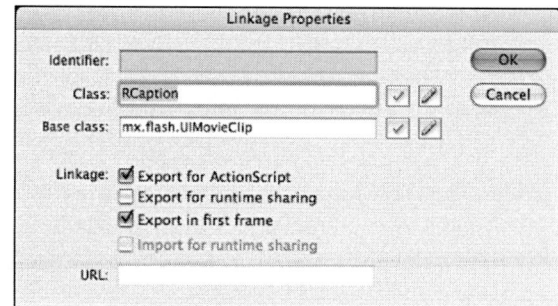

Figure 15-11. The linkage settings of the RCaption movie clip after exporting the Flex component

On this panel, click Add SWC, click Browse to navigate to the CaptionComponent.swc you just created, and then click OK. Once you do, your Library paths should be updated to look something like Figure 15-13.

Back in the project source code, you now need to add a new namespace reference. So include xmlns:myComps="*" as a new attribute in the <mx:Application/> tag. This refers to the default namespace created by Flash, unless you override the namespace settings in Flash.

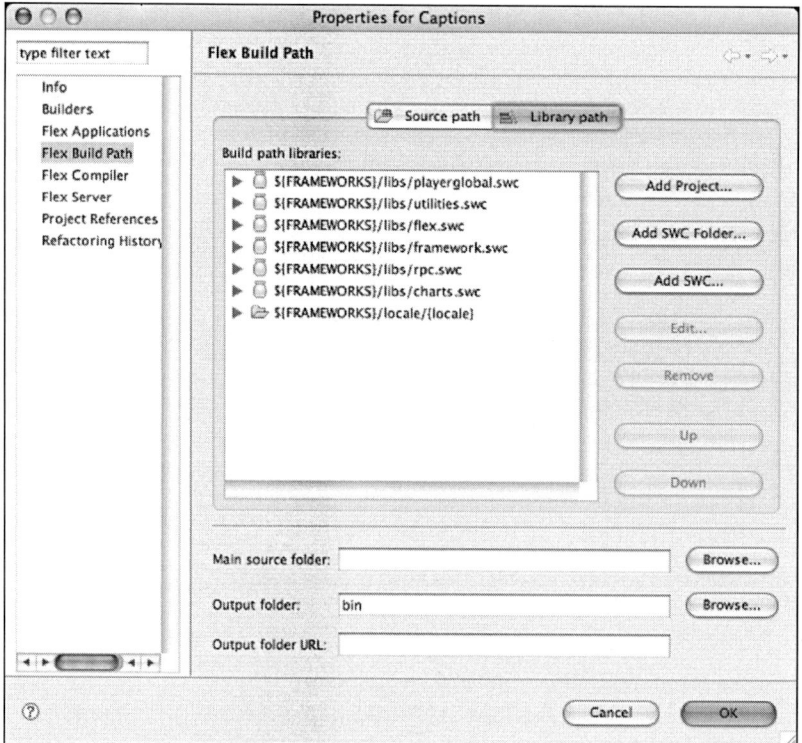

Figure 15-12. The Library paths of your project

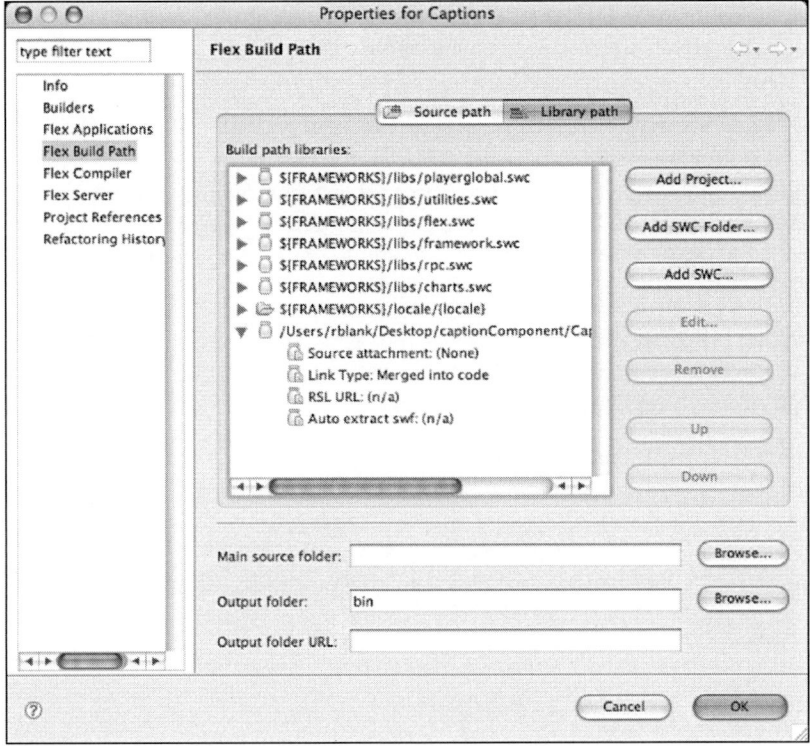

Figure 15-13. The Library paths after adding CaptionComponent.swc

So, to add an instance of your new component to the application, simply begin typing `<myComps:`, at which point Flex will help you complete the tag, as you see in Figure 15-14.

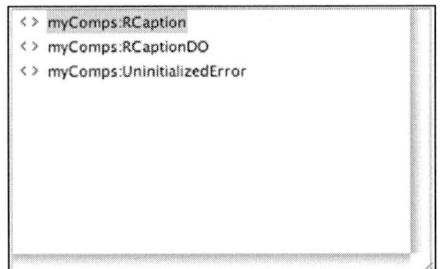

Complete the tag with an `id` attribute (for easy ActionScript reference) so it reads as follows:

```
<myComps:RCaption id="rVid"/>
```

Figure 15-14. The code hints that appear because Flex recognizes your component

Now, recall you took all the code that kicks off your video playback and placed it in a function called `setupVideo`, which is part of the `RCaptionDO` class. You can talk directly to the instance of `RCaptionDO` by running the `getCap()` method on your RCaption component.

Now you can add a bit of ActionScript to begin the playback of video in your component. So write a `<mx:script/>` tag like the following:

```
<mx:Script>
  <![CDATA[
    public function beginPlayback():void
    {
      rVid.getCap().setupVideo("SkinUnderPlayStopSeekCaptionVol.swf",
```

```
                                320,240,"kennedyCaptions.xml",
                                "kennedy2.flv");
        }
    ]]>
</mx:Script>
```

In this code, you run the getCap() method on the rVid instance of your custom component, returning a pointer to the RCaptionDO instance. In the same statement, you call the setupVideo() method on the returned instance, passing it the information about which skin, video, and captions file to load, and what dimensions to display at.

To get this all rolling properly, add a call to the beginPlayback() method from the creationComplete attribute of your <mx:Application/> tag. You'll also force-suppress scrolling. In the end, the code for your complete application should look like the following:

```
<?xml version="1.0" encoding="utf-8"?>
<mx:Application xmlns:mx="http://www.adobe.com/2006/mxml"
                xmlns:myComps="*" layout="absolute"
                creationComplete="beginPlayback()"
                horizontalScrollPolicy="off"
                verticalScrollPolicy="off">
<mx:Script>
  <![CDATA[
    public function beginPlayback():void
    {
      rVid.getCap().setupVideo("SkinUnderPlayStopSeekCaptionVol.swf",
                               320,240,"kennedyCaptions.xml",
                               "kennedy2.flv");
    }
  ]]>
</mx:Script>
<myComps:RCaption id="rVid"/>
</mx:Application>
```

And when you run this code, you'll see it works just fine, just like in Figure 15-15.

Remember, based on this code, you have to transfer three files to your bin directory:

1. kennedy2.flv (your FLV to play back)

2. SkinUnderPlayStopSeekCaptionVol.swf (your FLVPlayback skin)

3. kennedyCaptions.xml (your XML file with captions)

And, because you created this component to accept paths to any FLV, XML file, and skin, you can easily reuse this component without ever opening Flash.

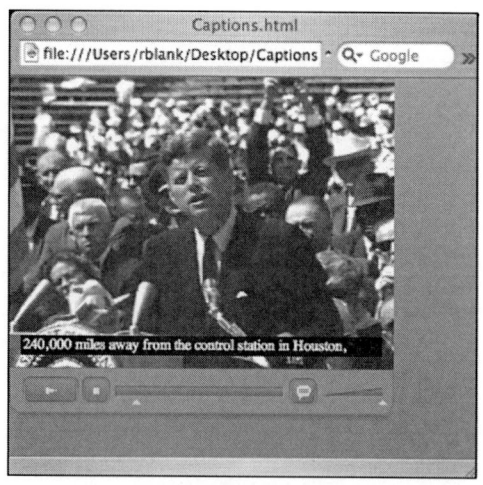

Figure 15-15. The result of your new component compiled in Flex

So that's a neat look into the Flash-Flex Integration Kit, illustrating a great use of the abilities to create Flex components right out of Flash. But I sort of glossed over how exactly you could possibly automate the generation of captions files. This brings us to transcribing audio.

Transcribing your audio

How do you go about converting your audio tracks into text transcripts? Well, there's no doubt that the options are still quite young and few.

Many people are used to voice recognition on the desktop, with applications like Dragon NaturallySpeaking (www.nuance.com/naturallyspeaking). But for an application like the RMX, of course, we need a server-based automated system.

One option that is currently available is WizzScribe SI for Linux, at www.wizzardsoftware.com/ wizzard_wizzscribe_si.php, which is powered by IBM's large vocabulary SPEAKER INDEPENDENT voice recognition technology. By integrating software such as this into your server application environment, you can queue all media for automated transcription.

Of course, converting an audio track to a transcript only handles part of the information in a video— it still leaves the video information obscured. And it doesn't help at all with video files with no audio or unintelligible audio (such as background noise at an event or music). For a video search to have optimal power for searchability, visual pattern recognition software already exists—some of it is amazingly powerful. But it has not evolved to become widely available. In the future, as computing increases in power and new software algorithms are developed to exploit the growing processor capacities, you can expect to add visual pattern analysis to the same transcripts, so users can search the actual contents of a video. But that is much further off.

So, in short, there is a lot we can do when we have transcripts of all media uploaded to the RMX. But this is just an example of how better and more detailed meta information increases the value of the source information.

Now I'll show you another example of this same dynamic: folksonomy.

Robust user-generated folksonomy

As discussed earlier in this book, categorizing content based on keywords is a key mechanism for increasing the usability and value of information. On the RMX, we allow content creators to tag any content (such as a blog post or a video) when the content is created on the network.

But creators often do not tag content fully—there could be dozens of additional tags that would improve the value of the media within the network. Anyone who views the content might think of several additional tags to label the content. So, why not let them?

At its simplest, we can allow someone viewing a blog post to apply additional tags to the post. In a more complex implementation, we can allow viewers to apply tags to video by specifying precise positions in the video the tag refers to. Again, recognizing that media like video includes the dimension of time, allowing time-based viewer tagging enables the members of your network to improve the value of the content even after it's been created. When properly implemented, robust, user-generated folksonomic tagging sort of "wiki-izes" all media on the network, by enabling all users to participate in the continued generation of content based around an initial content posting.

Fortunately, this is one of those ideas for which no new technologies need to be built—we just need some more time to consider how best to utilize viewer tagging and to then build that into the application.

Improved syndication controls

We have different ways of syndicating content on the RMX, as we've described in this book. For instance, when I create a post on my blog, that post can be automatically syndicated to the group blogs for all user groups to which I belong. Similarly, as an administrator, I can specify other groups from which I wish to syndicate content.

These data structures improve the experience of the RMX to the groups and members that form the network. But they are also complex. Let's take the simple example of video that has been syndicated from one RMX group (LA Flash) site to another (FiTO). Now let's say a viewer of the video on FiTO flags the video as inappropriate, and the FiTO moderator agrees (for the purposes of this example, assume those Canadians have a lower tolerance for inappropriate content). So the FiTO moderator deletes the video. But, of course, the FiTO moderator does not have the power to actually delete the video, since LA Flash is the originating site. All FiTO can do is block that video from the FiTO site. So, not only do we need to handle the syndication, we need to handle group-specific exceptions to the syndication.

If, instead, the viewer on the FiTO site really likes the video from LA Flash, and decides to copy the embed code and post it on another site, what branding should the video player reflect? LA Flash's or FiTO's? And then what happens if the original video is deleted?

These are just two of hundreds of possible use cases of the feature. The point is that dealing with these syndication issues rapidly becomes quite a complex endeavor in which it is vital to consider all use cases and relational dependencies and handle them appropriately.

But, despite their complexity, the syndication features we have enabled represent just the tip of the iceberg. For instance, one possibility is creating smart syndication rules. Just like you can create smart playlists in iTunes, which automatically aggregate music based on criteria you specify (for instance, all music in the Rock genre with at least a three-star rating), we can envision allowing the administrator of an RMX group to specify that he wants to receive all content from across the RMX that has specific tags and a minimum average rating with a minimum number of views. For example, as the administrator of LA Flash, I could choose to automatically aggregate via syndication all blog posts across the RMX that have "Flash," "ActionScript 3," and "video" as tags, with a minimum rating of 3 stars and a minimum number of views of 400. Similar rules could be applied to all media, including forum posts, videos, and calendar events.

But each one of these features requires interfaces for the configuration and management of the syndication rules, as well as the back-end logic to handle all the ramifications of the relationships that are established. So, with these features, we'll take it step by step over time.

Advertising

Advertising is a core component of most any Internet application. Unless the application is for corporate internal use or incurs a subscription fee, it is almost certain that advertising comprises a large part of the revenues for the application—and therefore the business justification for the application. In

Chapter 11, I provided some guidance on how to go about integrating banner and instream advertising into your application.

Banner advertising is, in essence, a mature set of technologies, business models, and processes. Instream advertising, on the other hand, is not. The only mainstream options right now for instream advertising include preroll (instream ads delivered prior to the main video content) and postroll (instream ads delivered after the completion of the main video content). It feels very much like squeezing a square peg (the television advertising model) into a round hole (Internet viewing patterns).

Since video is a large part of the RMX—and an even larger part of our bandwidth and server consumption (and therefore our costs)—having a set of mature technologies and standard practices to monetize our video content is vital to maximizing the value of our network.

So, we have a few ideas on where we want to take our instream advertising features moving forward. Some of these are ideas that are currently implemented or discussed in different settings across the Internet, but again there are no standards, and the concepts themselves are still evolving.

Interstitials

One of the most basic improvements that can be made to video delivery is the use of interstitial advertising. As I just explained, instream advertising consists largely of preroll and postroll ads. Why not add in an interstitial? For example, say you have a video that is four minutes long. It is much more likely that a viewer will sit through the instream ad if it is delivered three-and-a-half minutes into the video—that is, at some point in the middle of the video, when the viewer is already into the content and wants to see the end—rather than either before the video as a preroll, when the viewer hasn't yet formed an attachment to the content or a desire to see it all the way through, or after the video as a postroll, when there's absolutely no incentive to keep watching. That's what an interstitial is. You may encounter interstitials on some video-heavy sites (I recall seeing many a Nissan Versa interstitial while catching up on season 1 of *Heroes* with NBC's free video on demand, which is, of course, built in Flash), but there are very few, and there are no real standards for that type of ad delivery yet.

Overlays

Well, now that I think about it, why are we divorcing the ad from the content so definitively? When a preroll, postroll, or interstitial ad is playing, there is no other content to keep the viewer's attention. Wouldn't it be more effective to deliver some type of advertising *during* the playback of the video?

Overlays are similar to interstitials in that they occur during the video. But they are transparent and cover only a portion of the content, and most importantly, the video does not stop for an overlay and the playback controls are not disabled. We envision supporting both transparent video and transparent still formats for overlays. Overlays will be fully interactive and can consist of graphics, bitmaps, animations, and even other transparent FLVs (anything that can be done in Flash should be supported in an overlay, even to the extent of loading mini-games over certain videos or ads). Now, that's a way to make the ad engaging.

Of course, content for overlays need not be limited to advertising. They can also be exploited for branding purposes. We are all used to the "bugs" that video distributors superimpose on their images (this includes TV stations and cable broadcasters, as well as video-sharing services like YouTube). In an online context, why should bugs be totally static images? Why can't they be animations—or even better, interactive widgets? Of course, they can with Flash and Flex.

Since overlays display during the playback of the video content, we can also seek ways to exploit the timecoded transcripts I talked about creating earlier in this chapter. Capturing that data, we can change the overlay at various points during the video, or highlight and accentuate the overlays at other points in the video.

Hotspots

Hotspots are designated areas within videos and ads that have full support for interactivity. Hotspots may display custom cursors, link to another page, or load other content into the player (either as an overlay or as a new video). The great thing about hotspots is that they don't have to be ads per se. Think *The Truman Show*. For instance, let's assume I'm watching a tutorial on shooting great green-screen video footage (for processing into transparent FLVs), and I see a lighting gear that looks really good. With hotspots enabled, I can mouseover the lighting gear, and a dialog box with more information about the product appears. I can click a link to learn more at the manufacturer's web site, or even automatically add the gear to my cart. The advertising value is clear, and the product placement potential is tremendous (recall the Heineken tie-in in the second *Austin Powers* movie).

Just like prerolls, postrolls, interstitials, and overlays, hotspots may be integrated with external banners—so, for instance, in the preceding example, when I mouseover the lighting gear, all banner ads in the page could update to ones for that manufacturer. And, just like the other forms of instream advertising I've discussed here, the power of FLV cue points and ActionScript mean they are not technically challenging. The challenge again is in the establishment of some widely adopted standards. Detailed hotspots, like the lighting gear example, are certainly the most resource-intensive type of ad to create, but less specific, basic hotspots could be implemented with relative ease.

Bug-me-later ads

One final note on advertising is that, in the Web 2.0 universe, it is important to account for the MySpace effect. Any video-sharing site, including the RMX, includes shared or embedded players for users to easily post single videos on other sites such as their MySpace member pages or Blogger blogs. But, once the Flash is embedded in HTML that you do not control, you cannot control the `allowNetworking` parameter, which means that the site may disable all links in your Flash application (as well as full-screen functionality through the separate `allowFullScreen` parameter). While your Flash app can still function (for instance, it can continue to load videos and send metrics back to your server), links to URLs within your application may not function. Of course, if links in your shared media are disabled, this can really destroy advertising revenue, which can depend on not only views, but also clicks.

We envision implementing bug-me-later ads in the shared RMX players. These ads would deliver a message such as "Click here to get an e-mail with a coupon for x" or "Click here to learn about y." Interacting with the ad doesn't take the user out of the app—instead, it sends a message to your server, upon which you and your advertiser may act on a later date. This provides an additional channel through which advertisers can communicate directly to a viewer's inbox through a simple opt-in interaction.

Bug-me-later ads enable users to interact with advertising without deviating from their current experience (so they stay and watch more content and get more ads), they provide far superior information to the advertiser, and they work even when the user is experiencing the advertisement on a third-party site in which external linking has been disabled.

Money

Of course, advertising is not the only source of revenue on a community like the RMX. There is also commerce. While we launched the RMX without commerce (in part to simplify launch requirements, and in part to assemble a sufficiently large membership before adding commercial features), we have a lot of plans on how to handle commerce in future versions of the application.

Paid content

We can foresee the possible addition of paid membership to enable members to utilize additional features not included with the base membership. But the more interesting commercial opportunities, in my opinion, are in the prospect of allowing members to generate revenue by charging for content they create on the network.

We are likely to implement a system like this first for video, to enable members to create paid tutorials. At least once, almost each and every member of the RMX, while working with his Adobe tool of choice, has thought, "Wow, that's a neat thing I just discovered." Some of the more motivated developers might write a quick forum or blog post, or even perhaps a tutorial. But, as text mediums, posts and written tutorials are not as effective a way to teach software and coding as video can be. So, we want to enable these members to rapidly create a video tutorial of their ideas, tips, techniques, or full lessons.

But the moment we create a system such as this, we face two fundamental questions: how do consumers pay, and how do creators get paid?

Payment models

There are three main options when considering a payment system for content: unit based, subscription based, and points based. When considering these models, it is important to remember the nature of the content we are aiming to sell. These video tutorials (like all educational content) will be of varying length, quality, and difficulty. Some will be quite short—perhaps a minute or so—covering a quick tip, and others will be much longer and cover the topic in much more depth.

Unit-based model

Unit-based commerce is very simple—it's how we pay for almost everything in our lives. The consumer pays a given price for a specific piece of content. However, we must remember that not all content has the same value or should cost the same price. What's more, the shorter ones may be worth $0.50 each, and enabling transactions (called *micro-transactions*) for that low a price is difficult to do profitably. In short, unit-based pricing will not suit our needs.

Subscription-based model

In a subscription-based payment model, consumers pay a set price for access to all content on the system. This is very common online. For example, *The Wall Street Journal* places much of the paper's content behind a firewall and grants access only to those who pay an ongoing subscription fee.

We did not take to the idea of implementing a subscription model, at least at launch, for a couple of reasons. First, for a subscription to make sense, consumers need to feel there is a lot of content available behind that firewall. However, it takes time to build a library of valuable content. Second, subscription models make the accounting for royalty purposes much more complex. Let's say that users A and B pay the same subscription fee. User A and user B both watch video C. But, that month, video C was the only paid-content user A watched, while user B watched a lot of other paid content. How do we decide how much to give the creator for each view? So, for those two reasons, we opted against a subscription model, at least to start.

Points-based model

So, we did not like unit-based or subscription-based pricing models for the RMX, which brings us to the points-based model. In a points-based model, consumers pay upfront for a given number of points that may be spent over time on individual pieces of content. While less common than unit-based or subscription-based models, points-based pricing is gaining popularity, especially in the console gaming world. Both Xbox LIVE and Nintendo Wii use points for their online marketplaces.

Unlike with unit-based pricing, we do not need to support micro-transactions, since points are purchased in bulk. And, unlike with subscription-based models, accounting and royalties are simpler, because we can easily track the value of a purchase based on the points the content costs.

This brings us to the next topic: royalties.

Royalties system

Royalties are the portions of profits that go back to those who participated in creation of the content. In this section, I will also add in the topic of commissions, which is the revenue sharing for those who participated in the distribution and sale of the content, because the relationships are quite similar. To enable content creators and member sites to generate revenue, we need an accounting system in place to manage royalties and commissions.

Building a royalties system can actually be staggeringly complex, depending on how many ways you wish to split the revenue, and how many ways you wish to sell and distribute the content. For instance, on the RMX, a member of LA Flash could purchase content generated by a member of FiTO. In that transaction, I can see distributing royalties to the original uploader and commissions to both LA Flash and FiTO. If, on the other hand, a member of LA Flash paid to watch content generated by another on LA Flash, there are fewer commissions to distribute (and likely higher shares for the creator and for LA Flash). If we then add in the ability for members of different RMX groups to collaborate on video training tutorials, the web of payments grows even more complex.

It is for this reason that we did not implement these features at launch, but we plan to soon. And, of course, the accounting application interface will be built entirely in Flex, utilizing the charting components.

User group features

Of course, many of the features of the RMX, such as the blogs, forums, and user-generated video sharing, are features that are common to many web communities (although we are perhaps organizing them in a manner to provide more value to our specific members). But, at the same time, many of the current features of the RMX, such as the event calendar and the jobs board, have been designed specifically with the needs of user groups in mind. We have more ideas on how we can customize the RMX offering and increase its value to Adobe communities.

Physical library management

Many user groups have libraries. In the case of LA Flash, we have a library of a few hundred books and some DVDs, many donated from publishers like Apress and friends of ED, and many donated from our members who have finished using them. Since we allow our members to borrow the titles, managing the library is a huge hassle. Knowing which titles are in and which members have had which books for how long is too much of a pain to deal with.

Fortunately, there is a Mac-based tool called Delicious Monster, which you can learn more about and download at www.delicious-monster.com, that makes library management incredibly easy—it even uses the Mac's built-in iSight cameras to scan ISBN codes to enter new titles into a library quickly and automatically (among its many impressive features). But, while Delicious Monster makes library management much easier, integrating those records into your membership records can be difficult. So, if you want to send an e-mail blast to all members with overdue books or prevent members with overdue books from borrowing others, it's a cross-referencing hassle.

So, one UG-specific feature we will build into a future version of the RMX is integration with Delicious Monster, so library records and membership records (along with all other site activity) can be easily cross-referenced. This will not only allow user groups to manage larger libraries more efficiently, but also allow user groups to utilize borrowing statistics. Publishers donate books to user groups because they want to promote their offerings—not because they want the books gathering dust on never-accessed shelves. As the administrator of LA Flash, I could provide a report to friends of ED stating how many times each title was borrowed (we, of course, wouldn't share the membership information—just the raw borrowing numbers). What's more, I could forward a coupon from friends of ED for 10% off another book to everyone who has borrowed a friends of ED title in the past six months.

RSVP

While many user groups do not require RSVPs for their events, some groups do on occasion. For example, if a group manager needs to secure a meeting space and purchase refreshments for a special event, the manager needs to know how many people to expect. The big problem with RSVPs is that many people will RSVP and then not attend, because they know there is no penalty for doing so. This, of course, throws off the attendance numbers.

In a future version of the RMX, we plan to build in an RSVP module, or customize the Drupal RSVP module, which would enable user groups to accept RSVPs through the event calendar system. The manager would have an accurate list at all times of expected attendance and could easily generate e-mail blasts to those who have RSVPed. What's more, if the manager requires attendees to sign in at the event, he can track through the RMX membership records which members repeatedly RSVP for events but don't attend those events. The manager could warn the offending members or even prevent them from RSVPing for future events for a period of six months.

Distribution

As the RMX is a Web 2.0 application, its content is designed to be viewed both within the application and external to the application. Text-based content, such as the blogs, forums, and job postings, can be easily syndicated through RSS. And other content like video can be easily shared through the embedded players.

However, there are some really exciting new products from Adobe that are expanding the ways Flash Platform developers can think about building platforms for the distribution of content that was previously accessible only through web sites and web-based RIAs. While it's still too early to talk specifics on how we plan to utilize these platforms for the RMX, it is important to begin considering what these platforms offer.

Planning for AIR

You already know what AIR is, but as a refresher, AIR stands for Adobe Integrated Runtime (so Adobe AIR Runtime is really an acronym for Adobe Adobe Integrated Runtime Runtime). Users must install AIR, just as they must install Flash Player or Acrobat Reader, by downloading it from Adobe's web site. With AIR installed, users may install any AIR application onto their computer and have it perform just like any other desktop application.

What makes this special is that AIR is different from other runtimes, because it has been designed to enable full desktop applications built using SWF, HTML, PDF, and JavaScript. This means, among other things, the application can be directly launchable from the Windows Start menu or the Mac Dock, it can launch multiple windows (with or without chrome), and it has file system access. Applications running in AIR also have support for occasional connectivity (running online and offline).

The great thing is that Adobe developers do not need to learn a whole new language or set of technologies to do this—Flex, Flash, and Dreamweaver developers can utilize the same skills they've honed building web applications to now build cross-platform desktop applications. And with hundreds of thousands of Flash applications already on the Internet, there are a lot of existing projects to choose from.

Of course, it is important to realize that AIR is different from the Web, which means that it doesn't necessarily make sense to take the same application that you've built for the Web and simply reexport it for the desktop. Instead, you want to take time and consider how a desktop component can add value to your overall application.

At the time of writing, we have deployed one AIR application for use on the RMX (in addition to other FlexTube.tv clients), the AB Batch Uploader (the alpha release is pictured in Figure 15-16 and the design of the full release is shown in Figure 15-17).

The AB Batch Uploader comes directly from our experience implementing the FlexTube.tv video-sharing solution. One of the most common hassles for our clients is the media creation process. The system we have built for ingesting video through the web site is designed to take in a single video at a time, along with all the metadata for that video (title, tags, description, etc.). But, when a client launches a new FlexTube.tv implementation, he might have an existing catalog of over 1,000 videos. Uploading those, one at a time, can be a tremendously time-consuming hassle.

This is why we built the AB Batch Uploader. Running as an Internet-connected desktop application, the AB Batch Uploader enables users to upload any number of video files in a sequential queue. If the user loses Internet connectivity or quits the uploader, the queue will resume as soon as the uploader is running online again. User authentication is integrated into the application, so we know who is doing what on the system, and we sniff the files on the server to see if the videos need to be encoded (in which case they are queued for encoding) or are already in FLV format (in which case they proceed directly to upload moderation). We developed the AB Batch Uploader as a Flex SWC that can be painlessly compiled into an AIR application, along with an easily updatable configuration file to customize the URLs (where the files go, where users are authenticated, etc.), so that we can quickly compile new versions for various clients.

Figure 15-16. The alpha release of the AB Batch Uploader AIR application

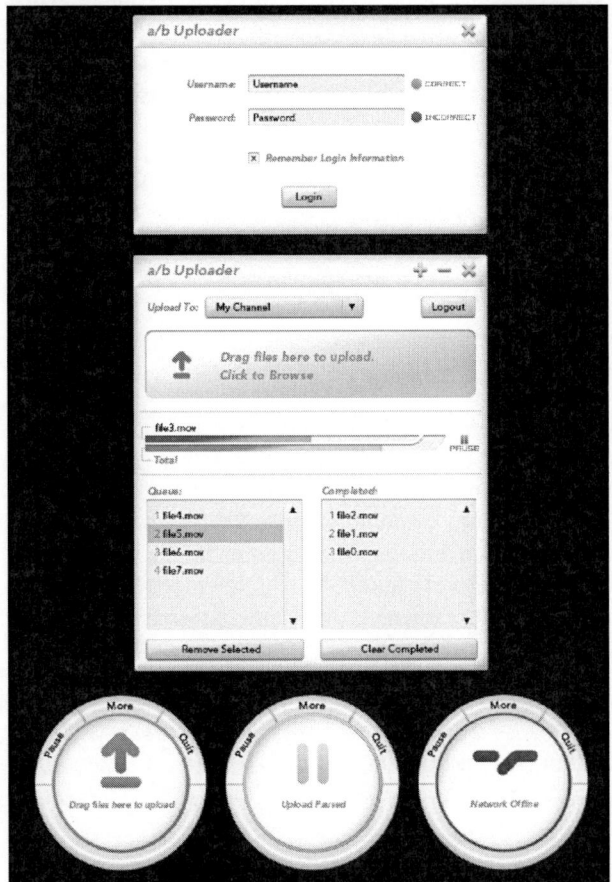

Figure 15-17. The designs for the full release of the AB Batch Uploader

At its core, this is a really simple application. In fact, we built a similar mechanism in a web-based Flex application for Live Nation to batch upload pictures into a content management system. But pictures are small, and uploading hundreds can take just a few minutes. Considering the file size of videos (and the resulting duration of uploading dozens or hundreds of videos at once), executing this same functionality for video files within a web page, and without direct and easy local file system access, would have been tremendously difficult; you simply cannot rely on a web session being persistent for 24 hours or more, and saving and resuming queues of local files through web sessions is remarkably difficult. And yet, with AIR, it was remarkably simple.

I cite this as an example of the type of AIR application we will seek to develop in the future: simple, focused applications that complement—not duplicate—the functionality of our web-based applications. For example, on the RMX, I can easily see aspects of the administrative control panel running as AIR applications, enabling administrators and moderators to easily manage network content from their desktops. If the administrator's computer is offline, he can use the desktop application to queue other actions for the next time the computer is online.

For consumers, we feel the aspects of the RMX with the highest potential value on the desktop to be the jobs board and the event calendar. Both of these applications are high-value applications, and having the ability to work from the desktop and offline can add even more value. For example, let's say you have ten jobs to post. You could enter all the information for those posts quickly, without waiting for the server to log each individually—even doing so offline. Then, when you're done entering all the information and you're back online, the application will automatically post the information to the server. Or, if a user is running the RMX event calendar as a desktop application, he can easily be informed when new events are posted or reminded with an alert when an upcoming event for which he has RSVPed is coming up.

There is, of course, a lot of potential in bringing the RMX video network to the desktop. To discuss this, let's take a look at the Adobe Media Player.

Planning for the Adobe Media Player

The Adobe Media Player is actually an AIR application. Just like the Windows Media Player and QuickTime, it can deliver Flash media to viewers through a desktop application.

In essence, the Adobe Media Player is a way for Flash content providers to syndicate their content easily to users' computers, using RSS. At the RMX, we can create a specialized feed for Adobe Media Player consumption, and then our members could add the RMX channel (which we can design with custom graphics defined in the RSS) to the Adobe Media Players on their desktops. Then, users will be able to view the RMX video content even when they are not on our web site. In fact, we can structure the media delivery so that the videos are automatically downloaded to a viewer's computer, so the viewer doesn't even need to be online when he's watching our video.

For those delivering Flash media using a Flash Media Server, the Adobe Media Player also integrates into the new content management mechanisms in FMS. This enables you to manage and track FLV and H.264 content even when it is distributed to your viewers' computers. The Adobe Media Player offers two types of DRM: **content integrity protection**, which guarantees that advertising remains attached to content, and **identity-based content protection**, which prevents media playback on unauthorized computers.

While the Adobe Media Player is a powerful new distribution platform for Flash media, because it is little more than a custom RSS reader (and, as you read in Chapter 6, we are already generating a lot of RSS), planning for and exploiting AMP will be much easier than executing on many of the other ideas in this chapter.

Summary

In this chapter, I outlined some of the thinking that we've put into ways we want to grow the RMX in the future. And I also took the opportunity to explore the Flash-Flex Integration Kit, which enables effective (and simple) development of Flash applications across both IDEs. This closes out Part 3 of the book, describing some of the larger RMX features available at launch. In Part 4 of the book, we'll look at some special topics, ranging from using runtime shared libraries to building an audio visualizer in Flex.

Part 4

SPECIAL TOPICS

In the first three parts of this book, we've walked you through the conception, planning, and development of several core parts of the Rich Media Exchange. In Part 4, we will walk you through a few more topics that didn't quite fit into the chapters on the development of the RMX, but cover important concepts for Flex developers, including persistent framework caching and optimizing your Flex applications and web sites for search engine placement.

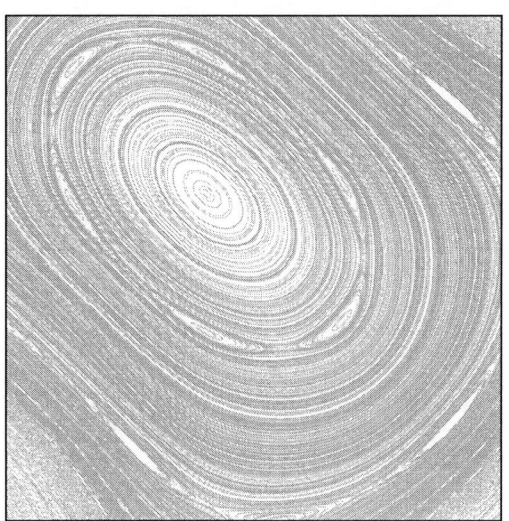

Chapter 16

RSLS AND PERSISTENT FRAMEWORK CACHING

By Omar Gonzalez

The Flex framework has become popular for many reasons, two of the main ones being it's open source, and it provides a strong foundation for rapid application development. Like all things that seem too good to be true, there is a catch. When you develop your Flash applications in Flex, your files include the framework, meaning that even with just an empty <mx:Application/> tag, your compiled project is already up to 142K. This limitation of Flex has meant that Flex has been ill suited for many Flash applications such as shared video players (which must be as small as possible—the YouTube player is only 40K, less than a third of the size of the Flex framework without even starting to build a video player).

Enter runtime shared libraries (RSLs) and persistent framework caching (PFC)! In this chapter, I will talk about the challenges that are posed by the inherent size of SWFs compiled in Flex and how to overcome those challenges with the new tools and techniques available in Flex 3. I will also talk about building your own SWC files for code portability and cover loading your custom libraries as RSLs.

Why are Flex SWF files big?

As R explained in Chapter 1, anything that can be produced in Flex can also be produced in Flash. But what he didn't add is that the version of the application written and compiled in Flex will almost certainly be larger than the one created in Flash—sometimes significantly larger. The reason for the size difference is the Flex framework. When you start a new Flex project, Flex Builder makes a new MXML file with an empty <mx:Application/> tag in it. If you compile that application, the outputted SWF should be just about 140K with the -debug compiler argument set to false; with -debug set to true, it should be just about 230K. This increase is caused by the debugging classes being compiled into your application. For deployment, the debugging classes should no longer be needed, so it's not necessary to carry the extra weight. If you compile an empty FLA to SWF, the resulting file will be approximately 34 bytes (that's bytes, not kilobytes). So an empty SWF produced in Flash will be over 99% smaller than an empty SWF produced in Flex.

The Application class (which is unique to Flex and not available in Flash) aggregates many other classes used by the Flex framework, which are exploited by the components you instantiate inside your Flex source. Some of these classes, which enable you to build advanced applications rapidly in Flex, are required by default, whether or not they are actually utilized; other parts of the framework will be added to your SWF as your code requires them. The extra file size—even 140K to start—might seem trivial as more and more households upgrade to broadband connections. And if your Flex app is a single dashboard-style application, that file size overhead really isn't a problem.

The problem with the extra overhead from the framework emerges with applications in which file size is essential (such as shared video players or banner ads) or in which multiple SWF files are embedded in a single HTML page. When the application requires this type of architecture, each SWF on the page includes the overhead of the framework.

This is exactly why Adobe has improved runtime shared libraries and added persistent framework caching with Flex 3 and Flash Player 9.0.60. These two features allow your SWFs to share framework libraries and to cache those frameworks on viewer machines independent of the browser caching system.

Runtime shared libraries

Runtime shared libraries, or RSLs, are SWF files that are loaded at runtime. They can contain any code or assets required for your application—including the Flex framework itself—so you can easily add the Application class and any other classes that are part of the framework.swc file. An SWC file is an archive file, similar to a ZIP archive. The SWC contains a SWF with compiled code and assets in it, and XML files used by Flex Builder to read the catalog of classes and assets included in the SWF. The SWF in the SWC file is the actual RSL that gets loaded at runtime The SWC file is usually somewhere around 1MB big, half the size usually coming from the RSL SWF file itself. These SWF files are designed to be used by Flex applications to share code libraries and assets, so these SWFs by themselves do not do anything functional.

Persistent framework caching

Starting with Flash Player 9.0.60, the Flash Player has support for caching Adobe signed RSLs using the Flash Player cache, instead of the regular browser cache. This means that the Flash Player now has a caching mechanism separate from the one used in web browsers. Why is this even necessary? I mean, if every browser on this great planet of ours already includes a cache, why do we need another?

The short answer is that the browser cache doesn't help as much as you might think when it comes to assets like the framework RSLs, for a few reasons. First, since browser caching is customizable, users may not even have it enabled—meaning that you cannot rely on its presence. Second, even if it is enabled, it may be purged at any point by the user with the click of a mouse. And third, when dealing with browser cache systems, you are dependent on the browser-specific caching policy; for example, Safari 2 absolutely refuses to cache anything greater than 1MB (very annoying, especially given the fact that the larger a file is, the more you need it to be cached).

Fourth, you cannot easily control load order in a browser; for example, let's say that you have five Flex-generated SWFs in the same HTML page (one of the use cases I mentioned earlier in this chapter) all sharing the same framework file. The first time someone visits that page, their browser will load the framework five times, because the browser cannot recognize a file in cache until it is completely downloaded, and each of the five SWFs requests the framework upon initialization. Writing code to daisy-chain the load order is really annoying and sometimes unreliable.

Finally, people have multiple browsers on their systems. You might use any combination of applications like Internet Explorer, Firefox, Safari, Opera, Camino, Avant, and so forth. Of course, each browser maintains its own cache, so even if your framework is successfully stored in your visitor's cache, it might be in a different browser than the one he is currently using, forcing a redownload. And, of course, these problems compound each other, making the situation far more annoying and frustrating for us as developers to address satisfactorily.

Persistent framework caching means that the Flash Player now has a caching mechanism separate from the web browser cache—which means that the PFC does not conform to the same browser-specific caching policies, this cache is not cleared when users clear their browser cache, and this cache is shared among all browsers. Wow! But wait, there's more.

Unlike a browser cache, PFC is not domain dependent. This means that if SWFs on two separate sites utilize the same Adobe signed framework, the Flash Player will recognize that fact and use the cached framework for the SWFs on both sites. OK, so maybe now you see how serious a feature I am talking about here. PFC is truly a game-changer when it comes to the opportunities for Flex in development for the Flash Platform—with one single feature, that file size differential between Flash-generated SWFs and Flex-generated SWFs becomes almost irrelevant.

Setting up an application to use RSLs

By default, Flex applications are configured to be compiled with the classes in the framework.swc file merged into the application SWF. This means that any Flex component that you add to your application, be it a Button or Accordion, increases the size of your application. This happens because the Link Type, or Framework linkage of the framework.swc in the Flex Build Path settings panel, is set to Merged into code by default. As your application makes use of these classes this setting causes the component code to be "baked" into the application SWF file. (Note: Link Type and Framework linkage are the same setting. Changing the Framework linkage setting changes the Link Type of the framework.swc entry; alternatively, you can explicitly set the Link Type of a particular SWC in the list, overriding the Framework linkage property.) When you use RSLs, those classes are carried and shared using an RSL, including the classes that the <mx:Application/> tag requires to run, causing the main application SWF file to be much smaller; also, if needed, other applications can use the same RSL. This is where the benefits of RSLs become most real.

To see the configuration setting for the Link Type and Framework linkage properties of the framework.swc, right-click/Ctrl-click the project folder and click Properties, or click the Project menu of Eclipse or Flex Builder and select the Properties option there. A dialog box will appear; in the menu on the left, click Flex Build Path, and then click the Library path tab in the right-hand panel, revealing any SWCs you already have installed. Near the top you will see a drop-down menu (new in Flex 3) labeled Framework linkage. By default, it should be set to Merged into code. Click the SWC folder—in the beta version I used while writing this chapter, it is labeled Flex Moxie M3 with a path to the SDK folder. Click the jar icon beside framework.swc to open it and see its configuration. The second line down should be labeled Link Type; the default is most likely Merged into code. Your dialog box should look like the one in Figure 16-1.

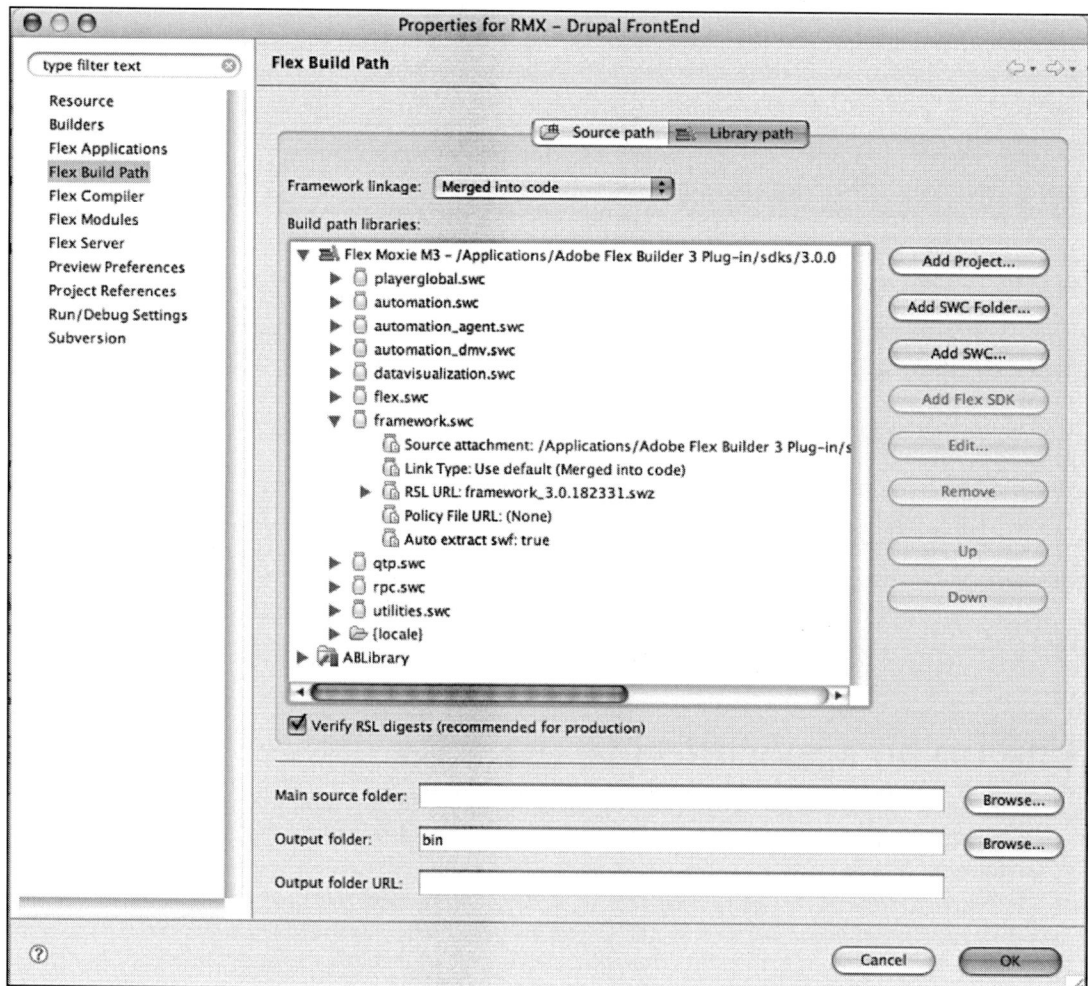

Figure 16-1. Default settings for framework.swc

Here you can make changes to create RSLs and configure how they are loaded. The Link Type has three options: Merged into code (the default), Runtime shared library, and External. External is not listed in the Framework linkage menu; I believe this option is a legacy option, but I could not find any documentation on it. Now let's look at how to set up an application to use an RSL and take advantage of the new Flash Player feature, persistent framework caching.

The signed RSL files are located in the Flex installation directory, at {installation_directory}/ sdks/3.0.0/frameworks/rsls. There are several pairs of SWZ and SWF files there, one pair for each Flex framework revision that Adobe has supplied signed RSLs for in your Flex installation. The SWZ is the Adobe signed version of the SWF RSL, which can only be used with Flash Player 9.0.60+.

Referring back to Figure 16-1, recall the option I pointed out at the top of the Library path tab, Framework linkage. This option is what tells the Flex compiler how to handle references to classes in the application. The default selection, Merged into code, compiles all the classes into the application SWF file. To keep those classes external and shareable by multiple SWF files, the option needs to be changed to Runtime shared library. If you still have the framework.swc branch open in the list of SWCs, you will see it automatically change to Runtime shared library when the Framework linkage option is changed in the drop-down menu (see Figure 16-2). This is not the case for all the SWC files referenced in the list; this only changes the framework.swc settings. However, most of the file size is added by classes referenced in the framework.swc file, so this is the only one that is actually externalized in the RSL that the application will load.

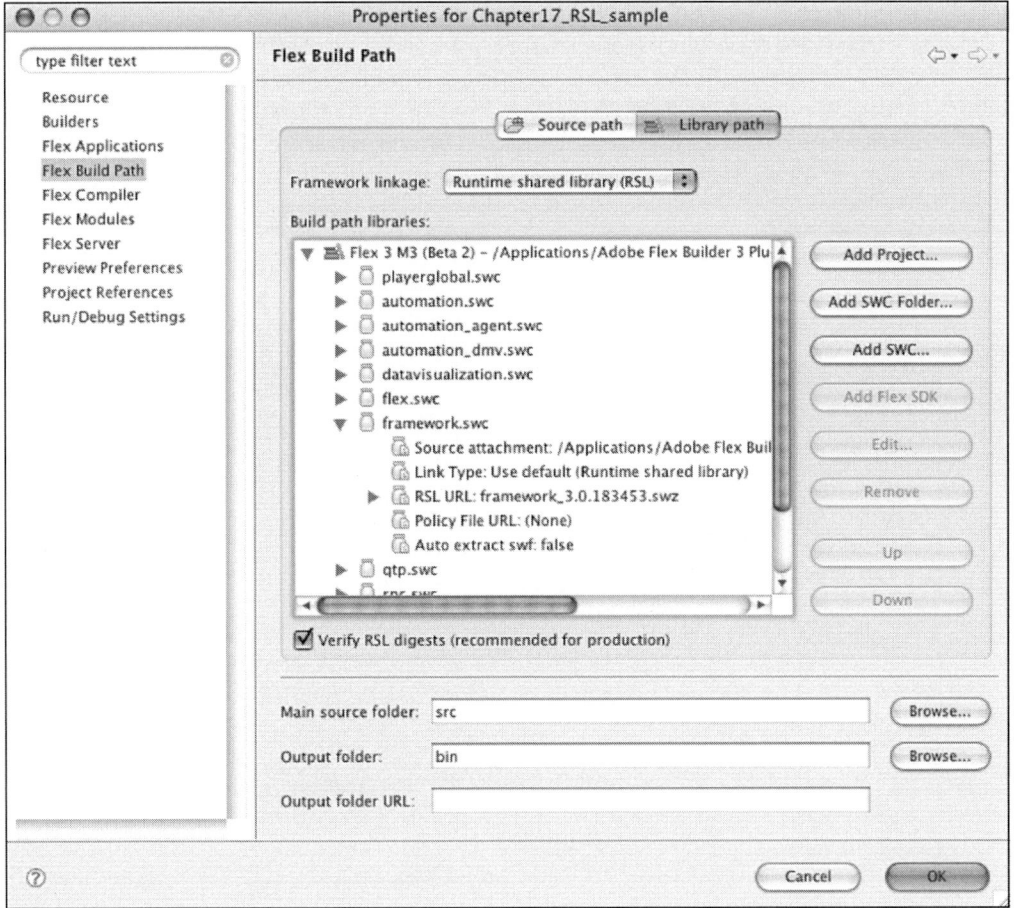

Figure 16-2. The framework.swc linkage settings are set through the Framework linkage drop-down menu.

This is all of the setup needed to get the application loading an RSL. At the bottom of the list is a check box option, Verify RSL digests. This option turns on verification of the RSL, which is the key in the RSL that is inserted by Adobe. Because this option is checked, the application will require Flash Player 9.0.60 or higher to load the signed RSL. However, a failover RSL is provided for backward compatibility. This is why there are pairs of files in the {installation_directory}/sdks/3.0.0/frameworks/rsls directory for each version of the Flex framework SWC file. Using the Verify RSL digests option also means that the SWF and SWZ files produced at compile time in the bin folder will not be valid RSLs and will cause an RSL digest mismatch error if you try to use them. Because the Verify RSL digests option is on, you must use the SWF and SWZ located in the rsls directory I just mentioned. They are useful, however, to reference the framework version number that you should be using from the {installation_directory}/sdks/3.0.0/frameworks/rsls directory. The RSL files follow a naming convention: the template is framework_3.0.{build}.swz and framework_3.0.{build}.swf. The pair in the bin folder lets you know which version of the Adobe-provided RSLs should be used with the application.

If you haven't yet loaded any applications in Flash Player 9.0.6+ and you try to run the Flex application from the Flex Builder IDE, the Flex application will likely output an RSL error that says that the digest verification failed. This will be the case because the RSL in the bin folder doesn't have the correct digest. Simply copy the SWZ and SWF file from the {installation_directory}/sdks/3.0.0/frameworks/rsls directory to the bin folder to make the application run. However, by default the compiler auto-extracts the framework files each time you run the application and overwrites any files currently in the bin directory. To get the auto-extracting feature to not overwrite the correct RSLs, open the Properties window of the project and go to Flex Build Path ➤ Library path. In the list of SWCs, open the framework.swc branch, and click the RSL URL line to bring up the window shown in Figure 16-3.

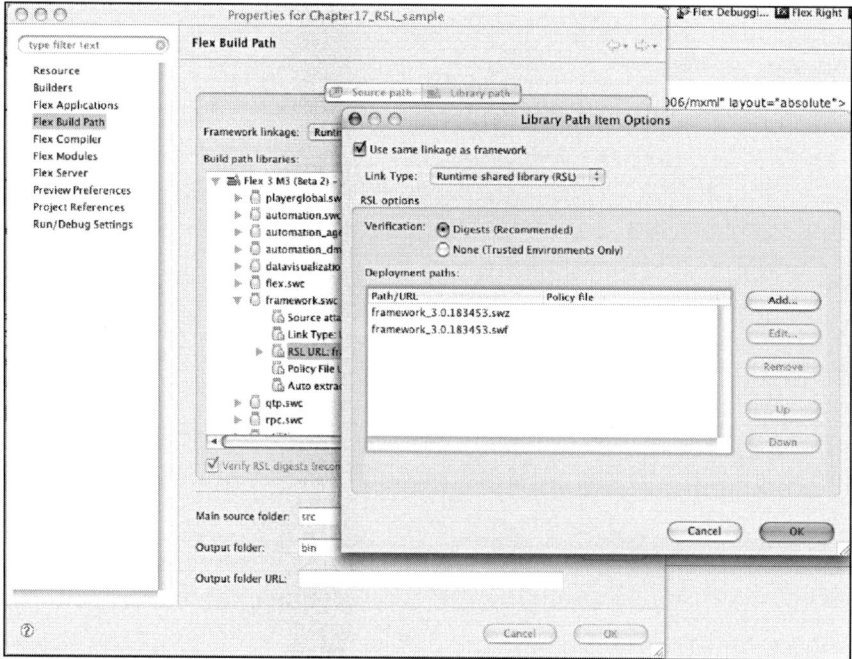

Figure 16-3. Setting up the extraction options

The Library Path Item Options window is where the compiler can be configured to not automatically generate the framework files and thus overwrite the Adobe-provided RSLs. To change this, select the SWZ file and click the Edit button. Another dialog window titled Edit RSL Deployment Path will pop up with a URL to the location of where the application should look for the framework file, the name of the file, and whether or not to copy the library file to the deployment path. By default the Copy library to deployment path option should be checked. Uncheck it for both the SWZ and SWF files (see Figure 16-4).

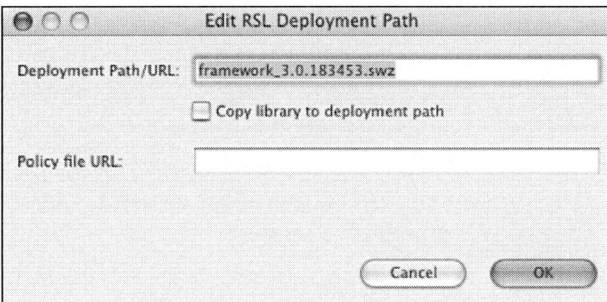

With the check box option turned off, you can now recompile the application, and this time the verify digest Flex error should no longer occur and the application should load properly.

Figure 16-4. Turning off auto-extraction on the framework files

Testing the caching

If you want to test the persistent framework caching, you can do so pretty easily. Since you have now successfully loaded your RSL test and you have Flash Player 9.0.60 or higher, you can simple rename or move the framework RSL files from the bin folder, and launch the application's HTML page. The framework should be cached in the player now, and you should still be able to launch your application without the SWZ and SWF framework files in the file system. The application has also shrunk from about 140K or so to 48K—a considerable difference in file size. Look at Figure 16-5 for a file size comparison.

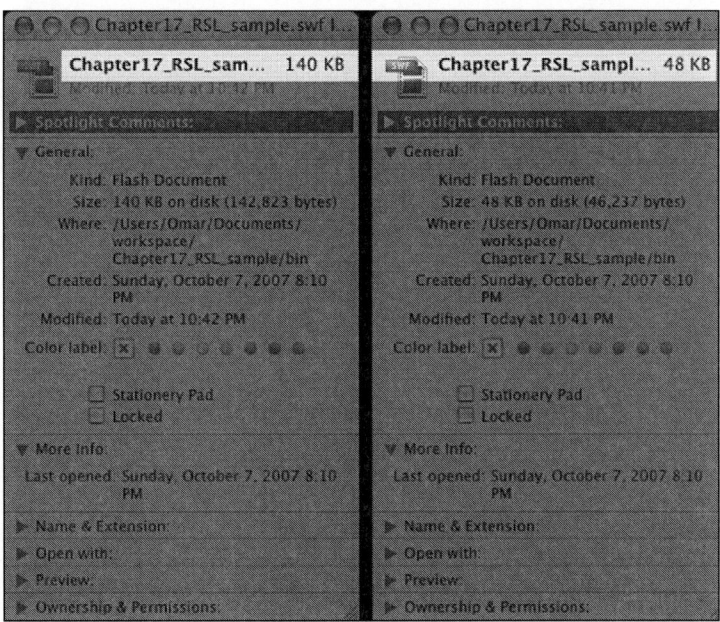

Figure 16-5. Before and after RSL file size comparison without debugging classes for an empty application

You don't have to use the Verify RSL digest option and the Adobe-supplied RSL files, but it's recommended that you do. They are created and signed by Adobe, they are reliable, many other developers around the world will be using the same RSLs, and many of your visitors will already have the required files cached—and after all, isn't that the whole point? And if they haven't they will only need to download it once!

Custom SWCs and RSLs

Although not cacheable by PFC, custom SWC and RSL files can also help to lighten the load of the main application file, as well as provide code portability for use among teams and be easily implemented from project to project.

In Figure 16-1, at the bottom, you can see an entry for a custom SWC named ABLibrary. This SWC contains classes and custom component classes we've built at Almer/Blank to use in our Flex projects. To create the SWC for use this way is quite simple actually. To build the SWC, I created a new Flex Library project in the Flex Builder Navigator pane. Place your "com" folder with all the classes you'd like to compile into a SWC on the root of your Library project folder. In the project properties for the Flex Library project, you can set which classes to include in the compile in the Flex Library Build Path section. Once all classes are chosen, simply right-click the project folder and click Build Project. In the bin folder will be your compiled SWC file to link to from other projects.

For the project you want to link your custom library, right-click the project folder and click Properties. In the Flex Build Path option, in the Library path tab, click the Add SWC button. Navigate to your SWC file and add it. The classes from the library will now be available in your project as if the class files themselves were in your source files folder.

The default option for the SWC Link Type setting will be Merged into code. If this is not what you want, you can change this to Runtime shared library and have your application load the SWC's RSL at runtime. To get the RSL SWF, simply open the SWC using a standard decompression tool, and a SWF file will be inside with the same name as the SWC. That file is your RSL to load.

Summary

In this chapter, I have covered how to reap the benefits of the new and improved runtime shared libraries and the new Flash Player persistent framework caching feature. In applications where multiple Flex SWF files are needed, runtime shared libraries help immensely to optimize the delivery of the application. Together with persistent framework caching, Adobe has finally come up with a good way to alleviate the hit that an application takes in file size by employing the Flex framework. And to make sure that applications stay safe, the verify digest feature is a good way to have some protection from a middle-man attack on your application. Plus the file sizes are great!

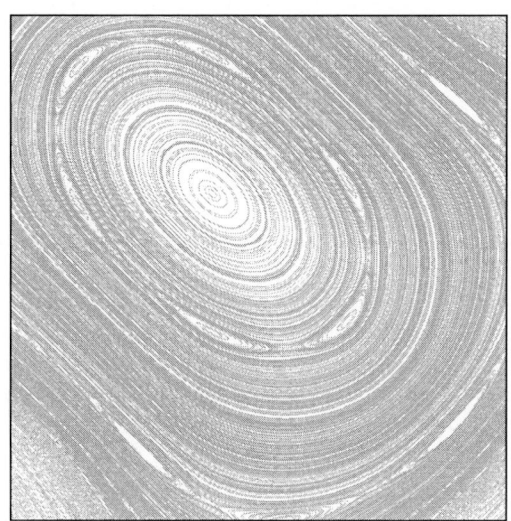

Chapter 17

SEARCH ENGINE OPTIMIZATION FOR FLEX

by Chris Charlton

Search engine optimization (SEO) is essentially a marketing strategy where the goal is to improve your site's traffic volume as well as the quality of that traffic. SEO can be a key requirement for some projects to be deemed successful, especially for content-based sites. The RMX, being one such site, has a lot of content, some of which is in formats that are easily accessible to search engines—our blogs, forums, and RSS feeds. But we also have event calendars, job postings, and videos that are exposed through rich Flex interfaces. These elements are not as accessible as plain HTML, but we want to ensure that the various search engines can easily find them too, and that's where SEO fits in.

Search engine friendliness is an important requirement for applications like the RMX, and it is often one reason why decision makers opt against Flash/Flex interfaces for these kinds of uses. But even if you use a Flash or Flex interface (which we think provides much better user experiences), you can include search engine optimization techniques to improve your visibility, rankings, and usefulness.

Now that's not to say that you'll always want your content exposed to the public. Sometimes your content is private—you want it found, but you don't want it directly accessible. In these situations, you might route users to a registration page first before they can access the content. In this chapter, I'll cover some of the traditional SEO techniques and explore how combining those with some of the new advances in this area can help make your Flex and Flash sites more accessible to the masses.

Using semantic markup to define content

Since Flex's inception (early 2004), content developers have been asked to make their creations index-able by the search engines. This is definitely not a foreign request, since those same demands have been made of Flash developers for several years prior to that. In the beginning, a lot of us were concerned with how the search engines would index our content, when the important question was and still is, *what* should the search engines index?

Since HTML pages are static, even with all the JavaScript in the world, it is second nature for a search engine's web crawler, or spider, to index and cache content when allowed. Unlike HTML, Flex applications have various states and views of the application, not separate pages. Are you at a disadvantage? Not really. The states and views mentioned are Flex's "pages," so you just need to feed the crawlers the right content to take back home with them, and then it's literally "Hello, World."

Head content

The first level of SEO for our Flex application is the HTML page in which it is embedded. When it comes to basic SEO, everyone knows about a page's <meta> tags, right? The famous keywords and description <meta> tags are your first steps of SEO. Think of your keywords list like a del.icio.us tag cloud: it's a list of words that organizes or groups your content so that people have a better chance of finding that content when performing their searches. Your description is a just brief summary of the page's content and should include some of your keywords for optimal impact. Here's a sample set of <meta> tags from our company web site to help illustrate:

```
<meta name="keywords" content=" Almer/Blank, R Blank, Markus Almer,
Macromedia Flash, Macromedia Flex, Macromedia Breeze, Flash
Actionscript, Flash Video, Flash Platform, Flash Application ➥
Development, Flash Animations, Configurators, Virtual Planning Tools,
Macromedia Certified Developers, Macromedia Alliance Partner,
Macromedia Solutions Provider, Flash Consulting, Flash Training, ➥
Flash Banners, Flash Design, Flash Designers, Flash Developer,
Flash Developers, Interactive Advertising, Interactive Marketing,
Interactive Application Development,
Action script, Rich Internet Applications, Broadcast Video, 3D, Rich
Entertainment Applications, XML, Motion Graphics, ➥
E-learning, Simulation Training,
User Experience, Usability, Interface Development, Interface Design,
Banner Design, Banner Development, Video Banner, Digital Marketing,
Digital Branding, EBusiness, EBusiness Consultant, Ecommerce,
ECommerce Implementation, Ecommerce Solutions, Best Flash
Developers, Best Flash Applications, Internet Advertising Services,
Internet Agency, Internet Consultants, Internet Branding, Internet
Marketing, Internet Services, Internet Solutions, Kiosk Development,
Flash Mobile, Online Advertising, Online Branding, Online Marketing,
Rich Media Banners, Viral Marketing, Web Design, Web Developer,
Web Developers, Web Development, Web Development Firm, Web
Development Agency, Web Site Development, Website Development,
Website Developer, Software Development, LA Flash User Group,
Interactive Media Agency in Los Angeles, Leading Flash Agency in
```

```
Los Angeles, Flash Programmers, Flash Content, " />
<meta name="description" content="Almer/Blank is an award-winning
application and video development agency. We offer consulting,
development and training services for the Flash Platform. "/>
```

If you're not comfortable compiling this info on your own or are just rusty, there are tools that can help you choose the right group of keywords. The best known of these come from Overture, a search engine company owned by Yahoo!, which offers a set of tools that allow you to query keywords and receive statistics on search popularity. The tools even provide recommendations, giving you insight on the best words for your money. Figure 17-1 shows partial results from a search on Flex.

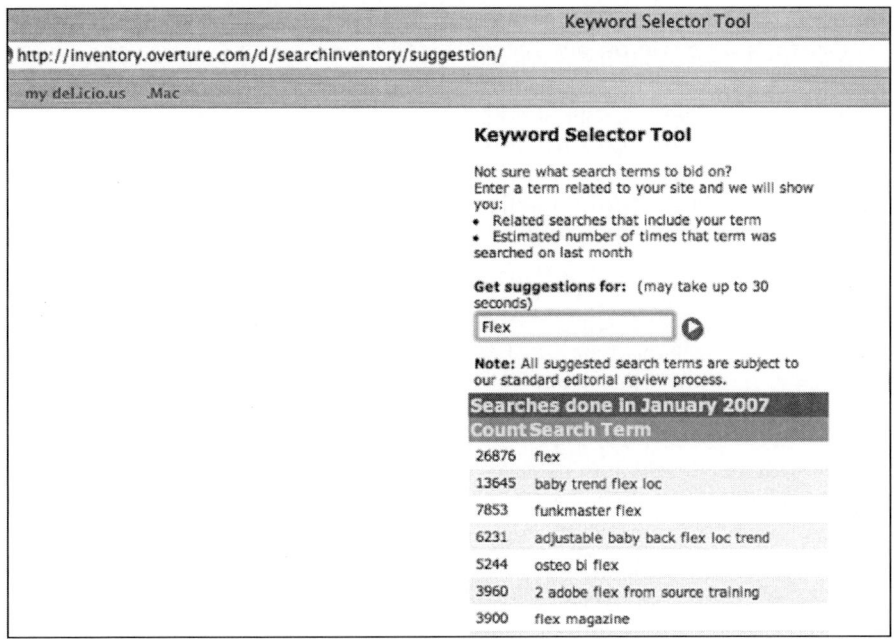

Figure 17-1. Results from Overture's keyword tool

> *The keywords list is limited to 1,024 characters, while descriptions should be between 120–150 characters. Staying within these limits will give you the widest reach among search engines, as each has different limit requirements.*

Are keywords and description <meta> tags by themselves enough? Some people like to think so. We'll cover deeper SEO techniques in a second, but before we're done with <meta> tags, you should know they don't end with just keywords and description. There are many uncommon <meta> tags like PICS-Label, Dublin Core, and rating. These tags can be used to further distinguish your content to, for example, mark your content safe for families and work. This could ensure that people using the Internet would be allowed to see your work with parental controls turned on.

The head content is not complete without a good page title to provide users with a "you are here" at the top of their browser window. The <title> tag is important head content too, since it's also an indexable element. Oftentimes, the title is interspersed with select keywords forming a brief one-line description. Use the same careful approach you use in defining your keywords and description when crafting your page titles, and your SEO becomes that much stronger.

I've covered a page's <head> element, now it's time to give the <body> its due.

Body content

Is there more to search engine placement than <meta> tags? Definitely. Careful crafting of the <body> content can really help with SEO. Even if you're not creating content-based sites, you still should pay attention to content in the <body> element although nothing may ever be seen by human eyes. This is an important concept to grasp as Flex developers, because we tend to specialize in Single Page Architectures (SPAs). In other words, our SWF is loaded once, and all subsequent views are served from that one HTML page. And, more often than not, that HTML page has nothing more than <OBJECT/> and/or <EMBED/> tags comprising the <body> element. One approach to overcome this deficiency is to provide alternate text content that is to be used in the event that the SWF can't be. Think of this extra content like the ALT attribute on an <IMG> tag. If the image can't be displayed for whatever reason, the text value of the ALT attribute is displayed instead. This is just good accessibility design and is also of tremendous benefit to SEO.

Search engine spiders don't care if something is blinking or turns red as they traverse a web page. Elements like these are of less importance to them. They just read and read until their bellies are full—which is never. Since we now know that their favorite food is textual content, we either want to feed the spiders that content or guide them through content that is there for them already.

Showing spiders what to read first and what other content exists on the page is really important. There is no black magic or JavaScript voodoo here. All this is accomplished by using only pure HTML tags. Remember HTML's heading tags, <h1>, <h2>, <h3>, <h4>, <h5>, and <h6>? How about the standard paragraph tag (<p>) and the common markup styles we take for granted like bold (<strong>) and italic (<em>)? All these have weight and add meaning for spiders. This information can be beneficial as you develop your SEO strategies for your Flex applications. For example, <h1> tags are heavier in weight than other heading tags, so you use those kinds of delineations to your advantage. Knowing that words that appear in a heading get more attention from the spiders can help you to really apply emphasis in places that will yield the most benefit. Each heading tag level defines an outline of a page's content as well as the weight of the content that it wraps. And, since spiders read a page top-down, this is one way that you can guide the spiders to the content you want noticed and to specify the order in which it's noticed.

As you structure your content in an ordinal fashion, you want to not only highlight the best content for the spider, but also deemphasize or obscure content of lesser or no search value. You also need to possibly include content that is helpful only for search purposes, but not for your human viewers.

So, if you're creating this spider-only content, how do you hide it from human users? The answer is CSS. You can easily use the following simple style declaration (CSS class) to hide any content on the page that you only want to be seen by spiders:

```
.hiddenContent
{
        visibility: none;
        display: none;
}
```

And any HTML on the page that you want to be "invisible" could apply the class like so:

```
<h1 class="hiddenContent">Very relevant content for my Flex ➡
application</h1>
```

Now you have content that you've tagged as "high priority" for the spiders without interfering with the user experience you've designed for your human visitors. With this, you definitely start to establish a "bridge" from your Flex content to the search spiders. Over the next couple of sections, I'll discuss XML and its role in SEO.

XML

A long-standing cousin to HTML is XML. In fact, XHTML is really XML, and so are all the popular syndication formats like RSS, ATOM, and RDF. There isn't a whole lot of buzz around search engines indexing XML files, but it's been going on for years. XML is just text, so why shouldn't search engines hunt for content in those files too? Have you ever clicked a search result link that took you to an RSS feed? Odds are you have. Some Flash-based sites are starting to utilize external XML for their content for some of the reasons that we've exposed thus far, like to offer a structured consumption "menu" to the spiders and to truly separate content from design. Using this concept, you could effectively offer an XML feed for your site or application.

XML feeds

Spiders consume XML like standard XHTML pages, but larger engines can recognize certain XML files by their formats and treat them accordingly. Syndication feeds (RSS, RDF, ATOM) are very popular, and search engines like this type of content because there's no fluff, just text. Not only does providing a feed for your content help humans who like that stuff, but it helps spiders who take full advantage of methods like auto-sensing feeds in your page and following them for more content. Auto-sensing is easy since you just point to a feed in a <link> tag, at the top of a page, in your <head> content with all that metadata you made sure was there. Here's an example of what one of those tags can look like:

```
<link rel="alternate" type="application/atom+xml" title=➡
"Will Graves" href="http://www.willgraves.com/blog/atom.xml" />
```

Smart spiders notice it's a feed and follow it and its links. So, do your best to inject relevant tags, data, and links in those feeds.

OPML is another neat format. Used for lists and outlines, OPML allows you to generate a list of feeds that spiders would follow indefinitely. Imagine search engine relevance when content is on your blog, forum, feeds, and even in a PDF on your site—all that would be indexed, and relevance would be taken into account. The OPML format is most commonly used by feed aggregators to exchange lists of feeds (e.g., FeedBurner, Firefox, and NewsGator). I believe that these creative uses of XML data are what gave birth to the newly popular Sitemaps Protocol format.

XML sitemaps

You should be familiar with a sitemap or site index. Way back when all web developers developed were HTML sites, a sitemap was a required page. Once these developers started developing complete sites in Flash/Flex, the sitemap became neglected. Well, it's time for Flash/Flex developers to rebuild that relationship thanks in part to the Sitemaps Protocol. Sitemaps are the best way for web masters to inform search engines about "pages" on their sites that are available for crawling. If you substitute your Flex "view states" for "pages," it would stand to reason that you should also be able to make use of sitemaps in your Flex SEO. In its simplest form, a sitemap is an XML file that lists URLs for a site, including additional metadata about each URL—when it was last updated, how often it usually changes, and how important it is relative to other URLs in the site. Using this data, search engines can crawl more intelligently through the site.

The Sitemaps Protocol was originally introduced by Google in 2005 and now has even wider adoption with Ask, Microsoft, and Yahoo! all offering support for it. What that means to us as Flex developers is that the biggest search engines around can all tap into the page information contained in that one sitemap file. So, let's look at a simple XML sitemap for the RMX:

```xml
<?xml version="1.0" encoding="UTF-8"?>
<urlset xmlns="http://www.sitemaps.org/schemas/sitemap/0.9">
    <url>
        <loc>http://www.richmediax.com/</loc>
        <lastmod>2007-01-01</lastmod>
        <changefreq>hourly</changefreq>
        <priority>1.0</priority>
    </url>
    <url>
        <loc>http://www.richmediax.com/news/</loc>
        <changefreq>daily</changefreq>
    </url>
    <url>
        <loc>http://www.richmediax.com/videos/</loc>
        <lastmod>2007-05-17</lastmod>
        <changefreq>daily</changefreq>
    </url>
    <url>
        <loc>http://www.richmediax.com/jobs/</loc>
        <lastmod>2007-05-18T18:12:15+00:00</lastmod>
        <priority>0.8</priority>
    </url>
    <url>
        <loc>http://www.richmediax.com/events/flex</loc>
        <lastmod>2007-05-20</lastmod>
    </url>
</urlset>
```

From this, you can see how I'm providing details about the content I'm linking to. Liken this to the HTML embellishments made earlier with the <h1> tags. Here I am saying that the home page is updated on an hourly basis and should have highest priority when it comes to crawling order. With the advancements made in generating bookmark-able Flash content, Sitemaps offers some pretty good insurance to supplement all your other SEO efforts. There's a lot more that Sitemaps can offer, and to cover it all would definitely be outside the scope of this book. To learn more about Sitemaps, visit http://sitemaps.org.

SWF metadata

Adding metadata to your SWF files is yet another way to improve your SEO. If you've used Flash 8 or CS3, I'm sure you're familiar with the window displayed in Figure 17-2.

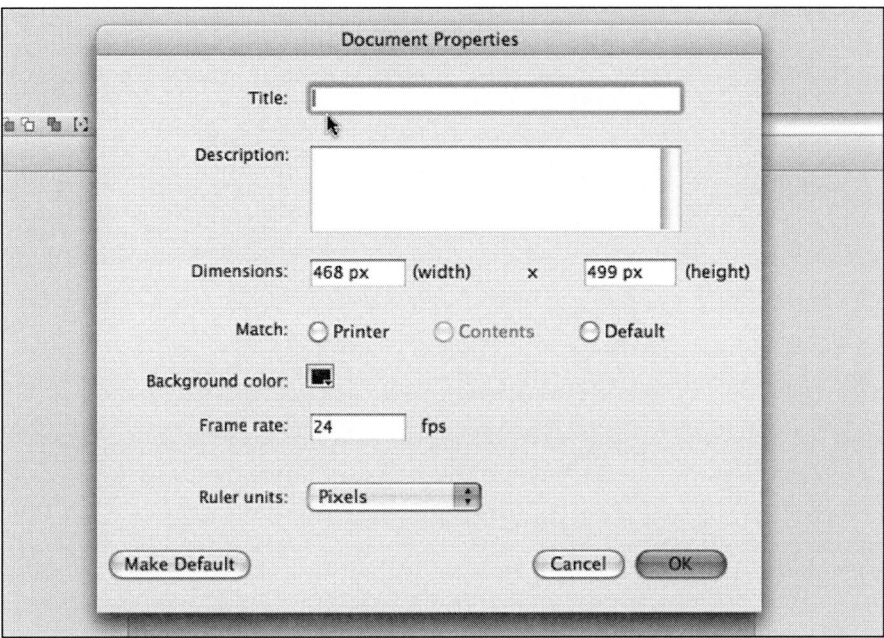

Figure 17-2. Adding metadata in Flash CS3

The title and description that you add via this dialog box is placed in the metadata of your SWF file and allows the search engines to make use of it when they index your SWFs. The process is a little more involved from the Flex side, though. You basically have three options: edit the <metadata> tag in your flex-config.xml file, add the extra metadata via the compiler options for your Flex project, or use a [SWF] metadata tag. The following is the default meta information found in your flex-config.xml:

```
<!-- Metadata added to SWFs via the SWF Metadata tag. -->
<metadata>
  <title>Adobe Flex 3 Application</title>
  <description>http://www.adobe.com/products/flex</description>
  <publisher>unknown</publisher>
  <creator>unknown</creator>
  <language>EN</language>
</metadata>
```

You can modify this and have it applied to all your projects, which may be a good option in an enterprise environment. In contrast, Figure 17-3 shows how you can add this information on a per-project basis inside of Flex Builder by simply pulling up the project Properties panel.

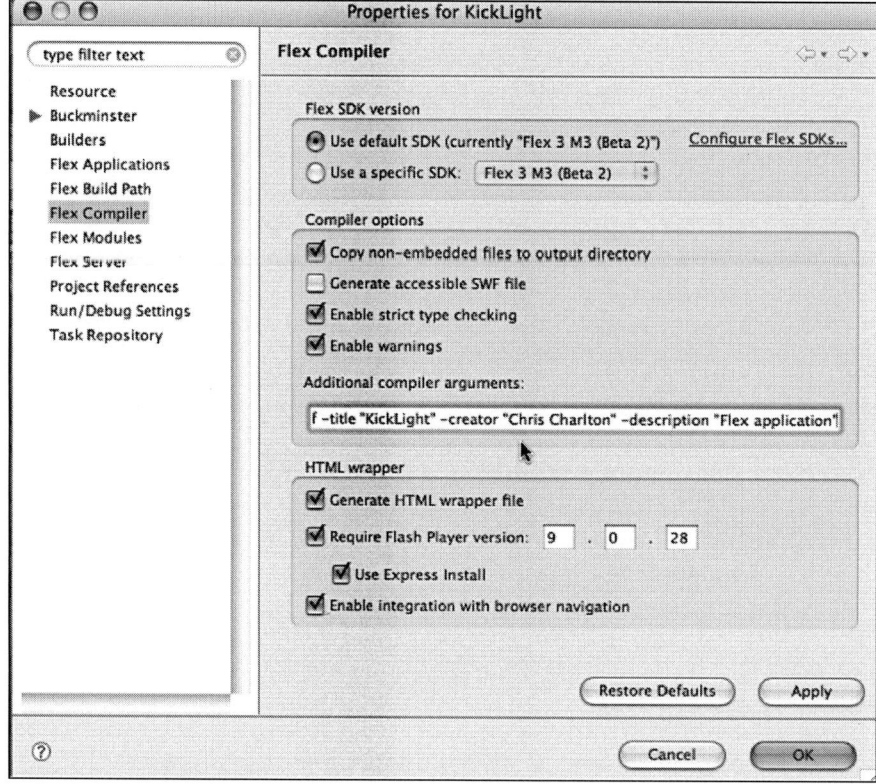

Figure 17-3. Adding metadata in Flex Builder

To make use of the third option, you can add a [SWF] metadata tag just before your class definition if you're using an ActionScript project or a custom ActionScript class as the base class for your MXML application.

```
[SWF(title="RichMediaX", description="Flex application", ➥
publisher="Almer/Blank")]
public class RmxBlog extends Application
{
  //rest of code...
```

Something to keep in mind with all of these options is you shouldn't rely solely on search engines actively consuming this information. Instead, be sure to also include this kind of information in your HTML page using any of the techniques covered earlier.

Clean URLs

Clean URLs, such as the ones I discussed in the section "Sharing permalinks" in Chapter 6, are great for legibility, bookmarking, and helping disguise server technology from the curious. Almost a decade ago, Google didn't properly index pages with URLs like page.php?id=1. Today that is not the case, but you should take notice that page.php?id=1 is not attractive or friendly. So, how do you clean that URL up? Well, if you're hosting your site on an Apache server, you can make use of the mod_rewrite module. This little engine will take in a clean URL that you've passed out and translate that into the actual URL. To implement this feature, you can create an .htaccess file and place that in the root directory of your web site. That file is a directory-level configuration file and just provides instructions on how to deal with the content in the directory it's located in. Inside of the .htaccess file you'll need a RewriteRule to instruct the server on how to handle your clean URLs. Here's a sample rule that will turn http://yoursite.com/page/1/ into *http://yoursite.com/page.php?id=1*:

```
<IfModule mod_rewrite.c>
  RewriteEngine on
  RewriteBase /
  RewriteRule ^([A-Za-z]+)/([0-9]+)/$ $1.php?id=$2 [L]
</IfModule>
```

What this does is it first checks whether or not the mod_rewrite module is available. If it is, it turns the module on. RewriteBase tells the server the starting point from which to process the rewrites. The rule says that anytime someone comes to this site looking for /page/1/, they need to be redirected to page.php?id=1. The caret, parentheses, and brackets are regular expression syntax that allows the string to be any string and the number to be any number within the ranges specified. Lastly, the [L], which stands for "LAST," is a parameter that tells the server how to perform the rewrite. A simple explanation is that this parameter tells the server to leave the clean URL in the user's address bar. It's a full URL mask. If you want to display the actual URL, just change that to an [R] to perform a hard redirect. For the complete 411 on mod_rewrite, you should check out Apache's documentation at http://tinyurl.com/a6a35. Sorry, couldn't resist that one. You'll get it after you visit the link.

The bottom line is this—help search engines by helping yourself. By using simple, clean URLs, your sites will not only be appreciated by all the humans who pass through, but also gain greater visibility as the spiders can index the text in your clean URLs much more efficiently. Just think of your URLs as another location to inject some solid keywords, and say hello to stronger SEO.

Deep linking

Everything that I've covered so far should be viewed as part of an overall strategy in making your Flex applications more searchable. And, thanks to Flex's new deep-linking support, you can use those clean URLs that you've just created to add URL mapping, or "bookmarking," capabilities to your Flex-based RIAs—meaning you can actually pretend you're surfing through separate pages when you move between states in your application, and the browser's address bar gets updated. There's work involved, but it's nice when it's done.

Flex 3 provides improved interaction between the Flex application and the browser to support the following use cases:

- When the application state changes, the browser URL can be updated to reflect the current state.
- The user should be able to bookmark the current URL, allowing the user to return to a specific state in the application.
- The user should be able to e-mail the current URL to another user, who could then enter the application at the specified state.

- The Back and Forward buttons should allow the user to navigate to recently visited application states.

- The application should receive notifications when the user has changed the address bar himself.

Flex 3 should solve these low-level browser interaction problems, enabling developers to build higher-level functionality on top. You can find more info on and see an example of this new feature in the Appendix.

Using FXT

Ted Patrick from Adobe has compiled a neat method for SEO in Flex that works very well. Known as FXT or Flex Templating (www.onflex.org/FXT/), this combination of XML, XSL, XHTML, and JS brings a whole new level of SEO-friendly data you can use in your Flex apps. What FXT does is it takes a Model-View-Controller (MVC) approach to serving up Flex apps in that the model (HTML page) drives the view of the Flex app. The data model remains untouched until it reaches the client, where it gets templated at runtime by an XSL style sheet instead of being compiled on the server. And since the page model is contained within the HTML, this solution ensures SEO compatibility by allowing search engine indexing, page ranking, and so forth.

At the core of this method are XML and XSL. Here's an example complete with metadata (XSL) and the data model (XML) combined:

```
<?xml version="1.0" encoding="ISO-8859-1"?>
<?xml-stylesheet type="text/xsl"
  href="http://directory.onflex.org/template002.xsl"?>
<html>
  <head>
    <title>Flex Directory - The consulting directory for
    Adobe Flex</title>
    <meta name="Description" content="An open listing
  of consulting firms providing development services for
Adobe Flex. Locate developers your your Flex projects."/>
    <meta name="Keywords" content="Adobe, Flex,
    ActionScript, Flash, consulting, development, services,
  outsourcing, RIA, Rich Internet Applications"/>
  </head>
  <company name="Almer/Blank"
contact="info@almerblank.com" url="www.almerblank.com"
partner="1" country="US" location="Venice CA US"
developers="10"/>
  <company name="Otuome Labs" contact=labs@otuome.com
  url="www.otuome.com" partner="0" country="US"
location="Los Angeles CA US" developers="1"/>
  <company name="Fingerprint Media"
    contact="info@fingerprintmedia.com "
url="www.fingerprintmedia.com" partner="0" country="US"
location="Los Angeles CA US" developers="2"/>
</html>
```

The preceding code is a pure XML representation of the example HTML content. First, I have my XML declaration specifying my version and encoding choices. Next, I load or attach an XSL style sheet to my content (more on that in a minute). After the style sheet is the root node, <html>, which is where I start defining the content. To keep it simple and relative, I'm using the same tags that I would if coding HTML. The <head> tag contains all the data that I want to appear in the <head> of the HTML page: title plus description and keywords <meta> tags. Following that is a series of <company> tags. Think of these as the HTML body. This is the data that will be rendered inside the Flex application. Now, back to the style sheet. Here's the code for that:

```
<?xml version="1.0" encoding="ISO-8859-1"?>
<xsl:stylesheet version="1.0"➥
  xmlns:xsl="http://www.w3.org/1999/XSL/Transform">
  <xsl:output method='html' version='1.0' encoding='UTF-8'/>
  <xsl:template match="/">
    <html>
      <head>
        <meta http-equiv="Content-Type" content="text/html; ➥
  charset=utf-8" />
        <title>Flex Directory</title>
        <script type="text/javascript"➥
    src="http://directory.onflex.org/swfobject.js"></script>
        <script type="text/javascript">
        // <![CDATA[
          function writeView(){
            var so = new➥
    SWFObject("http://directory.onflex.org/template002.swf", ➥
  "fxtxsl" , "100%" , "100%" , "9" , "#191919");
            so.addParam("scale" , "noscale");
            so.addVariable("xmlurl", document.location);
            so.useExpressInstall("http://directory.onflex.org/➥
  expressinstall.swf");
            so.write( 'flexcontent' );
            document.getElementById('logger').src= "/log.html"
          }

        // ]]>
        </script>
        <style type="text/css">
          /* hide from ie on mac \*/
          html {
            height: 100%;
            overflow: hidden;
          }
          #flexcontent {
            height: 100%;
          }
          /* end hide */
          body {
            height: 100%;
```

```
                    margin: 0;
                    padding: 0;
                    background-color: #191919;
                }
            </style>
            </head>
            <body scroll="no" onload="writeView()">
                <div id="flexcontent"></div>
                <iframe id="logger" style="visibility:hidden"/>
            </body>
        </html>
    </xsl:template>
</xsl:stylesheet>
```

This style sheet instructs browsers on how to render the XML data model. Notice the JavaScript in this XSL because that is what takes care of outputting the Flex application, as well as passing in a FlashVar path to the data model of the application. I activate the writeView() method following the onLoad() event of the <body> element. Inside that method I use SWFObject to render the application. SWFObject's addVariable() method passes in the URL of our data model (XML) to Flex for processing. Using this method, the browser will render the Flex, but search engine spiders don't even know or care about it. They get what they want, just the content, which should already be cached.

Summary

In this chapter, I talked about SEO: what it is, its importance to Rich Internet Application developers, and some of the techniques that Flex developers can use to achieve this often-elusive goal. Armed with these kinds of tools, there's no reason why the quantity and quality of the search traffic to your Flex applications wouldn't improve.

Now that you've got more traffic coming in, you'll see how you can pimp out your front end with an ActionScript 3 audio visualizer in the next chapter.

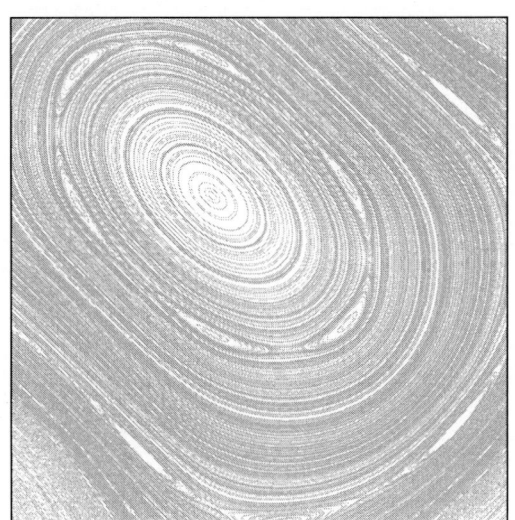

Chapter 18

BUILDING AN AUDIO VISUALIZER IN FLEX

By Hasan Otuome

Prior to Flash Player 9, Flash developers had to rely on third-party applications to create equalizer-type displays or audio visualizers. Now, thanks to improvements to the ActionScript language, you can create these experience enhancers natively. Combine that with the relative ease of use of the Flex framework, and you can come up with some pretty amazing visualizations with minimal effort. But before getting into exactly how to create one, I'll show you how the landscape has changed from ActionScript 2 to ActionScript 3.

In addition, this chapter introduces you to the SoundMixer class and the new ByteArray class, and discusses design planning and implementation.

AS2 vs. AS3

Before ActionScript 3, if you wanted or needed to include an audio visualizer in your Flash app, you had to use something like FlashAmp Pro, which examined your audio file and printed an array of amplitude values to a text file that you would then import into your FLA and use the values to animate your equalizer (EQ) movie clips. Figure 18-1 shows an example output file.

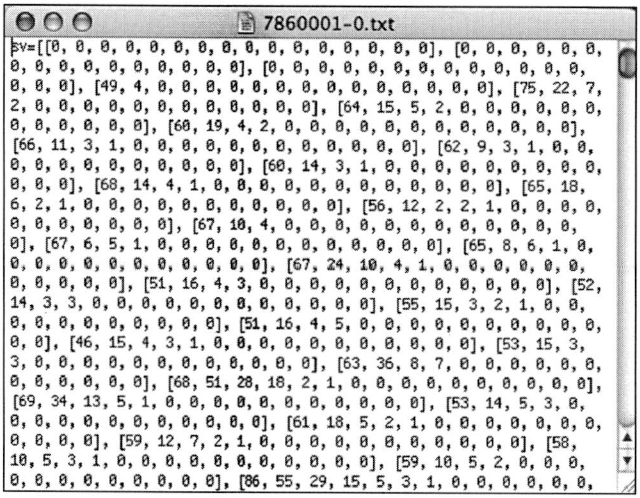

7860001-0.txt

```
sv=[[0, 0, 0, 0, 0, 0, 0, 0, 0, 0, 0, 0, 0, 0, 0, 0], [0, 0, 0, 0, 0, 0,
0, 0, 0, 0, 0, 0, 0, 0, 0, 0], [0, 0, 0, 0, 0, 0, 0, 0, 0, 0, 0, 0, 0,
0, 0, 0], [49, 4, 0, 0, 0, 0, 0, 0, 0, 0, 0, 0, 0, 0, 0, 0], [75, 22, 7,
2, 0, 0, 0, 0, 0, 0, 0, 0, 0, 0, 0, 0], [64, 15, 5, 2, 0, 0, 0, 0, 0, 0,
0, 0, 0, 0, 0, 0], [60, 19, 4, 2, 0, 0, 0, 0, 0, 0, 0, 0, 0, 0, 0, 0],
[66, 11, 3, 1, 0, 0, 0, 0, 0, 0, 0, 0, 0, 0, 0, 0], [62, 9, 3, 1, 0, 0,
0, 0, 0, 0, 0, 0, 0, 0, 0, 0], [60, 14, 3, 1, 0, 0, 0, 0, 0, 0, 0, 0, 0,
0, 0, 0], [68, 14, 4, 1, 0, 0, 0, 0, 0, 0, 0, 0, 0, 0, 0, 0], [65, 18,
6, 2, 1, 0, 0, 0, 0, 0, 0, 0, 0, 0, 0, 0], [56, 12, 2, 2, 1, 0, 0, 0, 0,
0, 0, 0, 0, 0, 0, 0], [67, 10, 4, 0, 0, 0, 0, 0, 0, 0, 0, 0, 0, 0, 0,
0], [67, 6, 5, 1, 0, 0, 0, 0, 0, 0, 0, 0, 0, 0, 0, 0], [65, 8, 6, 1, 0,
0, 0, 0, 0, 0, 0, 0, 0, 0, 0, 0], [67, 24, 10, 4, 1, 0, 0, 0, 0, 0, 0,
0, 0, 0, 0, 0], [51, 16, 4, 3, 0, 0, 0, 0, 0, 0, 0, 0, 0, 0, 0, 0], [52,
14, 3, 3, 0, 0, 0, 0, 0, 0, 0, 0, 0, 0, 0, 0], [55, 15, 3, 2, 1, 0, 0,
0, 0, 0, 0, 0, 0, 0, 0, 0], [51, 16, 4, 5, 0, 0, 0, 0, 0, 0, 0, 0, 0, 0,
0, 0], [46, 15, 4, 3, 1, 0, 0, 0, 0, 0, 0, 0, 0, 0, 0, 0], [53, 15, 3,
3, 0, 0, 0, 0, 0, 0, 0, 0, 0, 0, 0, 0], [63, 36, 8, 7, 0, 0, 0, 0, 0, 0,
0, 0, 0, 0, 0, 0], [68, 51, 28, 18, 2, 1, 0, 0, 0, 0, 0, 0, 0, 0, 0, 0],
[69, 34, 13, 5, 1, 0, 0, 0, 0, 0, 0, 0, 0, 0, 0, 0], [53, 14, 5, 3, 0,
0, 0, 0, 0, 0, 0, 0, 0, 0, 0, 0], [61, 18, 5, 2, 1, 0, 0, 0, 0, 0, 0, 0,
0, 0, 0, 0], [59, 12, 7, 2, 1, 0, 0, 0, 0, 0, 0, 0, 0, 0, 0, 0], [58,
10, 5, 3, 1, 0, 0, 0, 0, 0, 0, 0, 0, 0, 0, 0], [59, 10, 5, 2, 0, 0, 0,
0, 0, 0, 0, 0, 0, 0, 0, 0], [86, 55, 29, 15, 5, 3, 1, 0, 0, 0, 0, 0, 0,
```

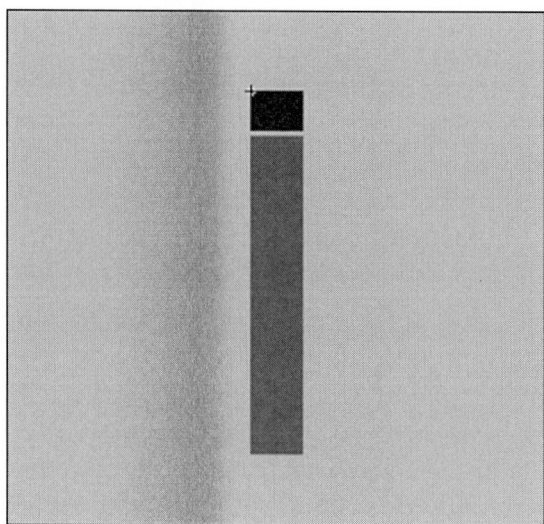

Figure 18-1. Sample FlashAmp Pro output file

If you wanted a visualizer that actually responded to the audio spectrum of a track, this was the only way. Although this method works, it is not the most streamlined, as you have to scan and create a peak file for each MP3, and then do some ActionScript coding to actually read these values on the fly and animate your clips accordingly. Following is a basic example of the process of creating an audio visualizer in AS2 using Flash 8.

Start off by creating a new Flash document and set the frame rate to 24 frames per second. Next, create a simple EQ band like the one in Figure 18-2.

Figure 18-2. Basic EQ-band graphic

After you've created your EQ graphic, convert it to a movie clip and start laying duplicates out on the stage until you have 16 of them like in Figure 18-3.

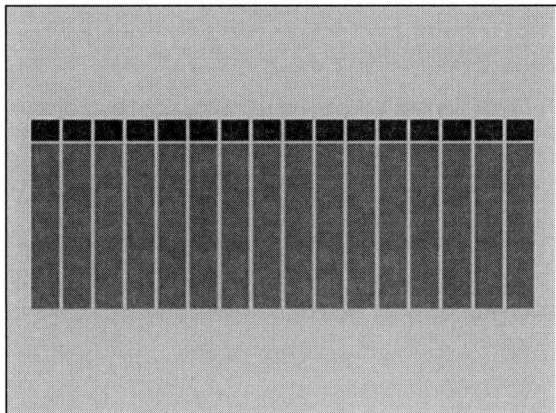

Figure 18-3. 16-band EQ

Once you've completed the EQ layout, give all instances names like s0, s1, and so on until all clips have instance names. After the naming phase, you can open your Actions panel by hitting Option+F9 (Mac) or Alt+F9 (Windows). Here you'll simply be including a reference to an external ActionScript file that you'll create in a minute. So, make sure that Layer 1 is selected, and then insert an include directive into your Actions panel:

```
#include flashamp.as
```

Now, in your favorite text editor, create a new text file and save it as flashamp.as. This is where all the ActionScript magic will happen. Note that the use of an external ActionScript file is completely optional. The code you are about to write can just as easily be inserted into your Actions panel inside of the Flash IDE.

As a matter of habit, I always start off my scripts with a variable declarations section. This serves as my dictionary that I can quickly reference as the code continually grows. So, the first few lines of our external script file are dedicated to just that purpose.

```
var i:Number;
var j:Number;
var index:Number;
var tl:MovieClip = this;
var alb:Number = 7860001;
var fps:Number = 24;
var numBands:Number = 16;
var titles:Array = new Array();
var tracks:Array = new Array();
var muzak:XML = new XML();
var spectrumInt:Number;
var spectrumUpdateInt:Number;
var spectrumArray:Array = new Array();
```

Here's a brief description of what these variables do:

- The first two are counter variables to be used later on in some looping construct.
- index is a counter variable for stepping through the XML playlist.
- tl is a reference to the main timeline.
- alb is a placeholder for the currently loaded album's ID.
- fps is the frame rate of the SWF.
- numBands is the number of EQ bands you're dealing with.
- titles will hold all the song titles for the playlist.
- tracks will hold all the URLs for the playlist.
- muzak will be the name for our XML object.
- spectrumInt will be used as the interval in the setInterval() function that spectrumUpdateInt will serve as the ID for.

Next, create a new Sound object for the MP3 you're going to load, and define what you want to happen when the song has loaded.

```
var snd:Sound = new Sound();
snd.onLoad = function(){
  snd.setVolume(50);
  snd.start(0, 1);
}
```

There's nothing fancy here. You're loading the song, cutting the volume in half so you don't blow any speakers, and starting playback. The next dilemma comes from how you process that spectrum data that FlashAmp Pro created for you. If you look at Figure 18-1 again, notice the double brackets after sv=. This means that FlashAmp Pro is outputting those spectrum values as a multidimensional array or arrays inside of an array. So, each EQ band has an array of values representative of that bandwidth's activity at a given point of the song. It's these values that you'll use to animate your movie clips, but first you have to get the values into Flash in a format that Flash can use. Enter the str2array function. This utility will parse that text file with the spectrum values and return an array formatted for use in your visualizer.

```
String.prototype.str2array = function(char){
  var spectrumValues:Array = this.split(" ").join("").split(char);
  var spectrumIndex:Number = 0;
  while(spectrumIndex < spectrumValues.length){
      spectrumValues[spectrumIndex] =
spectrumValues[spectrumIndex].split(char.split(",")[0]).join("")
.split(char.split(",")[1]).join("").split(",");
      spectrumIndex++;
  }
  return(spectrumValues);
}
```

That takes care of one of the hardest parts of the whole process. Now, you need to zero out all the EQ band clips. This gives your animation that home stereo quality.

```
for(i=0, i < numBands; i++){
  setProperty("tl.s"+i, _yscale, 0);
}
```

Here you use the global function setProperty(target:Object, parameter:Object, expression:Object) to change the _yscale of all your EQ clips from their defaults to 0. Now they will be hidden until audio playback begins. Next, you need to put the pieces in place to actually load the spectrum data. For this, the LoadVars object is perfect. Define a new LoadVars and set up a callback function for the onLoad event of the LoadVars like the following:

```
var spectrumLV:LoadVars = new LoadVars();
spectrumLV.onLoad = function(success){
  if(success){
    sv = this.sv.str2array("],[");
    return(sv);
  } else {
    trace("Error loading/parsing data");
  }
}
```

With your "spectrum reader" set up, you can now focus on loading the XML playlist.

```
muzak.ignoreWhite = true;
muzak.onLoad = getTrax;
muzak.load("playlist-7860001.xml");
```

You want to ignore any whitespace in the XML file and execute the getTrax() function once the file has been loaded. getTrax() is a key function, as it builds the playlist, loads the first track, loads the spectrum data for that track, and starts the spectrum animation.

```
function getTrax():Void{
  var trax:Array = this.firstChild.childNodes;
  for(i=0; i < trax.length; i++){
    titles.push(trax[i].attributes.lbl);
    tracks.push(trax[i].attributes.src);
  }
  index=0;
  snd.loadSound(tracks[0]);
  file = alb+"-"+index+".txt";
  spectrumLV.load(file);
  setStatus();
}
```

You see the last line of the getTrax() function makes a call to the setStatus() function. This function will set the initial positions for the EQ clips and set an interval by which to update the EQ display with new spectrum data.

```
function setStatus(){
  spectrumInt = Math.floor(snd.position/1000*fps);
  spectrumUpdateInt = setInterval(updateSV, spectrumInt, snd);
}
```

So, you use spectrumInt to figure out the frequency or how often you want the animation to be updated. Next, you tell Flash that you want to call the updateSV() function every spectrumInt and you're passing your Sound, snd, as an optional parameter to updateSV(). The updateSV() function will take care of the actual clip animations by reading the spectrumArray and updating the corresponding _yscale property of each clip based on the current spectrum value multiplied by the volume to account for user-initiated volume adjustments.

```
function updateSV(){
    var spectrumPos:Number = Math.floor(snd.position/1000*fps);
    vol = snd.getVolume()/100;
    for(i=0; i < numBands; i++){
        setProperty("tl.s"+i, _yscale, spectrumArray[spectrumPos][i]*vol);
    }
}
```

Now, that wasn't extremely painful, but it wasn't exactly painless either. Thanks to the advancements made to the ActionScript language and the new ActionScript Virtual Machine in Flash Player 9, you can bypass some of these steps and still produce some really cool user experiences. The first improvement worth exploring is the new SoundMixer class.

Introducing the SoundMixer

The SoundMixer class, found in the flash.media package, contains static properties and methods for global sound control in a SWF file. The SoundMixer class controls embedded streaming sounds in a SWF; it does not control dynamically created Sound objects or Sound objects created in ActionScript. It's a top-level class inheriting directly from Object, and it has a few properties and methods that you'll be tapping into to build your Flex visualizer. The most important method of the SoundMixer class is computeSpectrum(outputArray:ByteArray, FFTMode:Boolean, stretchFactor:int). What this method does is it takes a snapshot of the current sound wave and places it into the specified ByteArray object. This process is very similar to what FlashAmp Pro does when it creates that text file for you. Here, you're able to keep it all in-house.

The computed values are formatted as normalized floating-point values that range from −1.0 to 1.0 and are stuffed into the outputArray parameter, a ByteArray object that holds the values associated with the sound. The size of this ByteArray object is fixed at 512 floating-point values, with the first 256 representing the left channel of audio and the second 256 values representing the right channel. FFTMode is a Boolean value indicating whether a Fourier transformation is performed on the sound data first. A **Fourier transformation**, named after French mathematician and physicist Joseph Fourier, is a mathematical operation where you break something (technically referred to as the **function**) down into a series of related elements (aka the components). A good example is a musical chord (function) and the individual notes that make up the chord (components).

Setting the FFTMode parameter to true causes the method to return a frequency spectrum instead of the raw sound wave. In the resulting frequency spectrum, low frequencies are represented on the left, and high frequencies are on the right. The stretchFactor parameter deals with the resolution of the sound samples. The default is 0, which equates to data being sampled at 44.1 kHz. A value of 1 cuts that in half, reducing it to 22.05 kHz and so on.

> *This method is subject to local file security restrictions (aka restrictions on cross-domain loading). If you're working with sounds loaded from a server in a different domain than the calling SWF, you might need to utilize a cross-domain policy file.*

All of this newly built-in functionality will prove very handy. But before moving any further, you need to get an understanding of the seemingly mysterious ByteArray.

Understanding the ByteArray

The ByteArray class, found in the flash.utils package, offers methods and properties that optimize reading, writing, and working with data on a binary level (1s and 0s). To understand how cool this is, consider how the new ActionScript Virtual Machine in Flash Player 9 deals with things behind the scenes. The most compact representation of in-memory data is a **packed array**, or an array of bytes packed into a specialized format to improve computational performance. That's why this class is perfect for creating audio visualizers. You can perform a complex computational analysis on an audio file via SoundMixer.computeSpectrum() and easily gain access to the results through a ByteArray instance using standard ActionScript array access operators [].

Now, while the ByteArray class has a bevy of properties and methods that enable you to really optimize your data storage, streaming, and performance, you'll be using just one method for this project, readFloat(). readFloat() reads an IEEE 754 single-precision floating-point number from the byte stream and returns that number. Don't freak out about IEEE 754. It's just the standard for binary floating-point arithmetic. It defines the formats for representing floating-point numbers. "Single-precision" just means the number occupies 32 bits or 4 bytes of data.

So, what this means for your visualizer is that you'll use computeSpectrum() to take the audio stream and stuff the analysis of it into a ByteArray instance, and then you'll use readFloat() to return numerical data from the stream that will be used to create an accurate animation of the audio spectrum. Armed with knowledge of the tools required, you should now be ready to build it, so let's get started.

Design planning

When it comes to architecting your Flex applications, you have a lot of options. You can build them out using just MXML markup, ActionScript, or various combinations of the two. For this sample project, you'll need to use a combination. This visualizer will implement the code-behind technique, which is basically MXML markup powered by an ActionScript class.

To get started, open up your copy of Flex Builder or Eclipse. Next, create a new project either by right-clicking in the Navigator panel and selecting New ➤ Flex Project or by selecting File ➤ New ➤ Flex Project from the application menu. In the New Flex Project window that pops up, you want to keep the default selection for how the application will access data since you won't be using any of the options in this project. Click Next and name the project visualizer. After you've named it, click Finish.

Flex will create a main application file with the same name as your project that's empty and ready to be filled. Leave that alone for the time being, as you're going to create your Equalizer component and your Visualizer class first. In the Navigator panel, right-click your new project and select New ➤ Folder. Name this new folder components, make sure it's selected, right-click, and choose New ➤ MXML Component. Name this new component Equalizer and base it on Canvas. Once the file is opened, input the following into the file:

```
<?xml version="1.0" encoding="utf-8"?>
<mx:Canvas xmlns:mx="http://www.adobe.com/2006/mxml">

    <mx:HBox id="bands"/>

</mx:Canvas>
```

Save the file and set it to the side for now. In your main file, add a namespace that points to that components folder you created earlier by inserting this line into the root tag of your main application file:

```
xmlns:com="components.*"
```

This informs the compiler that you plan to have XML tags in your application that start with com and that these tags are pointed at files located in the components subdirectory. Now that you've added that namespace, you can add an instance of your Equalizer component to the application by inserting the following line into visualizer.mxml:

```
<com:Equalizer id="eq" horizontalCenter="0" verticalCenter="0"/>
```

The most important of the three attributes in this tag is the id since that's how you'll be able to talk to the component from the Visualizer class that you'll soon create. The other attributes relate to the layout of the Equalizer component, which in this case is pinned to the center of the browser window. Your modified main application file should now look like the following:

```
<?xml version="1.0" encoding="utf-8"?>
<mx:Application
    xmlns:mx="http://www.adobe.com/2006/mxml"
    xmlns:com="components.*"
    layout="absolute">

    <com:Equalizer id="eq" horizontalCenter="0" verticalCenter="0"/>

</mx:Application>
```

Now that you've created your EQ component and added it to your application, you're ready to bring this project to life by creating your Visualizer class, which will be responsible for loading the MP3 and drawing the visualizations.

The visualization

This is where you'll breathe life into your project by writing a Visualizer class that will serve as the backbone of your entire application. Your application will literally become an instance of the Visualizer class thanks to code-behind. So, first thing you want to do is create the location where the class will reside, aka the package. In the Navigator panel, right-click, choose New ➤ Folder, and name the folder com. With the com folder selected, create another new folder and name it almerblank. Now, with the almerblank folder selected, create another new folder named media. Once you're done, you will have created the package where the Visualizer class will live. Now, it is time to create your class, so, with the media folder selected, select New ➤ ActionScript Class, name the new class Visualizer, and ensure that it extends Application.

Flex Builder will then open the new class file complete with some basic stub code. Now would be a good time to import all the necessary classes that you'll be making use of in this class. So, make sure your import section looks as follows:

```
package com.almerblank.media {
  import mx.core.Application;
  import flash.media.Sound;
  import flash.media.SoundChannel;
  import flash.media.SoundMixer;
  import flash.utils.ByteArray;
  import flash.net.URLRequest;
  import flash.events.*;
  import flash.filters.*;
  import mx.events.*;
  import components.Equalizer;

  public class Visualizer extends Application {
```

That takes care of all of your external requirements, so you can now start declaring and defining your public and private variables. This class will only have one public, or externally accessible, property, and that's the file property, which will hold the URL to the MP3. You'll use a public setter and getter to retrieve the externally defined value and set the private variable _mp3. So, add the following lines inside of your class definition:

```
public class Visualizer extends Application {
  [Inspectable]
  private var _mp3:String;

  public function get file():String {
    return _mp3;
  }

  public function set file(str:String):void {
    _mp3 = str;
  }
```

Next, you want to create private variables for your Sound and SoundChannel objects, variables for the left and right audio peaks, and a public variable for your Equalizer component. For the code-behind to work, this variable's name needs to be the same as the ID that you gave your component when you added it to the main application file. Since it's named eq, this class variable should be named eq. Your variable declaration section should now look like the following:

```
public class Visualizer extends Application {
  [Inspectable]
  private var _mp3:String;

  public function get file():String{
    return _mp3;
  }

  public function set file(str:String):void{
    _mp3 = str;
  }

  private var _sound:Sound;
  private var _channel:SoundChannel;

  private var _leftStereoBarX:int = 131;
  private var _rightStereoBarX:int = 140;

  public var eq:Equalizer;
```

If you're wondering about the values for _leftStereoBarX and _rightStereoBarX, they're nothing special. These values were reached through trial and error. Feel free to play around with them to achieve your desired effect. With your variables declared, it's safe to move on to the constructor function. Your constructor should already have a call to its superclass, which in this case is Application. You now need to do two things; set the background color of the app and add an event listener for the creationComplete event. Your constructor should look like the following:

```
public function Visualizer() {
  super();
  this.setStyle("backgroundGradientColors", [0x0033cc, 0x191970]);
  addEventListener(FlexEvent.CREATION_COMPLETE,➡
    _creationCompleteHandler);
}
```

Here you've set the background color to a blue gradient and are delaying any further processing until Flex fires a creationComplete event for the application. This is clearly a matter of preference, as I don't like to have a whole lot going on in my constructors. Next thing you need to do is create the event handler for that Flex event. This handler will create a listener for the ENTER_FRAME event, initialize the Equalizer component, and load and play the chosen MP3 file. Following is the code for that event handler:

```
private function _creationCompleteHandler(event:FlexEvent):void {
  addEventListener(Event.ENTER_FRAME, _onEnterFrame, false, 0, true);
  _initEQ();
```

```
    _sound = new Sound(new URLRequest(_mp3));
    _channel = _sound.play();
}
```

Next, you want to create your initEQ() method, which is responsible for drawing all the background lines inside of your Equalizer component.

```
private function _initEQ():void {
  var eqX:uint;
  var eqY:uint;

  //draw background lines for the eq
  eq.bands.graphics.lineStyle(.1, 0xcccccc, .1);

  for(var i:uint = 2; i < 26; i++) {
    eqX = i*5;
    for(eqY = 0; eqY < 40; eqY+=2) {
      eq.bands.graphics.moveTo(eqX, -eqY);
      eq.bands.graphics.lineTo(eqX+4, -eqY);
    }
  }

  //draw the background lines for the left/right peaks
  for(eqY = 0; eqY < 60; eqY +=2) {
    eq.bands.graphics.moveTo(_leftStereoBarX, - eqY);
    eq.bands.graphics.lineTo(_leftStereoBarX+8, - eqY);
  }

  for(eqY = 0; eqY < 60; eqY +=2) {
    eq.bands.graphics.moveTo(_rightStereoBarX, - eqY);
    eq.bands.graphics.lineTo(_rightStereoBarX+8, - eqY);
  }
}
```

First, you declare two variables, eqX and eqY, that will be used as *x*- and *y*-coordinates when you start drawing your lines. The third line of code is where you define the characteristics of your drawing pencil. It also demonstrates another difference between AS2 and AS3. In ActionScript 2, you draw directly on your movie clips; but in ActionScript 3, all methods that you can use to create a vector shape are part of a new Graphics class, and your display objects, like Sprites and MovieClips, have a graphics property, which is a Graphics object. So, think of this property as your new sketchpad.

The first for loop is responsible for drawing all the EQ background lines. The inner for loop found inside this one is used to determine the bars' height. The += notation just provides the gaps between the bars. The other two for loops draw the background lines for the left and right peaks, respectively. With the EQ initialization completed, you can add the event handler for the ENTER_FRAME event, which will simply call the drawEQ() method every frame.

```
private function _onEnterFrame(event:Event):void {
  _drawEQ();
}
```

Now, you're ready for the drawEQ() method, which is where it really gets magical. Here you'll run computeSpectrum on the audio every frame and use the readFloat() method to get the numerical data necessary to animate your graphics.

```
private function _drawEQ():void {
  var singleBand:Number = 0;

  //create the byte array
  var eqBytes:ByteArray = new ByteArray();

  //fill it with data
  SoundMixer.computeSpectrum(eqBytes);

  //clear the graphics object every trip
  eq.bands.graphics.clear();

  eq.bands.graphics.beginFill(0xff6600, .1);

  //create the left channel visualization
  for(var i:uint = 0; i < 256; i++) {
    singleBand += eqBytes.readFloat()*2;

    if(i%10==0 && i > 0 && i != 10) {
      for(var a:uint = 0; a < singleBand; a++){
        eq.bands.graphics.beginFill(0xff6600, a/4);
        eq.bands.graphics.drawRect(i/2, -(a*2), 4, .2);
      }
      singleBand = 0;
    }

    if(i == 10){
      singleBand = 0;
    }
  }

  //draw the stereo bars
  for(a = 0; a < _channel.leftPeak*20; a++) {
    eq.bands.graphics.beginFill(0x66CC00, a/10);
    eq.bands.graphics.drawRect(_leftStereoBarX, -(a*2), 8, .5);
  }

  for(a = 0; a < _channel.rightPeak*20; a++) {
    eq.bands.graphics.beginFill(0x66CC00, a/10);
    eq.bands.graphics.drawRect(_rightStereoBarX, -(a*2), 8, .5);
  }
  eq.bands.graphics.endFill();
}
```

In this method, you define two variables, singleBand and eqBytes. singleBand deals with each individual EQ bar, and eqBytes is the ByteArray that is used to store the data retrieved with computeSpectrum(). The for loops in this method are very similar to the ones from initEQ(). They are responsible for drawing the EQ bars and peak bars. Instead of drawing lines, here you're drawing rectangular fills.

That completes the Visualizer class. All that's left to do is convert the main application file from an instance of the Application class to an instance of the Visualizer class. First, add a new namespace to the main tag that points to the package that Visualizer lives in, and then add a file property and set its value to the URL where your MP3 is located. Your modified application file should appear as follows:

```
<?xml version="1.0" encoding="utf-8"?>
<almerblank:Visualizer
  xmlns:mx="http://www.adobe.com/2006/mxml"
  xmlns:almerblank="com.almerblank.media.*"
  xmlns:com="components.*"
  layout="absolute"
  file="http://www.almerblank.com/songs/1/01.mp3">

  <com:Equalizer id="eq" horizontalCenter="-40" verticalCenter="0"/>

</almerblank:Visualizer>
```

You can now run the application to see what it looks like by choosing Run ➤ Run, clicking the Run icon on the toolbar, or pressing Ctrl+Enter (Windows) or Cmd+Enter (OSX).

Summary

In this chapter, I covered one method of building an audio visualizer in Flex. I shared with you some of the differences between accomplishing this task in Flex vs. older versions of Flash. I also explored the two ActionScript classes that allow you to easily create these visualizations without the use of third-party tools. You have many more options available to you like creating waveform analyses, and so forth, and with the power of ActionScript 3 behind you, the sky's the limit. Now, it's up to you to take what you've learned, extend it, and create some truly amazing visual effects.

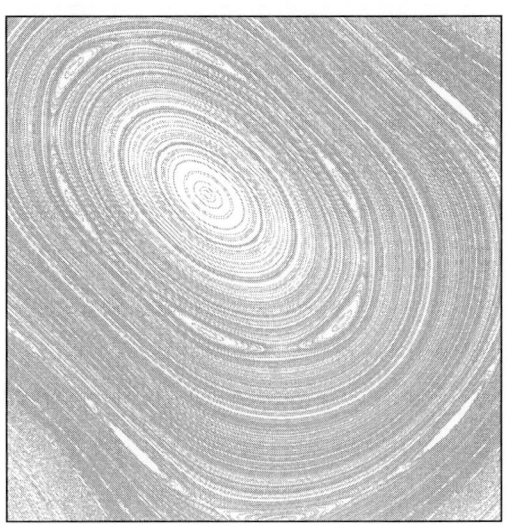

Appendix

THE EVOLVING FLEX SCENE

By Hasan Otuome

As if Flex 2 wasn't groundbreaking enough, Adobe has raised the bar even higher with the next release of the Flex framework. Chock-full of new development-enhancing features, Flex 3 promises to change the way we all develop Rich Internet Applications (RIAs). Some of the improvements that Flex 3 introduces are improved designer and developer workflow, code enhancements, component and Software Development Kit (SDK) enhancements, and smaller SWF sizes.

In this chapter, I'll cover what's different in Flex 3, the Flash-Flex Integration Kit, and what open sourcing Flex means.

Designer/Developer workflow

Flex 3 introduces many enhancements that aid in the workflow between developers and designers as well as improves skinning of all aspects of a Flex app. Some of those enhancements include the new Skin Importer and CSS outlines.

Skin Importer

With the new Skin Importer, you can select a folder of bitmaps or a SWF or SWC file and import them into a Flex project. The Import wizard will take care of mapping your assets to skin-able elements in the Flex 3 SDK. To import a folder of bitmaps, follow these steps:

1. Select File ➤ Import.

2. Select Skin Artwork from the Flex import category, as shown in Figure A-1, and click Next.

3. Choose your source and destination folders, as shown in Figure A-2, and click Next.

4. Select the skins to import and set their style and part names (see Figure A-3). When you're done, click Finish.

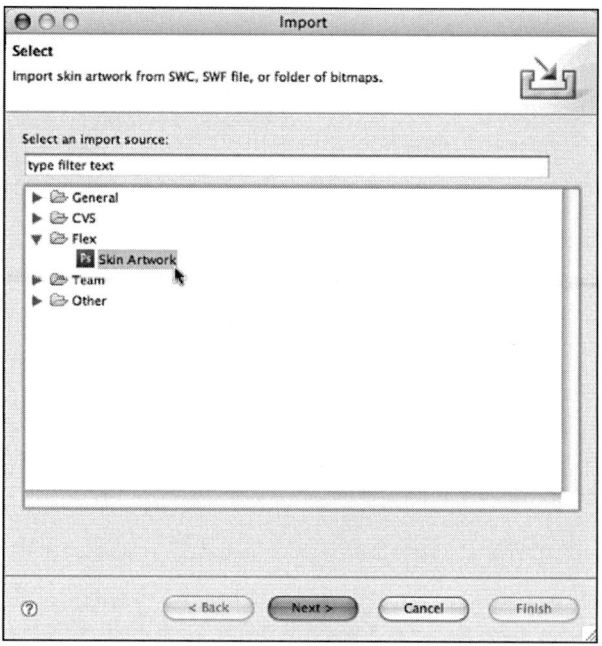

Figure A-1. Selecting Skin Artwork

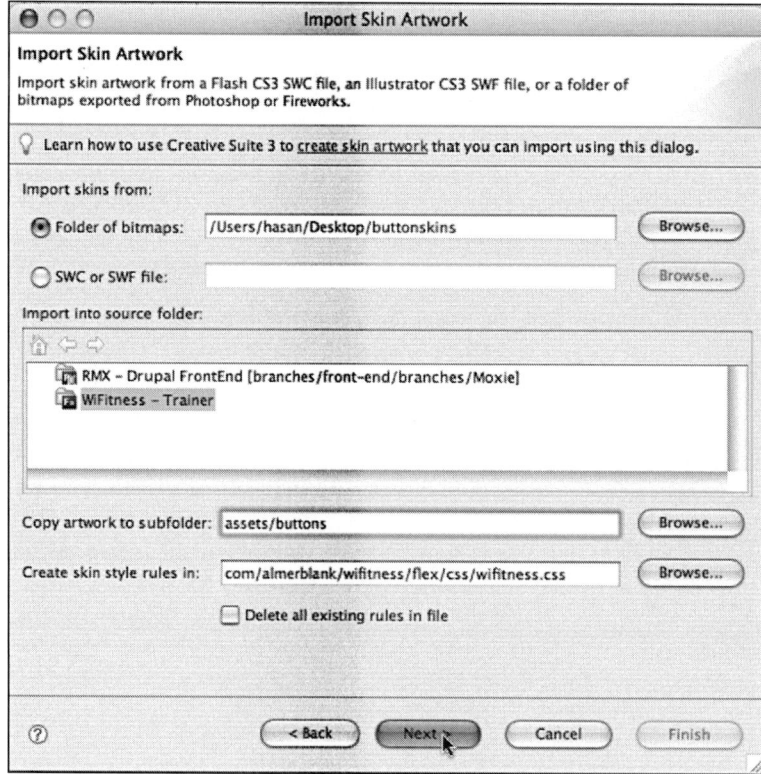

Figure A-2. Choosing source and destination folders

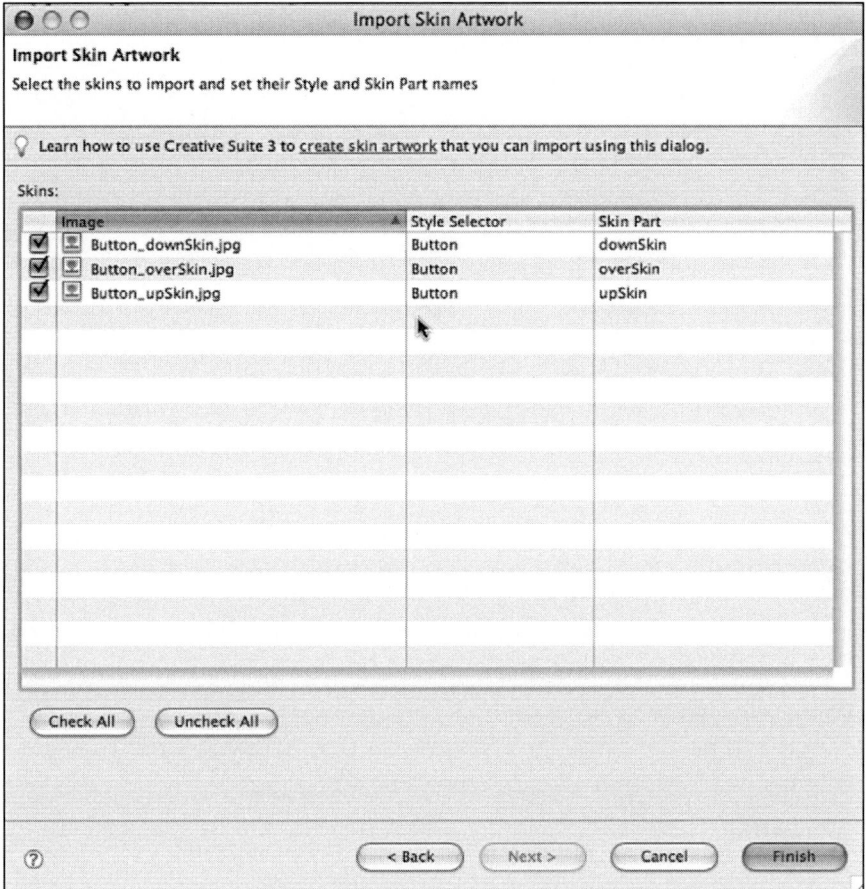

Figure A-3. Selecting the skins to import and setting their style and part names

CSS outlines

I really appreciate the CSS outlines feature, as I personally try to keep all of my styling information in external CSS files. With this feature, I can traverse my CSS document and find a style definition quickly and easily just as I have grown accustomed to doing in code view with my MXML and ActionScript files. From CSS outline view (see Figure A-4), when I select a style property, Flex 3 automatically navigates to that property, as Figures A-5 and A-6 illustrate.

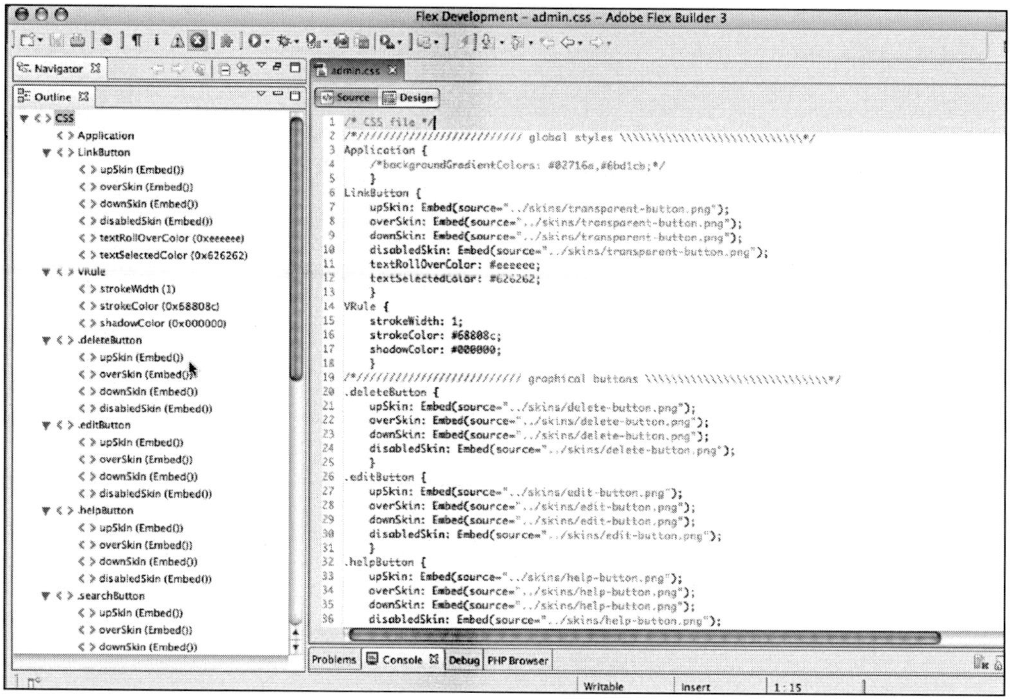

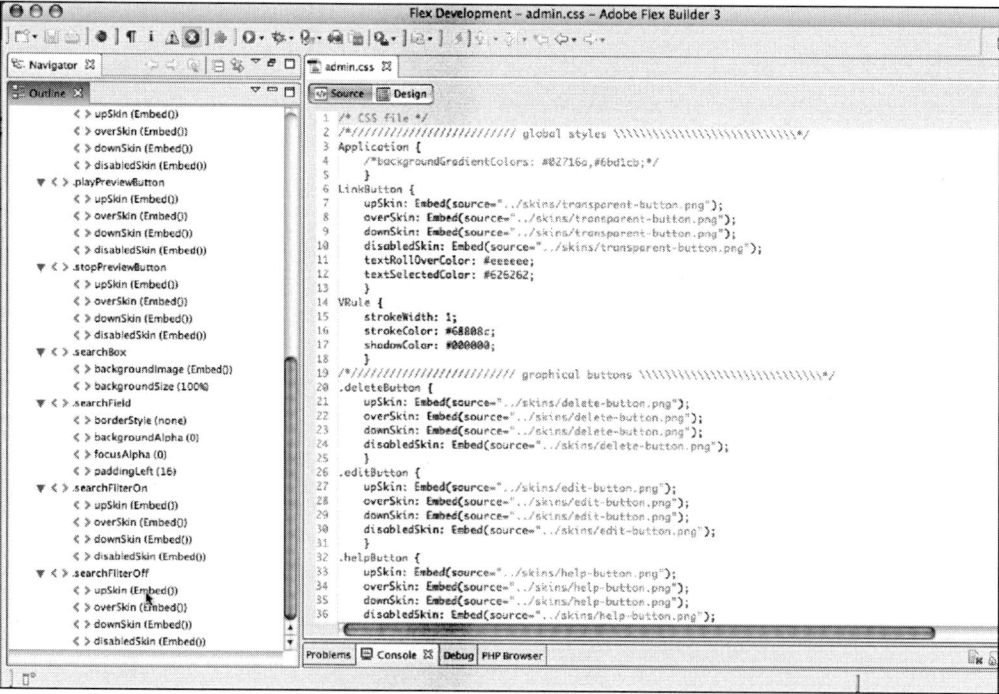

Figure A-4. CSS outline view

Figure A-5. Choosing a style property

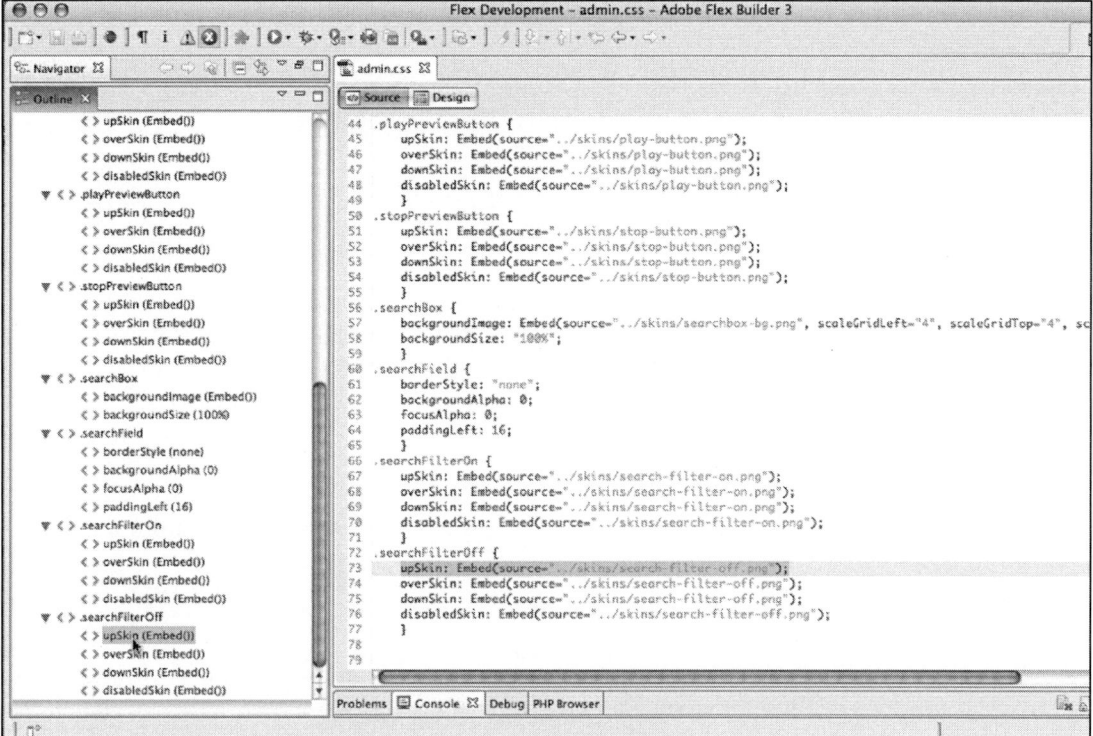

Figure A-6. Flex 3 automatically navigates to the selected style property.

Code enhancements

The following sections discuss new Flex 3 features designed to help make your coding easier.

Refactoring

The new refactoring feature in Flex 3 has to be one of my personal favorites. This feature enables method, class, and variable renaming at the project level and does so pretty quickly. Case in point: I was working on a section of the RMX application and started to develop a custom component for one of the views. After I completed the component, I realized I wanted to change the name of the component, but I didn't want to go through the chore of opening up all of the various files that made up the component or used the component—enter refactoring. To refactor my custom component throughout the project, I chose the class to refactor and then specified a new name, as illustrated in Figures A-7 and A-8. Figures A-9 and A-10 show the updated MXML and ActionScript after refactoring.

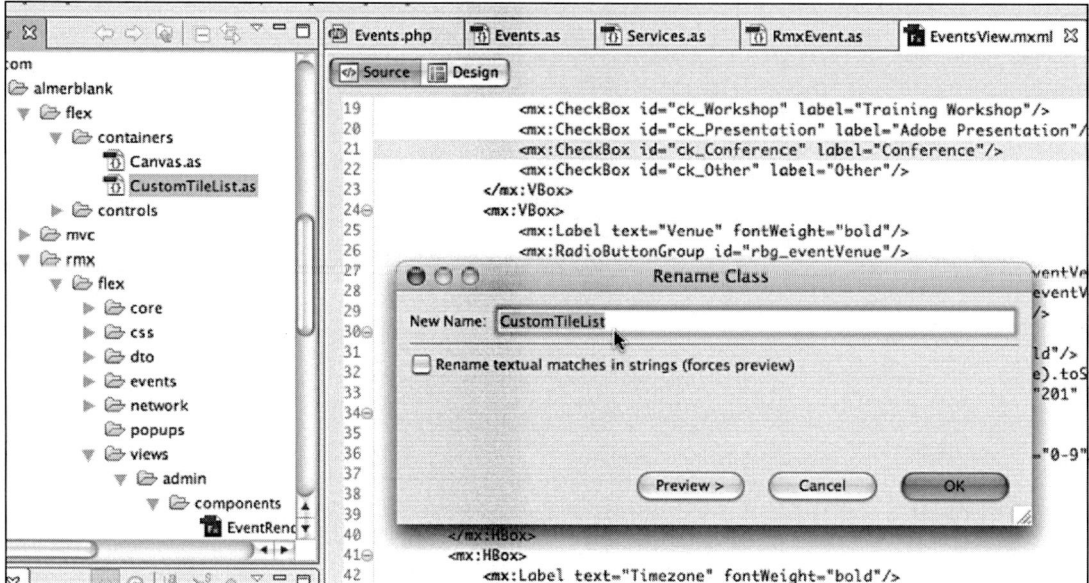

Figure A-7. Choosing the class to refactor

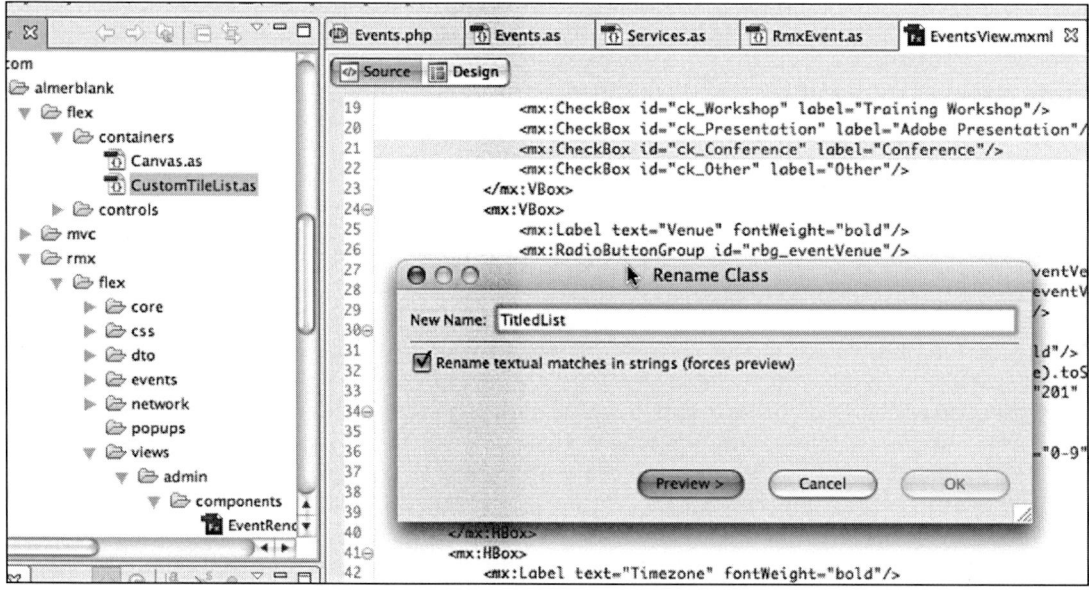

Figure A-8. Choosing the new class name

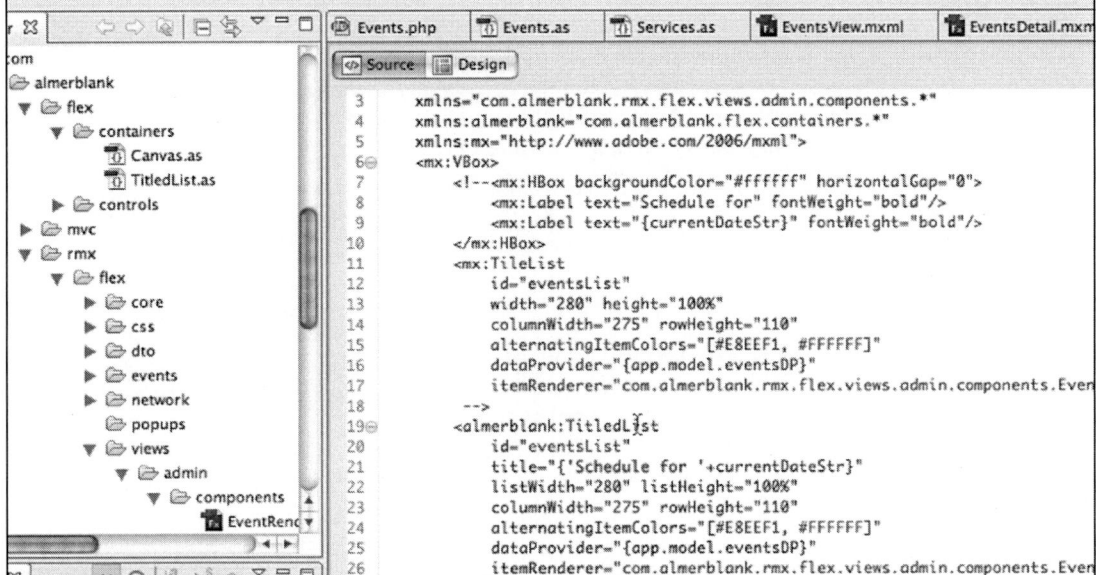

Figure A-9. MXML updated after refactoring

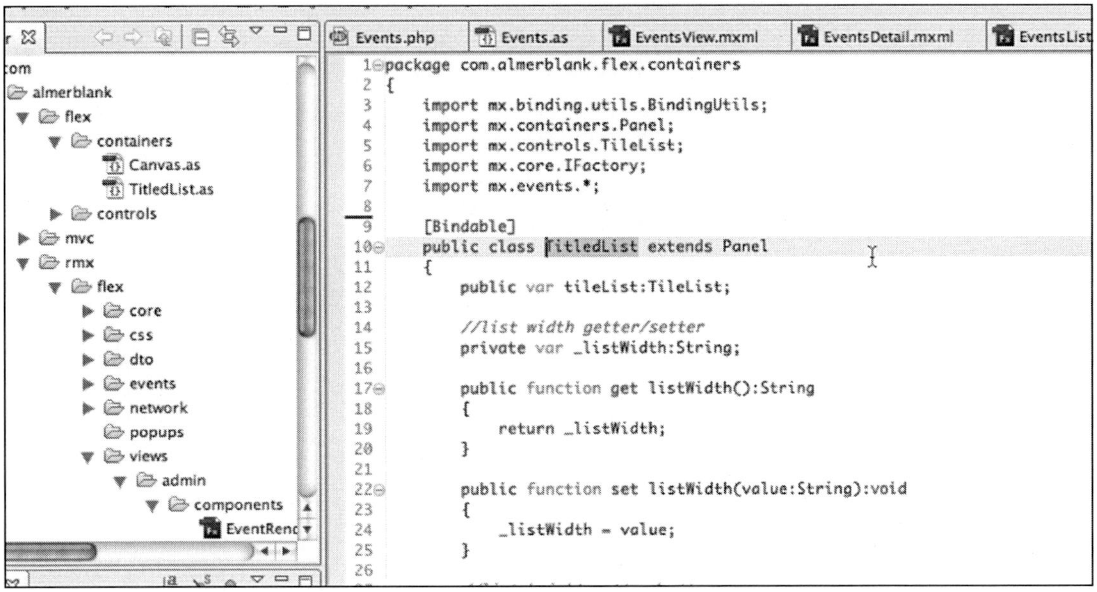

Figure A-10. ActionScript updated after refactoring

Class outlines

The outline view (see Figure A-11) now includes support for imports, so you can easily explore and develop massively large projects with ease when you combine this with the code search and code hints/completion features. I find myself using outline view a lot when a class contains a couple thousand lines of code and I need to find an import, property, or method quickly.

Code search

Flex 3 now includes a global search feature. I cannot begin to express how useful this feature is. While you're developing your project, select a property or method

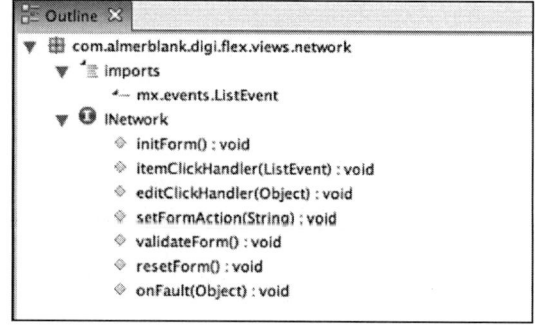

Figure A-11. Class outlines

name and press Ctrl+G (Windows) or Cmd+G (OSX) to search for all instances of that property or method in your project. Figure A-12 shows what the Search results panel will look like after performing a global search.

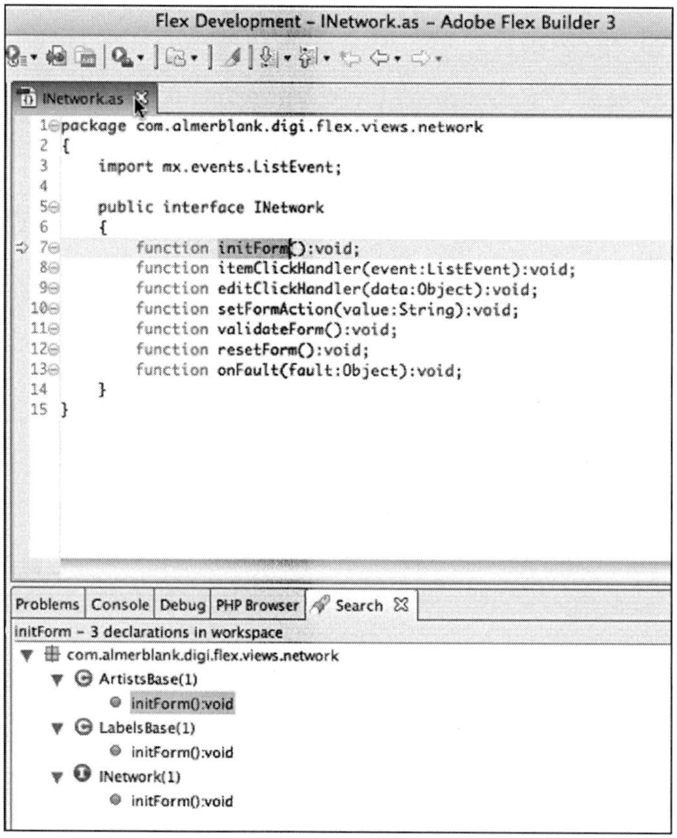

Figure A-12. Global search results panel

Multiple SDKs

With multiple SDK support, you can use Flex Builder 3 to develop and support not only your Flex 3 apps, but also your legacy 2.0.1 apps as well. And, when you're ready, you can easily update your project to use a different SDK version (see Figure A-13). You can even customize the SDK and use your custom SDK across all of your projects. That's a pretty cool advancement, because that custom SDK can even be shared across teams, and the projects using those settings will just work.

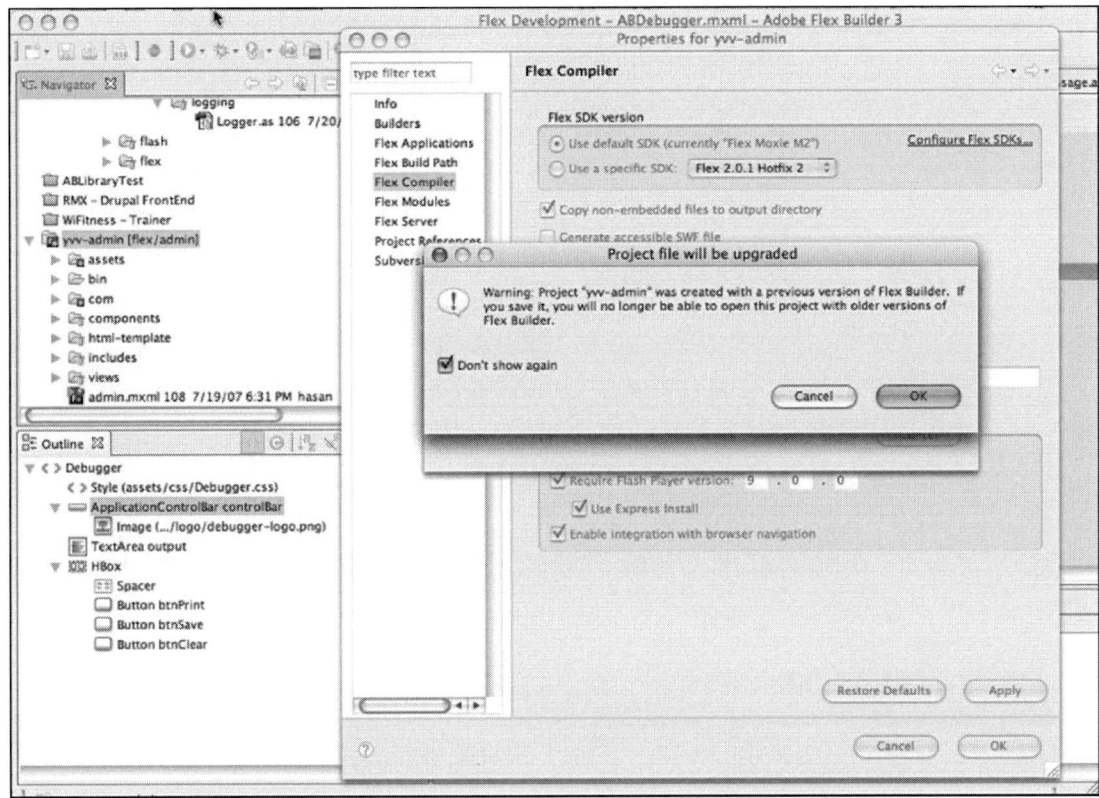

Figure A-13. Switching Flex SDKs for a project

Profiler

The new Profiler alone may be worth the price of admission to Flex 3. This feature allows you to see the guts of your applications running in the Flash Player. You'll easily be able to see what the internals of your application are actually doing as well as how much memory is allocated to each instance within your application. To use this feature, select your project and choose Profile As ➤ Flex Application from the project context menu, set your profiler options, and click Resume (see Figure A-14), and see what your application is doing behind the scenes (Figure A-15).

Compilation

The compilers in Flex 3 have been improved to include class-caching support during the compilation process, and this optimization results in much faster compile times. You can think of this as basically incremental compilation, as all subsequent compilations past the initial one will be limited to the classes that have been recently modified.

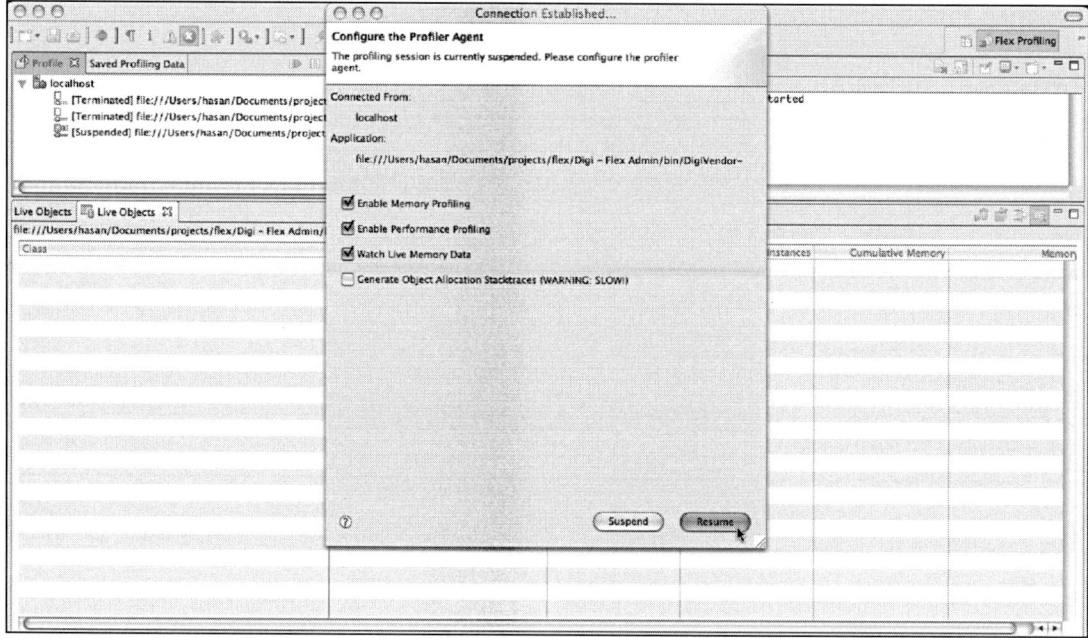

Figure A-14. Configuring the Profiler

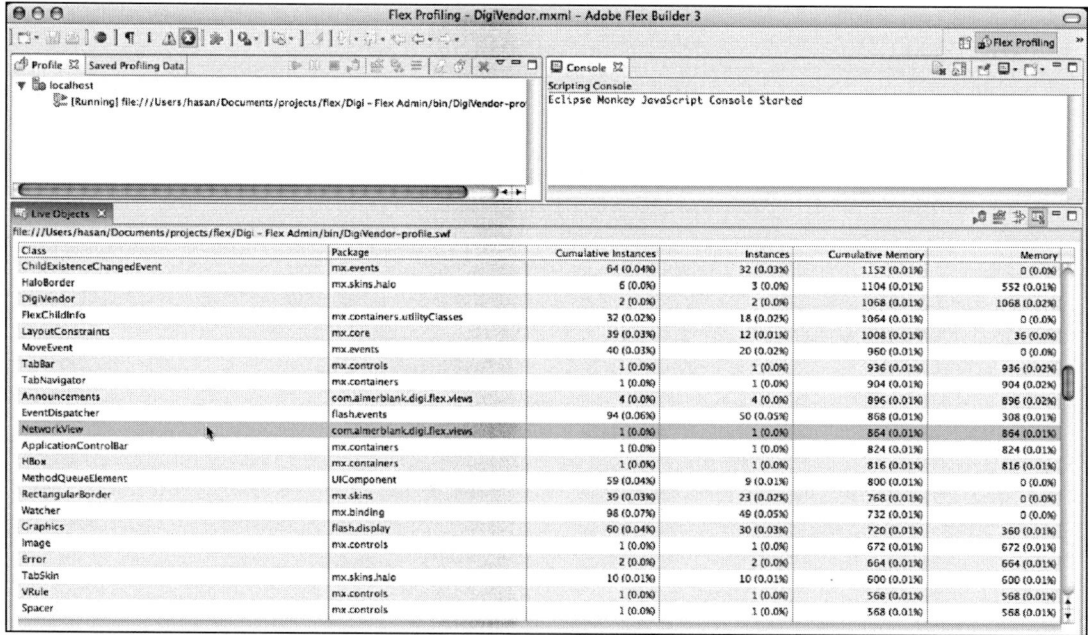

Figure A-15. The profiler is now profiling your application.

Component and SDK enhancements

Here I'll talk about a couple of the new Flex 3 features that affect working with components and the SDK: deep linking and runtime localization.

Deep linking

Flex 3 now includes deep-linking support, which allows your Flex application to both set and detect changes in the URL using the new BrowserManager class without closing the application as the URL changes. In this way, you can still develop using Single Page Architecture (SPA) while providing your users the multipage experience that they are accustomed to with traditional HTML applications. This enables you to easily set up bookmarks to the various parts that might make up your Flex app, thereby allowing a user to go directly to a products page or view directly. You also gain Back button support to allow navigation of your Flex app using the web browser's controls.

Here's some sample code that you can use to play around with this feature and see how best to use it in your applications:

```
<mx:Application
  xmlns:mx="http://www.adobe.com/2006/mxml"
  creationComplete="initApp()"
  historyManagementEnabled="false">
<mx:Script>
<![CDATA[
  import mx.events.BrowserChangeEvent;
  import mx.managers.IBrowserManager;
  import mx.managers.BrowserManager;
  import mx.utils.URLUtil;

  public var browserManager:IBrowserManager;
  private var parsing:Boolean = false;

  private function initApp():void
  {
    browserManager = BrowserManager.getInstance();
    browserManager.addEventListener(➡
        BrowserChangeEvent.BROWSER_URL_CHANGE, parseURL);
    browserManager.init("", "Products");
  }

  private function parseURL(event:Event):void
  {
    parsing = true;

    var o:Object = URLUtil.stringToObject(browserManager.fragment);
    if (o.view == undefined) o.view = 0;
    tn.selectedIndex = o.view;
    browserManager.setTitle((tn.selectedIndex == 0) ? ➡
        "Products" : "Services");
    tn.validateNow();
```

```
        var details:Boolean = o.details == true;
        if (tn.selectedIndex == 0)
            productDetails.selected = details;
        else
            serviceDetails.selected = details;

        parsing = false;
    }

    private function updateURL():void
    {
        if (!parsing) callLater(actuallyUpdateURL);
    }

    private function actuallyUpdateURL():void
    {
        var o:Object = {};
        var t:String = "";

        if (tn.selectedIndex == 1)
        {
            t = "Services";
            o.view = tn.selectedIndex;
            if (serviceDetails.selected) o.details = true;
        }
        else
        {
            t = "Products";
            o.view = tn.selectedIndex;
            if (productDetails.selected) o.details = true;
        }
        var s:String = URLUtil.objectToString(o);
        browserManager.setFragment(s);
        browserManager.setTitle(t);
    }

]]>
</mx:Script>
<mx:TabNavigator
    id="tn"
    change="updateURL()"
    width="300">
    <mx:Panel label="Products">
    <mx:CheckBox
        id="productDetails"
        label="Show Details"
        change="updateURL()"/>
    </mx:Panel>
    <mx:Panel label="Services">
```

```
        <mx:CheckBox
          id="serviceDetails"
          label="Show Details"
          change="updateURL()"/>
      </mx:Panel>
    </mx:TabNavigator>
  </mx:Application>
```

Runtime localization

In Flex 2, if you want to include localized content for your app, you have to build multiple SWFs for each locale that you want to support. That's not the case in Flex 3. You can incorporate multiple locales into your application in much the same way that you do with runtime CSS. This will allow you to preload a locale at application initialization and change to different locales on the fly. This will all be accomplished through the new ResourceManager class, which is the centerpiece of this new feature.

Smaller SWFs

Flex 3 really delivers on this long-awaited and much-needed feature. In the very near future, the Flex framework will be cached inside of the Flash Player itself. So, your compiled SWFs will see a dramatic reduction in size as a result. You can say "goodbye" to application bloat as your applications will now only contain your code plus Flex's preloader, which will handle the framework caching and loading logic for you under the hood. It gets better though, because this new caching feature supports versioning. Say, for example, you built a Flex 3 app that uses the 3.0 framework, but the current framework version is 3.2 or greater. Your legacy app will still work because each framework is stored in the Flash Player in its own space. And, with built-in support for cross-domain caching, Adobe is providing the community with a secure distributed component model that works across domains. So, everyone using Flex 3 to develop RIAs will benefit from much smaller and swifter SWFs.

Flex and Flash integration

With Flex 3, you gain the ability to create slick components in Flash CS3, compile them, and use them inside of Flex. A little known fact though is that you can create custom containers in Flash CS3 and also use those in Flex 3. This is pretty cool because you can have a Flex application that houses Flash-authored content that in turn houses Flex content. So, either you or the Flash gurus at your firm can roll out custom containers complete with signature Flash animations, pass off the SWC to you, and have the two worlds play together seamlessly. So with that in mind, I thought I'd show you how I built such a custom container for use in the RMX.

The process is very similar to the one detailed in Chapter 15 for the FLVPlaybackCaptioning component. The only real difference is that I'm making use of a new Flash JavaScript (JSFL) command provided by the Flex Component Kit (FCK), and I'm designing the CS3 component to utilize Flex's states and transitions mechanism. What I had in mind was a collapsible panel that I could design in Flash and use in Flex to house various data controls throughout the application. Figure A-16 shows the component in its collapsed state.

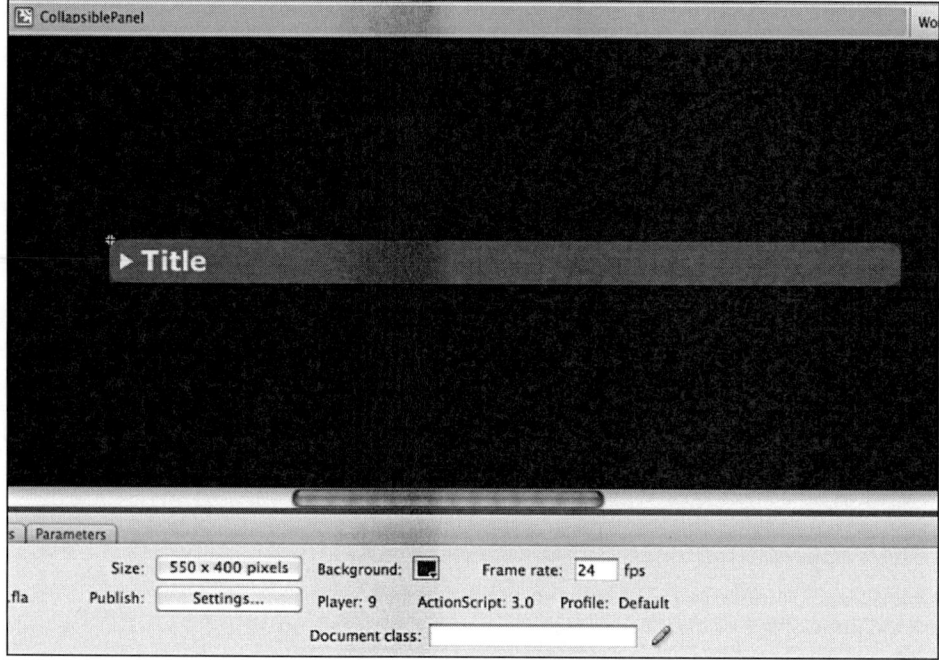

Figure A-16. Collapsible panel

At this point, it's just a rounded rectangle (cornerRadius = 5) along with an arrow graphic, a dynamic text field for the panel's title, and a 300X16 rectangle used as the boundingBox for the component. If you're unfamiliar with that last term, boundingBox is the instance name that you give the MovieClip that you wish to use to establish the physical space that your component takes up. This is very important to Flex because if your component does any resizing as a result of animations, and so forth, Flex will reposition everything in your application to compensate for this adjustment should you choose not to use a boundingBox MovieClip.

After creating the initial state of the component, I selected everything on the stage and converted this content to a MovieClip (F8 Windows/Mac). Once that was done, I started distributing everything to its own layer so I could keep it all organized and clearly see what's going on. Figure A-17 shows that layer setup.

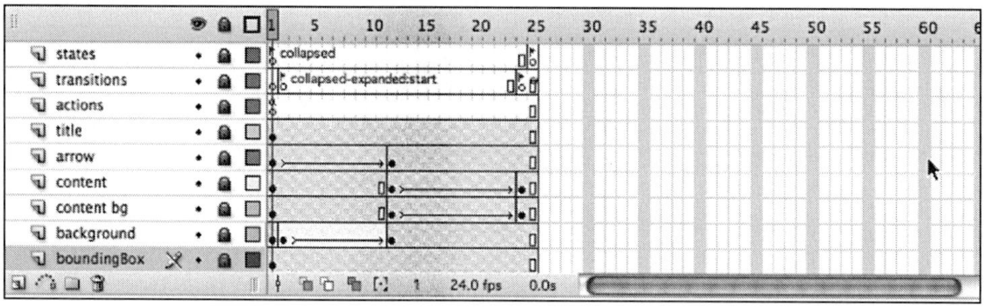

Figure A-17. Component layers

As you can see, I've given all the physical content its own layer and added layers for my actions, as well as ones for Flex's states and transitions. This is also a very cool feature because by just giving those frames labels, I've essentially defined Flex states and transitions. This magic happens courtesy of the UIMovieClip class that's installed by the FCK. That class takes care of mapping your Flash frame labels to Flex states. For the transitions, UIMovieClip looks for your frame labels that mark the start (state1-state2:start) and end (state1-state2:end) of your transition animation. In the case of my component, those labels are collapsed-expanded:start and collapsed-expanded:end, respectively. So, everything that happens between those two frame labels will be played as the transition between my collapsed state and my expanded state. What's even cooler is that when you want to return to the default state, you just instruct Flex to do so, and your transition will play in reverse, thus saving you the need to create another transition for that event unless you desire to do so.

Now, here's where it gets interesting. Thanks to Glenn Ruehle and the Flex engineering team, we now have access to a JSFL command as part of the FCK whose sole purpose is to convert your Flash CS3 movie clip into a container suitable to house Flex content. It's super easy to use, too. Just select your container clip in the Library panel and run Commands ➤ Convert Symbol to Flex Container.

Once the conversion is complete, you'll find a new movie clip, FlexContentHolder, that you can now drag to the stage and size/position it how you'd like your Flex content to appear. Don't worry about the Flex symbol included in the clip (see Figure A-18); it's for development purposes only and won't be visible once you import the component into Flex.

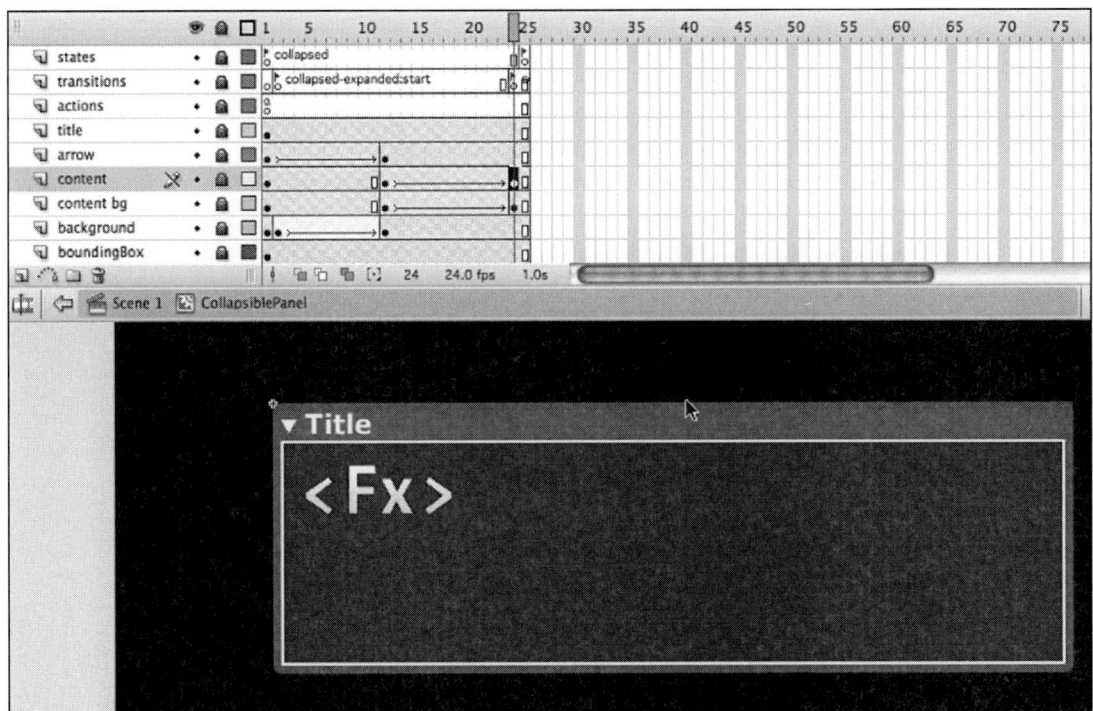

Figure A-18. FlexContentHolder movie clip

Now, all you need to do is publish the FLA to create your SWC for use in Flex. After you've created your SWC file, you use the same process described in Chapter 15 to add the SWC to the library path of your Flex project. Once you do, the component becomes accessible to you in the IDE (see Figure A-19).

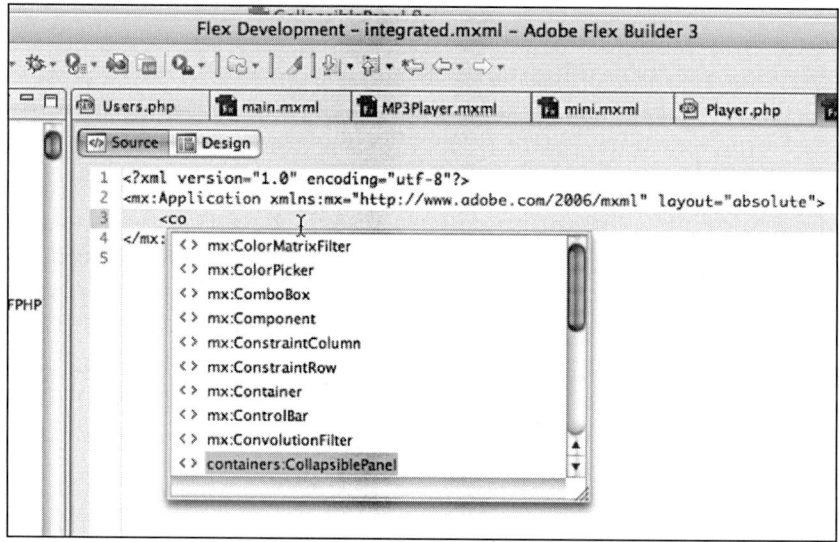

Figure A-19. Using the CS3 container

After inserting an instance of your custom container, you just place your Flex content in between the open and close tags of your custom container just as you would when using the built-in containers. There is one caveat to be aware of, though, and that's the fact that your CS3 containers can have only one Flex child (the child can have children, however). If you forget this, you'll get the error displayed in Figure A-20.

```
    Users.php    main.mxml    MP3Player.mxml    mini.mxml    Player.php

    Source    Design

1   <?xml version="1.0" encoding="utf-8"?>
2   <mx:Application
3       xmlns:mx="http://www.adobe.com/2006/mxml"
4       xmlns:containers="com.almerblank.flash.containers.*"
5       layout="absolute">
6       <containers:CollapsiblePanel
7           id="flashPanel"
8           title="Event Type">
9
10      Multiple markers at this line:
11       -In initializer for 'content': multiple initializer values for target type mx.core.IUIComponent.    "/>
12       -1 changed line, 1 added
13           <mx:CheckBox label="Adobe Presentation" labelPlacement="right"/>
14           <mx:CheckBox label="Conference" labelPlacement="right"/>
15           <mx:CheckBox label="Other" labelPlacement="right"/>
16       </mx:Canvas>
17
18      </containers:CollapsiblePanel>
19  </mx:Application>
20
```

Figure A-20. Only one child per CS3 container

This is just one example of how you can use the new FCK to add a little extra zing to your Flex applications, and when you see my collapsible panel around the RMX, you won't have to ask "How'd they do that?" because you'll know the secret.

Flex + open source = no limits!

In April 2007, Adobe announced its plans to move the development of Flex to an open source model under the Mozilla Public License (MPL). Now, if you've already been developing with Flex 2, you may be wondering what that means, since you already had access to the source of the ActionScript components in the SDK. Well, with this move, Adobe is strategically working toward releasing the Java source code for the ActionScript and MXML compilers, the ActionScript debugger, and the core ActionScript libraries from the SDK.

That's huge for the development community, because as a developer you'll be able to download, extend, and contribute to the source code for the Flex compiler and framework classes under the MPL. I would not be surprised to see the Flex community experience the same kind of explosive growth that the Drupal community has seen in recent years as a result of this move.

Adobe is rolling out this change incrementally with plans to have the public bug database and public daily builds for the SDK in place by summer 2007. The rest of the open source infrastructure, compiler source, and community contributions is expected by the end of 2007. So, in the early stages, Adobe plans to accept contributions in the form of attachments to bug reports and enhancement requests in the public bug database. From there, the Flex engineering team will review and approve those contributions. Once the complete infrastructure is in place, Adobe plans to open up the process to allow for external committers as well.

Summary

In this chapter, I covered some of what lies ahead on the Flex superhighway. I shared with you some of the cool new features available to you in Flex 3. I also explored the new Flash-Flex Integration Kit and how it helps you develop incredibly amazing applications where your imagination is the only barrier. Finally, I discussed how Adobe's decision to make Flex open source will forever change the RIA development landscape. Armed with all of this information and the lessons learned throughout this book, I, along with everyone at Almer/Blank, look forward to seeing the AdvancED Flex applications that you'll inevitably create!

INDEX

1-59059-543-2 $39.99 [US]

1-59059-518-1 $39.99 [US]

1-59059-542-4 $36.99 [US]

1-59059-517-3 $39.99 [US]

1-59059-651-X $44.99 [US]

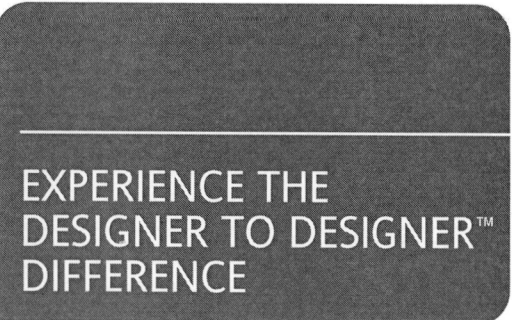

EXPERIENCE THE
DESIGNER TO DESIGNER™
DIFFERENCE

1-59059-558-0 $49.99 [US]

1-59059-314-6 $59.99 [US]

1-59059-315-4 $59.99 [US]

1-59059-619-6 $44.99 [US]

1-59059-304-9 $49.99 [US]

1-59059-355-3 $24.99 [US]

1-59059-409-6 $39.99 [US]

1-59059-748-6 $49.99 [US]

1-59059-593-9 $49.99 [US]

1-59059-555-6 $44.99 [US]

1-59059-533-5 $34.99 [US]

1-59059-638-2 $49.99 [US]

1-59059-765-6 $34.99 [US]

1-59059-581-5 $39.99 [US]

1-59059-614-5 $34.99 [US]

1-59059-594-7 $39.99 [US]

1-59059-381-2 $34.99 [US]

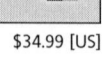

1-59059-554-8 $24.99 [US]